# American Foreign Policy

## Eighth Edition

# Glenn P. Hastedt

*James Madison University*

**Longman**

Boston   Columbus   Indianapolis   New York   San Francisco   Upper Saddle River
Amsterdam   Cape Town   Dubai   London   Madrid   Milan   Munich   Paris   Montreal   Toronto
Delhi   Mexico City   Sao Paulo   Sydney   Hong Kong   Seoul   Singapore   Taipei   Tokyo

Acquisitions Editor: Vikram Mukhija
Editorial Assistant: Toni Magyar
Marketing Manager: Lindsey Prudhomme
Production Manager: Kathy Sleys
Project Coordination, Text Design,
  and Electronic Page Makeup: Sadagoban Balaji/Integra Software Services Pvt. Ltd.
Photo Researcher: Rona Tuccillo
Creative Director: Jayne Conte
Cover Designer: Mary Siener/Bruce Kenselaar
Cover Illustration/Photo: © Chris Wattie/CORBIS All Rights Reserved
Printer and Binder/Cover Printer: Courier Companies

Library of Congress Cataloging-in-Publication Data

Hastedt, Glenn P.,
    American foreign policy / Glenn P. Hastedt. —8th ed.
      p. cm.
    Includes bibliographical references and index.
    ISBN-13: 978-0-205-79122-4 (alk. paper)
    ISBN-10: 0-205-79122-0 (alk. paper)
    1. United States—Foreign relations.    2. United States—Foreign relations—1945-1989
3. United States—Foreign relations—1989-    4. United States—Foreign relations
administration.    I. Title.
    E183.7.H27 2011
    327.73—dc22

                                                                    2009050873


1 2 3 4 5 6 7 8 9 10—CRS—14 13 12 11

**Longman**
is an imprint of

www.pearsonhighered.com

ISBN-13: 978-0-205-79122-4
ISBN-10:    0-205-79122-0

*To Cathy, Sarah, and Matthew*

# BRIEF CONTENTS

# CONTENTS

## CHAPTER 3
## The American National Style    55

## CHAPTER 4
## Learning from the Past    80

## CHAPTER 5
### Society            108

## CHAPTER 6
### Congress          143

## CHAPTER 7
### Presidency 175

# CHAPTER 10

## Diplomacy 256

# CHAPTER 11

## Economic Instruments 283

## CHAPTER 12

## Military Instruments: Big Wars                                       312

## CHAPTER 13

## Military Instruments: Small Wars                                     339

# PREFACE

American foreign policy had settled into a comfortable routine during the Cold War. The enemy was well known, both the United States and the Soviet Union had alliance systems that kept allies in place, and mechanisms were in place to manage superpower military, economic, and political relations. All of that ended with the fall of communism and the break up of the Soviet Union. The post–Cold War era that followed was confusing for the new type of challenges it presented the United States, but it was a world that seemed manageable and one in which the United States was comfortable in its position as the dominant world power. All of that ended on September 11, 2001. With the terrorist attacks of that day, the United States rediscovered how dangerous and unpredictable the world beyond its borders could be—and how porous its borders had become. No longer could the United States automatically rely on old habits of thought and action to guide its foreign policy to protect the national interest. The time had come to begin critically thinking about the issues confronting the United States and the options open to it.

*American Foreign Policy* is designed to help students develop the critical thinking skills they need to participate in this debate about the conduct and content of U.S. foreign policy. It does that in four specific ways. First, it raises the question, "what are the key components of foreign policy and what is the national interest?" Second, it looks to the past and asks, "how did we get here?" and "how do we learn from the past?" The answers are found in the nature of the contemporary international system, the American national style, and the actions of past administrations. Third, we ask "how is foreign policy made?" Answering this question leads us to an examination of American domestic politics on foreign policy, the intuitions that make it, how they all come together to make policy, and the policy instruments available to decision makers. Fourth, we ask, "what next?" Here, our interest is in getting students to think about tomorrow's headlines and how what we have talked about in *American Foreign Policy* will help them prepare for future policy debates.

## NEW TO THIS EDITION

This edition of *American Foreign Policy* contains all of the essential material found in previous editions. The number of chapters has been reduced to make it easier to use, leading to a reorganization of some discussions. In order to better help students become critical thinkers on American foreign policy, this edition has been significantly revised. Among its most important new features found in each chapter are the following:

- A short introductory section on a contemporary problem in U.S. foreign policy to get students involved in the topic.

- A "Historical Lesson" boxed insert that discusses a historical case relevant to understanding the problem raised by the introductory example and the chapter as a whole.
- Critical thinking questions found at the end of both the "Historical Lesson" case study and the chapter.
- A concluding "Over the Horizon" section that focuses student thinking on a few trends in American foreign policy they should begin to think about and anticipate.
- Glossary of key terms
- Suggested further readings

## FEATURES

Chapter 1 examines the nature of "Foreign Policy Problems" by introducing students to the need to make choices, consider costs, build a consensus, select policy instruments, and assess the results of one's action. Post–Cold War presidential doctrines are introduced to give substance to the discussion.

Chapter 2 looks at the "Global Setting of American Foreign Policy." The competing theoretical perspectives on international relations (realism, neoliberalism, and constructivism) are introduced first, followed by a discussion of the enduring and contemporary features that shape world politics. The chapter ends with a discussion of globalism, terrorism, and hegemony as the three competing core dynamics of world politics today.

Chapter 3 reviews the American national style with an eye toward highlighting its many sources and consequences. Emphasis is placed on the alternation between isolationism and internationalism. The chapter ends with a discussion of Wilsonianism as the dominant point of reference for contemporary discussions of the American national style.

The material presented in these three chapters is brought together in Chapter 4, which looks at the problem of learning from the past. It begins with an examination of how and what policy makers learn from the past and then goes into in-depth discussions of the Vietnam War and Iraq War to illustrate these points.

With Chapter 5 we turn our attention to how American foreign policy is made. Where once domestic factors received little attention in studies of American foreign policy, they now are a major subject of interest and provide a baseline from which Congress, the president, and bureaucracies make their decisions and interact. In this chapter, we examine public opinion, elections, interest groups, and protest. We also look at the role of the media and how policy makers view the public.

Chapter 6 deals with Congress. It begins by examining Congress' constitutional powers and then moves to a discussion of the institutional features that influence its ability to shape American foreign policy. It ends with a look at the changing relationship between Congress and the president in making American foreign policy.

Chapter 7 looks at the president. It begins by placing presidential action in the context of its constitutional powers and then moves to a discussion on presidential personality and the management of the presidential bureaucracy. Here we not only emphasize the National Security Council system but also look at other foreign policy voices within the White House.

In Chapter 8, we examine the "Foreign Affairs Bureaucracy." We give special attention to the State Department, Defense Department, and the intelligence community. For each we look at its growth and structure and their internal value system. We also look at Homeland Security and introduce some of the domestic bureaucracies that play a role in American foreign policy.

Our discussion of how American foreign policy is made is brought to a conclusion with the presentation of models of foreign policy making in Chapter 9 that help the students conceptualize the various ways we can understand the interaction of these actors and political forces. The Cuban missile crisis is used as a summary example to show how our understanding of a decision changes depending upon what model(s) we use to study it.

The next four chapters examine policy instruments. Chapter 10 looks at diplomacy, with both its classical and public diplomacy variations. It also examines the political use of force and arms transfers. Chapter 11 examines economic instruments, with an emphasis on free trade, sanctions, and foreign aid. Chapter 12 introduces students to military power as an instrument of foreign policy, beginning with nuclear weapons and ending with covert action. Chapter 13 reviews the history and issues involved in arms control and defense primarily against weapons of mass destruction, but it does touch on conventional weapons as well.

Chapter 14 is a brief concluding chapter. It places the various issues raised in the "Over the Horizon" sections of each chapter in a larger context by providing students with six alternative future American foreign policies to consider. They are put forward to spark debate and bring the critical thinking skills students have developed through reading *American Foreign Policy: Past, Present, Future* into sharper focus.

## SUPPLEMENTS

### For Instructors and Students

MyPoliSciKit Video Case Studies  Featuring video from major news sources and providing reporting and insight on recent world affairs, this DVD series helps instructors integrate current events into their courses by letting them use the clips as lecture launchers or discussion starters.

### For Instructors

Test Bank  This assessment resource includes multiple-choice, true–false, and essay questions for each chapter in this text. Available exclusively at the Instructor Resource Center (IRC), an online hub that allows instructors to quickly download book-specific supplements. Please visit the IRC welcome page at **www.pearsonhighered.com/irc** to register for access.

## For Students

**MySearchLab (0-205-71937-6)**   Need help with a paper? MySearchLab saves time and improves results by offering start-to-finish guidance on the research/writing process and full-text access to academic journals and periodicals. Order MySearchLab with this book and receive a 15% discount.

***Longman Atlas of World Issues* (0-321-22465-5)**   Introduced and selected by Robert J. Art of Brandeis University and excerpted from the acclaimed Penguin Atlas Series, the *Longman Atlas of World Issues* is designed to help students understand the geography and major issues facing the world today, such as terrorism, debt, and HIV/AIDS. These thematic, full-color maps examine forces shaping politics today at a global level. Explanatory information accompanies each map to help students better grasp the concepts being shown and how they affect our world today. Available at no additional charge when packaged with this book.

## ACKNOWLEDGMENTS

I thank the following reviewers for helping me to improve this book: Peter Bookmiller, Millersville University; Aaron Karp, Old Dominion University; Richard Nolan, University of Florida; and Timothy White of Xavier University. I also thank my editors at Longman: Vikram Mukhija and Toni Magyar.

# Defining American Foreign Policy Problems

"Y ou didn't have an approach against al Qaeda because you didn't have an approach against Afghanistan. And you didn't have an approach against Afghanistan because you didn't have an approach against Pakistan. And until we could get that right, we didn't have a policy."[1] This is how National Security Advisor Condoleezza Rice explained the problem the George W. Bush administration had in putting together an antiterrorism policy in her testimony before the 9/11 Commission in May 2004.

At the tactical level the answer the Bush administration ultimately settled upon to solve this riddle involved making an alliance with Pakistan, invading and overthrowing the Afghan Taliban government, and seeking to eliminate the leadership and sanctuaries of al Qaeda. At the strategic level, the administration's response involved declaring a war on terrorism and putting forward the Bush Doctrine as a document to guide its pursuit of that war. The need to find answers to the questions identified by Rice also faced the Obama administration. No easy answers presented themselves. Defining the situation in Afghanistan as likely resulting in failure, General Stanley McChrystal called in September 2009 for an increase in the size of the U.S. troop commitment. At the same time, many in the Obama administration favored a narrower war effort.

As Rice's comments highlight, foreign policy is a line of action. It is a set of activities designed to advance goals and protect them against threats. At least six distinct tasks are involved in constructing a foreign policy: (1) problems must be defined, (2) choices made, (3) costs assessed, (4) public support built, (5) a course of action designed, and (6) results assessed. We will review each of these in this chapter.

## TOWARD AN OBAMA DOCTRINE

Before doing so, it is important to note that foreign policies once in place also cast a shadow over what follows. George W. Bush entered office determined to distance his administration's foreign policy from that of Bill Clinton. Barack Obama has taken a similar position in putting together the outlines of his foreign policy. In his February 24, 2009, address to a Joint Session of Congress, Obama proclaimed that "a new era of engagement has begun. For we know that America cannot meet the threats of this century alone, but the world cannot meet them without America." Later that spring and in the summer, Obama traveled abroad and gave a series of speeches in which he outlined what some see as the beginnings of an Obama Doctrine.

Speaking in Russia on July 7, 2009, where he and Russian president Dmitry Medvedev agreed to engage in another round of nuclear disarmament talks, President Obama set out to define American national interests. He identified four areas of special concern: stopping the spread of nuclear weapons, isolating and defeating violent extremists, global prosperity, and the advance of democratic government and protection of citizen rights. Speaking in Ghana on July 11, 2009, Obama put forward four key features of his administration's foreign policy to the developing world: support for democracy, supporting economic development opportunities for people, strengthening public health, and the peaceful resolution of conflict. He returned to these themes in October when he addressed the United Nations and defined his foreign policy as consisting of four pillars: nonproliferation and disarmament, the promotion of peace and security, the preservation of our planet, and a global economy that advances opportunity for all people.

In the days following his Ghana speech, on July 16, Secretary of State Hillary Clinton gave a major foreign policy address in which she argued the United States could not go back to Cold War policies of containment, twentieth-century balance of power strategies, or nineteenth-century concert of powers strategies for dealing with the world. She asserted that the issues were now too complex and there were now too many actors to permit such strategies. What is needed is a new global architecture rooted in partnerships and not paternalism. In making this case, Clinton echoed a theme introduced by Obama in Russia when he said that "there was a time when Roosevelt, Churchill, and Stalin could shape the world in one meeting. Those days are over."

Just as with the Bush administration's policies toward al Qaeda, Pakistan, and Afghanistan, so too the Obama administration's effort to engage the world and tackle specific foreign policy problems will require meeting the six tasks we discuss in this chapter.

## THINKING ABOUT FOREIGN POLICY PROBLEMS

There is no such thing as a standard or typical foreign policy problem. Presidents discover three truths very quickly. First, most foreign policy problems contain within them a bundle of distinct policy problems or issues that intersect in complicated ways. This makes deciding how to approach a problem difficult because of uncertainty over just what the problem is or how attacking one aspect of the problem will affect its other dimensions. Consider the problem of AIDS (acquired immunodeficiency syndrome). The temptation is to treat it strictly as a health problem. But it is also an economic problem. The World Bank asserts that the spread of AIDS is in part responsible for the slowed growth rate experienced by the economies of sub-Saharan states. AIDS is also a military problem. Large numbers of HIV-infected personnel within a military reduce its ability to carry out assigned tasks. AIDS can also be viewed as a human rights problem. Fears exist that cultural norms and public laws place women and children who have contracted AIDS in a disadvantaged position in seeking help or treatment.

Second, foreign policy problems are seldom ever "solved." George Shultz, President Ronald Reagan's secretary of state, noted that policy making does not involve confronting "one damn thing after another . . . it involves confronting the same damn thing over and over."[2] Rarely is it the case that policy makers can close the book on a problem and move on to other matters. The invasion of Afghanistan was considered a major success.

A government under the direction of Hamid Karzai was installed, the North Atlantic Treaty Organization (NATO) was brought in to provide stabilizing troops, and the United States turned its attention to Iraq. Less than five years later the Taliban were making a political and military comeback, threatening to undermine this victory and presenting the new Obama administration with its first major foreign policy test.

Third, it is also important to realize that foreign policy problems differ in terms of their history and origin. Some foreign policy problems are inherited from previous administrations. The key dilemma faced by presidents is whether to continue the course of action and endorse the policy line of their predecessor or move in a new direction. A prime reason given by President Barack Obama's aides for his trip to Europe in March 2009 was "to confront those inherited challenges left over from the Bush administration." When George W. Bush came into office, he decided to reverse course on the Kyoto Protocol and end U.S. participation in this international effort to reduce environmental problems. He also decided to go ahead with deployment of the ballistic missile defense system, a decision that Bill Clinton had left to his successor. Clinton in turn inherited a military presence in Somalia from Bush's father and a NAFTA (North American Free Trade Agreement) that had yet to be ratified by the Senate.

Some foreign policy problems are new—the product of unfolding events beyond U.S. borders that earlier administrations never had to confront. With no track record of successes and failures against which to weigh their choices, presidents are left with only the informed judgment of their advisers and their own political instincts to guide them in selecting policy options. The most significant event of this type in recent times was the collapse of communism and the breakup of the Soviet Union that confronted the administration of George H. W. Bush in 1989. Except in the Eisenhower administration, when calls for "rolling back the Iron Curtain" were common (but never really acted on), it is difficult to remember when the United States even had a foreign policy toward Eastern Europe. Certainly, American foreign policy never contemplated the dissolution of its major Cold War rival. A similarly momentous new problem faced President George W. Bush in the war against global terrorism following the attacks of September 11, 2001.

Other foreign policy problems can be attributed largely to perceived or actual failings in an administration's own foreign policy. The problem may be either a specific policy or the administration's handling of foreign policy issues in general. George W. Bush was roundly criticized for his administration's policy toward Iraq after Saddam Hussein's forces were defeated. Bill Clinton's foreign policy was widely criticized for its inconsistency and his lack of decisiveness. Zbigniew Brzezinski, President Jimmy Carter's national security advisor, described Clinton's foreign policy as being an "enemy du jour" foreign policy.[3]

A last type of foreign policy problem consists of problems rooted in long-term structural features of the international system. One such problem is found in the existence of a trade-off between military power and economic growth. Paul Kennedy, in his book *The Rise and Fall of the Great Powers*,[4] argues that economic growth is the foundation of state power and that funds spent on the military invariably produce lower rates of economic growth. Historically, however, Great Powers continually overspend on the military. They succumb to "imperial overreach," a perceived need to protect their Great Power status through the possession of a dominant military establishment. In failing to curb their military spending, they do not address the long-term needs of their economic base. Thus, they begin their "fall" from Great Power status. Kennedy's declinist thesis is not universally accepted. Ronald Reagan rejected it in the 1980s, as do many today who see the United States' military and economic powers not as undermining each other but as complementing each other.

# CHOICES

Foreign policy is about choices: choices about what goals to pursue, what threats to protect against, what costs to bear, and who should bear those costs. Choices always exist. President George W. Bush, when asked if the president ever had a last card to play in foreign policy before having to walk away and accept defeat, replied "there is always another card." Just as there are always options once a conflict is underway, so too there are always choices about what problems to place on the foreign policy agenda. Two different lines of thinking have been used to make foreign policy choices: One involves asking what it is that Americans want, and the second involves asking what it is that the United States should do. Answers to the first are generally found in public opinion polls. Answers to the second are typically sought in the concept of the national interest.

## What Do Americans Want in Foreign Policy?

Table 1.1 presents a sampling of what Americans have considered to be the major foreign policy problems at different times. The 2008 survey saw Americans cite the importance of improving America's standing in the world. This was a new addition to the list of priorities. In other respects, the 2008 survey was consistent with its predecessors. In 2006 Americans rated protecting the jobs of American workers as the most important foreign policy problem, followed closely by preventing the spread of nuclear weapons, combating international terrorism, and securing adequate supplies of energy. Only protecting the jobs of American workers, preventing the spread of nuclear weapons, combating world hunger, and strengthening the United Nations were consistently cited as very important foreign policy goals over the span of three decades. Other foreign policy goals, such as defending our allies' security and promoting human rights, came and went. And some others, such as combating terrorism, controlling illegal immigration, and improving the global environment, joined the list.

## TABLE 1.1

### Top U.S. Foreign Policy Goals

| Foreign Policy Goal | 2008 | 2006 | 1999 | 1986 | 1978 |
|---|---|---|---|---|---|
| Improving America's standing in the world | 83 | | | | |
| Protecting the jobs of American workers | 80 | 76 | 80 | 73 | 78 |
| Preventing the spread of nuclear weapons | 73 | 74 | 85 | 79[a] | 64[a] |
| Combating international terrorism | 67 | 72 | 79 | | |
| Securing adequate supplies of energy | 80 | 72 | 64 | 69 | 78 |
| Promoting economic growth | | 62 | | | 86[b] |
| Controlling and reducing illegal immigration | 61 | 58 | 55 | | |
| Maintaining superior military power worldwide | 57 | 55 | 59 | 53[c] | |
| Improving the global environment | 42[d] | 54 | 53 | | |
| Combating world hunger | 46 | 48 | 62 | 63 | 59 |
| Strengthening the United Nations | 39 | 40 | 45 | 46 | 47 |
| Stopping the flow of illegal drugs | | | 81 | | |
| Combating communism | | | | 57 | 60 |
| Defending allies' security | | | 44 | 56 | 50 |
| Promoting and defending human rights | 31 | | 39 | 42 | 39 |

[a] Worldwide arms control.
[b] Keeping up the value of the dollar.
[c] Matching Soviet military power.
[d] Limit climate change.
Blank cells indicate not reported. The data are in percentages.
*Source:* Data from Chicago Council on Foreign Relations Public Opinion Surveys, www.ccfr.org/past_pos.php. The data are drawn from 1978, Table II-2; 1986, Table II-4; 1999, Table 2-8; 2006, Figure I-5; and 2009, Global Views, 2008, Figure 1.

## The National Interest

For those who pose the question of selecting goals in terms of "what should the United States want?" the answer is found in defending and pursuing the American **national interest**, the fundamental goals and objectives of a country's foreign policy. The term *national interest* is unmatched in its emotional impact and ability to shape a foreign policy debate. It conveys a sense of urgency, eminent threat, and higher purpose. All other foreign policy objectives pale in comparison to those promoting the national interest. It is advanced with great certainty and talked about as if there could be no doubt as to its meaning.

In fact, students of world politics have struggled with little success to give concrete meaning to the term *national interest*. They have turned to various formulations in an effort to separate threats and problems into different categories. Some employ a pyramid in which core national interest problems are found at its apex and are few in number. Beneath it are found larger numbers of long-range societal goals and goals that advance the interests of specific groups within a country. Others using the same logic divide foreign policy problems into three categories: "A" list threats are those that pose a direct and immediate challenge to U.S. survival. "B" list threats involve challenges to immediate U.S. interests but not to U.S. survival. "C" list threats indirectly affect U.S. national interest but are not immediate or direct.

The implication of both frameworks is the same. Policy makers need to concentrate resources on addressing the most important foreign policy issues. If they do not, and if they concentrate on lower-ranking issues or those on the B and C lists, they risk jeopardizing the U.S. national interest. The ever-present danger is that not enough resources will be available to successfully deal with a core or A list threat should it appear. Having said this, not all of those interested in foreign policy problems place them in the same category. When the Central Intelligence Agency (CIA) began issuing intelligence reports on the condition of the global environment, it was criticized by some for paying too much attention to a relatively unimportant problem.

A dissenting approach to defining the national interest argues that it is not possible to rank order foreign policy goals in some abstract fashion where by definition some are more important than others. They argue that the national interest should be defined by a country's actions. If it is willing to allocate significant resources to a problem, then solving that problem is in the national interest.

## COSTS

Foreign policy comes with a price tag. This is true whether we are dealing with **declaratory policy** or **action policy**. The former consists of proclamations that state the intent of the United States to pursue a line of action but in and of themselves do not produce action. Pledges to promote peace in the Middle East, end poverty in Africa, and protect the global environment are prominent examples of declaratory policy. Action policy is what the United States actually does. It is what we tend to think of when we study U.S. foreign policy: sending troops to Iraq, placing an economic embargo on Iran, and refusing to participate in the Kyoto Protocol on protecting the environment.

Both are important to the conduct of U.S. foreign policy. The positive and negative consequences of actions are intuitively clear. They can solve problems or make them worse. Declaratory policy has the same effect. This point was recognized by the Nobel committee when it awarded President Obama the Nobel Peace Prize in 2009, singling out his speeches in Prague and Cairo for special mention as evidence of his efforts to strengthen international diplomacy and cooperation among peoples.

The perennial danger exists that declaratory and action policies will be out of sync with one another, creating what some refer to as the "say–do" problem.[5] Declaratory policy establishes and raises expectations about what the United States will do. When peace does not come to the Middle East, poverty continues to plague Africa, or the global environment continues to worsen, the United States loses legitimacy and respect. This potentially makes it more difficult to get other nations to believe United States's rhetoric in the future and raises the cost to the United States in conducting its foreign policy, as others adopt a wait-and-see attitude or demand side payments such as increased foreign aid from it to act. The costs of action policy are often very clear. They can be measured in very concrete ways: lives lost, money spent, and jobs lost. Spanning from 1965 to 1975 the Vietnam War cost an estimated $111 billion ($686 billion in 2008 dollars). Over 58,000 U.S. soldiers lost their lives in the war, as did 3–4 million Vietnamese. From 2001, when China joined the World Trade Organization with the support of the United States, through 2007, Florida estimates it lost 100,00 jobs due to firms moving their operations to China.

Here we wish to introduce two additional dimensions of the cost problem that need to be taken into account when looking at action policy. The first is **opportunity cost**. Resources devoted to one foreign policy problem cannot be used on another or on domestic problems. In a world where resources are plentiful such dilemma does not exist. The reality, however, is quite different. Not only are resources not unlimited but the foreign and domestic policy goals which policy makers may decide to pursue have no natural limit. A fear has been raised that the global financial crisis of 2008 will result in a resource shortfall that will stop the United States and other Western powers from undertaking major foreign policy initiatives that are needed to bring stability back to the international system. Instead they will address domestic concerns first or pursue "band-aid" policies to deal with serious problems.

The difference between the resources available to pursue goals (power) and the list of goals being pursued is often referred to as **"the Lippmann Gap"** in honor of columnist Walter Lippmann, who in 1947 observed that a recurring problem in American foreign policy was an imbalance between American power and the goals it sought.[6] When this occurred he found American foreign policy to be mired in domestic conflict and ineffectual abroad. Most notably conflicts were not adequately prepared for, and peace agreements were too hastily constructed.

The second additional dimension to the cost problem is that policies have unintended consequences. **Blowback** is the term commonly used to capture the essence of this phenomenon.[7] It was first used by the CIA to characterize problems that came about as a result of covert action programs. In the eyes of some, we have already seen blowback in the war against terrorism. They see the 1988 bombing of Pan Am Flight 103 over Lockerbie, Scotland, which killed 270 people, as retaliation for President Ronald Reagan's bombing of Libya in 1986, which killed President Qaddafi's stepdaughter. Others see blowback in the surge of terrorism in Iraq following the ouster of Saddam Hussein. Rather than further weaken international terrorism, it made Iraq a lightning rod attracting terrorists to it.

# BUILDING CONSENSUS

In order to succeed a foreign policy must be supported by the American public. American policy makers have long recognized this reality. Dean Acheson, who served as secretary of state from 1949 to 1953, once commented that 80 percent of the job of conducting foreign policy was managing one's domestic ability to make policy.[8] The term long used to convey this sense of support was **bipartisanship**. It referred to the ability of both Democrats and Republicans to unite behind a course of action. Unity at home is seen as sending a message to adversaries that they cannot "wait out" a president in hopes of getting a better deal with his successor or to try and appeal to Congress to undercut his foreign policy. An ongoing point of debate in U.S. foreign policy is the question of how normal or natural bipartisanship is. Should we be worried when the American public is divided over how to conduct foreign policy, or is the periodic lack of consensus to be expected? Richard Holbrooke, who served as U.S. ambassador to the United Nations, authored the Dayton Peace Agreement in the Balkans, and is Obama's representative to the Middle East peace process, wrote prior to the 2008 election that the core challenge of the next president "will be nothing less than to re-create a sense of national purpose."[9]

As noted earlier, a key instrument that presidents and others have used to build public support for foreign policies is to invoke the national interest. While it may not dictate a specific course of action, the concept of national interest is a powerful political symbol that is capable of controlling the language of U.S. foreign policy—setting its reference points, assumptions, and symbols—and, in the process, steering it in a particular direction by building support for one policy option and placing opponents on the defensive.[10] The George W. Bush administration recognized this truth as it moved quickly to define the terrorist attacks on the World Trade Center and Pentagon as acts of war rather than criminal acts.

It is important to note that the concept of national interest can not only help steer foreign policy in a certain direction but also trap policy makers into lines of action. Having justified a course of action as being in the national interest, it is politically difficult to do an about-face and declare that this is no longer the case. Typically, in these cases we find policy makers insisting that their policy is correct but altering the definition of the national interest used as a justification. In March 2003, President George W. Bush stated that the purpose of the Iraq War was "to disarm Iraq, free its people and defense [sic] the world from grave danger [of weapons of mass destruction]." In June 2005, he characterized the Iraq War as one of quarantining terrorist groups that might otherwise attack the United States. In his 2006 State of the Union address he spoke of Iraq in the broader context of a U.S. mission to end tyranny and light the flame of freedom. The following year, in seeking to bolster public support for his foreign policy in Iraq and against terrorism, Bush compared America's enemies to communists, asserting: "Like the communists, the terrorists and radicals who have attacked our nation are followers of a murderous ideology that despises freedom, crushes dissent, has expansionist ambitions, and pursues totalitarian aims."[11]

The excessive focus on Iraq began to trouble Secretary of State Rice and others in Bush's second term, and they sought to get the president to tone down his rhetoric. They feared that by making Iraq the "end-all, be-all test" of American strength, U.S. standing and interests in other parts of the world were being harmed.[12]

## SELECTING A POLICY INSTRUMENT

Policy makers must decide not only what goals to pursue but also how to pursue them. A prime consideration to be kept in mind in selecting a policy instrument is the context in which it will operate. Economic strategies that worked well in an era when the United States was a hegemonic or predominant economic power may prove less useful in an era of economic decline or parity. Similarly, policy tools that were effective in a Cold War international system will not necessarily be as effective in a post–Cold War system.

### Hard Power and Soft Power

Looked at in narrow terms policy makers choose between miliary, economic, diplomatic, and covert action policy tools. Looked at more broadly, the choice is between employing hard or soft power (or some mixture of the two) in carrying out foreign policy. Secretary of Defense Robert Gates, who has served in both the George W. Bush and Obama administrations, is a strong advocate of **soft power** and has warned of the dangers of the "creeping militarization" of U.S foreign policy.[13] Observing that "we cannot kill our way to victory," Gates and others point with concern to the discrepency between the size of the Defense Department and other foreign policy agencies. The State Department has 6,000 Foreign Service officers, less than the number needed to staff an aircraft carrier battle group. In 2009 the Defense Department requested a $515 billion budget. The State Department, the Agency for International Development, and related agencies collectively sought a total of $39.5 billion.

**Hard power** is coercive power. It is the traditional means by which states protected and advanced their national interests. While most often employed against an enemy hard power can also be used against a reluctant ally. Hard power is designed to force or compel another state to act in a prescribed fashion. As much as possible it tries to limit the range of choice open to it so that it will act in accordance with U.S. wishes. Hard power is most often associated with military power, but virtually all instruments of foreign policy can be employed in this fashion.

Soft power is the power to influence and persuade. It is rooted in the power of attraction seeking to convince states to willingly identify with the United States and support the U.S. position. Domination is replaced by cooperation. Examples would include using the military for disaster and humanitarian relief efforts, providing economic and medical assistance to those in need, and strengthening democratic institutions and civil society in states making the transition to democracy. In each of these cases, a reservoir of goodwill is created, which the United States can draw upon in carrying out its foreign policy. A 2008 study of Asian public attitudes revealed the considerable strength the United States has in soft power. It ranked first in the responses of Japanese, South Koreans, and Chinese and second according to Vietnamese and Indonesians.[14]

Observers of U.S. foreign policy are divided as to whether hard power or soft power is preferable. Soft power supporters note that while hard military power can defeat an enemy it cannot produce peace. Hard power supporters note that soft power is just as difficult to use. Many of the resources associated with it, such as the appeal of American values and American democracy, are beyond the control of policy makers and not easily mobilized in support of the United States. Hard power places limits on what the United States can do. If it acts—or speaks—in contradiction to these values, soft power will be of little use.

## Grand Strategy

No matter how wisely or carefully they are chosen, selecting a set of foreign policy instruments in and of itself will not result in a successful foreign policy. It is also necessary to devise an overall course of action that brings these policy instruments together into a unified and coherent whole. **Grand strategy** is the lynchpin that unites goals and tactics. Grand strategy differs from military strategy or diplomatic strategy by its scope. Where they are concerned with the effective use of hard power or soft power, grand strategy is concerned with a governmentwide approach that brings together all elements of power.

Constructing an effectivce grand strategy is not an easy task. The Rand Corporation in a 2008 study of over 600 terrorist movements concluded that in spite of its emotional appeal, the Bush administration's decision to cast the struggle against terrorism as a war was a mistake. Doing so suggested that a battlefield solution existed and gave warrior status to the terrorists.The report's authors argued that a strategy that emphasized police work and law enforcement activities was preferable.[15] The administration fared little better in constructing a strategy for postwar Iraq. In 2005 Secretary of State Rice told the Senate Foreign Relations Committee that the U.S. strategy in Iraq was "clear, hold, and build." To others, including General George Casey, who was the Commanding General in Iraq at the time, it was not a strategy and amounted to little more than a bumper sticker.[16]

Some believe that we should not try and construct a grand strategy. Supporters of this perspective argue it is more appropriate to proceed on a case-by-case method in which pragmatism rather than broad principles rule. Still others believe it cannot be done. Several factors contribute to this most pessimistic view.[17] One limitation on the effectiveness of strategy is our incomplete knowledge of cause and effect and lack of control over key variables when trying to manipulate the course of international events. In this view we do not understand democratization, terrorism, or other challenges well enough to formulate overarching grand strategies to deal with them. A second limitation is found in the organizational and political barriers one encounters in trying to implement grand strategy. Iraq is the most recent example of the inefficiencies and problems that have arisen as the State Department, Defense Department, and others have tried to coordinate their plans. Because of this, grand strategy on paper always seems to fall short of grand strategy as put into practice. Third, there are perceptual and psychological barriers to how accurately policy makers see the world and understand their own motives. In a conversation about the changing balance of power in the Middle East following the Iraq War, President Bush spoke of the United States having "freedom hegemony" in the region, a condition many critics of U.S. policy in other countries would characterize quite differently.[18] Still, most believe that there is little choice but to try and craft grand strategies if for no other reason than it forces us to look at the big picture and ask big questions.

One prominent planning tool used by the military to formulate strategy is the Quadrennial Defense Review (QDR). The first QDR was mandated by Congress in 1996 following the end of the Cold War. Today the State Department, intelligence agencies, and other government offices involved in foreign policy also conduct their own QDRs as part of a broader effort to formulate national security policy.

## HISTORICAL LESSON

### The Monroe Doctrine

In the early 1820s the United States faced a new challenge for which it needed a foreign policy. Napoleon had been defeated and the conservative states of Europe were successfully putting down a series of revolutions in southern Europe. The possibility now presented itself that France and Spain together might try to reestablish their influence in the Western Hemisphere, where states throughout Central and South America had taken advantage of the conflict in Europe to declare their independence.

In August 1823 the British contacted the U.S. Minister to Great Britain and suggested a joint American–British declaration intended to prevent France from interfering into the affairs of these new democracies or to gain territory in the Americas through conquest or cession. The U.S. Minister welcomed the idea, but lacking the authority to accept the British proposal he sent it on to Washington.

President James Monroe was inclined to accept the British offer. He consulted with former presidents James Madison and Thomas Jefferson, both of whom supported it. Secretary of State John Quincy Adams opposed the idea. He felt that the possibility of a European intervention into Latin America was remote. Adams was also confident that if France and Spain tried to do so, Great Britain would be forced to counter it with or without an agreement with the United States. Adams was also concerned that language in the proposed statement could also be interpreted to mean the United States had to abandon hope of acquiring Texas, California, and Cuba. Finally, Adams resisted the idea of playing a secondary role to Great Britain in a matter involving the defense of the Western Hemisphere.

Adams' position carried the day, and the question now became how to proceed with a unilateral American statement. Adams preferred a series of diplomatic notes. Monroe preferred including it in his regular message to Congress. The first draft presented to the cabinet in November 1823 was defiant in tone. Adams objected and succeeded in having the speech toned down substantially.

As presented to Congress on December 2, 1823, the Monroe Doctrine had three parts. The first part was primarily directed at Russia and warned it not to try and establish a colonial presence in North America by moving down southward from Russian Alaska. In the next section Monroe warned the European monarchies that the United States would view "any attempt on their part to extend their system to any portion of this hemisphere as dangerous to our peace and safety." He continued, "we could not view any interposition for the purpose of oppressing them, or controlling in any other manner their destiny . . . in any other light as the manifestation of an unfriendly disposition toward the United States." Monroe concluded that the policy of the United States continued to be one of not interfering in the internal concerns of any European power.

Monroe's pronouncement met with widespread approval within the United States, although some questioned his positioning of the United States as protector of newly established democracies and feared that this position would involve the United States in foreign conflicts. European powers reacted with displeasure, terming it arrogant and blustering. Great Britain reacted with a mixture of support and muted anger. It knew that it would be the British navy and not the U.S. navy or army that would guarantee the independence of the former Spanish colonies. For their part the newly independent states of Latin America responded with caution. They too recognized the importance of the British navy. Moreover, when Colombia, Brazil, and Mexico proposed an alliance with the United States based on Monroe's address, they were turned down.

Some 80 years later in December 1904 President Theodore Roosevelt added what came to be known as the Roosevelt Corollary to the Monroe Doctrine. It stated that it was now necessary for the United States to act as a hemispheric policeman punishing wrongdoing and establishing domestic order when governments were incapable of doing so. Roosevelt was moved to announce his Corollary because European states were becoming angry with Latin American states for their failure to pay debts owed to them and began to use force to obtain payment. Roosevelt at first approved of their plans but then became concerned with the precedent they set.

### Applying the Lesson

1. Some argue that the Bush Doctrine is based on the Monroe Doctrine and turns it into a global document. Do you agree or disagree?
2. Is the original Monroe Doctrine or the Roosevelt Corollary most important for U.S. foreign policy today?
3. Which foreign policy problem was more difficult to create a response to, that faced by Condoleezza Rice or that faced by James Monroe? ■

## PRESIDENTIAL FOREIGN POLICY DOCTRINES

The earliest grand strategy in American diplomatic history was put forward in President George Washington's Farewell Address, when he called for avoiding entanglement in foreign alliances. It provided the conceptual foundation for a policy of isolationism that in various forms was embraced by many of his successors. The Monroe Doctrine, calling for a policy of activism and domination in Latin America and abstention in European affairs, Manifest Destiny, or a policy of continental expansion, and the Open Door, as a strategy for establishing an American presence in Asia, are other examples of notable early American foreign policy grand strategies.

Beginning with the earliest years of the Cold War, U.S. foreign policy grand strategy has come to be associated with a series of presidential doctrines that set forward the goals and objectives of U.S. foreign policy and the means that would be used to achieve them. In Box 1.1 we highlight five doctrines that have been particularly important for signaling shifts in the agenda of U.S. foreign policy. We discuss them in more detail below and then turn to the challenge of evaluating foreign policy.

### The Truman Doctrine

On March 12, 1947, in a speech to a special joint session of Congress, President Harry S. Truman asked for $400 million for economic assistance to Greece and Turkey to help them resist Soviet-inspired aggression. In making his request, he asserted that "it must be the policy of the United States to support free peoples who are resisting attempted subjugation by armed minorities or outside pressures." Prior to the speech, Secretary of State Dean Acheson met with congressional leaders and outlined the need for action, citing "a highly likely Soviet breakthrough" in Greece and the danger of "infection" elsewhere by this "eager and ruthless opponent." Congressional leaders agreed to support the request provided Truman made his case to the full Congress and the American people.

Greece was involved in a civil war that pitted a pro-British government against leftist rebels. A truce signed in 1945 unraveled in 1946 when the Greek government attempted to eliminate its political opposition. Corruption, inefficiency, and brutality were hallmarks of this regime, and the communist-controlled opposition National Liberation Front had many supporters. Turkey was involved in an ongoing dispute with the Soviet Union over control of the Dardanelles Straits. These straits controlled access to the Black Sea. From the Soviet point of view, unfettered transit through the Dardanelles to the Mediterranean was crucial to its ability to act as a Great Power. At the same time, the Dardanelles served as an entry point for hostile naval forces to enter the Black Sea. During World War II, Turkey had permitted German naval forces to do so, and the Soviet Union felt its security threatened. Stalin now insisted on international control over the straits, a demand that Turkey interpreted as a threat to its national sovereignty.

## Box 1.1  SELECTED PRESIDENTIAL FOREIGN POLICY DOCTRINES

### The Truman Doctrine

The gravity of the situation which confronts the world today necessitates my appearance before a joint session of the Congress. The foreign policy and national security of this country are involved. One aspect of the present situation, which I wish to present to you at this time for your consideration and decision, concerns Greece and Turkey. . . . The United States has received from the Greek government an urgent appeal for financial and economic assistance. . . . The very existence of the Greek state is today threatened by the terrorist activities of several thousand armed men, led by Communists. . . . The United States must supply that assistance. . . . There is no other country to which democratic Greece can turn. . . . The future of Turkey as an independent and economically sound state is clearly no less important to freedom-loving peoples of the world. . . . [its] integrity is essential to the preservation of order in the Middle East. . . . I am fully aware of the broad implications involved if the United States extends assistance to Greece and Turkey. . . . One of the primary objectives of the foreign policy of the United States is the creation of conditions in which we and other nations will be able to work out a way of life free from coercion. . . . I believe that it must be the policy of the United States to support free people who are resisting attempted subjugation by armed minorities or outside pressures. I believe that we must assist free people to work out their own destinies in their own way. . . . If we falter in our leadership, we may endanger the peace of the world—and we shall surely endanger the welfare of our own nation. . . .

Address before a joint session of Congress, March 17, 1947

### The Nixon Doctrine

A nation cannot remain great if it betrays its allies and lets down its friends. Our defeat and humiliation in South Vietnam without question would promote recklessness in the councils of those great powers who have yet to abandon their goals of world conquest. . . . I laid down in Guam three principles as guidelines for future American foreign policy toward Asia. First, the United States will keep its treaty –commitments. Second, we shall provide a shield if a nuclear power threatens the freedom of a nation allied with us or of a nation whose survival we consider essential to our security. Third, in case involving other types of aggression, we shall furnish military and economic assistance when requested in accordance with our treaty commitments. We shall look to the nation directly threatened to assume primary responsibility of providing the manpower for its defense. . . . The defense of freedom is everybody's business, not just America's business. . . .

President Nixon's address to the nation, November 3, 1969

### The Carter Doctrine

The 1980s have been born in turmoil strife, and change. This is a time of challenge to our interest and our values and it's a time that tests our wisdom and our skills. . . . I am determined that the United States will remain the strongest of all nations,

*(Continued)*

*(Continued)*

but our power will never be used to initiate a threat to the security of any nation or to the rights of any human being. We seek to be and to remain secure—a nation at peace in a stable world. But to be secure we must face the world as it is. . . . The region which is now threatened by Soviet troops in Afghanistan is of great strategic importance. . . . Let our position be absolutely clear: an attempt by any outside force to gain control of the Persian Gulf region will be regarded as an assault on the vital interests of the United States of America, and such an assault will be repelled by any means necessary, including military force. . . .

State of the Union address, January 23, 1980

### The Reagan Doctrine

We must stand by all our democratic allies. And we must not break faith with those who are risking their lives—on every continent from Afghanistan to Nicaragua—to defy Soviet-supported aggression and secure rights which have been ours from birth. . . . The U.S. must rebuild the credibility of our commitment to resist Soviet encroachment on U.S. interests and those of its allies and friends, and to support effectively those Third World states that are willing to resist Soviet pressures or oppose Soviet initiatives hostile to the United States, or are special targets of Soviet policy.

Reagan Doctrine, U.S. Department of State

### The Bush Doctrine

Today, at the start of a new century, we are again engaged in a war unlike any our nation has fought before—and today like Americans in Truman's day, we are laying the foundations for victory. The enemies we face are different in many ways from the enemy we faced in the Cold War. In the Cold War, we deterred Soviet aggression through a policy of mutually assured destruction. . . . The terrorists have no borders to protect, or capital to defend. They cannot be deterred—but they will be defeated. . . . In this new war we have to set a clear doctrine. . . . America will not wait to be attacked again. We will confront threats before they fully materialize. We will stay on the offense against the terrorists, fighting them abroad so that we do not have to face them at home. . . . The security of our nation depends on the advance of liberty in other nations. . . . So we are pursuing a forward strategy of freedom in the Middle East. I believe the desire for liberty is universal, and by standing with democratic reformers across a troubled region we will extend freedom to millions who have not known it—and lay the foundation of peace for generations to come. . . .

Commencement address at the United States Military Academy at West Point, May 27, 2006 ■

Truman's speech is widely seen as the equivalent to a U.S. declaration of Cold War against the Soviet Union. It firmly rejected the pre–World War II U.S. foreign policy of isolationism and provided a rationale for U.S. activism in world affairs by declaring that the world was "divided between two antithetical ways of life: one based on freedom, another on coercion" and that "we shall not realize our objectives . . . unless we are willing to help free peoples to maintain their free institutions and their national integrity." The Truman Doctrine, as the contents of this speech came to be known, also identified a universal enemy with its references to aggression by "totalitarian regimes." This phrase was applied almost exclusively to the Soviet Union and its allies.

Although the Truman Doctrine did not specify a set of actions to be taken in this struggle to protect free peoples around the world, its implementation quickly came to center on two concepts: containment and deterrence. Central to both the concepts was a status quo orientation to the events in the world. U.S. foreign policy would not actively seek to roll back the Iron Curtain so much as it would work to stop the further expansion of the Soviet Union and its sphere of influence. Containment became identified with three sets of policies. The first was encircling the Soviet Union and its allies in a ring of alliances and bilateral security agreements that would contain it. The most significant alliances were the NATO in Europe, the Central Treaty Organization (CENTO) in the Middle East, and the Southeast Asia Treaty Organization (SEATO) in Southeast Asia. Important bilateral agreements were signed with Japan, the Philippines, and South Korea. Covert military action was a second important instrument of containment. It was directed at key countries that were being threatened by communist takeovers or had just fallen victim to them, such as Iran, Guatemala, Cuba, and Indonesia. Finally, foreign aid was used to help assure the loyalty and support of key governments and to promote economic prosperity as a way to dampen the appeal of communism. Deterrence came to be associated with nuclear weapons and the recognition that they were no longer effective instruments of war. Instead, their primary purpose was to stop conflicts from erupting to reach the highest levels of violence.

## The Nixon Doctrine

The logic of containment dictated a U.S. military presence in South Vietnam. The process began in the early 1950s, when Truman began to provide financial support to the French effort to challenge Ho Chi Minh for political control of its former colony. Under President Dwight Eisenhower, American military advisors began to arrive in South Vietnam in large numbers, and then President Lyndon Johnson sent American combat troops to Vietnam and began a policy of bombing North Vietnam. The inability of American and South Vietnamese forces to secure victory and steadily mounting American casualties gave birth to an antiwar movement in the United States that eventually led Johnson to announce in March 1968 that he would not seek reelection to the presidency. Richard Nixon was elected president.

The Nixon Doctrine was part of an attempt by President Richard Nixon to formulate a policy that would allow the United States to remain the dominant power in the international system after Vietnam but would not require that it send troops abroad to contain the spread of communism. First announced in 1969 and then elaborated in his 1971 foreign policy report to Congress, the Nixon Doctrine stated that the United States would help free countries defend themselves, but that these countries must provide for their own military defense, with the United States providing both military and economic assistance. In short, there would be no more Vietnams.

In addition to the Nixon Doctrine, the Nixon administration pursued two other initiatives as part of its strategy to redirect American foreign policy. The most narrowly constructed was *Vietnamization,* which sought to turn over responsibility for defending South Vietnam to the South Vietnamese. In an effort to buy sufficient time for Vietnamization to work, Nixon ordered the invasion of Cambodia and Laos in order to eliminate communist sanctuaries there. That strategy failed when, in spring 1972, North Vietnamese forces attacked across the 17th Parallel into the South, forcing Nixon to "re-Americanize" the war. The second and more broadly conceived policy initiative was détente. It sought to engage the Soviet Union and China in a dialogue that would transform their relationship with the United States from one of competition and open distrust to one of limited cooperation and muted conflict. It thus marked a significant step away from a military-oriented and confrontational approach to containment. The most significant accomplishments of détente with regard to American dealings with its former adversaries were the opening to China, which led to the normalization of relations in 1979 in the Carter administration, and the signing of Strategic Arms Limitation Talks (SALT) arms control agreements with the Soviet Union.

A major consequence of the Nixon Doctrine was a massive increase in the level of arms transfers to regional powers, which Nixon hoped would serve as surrogate powers to contain the spread of communism. Providing allies with military aid was seen as necessary because, while détente reduced the level of tension between the United States and the Soviet Union, it did not do away with the fact that they were the world's two superpowers and were still engaged in competition for global influence. Indonesia, the Philippines, Saudi Arabia, Iran, Pakistan, and South Korea became prime recipients of this aid. A particularly troubling situation developed in the Middle East. The rapid increase in oil prices brought on by the Organization of Petroleum Exporting Countries (OPEC) allowed these states to purchase weapons rather than receive them as foreign aid. This resulted in ever-more sophisticated weapons flowing into the region. The close political identification between these regimes and the United States that accompanied these arms transfers became an important factor in the downfall of the Shah of Iran and the development of anti-American sentiment elsewhere. The Nixon administration did not remain totally faithful to the spirit of the Nixon Doctrine. Along with the invasions of Cambodia and Laos, it orchestrated a covert action program against popularly elected Chilean President Salvadore Allende that was designed to remove him from power.

## The Carter Doctrine

The Carter Doctrine is the name given to the policy announced by President Jimmy Carter in response to the Soviet Union's December 1979 invasion of Afghanistan. Carter stated that the United States would treat an "attempt by any outside force to gain control of the Persian Gulf region as an assault on the vital interests of the United States and such force will be repelled by any means necessary, including military force."

The Carter Doctrine represented a virtual about-face for Carter's foreign policy toward the Soviet Union. Carter had campaigned on a platform that rejected power politics and promised to replace it with one that emphasized human rights and morality. He quickly moved to negotiate a new Panama Canal Treaty, and in September 1977 two treaties were signed that would transfer sovereignty over the canal to Panama on January 1, 2000. The following year, in September 1978, Carter arranged for a summit conference at the presidential retreat at Camp David between Israeli Prime Minister Menachem Begin and Egyptian President Anwar Sadat, at which both leaders agreed to a "just, comprehensive and durable settlement for the Middle East conflict."

The inevitable consequence of Carter's foreign policy was to de-emphasize the importance of the Soviet Union to U.S. foreign policy and to draw attention to how the Soviet Union treated its citizens. Both moves offended Soviet leaders, who continued to view world politics through a prism that emphasized the importance of power politics and traditional security concerns. They responded by rejecting Carter's efforts to abandon the Vladivostok Accords as the basis for a SALT II arms control agreement. This agreement had been negotiated with the Ford administration, and Carter wished to jettison it in favor of deeper reductions in each side's nuclear inventory, a move that Soviet leaders saw as a veiled effort to reestablish American nuclear superiority. Only after two-and-one-half years of difficult negotiations was a SALT II agreement reached at a meeting between Carter and Soviet leader Leonid Brezhnev in Vienna in 1979. That agreement, already controversial, was never voted on by the Senate. Carter withdrew it from consideration because of the Soviet invasion of Afghanistan.

A 1973 coup d'état deposed the king of Afghanistan. Soon thereafter the new government came under attack from Maoist and pro-Soviet factions of the Marxist People's Democratic Party. In April 1978 the pro-Marxist wing took control of the government and began to impose a series of radical social and economic reforms. In September 1979 another rival Maoist group seized power and set out on a path of even more radical social reforms. Throughout this time the Soviet Union had been urging caution while still supplying the new communist government with military weapons. In December 1999, faced with a chaotic situation in Afghanistan and the possible triumph of opposition Islamic forces that were resisting these reforms, the Soviet Union sent an invasion force of over 50,000 soldiers into Afghanistan and placed exiled pro-Soviet Communist Party leader Babrack Karmal in power.

The Soviet action caught the Carter administration off guard and called into question the wisdom of Carter's foreign policy agenda. As part of his response, Carter requested a 5 percent increase in annual defense spending (up from the 3 percent increase he had been requesting) and expanded the American naval and air presence in the Persian Gulf. Though this action was generally applauded, some commentators criticized Carter's response as over-reacting and motivated by domestic political concerns. They argued that while the Soviet invasion of Afghanistan was deplorable, it did not represent a calculated Soviet move to control the Persian Gulf. This debate, however, was soon overshadowed by the Iranian hostage crisis and the Carter administration's inability to secure the release of the Americans taken hostage in the American Embassy.

With only a slight period of interruption, Iran had been ruled since 1941 by one of the United States's most loyal Third World allies, Mohammed Reza Shah Pahlavi. That interruption came in 1953, when the Shah was forced into exile as Iranian nationalists seized power. He was restored to the throne largely through the efforts of a CIA-inspired coup. Over time the corruption and repression of the Shah's rule reached a point at which he became dependent on the military and his ruthless secret police, the SAVAK, to stay in power. Even this proved insufficient as the 1970s drew to a close and Iranians took to the streets demanding reform. After initially backing the Shah, the Carter administration unsuccessfully urged him to negotiate with his opponents. The most important opposition leader was Ayatollah Khomeini, who was in exile in France. Khomeini returned to Iran on January 31, 1980, to assume control of the government. The Shah had left Iran in the middle of the month, paving the way for Khomeini's return. Initially the Carter administration had denied the Shah entry into the United States for fear of provoking a violent reaction in Iran, but in October, at the urging of Henry Kissinger, David Rockefeller, and National Security Advisor Zbigniew Brzezinski and over the objections of the embassy in Tehran, the Carter administration changed its policy on the grounds that the Shah required potentially life-saving medical care. Two weeks later the American embassy in Tehran, Iran, was seized and hostages taken. Demands were issued for the return of the Shah to stand trial in Iran. Neither economic sanctions nor a (failed) military rescue mission was able to secure the release of the hostages. They would not be freed until after Ronald Reagan's inauguration, spending 444 days in captivity.

## The Reagan Doctrine

The outlines of President Reagan's foreign policy were well in place by the time what became known as the Reagan Doctrine was put forward in his February 1985 State of the Union address. Unlike Nixon and Carter, for most of his presidency, Reagan saw the Soviet Union as a state to be challenged and not worked with. Early in his administration he referred to the Soviet Union as an "evil empire," charging that "the only morality they recognize is what will further their cause; meaning they reserve unto themselves the right to commit any crime, to lie, to cheat." A perquisite for dealing effectively with such a state was a major buildup of American military strength and a toughened stance toward arms control. To these ends, Reagan called for a $16 billion increase in defense spending over five years, the deployment of the MX missile system, the renewed production of poison gas, the development of the neutron bomb, and the beginning of a long-term research plan, the Strategic Defense Initiative ("Star Wars"), to build a missile defense system. On arms control, his administration went public with a series of accusations of Soviet arms control cheating.

In his 1985 State of the Union speech, Reagan asserted, "We must not break faith with those who are risking their lives—on every continent from Afghanistan to Nicaragua—to defy Soviet aggression and secure rights which have been ours from birth. Support of freedom fighters is self-defense." By speaking in this manner, Reagan signaled an important shift in his foreign policy from that of his predecessors. The United States would now do more than contain the spread of communism; it would also work actively to remove communists and their allies from power. In fact, the Reagan administration was already doing so.

Reagan saw Central America as a major front in the conflict between the United States and Soviet Union. His administration considered El Salvador a textbook case of communist aggression. Large-scale fighting had begun there in 1979 when reform-minded elements of the El Salvador military seized power and installed Jose Durate as president. This set off a wave of right-wing violence targeting radical and reformist political groups. Centrist and leftist forces united to form the Revolutionary Democratic Front to oppose Durate, who was unable to control this rising tide of violence. The Reagan administration contended that a large part of the problem in El Salvador was due to Russian and Cuban military support for leftist rebel forces, which was being funneled through Nicaragua. In a move to cut off the supply of weapons, Reagan signed a presidential finding in March 1981 authorizing the CIA to organize and fund moderate opponents of the Sandinista Nicaraguan government. These forces became known as the Contras.

The administration's unwavering support for the Contras became one of the most controversial features of its foreign policy. Where Reagan characterized the Contras as the "moral equivalent of the founding fathers," human rights groups complained at length about their brutality. In 1984, Congress cut off funding for the Contras. In an effort to circumvent this ban the Reagan administration undertook a failed secret initiative that became known as the Iran–Contra Affair. It proposed that American weapons intended for Israel would be sold to Iran. Israel would receive new weapons. In return, Iran would help secure the release of American hostages in Lebanon. Money from the weapons sales would be used to fund the Contras.

The Reagan administration was also already deeply involved in Afghanistan by 1985. The original Soviet invasion plan called for the Afghan army to pacify the Afghan population. Wholesale defections in the Afghan army negated this strategy and required the introduction of large numbers of Soviet forces, which had to bear the responsibility of fighting the Afghan guerrillas or Mujahadin. They proved to be a formidable fighting force, not only because of their tenacity but also because of the American aid they received. In 1984 the Reagan administration was underwriting the Mujahadin to the tune of $120 million. By 1987 this figure had increased to $630 million, bringing the total value of U.S. military aid to that point to $2.1 billion. The success achieved by the Reagan administration in tying down the Soviet Union in Afghanistan was not without its long-term costs, however. This policy resulted in a large amount of U.S. arms flowing into the hands of Afghan groups that combined forces with the Taliban-led government that came into power after the Soviet Union left and were later used against U.S.-supported interests.

Near the end of his administration, Ronald Reagan did a seeming about-face in his foreign policy. He and Soviet leader Mikhail Gorbachev became regular partners at summit conferences, meeting five times during Reagan's last term. It was their second summit at Reykjavik, Iceland, that provoked the most controversy. Given insufficient preparation, the Reagan administration was caught off guard by Gorbachev's proposal that both sides eliminate all offensive strategic nuclear weapons. Reagan accepted the proposal, only to back off later because of his personal attachment to the Star Wars program.

## THE BUSH DOCTRINE

Although the Bush Doctrine first appeared as a unified statement in the September 2002 *National Security Strategy of the United States of America,* its key themes were already visible by then.[19] Speaking to a joint session of Congress following the 9/11 terrorist attacks, President George W. Bush stated that the United States "would make no distinction between the terrorists who committed these acts and those who harbor them" and that "we will pursue nations that provide aid or safe haven to terrorism. Every nation, in every region, now has a decision to make. Either you are with us or you are with the terrorists." In a June 2002 speech to the graduating class at West Point, Bush stated, "Our security will require all Americans to be forward-looking and resolute, to be ready for preemptive action when necessary to defend our liberty and to defend our lives." He also asserted that "the gravest danger to freedom lies in the crossroads of radicalism and technology." To these observations the *National Security Strategy* added, "We cannot let our enemies strike first," that the United States will use its power to encourage free and open societies, and that it will never allow its military supremacy to be challenged.

The Bush Doctrine provided the intellectual framework for launching the Global War on Terrorism, including the overthrow of the Taliban government in Afghanistan and the Iraq War. It also provided the context for identifying Iran, Iraq, and North Korea as an "axis of evil" in Bush's January 2002 State of the Union address. Air strikes on Taliban military targets and terrorist facilities in Afghanistan began on October 7, 2001. Ground forces were supplied largely by the Northern Alliance, a coalition group that opposed Taliban rule and who were aided by the CIA. The first U.S. Special Forces entered Afghanistan on October 19. Conventional forces arrived on November 25, and the last Taliban stronghold fell on December 16. Osama bin Laden, whose group al Qaeda was held responsible for the 9/11 attacks, remained at large. By year end a multiethnic interim government led by Hamid Karzai was in place.

U.S. forces invaded Iraq on March 20, 2003. The months leading to the invasion were marked by a steady buildup of U.S. forces in the region and diplomacy at the United Nations, where the Bush administration sought to obtain UN support for removing Saddam Hussein from power. Central to the administration's argument was Iraq's possession of weapons of mass destruction. In the end, the United Nations refused to support the war, with Security Council members France, Germany, and Russia voting no and China abstaining. At this point the Bush administration issued a 48-hour ultimatum to Saddam Hussein to leave Iraq. Baghdad fell on April 9, and on May 1 President Bush declared an end to major combat operations. Operation Iraqi Freedom was based on the principle of relying on rapidly advancing forces to overwhelm the Iraqi military. Although this strategy brought about a swift military victory, it also created problems for the administration in the form of an unstable post–Saddam Hussein Iraq.

Expecting to be greeted as liberators, U.S. forces soon came to be viewed as occupiers and became the target of terrorist attacks. Looting and vandalism were common. In September 2004 U.S. casualties had reached the 1,000 mark. As American casualties mounted, the nature of the conflict changed as well. Terrorist attacks directed at the United States and its Iraqi allies now took place alongside a heightened sectarian conflict between the Shias and Sunnis, which increasingly took on the character of a civil war. The conflict also brought forward vivid images of mistreatment of prisoners by American military personnel at Abu Ghraib prison, which served to enflame anti-American sentiment in Iraq and antiwar feelings in the United States. American casualties reached the 3,000 mark by the end of 2006; the United Nations estimated that 34,452 Iraqi civilians died in 2006 and 30,842 people were detained in Iraq, including 14,534 in U.S. military–run prisons.

Two years later the political-strategic landscape of Iraq looked very different. The Bush administration's decision after the November 2006 midterm elections to send additional forces to Iraq, popularly known as the "surge," along with a change in strategy put into place by General David Petraeus that emphasized counterinsurgency tactics against U.S. enemies and working with Iraqis rather than trying to secure victory through battlefield successes against them led to a reduction in the violence and increased political stability. By the time President Barack Obama took office there was widespread agreement that U.S. troop withdrawals from Iraq could take place.

What did not look different in 2008 were continued problems with Iran and North Korea, the two other members of the axis of evil identified by President Bush. Neither had been dissuaded from their pursuit of nuclear power by attempts at diplomatic isolation, economic sanctions, or veiled threats of preemptive military action. Problems also began to resurface in Afghanistan, where the Taliban had regrouped and were now once again viewed as a significant national security threat that demanded a U.S. military presence there. More generally a sense had developed that the administration's goal of spreading democracy through the region had been replaced by a support for stability. Finally, because the Bush Doctrine had been so heavily focused on terrorism, it seemed to provide little guidance for other national security threats. A case in point was Russian intervention into Georgia during the 2008 Summer Olympics on the side of pro-Russian separatists. The U.S. response was little more than a series of declaratory policy statements of disapproval and support for Georgia. Nothing was done to change the situation on the ground.

## ASSESSING RESULTS

Judging the consequences of a foreign policy undertaking is a complicated task. A major problem is that success and failure are often treated as absolute categories, yet this is seldom the case. Far more typical are situations in which success and failure are both present in varying degrees. A state rarely has only one goal when it undertakes a course of action, and the reality of multiple goals further complicates the calculations of costs and benefits. Estimates of success and failure also depend on one's time frame. Economic sanctions work slowly, but that does not mean that they are any less effective than fast-acting ones. They might even be preferable, because they minimize the risk of miscalculation that occurs during crisis situations. Finally, political considerations also cloud any evaluation of the effectiveness of a policy instrument. In 2003, Libya announced that it was giving up its pursuit of nuclear weapons. The George W. Bush administration quickly hailed the announcement as evidence that its tough post–9/11 military stance, including the doctrine of preemption, was succeeding. Others countered that the success really should be attributed to years of behind-the-scene diplomacy and economic sanctions.[20]

Beyond questions of success or failure we can also judge past, present, and future U.S. foreign policies in terms of their underlying characteristics. Below we introduce three such standards: (1) their intellectual coherence, (2) the extent to which they are motivated by domestic politics rather than foreign events, and (3) the consistency with which they are applied to foreign policy problems. To a greater or lesser extent each of these reference points has been found to be a problem in the five foreign policy doctrines we examined earlier.

**INTELLECTUAL COHERENCE**   The foreign policy of containment that grew out of the Truman Doctrine was grounded in two very different views of the Soviet Union within the Truman administration, both of which could not be correct. One view, championed by George Kennan, saw Soviet expansion largely as defensive and reactionary. This view saw Soviet leaders as more concerned with staying in power than with spreading communism. The authors of National Security Council document #68 (NSC-68) rejected this perspective. They saw Soviet hostility to the United States as unrelenting and based on Marxist–Leninist ideological principles. Moreover, its leadership was committed to spreading communism throughout the world. For Kennan, American power could be applied selectively around the world. From the perspective of NSC-68, it had to be applied wherever communists were present or threatened.

Nixon's policy of détente was rooted in National Security Advisor Henry Kissinger's belief that the most stable international system was one in which all major powers viewed the international system as legitimate, something the Soviet Union and China could not do so long as they were the target of American containment efforts.[21] Conservative critics took exception to Nixon's willingness to accept the Soviet Union as a full partner in the family of nations, given the revolutionary and anticapitalist creed to which it adhered. They maintained that little if anything had changed in communist foreign policy other than the Nixon administration's evaluation of it. Others questioned the ability of the United States to continue to play the role of a superpower with global interests while operating primarily through allies and regional substitutes.

Carter's foreign policy was characterized by sympathetic observers as "the hell of good intentions" for its immature and mistaken belief that it could push U.S.–Soviet relations to the sidelines while addressing human rights problems.[22] Jeanne Kirkpatrick, who would go on to serve as ambassador to the United Nations in the Reagan administration, criticized the intellectual foundations of Carter's human rights policy, arguing that it did not recognize the difference between right-wing governments and totalitarian governments such as that of the Soviet Union.[23] The former could make a transition to democracy, whereas the later could not. Accordingly, far greater pressure needed to be put on totalitarian governments than on right-wing dictatorships. Reagan's view of the Soviet Union was challenged by most on the political left, as was the presumed linkage in the Reagan Doctrine between a renewed Cold War and the fall of communism. One observer asserted that the principal reasons for Reagan's success had little to do with administration policy but rather resulted from "forces and trends outside the control of the United Sates and of measures undertaken by others and occasionally even opposed by Mr. Reagan."[24] Interestingly, Reagan's foreign policy near the end of his administration, with its interest in arms control and willingness to push American allies such as Philippine President Ferdinand Marcos on human rights and pro-democracy issues, led some conservatives to characterize it as Carterism without Carter.

Several aspects of the Bush Doctrine brought forward questions about the strength of its intellectual foundations, with some asserting that it was not a strategic road map that guided policy but an opportunistic response to the events of 9/11 that allowed the administration to address real and long-standing foreign policy problems in the Middle East.

At its most general level, the debate over the Bush Doctrine has pitted conservative realists against neoconservatives. Five key themes form the foundation for neoconservative thinking about world politics.[25] First, the internal character of regimes matters. Second, American power should be used for moral purposes. Third, neoconservatives are skeptical about the legitimacy and effectiveness of international law and institutions to achieve security and justice. Fourth, the United States should act unilaterally whenever possible. And fifth, military power ought to be considered as a primary instrument of American foreign policy. Conservative realists are in partial agreement with neoconservatives on such matters as the importance of military power in world politics and a de-emphasis on the role of international organizations and international law in world politics. But they take exception elsewhere.

For realists there is a fundamental difference between national interest and global interest. Any foreign policy that does not recognize the difference will result in overreaching and in the long run result in dilution of a country's power, which will, in turn, threaten its ability to protect its national security. Moreover, what matters in world affairs is the nature of a country's foreign policy and not its domestic policies in areas such as human rights and democracy. They argue that the link between democracy and peace is not as iron-clad as many would consider it to be. New democracies, for example, tend to be prone to war. Finally, realists assert that although international law and institutions cannot protect countries from national security threats, they do provide a means for legitimizing the use of power, thus reducing both resistance to it and the costs of using it.

Specific aspects of the Bush Doctrine have also brought forward challenges. The most prominent point of controversy is the concept of preemption. At issue here was the blurring of a long-standing distinction in international politics between preemption and prevention.[26] Both are based on the principle of striking first in self-defense. In the case of preemption, the feared attack is imminent. In the case of prevention, it is more general and future oriented. International law recognizes the legitimacy of preemptive strikes but not necessarily of preventive strikes on an enemy. Critics argued that in casting the Iraq War as a preemptive one, the Bush administration used the imagery of preemption in a situation that was more legitimately characterized as prevention, especially when it was later found that Iraq did not possess weapons of mass destruction. Another line of criticism questioned the assertion that containment deterrence could not work against rogue regimes and supporters of international terrorism.[27] Defenders of these strategies argued that they continued to be useful, and they attributed Libya's decision to abandon its quest for weapons of mass destruction to them. Critics also questioned the assertion that deterrence could not work because of the irrational nature of these regimes, making the argument that rationality is a matter of degree and not an all-or-nothing quality. Rogue regimes concerned with their survival could be expected to act rationally enough in the face of U.S. deterrence threats.

**THE DOMINANCE OF DOMESTIC POLITICS** Truman resisted adopting the changes suggested in NSC-68 because of their budgetary implications, especially the need to fight communism everywhere in the world. Only after the outbreak of the Korean War and the changed domestic climate at home did he embrace a more expansive and expensive definition of containment. Nixon's embrace of détente and the shifting of defense responsibilities on to allies was likewise heavily influenced by the unwillingness of the American public to pay for the Vietnam War. Carter announced his doctrine and abandoned détente with the Soviet invasion of Afghanistan and a reversal in American thinking about what it was willing to pay for national security. Reagan and Bush present interesting cases. Both pursued aggressive foreign policies that required large-scale military spending. Yet, as even sympathetic critics of each pointed out, neither called on the American public to sacrifice. As one observer put it about Reagan's foreign policy, its great appeal was that it demanded so little from the public while promising to deliver so much.[28] When costs were encountered, such as the attacks on the marine barracks in Lebanon in 1983 that killed 241 marines, the policy was quickly terminated by Reagan. Bush, by contrast, held firm in his commitment to victory in Iraq (although he did change his policy) even after the 2006 midterm elections indicated widespread public disapproval for the war. Still there was no call for greater public sacrifice.

**INCONSISTENCY OF APPLICATION**   Critics have charged that no administration fully succeeded in using its doctrine as an organizing device to guide all of its foreign policy decisions. Inconsistencies are always present. Nixon ordered the invasion of Cambodia and Laos. Carter succumbed to offering arms sales to states whose human rights record his administration had criticized. Reagan did little to aid Eastern European states seeking to break away from the Soviet Union, and he entered into negotiations with supporters of terrorism as part of the Iran–Contra affair. He also entered into arms control talks with the Soviet Union near the end of his presidency. Bush engaged in a preemptive war with one member of the "axis of evil" (Iraq), but found it necessary to enter into negotiations with another that obtained nuclear weapons (North Korea) and struggled to get support from the international community to block the efforts of the third to get nuclear weapons (Iran).

On one level the existence of a gap between declaratory policy and action policy, between what is announced and what is implemented, is unavoidable and comes as no surprise. The world is too complex for a one-size-fits-all solution, and it is natural to expect that foreign policy strategies will evolve and change over time. Bush's 2006 National Security Strategy, for example, makes three times as many references to democratization as did the 2002 version and speaks less forcefully to the concept of preemptive war.[29] Presidents walk a fine line in putting forward a doctrine to guide their foreign policy. George H. W. Bush and Bill Clinton were often criticized for their lack of a guiding foreign policy doctrine in the early years of the post–Cold War international system. Many defended Bush's failure to do so, arguing that, given the uncertainty associated with this new world, the benefits of pragmatism far outweighed the benefits of an overarching vision of American foreign policy that would guide decision making. Clinton, by contrast, was roundly criticized for his indecision and frequent changes of direction over the use of military force in Somalia, Haiti, and Bosnia.

Even under the best of circumstances, the existence of a gap between what is said and what is done points to a potential problem. Such a gap can undermine the effectiveness of a country's foreign policy, leaving it open to charges of hypocrisy and self-serving behavior. The George W. Bush administration found itself in this position in 2006. Secretary of State Condoleezza Rice, on a trip to Southeast Asia, condemned Myanmar (Burma) for its oppressive policies toward democracy and human rights while praising Indonesia as an example of moderation, tolerance, and inclusiveness. A few months later, Vice President Dick Cheney described Russian President Vladimir Putin as an opponent of democratic reform and praised Kazakhstan for its efforts at democratic reform even though the State Department had stated that the latter's most recent presidential elections fell short on a number of international standards and also criticized Kazakhstan's security forces for human rights abuses.

## OVER THE HORIZON

The challenges identified by Condoleezza Rice at the beginning of this chapter are not unique to the problem of counterterrorism. At a minimum, formulating a foreign policy toward North Korea requires a policy to China, which in turn requires a foreign policy to Japan and also requires a foreign policy to South Korea. Simply put, there is nothing simple about foreign policy problems.

Thinking critically about U.S. foreign policy requires not only understanding the past and present but also anticipating and preparing for the future. In looking over the horizon in an effort to anticipate the future we are not interested in fortune-telling or predicting specific events. Rather, our goal is to highlight possible trends and become sensitive to possible challenges and opportunities that lie ahead for U.S. foreign policy. Here we highlight three ideas that are central to the very concept of foreign policy that may change.

First, we can anticipate a reordering of foreign policy problems from the A, B, and C lists which they are now on. It is already becoming clear that terrorism will not dominate the foreign policy agenda of the United States in the years to come the way it did in the years after 9/11. In 2008 the National Intelligence Council released an unclassified report, *Global Trends 2025: A Transformed World*, in which it sought to stimulate thinking about the future.[30] Among its core arguments were that the whole international system will be revolutionized. Not only will new powers arise but the rules governing foreign policy and global interactions will change. The report anticipates the continued transfer of wealth from the West to the East and sees the combination of global economic and population growth as placing tremendous pressure on resources. This in turn raises the possibility of conflict as demand exceeds supply. Through all of this, the report sees the United States remaining as the world's most powerful country, although it will be less dominant and may be forced to make hard choices between foreign and domestic policy priorities.

Second, we can expect to see new forms of power develop. One possibility put forward is the power of connectedness. Rooted in globalization the power of connectedness provides leverage to those states that can place themselves at the center of global information and communication networks that link people and countries around the world together. Anne-Marie Slaughter argues that the United States is ideally positioned to lead in a connected world because American firms, individuals, and nonprofit organizations are at the center of many of the most prominent global networks. Slaughter cautions that connectivity does not lend itself to direction and control. Rather the United States will have to become a manger and orchestrator in which it harnesses knowledge and skills to achieve a common purpose.[31]

Third, we can expect to see lively discussions about how to define the national interest. Historically the concept of national interest has most often been used in the context of protecting states from direct threats. Joseph Nye argues that the United States must take a broader view of its national interest to include providing international **public goods**.[32] Public goods do not belong exclusively to anyone. All members of a community benefit from them. The age-old problem is that since public goods do not belong to anyone, no one takes responsibility for providing them, and they go neglected. Nye argues that as the global leader, it is the United States' responsibility to do so. He identifies three public goods to place at the top of a list of U.S. national interests: international stability, open markets, and the global commons.

## CRITICAL THINKING QUESTIONS

1. Identify 10 foreign policy problems facing the United States today. Divide them into A, B, and C list problems. On what basis did you make your decisions?
2. What type of foreign policy problems do hard power and soft power work best on?
3. Pick a foreign policy problem. What standards should be used to evaluate U.S. efforts to address it?

## KEY TERMS

action policy   7
bipartisanship   9
blowback   8
declaratory policy   7

grand strategy   11
hard power   10
Lippmann Gap   8
national interest   6

opportunity costs   8
public goods   29
soft power   10

## FURTHER READING

Richard Betts, "Is Strategy an Illusion?" *International Security*, 25 (2000), 5–50.
Ted Galen Carpenter, *Smart Power. Toward a Prudent Foreign Policy for America* (Washington, DC: CATO Institute, 2008).
Terry Deibel, *Foreign Affairs Strategy Logic for American Statecraft* (New York: Cambridge University Press, 2007).
Joseph Nye, "Recovering American Leadership," *Survival*, 50 (2008), 55–68.
Condoleezza Rice, "Rethinking the National Interest," *Foreign Affairs*, 87 (2008), 2–26.

## NOTES

1. Steve Strasser ed., *The 9/11 Investigations* (New York: Public Affairs Press, 2004), p. 233.
2. Jim Hoagland, "Why Clinton Improvises," *The Washington Post*, September 25, 1994, p. C1.
3. Zbigniew Brzezinski, *Second Chance: Three Presidents and the Crisis of American Superpower* (New York: Basic Books, 2007), p. 183.
4. Paul Kennedy, *The Rise and Fall of the Great Powers* (New York: Random House, 1987).
5. Humphrey Taylor, "The Not-so-Black Art of Public Diplomacy," *World Policy Journal*, 24 (2007/08), 51–59.
6. Walter Lippmann, *The Cold War: A Study in US Foreign Policy* (New York: Harper, 1947).
7. Chalmers Johnson, *Blowback* (New York: Owl Books, 2000).

8. Charles Kupchan and Peter Trubowitz, "Grand Strategy for a Divided America," *Foreign Affairs,* 86 (2007), 82.

9. Richard Holbrooke, "The Next President," *Foreign Affairs,* 87 (2008), 2.

10. John P. Lovell, "The Idiom of National Security," *Journal of Political and Military Sociology,* 11 (1983), 35–51.

11. Glenn Kessler and Robin Wright, "A Case for Progress amid Some Omissions," *The Washington Post,* June 29, 2005, p. A1; Dan Fromkin, "White House Briefing," January 24, 2005, www.washingtonpost.com/wp-dyn/politics/administration/briefing; and Omar Fekeiki, "The Toll of Communism," *The Washington Post,* June 13, 2007, p. C1.

12. Bob Woodward, *The War Within* (New York: Simon & Schuster), p. 189.

13. Ann Scott Tyson," Gates Warns of Militarized Policy," *Washington Post,* July 16, 2008, A6.

14. *Soft Power in Asia: Results of a 2008 Multinational Survey of Public Opinion,* Chicago Council of Global Affairs, 2008.

15. Joby Warwick, "Strategy Against Al-Qaeda Faulted," *Washington Post,* July 30, 2008, A4.

16. Woodward, *The War Within,* p. 32.

17. Richard Betts, "Is Strategy an Illusion?" *International Security,* 25 (2000), 5–50.

18. Woodward, *The War Within,* p. 425.

19. *National Security Strategy of the United States, 2002,* www.whitehouse.gov/nsc/nss.html.

20. George Joffe, "Libya: Who Blinked and Why," *Current History,* 103 (May 2004), 221–25.

21. Henry Kissinger, *A World Restored* (New York: Grosset & Dunlap, 1964).

22. Stanley Hoffmann, "Requiem," *Foreign Policy,* 42 (1981), 3–26.

23. Jeanne Kirkpatrick, "Human Rights and American Foreign Policy: A Symposium," *Commentary* (November 1981), 42–45.

24. Michael Mandelbaum, "The Luck of the President," *Foreign Affairs,* 64 (1986), 393–413.

25. G. John Ikenberry, "The End of the Neo-Conservative Moment," *Survival,* 46 (2004), 7–22; Francis Fukuyama, *America at the Crossroads* (New Haven: Yale University Press, 2006).

26. On the distinction between preemption and prevention, see Lawrence Freedman, "Prevention, Not Preemption," *Washington Quarterly,* 26 (2003), 105–114.

27. Robert F. Trager and Dessislava P. Zagorcheva, "Deterring Terrorism: It Can Be Done," *International Security,* 30 (2005/6), 87–123; and Jeffrey Record, "The Bush Doctrine and War with Iraq," *Parameters* (Spring 2003), 4–21.

28. Robert Tucker, "Reagan's Foreign Policy," *Foreign Affairs,* 68 (1989), 1–27.

29. *National Security Strategy of the United States, 2006,* www.whitehouse.gov/nsc/nss/2006.

30. National Intelligence Council, *Global Trends: A Transformed World* (Washington, DC: Government Printing Office, 2008).

31. Anne-Marie Slaughter, "America's Edge: Power in the Networked Century," *Foreign Affairs* 88 (2009), 94–112.

32. Joseph Nye, "Recovering American Leadership," *Survival* 50 (2008), 55–68.

# CHAPTER

## 2

# The Global Context

On April 9, 2009, Somali pirates captured the *Maersk Alabama* and took its captain hostage. Three days later U.S. Navy SEALS rescued him, killing three of the pirates who were holding him. A fourth pirate surrendered. The months preceding this attack had seen a spike in pirate attacks off the Somali coast. In 2008, there were a total of 111 attacks, of which 42 resulted in successful hijackings. At least five pirate gangs operate in the Indian Ocean, with most pirates being between 20 and 35 years of age. They are supported by ex-militia soldiers and technicians who operate Global Positioning Systems to track their prey. Those taken hostage wait 45 days or more to be released. Those in captivity are generally treated well. They and their cargo are turned over promptly after payment is received. In 2008 an estimated $80 million was paid in ransom, most of it in U.S. dollars. The *Maersk Alabama* carried 17,500 metric tons of cargo, 5,000 of which were relief supplies intended for Somalia, Kenya, and Uganda.

Somali piracy has been going on since the early 1990s, when Somalia fell into civil war. The collapse of the Somali central government, the clan-based organization of Somali society, and the extreme poverty of the country are all cited as factors contributing to the appeal of piracy. As the pirate attacks increased in number and the costs to international shipping grew, the international community began to mobilize a response. In August 2008, a multilateral Combined Task Force began operating in the Gulf of Aden to combat piracy there. In October 2008, the United Nations Security Council adopted a resolution calling on states to use military force against the pirates. The next month it passed another resolution applying sanctions against the Somali government for failing to take steps to effectively address the piracy problem. The United States, Russia, France, China, Japan, and India have all sent vessels to the region to combat piracy or have pledged to do so.

## THINKING ABOUT THE WORLD

Foreign policy looks outward. It looks beyond American borders. But what it sees is anything but predetermined or universally agreed upon. Are Somali pirates a foreign policy problem or just a minor nuisance? One reason for disagreements about the foreign policy challenges facing the United States is that observers hold different theoretical perspectives about the fundamental nature of world politics. Three perspectives are particularly important for understanding the larger debate over what American foreign policy should be and what it can be.

### Realism

The first theoretical perspective is **realism**. Realism was the dominant intellectual perspective used for studying world politics in the twentieth century.[1] It began to emerge as a powerful perspective in the United States after World War I as the euphoria of victory gave way to distress over Hitler's rise to power and the increasingly conflictual tone of world politics. For realists, world politics involves a constant struggle for power that is carried out under conditions that border on anarchy. There is little room for embracing universal principles or taking on moral crusades. The acknowledged founding voice of American realism was Hans Morgenthau, who captured the essence of realism in stating that leaders "think and act in terms of interests defined as power." Henry Kissinger, who served as national security advisor and secretary of state under President Nixon, is its best known contemporary proponent. For realists, peace defined as the absence of war is possible only when states (leaders) follow their own narrowly defined national interests. Where early realists stressed human nature as the central driving force in world politics, later realists focused their attention on the central role played by the structure of the international system. Once in place, international systems become a force that states cannot control but one that controls states instead. It was Kissinger's hope to reconstruct the international system after Vietnam in such a way as to protect American national interests in a world where it could no longer dominate others.

## Neoliberalism

A second theoretical perspective is **neoliberalism**.[2] While conceding that in many respects the international system is anarchic, it rejects the pessimistic conclusion reached by realists that world politics is essentially a conflictual process from which there is no escape. Instead neoliberalism sees world politics as an arena in which all participants (states and nonstate actors) can advance their own interests peacefully without threatening others. This becomes possible when conditions are created that allow the inherent rationality of individuals to come to the forefront. Among the primary factors that promote peaceful intercourse are democracy, respect for international laws, participation in international organizations, restraints on weapons, and free trade. President Woodrow Wilson, who championed the League of Nations after World War I, is the American statesperson most associated with neoliberalism. Long dismissed by realists as idealistic, Wilsonianism began to reassert itself as a powerful voice in American thinking about foreign policy after Vietnam.

## Constructivism

The third theoretical perspective is **constructivism**.[3] Where realism and neoliberalism differ in their interpretations of the essential features of world politics, they both share the conviction that these features do exist and that objective rules for conducting foreign policy can be derived from them. Constructivism takes issue with this. Constructivists assert that international politics is not shaped by underlying forces but by our perceptions of them. Ideas, and cultural and historical experience give meaning to what we see. Moreover, our ways of looking at the world are capable of changing over time as we interact with others. Free trade is not inherently a force for peace or a cause of war. Which of these it is depends on our personal experiences with free trade, the experiences of those we interact with, and how free trade is depicted in our collective memory as group or nation. Consider that, as one scholar notes, an entire generation of Americans has grown up after the end of the Cold War and sees unipolarity and American global dominance as natural. He also notes that we have trouble understanding how revolutionary and unnatural this can appear to others.[4] The importance of images and language is also evident in the caution urged by Brent Scowcroft and Zbigniew Brzezinski, national security advisors to Presidents George H.W. Bush and Jimmy Carter, respectively. In 2008, they urged President George W. Bush not to talk about bombing Iran, noting that doing so "legitimizes the use of force" and "convinces Iran it is being threatened."[5]

# INTERNATIONAL SYSTEM: STRUCTURAL CONSTANTS

In this and the following two sections we present a survey of those forces in the international system that are most often seen as driving state behavior. We group them into three categories: structural constants, Cold War trends, and the dominant features of the contemporary international system. While realists, neoliberals, and constructivists would disagree on how to rank their relative importance, all would agree that constructing an effective U.S. foreign policy requires thinking critically about them. In this section, we examine three frequently cited structural features that have endured over time and continue to shape foreign policy today.

## Decentralization

The first enduring feature of the international system is its decentralized nature. Unlike in highly developed domestic political systems, there exist no central political institutions to make laws or see to their enforcement in the international arena. In addition, there is no common political culture in which to anchor an agreed-on set of norms governing the behavior of states. The combined result is a highly competitive international system in which there is a constant expectation of violence and very little expectation that either international law or appeals to moral principles will greatly influence the resolution of an issue.

Decentralization does not mean that the international system operates in a state of anarchy. "Ordered anarchy" would be a more apt characterization. Enforceable laws and common values may be absent, but rules do exist that lend a measure of predictability and certainty to international transactions. They do so by indicating the limits of permissible behavior and the directions to follow in settling disputes. Rules are less permanent than laws, are more general in nature, and tend to be normative statements rather than commands. Different international systems operate according to different rules and therefore place different opportunities and challenges before policy makers depending upon whether they are **bipolar, multipolar,** or **unipolar.** Neutrality, for example, is generally held to be permissible according to the rules of loose bipolarity but impossible under the rules of tight bipolarity.

## HISTORICAL LESSON

### Barbary Pirates

In the first two decades of the nineteenth century, the United States fought two wars with the Barbary pirates. Pirates had roamed the Mediterranean, threatening European shipping since the early 1300s. The severity of the problem had been held in check by the Knights of Malta, who both acted as Europe's first line of defense against piracy and profited greatly from it as the pirate's treasures were often brought to Malta, where they were sold. In 1798 all of this changed. Napoleon captured Malta and defeated the Knights, creating a power vacuum in the Mediterranean Sea. With no military force to stop it, piracy blossomed.

While piracy was an age-old foreign policy problem for Europe, it was a new problem for the United States. As a colony, American merchant vessels in the Mediterranean Sea had benefited from the protection offered by British treaties with Morocco, Algiers, Tunis, and Tripoli, the four major independent North African states sponsoring piracy. The 1778 Treaty of Alliance with France provided protection during the American Revolution. Once independent, the United States had to protect its own ships from being seized and held for ransom, with its crew being sold into slavery.

In 1786, Thomas Jefferson and John Adams, both future presidents, traveled to London to negotiate with Tripoli. They did so after Congress had appropriated funds for a yearly tribute that would be paid to protect U.S. shipping. Upon their return to the United States, Jefferson argued against paying the requested yearly tribute. He proposed creating an international alliance of small states to patrol the Mediterranean, but since the United States had no ships to contribute to such a force, the idea floundered. Adams agreed in principle that tribute should not be paid to the Barbary pirates, but citing the lack of a navy and the poor finances of the new Republic, he argued that the United States had no choice but to pay it. His position held the day, and over the next 15 years the United States paid up to $1 million per year in tribute money. Still, by late 1793, 12 American merchant ships had been captured by Barbary pirates and its crew and cargo held for ransom. The following year Congress appropriated funds for a navy.

Upon becoming president in 1801 and now in possession of a small navy, Jefferson was able to act on his instincts and rejected Tripoli's demand for $225,000 in tribute. Tripoli responded by declaring war on the United States. Algiers and Tunis soon did so as well. Congress supported Jefferson's decision but never declared war.

This first Barbary War lasted from 1801 to 1805. During the war the U.S. Navy and Marines acquitted themselves well, and the United States demonstrated the ability to project power far from its continental shores. The peace treaty itself was controversial, with the United States agreeing to pay a $60,000 ransom to free American prisoners held by Tripoli. The fruits of this victory were short lived. Two years later, in 1807, Algiers was engaging in piracy against American ships and holding sailors hostage for ransom. Rather than send the navy back to the North African coast, the United States returned to the practice of paying ransom. Algiers was able to do so because the United States had shifted its foreign policy attention elsewhere. It would go to war with Great Britain in 1812, and already this conflict was pushing other problems off the foreign policy agenda. Once the War of 1812 broke out, Algiers declared war on the United States for its failure to pay the required tribute. This became the second Barbary War (1812–1816).

The United States was in no position to take action against the Barbary pirates during the War of 1812. With the conclusion of that war, President James Madison acted. In March 1815, Congress authorized deploying U.S. naval forces to the Mediterranean Sea. Once again it did not declare war. Unlike the first Barbary War the United States did not act unilaterally now. Its naval forces were eventually joined by ships from Great Britain and the Netherlands.

Military victory was quickly achieved, and on July 3, 1815, a peace treaty was signed. By its terms, prisoners were exchanged and the United States received full shipping rights in the region with no further tribute being due to the Barbary pirates. Algerian leaders, however, quickly repudiated the treaty. A second treaty containing similar terms was signed in 1816 after the arrival of an Anglo-Dutch fleet that engaged in a heavy and effective bombing of Algiers.

### Applying the Lesson

1. To what extent do the Barbary and Somali pirates present the United States with a similar foreign policy problem?
2. What lessons do the Barbary Wars hold for the United States today in fighting Somali pirates?
3. Using the language of hard power and soft power that we introduced in Chapter 1, which do you think would be more effective in dealing with pirates? ■

## Self-Help System

The second structural constant in the international system grows out of the first: The international system is a self-help system. States must rely only on themselves to accomplish their foreign policy goals. To do otherwise runs the risk of manipulation or betrayal at the hands of another state. It is important to stress that Great Powers as well as smaller powers need to heed the admonition to avoid excessive dependence on others. During the Reagan administration, for example, it was proposed to use Israel as a go-between to sell weapons to Iran in hopes of gaining the release of American hostages in Lebanon. One of the points stressed by opponents of this plan was that Israeli and U.S. national interests were not identical, and that, in some cases, they were in direct conflict.[6]

The self-help principle challenges policy makers to bring goals and power resources into balance. Pursuing more goals than one has the resources to accomplish or squandering resources on secondary objectives saps the vitality of the state and makes it unable to respond effectively to future challenges. Vietnam is argued by many to be a classic example of the inability to balance goals and resources and its crippling consequences. American policy makers entered into the Vietnam conflict with little understanding of the history of the region or of the Vietnamese struggle for independence. Once the United States was involved, American policy produced steady increases in the level of the U.S. commitment to the war, but it did not bring the United States any closer to victory. Instead, the reverse occurred: The longer the United States remained in Vietnam and the greater its commitment, the more elusive victory became. Perhaps most frustrating was the inability to devise a workable exit scenario. The Vietnam experience continues to cast a long shadow over U.S. foreign policy. Many conservatives argue that the Vietnam syndrome has prevented the United States from acquiring either the capability or the will to protect its vital interests in the Persian Gulf, Angola, or Central America.

## A Stratified System

The third structural constant in the international system is its stratified nature. The equality of states embedded in the concept of **sovereignty** is a legal myth. The principle of sovereignty dates back to the Treaty of Westphalia and the beginnings of the modern state system in 1648. It holds that no legal authority exists above the state except that which the state voluntarily accepts. The reality of international politics is quite different, and sovereignty is a matter of degree rather than an absolute condition. States are "born unequal."[7] The resources they draw on for their power are distributed unequally across the globe. As such, the ability of states to accomplish their foreign policy objectives (as well as their very choice of objectives) varies from state to state.

Two key areas of disagreement among recent administrations have been over how great a degree of power inequality exists in the international system and the identity of the power centers. Reagan's foreign policy was based on the assumption that the international system is essentially bipolar. The Soviet Union and the United States were held to be the two central actors in a global power struggle. Furthermore, it was a struggle in which incompatible ideologies were a powerful force affecting foreign policy decisions. The Carter, Ford, and Nixon administrations all saw power distributed more broadly, and ideology was seen as a less important factor for the operation of the international system. The Nixon and Ford foreign policies stressed the ability to coexist with the Soviet Union (the policy of détente) and alluded to using other powers as counterweights to the USSR (the "China card"). The early Carter administration also felt that the United States could coexist with the Soviet Union. Its foreign policy differed from its predecessors in its emphasis on human rights and economic issues. This switch in concerns brought with it a shift in the identification of power centers, away from the Soviet Union and toward Western Europe, Japan, and key Third World states. With the invasion of Afghanistan, Carter's priorities changed, and once again the Soviet threat became the primary foreign policy problem for the United

States. The dramatic easing of Cold War hostilities that took place early in the George H. W. Bush administration left unchanged the stratified nature of world politics. Instead of a world with two superpowers, there now existed only one: the United States.

## INTERNATIONAL SYSTEM: COLD WAR TRENDS

In addition to the underlying structural features just discussed, a series of trends in the international system began to exert an important influence on U.S. foreign policy during the Cold War. They continue to exert an influence on U.S. foreign policy even though the Cold War has ended by shaping the context within which power is exercised and the problems faced.

### Diffusion of Power

Although the basic structure of the international system has endured over time, the system itself is not unchanging. Four post–World War II trends are especially notable: a diffusion of power, issue proliferation, actor proliferation, and regional diversity. Power is the ability to achieve objectives. It is typically viewed as something one possesses—a commodity to be acquired, stored, and manipulated. But power must also be viewed as a relational concept. What is ultimately at issue is not how much power a state has, but how much power it has in a specific issue compared to those with whom it is dealing.

The postwar era has seen a steady diffusion of power. This in turn has created a frustrating gap between the ends and means of U.S. foreign policy. It is not so much that the quantity of power possessed by the United States has declined. U.S. dominance in nuclear weapons remains unchallenged. The same holds true for conventional weapons. What has changed is the utility of certain types of power, the issues being contested, and the ability of other states to exploit points of sensitivity and vulnerability. The international distribution of power no longer resembles a steep pyramid. It now is one with a bulge in the middle, made up of states that possess sufficient power resources to block or resist American initiatives. A prime example is the emergence of the BRICS (Brazil, Russia, India, and China) as strong voices in international economic policy making. Their emergence signifies the shifting of economic power away from the United States, Europe, and Japan. Together these four states hold 42 percent of the world's population. They held their first international summit conference in June 2009, ending it with a call for the establishment of a multipolar international system.

The causes for the diffusion of power can be found both in the specifics of American foreign policy and in the more universal cycles of hegemonic decline. Robert Gilpin, after examining the decline of empires throughout history, asserts that we can identify a cycle of hegemonic decline.[8] As the cycle progresses, a combination of the burdens of imperial leadership, increased emphasis on the consumption of goods and services, and the international diffusion of technology conspire to sap the strength of the imperial state and bring about its decline.

A primary contributing factor to the diffusion of power is the very successes and failures of postwar American foreign policy. The effect of foreign policy failures is relatively easy to anticipate. In the wake of defeat follow the search for scapegoats, disillusionment with the task undertaken, and a desire to avoid similar situations. Vietnam stands out as the most significant military failure in recent U.S. history, and it is held by many to have been responsible for destroying the postwar domestic consensus on the purpose of American power.

Economic failures have also contributed to the diffusion of power. Economic sanctions directed against Fidel Castro in Cuba in the 1960s failed to bring down his regime and only made him more dependent on Soviet support. Repeated efforts at bringing about economic and social development in the Third World, such as Truman's Point Four Program and Kennedy's Alliance for Progress, have also failed. The continued existence of widespread poverty has proven to be a fertile breeding ground for anti–U.S. nationalist and revolutionary forces.

American foreign policy successes have also hastened the decline of U.S. dominance. The reconstruction of the Japanese and Western European economies ranks as two truly remarkable achievements. In a sense, U.S. foreign policy has been almost too successful here. These economies are now major economic rivals of the U.S. economy and often outperform it. The North Atlantic Treaty Organization (NATO) is another success that has had a dual impact. Its creation in 1949 did succeed in erecting a military shield for Western Europe and in stopping further Soviet expansion into Europe. At the same time, NATO offered U.S. European allies, most notably the French, the opportunity to pursue their own foreign policy objectives, often at the expense of U.S. interests.

## Issue Proliferation

The second area of evolutionary change in the international arena is issue proliferation. Not long ago, one could speak of a clear-cut foreign affairs issue hierarchy. At the top were a relatively small number of high-politics problems involving questions of national security, territorial integrity, and political independence. At the bottom were the numerically more prevalent low-politics issues of commerce, energy, environment, and so on. Although largely intuitive, the line between high and low politics was well established. The positions occupied by issues in this hierarchy were also relatively fixed. This allowed policy makers to develop a familiarity with the issues before them and the options open to them. Today this is no longer the case.

The high-politics category has become crowded. The oil crisis and fear of resource scarcity elevated economic issues to the status of national security issues. Economic recession and high unemployment have made the existence of an open international system a question of high politics. There is now also a great deal of movement within the high–low ranking system. Under President

Jimmy Carter, human rights for a time became a pivotal concern for the United States. During the Reagan administration, it returned to a low-politics position when the emphasis shifted to international **terrorism**.

The high–low politics distinction was implicitly based on the existence of a prior distinction between foreign and domestic policy. This distinction has become increasingly difficult to maintain. How, for example, do we classify attempts to get China to agree to export restrictions on goods shipped to the United States, or the negotiations over the damage done in Canada by acid rain originating in U.S.-based industries? The term that is used increasingly to characterize these and other issues with significant domestic and international dimensions is **intermestic** (*inter* from international and *mestic* from domestic).[9] A prime example of an emerging intermestic policy area is food safety. Traditionally, food safety issues have been treated as a domestic policy matter. This is no longer realistic. Food production has become globalized. Between 2000 and 2006 the value of food imports doubled, to $2.2 trillion, yet traditionally the FDA inspects less than 1 percent of the imported food products under its jurisdiction. Both Congress and the George W. Bush administration moved to change this situation by toughening inspection standards on imported food. Issue proliferation has thus brought with it added complexity. Policy makers must judge not only the ranking of an issue but also the extent of its domestic impact. They then must be constantly prepared to reevaluate their thinking in light of changing circumstances. Figures 2.1 and 2.2 illustrate how the high–low scale and the foreign–domestic scale can be used to classify issues and show how issues have changed position over time.

| | High | | | |
|---|---|---|---|---|
| | | | Vietnam War | Nuclear strategy<br>Arms control |
| | | | Recognizing China | Covert actions<br>Foreign aid |
| FOREIGN<br>POLICY<br>"IMPORTANCE" | | | | Test Ban Treaty<br>Tariffs<br>Energy<br>Grain sales |
| | | Interest rates<br>Environmental<br>standards | Negotiations | Routine diplomatic |
| | Low | | | |
| | | 100%<br>Domestic | 50/50<br>Intermestic | 100% Foreign<br>Policy |

RELATIVE IMPORTANCE OF FOREIGN
AND DOMESTIC CONSIDERATIONS
TO RESOLUTION OF ISSUE

**FIGURE 2.1**
Illustrative Distribution of Issues in the Late 1960s

| FOREIGN POLICY "IMPORTANCE" | High | Arms control/ Nuclear freeze | MX | |
| | | Panama Canal Treaty | Covert action | Human rights— Carter |
| | | Energy policy Tariffs/Quotas | Foreign aid | International terrorism— Reagan |
| | | Grain sales | | |
| | | | China/Taiwan | |
| | | Interest rates | | Human rights— Reagan |
| | | Environmental standards | | Routine diplomatic negotiations |
| | Low | | | |
| | | 100% Domestic | 50/50 Intermestic | 100% Foreign Policy |

RELATIVE IMPORTANCE OF FOREIGN
AND DOMESTIC CONSIDERATIONS
TO RESOLUTION OF ISSUE

**FIGURE 2.2**
Illustrative Distribution of Issues in the Early 1980s

## Actor Proliferation

The third evolutionary feature of the international system is actor proliferation. On the one hand, actor proliferation has taken the form of an expansion in the number of states. Today the United States has diplomatic relations with some 180 states. This compares to 58 states in 1930. This expansion in the number of states has brought with it a corresponding expansion in the number of views that can be found on any given problem. Quite often these views are based on different starting premises and assumptions from those held by the United States. The United Nations Conference on the Law of the Sea (UNCLOS) illustrates the effect that the proliferation of states has had on U.S. foreign policy. Whereas 84 states attended UNCLOS I in 1958, 148 states attended UNCLOS III in 1973. The very number of states participating presented great obstacles to achieving an agreement, as did the diversity of views expressed. The decision-making rules for the proposed International Seabed Authority that would oversee seabed mineral exploration emerged as a major point of contention. The United States insisted on some form of weighted voting. It refused to participate in a system in which it could be outvoted by an alliance of small states. In the end, the United States was the only Western industrialized state that refused to sign the treaty. One-hundred-thirty states voted to sign it.

Although the growth in the number of states has nearly run its course, continued growth is taking place in a second area: nonstate actors. States have never been the only actors in world politics. Yet it is only comparatively recently that nonstate actors have appeared in sufficient numbers and possessed control over enough resources to be significant actors in world politics. Three categories of nonstate actors may be identified. They are intergovernmental organizations (IGOs) such as the United Nations, NATO, and the Organization of American States; nongovernmental organizations (NGOs) such as General Motors, the International Red Cross, the Catholic Church, the Palestine Liberation Organization, and terrorist groups; and subnational actors such as the Central Intelligence Agency (CIA), the Defense Department, New York City, and Texas.

Statistically, the growth in the number of nonstate actors has been explosive. On the eve of World War I there were only 49 IGOs and 170 NGOs. In 1940 the numbers had grown to over 80 IGOs and about 500 NGOs. In 2004 the Union of International Associations listed 7,350 IGOs and 51,509 NGOs.[10] The emergence of nonstate actors as a significant force in world politics is generally tied to the inability of the state to respond adequately to the demands that citizens place on it. In some cases, nonstate actors have emerged as by-products of state efforts to meet citizen demands. In other cases, they have emerged as challenges to the state for the loyalties of its citizens.

Actor proliferation has also altered in three ways the context within which American foreign policy decisions are made. First, the presence and actions of nonstate actors have altered the language used in thinking about foreign policy problems. The language of the Cold War now competes with the imagery of interdependence for the attention of policy makers. Second, nonstate actors often serve as potential instruments of foreign policy. There are major advantages to using nonstate actors to advance state objectives. By not being identified as part of a state, their actions may be better received by other actors. Decisions made by the International Monetary Fund or the World Bank tend to be more readily accepted by Third World states than if they had come directly from the United States. The third impact that nonstate actors have on U.S. foreign policy is that they often limit the options open to policy makers. Their ability to resist and frustrate state initiatives necessitates that policy makers consider courses of action they otherwise would likely reject.

## Regional Diversity

As a superpower, the United States is concerned not only with the structure and operation of the international system as a whole but also with the operation of its subsystems. Three subsystems are especially important to the United States. Each presents it with different management problems and thus requires a different solution.[11] It should be stressed that U.S. policy makers have not always viewed the world from this perspective, nor do they uniformly do so today. For much of the Cold War era, the international system was viewed as an undifferentiated whole in which competition with the Soviet Union was the key management problem. The first subsystem is the Western system, which is made up of the advanced industrial states of the United States, Canada, Western Europe, and Japan. The principal problem in the Western system is managing interdependence. At issue is the distribution of costs and benefits. U.S. leadership and initiative, once so eagerly sought by its allies, is now often resisted. For its part, the United States has begun to question the costs of leadership and seeks to have its allies pick up a larger share of the defense burden. A similar situation holds for economic relations. Many in the United States are no longer willing to underwrite a free trade system or to accept economic discrimination in the name of alliance unity, whereas U.S. allies have become increasingly disenchanted with U.S. economic policies.

The second subsystem is the North–South system. A quite different set of perspectives governs interactions in this system from that in the Western system. Instead of expectations of sharing and mutual gain, the South perceives exploitation. The fundamental management problem in the North–South system is coping with military and economic dependence. Whereas solutions to the problems of interdependence lie in the fine-tuning of existing international organizations and practices, solutions to the problems of dependence require constructing a new system that the South is willing to accept as legitimate and in which it is treated as an equal.

The third subsystem of concern to the United States is the remnants of the Cold War East–West system. The fundamental management problem here is one of reintegration. The Cold War divided the East and West into two largely self-contained, competing military and economic parts. Détente brought about a limited reintegration of the East and West in the 1970s through arms control and trade agreements. The demise of communism in the Soviet Union and Eastern Europe together with the collapse of the Soviet Union greatly complicated this task and lent an aura of urgency to it. The task is now seen as urgent because of fears for what a Russian economic collapse could mean for the global economy and its ability to control its remaining nuclear forces. The task is complicated by the fact that there still exists a great military and economic power in the "East" (China), whose reintegration into a Western-centered international military and economic system appears to be fraught with domestic and international difficulties.

## DOMINANT FEATURES TODAY

Up until the terrorist attacks of 9/11, the contemporary international system lacked a defining identity. Just as the late 1940s were referred to as the "post–World War II" period, so the 1990s were the "post–Cold War" period. It may be that in the future we will come to see the terrorist attacks of that day as inaugurating a new era of world politics with its own temperament. Or we may not. Some commentators looking back at 9/11 argue that not much has changed in world politics.[12] From this perspective, the fundamental national security threats continue to come from aspiring Great Powers, and the United States continues to be the world's dominant or hegemonic state. Others see continuity in the continued growth and spread of globalization. We look at each of these in turn.

## Terrorism

To many the most prominent feature of the contemporary international system is terrorism. The July 2007 National Intelligence Estimate lent support to this perspective by concluding that the U.S. homeland will face a persistent and evolving terrorist threat over the next three years, with al Qaeda being the primary enemy. Used in its most value-free and politically neutral sense, terrorism is violence for the purpose of political intimidation. It is not the exclusive tool of any political ideology or political agenda. It does not specify an organizational form. Governments may engage in terrorism, but so too can NGOs such as al Qaeda. Terrorism is not a new phenomenon. All of this makes terrorism a difficult enemy. Today's brand of terrorism dates from 1979 and is the fourth wave of terrorism that has arisen since the 1880s.[13]

The preceding three waves each lasted a generation. If this pattern holds, the current wave of terrorism will not lose its energy until around 2025. The first, anarchist wave of terrorism began in Russia and was set in motion by the political and economic reform efforts of the Czars. The second, anticolonial wave of terrorism began in the 1920s and ended in the 1960s. These terrorists sought to obtain independence for those parts of the European empires where the ruling colonial power would not leave on its own. The third, New Left wave of terrorism was set in motion by the Vietnam War. It was made up of Marxist groups such as the Weather Underground (United States) and the Red Brigade (Italy) and separatist groups that sought self-determination for minority groups trapped inside larger states. A prominent example is the Palestine Liberation Organization (PLO).

The defining features of the current wave of terrorism are twofold. The first is its religious base, and Islam is at its core. Its initial energy was drawn from three events in 1979: the start of a new Moslem century, the ouster of the Shah in Iran, and the Soviet invasion of Afghanistan. The United States is the special target of this religious wave of terrorism. Iranian leaders have long referred to the United States as the "Great Satan," and the common goal shared by Islamic terrorist groups was to drive the United States out of the Middle East. Before 9/11, this wave had produced a steady flow of terrorist attacks on U.S. facilities. Marine barracks were attacked in Lebanon in 1983, the World Trade Center was struck in 1993, American embassies were attacked in Kenya and Tanzania in 1998, and the USS *Cole* was attacked in 2000. The second defining attribute is the specter of mass casualties. Whereas earlier waves of terror focused on assassinating key individuals or the symbolic killing of relatively small numbers of individuals, today we also see terrorist attacks resulting in large numbers of deaths.

Understanding how terrorism might be seen as the dominant feature of the contemporary international system requires more than placing it in a historical context. It also requires an understanding of its organizational characteristics. This is not easily done since terrorist groups change in structure frequently. Al Qaeda today is not the same organization as it was on 9/11. One way to think about how al Qaeda is organized is to view it as composed of a series of concentric rings, each of which presents different foreign policy challenges to the United States.[14] In the center is al Qaeda central, which comprises the organizational and leadership remnants of the pre–9/11 al Qaeda along with new recruits. It is believed to operate out of Afghanistan and parts of Pakistan. In the next ring are al Qaeda affiliates and associates. These are established terrorist groups found largely in the Middle East, Asia, and Africa; they have worked with al Qaeda central and received money, training, and guidance from it. In the third ring are al Qaeda locals. This category comprises individuals with active or dormant ties to al Qaeda who engage in terrorist activities that support its overarching goals. Finally, in the outermost circle is found the al Qaeda network. It is made up of home-grown radicals with no direct connection to al Qaeda but who are drawn to its ideology and act in support of it. They are not members of organized terrorist groups and often have few uniting ties. Members of the al Qaeda network have become increasingly visible in Europe. The al Qaeda network presents a significant challenge to American antiterrorism policy because military force is of limited value in negating the threat they pose.

The complex organizational structure of terrorist organizations along with the tactics they employ make formulating a counterterrorism strategy a difficult task. Perhaps the most fundamental question is whether or not we can fight a global war against terrorism. Some favor thinking of counterterrorism in terms of law enforcement activities, as was the case in London with the subway bombers and the would-be airplane hijackers. This might be particularly critical, as terrorism moves into the fourth circle of activity we noted earlier. Viewing terrorism in global or monolithic terms runs the risk of overstating its significance and potentially involving the United States unnecessarily in local conflicts in places such as Central Asia, Africa, and Pacific Asia.

There is also the question of how terrorist groups end. Much attention has been paid to the factors that might lead to terrorism, but what factors perpetuate terrorism and what factors bring about the end of terrorist groups? There is no reason to expect them to be the same.[15] This question is of special importance, given the emphasis placed by the United States on creating democracy as a long-term solution to the problem of terrorism. One scholar argues that the data show no link between democracy and terrorism and that they instead suggest a link between perceived foreign domination and terrorism.[16]

## Globalization

**Globalization** is the term used most frequently to characterize the structure of the international economic system today. For those who see it as the primary structural feature of the emerging international system, globalization is a reality and not a choice.[17] The problem facing the United States is not whether to participate in a globalized economy but how to participate. And, as with all underlying structural aspects of the international system, it places limits on state behavior—rewarding correct foreign and domestic policies and punishing states for adopting inappropriate ones. Having said that, *globalization* is an ill-defined term that is sometimes used interchangeably with *internationalization, Westernization,* and

*Americanization.* In trying to give more specific meaning to the term, most commentators define globalization as an economic process. For most commentators, globalization is an economic process that centers on the speed with which economies interact with one another and the intense and all-encompassing nature of those interactions. Economies do not simply trade with one another; they are transformed by their interactions. For its supporters, this transformation will lead to economic benefits and prosperity.

Globalization did not arrive on the scene suddenly or in one fell swoop. It emerged bit by bit over time. Although some commentators trace its foundations back to the eighteenth century, most identify its beginnings with the post–World War II era and the establishment of the Bretton Woods monetary system and its core institutions: the World Bank, the International Monetary Fund, and the General Agreement on Tariffs and Trade (GATT). Together they laid the foundation for an international economic system that facilitated and encouraged an ever-expanding and accelerating cross-border flow of money, commodities, ideas, and people. This foundation set in motion a chain reaction in the mid-1990s that led to what Thomas Friedman refers to as the "flattening of the world."[18]

Globalization, however, is much more than just an economic process. It is a dynamic mix of economic, political, social, and cultural forces. Not only does it alter the manner in which international economic transactions are conducted, it also affects the ability of governments to control their domestic economies and the ability of publics to hold their elected officials accountable, the solidarity and values of cultures, and the homogeneity of societies. In doing so, it holds the potential for bringing about both positive and negative changes within states and between them. Globalization may unleash the forces of democracy, but it may just as easily unleash a fundamentalist and defensive cultural backlash by those who feel threatened. Similarly, globalization accelerates the diffusion of technology and knowledge among people that may help solve global health and environmental problems, but it also allows terrorist groups to communicate with one another and to travel more efficiently as well as potentially to gain access to weapons of mass destruction.

Those who embrace globalization as the dominant structural feature of the contemporary international system see it as an irreversible process. Others are not convinced of this, raising the possibility that at some point globalization may collapse and we may enter into a postglobalist era. One of these contrarians is historian Niall Ferguson.[19] He sees echoes of the past in today's globalization, echoes that led to World War I and the Great Depression of the 1930s. The reasons for his pessimism are found not so much in the economic similarities between today and the pre–World War I era as they are in the global political similarities of the two periods. Economically, then as now, the United States possessed the world's biggest economy, China was opening up to the West, free trade was prevalent, there were few restrictions on immigration and capital flows, and a wave of technological innovation was sweeping the world. War was impossible: It was the "great illusion."[20]

War did happen then, and Ferguson argues that a similar fate could befall this era of globalization. He identifies five precipitating factors that led to the demise of globalization in the first part of the twentieth century. First is imperial overstretch: Great Britain was showing signs of tiring in its role as the keeper of global peace and prosperity. Second, signs pointed to a growing imperial rivalry between Germany and Russia. Third, existing alliance systems were unstable. Alliance leaders could not count on allies to follow them. Fourth, rogue regimes (e.g., Serbia) supported international terrorism (the assassination of Archduke Ferdinand). And fifth, there was in the emergence of the Bolsheviks the rise of a revolutionary terrorist group that was hostile to capitalism. Ferguson argues that similar conditions exist today. The United States is overstretched militarily, and the American public is on edge. China appears to many as a rising challenger to the United States. Neither NATO nor the United Nations provides the United States with a stable alliance system that will help it carry out preemptive strikes or peacekeeping operations. Syria and Iran are identified as sponsors of international terrorism, whereas other players, such as Pakistan, are less than enthusiastic in their pursuit of terrorists. Finally, Ferguson argues that al Qaeda is much more of an Islamo–Bolshevist terrorist group than it is an Islamo–fascist group.

## American Hegemony

In the early 1990s, in the first years after the end of the Cold War, a great debate raged over the direction in which the international system would evolve. Few questioned the assertion that the United States had won the Cold War, but many doubted that it could remain the sole superpower for very long. The logic of world politics seemed to dictate that other states would try to balance U.S. military power and that, as a result, we would soon see the emergence of a bipolar or, more likely, a multipolar system. Today, there is little life in this debate. Virtually all observers speak of unchallenged American military **hegemony**. The international military system is solidly unipolar. Some go so far as to argue that the United States is so strong that it cannot be balanced in the foreseeable future.[21]

What is less clear to observers is the character of American hegemony. The terms *Superpower* and *Great Power* seem not to be sufficient. Quite often today the United States is referred to as an *empire*. Not surprisingly, this characterization is controversial.[22] In its most neutral sense, an *empire* is a state with "a wide and supreme domain." The political, economic, and military reach of the United States fits that criterion, leading some to argue that in studying American foreign policy the most instructive point of reference is past empires. However, the term *empire* also carries very negative connotations. An empire is viewed as a state that imposes its will on others and rules through force and domination. Military occupation and the arbitrary use of military power typify their foreign policies. These are charges that have frequently been leveled at American foreign policy with regard to Iraq, where U.S. forces were greeted not as liberators but as occupiers, and with the George W. Bush administration's military doctrine of preemption. Critics of the *empire* label assert that what is being confused today is a negative reaction to the reach of American foreign policy, which is imperial in the sense that it is global, and the political ambition of the United States to directly or indirectly rule vast expanses of territory beyond its borders, which does not exist.

A competing view to the U.S.-as-empire vision of the contemporary international system is that America's unchallenged dominance allows it to act as the functional equivalent of a world government. It provides services that are needed for the effective functioning of the international system, such as military security, stewardship of the global economy, and emergency humanitarian aid. Were the United States not to carry out these and other crucial tasks, the international system might cease to function effectively, because no other state possesses the resources to do them, and a true world government is not likely to come into existence. One need not go this far to see American hegemony as being beneficial rather than exploitive. As one supporter of this position noted, it is in America's interest and the world's interest for American primacy to last as long as possible.[23]

But can it? Empires come with expiration dates. They do not last forever. And modern empires tend to have much shorter life spans than did ancient and early modern ones. The average Roman Empire lasted 829 years. The average Egyptian Empire lasted 365 years, and the British Empire lasted 336 years. Twentieth-century empires, in contrast, have lasted on average only 57 years.[24]

Pessimists assert that balancing by other major powers is to be expected and the end of American hegemony is inevitable. A variety of options exist for countries to follow in trying to counter American hegemony. At one extreme are direct military challenges to the United States, and at the other are soft balancing strategies of "leash slipping," by which countries try and maximize their ability to conduct independent foreign policies without challenging the United States directly.[25] Optimists hold that American hegemony can endure long into the future and that countries will stay on the American bandwagon indefinitely out of self-interest. Key is that the United States acts with restraint and pursues limited objectives so as not to stampede other countries into pulling away from the United States. Moreover, no credible challenger exists. Still, these observers recognize that hegemony is not without its costs to the United States and that it pays a price for primacy.[26] Allies may also pay a price in supporting the United States. Fouad Ajami observed of the United States's role in the Middle East shortly after 9/11, "a foreign power that stands sentry in that world cannot spare its local allies the retribution of those who brand them 'collaborators' and betrayers of the faith."[27]

A parallel debate exists over the location of the primary threat to American hegemony. Is it external, to be found in the actions of other states, or will hegemony pass because of the unwillingness of Americans to bear the economic and political burdens of being the world's only superpower? For those who see the threat to American hegemony as coming from within, the fear is of the emergence of an "Iraq syndrome" that—just as the Vietnam syndrome did—will cause policy makers to shy away from committing to the use of American military power. For those who look abroad for a threat to American hegemony, the primary candidates to play the role of challenger to American hegemony are authoritarian Great Powers such as Russia or China. In this view, while global capitalism is secure, the hold of democracy is not.[28] China, more so than Russia, tends to be identified as the most likely threat. Box 2.1 summarizes the view of China presented in a 2006 report to the U.S. Congress. It identifies China's rise in military power as having significant implications for U.S. security interests, noting that it could, over time, offset traditional American military advantages. Furthermore, it cautions that Chinese leaders have yet to explain the rationale

## Box 2.1  MILITARY POWER OF THE REPUBLIC OF CHINA, 2006

China's rapid rise as a regional political and economic power with global aspirations is an important element of today's strategic environment—one that has significant implications for the region and the world. The United States welcomes the rise of a peaceful and prosperous China. U.S. policy encourages China to participate as a responsible international stakeholder by taking on a greater share of responsibility for the health and success of the global system from which China has derived great benefit. . . .

The People's Liberation Army (PLA) is in the process of long-term transformation from a mass army designed for protracted wars of attrition on its territory to a more modern force capable of fighting short duration, high-intensity conflicts against high-tech adversaries. Today, China's ability to sustain military power at a distance is limited. However, as the 2006 Quadrennial Defense Review notes, "China has the greatest potential to compete militarily with the United States and field disruptive military technologies that could over time offset traditional U.S. military advantages."

In the near term, China's military build-up appears focused on preparing for Taiwan Strait contingencies, including the possibility of U.S. intervention. However, analysis of China's military acquisitions suggests it is also generating capabilities that could apply to other regional contingencies, such as conflicts over resource or territory.

The PLA's transformation features new doctrine for modern warfare, reform of military institutions . . . and the acquisition of advanced foreign (especially Russian) and domestic weapons systems. Several aspects of China's military development have surprised U.S. analysts, including the pace and scope of its military forces modernization. China's military expansion is already such as to alter regional military balances. Long-term trends in China's strategic nuclear forces modernization and land- and sea-based access denial capabilities, and emerging precision-strike weapons have the potential to pose credible threats to modern militaries operating in the region.

China's leaders have yet to adequately explain the purposes or desired end-states of their military expansion. Estimates place Chinese defense expenditures at two or three times officially disclosed figures. . . .

Absent greater transparency, international reactions to China's military growth will understandably hedge against these unknowns.

*Source:* "Executive Summary," Military Power of the Republic of China, 2006, Annual Report to Congress, Office of the Secretary of Defense.  ■

behind this buildup and that consequently China's military growth has to be watched carefully. Advocates of this view that China represents the most significant threat to continued U.S. hegemony point with concern to joint military exercises between Russia and China in 2005 and to China's testing of a missile defense system in early 2006.

## AMERICA AND THE WORLD: ATTITUDES AND PERCEPTIONS

The global setting of American foreign policy involves more than just a series of contemporary problems and underlying structural features. It also consists of attitudes and perceptions about the world. And, it is increasingly evident that Americans and non-Americans do not always see the world the same way. A 2006 poll of Americans and Russians undertaken by the Program on International Policy Attitudes asked respondents to rank the most powerful countries in the world. Both agreed that the United States was the most powerful country, giving it virtually the same score. After that their lists differed significantly, as shown by Table 2.1. Americans saw China as the next most powerful country, but also saw it as a fairly distant second. Russia saw the European Union as a much closer second to the United States and ranked Russia third. Americans had Russia a much more distant sixth.

A poll carried out in late 2006 and released in January 2007 compared Iranian and American attitudes toward each other and on key international politics issues.[29] It found that most Iranians had a negative opinion of the United States, with 65 percent holding unfavorable views of it and 93 percent

### TABLE 2.1

WHO IS MOST POWERFUL?

| Most Powerful Countries According to Americans | Response on 1–10 Scale, with 10 Being the Highest | Most Powerful Countries According to Russians | Response on 1–10 Scale, with 10 Being the Highest |
|---|---|---|---|
| United States | 8.77 | United States | 8.74 |
| China | 6.63 | European Union | 7.14 |
| Great Britain | 6.61 | Russia | 6.57 |
| Japan | 6.2 | Great Britain | 6.2 |
| European Union | 5.78 | Japan | 6.18 |
| Russia | 5.67 | China | 6.1 |
| Germany | 5.06 | Germany | 6.1 |

Source: Data from "Americans and Russians Agree U.S. Is No. 1, but Disagree on the Up and Comers." worldpublicopinion.org/pipa/articles/views_on_countriesregions_bt/225.php?

holding negative views of the U.S. government. Most Americans held similarly negative views of Iran, with 80 percent saying it has a negative influence on world affairs and 78 percent holding a negative view of the Iranian government. Still, citizens of both countries rejected the inevitability of conflict. Twenty-four percent of Iranians did not believe that conflict was inevitable, and 54 percent thought it was possible to find common ground. Thirty-six percent of Americans thought it was possible to avoid conflict, and 56 percent felt it was possible to find common ground. In looking at specific issues, one finds areas of both agreement and disagreement. Majorities in both states saw terrorism as a critical threat (56 percent in Iran, 68 percent in the United States), but differed on the seriousness of global warming (61 percent in Iran saw it as critical, but only 48 percent did so in the United States), potential global epidemics (77 percent in Iran and 48 percent in the United States), and drug trafficking (85 percent in Iran saw it as a critical threat, while 47 percent in the United States saw it this way).

Differences in outlook between Americans and others potentially extend far beyond questions of who is most important or what to do about world problems. They also extend to more fundamental feelings about what is right and what is wrong and about who is good and who is bad. A July 2009 global public opinion poll found that citizens of one in four countries said the United States treated their country fairly, while two-thirds said it abused its power. Overall, majorities of those interviewed said that the United States uses the threat of military force to gain an advantage. Countries were evenly split on whether the United States was playing a mainly positive or negative role in world affairs.[30]

Looking beyond the answers to specific questions, it is possible to distinguish among four different types of anti-Americanism.[31] First, there is liberal anti-Americanism. It is commonly found in other advanced industrial societies. At its core is the charge that the United States repeatedly fails to live up to its own ideals in conducting its foreign policy. A second strain of negative feelings toward the United States is social anti-Americanism. Here the complaint is with the United States trying to impose its version of democracy and its definition of rights on others while being insensitive to local societal values and norms. Third, there is sovereign anti-Americanism. This version of anti-Americanism focuses on the threats the United States presents to the sovereignty and to the cultural and political identity of another country. It matters not whether the country is powerful or weak for there to be a nationalistic backlash. Finally, there is radical anti-Americanism. It defines American values as evil and subscribes to the notion that only by destroying them can the world be made safe.

The world is not solidly anti-American. Pro-American views tend to be most pronounced among those aged 60 and older, a factor many attribute to American foreign policy initiatives during the Cold War. Another group that has solidly pro-American sentiments is made up of individuals identified as "aspirational." They are upwardly mobile people or individuals who would like to be. They do not fit easily into any demographic category. In some cases these are people from low-income or low-education backgrounds, whereas in other cases they are among the younger and wealthier citizens of a country.[32]

## OVER THE HORIZON

Our Somali pirate anecdote highlights three important points that need to be kept in mind when thinking about the current international system and looking over the horizon to anticipate the future. First, the international system is multilayered. Some features, those we labeled as structural constants, have exerted their influence on foreign policy for generations. Other features, ones we labeled as Cold War trends and dominant features of the contemporary international system, are more recent and have been grafted on top of this base but are just as important to understanding U.S. foreign policy. Second, the dynamics these enduring and more recent features of the international system create can bring about unexpected foreign policy challenges and opportunities. They can be seen as acting much in the manner of the giant tectonic plates beneath the Earth's crust that can suddenly unleash tremendous pressures that transform the world's geography.[33] Few would have predicted that dealing with piracy would be a twenty-first-century foreign policy problem. Third, not everyone will define upcoming foreign policy problems the same way. These differences will be rooted both in theoretical perspectives on the nature of world politics and in normative value judgments about what is important and what needs to be done.

What then might the future hold? One possibility suggested is that the focal point of international relations might shift again. Where once U.S. foreign policy was heavily European oriented, it now focuses on Asia Pacific, China, Japan, and the Korean Peninsula. The next focal point may be the Indian Ocean due to the combined importance of terrorism, Islam, oil, and the rise of India and China.[34]

A second trend that might emerge is an increased concern for the way in which domestic politics affects international relations. The idea behind intermestic politics is that international events influence domestic policy. We are starting to see the reverse. The increasingly violent situation along the U.S.–Mexico border is a case in point. Secretary of State Hillary Clinton observed that the repeated failures of U.S. antinarcotics policies at home have contributed greatly to the explosion of drug violence along the border. Others have noted that one factor complicating U.S. efforts to eliminate or control the activities of Mexican drug cartels is the ease with which they can cross into the United States and buy guns at gun shows. One gun dealer alone was found to have sold more than 700 AK-47 assault rifles and pistols to individuals known to be buying for drug cartels. The case was thrown out of court.

## CRITICAL THINKING QUESTIONS

1. Which of the three theoretical perspectives we introduced (realism, neoliberalism, and constructivism) is best suited for guiding thinking about U.S. foreign policy today?
2. Is globalism or hegemony the most important current feature of the international system today for U.S. foreign policy?
3. Which features of the international system are most influential in determining the success or failure of U.S. foreign policies, Cold War trends or structural constants?

## KEY TERMS

bipolar 34
constructivism 33
globalization 45
hegemony 47

intermestic 40
multipolar 34
neoliberalism 33
realism 32

sovereignty 37
terrorism 44
unipolar 34

## FURTHER READING

Stephen Brooks and William Wohklforth, *World Out of Balance: International Relations and the Challenge of American Primacy* (Princeton: Princeton University Press, 2008).

Buzan Barry, *The United States and the Great Powers: World Politics in the Twenty-First Century* (Malden, MA: Polity Press, 2004).

John Lewis, Gaddis, *The United States and the End of the Cold War: Implications, Reconsiderations and Provocations* (New York: Oxford University Press, 1992).

John, Ikenberry, (ed.), *America Unrivaled* (Ithaca: Cornell University Press, 2002).

Alexander Wendt, *Social Theory of International Relations* (New York: Cambridge University Press, 1999).

## NOTES

1. See Kenneth Waltz, *Theory of International Politics* (New York: McGraw-Hill, 1979).
2. See Andrew Moravcsik, "Taking Preferences Seriously: A Liberal theory of International Politics," *International Organization* 51 (1997), 513–553.***
3. See Alexander Wendt, *Social Theory of International Politics* (New York: Cambridge University Press, 1999).
4. David Calleo, "The Tyranny of False Vision: America's Unipolar Fantasy," *Survival* 50 (2008), 61–78.
5. Walter Pincus, "Ex-Advisers Warn Against Threatening to Attack Iran," *Washington Post*, July 23, 2008, A11.
6. The New York Times, *The Tower Commission Report* (New York: Bantam, 1987), p. 137.
7. Robert Tucker, *The Inequality of Nations* (New York: Basic Books, 1977).
8. Robert Gilpin, *War and Change in World Politics* (New York: Cambridge University Press, 1981). For a dissenting view on the decline of U.S. power, see Bruce Russett, "The Mysterious Case of Vanishing Hegemony; or, Is Mark Twain Really Dead?" *International Organization*, 39 (1985), 207–32.
9. Bayliss Manning, "The Congress, the Executive and Intermestic Affairs: Three Proposals," *Foreign Affairs*, 56 (1977), 306–24.
10. For discussions of the growth of nonstate actors, see Werner Feld, *International Relations, A Transnational Approach* (Sherman Oaks, CA: Alfred, 1979); and Harold K. Jacobson, *Networks of Interdependence* (New York: Knopf, 1979). For statistics, see the Yearbook of International Organizations, www.uia.org/statistics/organizations/types. The data for 2004 are found in appendix 3, table 1.
11. The three subsystems as well as the management problems they present are taken from Joan Edleman Spero, *The Politics of International Economic Relations*, 3rd ed. (New York: St. Martin's, 1985), pp. 13–19.
12. William Dobson, "The Day Nothing Much Changed," *Foreign Policy,* 156 (2006), 22–25.

13. David C. Rapoport, "The Four Waves of Modern Terrorism," and Audrey Kurth Cronin, "The Sources of Contemporary Terrorism," in Audrey Kurth Cronin and James Ludes (eds.), *Attacking Terrorism* (Washington, DC: Georgetown University Press, 2004).

14. Bruce Hoffman, "From Global War on Terror to Global Counterinsurgency," *Current History,* 105 (December 2006), 423–29.

15. Audrey Kurth Cronin, "How al-Qaida Ends: The Decline and Demise of Terrorist Groups," *International Security,* 31 (2006), 7–48.

16. F. Gregory Gause III, "Can Democracy Stop Terrorism?" *Foreign Affairs,* 84 (2005), 62–76.

17. Richard Haass and Robert Litan, "Globalization and Its Discontents: Navigating the Dangers of an Entangled World," *Foreign Affairs,* 77 (1998), 2–6.

18. Thomas Friedman, *The World Is Flat* (New York: Farrar, Straus & Giroux, 2005).

19. Niall Ferguson, "Sinking Globalization," *Foreign Affairs,* 84 (2005), 64–77.

20. Roger Angell, *The Great Illusion* (London: William Heinemann, 1912).

21. William Wohlforth, "U.S. Strategy in a Unipolar World," in G. John Ikenberry (ed.), *America Unrivaled* (Ithaca, NY: Cornell University Press, 2002), pp. 98–118.

22. Alexander Motyl, "Empire Falls," *Foreign Affairs,* 85 (2006), 190–94.

23. Michael Mandelbaum, *The Case for Goliath* (New York: Public Affairs Press, 2005).

24. Niall Ferguson, "Empires with Expiration Dates," *Foreign Policy,* 156 (2006), 46–52.

25. Christopher Layne, "Impotent Power?" *The National Interest,* 85 (September/October 2006), 41–47.

26. Bradley Thayer, "In Defense of Primacy," *The National Interest,* 86 (November/December 2006), 32–37. See also Ethan Kapstein and Michael Mastanduno (eds.), *Unipolar Politics* (New York: Columbia University Press, 1999).

27. Fouad Ajami, "The Sentry's Solitude," *Foreign Affairs,* 80 (2001), 15.

28. Azar Gat, "The Return of Authoritarian Great Powers," *Foreign Affairs,* 86 (2007), 59–69.

29. *Public Opinion in Iran and America on Key International Issues*, January 24, 2007, World Public Opinion.Org, www.worldpublicopinion.org/pipa/articles/home_page.

30. *Though Obama Viewed Positively, Still Much Criticism of US Foreign Policy: Global Poll,* WorldPublicOpinion.org. July 7, 2009.

31. Peter Katzenstein and Robert Keohane, "Anti-Americanisms," *Policy Review,* 139 (2006), 25–37.

32. Anne Applebaum, "In Search of Pro-Americanism," *Foreign Policy,* 149 (2005), 32–40.

33. John Lewis Gaddis, "Toward the Post–Cold War World," *Foreign Affairs,* 70 (1991), 102–22; and "Tectonics, History, and the End of the Cold War," in John Lewis Gaddis, *The United States and the End of the Cold War: Implications, Reconsiderations, Provocations* (New York: Oxford University Press, 1992), pp. 155–67.

34. Robert Kaplan, "Center Stage for the Twenty-first Century: Power Plays in the Indian Ocean," *Foreign Affairs,* 88 (2009), 16–44.

# The American National Style

The U.S.–Mexico border is 1,969 miles long and is the world's most frequently crossed international border, with some 250 million people moving across it. While many enter and exit the United States legally, it also has the highest number of illegal border crossings, with an estimated 500,000 illegal entries into it taking place every year. It is also a deadly border. From 1998 to 2004, 1,954 migrants died trying to cross it.

In 2005, members of Congress proposed constructing a fence along the entire U.S.–Mexican border to stop illegal immigration and prevent terrorists from entering the United States. The following year, in October 2006, President George W. Bush signed the Secure Fence Act, which called for creating a double-reinforced fence along 700 miles of the border where illegal drug trafficking and immigration were most common. In signing the bill, he stated, "this bill will help protect the American people. This bill will make our borders more secure. It is an important step toward immigration reform."

The "fence" is actually made up of several different barrier projects. In some locations it is a physical structure. In others it is a virtual fence made up of mobile towers, radar, cameras, and vehicles retrofitted with laptops, satellite phones, or handheld devices that are linked to a near-real-time maplike projection of the frontier. Just prior to President Barack Obama's inauguration in January 2009, more than 580 miles of fence was in place.

The project has proven to be controversial on a number of counts. It has experienced significant cost overruns, with the Bush administration asserting in fall 2008 that they were running out of money to complete the fence. Technical problems arose, forcing changes in plans, and more than thirty legal waivers were used to bypass existing laws and regulations. Among those Acts for which the project received exemptions from were the Endangered Species Act, the Clean Water Act, the Clean Air Act, and the National Historic Preservation Act. Michael Chertoff, Secretary of the Department of Homeland Security Department justified the legal waivers, stating, "criminal activity does not stop for endless debate or protracted litigation." States and communities along the border registered objections to the concept of a fence because of the negative impact it had on the economic health of their areas.

No one can doubt the complexity of illegal immigration as a foreign policy problem, and it is unlikely that any one solution exists for it. In this chapter, we explore the American national style of thinking about foreign policy in order to understand why it is that the United States repeatedly embraces some types of policies and rejects other lines of action that are open to it. We begin by looking at the importance of ideas and then turn to the sources and consequences of the American national style. We pay special attention to the alternation between isolationism and internationalism. Finally, we look to Wilsonianism and its competitors for insight into how the United States defines its role in the world today.

# THE IMPORTANCE OF IDEAS

Policy makers come and go, but ideas and ways of thinking endure. George W. Bush's major foreign policy innovation, moving from **containment** and **deterrence** to **preemption,** strikes many casual observers of U.S. foreign policy as a radical departure from the past, but others see in it the long reach of American history.[1] The same holds true for **neoconservatism** more generally. It is the set of foreign policy ideas that formed the core of the administration's view of world politics and was the conceptual foundation for the Bush doctrine, with its emphasis on preemption, unilateral action, and support for democratization. To many it is neither "neo" nor "conservative." Its core ideas of moralism, idealism, exceptionalism, militarism, and global ambition have deep intellectual roots in the American foreign policy tradition.[2]

The importance of ideas as a force in foreign policy decision making stems from both their immediate and long-term effects.[3] In the short run, shared ideas help policy makers and citizens cope with the inherent uncertainty involved in selecting among competing policy lines. Consistency with the principles of free trade or isolationism may not produce the "correct" policy, but these criteria do provide a basis for the selection or rejection of one. Ideas also become institutionalized, as organizations and laws are designed around them. Because organizations and laws are slow to change, they become an anchor for any future reform debate. And once they are in place, political constituencies coalesce around policies rooted in these ideas and lobby for their continued existence. As a result, ideas continue to exert an influence on policy long after they have lost their vitality and after those who espoused them have passed from the scene. Viewed over the long term, the result of this interplay of policies and ideas is a layered pattern in which policies reflecting different sets of ideas and pulling in different directions are combined, with little overall coherence.

This pattern is very much evident in American commercial policy. Conventional attempts to explain American trade policies focus on the political leverage of societal interest groups or the demands of the international system.[4] Others argue that only by looking at ideas, the "political salience of economic theories," can one explain America's movement from a protectionist cycle that began in the early nineteenth century and culminated in the highly protective tariffs of the 1930s to a free-trade cycle that now contains elements of both free trade and fair trade.

The national security policy arena provides an even clearer picture of the influence of shared ideas and ways of acting on American foreign policy. Throughout most of the Cold War period, these ideas and actions were embodied in the concept of containment. The first public statement of containment came in an article in *Foreign Affairs* written by George Kennan. In it he argued:

> Soviet pressure against the free institutions of the western world is something that can be contained by the adroit and vigilant application of counter-force at a series of constantly shifting geographical and political points, corresponding to the shifts and maneuvers of Soviet policy but which cannot be charmed or talked out of existence.[5]

The logic of containment became embodied in a wide range of U.S. foreign policy initiatives. The Truman Doctrine, which pledged U.S. support to all states coming under pressure from international communism, was faithful to it. So too were early U.S. foreign aid programs intended to rebuild the economies of Western Europe (the Marshall Plan) and bring economic development to the Third World (the Four Point Program). It was U.S. military policy, however, that became the primary vehicle for implementing containment, in the form of a series of encircling alliances around the Soviet perimeter: the North Atlantic Treaty Organization (NATO), the Southeast Asia Treaty Organization (SEATO), and the Central Treaty Organization (CENTO). What disagreements existed within policy-making circles arose largely over the tactics and strategies to be used and not the ends of U.S. foreign policy. Such disputes were possible in part because in his article Kennan did not specify the means of containment. He would later become a critic of containment, arguing that his ideas had been misinterpreted and misapplied. Kennan specifically objected to the heavy reliance on military force and the perceived need to practice containment everywhere and anywhere that communist expansion was encountered.

Even the Nixon administration's much heralded shift to a policy of **détente** could be comfortably fitted into the larger strategy of containment. Détente was designed to protect U.S. influence as much as possible in an era of lessened power abroad and increasingly isolationist feeling at home. Confrontation and crisis management were now too expensive to be the primary means for stopping Soviet expansion. Détente sought to accomplish this end by creating a framework of limited cooperation within the context of an international order that recognized the legitimacy of both U.S. and Soviet core security goals.[6]

This long-term continuity in U.S. foreign policy goes back to before the period of containment. It stretches back to the very beginnings of the United States. In this chapter we examine the foundations of the American **national style** of foreign policy. First, we look at the tendency for U.S. foreign policy to fluctuate between **isolationism** and **internationalism**. Second, we examine the patterns of thought and action that provide the building blocks for both of these general foreign policy orientations. Finally, we look to the post–Cold War era.

## ISOLATIONISM VERSUS INTERNATIONALISM

U.S. foreign policy is frequently discussed in terms of a tension between two opposing general foreign policy orientations: isolationism and internationalism. From the isolationist perspective, American national interests are best served by "quitting the world" or, at a minimum, maintaining a healthy sense of detachment from events elsewhere. It draws its inspiration from Washington's Farewell Address, in which he urged Americans to "steer clear of permanent alliances with any portion of the foreign world" and asserted that "Europe has a set of primary interests which to us have none or very remote relations."[7] Among the major foreign policy decisions rooted in the principles of isolationism are the Monroe Doctrine, the refusal to join the League of Nations, the neutrality legislation of the 1930s, and, more loosely, the fear of future Vietnams. The internationalist perspective sees protecting and promoting American national interests as requiring an activist foreign policy. Internationalists hold that the United States cannot escape the world. Events abroad inevitably impinge upon U.S. interests, and any policy based on the denial of their relevance is self-defeating.

The global depression of the 1930s, Hitler's rise to power, the outbreak of World War II, and the constant outward thrust of post–World War II communism are proof to the internationalists that Washington's advice is no longer relevant. Such widely divergent undertakings as membership in the United Nations (UN) and NATO, the Marshall Plan, the Alliance for Progress, covert action by the Central Intelligence Agency (CIA), the Helsinki Human Rights Agreement, and involvement in Korea and Vietnam can be traced to the internationalist perspective on world affairs. The oscillation between isolationism and internationalism has not been haphazard. An underlying logic appears to guide the movement from one to the other. Five different periods of U.S. foreign policy of 20–30 years' duration have been identified.[8] Each combines an introvert (isolationist) and extrovert (internationalist) phase. According to this line of analysis, the United States is currently in an internationalist phase, with the next isolationist phase set to begin around 2014.

| Introvert | Extrovert |
|-----------|-----------|
| 1. 1776–1798 | 1798–1824 |
| 2. 1824–1844 | 1844–1871 |
| 3. 1871–1891 | 1891–1918 |
| 4. 1918–1940 | 1940–1967 |
| 5. 1967–1987 | 1987–2014 |

In each period, U.S. policy makers were forced to confront a major foreign policy problem. In period 1, it was independence; in period 2, issues involving manifest destiny were dominant; and in period 3, it was the process of becoming an industrial power. The crisis of world democracy dominated period 4, and today the need to create a stable world order lies at the heart of the challenges facing U.S. foreign policy. In each period, the dominant cycle (introversion or extroversion) imposes limits on the types of solutions that can be considered by policy makers and predisposes the public to accept certain courses of action. The cyclical movement between isolationism and internationalism is seen as being spiral in nature. Each movement toward internationalism is deeper than the one before it, and each reversal to isolationism is less complete than the one preceding it.

Disagreement exists over the mechanism that triggers a shift from one phase to the next. A number of possibilities have been suggested. A possibility is that shifts in foreign policy orientations may be tied to the business cycle.[9] Some have found that in periods of economic recovery after a period of stagnation and decline U.S. foreign policy takes on a belligerent tone. Similarly, the more stable the economy, the more moderate is U.S. foreign policy. In a similar vein it has been argued that the periodic outward thrust of U.S. foreign policy is a product of domestic frustrations and disappointments.[10] Foreign policy successes are sought as a sign that the American dream is still valid and capable of producing victories.

Whatever the specific trigger, the movement from isolationism to internationalism and back again is made possible because both general foreign policy orientations are very much a part of the American national style. One does not represent the American approach to world affairs, and the other its denial. They are two different ways in which the patterns of American foreign policy, its fundamental building blocks, come together.[11] Both are united in the conviction that the institutions and ideals brought forward by the American experience need protection. The approaches differ on how best to provide for their continued growth and development. Isolationism seeks to accomplish this end by insulating the American experience from corrupting foreign influences. Internationalism seeks to protect them by creating a more hospitable global environment. For both, world affairs gain meaning and importance (or irrelevance) primarily in terms of how they affect the American historical experience and American ideals.

## SOURCES OF THE AMERICAN NATIONAL STYLE

The sources of the American national style are found in many places.[12] One of the most frequently talked about influences is the conditions under which earlier generations of American policy makers operated and the ideas that guided their thinking. Few nations can look back on as favorable a set of conditions in which to grow and develop. The vast size of the United States brought with it an abundance of natural resources on which to build a prosperous economy. Between the mid-1600s and the mid-1800s, America grew from a series of isolated settlements into an economic power rivaling its European counterparts. Just as important for the development of the American national style is the fact that this growth took place without any master plan. Individual self-reliance, flexibility, and improvisation were the cardinal virtues in developing America. Guided by these principles, the United States has become a "how-to-do-it" society, whose energies are largely directed to the problem at hand and whose long-range concerns receive scant attention.[13]

It also needs to be noted that this growth occurred in an era of unparalleled global harmony. With the exception of the Crimean War, from the Congress of Vienna in 1815 until the outbreak of World War I in 1914, the Great Powers of Europe were largely at peace with one another. Closer to home, the defense of America's continental borders never required the creation of a large standing army or navy. For more than a century, America's peace and security required very little effort on its part. Peace and security seemed to come naturally, and they were widely accepted as the normal condition of world affairs. The links between American security and developments abroad went unnoticed. Democracy, rather than the strength of the British navy or the European balance of power, was seen as the source of American security.

The faith in the power of democracy reflects the extent to which American political thought is rooted in the eighteenth-century view of human nature. Most important to the development of the ideas that have guided U.S. policy makers is the work of John Locke, who argued that people are rational beings capable of determining their own best interests. The best government was held to be that which governed least. To Locke, the historical record indicated that the exercise of power led inevitably to its abuse and corrupted the natural harmony that exists among individuals. Conflicts between individuals could be settled without the application of concentrated state power. The wastefulness and destructiveness of war disqualified it as a means of conflict resolution. Negotiation, reason, and discussion are sufficient to overcome misperceptions and reconcile conflicting interests.

In contrast to war, trade is seen as a force promoting the peaceful settlement of disputes. The dynamics of the marketplace bind individuals together in mutually profitable exchanges. The power of the marketplace and the power of governments are seen as being in direct competition with one another. The greater the power of one over society, the lesser the power of the other. Because commerce creates a vested interest in peace, logic again points to limiting government powers. The American historical experience seemed to offer vivid proof of the correctness of the liberal outlook on human affairs.

Much attention, of late, has also been given to the influence of religion on American foreign policy.[14] Four components of this religious frame to American foreign policy are especially important. First is the idea of America as God's "chosen nation." Second, America has a special mission or calling to transform the world. Third, in carrying out this mission, the United States is engaged in a struggle against evil. Finally, American foreign policy has come to be characterized by an apocalyptic outlook on world affairs. Change will come about not through gradual or subtle changes but through a cataclysmic transformation in which evil is encountered and then decisively and permanently defeated.

One must be careful, however, to recognize that not all religions necessarily view world politics or America's role in the world in the same way. For example, within Protestantism, three different schools of thought speak to the conduct of American foreign policy.[15] They are fundamentalism, evangelicalism, and liberal Christianity. Though long established, what has drawn attention to them today are their changing political fortunes. Liberal Christianity provided the worldview for such key members of the founding generation of "Cold Warriors" as Dean Acheson, John Foster Dulles, Harry Truman, and Dwight Eisenhower. It is now in decline and has been replaced by fundamentalism and evangelicalism as the politically dominant forces among Protestantism. Fundamentalism had been pushed to the margins of American politics during the 1920s and 1930s. Before its recent return to influence, the heyday of political influence for evangelicals was the later part of the nineteenth century and the early decades of the twentieth century.

Fundamentalism and evangelicalism each provide a different sort of lens for looking at America's place in the world. Fundamentalists are deeply pessimistic about the possibility of bringing about a new world order and see a deep divide separating believers and nonbelievers. At the same time defensive and self-confident, they hold an apocalyptic view of the future and are not particularly interested in cooperating with those with whom they disagree. Liberals, in contrast, are optimistic about the potential for establishing a new world order and do not stress the differences between Christians and nonbelievers. They have little trouble cooperating with those who represent other religious traditions. In between these two extremes are the evangelicals. Like fundamentalists, they divide the world into believers and nonbelievers. Evangelicals are far more optimistic than fundamentalists in their view about the potential for progress and cooperation among different people. They do so, however, not out of a sense that it is the correct thing to do because of a shared humanity, but because of their mission to create a carry out God's will and create a new Puritan commonwealth. Here again, of course, caution must be exercised in making generalizations. Some sixty or seventy different evangelical/fundamentalist groups exist, and they do not all hold identical foreign policy positions. In fact, for many of these groups, foreign policy is quite secondary in importance to domestic social policy.[16]

American exceptionalism, regardless of its source, is taken to demand a leadership role in world affairs.[17] During isolationist periods, leadership takes the form of standing apart from international politics and leading by example. In internationalist periods, it is revealed in attempts to transform the international system. Defending the Clinton administration's use of cruise missiles against Iraq in 1998, Secretary of State Madeline Albright asserted that "if we use force, it is because we are America. We are the indispensable nation. We stand tall. We see farther into the future." Vice President Dick Cheney spoke in equally expansive terms in 2002, stating, "America has friends and allies in this cause, but only we can lead it. . . . The responsibility did not come to us by chance. We are in a unique position because of our unique assets, because of the character of our people, the strength of our ideals."

Before proceeding, a caveat is in order. This is not the only way to characterize the American historical experience, value system, or national style.[18] For some, the United States has been antirevolutionary, seeking to prevent social change and Third World revolutionary movements that might threaten its dominant position in world affairs. This view is often found in the writings of revisionist historians who find U.S. foreign policy to be imperial in nature and rooted in the expansionist needs of capitalism. Others see U.S. foreign policy as racist, as evidenced by its immigration policy, which systematically discriminated against the Chinese and other non–Western Europeans; its hesitancy to support international human rights conventions; and its attitude toward the suitability of Hawaii, Puerto Rico, and the Philippines for either statehood or independence. Finally, some argue that what we have called internationalism is better defined as interventionism: a tendency to intervene in the affairs of other states to a degree far beyond what is required by any reasonable definition of

U.S. national interest. In this view, there is no competing theme of isolationism but only an opposition to specific cases of intervention (such as Vietnam) on pragmatic or tactical grounds.

## PATTERNS

### Unilateralism

Three patterns of thought and action provide the building blocks from which the American national style emerges. The first pattern is **unilateralism**, or a predisposition to act alone in addressing foreign policy problems.[19] Unilateralism does not dictate a specific course of action. Isolationism, neutrality, activism, and interventionism are all consistent with its basic orientation to world affairs. The unilateralist thrust of U.S. foreign policy represents a rejection of the balance-of-power approach for providing national security. This approach, which is second nature to European diplomats, is alien to the American experience. Security could largely be taken for granted, and collaborative efforts were unnecessary. The willingness to apply the American approach to security on a global basis also reflects the American sense of exceptionalism and is often perceived by others to be an insensitive and egoistic nationalism.

The best-known statement of the unilateralist position is the Monroe Doctrine. With the end of the Napoleonic Wars, concern arose that Spain might attempt to reestablish its control over the newly independent Latin American republics. Great Britain approached the United States about the possibility of a joint declaration to prevent this from happening. The United States rejected the British proposal, only to turn around and make a unilateral declaration to the same end: The United States would not tolerate European intervention in the Western Hemisphere, and in return it pledged not to interfere in European affairs. In 1904, the Roosevelt Corollary to the Monroe Doctrine was put forward. Spurred into action by the inability of the Dominican Republic to pay its foreign lenders, President Theodore Roosevelt sent in U.S. forces. The Roosevelt Corollary established the United States as the self-proclaimed policeman of the Western Hemisphere. It would play that role many times. The years 1904–1934 saw the United States send eight expeditionary forces to Latin America, conduct five military occupations ranging in duration from a few months to 19 years, and take over customs collections duties twice. The legacy of the Monroe Doctrine continues into the post–World War II era. The CIA-sponsored overthrows of the Arbenz government in Guatemala and the Allende government in Chile, U.S. behavior in the Bay of Pigs and the Cuban missile crisis, the 1965 invasion of the Dominican Republic, the 1983 invasion of Grenada, and the 1989 invasion of Panama testify to the continued influence of unilateralism on U.S. behavior in the Western Hemisphere.

The nature of the American participation in World War I and the subsequent U.S. refusal to join the League of Nations also reflect the unilateralist impulse. Official World War I documents identify the victors as the Allied and Associated Powers. The only Associated Power of note was the United States. For U.S. policy makers, this was more than a mere symbolic separation from its European allies. Woodrow Wilson engaged in personal negotiations with Germany over ending the war without consulting the allies about the terms of a possible truce. The United States was also the only major victorious power not to join the League of Nations. This abstention is often attributed to isolationism, but Robert Tucker argues that the U.S. refusal represented a triumph of unilateralism.[20] Membership would have committed the United States to a collective security system that could have obliged it to undertake multilateral military action in the name of stopping international aggression.

The impact of unilateralist thinking also comes through clearly in the neutrality legislation of the 1930s. These acts placed an embargo on the sale of arms to warring states. Because arms sales were seen as the most likely method of U.S. entry into a war, they had to be prohibited regardless of the consequences that the embargo might have on events elsewhere. The post–World War II shift from isolationism to internationalism did not bring about an abandonment of unilateralism; it only placed a multilateral façade over it. Control over NATO's nuclear forces remains firmly in the hands of the United States. The presence of the UN flag in Korea and references to SEATO treaty commitments in Vietnam could scarcely conceal the totally U.S. nature of these two wars. In the United Nations, the United States' veto power protects its vital interests from the intrusion of other powers, and the system of weighted voting used in international financial organizations guarantees the United States a preponderant voice in their deliberations.

The American penchant for unilateralism was never far beneath the surface in its dealings with allies during the later years of the Cold War. Nowhere was this more evident than in the Reagan administration's secret effort to sell arms to Iran in return for the freedom of American hostages in Lebanon at a time when its public stance was one of pressuring allies not to negotiate with terrorists. Unilateralism was also evident in its approach to summitry. James Schlesinger argues that at the Reykjavik summit meeting with Soviet leader Mikhail Gorbachev, "The administration suddenly jettisoned 25 years of deterrence doctrine . . . without warning, consultation with Congress or its allies."[21]

Unilateralism continued to characterize U.S. foreign policy in the post–Cold War era. President George H. W. Bush embraced unilateralism in assembling a global coalition against Saddam Hussein. It was the United States that decided when to launch air strikes; it was the United States that decided when to begin ground operations; it was the United States that ended the ground war; and it was the United States that declared the coalition's objectives to have been met. A vivid reminder of the continued pull of unilateralist thinking in the post–Cold War era came early in the Clinton administration when, as a price for congressional approval of the GATT (General Agreement on Tariffs and Trade) agreement, Clinton agreed to insert an "escape hatch" into the treaty that would allow the United States to withdraw if the World Trade Organization's arbitration process consistently violated U.S. rights. President George W. Bush acted unilaterally several times in the first months of his presidency. The most notable examples included his decision not to participate in the Kyoto Protocol or the international criminal court and to proceed with the ballistic missile defense system. Both decisions were made in the face of protests by U.S. allies.

The global war against terrorism did not change this unilateralist impulse; if anything, it reinforced it. In December 2001, George W. Bush unilaterally gave notice that the United States was withdrawing from the 1972 Antiballistic Missile Treaty. In his State of the Union address the following month, he gave notice to the world that he was prepared to act unilaterally against terrorism. "Some governments will be timid in the face of terror. . . . If they do not act, America will." Unilateralism became part of the CIA's standard operating procedure in Pakistan, as it first sought to eliminate al Qaeda hiding in that country and later attack Taliban forces using the border region as a sanctuary. Frustrated by Pakistan's refusal to permit missile strikes against these targets, it began simply to inform Pakistani officials that a strike was underway.

## Moral Pragmatism

The second pattern in American foreign policy is **moral pragmatism**.[22] The American sense of morality involves two elements. The first is that state behavior can be judged by moral standards. The second is that American morality provides the universal standard for making those judgments. By definition, American actions are taken to be morally correct and justifiable. Justifying the invasion of Panama as being necessary to protect democracy is a case in point. Flawed policy initiatives are routinely attributed to leadership deficiencies or breakdowns in organizational behavior and not to the values that guided that action. In the aftermath of World War I, the Nye Committee investigated charges that the United States had been led into war by banking interests, and the McCarthy investigations followed the "loss of China."

In judging state behavior by moral standards, the United States typically makes the leap of placing responsibility for foreign policy problems on the evil nature of the opponent rather than on the underlying dynamics of world politics or its own actions. George Kennan, the author of the containment doctrine, put it this way: "There seems to be a curious American tendency to search, at all times, for a single external evil, to which all can be attributed." Some 50 years later, a neoconservative columnist writing shortly after the 9/11 attacks, asserted, "America is no mere international citizen. . . . America is in a position to reshape norms, alter expectations, and create new realities. How? By unapologetic and implacable demonstrations of will."[23]

American pragmatism takes the form of an "engineering approach" to foreign policy problem solving.[24] U.S. involvement is typically put in terms of "setting things right." It is assumed that a right answer does exist and that it is the American answer. Moreover, the answer to the problem (be it Lebanon, Nicaragua, the defense of Europe, economic growth in the Third World, or arms control) is seen as being permanent in nature. Problems arise when others do not see the problem in similar terms. To some this has been especially evident in U.S.–Soviet arms control talks, where the American approach to strategic thinking treated nuclear war as a "mathematical exercise" and its basic concepts (deterrence, sufficiency, and retaliation) are supposed to "guarantee" continued U.S. security.[25] Operating on the basis of a very different historical experience, the Soviets developed concepts (victory, superiority, and offensive action) that "are goals to be striven for, not conditions to be guaranteed." To the Soviets, uncertainty remained inherent in the nature of warfare, for which no engineering solution exists.

The preferred American method for uncovering the solution is to break the problem into smaller ones—the same way an engineer may take a blueprint and break it down into smaller tasks. An organizational or mechanical solution is then devised for each of the subproblems. In the process, it is not unusual to lose sight of the political context of the larger problem being addressed. When this happens, the result can be the substitution of means for ends, improvisation, or reliance on canned formulas to solve the problem.

Both the Monroe Doctrine and its Roosevelt Corollary show the influence of moral pragmatism. "The major purpose of the Monroe Doctrine was to preserve the fundamental distinction between old and new world political systems."[26] This goal and its premises went unquestioned. Attention instead focused on how to accomplish this end. The option seized did not reflect the realities of international politics. The Monroe Doctrine was a success because it reflected both British and American interests and because of the power of the British navy. It did not succeed because of American power. Roosevelt justified his corollary to the Monroe Doctrine on the grounds that if nations near the United States could not keep order within their own borders, then the United States had a moral obligation to intervene. Once again the question was largely defined as an engineering problem—how best to intervene.

The neutrality legislation of the 1930s provides an example of moral pragmatism at work in a quite different setting. Here, the concern was not with asserting U.S. influence but with detaching the United States from world affairs. As first put forward, the legislation was easy to implement but paid little attention to the political realities of the day. Weapons were not to be sold to either side. Yet, refusing to sell weapons to either participant guaranteed victory to the stronger side and invited its aggression. The neutrality legislation was repeatedly amended in an effort to close the gap between technique and political reality. In 1937, the president was given the authority to distinguish between civil strife and war. In 1939, the neutrality legislation permitted the cash-and-carry purchase of weapons by belligerents. This allowed the United States to sell weapons to Great Britain, but made a mockery of the neutrality principle.

The overreliance on formulas by the United States in the post–World War II era has frequently been commented on. Among the most prominent have been (1) opposition to aggression, (2) containment of communism, and (3) defense of free nations. All three have been criticized for being moral abstractions, failing to provide concrete guidance on how to tailor goals to the situation at hand, select the proper approach to solve the problem, or weigh the costs and benefits of a course of action.[27] One author argues that the anticommunist impulse in particular has been used to sanction almost any course of action, no matter how immoral, if it brings about the greater goal of stopping communism.[28]

Right-wing dictators have been supported as the lesser of two evils, governments overthrown, states invaded, international law violated, and the rights of American citizens compromised in the pursuit of this end.

The potential dangers of rooting U.S. foreign policy on a foundation of moral pragmatism came through quite clearly in the Iran–Contra fiasco. Convinced of the moral correctness of the goal of freeing American hostages in Lebanon, the Reagan administration proceeded to sell arms to Iran and then diverted monies gained through these sales to the U.S.-backed Contras fighting the Sandinista government in Nicaragua. The reliance on engineering solutions and formulas to solve problems also reached excess here, as witnessed by National Security Council (NSC) staffer Lieutenant Colonel Oliver North's equation for achieving the release of the American hostages, part of which read: 1 707 w/300 TOWs (Tube-launched Optically tracked Wire-guided missiles) = 1 AMCIT (American citizen). More recently this tendency to see the solution to foreign policy problems as lying in designing blueprints and putting them in place is evident in the American tendency to equate building democracy with holding elections and writing a constitution.

In carrying out his most ambitious foreign policy initiative, the war against Iraq, George H. W. Bush demonstrated a penchant for moral pragmatism. Saddam Hussein was defined as the embodiment of evil and a threat to American national interests. The justness of the American cause was unquestioned. Attention focused solely on how to accomplish the stated goal of bringing about a removal of Iraqi forces from Kuwait with a minimum loss of American lives. The centerpiece of the chosen solution was airpower and, as one observer has noted, "reliance on air power has set the American way of war apart from all others . . . it plays to the machine-mindedness of American civilization."[29] George W. Bush continued in this tradition. The classic expressions of moral pragmatism in his administration came in the war against terrorism. In his address to the American people following the 9/11 attacks, he declared, "either you are with the U.S. or you are with the terrorists." He would go on to call for Osama bin Laden's capture "dead or alive." Others find evidence of it not in his language, which often invoked images of the American frontier, but in his administration's shifting rationales for the Iraq War. The failure to find weapons of mass destruction or links between Iraq and al Qaeda did not bring about an admission of error. Rather it brought forward new rationales for why the war was necessary.

## Legalism

The third pattern in U.S. foreign policy is **legalism**. It grows out of the rejection of the balance of power as a means for preserving national security and the liberal view that people are rational beings who abhor war and favor the peaceful settlement of disputes.[30] A central task of U.S. foreign policy, therefore, is to create a global system of institutions and rules that will allow states to settle their disputes without recourse to war. The primary institutional embodiments of the legalist perspective are the League of Nations and the United Nations. Also relevant are the host of post–World War II international economic organizations that the United States joined (i.e., the World Bank, International Monetary Fund, and the GATT). Just as commerce between individuals binds them together, international trade is assumed to bind states together and reduce the likelihood of war.

The rule-making thrust to legalism is found in the repeated use of the **pledge system** as an instrument of foreign policy.[31] In creating a pledge system, the United States puts forward a statement of principle and then asks other states to adhere to it either by signing a treaty or by pledging their support for the principle. Noticeably absent is any meaningful enforcement mechanism. The Open Door Notes exemplify this strategy for world affairs problem solving. In the Notes, the United States unilaterally proclaimed its opposition to spheres of influence in China and asked other powers to do likewise, but it did not specify any sanctions against a state that reneged on its pledge. The Washington Naval Disarmament Conference of 1922 and the 1928 Kellogg–Briand Pact are also part of the pledge system. The Washington Naval Disarmament Conference sought to prevent war by establishing a fixed power ratio for certain categories of warships. The agreement failed to include inspection or enforcement provisions. Its restraining qualities were soon overtaken by a naval arms race in areas left uncovered by the agreement and by a general heightening of international tensions. The Kellogg–Briand Pact sought to outlaw war as an instrument of foreign policy. Yet, true to its unilateralist impulse, the United States stated that signing the pact would not prevent it from enforcing the Monroe Doctrine or obligate it to participate in sanctions against other states. The SALT I and SALT II (Strategic Arms Limitation Talks) agreements followed in the tradition of the pledge system. They specified in broad terms the nuclear inventories that the Soviet Union and the United States were permitted to have, but without creating any enforcement provisions.

A variation of the pledge system has become a prominent feature of U.S. bilateral and multilateral trade policy. Confronted with an intransigent Japan in 1993, U.S. negotiators settled for a "framework" agreement that specified how future agreements would seek to resolve issues of trade imbalances and barriers to trade without detailing the particulars of the agreement. On the multilateral level, agreements were signed in 1994 that pledged the United States and thirty-three other Western Hemisphere states to create a free trade zone by 2005 and that pledged the United States and seventeen Pacific Basin countries to create their own free trade zone by 2020. In neither case were organizational blueprints or detailed schedules for creating these free trade areas presented.

Legalism has also placed a heavy burden on U.S. foreign policy. In rejecting power politics as an approach for providing for U.S. national security, policy makers have denied themselves use of the "reasons-of-state" argument as a justification for their actions. Instead, they have sought to clothe their actions in terms of legal principles. Post–World War II examples include fighting the Korean War under the UN flag, seeking the Organization of American States's approval for a blockade during the Cuban missile crisis, and citing a request by the Organization of Eastern Caribbean States as part of the justification for going into Grenada. This pattern has continued in the post–Cold War era.

George H. W. Bush obtained UN endorsement for his military campaign against Iraq, and Clinton did the same for his use of force in Haiti. George W. Bush continued this reliance on legalism even though he acted without UN support. His administration argued that no new UN resolution was necessary, because Saddam Hussein had violated previous UN resolutions and was thus in violation of an international agreement. In Bush's words, Iraq "had answered a decade of UN demands with a decade of defiance.... We want the resolutions of the world's most important multilateral body to be enforced."

While he sought to steer a new course in U.S. foreign policy, President Obama's early foreign policy initiatives fit well within the boundaries of the American national style. American exceptionalism may have been downplayed, but there was no doubting the importance of American leadership or need for global involvement. This was fully evident in his major foreign policy speeches to the United Nations and in Europe and Africa. Unilateralism was visible in his abandoning the Bush administration's plans for an anti-Iranian missile defense system that was to be built in Poland. Moral pragmatism surfaced in his support for human rights coupled with a decision prompted by Chinese protests to postpone a scheduled meeting with the Dalai Lama until after Obama met with Chinese leaders. Legalism could be seen in his administration's quick statement of support for the International Criminal Court and its signing of an international agreement on the rights of disabled persons.

## CONSEQUENCES OF THE AMERICAN NATIONAL STYLE

As we suggested earlier, these three patterns come together to support both isolationism and internationalism. They also produce four consequences for the overall conduct of U.S. foreign policy regardless of which general foreign policy orientation is dominant. The first consequence is a tendency to "win the war and lose the peace." As Robert Osgood wrote in 1957:

> The United States has demonstrated an impressive ability to defeat the enemy. Yet . . . it has been unable to deter war; it has been unprepared to fight war; it has failed to gain the objectives it fought for; and its settlements have not brought satisfactory peace.[32]

This condition stems from the American tendency to see war and peace as polar opposites. War is a social aberration, whereas peace is the normal state of affairs. Strategies and tactics appropriate for one arena have no place in the other. The two categories must be kept separate to prevent the calculations of war from corrupting the principles of peace. In times of peace, reason, discussion, and trade are relied on to accomplish foreign policy objectives. In times of war, power is the appropriate tool. The absence of a conceptual link between war and peace means that war cannot serve as an instrument of statecraft and that war plans will be drawn up in a political vacuum. The objective of war is to defeat the enemy as swiftly as possible. Only when that is accomplished can one return to the concerns of peace. The closing stages of World War II illustrate the problem inherent in the war–peace dichotomy.

## HISTORICAL LESSON

### The Bracero Program

World War II led to a significant demand for additional workers in the United States, most notably in agriculture and the railroad industry. This demand was filled by Mexican workers, "braceros," who crossed into the United States as part of a guest worker program negotiated between the two countries. Officially known as the Mexican Contract Labor Program, it existed from 1942 to 1964. The wartime years produced the smallest migrant flow of any of these years, with 49,000–82,000 Mexican workers crossing the border. From 1947 to 1954, the average annual migration was 116,000–141,000 per year. In the last 10 years of the Bracero Program, there were on average 333,000 migrant worker contracts.

This was not the first attempt to regulate the entry of Mexican labor. In 1909, President William Howard Taft signed an executive agreement with Mexico permitting thousands of Mexican contract workers to harvest sugar beets in Colorado and Nebraska. When the United States entered World War I, restrictions on the number of contract workers permitted into the United States were eased, and the number of Mexican workers swelled to 73,000. The Mexican government viewed this situation with some alarm. The Mexican Constitution of 1917 contained a provision that sought to safeguard the rights of emigrant workers, and it attempted to discourage workers from going to the United States unless they already had contracts that provided such protections. These efforts were largely ineffective. In 1929, with the depression under way in the United States and large numbers of Mexicans returning home due to lack of jobs, the Mexican government sought but failed to obtain a bilateral agreement with the United States that would allow them to jointly manage the flow of workers across the border.

At the outset of the Bracero Program, Mexico possessed significant bargaining strength that allowed it to insert provisions protecting migrant rights, such as insisting that the braceros be paid the prevailing wage in the community they were working in and prohibiting Mexicans from being rejected at "white" restaurants and other facilities in the American South. Mexico blacklisted Texas because of its discrimination policies and would not allow braceros to go there. Gradually, however, Mexico's leverage began to weaken.

One important reason for this was the growing phenomenon of illegal, or wetback, immigration into areas such as Texas, where demand for migrant labor was great. In 1943, Congress passed Public Law 45 that gave legal status to the agreement reached with Mexico in 1942. One of its key provisions was that the United States could unilaterally declare an "open border" if need be. This power was used in May 1943 to grant one-year entrance permits. Texas farmers rushed into Mexico and began recruiting migrants and in the process undermined the orderly bilateral recruitment of workers. Lax border control enforcement in the early 1950s further contributed to the flow of illegal migrant workers.

In the late 1940s and early 1950s, the United States sought to deal with the problem of illegal migrant labor by transforming it into legal labor. This was done by mass deportations and mass legalizations. The scope of the problem was immense. From 1955 to 1959, 18 percent of all seasonal farm laborers were braceros. In New Mexico, braceros made up 70 percent of the seasonal labor force. From1947 to 1949, the President's Commission on Migratory Labor estimated that 142,000 deportable Mexicans in the United States were legalized as braceros. In 1950, slightly more than 19,800 new bracero contracts were awarded, but an estimated 96,200 illegal Mexicans were working in the United States.

The legacy of the Bracero Program is found in many areas. Seasonal and regional concentrated agricultural jobs, as opposed to establishing permanent residences, became the norm for Mexicans coming to the United States. Part of the Mexican government's response to the end of the Bracero Program was to create jobs along the U.S. border for returning migrants. This became the Border Industrialization or Maquiladora Program. It has not worked as expected, since these firms have preferred to hire young Mexican women rather than returning braceros.

Within the United States, the end of the Bracero Program has not ended the debate over how to address the problem of illegal Mexican workers in the United States or how to provide sanctioned labor to employers. The Reagan administration proposed a pilot program giving 50,000 Mexicans temporary work permits each year. The George W. Bush administration floated the idea of a massive amnesty program for illegal Mexican migrants in the months prior to the 9/11 attacks. When the administration dropped these plans, Mexico called for establishing a new guest worker program.

**Applying the Lesson**

1. What elements of the American national style can be found in the idea of a fence to control immigration and the Bracero Program?
2. Rate the importance of foreign policy and domestic policy considerations in these two policies.
3. Should we think about immigration primarily as an economic problem or a national security problem? ■

Should U.S. forces have pushed as far as possible eastward for the political purpose of denying the Red Army control over as much territory as possible, or should they have stopped as soon as the purely military objectives of the offensive were realized and not risked the lives of U.S. soldiers on nonmilitary goals? The latter course of action was selected, and the Cold War East–West boundary in Europe reflected this choice. The George W. Bush administration was not immune from this artificial separation of war and peace. Only one month into the war in Afghanistan, in 2001, Secretary of State Donald Rumsfeld stated that victory was nonnegotiable so there was no reason to talk with the Taliban.

The second consequence is the existence of a double standard in judging the behavior of states. Convinced of its righteousness and the universality of its values, and predisposed to act unilaterally, the United States has often engaged in actions that it condemns when they are practiced by other states. The United States can be trusted to test and develop nuclear weapons, but other states, especially Third World states, cannot. Soviet interventions in Afghanistan and Czechoslovakia are condemned as imperialism, while U.S. interventions in the Dominican Republic, Grenada, and Panama are held to be morally defensible. The United States urges its allies not to sell weapons to terrorists or those who support them, while it is selling weapons to Iran in the hopes of securing the release of U.S. hostages in Lebanon. The reverse condition also holds. Activities considered by most states to be a normal part of world affairs have been highly controversial in the United States. The clandestine collection of information and covert attempts to influence developments in other states are cases in point. Both are long-standing instruments of foreign policy. Yet the United States has always exhibited a reluctance to employ them for fear of their potentially corrupting effect on American freedoms.

The third consequence is an ambivalence toward diplomacy. In the abstract, diplomacy is valued as part of the process by which states peacefully resolve their disputes. Along with international law and international organizations, diplomacy occupies a central place in liberal thinking about the proper forums for conducting foreign relations. The product of diplomacy, however, is viewed with great skepticism. If the U.S. position is the morally correct one, how can it compromise (something vital to the success of diplomacy) without rejecting its own sense of mission and the principles it stands for? As John Spanier notes, under these conditions compromise is indistinguishable from appeasement.[33] It does not matter whether the other party to the negotiations is a twentieth-century communist state or an eighteenth- or nineteenth-century European state. In either case, the fruits of diplomacy have been looked on with suspicion.

For the George W. Bush administration, this skepticism over the value of negotiating with the enemy was evident in its dealings with North Korea over its violation of the Agreed Framework it had negotiated with the Clinton administration and its open pursuit of a nuclear capability. "Talking" with North Korea was seen as tantamount to "caving in" to a government that the administration had labeled as being part of an "axis of evil." It came as no surprise that when the Bush administration did reach an agreement with North Korea in February 2007, it found it necessary to assure conservative Republicans that it had not gone too easy on North Korea and that the agreement was not fundamentally flawed, as argued by the administration's former ambassador to the UN, John Bolton. Similar assurances that it was not rewarding an enemy were necessary later that year when the administration entered into low-level talks with Iran, another member of the axis of evil and on whom the administration laid much of the blame for the violence in Iraq.

The fourth consequence is impatience. Optimistic at the start of an undertaking and convinced of the correctness of its position in both a moral and a technical sense, Americans tend to want quick results. They become impatient when positive results are not soon forthcoming. A common reaction is to turn away in frustration. The next time a similar situation presents itself and U.S. action is needed, none may be taken. Calls for "no more Vietnams" reflect this sense of frustration. So, too, did the demand to get U.S. Marines out of Lebanon following the terrorist attacks on the U.S. compound during the Reagan administration.

The desire for quick and visible results is seen by many as creating a bias for the use of the military as an instrument of foreign policy. Neither diplomacy nor economic power offers quick results. Both are slow working and work best when used out of the public eye. A vicious circle thus can be created. The demand for quick results leads to a reliance on military power, but the rigid distinction between war and peace makes it difficult to use that power effectively. Its use may be marked by a double standard or, as Osgood observed, may simply fail to meet its political objectives. If that is the case, then diplomacy may be turned to. Yet here again the results are likely to be slow in coming, and the settlement will be looked on with skepticism. Frustration will set in and dominate U.S. foreign policy until a consensus exists supporting new foreign policy initiatives.

All four of these consequences have already shown themselves in the buildup to the Iraq War and its aftermath, including the war on terrorism. One of the most frequent observations made by commentators was the disconnect between planning for the Iraq War and planning for the ensuing occupation and transition to democracy. The original war plan expected that U.S. troops would be withdrawn within six months of the invasion. The notion that different rules might apply to the United States than to other states surfaced after revelations of widespread abuse by American interrogators at Abu Ghraib prison led to the release of internal memos by the administration (since disavowed) that the Justice Department had asserted and the president agreed that he had the power to sanction torture and suspend the application of international protections for detainees, and that those acting on his authority would be immune from prosecution. In May 2005, President Bush dismissed as "absurd" an Amnesty International report charging the administration with having created a gulag at the Guantanamo Bay detention facility, and said that those who made allegations of mistreatment were detainees who "hate America" and are trained to lie.[34] An ambivalence to diplomacy was evident in the reluctance of the administration first to go the UN and obtain its support for the use of force against Saddam Hussein and then in its unwillingness to back continued weapons inspections or make the compromises necessary to obtain UN support. The ambivalence continued to be felt in the administration's reluctance to follow the advice of the 2006 Baker–Hamilton Commission to engage in a diplomatic dialogue with Iran and Syria and seek a way of ending the U.S. presence in Iraq. Finally, impatience was evident in the expectation that the United States could oversee an election for an interim Iraqi government, the writing of a constitution, its ratification, and the election of a permanent government in twelve months. Impatience could also be seen in the notion that a surge of 21,500 U.S. troops in 2007 would permit the United States to exit Iraq before the 2008 election. The problem is, as one columnist noted, that Iraq does not operate on Washington's clock.[35]

## A REVIVAL OF WILSONIANISM?

What, then, of American foreign policy in an age of terrorism? Will it move forward on new foundations or continue to build on the traditions of the past? During the 2000 presidential campaign, candidate George W. Bush spoke of the need to adopt a humble foreign policy, suggesting that a change might be in the offing (although, as we shall see in the next section, he would not be the first American statesperson to call for such a policy). After 9/11, his foreign policy was anything but modest and unassuming. In fact, George W. Bush began to sound very much like Woodrow Wilson. In his 2002 State of the Union address, Bush stated, "America will lead by defending liberty and justice because they are right and true and unchanging for people everywhere. . . . We have no intention of imposing our culture. But America will always stand firm for the nonnegotiable demands of human dignity." Speaking at West Point later that year, he spoke of the "time of opportunity for America" and how "we will work to translate this moment of influence into decades of peace, prosperity, and liberty." And, in his 2005 Inauguration Day address, he spoke of "ending tyranny in our world." This embrace of **Wilsonianism** is reflective of a broader rediscovery and admiration for Wilson's foreign policy that has arisen since the end of the Cold War. A standard ingredient in postmortems of Wilson's foreign policy was that it was naively idealistic. The implication was that it was a fundamentally flawed vision that offered little guidance to future generations of American foreign policy makers. This is no longer the case. Many now concede that the Wilsonian vision was ill-suited to the first decades of the twentieth century but assert that it is quite relevant to the conditions of the post–Cold War era. Rather than characterizing Wilson as an idealist, many see him as a vindicated visionary.[36]

Proponents of neo-Wilsonianism as the basis for post–Cold War American foreign policy center their attention on his Fourteen Points. Presented in a speech Wilson delivered before Congress in 1918, the Fourteen Points constituted an outline for constructing a new world order. The first five points would lay the foundation for a new, "open" era of international politics. Points Six through Thirteen addressed the problems of national self-determination and drawing national boundaries in Europe. Point Fourteen asserted that "a general association of nations must be formed under specific covenants for the purpose of affording mutual guarantees of political independence and territorial integrity to great and small states alike." Looking beyond the Fourteen Points themselves, the Wilsonian vision of world politics rested on four elements: first, promoting democracy; second, encouraging free trade; third, controlling weapons. Together, these three elements would place restraints on the exercise of power by governments and provide space for the development of individual liberty. The fourth element was the League of Nations. It would provide an alternative to balance-of-power politics as a means of providing for national security.[37]

That Wilson's proposals did not fare well at the Paris Peace Conference and that the United States did not join the League of Nations are acknowledged as great failures, but are no longer treated uniformly as signs that the ideas Wilson espoused were defective. Many now echo historian and Wilson biographer Arthur S. Link's conclusion that Wilson possessed a "higher realism" in his handling of foreign affairs.[38] Link characterizes Wilson as a quick learner in foreign policy matters who took personal control over foreign policy making because of the incompetence of those in high-ranking State Department positions. He was a man who recognized the need for give-and-take in treaty negotiations. He was all of this while remaining loyal to his fundamental Christian principles and belief in democracy.

Those who advocate a neo-Wilsonian foreign policy have not gone unchallenged. Some opponents have reexamined the Wilsonian legacy and asked, "Are we all not Wilsonians?" Others have asserted that advocates of a neo-Wilsonian foreign policy have drawn too narrow a picture of Wilsonianism. Robert Tucker asks the first question.[39] Rare is the modern president, he observes, who does not claim to be a Wilsonian. Some argue that the Reagan Doctrine could be seen as the ultimate embodiment of the Wilsonian legacy, given its commitment to expand democracy, and that Reagan was the "most Wilsonian of presidents since Wilson's time."[40] This overextension of the Wilsonian label leads Tucker to reexamine the roots of Wilsonian thought. He concludes that Wilson's approach to foreign policy shares much in common with that of Jefferson, who is cited by many as an early advocate of isolationism. They both rejected amoral European-style diplomacy and sought to replace it with a new diplomacy that rested on the will of the people. They were united in the belief that American interests could only be safeguarded by a reformed international system. Tucker asserts that only force could bring about this condition. Rejecting this course of action led Jefferson to embrace isolationism. For Wilson, it came to mean creating a global concert of powers that would bring such a reformed international system into existence. Where the Wilsonian vision encountered problems was in the relationship between ends and means. Could a reformed international system be created with only limited costs and demands being placed on the United States? If not, then the Wilsonian vision of a democratic world could only be purchased at an excessive price, one that threatened to undermine the very American values it was designed to foster. It is these questions of the relationship between means and ends and between force and peace that Tucker sees as representing the core challenge facing the Wilsonian vision today.

David Fromkin raises the second question posed above: What is Wilsonianism?[41] He concludes that it is a mistake to equate Wilsonianism with collective security. At a minimum, attention must be given to several other aspects of Wilson's thinking. Foremost among these is his belief in a strong presidency. Wilson saw the president's control of foreign policy as "very absolute." He believed that the Senate had no choice but to ratify any treaty submitted to it by the president, regardless of any doubts about its wisdom or the secrecy with which it may have been negotiated. Also critical to any definition of Wilsonianism, Fromkin argues, is a close examination of the relationship between words and deeds in Wilson's decision making. Fromkin sees a pattern in which Wilsonian principles followed his actions rather than preceding them. As a consequence, Wilsonian principles served to rationalize policy made for very different reasons, rather than to direct it. He freely changed sides on an issue or applied standards unevenly. Fromkin concludes that Wilsonianism can only be taken to mean "a certain way of talking and thinking about international relations in terms of concepts that are inspiring and high minded but impractical application provides no guidance."

## OTHER VOICES FROM THE PAST

Woodrow Wilson's is not the only voice from the past being rediscovered as the United States searches to define its place in the world today. Isolationists point to the writings of John Adams. According to Adams, American foreign policy should be based on the principle that the United States is "the well-wisher to the freedom and independence of all" but "the champion and vindicator only of her own."[42] Adams was putting forward an argument for nonintervention into the affairs of others and advocating a foreign policy that was to be based on the "power of example." To go further, he warned, would involve the United States in "wars of interest and intrigue, of individual avarice, envy, and ambition." Conservative internationalists point to Theodore Roosevelt's writings.[43] They would replace liberal internationalism's conception of humanitarian intervention as a philanthropic exercise with one rooted in a sense of nationalistic patriotism. Writing before the Spanish–American War, Roosevelt wrote that "the useful member of a community is the man who first and foremost attends to his own rights and duties . . . the useful member of the brotherhood of nations is that nation which is most thoroughly saturated with the national ideal."

In addition to these two, other voices from the past continue to exert an influence on the present.[44] Alexander Hamilton speaks to those who see the primary purpose of American foreign policy as the promotion of American economic strength at home and abroad. After World War II, this required an American foreign policy that worked with other states to promote and protect an open international economic order. Andrew Jackson's writings and actions provide a foundation for those who stress the populist principles of courage, honor, and self-reliance in the conduct of American foreign policy. Suspicious of outsiders and their values, Jacksonians champion a foreign policy of constant vigilance backed by overwhelming might that may be employed with few if any constraints.

## OVER THE HORIZON

What of the future? Will the United States seek to build more fences to keep out perceived threats or will it turn to other methods? The answer would appear to be a resounding "maybe." As we have seen, the patterns that make up the American national style, unilateralism, moral pragmatism, and legalism, support a variety of foreign policies ranging from internationalist to isolationist. It is thus not inevitable that more fences will be built, but at the same time it seems reasonable to expect that any policy put forward will be compatible with these fundamental ideas or those that have been advanced by other voices from the past.

Looking over the horizon, we might see the signs of the beginning of change in the American national style. The American national style is not frozen in place. In the eyes of one observer, legalism has already lost much of its influence.[45] Change might come about as a result of the increased presence of women, blacks, and Hispanics in the policy-making process.[46] Their histories read quite differently from those presented in the standardized accounts of the American past, and they may bring to the policy process a very different style of acting and thinking about solutions of foreign policy problems.

Additionally we can expect to see a search for other presidents to emulate beyond Wilson and the others we identified. Already Franklin Roosevelt is being suggested as a model at least in so far as dealing with the public is concerned. Where previous wartime presidents, most notably, Teddy Roosevelt, Woodrow Wilson, and George W. Bush, were seen as leading public opinion without transforming it, Franklin Roosevelt is credited by some as having shown true leadership in moving American public opinion on foreign policy forward.[47]

We may also see signs of a more traditional form of change in the American national style. If cycles of isolationism and internationalism do exist, we are more than halfway through our current extrovert or internationalist cycle. We may thus be on the lookout for signs of an impending isolationist phase to U.S. foreign policy.

## CRITICAL THINKING QUESTIONS

1. Could the United States become isolationist again?
2. What is the most important element in the American national style for understanding U.S. foreign policy?
3. How difficult would it be for the U.S. national style in foreign policy to change?

## KEY TERMS

| | | |
|---|---|---|
| containment 57 | legalism 67 | preemption 57 |
| détente 58 | moral pragmatism 65 | unilateralism 63 |
| deterrence 57 | national style 58 | Wilsonianism 74 |
| internationalism 58 | neoconservatism 57 | |
| isolationism 58 | pledge system 68 | |

## FURTHER READING

Andrew Bacevich, *The New American Militarism: how Americans are seduced by War* (New York: Oxford University Press, 2005).

Judith Goldstein, *Ideas, Interests, and American Trade Policy* (Ithaca: Cornell University Press, 1993).

David Fromkin, "What Is Wilsonianism?" *World Policy Journal*, 11 (1994), 100–12.
John G., Ikenberry, et. al., *The Crisis of American Foreign Policy: Wilsonianism in the 21ˢᵗ Century* (Princeton: Princeton University Press, 2009).
Walter Russell Mead, *Special Providence* (New York: Routledge, 2002).

## NOTES

1. See Michael Desch, "America's Liberal Illiberalism: The Ideological Origins of Overreaction in U.S. Foreign Policy," *International Security*, 32 (2007/8), 7–43.
2. Robert Kagan, "Neocon Nation: neoconservatism, c. 1776," *World Affairs* 170 (2008), 13–35.
3. Judith Goldstein, *Ideas, Interests, and American Trade Policy* (Ithaca, NY: Cornell University Press, 1993), pp. 1–18.
4. Ibid.
5. George Kennan, "The Sources of Soviet Conduct," *Foreign Affairs*, 25 (1947), 576.
6. For discussions of containment and détente, see John Spanier, *American Foreign Policy since WW II*, 10th ed. (New York: Holt, Rinehart & Winston, 1985), pp. 23–29, 189–200, 304–06, and 316–21; Charles W. Kegley, Jr., and Eugene R. Wittkopf, *American Foreign Policy: Pattern and Process*, 2nd ed. (New York: St. Martin's, 1982), pp. 48–69; and Henry T. Nash, *American Foreign Policy: A Search for Security*, 3rd ed. (Homewood, IL: Dorsey, 1985), pp. 44–48 and 249–50.
7. Quoted in Howard Bliss and M. Glen Johnson, *Beyond the Water's Edge: American Foreign Policy* (Philadelphia: Lippincott, 1975), pp. 52–53.
8. Frank Klingberg, *Positive Expectation's of America's World Role* (Lanham, MD: University Press of America, 1996).
9. Dexter Perkins, *The American Approach to Foreign Policy* (Cambridge, MA: Harvard University Press, 1962), p. 154.
10. Robert Dallek, *The American Style of Foreign Policy, Cultural Politics and Foreign Affairs* (New York: New American Library, 1983).
11. Max Lerner, cited in Cecil Crabb, Jr., *American Foreign Policy in the Nuclear Age*, 4th ed. (New York: Harper & Row, 1983), p. 47; and Richard Ullman, "The 'Foreign World' and Ourselves: Washington, Wilson and the Democratic Dilemma," *Foreign Policy*, 21 (1975/76), 97–125.
12. For a discussion of these points, see Stanley Hoffmann, *Gulliver's Troubles, or the Setting of American Foreign Policy* (New York: McGraw-Hill, 1968); Spanier, *American Foreign Policy since WW II*; Perkins, *The American Approach to Foreign Policy*; and Amos Jordan and William J. Taylor, Jr., *American National Security, Policy and Process* (Baltimore, MD: Johns Hopkins University Press, 1981).
13. Kenneth Keniston, quoted in Bliss and Johnson, *Beyond the Water's Edge*, p. 110.
14. John Judis, "The Author of Liberty," *Dissent* (Fall, 2005), 54–61.
15. Walter Russell Mead, "God's Country" *Foreign Affairs*, 85 (2006), 24–43.
16. Peggy Shriver, "Evangelicals and World Affairs," *World Policy Journal*, 23 (2006), 52–58.
17. Stanley Hoffmann, "Foreign Policy Transition: Requiem," *Foreign Policy*, 42 (1980/81), 3–26.
18. For a discussion of alternative interpretations of U.S. foreign policy and national style, see Kegley and Wittkopf, *American Foreign Policy*, pp. 69–81.
19. For a discussion of unilateralism, see Gene Rainey, *Patterns of American Foreign Policy* (Boston: Allyn & Bacon, 1975), pp. 19–43.
20. Robert Tucker, *The Radical Left and American Foreign Policy* (Baltimore, MD: Johns Hopkins University Press, 1971), p. 34.

21. James Schlesinger, "Reykjavik and Revelations: A Turn of the Tide?" *Foreign Affairs*, 65 (1987), 431.
22. For a discussion of American foreign policy highlighting these themes, see Arthur Schlesinger, Jr., "Foreign Policy and the American Character," *Foreign Affairs*, 62 (1983), 1–16.
23. Both Kennan and Krauthammer are quoted in Anatol Lieven and John C. Hulsman, "Neo-Conservatives, Liberal Hawks, and the War on Terror," *World Policy Journal* (Fall 2006), 64–74.
24. Hoffmann, *Gulliver's Troubles*, p. 150.
25. Freeman Dyson, "On Russians and Their Views of Nuclear Strategy,'" in Charles W. Kegley, Jr., and Eugene R. Wittkopf (eds.), *The Nuclear Reader* (New York: St. Martin's, 1985), pp. 97–99.
26. Crabb, *American Foreign Policy*, pp. 36–37.
27. Hoffmann, *Gulliver's Troubles*, pp. 141–43; and Frederick Hartmann, *The Relations among Nations*, 6th ed. (New York: Macmillan, 1983), pp. 421–26.
28. David Watt, "As a European Saw It," *Foreign Affairs,* 62 (1983), 530–31.
29. Elliot A. Cohen, "The Mystique of U.S. Air Power," *Foreign Affairs,* 73 (1994), 109–24.
30. For a critical discussion of the impact of legalism, see George Kennan, *American Diplomacy, 1900–1950* (New York: Mentor, 1951).
31. Rainey, *Patterns of American Foreign Policy*, p. 36.
32. Robert E. Osgood, *Limited War: The Challenge to American Strategy* (Chicago: University of Chicago Press, 1957), p. 29.
33. Spanier, *American Foreign Policy since WW II*, p. 11.
34. William Branigin, "Bush Calls Amnesty International Report 'Absurd," *The Washington Post,* June 1, 2005, p. A1.
35. Jackson Diehl, "War Against Time," *The Washington Post*, January 8, 2007, p. A15.
36. See Charles W. Kegley, Jr., "The Neoidealist Moment in International Studies: Realist Myths and the New International Realities," *International Studies Quarterly*, 37 (1993), 131–46.
37. Michael Mandlebaum, "Bad Statesman, Good Prophet: Woodrow Wilson and the Post–Cold War Order." *National Interest*, 64 (2001), 31–41.
38. Arthur S. Link, *The Higher Realism of Woodrow Wilson* (Nashville, TN: Vanderbilt University Press, 1971).
39. Robert W. Tucker, "The Triumph of Wilsonianism?" *World Policy Journal*, 10 (1993), 83–100.
40. Ibid.; and Tony Smith, "Making the World Safe for Democracy," *Washington Quarterly*, 16 (1993), 92–102.
41. David Fromkin, "What Is Wilsonianism?" *World Policy Journal*, 11 (1994), 100–12.
42. George Kennan, "On American Principles," *Foreign Affairs*, 74 (1995), 116–26.
43. The material and quotation in this section are found in Adam Wolfson, "How to Think about Humanitarian War," *Commentary*, 110 (July/August 2000), 44–48.
44. Walter Russell Mead, *Special Providence* (New York: Routledge, 2002). Mead also identifies two other American traditions; one is associated with Wilson and the other with Jefferson.
45. Rainey, *Patterns of American Foreign Policy*, p. 386.
46. Ernest J. Wilson III (ed.), *Diversity and U.S. Foreign Policy: A Reader* (New York: Routledge, 2004).
47. H.W. Brands, "FDR and GWB: Unlearned Lessons of a Wartime Presidency," *World Affairs* 170 (2008), 83–90.

# Learning from the Past

It is for good reason that Afghanistan is known as the "graveyard of empires." According to Michael Breeden, who ran the CIA's covert operations program in Afghanistan and Pakistan during the Reagan administration, it is a country that is easily conquered and then presents its conqueror with unyielding rebellions that drain its will and resources.[1] Alexander the Great found this to be the case, as did Mughals, Great Britain, and the Soviet Union. Even the first American experience in Afghanistan supports this view. The Taliban were quickly defeated by U.S. forces in the search for Osama bin Laden in 2001, but less than a decade later they were leading an ever-growing rebellion that challenged the power of Hamid Karzai, the U.S. handpicked Afghan leader, and it was the NATO occupation force that was going home. In its place were coming U.S. forces. Breeden observes that while the outcome of this second U.S. military involvement is by no means foreordained by the past, what is certain is that Afghanistan will be seen as Obama's war just as Iraq was Bush's war and Vietnam was Johnson's war.

If there are to be no more Vietnams (or Munichs, Pearl Harbors, Koreas, or Iraqs), policy makers must learn from past foreign policy failures. Yet remarkably little learning from the past takes place.[2] The same mistakes occur over and over. We begin this chapter by treating the problem of learning from the past as a generic one and asking how and what policy makers learn: the types of events they learn from, the types of calculations they make, and the lessons they learn. The bulk of the chapter presents two case studies drawing on post–World War II U.S. foreign policy to illustrate these points. The first is the Vietnam War. The second is the Iraq War.

## HOW DO POLICY MAKERS LEARN FROM THE PAST?

Policy makers learn by matching the known with the unknown.[3] This is not a passive act. They do not sit back and simply accept data as a given, but actively interact with them.[4] Much of the foreign policy debate during the presidency of Bill Clinton was over what to do about the military and humanitarian crisis in Kosovo.[5] On the surface, the issue at hand was straightforward: whether or not to intervene militarily. **Analogies** were drawn with at least four different events from the past, each of which suggested a different definition of the problem and response. These events were Vietnam, the Holocaust, Munich, and the outbreak of World War I.

In addition to selecting reference points for evaluating information, policy makers must make judgments about what is a piece of information (**signal**) and what is unimportant (**noise**). Discriminating between the two is no easy task. Having identified a piece of data as a signal does not tell the policy maker what to do; it only sets in motion the process of learning. Information received in the Philippines that Pearl Harbor was under attack did not tell policy makers there that they were the next target or what steps to take to defend themselves. In the period before Pearl Harbor, fifty-six separate signals ranging in duration from one day to one month pointed toward the Japanese attack, but there was also a good deal of evidence to support all of the wrong interpretations. Surprise occurred not because of a lack of signals, but because there was too much noise.[6]

Policy makers discriminate between signals and noise by making a series of assumptions about what motivates the behavior of others or what constitutes the underlying dynamics of a problem confronting them. Consider the intercepted Japanese directive to their U.S. embassy and consulates to burn their codes. In retrospect, this is taken as a clear indication that hostilities were imminent. But during the first week of December 1941, the United States ordered all of its consulates in the Far East to burn their codes, and no one took this to be the equivalent of a U.S. declaration of war against Japan.

The assumptions that policy makers bring to bear on foreign policy problems are influenced by their long-term experiences and immediate concerns. Long-term experience provides policy makers with a data base against which to evaluate an ongoing pattern of behavior. For Franklin Roosevelt and other U.S. policy makers, personal experiences and their reading of history led to a conclusion that the presence of the U.S. fleet at Pearl Harbor was a deterrent to a Japanese attack. They failed to appreciate that it also made a fine target. For their part, Japanese leaders drew on their 1904 war-opening attack in the Russo–Japanese War as the model for how to deal with a more powerful enemy. Immediate concerns largely determine what we expect to see.

Once they are in place, perceptual systems are not readily changed. They easily become obsolete and inaccurate. Holding on to one's views in the face of challenges is not necessarily irrational. No firm evidence exists that open-minded policy makers are better equipped to avoid surprises than are closed-minded ones. Some might even argue that a firm conceptual system is a necessary requirement for action—that in its absence one is condemned to indecision in the face of unfolding events. The principle involved here is **cognitive consistency**.[7] Individuals try to keep their beliefs and values consistent with one another by ignoring some information, actively seeking out other data, and reinterpreting still other information so that it supports the individuals' perception of reality. The result is that, instead of being a continuous and rationally structured process, learning is sporadic and constrained. Policy makers do not move steadily from a simplistic understanding of an event to a more complex one as their experience and familiarity with it build. New information and new problems are fitted into already well-established perceptual systems. Learning thus rarely produces dramatic changes in priorities or commitments, and changes in behavior tend to be incremental.

A well-documented case of this process at work is John Foster Dulles's perception of the Soviet Union.[8] Dulles was secretary of state for all but a few months of the Eisenhower administration and had a **closed belief system**. He saw the Soviet Union as a hostile state and interpreted any data that might indicate a lessening of hostility in such a way that it reinforced his original perceptions. Cooperative Soviet gestures were not a sign of goodwill but the product of Soviet failures and represented only a lull before they would engage in another round of hostilities.

# EVENTS POLICY MAKERS LEARN FROM

The sporadic and constrained nature of the learning process means that not all aspects of the past are equally likely to serve as the source of lessons. Two categories of events are turned to most often by policy makers in their search for lessons. The first is the dramatic and highly visible event. Policy makers turn to these events out of the conviction that because they are so dramatic and visible, they must contain more information about international politics than do more commonplace happenings. The scars they leave in defeat and the praises sung in victory are so deeply entrenched in the collective memory of society that the individual does not have to experience them personally in order to see them as providing lessons for the present. Events of this magnitude are often referred to as **generational events**, because an entire generation draws on them for lessons. War is the ultimate dramatic event. A policy maker need not have been involved in the negotiations at Munich in 1938 to invoke the analogy and point to the dangers of appeasement, or in Korea to cite the military and political problems of fighting a limited war.

The corollary to paying a great deal of attention to highly dramatic events is to all but ignore the nonevent. The crisis that almost happened but did not is not learned from. Warnings about the weakness of the Shah of Iran were heard as early as 1961, when members of the Senate Foreign Relations Committee warned the newly installed Kennedy administration that no number of weapons could save the Shah. Mass unrest and corruption, they argued, doomed him to defeat. Senator Hubert Humphrey declared: "This crowd they are dead. They just don't know it. . . . It is just a matter of time."[9] The more often the warning is given and no attack occurs, the easier it is for policy makers to dismiss the next warning. The November 27, 1941, warning to Pearl Harbor that a Japanese attack was possible was not the first time a warning was received. An alarming dispatch had been received in October, and no attack had followed. Also, several other warnings had been issued during the course of 1941 that the Japanese in Honolulu were burning their codes.

The second type of event typically searched for lessons is one that the policy maker experienced firsthand. Especially important are those experiences that took place early in the policy maker's career. The lessons drawn from events experienced firsthand tend to be overgeneralized, to the neglect of lessons that might be drawn from the careful analysis of the experiences of others. U.S. thinking about the post–World War II role of the atomic bomb provides an example of the pull of personally experienced events on policy making.[10] The initial decisions were made by the men who had defeated Germany and Japan. In formulating ideas about the uses to which the bomb might be put, they drew heavily on these experiences. From 1945 to 1950, the Soviet targets identified for destruction by the atomic bomb duplicated those emphasized in the U.S. World War II policy of targeting commercial and industrial centers. To these men the atomic bomb was not a qualitatively new weapon for which a new strategy had to be developed. It was only the latest and most powerful weapon developed to date. It would be left to politicians to put forward the first strategy tailored to the political and technological realities of the postwar era.

Firsthand experiences that occur early in a policy maker's career are especially important because perceptual systems are resistant to change. Individuals are most open to competing images of reality when they confront a situation for the first time. Once a label or category is selected, it establishes the basis for future comparisons. These early firsthand experiences are not necessarily related to foreign policy problems. They may be ways of thinking about problems that proved successful in the past, positions taken on issues that produced the desired outcome, or strategies used in winning political office.[11] Early firsthand experiences are also of special significance because of the conditions under which policy makers must try to learn from the past. Decisions must be made, and a policy maker's attention is constantly spread over a wide variety of situations demanding his or her attention. Henry Kissinger spoke to these problems in his memoirs when he stated that "policy makers live off the intellectual capital they have brought with them into office; they have no time to build more capital."[12]

## TYPES OF CALCULATIONS MADE

When an event is recognized as a possible source of lessons, policy makers frequently engage in three types of calculations. First, they pay attention to *what* happened and seldom to *why*. The Iron Curtain descended across Europe; Vietnam fell; and the American embassy was attacked and hostages were taken. Focusing on what happened rather than on why creates a type of tunnel vision that obscures from view the differences between the present situation and earlier ones. What can one conclude from the fact that for the 1968 invasion of Czechoslovakia, the 1979 invasion of Afghanistan, and the 1981 noninvasion of Poland, the Soviet Union required three months' preparation time? Betts suggests not very much.[13] Policy makers could not assume that the Soviets would need three months to prepare for the next invasion. None of these were extremely urgent cases; they do not preclude more rapid mobilizations or a mobilization starting at a higher stage of readiness.

Second, in examining what happened, policy makers tend to dichotomize the outcome into successes and failures. They tend to forget that most policy initiatives are designed to achieve multiple objectives, that success and failure are rarely ever total, and that neither success nor failure is permanent. Problems are not so much solved as redefined and transformed into new challenges and opportunities.

When a policy is defined as a success, policy makers are especially prone to ignore three considerations in applying it as a lesson: (1) its costs, (2) the possibility that another option would have worked better or produced the same result at less cost, and (3) the role that accident, luck, and chance play in affecting the outcome of events. When an event is defined as a failure, a different set of biases tends to grip policy-maker thinking. There is (1) the presumption that an alternative course of action would have worked better and that policy makers should have known this and (2) an unwillingness to admit that success may have been unattainable or that surprise is inevitable. The congressional investigation into Pearl Harbor takes up thirty-nine volumes, and the success of the Japanese attack continues to bring forward a never-ending series of books asserting that U.S. policy makers knew of the attack and permitted it to happen.

To the extent that policy makers do seek to discover explanations, they tend to treat the most visible features of the situation as having had the biggest impact on the outcome of events. Diplomatic and military histories are written in terms of personalities and actors' strategies. Rarely is organizational planning, careful staff preparation, or bureaucratic coordination placed at the center of analysis.

## LESSONS LEARNED

Three lessons are most often learned by policy makers from their studies of history. The first is to expect to see more of the same. The Shah of Iran was expected to continue in power in 1979 simply because he had ruled for so long. Iran without the Shah seemed inconceivable. The grain shortage of 1973 caught U.S. policy makers by surprise, because, for policy makers, "the grain problem" was always one of too much grain. It did not occur to them that the combination of large-scale Soviet purchases of grain plus global drought would send the price of grain in the United States skyrocketing.

A second lesson learned is to expect continuity in the behavior of other actors. In part this occurs because policy makers are insensitive to the perceived costs of inaction as viewed by another state. The United States made this mistake at Pearl Harbor. U.S. estimates of Japanese behavior were based on the cost of attacking the United States. Insufficient attention was given to the costs that the Japanese would experience if they did nothing and allowed the status quo to continue into the future. For similar reasons, the hostile acts or words of allies surprise policy makers more than the hostility of an enemy. Having labeled a state as an ally, policy makers tend to become insensitive to the continuing conflicts of interest between them and the possibility that the ally will act to resolve them.

Third, policy makers learn to avoid policies that failed and to repeat policies that brought success. This would be fine if two conditions did not work against the continued success of a policy. First, successful policies get overused. They are applied to problems and situations for which they were not intended. Second, a successful policy often changes the situation in ways that will frustrate its future use. In the 1960s, military aid to the Shah may indeed have been responsible for averting the coup predicted by members of the Senate Foreign Relations Committee; but it also changed the situation so that by the late 1970s continued military aid became part of the Shah's problem instead of the answer.

These three lessons cast a long shadow over U.S. foreign policy making in the lead-up to the Iraq War. First, policy makers expected to see more of the same. The dominant view was that nuclear proliferation is a "strategic chain reaction,"[14] with Iraq under Saddam Hussein being the most recent addition to this chain. Second, it was assumed that Saddam Hussein was evil and could not be trusted to change his policies or at a minimum be contained as a security threat. Moreover, Saddam Hussein was engaged in an ongoing game of deception and obstruction with UN weapons inspectors. Why would he do this unless he was trying to hide something? When no weapons of mass destruction were found, an unexamined possibility emerged as the best explanation.[15] Saddam Hussein was acting out of a fear that if his bluff was exposed his enemies within Iraq would be emboldened and his hold on power seriously weakened. Finally, the George W. Bush administration was determined to avoid what it saw as the central mistake made by George H. W. Bush in the Persian Gulf War. He would remove Saddam Hussein from power.

## HISTORICAL LESSON

### The Philippine–American War (1899–1902)

In October 2003, in the Philippines, President George W. Bush declared that "America is proud of its part in the great story of the Filipino people. . . . Together our soldiers liberated the Philippines from colonial rule." Contingency planning for a war over Cuba called for taking the Philippines. Accordingly, Commodore George Dewey destroyed the Spanish fleet in Manila harbor on May 1, 1898. Manila surrendered in August. The Treaty of Paris signed on December 10, 1898, made the Philippines a U.S. possession.

In the Philippines, the American takeover came in the midst of an ongoing war for independence whose roots can be traced back to 1892. Fighting began in 1896, but by 1897 an impasse had been reached. Armistice negotiations were begun between the Spanish governor-general and rebel leader Emilio Aguinaldo, who agreed to denounce the revolution and go into exile for a large sum of money. Shortly before the attack, Dewey reportedly met with Aguinaldo, urging him to return to the Philippines and take up the revolutionary cause again. In any event, Aguinaldo did return, and with Spanish forces there weakened by Dewey's victory, Aguinaldo's forces scored a series of major victories. On June 12, 1898, Aguinaldo declared the Philippines independent. On June 2, 1899, his government declared war on the United States.

The United States refused to recognize this declaration of independence and declared that an armed insurgency now existed. In December 1898, President William McKinley had already issued his Benevolent Assimilation Proclamation, which tasked the U.S. Army with what today would be called "Phase IV" activities: building schools, guaranteeing religious freedoms, creating a judicial system, and protecting private property. The ultimate goal was to create conditions that would make Filipinos support American sovereignty. On the one hand, the results were positive as living conditions improved markedly, but on the other hand, these successes were offset by acts of political repression.

Almost all of the U.S. generals in command had participated in the Indian Wars in the United States. Over 126,000 U.S. soldiers served in the war, with the average troop strength being 40,000 and peaking at 74,000. The first shots in the conflict were fired on February 4, 1899. Initially Aguinaldo chose to fight a conventional military war against the United States. In this his forces suffered heavy casualties and were defeated handily. He then turned to guerrilla warfare. This phase began in November 1899. The official State Department history of the war describes it as having been "brutal on both sides." Large numbers of civilians died as a result of the fighting and it also resulted in food shortages and health crises in the form of cholera and malaria epidemics. The United States burned villages and forcefully relocated Filipinos from their homes into camps in an effort to separate the insurgents from the population. Both sides engaged in torturing captured soldiers and suspected enemy sympathizers. As is characteristic of guerrilla warfare, part of the insurgents' strategy was designed to influence the U.S. public. William Jennings Bryant was running on an anti-imperialist platform in the 1900 election, and rebel leaders hoped his victory would aid their cause.

In 1900, William Howard Taft, who was now in charge of the U.S. colonial government in the Philippines, put forward a policy of attraction designed to split the insurgent movement. It created a system of limited self-government and introduced a series of economic and social reforms that benefited the middle class. Aguinaldo was captured on March 23, 1901, and on April 1, he swore an oath of allegiance to the United States. Officially fighting ended on July 4, 1902.

Actual fighting continued through 1913. This conflict pitted U.S. forces against the Moros, a Philippine Muslim group whose homeland was in southern Philippines. It had been controlled by Spain only in the loosest fashion. The Moros were neutral in the Philippine–American War. As the war progressed, U.S. forces began to establish garrisons in their homeland, and relations between the American "occupiers" and the Moros became unstable and often resulted in violence as the United States sought to defeat them militarily and transform Moro society. Among the reforms put into place by U.S. military authorities were the abolition of slavery and the introduction of private property and a reformed legal system. Military battles resulted in the deaths of between 10,000 and 20,000 Moros. U.S. forces suffered 130 combat fatalities, with another 500 dying of disease.

## Applying the Lesson

1. What would a Filipino think of President Bush's reading of history?
2. What lessons do the Philippines in 1902 hold for U.S. policy in Afghanistan today?
3. Did the United States have an exit strategy in the Philippines? Can it be used today? ∎

# CASE STUDIES

Our attention now shifts to an examination of Vietnam and the Iraq War. The primary purpose of examining Vietnam is twofold. First, Vietnam is used to provide a look at the range of lessons used by policy makers in making decisions. The second reason for looking at Vietnam is to illustrate the range of lessons that American elites have drawn from U.S. involvement. We examine the Iraq War because it serves as the most immediate lesson of the past for a U.S. military presence in Afghanistan, and at the same time, many now speak of the possible onset of an **"Iraq Syndrome"** that will cast a shadow over future U.S. foreign policy initiatives the way Vietnam did.

## The Vietnam War

America's involvement in Vietnam spanned the terms of six presidents. The cost of the war and its level of destruction were enormous: 55,000 American dead; a maximum American troop presence of 541,000 men; a total cost of $150 billion; untold numbers of Vietnamese dead and wounded; 7 million tons of bombs dropped; and 20 million craters left behind. Table 4.1 presents a chronology of major events in the history of the U.S. presence in Vietnam. Our purpose in examining Vietnam is not to establish responsibility but to highlight (1) the types and sources of lessons used by U.S. foreign policy makers in making decisions and (2) the lessons that emerged from this involvement. This type of evaluation is necessary both to better understand Vietnam and to evaluate assertions that Angola, Nicaragua, or country X is another Vietnam. The need for it is evident in the ignorance of the public and U.S. policy makers about what happened there. A public opinion poll taken between March 21 and March 25, 1985, revealed that only three in five Americans knew that the United States supported South Vietnam. In a press conference on February 18, 1982, in response to a question about covert operations in Latin America, President Reagan stated:

> If I recall correctly, . . . North and South Vietnam had been, previous to colonization, two separate countries [and] provisions were made that these two countries could, by the vote of their people together, decide whether they wanted to be one country or not. . . . Ho Chi Minh refused to participate in such an election. . . . John F. Kennedy authorized the sending of a division of Marines. And that was the first move toward combat troops in Vietnam.[16]

**VIETNAM CHRONOLOGY** The first president to have to deal with Vietnam was Truman. Initially, his views on Indochina resembled those held during World War II by Roosevelt, who was sympathetic to Ho Chi Minh's efforts to establish independence for the region and unsympathetic to French attempts to reestablish their prewar position of colonial domination. In 1947, Truman resisted French requests for U.S. aid and urged France to end the war against Ho Chi Minh, who, while being one of the founders of the French communist party, had proven himself a valuable ally and nationalist in defeating Japan.

## TABLE 4.1

CHRONOLOGY OF U.S. INVOLVEMENT IN VIETNAM

| | |
|---|---|
| September 1940 | France gives Japan right of transit, control over local military facilities, and control over economic resources in return for right to keep nominal sovereignty. |
| March 1945 | Gaullist French forces take over administration of Vietnam from pro-Vichy French troops. |
| September 1945 | Ho Chi Minh declares Vietnam to be independent. |
| February 1950 | United States recognizes French-backed Bao Dai government. |
| March 1954 | French forces defeated at Dien Bien Phu. |
| April 1954 | Geneva Peace Talks begin; end in July. |
| September 1954 | SEATO created. |
| July 1956 | No elections held in Vietnam. |
| October 1961 | Taylor–Rostow mission sent to Vietnam; 15,000 advisers sent in as a result. |
| November 1963 | Diem and Kennedy assassinated. |
| August 1964 | Gulf of Tonkin incident. |
| February 1965 | Pleiku barracks attacked; 8 U.S. soldiers dead and 60 injured; Operation Rolling Thunder launched in retaliation. |
| May 1965 | General Westmoreland requests 80,000 troops. |
| July 1965 | President Johnson announces an additional 125,000 troops to be sent to Vietnam. |
| January 1968 | Tet Offensive. |
| March 1968 | Bombing halted; Johnson steps out of presidential race. |
| April 1970 | Cambodia invaded. |
| March 1972 | Major North Vietnamese offensive launched. |
| April 1972 | B-52 bombings of Hanoi and Haiphong. |
| May 1972 | North Vietnamese harbors mined. |
| December 1972 | Peace talks collapse and then resume after heavy bombing. |
| January 1973 | Peace agreement signed. |
| March 1975 | North Vietnamese offensive begins. |
| April 1975 | South Vietnam surrenders. |

Truman's views were soon to undergo a stark and rapid transformation. By 1952, the United States was providing France with $30 million in aid to defeat Ho Chi Minh, and in 1953, when Truman's presidency ended, the United States was paying one-third of the French war cost. Ho Chi Minh was also redefined from a nationalist into a communist threat to U.S. security interests. Nothing had changed in Indochina to warrant this new evaluation of the situation. Dramatic events, however, were taking place elsewhere as Cold War competition took root. In the process, decisions on Indochina came to be viewed in a larger context. France was reluctant to participate in a European Defense System, something the United States saw as vital if Europe was to contain communist expansionist pressures. In a virtual *quid pro quo,* the United States agreed to underwrite the French war effort in Indochina on the same day France announced its intent to participate in plans for the defense of Europe.

The Eisenhower administration began by reaffirming Truman's financial commitment to France and then enlarged upon it. By the end of 1953, U.S. aid rose to $500 million and covered approximately one-half of the cost of the French war effort. For Eisenhower and Secretary of State John Foster Dulles, expenditures of this magnitude were necessary to prevent a Chinese intervention that they both felt was otherwise likely to occur. Unfortunately for the French, U.S. aid was not enough to secure victory, and Eisenhower was unwilling to go beyond financing a **proxy war.**

The end came for the French at Dien Bien Phu. With its forces under siege there, France informed the United States that unless it intervened, Indochina would fall to the communists. With no aid forthcoming, the process of withdrawal began. France's involvement in Indochina officially came to an end with the signing of the 1954 Geneva Peace Accords. According to this agreement, a "provisional demarcation line" would be established at the 17th Parallel. Vietminh troops loyal to Ho Chi Minh would regroup north of it, and pro-French Vietnamese forces would regroup south of it. Elections were scheduled for 1956 to determine who would rule over the single country of Vietnam. The Geneva Accords provided the French with the necessary face-saving way out of Indochina. Ho Chi Minh's troops controlled three-quarters of Vietnam and were poised to extend their area of control. All parties to the agreement expected Ho Chi Minh to win the 1956 election easily.

The United States did not sign the Geneva Accords but pledged to "refrain from the threat or use of force to disturb" the settlement. However, only six weeks after its signing, the Southeast Asia Treaty Organization (SEATO) was established as part of an effort to halt the spread of communism in the wake of the French defeat. Signatory states to this collective security pact were Great Britain, France, New Zealand, Pakistan, the Philippines, Thailand, Australia, and the United States. A protocol extended coverage to Laos, Cambodia, and "the free people under the jurisdiction of Vietnam." The Vietminh saw the protocol as a violation of the Geneva Accords because it treated the 17th Parallel as a political boundary and not as a civil war truce line. Political developments below the 17th Parallel supported the Vietminh interpretation. In 1955, the United States backed Ngo Dinh Diem, who had declared himself president of the Republic of Vietnam. With U.S. support, he argued that because South Vietnam had not signed the Geneva Accords, it did not have to abide by them and hold elections. The year 1956 came and went with no elections. By the time Eisenhower left office, U.S. military aid had reached 1,000 U.S. military advisers stationed in South Vietnam.

The landmark decision on Vietnam during the Kennedy administration came in October 1961 with the Taylor–Rostow Report. Receiving contradictory information and advice on how to proceed, Kennedy sent General

Maxwell Taylor and Walt Rostow to Vietnam on a fact-finding mission. They reported that South Vietnam could only be saved by the introduction of 8,000 U.S. combat troops. Kennedy rejected this conclusion, but while skeptical of the argument, he did send an additional 15,000 military advisers. Kennedy's handling of the Taylor–Rostow Report is significant for two reasons. First, the decision was typical of those he made on Vietnam. He never gave the advocates of escalation all they wanted, but neither did he ever say no. Some increase in the level of the American military commitment was always forthcoming. Second, in acting on the Taylor–Rostow Report, Kennedy helped shift the definition of the Vietnam conflict from a political problem to a military one. Until this point Vietnam was seen by the Kennedy administration as a **guerrilla war** in which control of the population was key. From now on, control of the battlefield was to become the priority item.

Under President Lyndon Johnson, U.S. involvement in the war steadily escalated. Pressures began building in January 1964, when the Joint Chiefs of Staff (JCS) urged Johnson to put aside U.S. self-imposed restraints so that the war might be won more quickly. The JCS especially urged aerial bombing of North Vietnam. In August 1964, this bombing began, in retaliation for an incident in the Gulf of Tonkin. The United States stated that two North Vietnamese PT boats fired on the *C. Turner Joy* and the *Maddox* in neutral waters. President Johnson also went to Congress for a resolution supporting his use of force against North Vietnam. The Gulf of Tonkin Resolution passed by a unanimous vote in the House and by an 88-to-2 vote in the Senate. It gave the president the authority to "take all necessary measures to repel any armed attack against the forces of the United States and to prevent further aggression." The incident itself is clouded in controversy. Later studies suggest that the incident was staged or that it never occurred. These views hold that Johnson was merely looking for an excuse to begin bombing.[17] In the eyes of many, the Gulf of Tonkin Resolution became the functional equivalent of a declaration of war.

From that point forward, the war became increasingly Americanized. Operation Rolling Thunder, a sustained and massive bombing campaign, was launched against North Vietnam in retaliation for the February 1965 Vietcong attack on Pleiku. In June, the military sought 200,000 ground forces and projected a need for 600,000 troops. By 1967 U.S. goals were also changing. A Pentagon Papers memorandum put forward the following priorities: 70 percent to avoid a humiliating defeat; 20 percent to keep South Vietnam from China; and 10 percent to permit the people of South Vietnam to enjoy a better, freer way of life.[18]

The Tet Offensive in January 1968 brought yet another challenge to the Johnson administration, and in many ways it was the final challenge. In March 1968, Johnson announced a halt in the bombings against North Vietnam and that he was not a candidate for reelection. The Tet Offensive was a countrywide conventional assault by communist forces on South Vietnam. It penetrated Saigon, all of the provincial capitals, and even the U.S. embassy compound. The U.S. response was massive and expanded bombings of North Vietnam. In the end the communist forces were defeated. As a final thrust to take control of South Vietnam, the Tet Offensive had been premature, but it did demonstrate the bankruptcy of U.S. policy. Massive bombings and hundreds of thousands of U.S. combat troops had not brought the United States closer to victory.

Establishing détente was Richard Nixon's primary concern, and this policy could be threatened by any weakness or vacillation in U.S. policy on Vietnam. American commitments to Vietnam had to be met if the Soviet Union and China were to respect the United States in the post-Vietnam era. The strategy selected for accomplishing this was Vietnamization. Gradually, the United States would reduce its combat presence such that by 1972 the South Vietnamese army would be able to hold its own when supported by U.S. air and naval power and by economic aid.

The inherent weakness of Vietnamization was that the strategy could succeed only if the North Vietnamese did not attack in the transition period, before the South Vietnamese army was ready. Nixon and Kissinger designed a two-pronged approach to lessen the likelihood that this would occur. Cambodia was invaded with the hope of cleaning out North Vietnamese sanctuaries, and the bombing of North Vietnam was increased. Nevertheless, the potential danger became a reality when in the spring of 1972 North Vietnam attacked across the demilitarized zone (DMZ). At this point Nixon was forced to re-Americanize the war in order to prevent the defeat of South Vietnam. Bombing of North Vietnam now reached unprecedented levels, and North Vietnamese ports were mined.

Being carried out against the backdrop of this fighting were the Paris Peace Talks. They had begun in earnest in 1969 but had made little progress. With this escalation of the war Nixon also offered a new peace plan, which included a promise to withdraw all U.S. forces after an Indochina-wide cease-fire and exchange of prisoners of war (POWs). Progress was now forthcoming. Hanoi was finding itself increasingly isolated from the Soviet Union and China, both of which had become more interested in establishing a working relationship with the United States than in defeating it in Vietnam. It was now South Vietnam that began to object to the peace terms and stalled the negotiating process. In early December 1972, the "final talks" broke off without an agreement. On December 18, the United States ordered the all-out bombing of Hanoi and Haiphong to demonstrate U.S. resolve to both North and South Vietnamese leaders. On December 30, talks resumed, and the bombing was ended. A peace treaty was signed on January 23, 1973.

President Gerald Ford was in office when South Vietnam fell in 1975. What had begun as a normal military engagement ended in a rout. On March 12, 1975, the North Vietnamese attacked across the DMZ. On March 25, Hue fell. Five days later Da Nang fell. The United States evacuated on April 29, and on April 30, South Vietnam surrendered unconditionally.

**LESSONS USED BY POLICY MAKERS**   In examining the lessons used by policy makers in their decision making on Vietnam, our focus is on the Kennedy and Johnson administrations because it was during this period that the major escalations in the type and level of the U.S. commitment took place. We can identify two broad types of lessons of the past held by U.S. policy makers. The first are political lessons, and the second are strategic and tactical ones.

The political lessons of the past differed for elected and appointed policy makers only in their details. The bottom line was the same: Personal survival in the upper circles of decision making in Washington required creating an image of toughness. The source of this lesson for elected officials was the "loss" of China. The Republicans had successfully leveled this charge against the Democrats. Kennedy applied the same strategy against Nixon in 1960, accusing the Eisenhower administration of losing Cuba. Politically, Kennedy saw Vietnam as his China. Johnson saw the same lessons as did Kennedy. As Johnson stated many times, he did not intend to be the first U.S. president to lose a war.

The national security managers also drew on the fall of China for lessons. To this they could add lessons from decision making in the Korean War. In each case the implications were the same: A reputation for toughness was the most highly prized virtue that one could possess.[19] The bureaucratic casualties in the decision-making process on China were those who, even though they were correct, had become identified with the "soft" side of a policy debate. Those who had been hawkish—though wrong—emerged relatively unscathed from McCarthyism. To a lesser extent, Korea produced a similar pattern. Dean Rusk, who had failed to predict the Chinese entry into Korea but was staunchly anticommunist, did not pay a price for being wrong. In 1961, he became Kennedy's secretary of state.

Standing out among the host of strategic and tactical lessons of the past that were drawn on by policy makers on Vietnam was the Munich analogy and the danger of appeasement. Munich had become a symbol for a generation of policy makers.[20] Its impact was so great that even those with no personal contact with the European peace efforts in the late 1930s could draw on it for insight. Lyndon Johnson, for example, saw the central lesson of the twentieth century as being that the appetite for aggression is never satisfied. It was Dean Rusk who drew most openly and repeatedly on the Munich analogy. Although he recognized that differences existed between the aggressions of Ho Chi Minh and those of Hitler, the basic point remained the same: "Aggression by any other name was still aggression and . . . must be checked."[21]

Very different were the lessons drawn from the French experience in Indochina. It was on the mind of every participant in the debate on the Taylor–Rostow Report.[22] Yet it had a negligible effect on American thinking, falling far short of being a generational experience on the order of Munich. Only George Ball drew actively on this analogy. He had firsthand experience with the French war effort, having served as a lawyer for France during the Geneva negotiations. To him the war was unwinnable, and he warned Kennedy that if he sent the 15,000 combat troops to Vietnam as recommended, the commitment would escalate to 300,000 men.

Ball became concerned with U.S. policy in Vietnam because he feared that it was diverting attention from Europe. This Europeanist orientation to world politics was not unique within the Kennedy–Johnson administrations. McGeorge Bundy was "totally a man of the Atlantic." He was also very much a product of the 1950s and the Cold War, so when he entered the debate on Vietnam, he was an advocate of the U.S. presence. Kennedy's first ambassador to Vietnam, Fritz Nolting, and his top aide, William Trueheart, were also Europeanists who were totally ignorant of Asia and Asian communism. The predominance of Europeanists illustrates the interaction of political, strategic, and tactical lessons of the past. A president concerned with making sure Vietnam did not become his China had limited options in making appointments. A residue of doubt continued to hang over the credentials of most Asian experts. Even though they lacked knowledge about Asian affairs, a president could feel politically safe with Europeanists in key decision-making positions.

The lack of knowledge about Asia on the part of key policy makers comes through in the strategic and tactical lessons they drew from Asian events. In many respects Kennedy was more knowledgeable about Asia than most in his administration. He had taken a special interest in Indochina while he was in Congress and had read about guerrilla warfare. Yet for all of this, his views were not particularly sophisticated. They rested more on intuitive feel than on knowledge.[23] The inadequacy of this intuitive feel is evident in Kennedy's favored set of lessons of the past: Magsaysay's struggle against the Huk guerrillas in the Philippines and the British experience in Malaysia. Both contests were of a far different order from what was being contemplated in Vietnam. For example, the Malaysian analogy was flawed in at least five respects, according to the U.S. military:

1. Malaysian borders were far more controllable.
2. The racial characteristics of the Chinese insurgents in Malaysia made identification and segregation a relatively simple matter compared with the situation in Vietnam.
3. The scarcity of food in Malaysia compared to the relative plenty in South Vietnam made the denial of food to the guerrillas a far less usable weapon.
4. More important, in Malaysia the British were in actual command of military operations.
5. Finally, it took the British twelve years to defeat an insurgency that was less strong than the one in South Vietnam.[24]

The professional military also proved unable to draw on Asia for insights into how to fight in Vietnam. General Westmoreland was "a conventional man in an unconventional war." Vietcong challenges brought only a request for more and more men and more bombing. They did not produce innovative strategies or tactics. Robert McNamara was no different in this respect. Never challenging the assumptions of policy, he limited himself to translating ideas into workable processes. In the end, he was unable "to adapt his values and terms to Vietnam realities."[25] The approach of the chairman of the JCS, General Maxwell Taylor, was not very different. While he spoke of the challenge of brushfire wars, his cables from Vietnam and the Taylor–Rostow Report indicated that Taylor was not really talking in terms of fighting a guerrilla war. His concern was with the military problem in Vietnam, and he approached it in a very conventional manner. Additional troops were the answer; political reforms were not mentioned. Taylor's analogy was with

Korea and not with the Philippines or the French experience in Indochina. Looking at Korea, he drew favorable comparisons with battlefield conditions and terrain. Taylor overlooked the differing nature of the two wars. Korea had been a conventional war begun with a border crossing by uniformed troops who fought in large concentrations.[26] This was not Vietnam in 1964.

The lessons drawn by two other policy makers deserve mention. The first is Walt Rostow, who brought to Vietnam decision making a firm set of beliefs on how to win the war and of the necessity of winning it. In his eyes, communist intervention had taken place in South Vietnam, breaking the first rule of peaceful coexistence. The boundaries of the two camps were immutable, and any effort to alter them had to be resisted. His solution was air power.

Rostow had selected bombing targets during World War II and was convinced that massive bombing would bring North Vietnam to its knees. He was challenged on this point by George Ball, who had been a member of the Strategic Survey Group that studied the effect of the Allied bombing of Germany. It concluded that the bombing had been of limited value. Ball concurred in this conclusion and argued that bombing North Vietnam would be equally futile. The second person worth looking at is Lyndon Johnson, who drew heavily on his experience in Texas politics in formulating his Vietnam strategy. He had opposed the idea of a coup against Diem. That simply was not the way things were done in Texas. "Otto Passman and I, we have our differences, . . . but I don't plan his overthrow."[27] Beyond that, the United States had given its word to Diem, and you don't go back on your word. Johnson also felt that displays of toughness were prerequisites for dealing with the Vietnamese. Here he drew on analogies to his dealings with Mexicans. "If you don't watch they'll walk right into your yard and take it over . . . but if you say to 'em right at the start, 'Hold on just a minute,' they'll know they are dealing with someone who'll stand up. And after that you can get along just fine."[28]

**LESSONS LEARNED**  Vietnam had a tremendous impact on public opinion and elite attitudes. It destroyed the postwar consensus on the ends and means of U.S. foreign policy and left in its place three competing belief systems: Cold War internationalism, post–Cold War internationalism, and neoisolationism. That three competing belief systems have merged is an indication that the lessons of Vietnam are not self-evident or easily agreed on. The identification of three belief systems understates the extent of disagreement on the lessons of Vietnam. In identifying the lessons of Vietnam, we rely on a survey conducted by Ole Holsti and James Rosenau.[29] Respondents were asked to assess the lessons of Vietnam, the sources of failure, and the consequences of that failure. They were also asked to identify their positions on Vietnam when the war first became an issue for them and toward the end of the U.S. involvement. The sample was divided into three parts. The first was made up of a random sampling of names from *Who's Who*. The second group was selected on a quota basis from key groups in society (foreign service officers, clergy, women, labor, media, academics, and politicians). The third group was made up of military personnel.

On the basis of attitudes held at the beginning and end of American involvement in Vietnam, Holsti and Rosenau identify seven groups holding different notions about the sources, consequences, and lessons of Vietnam. These groups covered the entire range of opinion from consistent critics to consistent supporters. Fully 30 percent of the sample falls at the extremes, confirming the depth of the impact Vietnam had on American attitudes. Looking first at the sources of failure, Holsti and Rosenau were able to identify twenty-one reasons why the United States lost in Vietnam, according to those they polled. The depth of the disagreement is great. Not only are the sources of failure ranked differently by the various groups, no one explanation appears among all seven groups. Only three explanations appear among six of these groups: the United States' lack of clear-cut goals, the presence of Soviet and Chinese aid, and North Vietnamese dedication.

A more coherent picture emerges when we look at the consequences of Vietnam cited by the seven groups. Supporters cited international system–related concerns as the most important consequences of Vietnam. Critics cited Vietnam's domestic impact as most significant. Only one consequence was cited by all seven groups, but not with the same relative importance: The United States will limit its conception of its national interest. The picture becomes cloudy again when turning to the lessons of Vietnam. Thirty-four lessons were cited. No one lesson appears among all seven groups. Only two appear among six groups: Executive–legislative cooperation is vital; and Russia is expansionist.

## The Iraq War

Military planners describe six linked phases of military activity. They are depicted in Figure 4.1. In the Shape Phase (Phase 0), normal and routine military operations take place that are designed to solidify relations with allies and dissuade or deter potential enemies. In the Deter Phase (Phase I), military action is designed specifically to support or facilitate the execution of an upcoming military operation or campaign. It seeks to deter the enemy by demonstrating resolve and capabilities for action. In the Seize Initiative Phase (Phase II), military force is used to execute offensive operations at the earliest possible time, setting the stage for decisive operations to come.

This may require dislodging the enemy from its positions and thus creating the conditions for the ultimate destruction of its forces. In the Dominate Phase (Phase III), military forces focus on breaking the enemy's will for organized resistance. This phase involves the full deployment of force and the rapid sequencing of military operations. The Stabilize Phase (Phase IV) is required when there is no functioning legitimate government or there is only a minimally functioning one. Here military forces are required to perform limited local governance activities. As such, the focus shifts from sustained combat operations to stability operations, and the objective is to reduce the level of threat to manageable levels that can be controlled by civilian authorities. Finally, in the Enable Civil Authority Phase (Phase V), the objective of the military is to support the civil authorities. Redeployment

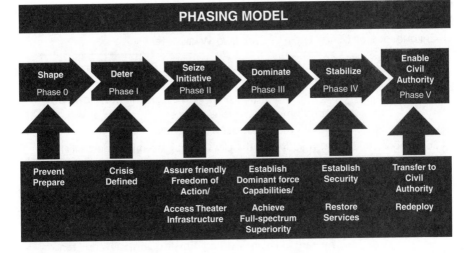

**FIGURE 4.1**
Phase Model of Military Activity.

of military combat forces begins in this phase, and the military end state is achieved with a return to a Shape Phase (Phase 0) military posture. Whereas great praise surrounded the initial military operation in Iraq, the lack of connections between the first three phases and Phase IV as well as the conduct of Phase IV became the subject of much criticism.[30]

**IRAQ WAR CHRONOLOGY** The prelude to the Iraq War found the United States engaged in diplomatic efforts at the UN Security Council to gain approval from that body for military action against Iraq. President George W. Bush addressed the UN General Assembly in September 2002, calling on it to move quickly to enforce the resolution demanding Iraq's disarmament while making it clear that the United States was prepared to act on its own. Secretary of State Colin Powell made a final presentation to the Security Council in February 2003 using electronic intercepts, satellite photos, and spies to make the case that Iraq possessed weapons of mass destruction and that high-level links existed between Iraq and al Qaeda. The United States was supported by Great Britain but opposed by France, Germany, Russia, and China. With the prospects for an affirmative vote by the UN Security Council virtually nonexistent, on March 16 President Bush met with British Prime Minister Tony Blair and leaders from Spain and Portugal in the Azores to announce that the "moment of truth" had arrived for Saddam Hussein. The following day Bush issued an ultimatum requiring Saddam to leave Iraq in 48 hours, and on March 19 Brush ordered the invasion of Iraq. A **"shock and awe"** military campaign was begun that was designed to overwhelm and demoralize Iraqi forces, allowing the coalition forces to move swiftly to Baghdad. On April 9, Baghdad came under the control of U.S. forces, and on May 1, President Bush declared an end to major combat operations. At this point the administration began Phase IV. A chronology of major events in the Iraq War is presented in Table 4.2.

## TABLE 4.2

CHRONOLOGY OF MAJOR EVENTS IN THE IRAQ WAR

| | |
|---|---|
| January 2002 | In his State of the Union address, President Bush identifies Iraq, Iran, and North Korea as an "axis of evil" and promises that the United States will not allow "the world's most dangerous regimes to threaten us with the world's most destructive weapons." |
| September 2002 | Bush addresses the UN General Assembly and challenges it to confront "the grave and gathering danger" of Iraq or become irrelevant. |
| December 2002 | Bush approves deployment of U.S. forces to the Persian Gulf. |
| February 2003 | The United States, Spain, and Great Britain introduce a resolution in the Security Council authorizing the use of military force against Iraq. Russia, Germany, and France oppose it. |
| March 17, 2003 | Bush gives Saddam Hussein a 48-hour ultimatum to leave Iraq. |
| March 19, 2003 | Operation Iraqi Freedom begins with a "decapitation" air strike against leadership targets in Baghdad. |
| March 21, 2003 | Major fighting begins. |
| May 1, 2003 | Bush declares an end to major combat operations. |
| December 2003 | Saddam Hussein is captured. |
| April 2004 | Photos are aired showing torture and mistreatment of prisoners by U.S. personnel at Abu Ghraib prison. |
| June 2004 | United States transfers power to a new interim Iraqi government. |
| September 2004 | U.S. casualties reach the 1,000 mark. |
| December 2004 | United States announces it plans to expand its military presence in Iraq to 150,000 troops. |
| January 2005 | Iraq holds its first multiparty election in 50 years. |
| May 2006 | Nouri al-Malaki forms Iraq's first permanent democratically elected government. |
| December 2006 | The Iraq Study Group Report (Baker–Hamilton Report) is released. |
| January 2007 | President Bush announces a surge of U.S. forces into Iraq to stem the violence and create conditions for peace. |
| March 19, 2008 | Fifth anniversary of the start of the Iraq War. |
| September 2008 | The U.S. transfers responsibility for security in Anbar Province, the heart of the Sunni insurgency, to the Iraqi military and police. |
| November 2008 | The Iraq cabinet approves a status of forces agreement that will govern the U.S. presence in Iraq through 2011. |
| January 2009 | Iraq holds local elections that are free from violence. |

By all accounts the Bush administration entered Phase IV without a great deal of forethought, expecting it to be completed in about six months. Calls for additional forces were rejected as unnecessary, and postwar planning carried out in the State Department and elsewhere received little attention in the Pentagon. On May 12, Paul Bremer arrived in Iraq as head of the new Coalition Provisional Authority (CPA). He replaced retired General Jay Garner, who had been named head of the Office for Reconstruction and Humanitarian Assistance on April 21. Bremer's first two orders prove to be highly controversial. CPA Order #1 attempted to "de-Baathify" Iraqi society. All full Baath party members were immediately dismissed from their government positions and banned from future government employment. CPA Order #2 dissolved the Iraqi army along with Saddam Hussein's bodyguard and special paramilitary. Originally the Ministry of Interior was also to be dissolved, but the decision was reversed when it became understood that the police were part of this ministry. The result of these two decisions was to drive into the opposition many highly trained individuals who were not necessarily supporters of Saddam Hussein and on whom the United States would have otherwise been able to rely on to help stabilize the military and political situation in Iraq.

Establishing political stability, much less creating a democratic government, proved an elusive goal. Political milestones were realized, but the creation of a functioning government supported by the all sectors of the Iraqi population was not achieved. On May 28, 2004, Iyad Allawi was selected as prime minister of the interim Iraqi government. One month later, sovereignty was transferred to this government, and Paul Bremer left Iraq. On January 30, 2005, elections for Iraq's National Assembly were held. On October 13 a national referendum was held on Iraq's constitution, and on December 15, voting began for Iraq's first permanent National Assembly under this constitution. In May 2006, Nouri al-Malaki formed Iraq's first permanent democratically elected government. President Bush praised his government as having "strong leaders that represent all of the Iraqi people" and signaling a "decisive break with the past." By the end of 2006, U.S. national security advisor Stephen Hadley was questioning the will and capacity of the al-Malaki government to take the necessary military and political steps to bring the sectarian violence in Iraq under control. Al-Malaki's ability to do so was central to the success of Bush's surge plan, announced in January 2007, which sent additional U.S. forces to Iraq. Bush's decision was controversial because it contradicted the central thrust of the Iraq Study Group's report.[31] Also known as the Baker–Hamilton Commission, it recommended a phased exit of U.S. forces from Iraq as well as talks with Syria and Iran. In June, it was announced that the surge was complete, with 28,500 more U.S. forces in country. This brought the total number of U.S. forces in Iraq to 165,000, the largest to date. It was not, however, significantly above the total level of coalition forces in Iraq in 2004 and 2005. Whereas once U.S. allies contributed about 25,000 soldiers to the Iraq operation, by 2007 only about 12,000 coalition forces were present.

U.S. strategy in Iraq began to move in a new direction in 2007 when General David Petraeus took command of the military operation there. Prior to assuming this post he oversaw the writing of the Army's new counterinsurgency manual.[32] It was the first new manual on counterinsurgency (COIN) operations produced by the army in 20 years and became the basis of U.S. operations in Iraq. The manual states that the central issue in insurgencies and counterinsurgencies is political power. The long-term success of COIN requires that people take charge of their own affairs and consent to the government's rule. Thus, the primary objective of COIN is to help establish a legitimate government. It continues by noting that "Armed Forces" cannot succeed in COIN alone and that an effective counterinsurgent force must be a learning organization. Among the pieces of advice it offers to U.S. commanders and soldiers are the following:

- Sometimes doing nothing is the best reaction
- Sometimes the more force is used, the less effective it is
- Some of the best weapons for counterinsurgents do not shoot
- If a tactic works this week, it might not work next week
- Sometimes the more you protect your forces, the less secure you may be

**LESSONS OF THE PAST AND THE IRAQ WAR**   Not long after 9/11, Deputy Secretary of State Richard Armitage asserted that "history starts today."[33] If he is correct, then the past offers us few lessons on how we should approach the Iraq War and the broader global war on terrorism. We have tried to suggest in the opening chapters that no such firm line separates U.S. foreign policy today from what has gone on before. However, even in rejecting Armitage's argument, it is clear that because the events in Iraq are so close to us, bringing together the words *learning* and *Iraq* is not easy. For this reason, our analyses of how the past will help us better understand the Iraq War is more speculative than was our discussion of the Vietnam. We will focus on two broad contextual questions. What insights can we gain from looking back at past conflict situations for improving our understanding of the Iraq War, and what are the lessons of the past for thinking about political occupations and for fighting counterinsurgencies?

### Contextual Lessons

*The Cold War.*   The George W. Bush administration has cast the global war against terrorism as a long war and identified Iraq as the central front in that war, thus inviting comparisons with the Cold War.

One factor that stands out in many analyses of how the Cold War was played, especially in the Third World, is the challenge that nationalism presented to U.S. foreign policy as it sought to counter the influence of the Soviet Union and communism.[34] Both sides were most effective when they cast their arguments in terms of local conditions and nationalist sentiment. They were least effective when trying to couch a local conflict in global terms—terms that were of little interest to those engaged in that particular struggle. Similarly, the United States found itself in a difficult position when it ignored the differences among local enemy forces, grouping them all together under the heading of "communists" or "communist sympathizers." The flip side is that the failure to understand the nationalist aspect of local conflicts that we incorporated into the global struggle against communism caused us to ally with leadership forces that were often seen by local political forces as part of the problem. This same problem of dealing with nationalism was central to the challenge faced in Iraq.

A rather ominous reading of the past is presented by Andrew Bacevich.[35] He sees the Cold War and the Iraq War as firmly linked. In his view, they are World War III and part of World War IV, respectively. Periodically during the Cold War, the Middle East and the Persian Gulf in particular had been a major concern of U.S. policy makers, but this concern was almost always overshadowed by other conflicts. This changed just as the Cold War was ending, with the Soviet invasion of Afghanistan and the Iranian hostage crisis. Bacevich sees President Jimmy Carter as virtually declaring the start of World War IV and Ronald Reagan as fully committing the United States to the region. The first phase of World War IV concluded in 1990. Iran and the Soviet presence in Afghanistan were the main U.S. enemies at this time. A second phase began with Iraq's invasion of Kuwait and ran through the 1990s. World War IV entered its third phase with the terrorist attacks of 9/11.

*The Vietnam War.* There is no shortage of comparisons between the Vietnam War and the Iraq War.[36] Nor is there any shortage of controversy over such comparisons. When President George W. Bush invoked the Vietnam comparison in 2007, stating that "one unmistakable legacy of Vietnam is that the price of America's withdrawal was paid by millions of innocent citizens," Senator Edward Kennedy (D. Mass.) countered, saying, "the president is drawing the wrong lessons from history."[37] Among the most often-noted differences are those involving the nature of the military conflict. In Vietnam, the United States entered into an ongoing national war of liberation. It was a war in which the enemy operated as a unified political–military force and engaged in conventional military battles as well as conducting insurgency operations. Violence rarely spread into major South Vietnamese cities. The United States also carried the war on the ground and in the air to neighboring states that it accused of aiding the enemy and, in the case of North Vietnam, being part of the enemy.

In Iraq the conflict began with an American invasion. Conventional war fighting soon ended, and the conflict now has become almost entirely a combination of terrorist and insurgency attacks. Opposition forces do not operate as a unified political–military front but as militias, terrorist bands, and death squads under the leadership of a host of leaders. In the process, cities have become the battleground and civilians frequent targets as the various sides fight for dominance and settle old and new feuds. The United States has not sought to expand the Iraq War beyond that country's borders, even though it asserts that Iran and Syria have been harboring and supporting Iraqi insurgents.

It is with the political side of the Iraq War that commentators see far more parallels with the Vietnam War, although not all agree on what they are. Melvin Laird, who served as secretary of defense under Nixon during Vietnam, observed that one point of similarity is that both wars were launched on the basis of faulty intelligence and "possibly outright deception."[38] In both cases the intelligence failures prevented the United States from getting a clear picture of what motivated the enemy. By "possible deception" he was referring to the weapons-of-mass-destruction charge leveled against Saddam Hussein by the Bush administration and the Gulf of Tonkin incident that became the basis for the congressional resolution used by the Johnson administration as a rationale for expanding the American presence in Vietnam. Similarities are also found in the decisions made by presidents early in the war and then as they encountered wars in which victory no longer seemed attainable. Kennedy and Bush saw Vietnam and Iraq, respectively, as testing grounds for new strategic doctrines.[39] For Kennedy, it was an opportunity to move away from Eisenhower's doctrine of massive retaliation to one of graduated escalation. Massive retaliation with its emphasis on the all-out use of nuclear weapons left presidents few options in dealing with regional threats like Vietnam. For Bush, Iraq provided a test case for preemption as the new American strategic doctrine and a replacement for deterrence, which was judged as too passive and unable to dissuade leaders of rogue states.

Both Johnson and Bush responded by deciding to increase the level of American forces in the hope, critics of these two wars argued, of passing it along to their successors so that history would not identify them as having lost Vietnam or Iraq. Nixon and Bush used similar language in explaining an American exit strategy to the public. Nixon said that "as South Vietnamese forces become stronger, the rate of American withdrawal can become greater." Bush asserted that "as the Iraqi security forces stand up, coalition forces can stand down."[40] Political differences are also present. The depth of support for the Vietnam War was far wider and deeper than it was for the Iraq War. In the early 1960s, few questioned the domino theory and the need for an American presence in Vietnam. No equivalent rationale for action existed at the outset of the Iraq War. This was unlike the war in Afghanistan that preceded it, in which the link to the global spread of terrorism seemed evident to most.[41]

*The Korean War.*   In June 2007, the Bush administration publicly raised the possibility of a long-term deployment of U.S. troops in Iraq after the present mission ends. The historical analogy put forward is South Korea, where U.S. forces continued to be based for decades after the Korean conflict formally ended. The Korean model was presented by both Bush and Secretary of Defense Robert Gates as superior to the Vietnam model, which U.S. forces left "lock, stock, and barrel." The analogy is attractive because of the economic prosperity and political stability that South Korea has experienced since the armistice was signed. Critics quickly pointed out, however, that given the animosity toward American forces in Iraq, the continued presence of U.S. troops would likely be a lightening rod in domestic Iraqi politics and a target of military and terrorist attacks. Beirut in the 1980s, where U.S. Marines established a presence after fighting between Lebanon and Israel, was cited as a better analogy. At first welcomed by all factions, a suicide bomber driving a truck struck the Marine barracks in 1983, killing 241 soldiers.

**Operational Lessons**

*Fighting Counterinsurgency Operations.* The recognized differences between the political and military battlefields of Vietnam and Iraq that we noted earlier have led to a major debate over the military lessons of Vietnam for Iraq when it comes to fighting counterinsurgency operations. At one end of the debate are those who argue that the most relevant strategy in Vietnam was the abandoned "strategic hamlet" program, in which the United States sought to pacify specific areas and then gradually expand control outward. In Iraq, this has been referred to as the "oil spot" strategy.[42] At the other end of the spectrum are those who argue that the different political situations in Iraq and Vietnam negate the relevance of any Vietnam counterinsurgency strategy for Iraq. They argue that in Iraq the issue is not the people against a government so much as it is a security problem driven by mutual fear of all people about what will happen if the opposing group(s) seizes control of the government. Winning the hearts and minds of the people does not address this problem; nor does promoting democracy. In fact, democratization may only further polarize the situation by increasing anxieties over what the new government will do.[43]

The search for lessons from the past that the United States can use in fighting insurgents in Iraq also yields a cautionary note. David Kilcullen argues that today's insurgents differ greatly from their predecessors in terms of policy, strategy, operational art, and tactics.[44] For example, given the global and instantaneous nature of communications today, the success of the insurgents may not ride on the legitimacy of the local government but on the ability to mobilize public support around the world for their cause. Kilcullen continues by saying that whereas it was once believed that counterinsurgency operations were 25 percent military and 75 percent political, they may be 100 percent political today. Kilcullen concludes by echoing the observation of Bernard Fall, a noted Vietnam-era counterinsurgency specialist: "If it works, it is obsolete."

*Rebuilding Iraq.* The post–World War II American occupations of Germany and Japan were put forward by the George W. Bush administration as the starting points for thinking about rebuilding Iraq. He observed, "America has made and kept this kind of commitment before . . . after defeating enemies, we did not leave behind occupying armies, we left constitutions and parliaments." A closer reading of the American experience in Germany and Japan would have provided reason for caution with regard to both process and outcome. Douglas Porch maintains that for nearly a full decade many of those involved in these reconstruction programs considered their efforts to be nearly a complete failure.[45] Rather than encounter a welcoming population, they found resentment and resistance. Actions taken to bring about reform were often counterproductive. General Lucius Clay, who was in charge of the American occupation zone in Europe, called de-Nazification his biggest mistake. It was in his mind a "hopelessly ambiguous procedure" that linked together small and big Nazis and engendered the hostility of the population at large because the implementation of this policy often appeared arbitrary and hypocritical. Yet the United States moved quickly to "de-Baathify" Iraq by dismissing party members from government positions and decommissioning the army.

It can be argued that the reasons for the ultimate success of the occupations of Germany and Japan had little to do with American policy or the presumed natural inclination of people liberated from tyranny for democracy. Rather, it had to do with such factors as enlightened domestic leadership, economic miracles fueled by the Marshall Plan in Europe and the Korean War in Asia, along with the prior experience of democracy and entrepreneurship in these two states. The key American contribution was creating domestic and regional security, laying the ground rules for democratic reform, and then getting out of the way.

Germany and Japan were not the only efforts at reconstruction (or, more broadly, nation building) that might have been looked to for lessons. Fourteen other cases exist including Cuba (1898–1902, 1906–1909, and 1917–1922), the Dominican Republic (1916–1924, 1965–1966), South Vietnam, Cambodia, and Afghanistan.[46] In only two of these cases, Panama (1989) and Grenada, was democracy in place after 10 years. The cases embodied a wide variety of interim administrations in the nation-building period. In seven cases, the United States established governments that almost totally depended on it for their survival. In none of these cases did democracy emerge. One lesson drawn from these experiences is that the ideal form of transition involves a quick transfer of power to legitimately elected local leaders, but he cautions that this presupposes a functioning electoral system and moderate local leaders who have genuine support among the populace.

## OVER THE HORIZON

Only time will tell if the United States becomes the latest foreign power to meet defeat in Afghanistan. Learning lessons from the past will be important if defeat is to be avoided. The Cold War, Vietnam, and the Iraq War show that learning from the past is not easily done. Not only are the events tremendously complex, the question of learning from them hides a host of less visible preliminary questions: What is it about the event you wish to learn? What phase of the event are you concerned with? Whose views are you concerned with? What set of values will you bring to your analysis? In looking at Vietnam or the Cold War, we have the luxury of time and distance from the event itself. This is not always the case, and when it is not, the task of learning from the past becomes even more complex.

In looking over the horizon for new efforts to learn from the past, we can expect to see efforts to examine two recent events for lessons. One is the Iraq War. The late turnaround in that war and the increased possibility that a stable political system may emerge may lead to renewed debate about the wisdom of the war and how it was fought. Three different schools of thought now exist and compete with each other for acceptance: (1) it was a war of choice and not necessity and should not have been fought, (2) it was a necessary war but fought badly, and (3) it was a necessary war whose ending vindicated the Bush administration strategy.

A second event we can expect to be looked closely at for lessons is the tragedy of September 11, 2001. Its tenth anniversary is not far away. At the same time, the closeness of this event in time and the deep emotions it stirs make 9/11 an especially difficult event from which to draw lessons. Among the dangers that observers say we must be on the lookout for in drawing lessons is letting potential threats determine U.S. interests rather than first determining U.S. interests and then identifying threats to them, seeking universal solutions to problems, and emphasizing immediate actions over developing long-term strategies.[47]

## CRITICAL THINKING QUESTIONS

1. What is the most important lesson that can be learned from the U.S. experience in Vietnam?
2. What lessons does Iraq hold for an involvement in Afghanistan?
3. What are the dangers of looking to the past for lessons on how to deal with current foreign policy problems?

## KEY TERMS

analogies   81
closed belief system   82
cognitive consistency   82
generational events   83

guerrilla war   91
Iraq syndrome   88
noise   81
proxy war   90

shock and awe   97
signal   81

## FURTHER READING

Robert Jervis, *Perception and Misperception in International Politics* (Princeton, NJ: Princeton University Press, 1976).

Yuen Foong Khong, *Analogies at War: Korea, Munich, Diem Bien Phu and the Vietnam Decision of 1965* (Princeton: Princeton University Press, 1992).

David Kilcullen, "Counter-insurgency Redux," *Survival*, 48 (2006–2007), 111–30.

Melvin Laird, "Iraq: Learning the Lessons of Vietnam," *Foreign Affairs*, 84 (2005), 22–43.

Ernest May, *"Lessons" of the Past: The Use and Misuse of History in American Foreign Policy* (New York: Oxford University Press, 1978).

## NOTES

1. Michael Breeden, "Curse of the Khyber Pass," *National Interest*, 100 (2009), 4–12.
2. Richard K. Betts, *Surprise Attack: Lessons for Defense Planning* (Washington, DC: Brookings, 1982), p. 8.
3. Richard Ned Lebow, *Between Peace and War: The Nature of International Crisis Behavior* (Baltimore, MD: Johns Hopkins University Press, 1981), p. 199.

4. Roberta Wohlstetter, *Warning and Decision* (Stanford, CA: Stanford University Press, 1962), p. 70.
5. Roland Paris, "Kosovo and the Metaphor War," *Political Science Quarterly*, 117 (2002), 423–50.
6. Wohlstetter, *Warning and Decision*, p. 388.
7. On cognitive consistency and its application to world politics, see Robert Jervis, *Perception and Misperception in International Politics* (Princeton, NJ: Princeton University Press, 1976); John D. Steinbruner, *The Cybernetic Theory of Decision: New Dimensions of Political Analysis* (Princeton, NJ: Princeton University Press, 1974); and Lebow, *Between Peace and War*.
8. Ole Holsti, "The Belief System and National Images: A Case Study," *Journal of Conflict Resolution*, 6 (1972), 244–52.
9. *The Washington Post*, December 23, 1984, p. 11.
10. These points are discussed in George Quester, *Nuclear Diplomacy, The First Twenty-Five Years* (New York: Dunellen, 1970); and Michael Mandelbaum, *The Nuclear Question: The United States and Nuclear Weapons, 1946–1976* (New York: Cambridge University Press, 1979).
11. Jervis, *Perception and Misperception*, pp. 249–50.
12. Henry Kissinger, *The White House Years* (Boston: Little, Brown, 1979), p. 54.
13. Betts, *Surprise Attack*, p. 8.
14. Scott Sagan, "Why Do States Build Nuclear Weapons?" *International Security*, 21 (1996–97), 58.
15. Kenneth Pollack, "Spies, Lies, and Weapons," *Atlantic Monthly*, 293 (January 2004), 78–92.
16. Results of the public opinion poll are found in *The New York Times*, March 31, 1985, sec. 6, p. 34. Reagan's comments can be found in the *Weekly Compilation of Presidential Documents*, 18 (February 18, 1982), 185.
17. John Stoessinger, *Why Nations Go to War*, 3rd ed. (New York: St. Martin's, 1982), p. 101.
18. *The Pentagon Papers* as published by the *New York Times* (New York: Quadrangle, 1971), p. 263.
19. On this point see Richard Barnett, *The Roots of War* (New York: Penguin, 1973), chaps. 4 and 5.
20. Ernest May makes this point in his treatment of Vietnam in *"Lessons" of the Past: The Use and Misuse of History in American Foreign Policy* (New York: Oxford University Press, 1978).
21. Robert Gallucci, *Neither Peace nor Honor: The Politics of American Military Policy in Vietnam* (Baltimore, MD: Johns Hopkins University Press, 1975), p. 33.
22. May, *"Lessons" of the Past*, p. 94.
23. David Halberstam, *The Best and the Brightest* (New York: Random House, 1969), p. 119.
24. May, *Lessons of the Past*, pp. 98–99.
25. Halberstam, *The Best and the Brightest*, p. 304.
26. Ibid., p. 212.
27. Ibid., p. 356.
28. Ibid., p. 643.
29. Ole Holsti and James N. Rosenau, "Vietnam, Consensus, and the Belief Systems of American Leaders," *World Politics*, 32 (1979), 1–56.
30. For a first wave of writings on the Iraq War see Larry Diamond, "What Went Wrong in Iraq," *Foreign Affairs*, 83 (2004), 34–56. Bob Woodward, *State of Denial* (New York: Simon & Schuster, 2006); Thomas Ricks, *Fiasco* (New York:

Penguin, 2006); and Rajiv Chandrasekaran, *Imperial Life in the Emerald City* (New York: Alfred A. Knopf, 2007).

31. *The Iraq Study Group Report* (New York: Vintage, 2006).
32. FM 3-24, Counterinsurgency. It is available at Army Knowledge Online. www.us. army.mil
33. Quoted in Andrew Bacevich, "The Real World War IV," *Wilson Quarterly* (Winter 2005), 60.
34. Anatol Lieven and John C. Hulsman, "Neo-Conservatives, Liberal Hawks, and the War on Terror: Lesson from the Cold War," *World Policy Journal* (Fall 2006), 64–74.
35. Bacevich, "The Real World War IV."
36. For comparisons of Vietnam and Iraq see Stephen Biddle, "Seeing Baghdad, Thinking Saigon," *Foreign Affairs*, 85 (2006), 2–14; Frederick Kagan, "Iraq Is Not Vietnam," *Policy Review*, 134 (2005–2006), 3–14; and Andrew Krepinevich, Jr., "How to Win in Iraq," *Foreign Affairs*, 84 (2004), 87–104.
37. Michael Fletcher, "Bush Compares Iraq to Vietnam," *The Washington Post*, August 23, 2007, p. A1.
38. Melvin Laird, "Iraq: Learning the Lessons of Vietnam," *Foreign Affairs*, 84 (2005), 22–43.
39. Lawrence Freedman, "Iraq, Liberal Wars and Illiberal Containment," *Survival*, 48 (2006), 51–65.
40. Quoted in Biddle, "Seeing Baghdad, Thinking Saigon," 4.
41. Leslie H. Gelb and Richard K. Betts, "We're Fighting Not to Lose," *The Washington Post*, January 14, 2007, p. B1.
42. Krepinevich, "How to Win in Iraq."
43. Biddle, "Seeing Baghdad, Thinking Saigon."
44. David Kilcullen, "Counter-insurgency Redux," *Survival*, 48 (2006–2007), 111–30.
45. Douglas Porch, "Occupational Hazards," *The National Interest* (2003), 35–46.
46. Minxin Pei, "From Victory to Success: Afterwar Policy in Iraq," *Foreign Policy*, 137 (July 2003), 1–55.
47. Christopher Hemmer, "The Lessons of September 11, Iraq and the American Pendulum," *Political Science Quarterly*, 122 (2007), 207–238.

# Society

In 2006, two well-respected U.S. foreign policy scholars, John Mearsheimer and Stephen Walt, published a report on the Israel lobby that set off a firestorm of debate over the extent of influence that Israel had on U.S. foreign policy.[1] They argued that "no lobby has managed to divert U.S. foreign policy as far from what the American national interest would otherwise suggest, while simultaneously convincing Americans that U.S. and those of the other country . . . in this case Israel, are essentially identical," something the authors argue is not the case. In fact, they argue Israel has become a strategic burden and often reneges on promises to the United States, such as promising not to engage in more building in contested areas or to target for assassination key Palestinian leaders.

Critics attacked the quality of the research, labeling it "paranoid and conspiratorial," "racist," and "anti-Semitic." Others claimed that the authors were arguing that the very survival of Israel was of little concern to the United States and that the U.S. terrorism problem was due to its support of Israel. In responding to their critics, the authors asserted that they never said the Israel lobby was a conspiracy, but they did maintain that without the lobbying of the American–Israel Political Action Committee, support for Israel in the United States would be less than it is.

As this debate over the power of the Israeli lobby on U.S. foreign policy indicates, great controversy exists over the proper role that the American public should play in making U.S. foreign policy. Should it come through the active participation of the public in making foreign policy decisions or should the public be largely passive, allowing policy makers a great deal of freedom of action in formulating foreign policy initiatives? James Billington argues the case for an active and involved public. "International affairs cannot be a spectator sport any more than policy making can be the preserve of a small group of elites. Many must be involved; many more persuaded."[2] Walter Lippmann presents the opposite position, stating "the people have imposed a veto upon the judgment of the informed and responsible officials . . . They have compelled the governments, which usually knew what would have been wiser, was necessary, or was more expedient, to be too late with too little, or too long with too much . . . "[3]

In this chapter, we examine the major avenues available to the public in exercising its voice on foreign policy matters: public opinion, elections, interest-group activity, and political protest. We also discuss how policy makers view the public voice in making foreign policy decisions and the role of the media.

## PUBLIC AWARENESS OF FOREIGN POLICY ISSUES

Before examining these avenues of influence open to those seeking to influence U.S. foreign policy, it needs to be recognized that not everyone is equally interested in or aware of foreign policy issues. A commonly used framework for dividing the American public into groups based on their level of awareness finds four groups that have remained relatively consistent in size over time.[4]

There is a large group, comprising 30 percent of the public, which is unaware of all but the most significant international events. Members of this group have at best vague and weak opinions. Second, there exists another large group, comprising 45 percent of the public, which is aware of many major international events but was not deeply informed about them. The remaining 25 percent are generally knowledgeable about foreign issues and holding relatively firm convictions. They are referred to as opinion holders. Within this group there is a smaller set of activists (1–2 percent) who serve as opinion mobilizers for the other segments of the public.

Polling done in the months following the invasion of Iraq is consistent with this picture of the American public. It found that many Americans were wrong about three "facts." First, 45–52 percent of Americans polled believed that evidence existed of a link between Iraq and al Qaeda. Second, some 23 percent believed that weapons of mass destruction (WMD) had been found. Third, about 25 percent of those who were questioned believed that the majority of people around the world supported the U.S. decision to go to war.

The sources of information about the war people relied upon played a major role in explaining these figures. When questioned as to where they received most of their news from, 19 percent said the print media and 80 percent said TV or radio. Fox was the news source of choice for those who had the most misperceptions, while National Public Radio listeners held the least misperception. Just as striking is the fact that there was no relationship between the degree to which people paid attention to the news and their holding misperceptions. In fact, the more one reported paying attention to Fox News, the more one was at least slightly more likely to hold a misperception.

The impact of one's news source on one's opinions about the Iraq War is consistent with another set of findings about the relationship between the media and public opinion: For those members of the public who are not very attentive to foreign affairs, exposure to soft news coverage of international events had a much greater impact on their thinking than did hard news coverage, and these individuals tended to hold isolationist attitudes.[5] Talk shows such as those hosted by Oprah Winfrey, Geraldo Rivera, Regis Philbin, Arsenio Hall, and Jay Leno are examples of soft news outlets. These news sources were found to be three times more likely than hard news reports to make comparisons between a current foreign policy crisis and past U.S. foreign policy failures such as Vietnam or terrorist attacks.

## PUBLIC OPINION

Public opinion provides a first avenue for the public to express its views on foreign policy. And while every president has claimed that he does not care what polls say the public thinks, every president since Richard Nixon has employed pollsters to learn just that.[6]

Interpreting a public opinion poll is not always easy. The public's response can easily be swayed by the wording of a question. For example, prior to the

Persian Gulf War, when asked if the United States should take all action necessary, including military force, to make sure Iraq withdrew from Kuwait, 65 percent said yes. Only 28 percent said yes when asked if it should initiate a war to force Iraq out of Kuwait.

## Trends and Content

Given these types of problems, analysts conclude that when taken out of context, answers to foreign policy questions seldom provide an accurate reading of public opinion. Far more valuable is trend analysis, in which responses to questions are traced over time for their content and stability. Approached this way, public opinion polls have captured several clearly identifiable changes in the structure of American public opinion about foreign affairs issues.

The pivotal event for the first change was World War II. Public opinion polls before World War II suggested a strongly isolationist outlook. In 1939, 70 percent of opinion holders said that American entry into World War I was a mistake, and 94 percent of those with opinions felt that the United States should "do everything possible to stay out of foreign wars" rather than try to prevent one. The outbreak of fighting in Europe had little impact on U.S. attitudes. Public support for war against Germany rose only from 13 percent to 32 percent between late 1939 and late 1941.[7] Following the attack on Pearl Harbor, this situation changed dramatically. Internationalist sentiment came to dominate public perceptions about the proper U.S. role in the world. Between 1949 and 1969, 60–80 percent of the American public consistently favored active U.S. participation in world affairs.[8]

Before the Vietnam War, virtually all internationalists were in fundamental agreement on the nature of the international system and the makeup of U.S. foreign policy. Among their core beliefs were that the United States had both the responsibility and the capability to create a just and stable world order, that peace and security are indivisible, that the Soviet Union was the primary threat to world order, and that containment was the most effective way to meet the Soviet challenge.[9] Foreign policy based on these beliefs could expect to receive the support of the American people. When disagreements arose, they tended to be about the process of making foreign policy rather than about its substance.

Vietnam was the next pivotal event shaping the direction of public attitudes.[10] Using polling data that began in 1964, researchers have found a steady and precipitous erosion of internationalist sentiment that continued for a decade. Internationalism only reemerged as the majority perspective in 1980. In 1964, 65 percent of the public was defined as internationalist. This fell to 41 percent in 1974. That year also saw a dramatic increase in the number of isolationist responses, from 9 percent in 1972 to 21 percent in 1974. Those who supported an active U.S. role rose in number to 61 percent in 1980. No single, pivotal event seems to be associated with this rebirth of internationalism. Instead, the American public gradually came to see the international system as threatening and out of control and developed a renewed willingness to use U.S. power and influence to protect U.S. national interests.

Pronounced changes have occurred in Americans' self-image since the end of the Cold War. A poll taken in late 1998 found that the American public appeared to have grown more self-confident as the Cold War receded.[11] Fifty percent felt that the United States now played a more important and more powerful role in the world than it had 10 years earlier. Seventy-nine percent of the public anticipated that the United States would play an even greater role in another 10 years, with 63 percent viewing economic strength as the key determining factor to overall power and influence in the world.

A 2006 poll painted a picture of an American public that had lost much of this sense of confidence.[12] It found a pervasive fear that U.S. international strategy had backfired and made the United States less secure. Sixty-three percent of those polled felt that people around the world had grown more afraid that the United States would use force against them, and a similar percentage felt that as a consequence countries would take aggressive military steps to protect themselves. Rejecting attempts to use military force to increase American security, 80 percent agreed with the statement that promoting goodwill in other countries was an essential part of any security strategy, and 82 percent opposed isolating and not talking to problem countries.

On a deeper level, however, neither the Cold War nor the war on terrorism seemed to have changed the underlying structure of American attitudes on foreign policy.[13] A 1992 study found little support among opinion leaders for a return to pre–World War II, across-the-board isolationism as the cornerstone of American foreign policy. Similarly, public opinion data suggest that the 9/11 terrorist attacks did not fundamentally alter the basic internationalist beliefs of Americans.[14] A poll conducted in November 2001 showed that 81 percent of Americans felt it was important for the United States to take an active role in the world. This was the highest level ever recorded since the question was first asked in 1947. Both before and after 9/11, a strong majority of Americans voiced support for sharing the burdens of international activism with others.

## Public Opinion and the Use of Force

A particularly important question to policy makers is the willingness of the public to support the use of military force. The conventional wisdom inherited from the Vietnam War era is that the public is unwilling to support the use of force if it resulted in casualties. Known as the Vietnam syndrome, the policy implication of this reading of the public led policy makers to either avoid the use of force altogether or to use it only in highly controlled settings where military force could be applied quickly and in an overwhelming fashion to ensure a short conflict with few American casualties.

The accumulated evidence on the use of force from the 1960s through the 1990s now points in a different direction and questions to policy implications of the **Vietnam syndrome**. The public is not totally gun shy. It will support the use of military force even when casualties occur, depending on (1) the policy purpose behind its use, (2) the success or failure of the undertaking, and (3) the degree of leadership consensus. In a related vein, other studies suggest that the public is sensitive to the domestic costs of foreign policy activism. The more serious the domestic problems relative to the external challenge, the more powerful will be the public's isolationist impulse. Thus, the weaker the economy, the less support a president is likely to find for an activist foreign policy. A similar dynamic appeared to be at work in terms of the Iraq War. Because spending on the Iraq War amounted to less than 1 percent of the gross domestic product or GDP (about one-half of what is spent at Wal-Mart), and because President Bush had not raised taxes to pay for the war, the cost was largely invisible. This is in contrast to the Vietnam War, which cost 9 percent of the GDP, and the Korean War, which at one point cost 14 percent of the GDP.[15]

Of particular interest for the question of purpose is a study undertaken by Bruce Jentleson,[16] who argues that the American public is most likely to approve military force when the purpose is to restrain the foreign policy actions of a hostile state and least likely to do so when the purpose is to bring about internal political change. A summary of his findings is presented in Table 5.1. This shows that all five uses of force that involved attempts to curb the foreign policy activities of another state ranked higher than any effort to use military force to bring about internal political change. Public support for the war against Iraq bears out Jentleson's argument. Support was highest for Operation Desert Shield and Operation Desert Storm, which were designed primarily to curb Iraqi foreign policy adventurism by defending Saudi Arabia

## TABLE 5.1

### POLICY OBJECTIVES AND PUBLIC SUPPORT

| Case | Principal Policy Objective[a] | Public Support Score (reranking)[b] |
|---|---|---|
| Libya: antiterrorism | FPR | 1 |
| Persian Gulf reflagging | FPR | 2 |
| Lebanon | Mixed | 3 |
| Afghanistan | Mixed | 4 |
| Nicaragua: military exercises | FPR | 5 |
| Panama (preinvasion) | IPC | 6 |
| El Salvador | IPC | 7 |
| Libya: get Qaddafi | IPC | 8 |
| Nicaragua: overthrow Sandinistas | IPC | 9 |

[a]FPR, foreign policy restraint; IPC, internal political change.
[b]Reranking excludes halo-effect cases. (The *halo effect* occurs when the use of force produces such quick success that everyone approves and no one remembers being opposed to the use of force at the outset. For that reason, public opinion polls are of little value in these situations.)
*Source*: Bruce W. Jentleson, "The Pretty Prudent Public," *International Studies Quarterly*, 36 (1990), 64.

and liberating Kuwait. The American public was distinctly less interested in using American military power to protect the Kurds or Shiites in southern Iraq after President George H. W. Bush announced the cease-fire. A similar pattern of public support emerged in 1999 for NATO's bombing in Kosovo to stop Serb aggression. This overall pattern held true in the early months of the Obama administration as it dealt with Afghanistan. According to an October 2009 Washington Post–ABC News poll, most Americans favored attacking al Qaeda and Taliban leaders in Pakistan but fewer endorsed building a stable democracy in Afghanistan as a priority goal.

The impact of race and gender also has been an important area of inquiry in the study of public opinion and the use of force. Distinct racial differences appear to exist. When the Iraq War started, only 29 percent of blacks polled supported it. This was significantly fewer than the 59 percent who supported the Persian Gulf War, but in both cases the percentages were below the level of support offered by whites. A Chicago Council of Foreign Relations poll in the mid-1990s found that the only hypothetical conflict situation in which nonwhites were more willing than whites to use military force was a South African civil war.[17] Research on gender also shows differences. On average, regardless of the purpose, women are less supportive of the use of military force. They are also more sensitive to humanitarian concerns and the loss of life. Having said this, women by and large are not pacifists. The differences between men and women on the use of force tend to occur at the margins and are a response to specific circumstances. This does not mean, however, that gender differences do not have the potential to be a significant factor in political decisions to use force.[18] Table 5.2 presents a snapshot view of how men and women responded differently to the use of force between 1990 and 2003.

Beyond race and gender a number of other factors appear to affect public opinion of foreign policy matters. Not surprisingly, one is party identification. By late 2004, public opinion had turned steadily against the Iraq War. Still, 69 percent of Republicans supported the war. This compared to 81 percent of Democrats and 65 percent of independents who felt that the Iraq War was not worth fighting. A similar divide existed among churchgoers and nonchurchgoers. Fifty-five percent of those who attend church weekly felt that the Iraq War was justified compared to 31 percent of those who never attend church. Partisan differences were also very much in evidence in the first year of the Obama administration. In October 2009, 71 percent of Republicans opposed his handling of Afghanistan, while about two-thirds of democrats rated it positively. Similarly, while more than two-thirds of Republicans favored increasing the U.S. military presence in Afghanistan, only about one-third of Democrats endorsed this line of action.

## Impact

The question of how much influence public opinion has on American foreign policy can be answered in two ways: One can look (1) to the type of impact it has and (2) to the conditions necessary for it to be heard. Public opinion can have three types of impact on the policy process and the nature of American

## TABLE 5.2

GENDER-BASED DIFFERENCES ON USE OF MILITARY FORCE

| Policy Issue | Female (% in favor) | Male (% in favor) |
| --- | --- | --- |
| **Conflict** | | |
| War against terror | 70.5 | 80.0 |
| Persian Gulf War | 49.8 | 66.8 |
| Somalia | 52.6 | 61.4 |
| Kosovo/Serbia | 47.0 | 54.4 |
| **Type of Military Action** | | |
| Air/missile strikes/bombing | 54.1 | 66.6 |
| Send troops abroad | 48.1 | 60.0 |
| **Policy Objective** | | |
| Foreign policy restraint | 54.9 | 68.1 |
| Humanitarian intervention | 63.4 | 68.1 |
| Internal political change | 43.8 | 53.2 |
| Peacekeeping | 43.4 | 49.6 |
| **Mention of Casualties** | | |
| War on terror/no casualties mentioned | 73.8 | 82.4 |
| War on terror/casualties mentioned | 58.0 | 71.5 |
| Haiti/no casualties mentioned | 31.3 | 42.5 |
| Haiti/casualties mentioned | 26.0 | 37.7 |

Source: Adapted from Richard Eichenberg, "Gender Differences in Public Attitudes Toward the Use of Force by the United States, 1990–2003," International Security, 28 (2003), 110–141, Tables 2, 3, 4, and 5.

foreign policy. It can serve as a constraint on policy innovation, a source of policy innovation, and a resource to be drawn on by policy makers in implementing policy. Public opinion acts as a constraint by defining the limits of what is politically feasible. Many regarded the existence of unstable moods as a powerful constraint on U.S. foreign policy. A case can also be made that the existence of too firm an outlook or too rigid a division of opinion is just as much a constraint. The deeply entrenched isolationist outlook of the American public during the 1930s made it extremely difficult for President Franklin Roosevelt to prepare the United States for World War II. A firm but divided opinion is cited by one major study as being responsible for the prolonged U.S. presence in Vietnam.[19] Faced by a "damned if they do and damned if they don't" dilemma, successive administrations are seen as having followed a strategy of perseverance until a public consensus developed for either a strategy of victory or withdrawal.[20]

Observers generally agree that public opinion rarely serves as a stimulus to policy innovation. Policy makers fear losing public support much more than they feel compelled to act because "the public demands it." One commentator argues that "no major foreign policy decision in the U.S. has been made in response to a spontaneous public demand."[21] Although this may be the case, public opinion today does appear to be capable of placing new items on the political agenda. The nuclear freeze movement demonstrates both the potential and the limitations of public opinion as a source of policy innovation. Springing spontaneously from the American public in the winter of 1982, the nuclear freeze movement did not produce a major breakthrough in arms control policy. It did, however, give renewed life to the arms control process that had stalled during the Reagan administration's first term. As an aide to Senator Edward Kennedy noted, Kennedy's legislative leadership on nuclear freeze matters was not a case of his mobilizing public opinion in opposition to Reagan's policies, but rather one of Kennedy's trying to "catch up with the country."[22]

With regard to the second point, the conditions that must be in place for public opinion to have an impact, the obvious starting point is that policy makers and political elites must be open to public opinion. One study found that great variation existed among presidents in terms of their beliefs that listening to public opinion was either desirable or a practical necessity in making decisions. Most presidents, it was found, tended to respond to how they anticipated the public would respond rather than to the public's actual views on a problem.[23]

More broadly, recent work by public opinion pollsters suggests that we might think about the influence of public opinion on foreign policy in terms of **"tipping points."**[24] Policies that have reached the tipping point at which public opinion begins to exert an influence share three characteristics: (1) a majority of the public is in support of or opposed to a particular policy, (2) they feel intensely about it, and (3) they believe that the government is responsible for addressing the problem. Public opinion on most foreign policy issues does not meet these requirements. Issues that are at the tipping point or crossed over it are the Iraq war, illegal immigration, dependence on foreign oil, outsourcing of jobs, and relations with other countries, especially Muslim countries.

## ELECTIONS

In December 2004, after being reelected, President George W. Bush proclaimed that the election was an endorsement of his foreign policy. He was not the first to make such a claim. Almost invariably, the winning candidate in an election cites the results as a mandate for his or her policy program. Yet is this really the case? Do elections serve as a mechanism for translating the public voice into policy? The evidence suggests that claims of popular mandates are often overstated and based on a flawed reading of election returns. A look back at the Lyndon Johnson–Barry Goldwater election of 1964 and the 1968 New Hampshire Democratic primary shows just how deceptive electoral outcomes can be. In both cases, Vietnam was the major issue. In 1964 Johnson won a landslide victory over Goldwater, who had campaigned on a platform of winning the war against communism in Vietnam "by any means necessary." The results were commonly interpreted as a mandate for restraint in the war effort. National surveys, however, revealed a far more complex picture: Eighty-two percent of those who wanted to maintain the U.S. presence in Vietnam supported Johnson over Goldwater, as did 63 percent of those who favored withdrawal and 52 percent of those who favored a stronger stand, such as invading North Vietnam.[25] In 1968, Eugene McCarthy "upset" Johnson in the New Hampshire primary, even though Johnson received more votes than he did (49–41 percent). McCarthy's strong performance was widely interpreted as a repudiation of Johnson's handling of the war and an endorsement of McCarthy's dovish position. Analysis reveals that in terms of overall numbers, McCarthy received more votes from dissatisfied hawks than from doves.

For elections to confer a mandate on the winner, three demands are made of the voters: (1) they must be knowledgeable, (2) they must cast their ballots on the basis of issue preferences, and (3) they must be able to distinguish between parties or candidates.

## Voting and Foreign Policy

Evidence on the first point is not encouraging. The lack of widespread public understanding about foreign affairs issues never ceases to amaze commentators. Consider the following:

1964: 38 percent know that Russia was not a member of NATO.

1966: Over 80 percent fail to properly identify the Vietcong.

1972: 63 percent could identify China as communist.

1979: 23 percent knew which countries were involved in the SALT (Strategic Arms Limitation Talks) discussions.

1983: 8 percent knew that the United States supported the government in El Salvador and the insurgents in Nicaragua.

1993: 43 percent could not identify which continent Somalia was on.

2003: 68 percent believed that Iraq played an important role in the terrorist attacks of 9/11.

2008: only 28 percent knew that about 4,000 American soldiers had died in Iraq.[26]

Do candidates win because of their policy preferences, or in spite of them? Much evidence supports the view that voters do not respond to issues when they cast their ballots.[27] Historically, foreign policy has not been a good issue on which to conduct a campaign.[28] Terrorism was a significant campaign issue in 2002 and 2004, when some 25 percent of the American public identified terrorism or national security as the top policy problem facing the United States. In 2008, this number had fallen to 4 percent. Party identification, candidate image, incumbency, or some other nonissue factors generally play the most important roles in deciding how the public votes. The influence of party on candidate evaluation is fully evident in how the public viewed the George W. Bush administration's prewar claims about Iraq's possession of weapons of mass destruction. Of those polled, 75 percent of Democrats said that Bush had lied or exaggerated on the subject. An equally large number of Republicans said that he had not.

Charles Whalen, a six-term Republican from Ohio who retired in 1980, sees the sporadic interest and low information level of constituents on foreign policy matters as a point of vulnerability to incumbents.[29] Challengers attempt to create an image of having policy differences with the incumbent and to cast the incumbent in a negative light. They find a powerful weapon in foreign affairs voting records. These issues are often complex, and when taken out of context, they can put the incumbent on the defensive. Examples of what concerns Whalen are easy to find. In 2000, the Cuban–American National Foundation, a powerful anti-Castro lobbying force, targeted members of Congress who supported lifting U.S. economic sanctions against Cuba. Advertisements asserted that by voting to lift these sanctions voters would be strengthening Castro and allowing him to continue to engage in forced child labor and child prostitution, sponsoring international terrorism, and imprisoning political prisoners.

The third prerequisite for elections to serve as a mandate is that voters must be able to distinguish between party and candidate positions. Compared to their European counterparts, American political parties do not offer voters a clear and consistent choice. They are neither ideologically distinct nor internally cohesive. Election campaigns generally find the two major parties on the same side of an issue. In the 2008 presidential campaign, aside from Iraq, few major differences existed between John McCain and Barack Obama. Both agreed on the need for sending military forces to Afghanistan, both expressed a willingness to commit the United States to humanitarian efforts, both said a nuclear Iran was unacceptable, and neither described how U.S. forces would leave Afghanistan.

Presidential candidates tend to stress **valence issues** that find most people on the same side of the argument out of the need to form and hold together broad electoral coalitions. Issues about which candidates may truly hold competing viewpoints, **positional issues,** are best suited to primary campaigns, where the candidates are trying to stand out from other competitors. General elections thus turn out to be less a debate on the issues and more a contest about whom the public feels is best capable of achieving the same goals.[30] In this respect, incumbents possess an electoral edge because they can use their time in office as proof of their leadership abilities. President George W. Bush was able to exploit this advantage in his 2004 reelection race against John Kerry, who was not able to establish strong foreign policy leadership credentials.

## Impact

What, then, is the impact of elections on U.S. foreign policy? Policies may change as the result of an election, but the link between this change and public attitudes is often tenuous. In the 2006 midterm elections, George W. Bush and the Republican Party suffered a defeat at the hands of the Democrats in what most referred to as a referendum on Bush's Iraq policy. Yet, rather than reduce the number of U.S. troops in Iraq, as polls indicated voters wanted him to do, he announced that he would increase the number of U.S. troops there as part of a short-term surge.

Many observers see one significant effect of elections on foreign policy that exists quite apart from its ability or inability to confer a mandate. "Foreign governments have long understood the difficulty of doing business with the U.S. in election years."[31] Foreign policy initiatives come to a halt as all sides await the outcome of the election, and U.S. foreign policy takes on a nationalistic and militant character.

The influence of American elections on foreign policy extends well beyond the presidential election year.[32] Some observers see an electoral cycle existing that influences noncrisis foreign policy decisions during a president's entire term in office. The first year in office generally is characterized by policy experimentation, false starts, and overly zealous goals. This is due to the continued influence of overly simplistic campaign rhetoric that comes about because presidents are forced to take positions on issues before they have mastered the intricacies of managing the presidency. Instinctively, they return to the themes that served them so well during the campaign. During the second year in office, pragmatism becomes more evident. This is because of both the increased knowledge and skill of the administration and the realization that a foreign policy mishap may lead to the loss of House and Senate seats in the midterm elections. In the third year, foreign policy issues are evaluated largely in terms of their potential impact on the presidential reelection campaign. Potential successes are pursued vigorously even if the price tag is high, while the administration will try to disengage itself from potential losses. As noted above, the final year brings stalemate to the foreign policy process. The most propitious time for foreign policy undertakings is the first year and a half of a second term. Here one finds an experienced president who knows what he or she wants to do in foreign affairs operating under the halo effect of a reelection victory. By late in the second year of a president's second term, electoral considerations begin to overwhelm foreign policy again, as jockeying begins in both parties for their respective presidential nominations. At some point, the president comes to be regarded both at home and abroad as a "lame duck," which limits his or her ability to conduct foreign policy.

An example of the influence of the election cycle comes from the George W. Bush administration's efforts to deal with Iraq in his second term.[33] The fear of an explosive news story before the 2006 midterm elections delayed a serious strategic review of Iraq policy, even though it was acknowledged within the White House that the current strategy was not working. Only after the election were military planners brought into the decision-making process. To the extent that Iraq policy was being reviewed, great care was taken that it proceeded undetected by the media.

## HISTORICAL LESSON

### The China Lobby

Over the course of the twentieth century, U.S foreign policy toward China went through many different phases. Up until the 1930s, Americans were largely sympathetic to the Chinese people due to the stories brought back by missionaries, but generally not inclined to adopt anything but an isolationist foreign policy. This began to change in 1937 with the outbreak of war between China and Japan in 1937 and changed completely after Pearl Harbor. The United States now saw China, and Chiang Kai-Shek in particular, as an ally. Accompanied by the charismatic Madame Chiang Kai-Shek, he came to the United States in 1943 to appear before Congress and drum up public support for China. A crowd of 17,000 greeted them in Madison Square Garden. World War II did not end as Chiang Kai-Shek planned. Instead of ruling China, he and his Nationalist Party were forced to flee to Taiwan as Mao Zedong and the Communists emerged triumphant in the long-running Chinese civil war. U.S. foreign policy now faced the dilemma of how to deal with two Chinas, each of which claimed to be the sole government of all of China.

Into this policy dispute stepped a diverse set of interest groups that collectively came to be known as the "China Lobby." With virtually no central guidance, they acted together to argue forcefully for refusing to recognize Communist China. Employing a wide variety of strategies and forming strong alliances with key members of Congress as well as with the Nationalist government, the China Lobby was virtually unchallenged from the late 1940s into the early 1960s. It was widely seen as having captured U.S. foreign policy on China. While it came to be regarded as a staunchly conservative group, many of those involved in its early activities were political liberals. Other early supporters included Henry Luce, publisher of *Time*.

The formal beginnings of the China Lobby are traced to a 1944 meeting in a private home in New York that was designed to discuss ways of countering the favorable image the Chinese communists were receiving in the U.S. press. In 1945, this group formed the American China Policy Association. It would work closely with Senator Joseph McCarthy in searching for communists within the State Department to hold responsible for the loss of China and lead the attack on the Institute for Pacific Relations, believing it to be overly sympathetic to communism. The attack on the State Department led to the resignations of most of its China experts, whose crime was accurately predicting Mao's victory. This left the State Department with few China experts as the United States began its involvement in Vietnam. The attack on the Institute for Pacific Relations resulted in an Internal Revenue Service investigation into its tax exempt status. Although the institute won its case, it was forced to dissolve in 1960 due to lack of funds.

In time, this organization and other early members of the China Lobby such as the Committee to Defend America by Aiding Anti-Communist China gave way to others. The most important of which was the Committee of One Million. Begun in 1953, this group organized a nationwide petition drive that garnered one million signatures in ten months calling upon the president to oppose communist Chinese membership in the United Nations (UN). It circulated another petition in 1961 that not only called for refusal to allow communist China into the UN but also rejected any move to diplomatic recognition by the United States. Once again it obtained over one million signatures. Armed with these petitions and putting forward a series of declarations of support for China, the Committee of One Million had no trouble obtaining the support of such diverse members of Congress as Barry Goldwater and Hubert Humphrey. In 1965, it circulated a petition in Congress that got 312 signatures from both Republicans and Democrats to oppose any steps that would increase the power or prestige of communist China.

The China Lobby with the financial support of the Nationalist government also engaged a public relations firm to aid it in its lobbying efforts. The firm of Hamilton Wright was to arouse public opinion in the United States and elsewhere by creating a sympathetic understanding of Nationalist China that would prevent communist China from being seated in the UN or having trade restrictions against it lifted. The cost of this program was $300,000 for each of four years beginning in 1957. Hamilton Wright promised to deliver at least $2.5 million worth of publicity in print media and television. This relationship unraveled as it became the subject of a Senate Foreign Relations Committee investigation in 1963.

**Applying the Lesson**

1. Is it possible for any lobbying group to "control" U.S. foreign policy?
2. In what ways are the China Lobby and the Israel lobby similar and different?
3. Are special rules needed to control lobbying on U.S. foreign policy? What should they be? ■

## INTEREST GROUPS

The third avenue open to the public for expressing its outlook on foreign policy issues is interest group activity. A wide variety of groups actively try to influence U.S. foreign policy. Consider U.S. policy toward China.[34] A representative list of interest groups active in this policy area includes such diverse groups as the AFL-CIO, Amnesty International, the Christian Coalition of America, the Committee of 100 for Tibet, the Emergency Committee for American Trade, the Family Research Council, the National Endowment for Democracy, the Asia Society, and the U.S.–China Business Council.

Groups wishing to influence U.S. foreign policy make their views known to policy makers either directly or through interest brokers. Not surprisingly former policy makers are among the most prominent interest brokers because of their access to policy makers and policy-making institutions. Among those who have established firms are former national security advisor and secretary of state Henry Kissinger, who founded Kissinger and

Associates, and Bill Clinton's secretary of state Madeline Albright, who formed Albright and Associates. When Northrop Grumman Corp. came under attack for having been awarded a lucrative contract to build a new fleet of tanker planes, it hired former Majority Leader Senator Trent Lott to lobby Congress on its behalf. The cost of employing such high-profile power brokers can be considerable. For example, fearing it might lose military installations as a result of decisions made by the Defense Base Realignment and Closure Commission, the city of Jacksonville, Florida, signed a $490,000 seven-month contract with the Cohen Group, founded by former secretary of defense William Cohen.[35]

## Types of Interest Groups

We can divide the most active foreign policy interest groups into four broad categories: business groups, ethnic groups, foreign interests, and ideological public interest groups.

BUSINESS GROUPS   The long-standing cliché at the heart of business lobbying is that "What is good for General Motors is good for the United States." It is a view endorsed both by those who feel threatened by foreign competition and seek protection, such as the auto, steel, and textile industries and farmers, as well as by those that depend on open access to foreign markets such as Wal-Mart. Nowhere is business foreign policy lobbying more controversial than when it is carried out by defense industries. Their activities bring forth images of what President Dwight Eisenhower referred to in his farewell address as the **military–industrial complex.**[36]

At the core of this negative image is the assertion that there exists within U.S. policy-making circles a dominating political force consisting of professional soldiers, industrialists, and government officials. Acting in unison, they determine policy on defense-related matters.[37] The resulting policies are based on an ideology of international conflict that requires high levels of military spending, a large defense establishment, and a belligerent, interventionist foreign policy. In the 1960s, the concept of a military–industrial complex became a major theme in writings of those who opposed the U.S. involvement in Vietnam. Concerns about its influence waned in the 1970s with the shift in emphasis from confrontation and containment to détente.

The Iraq War, with its heavy reliance on private-sector contractors to provide key services, brought forward new allegations about the existence of a military–industrial complex. At the center of the storm was Halliburton. One of the world's largest companies providing products and services to the oil industry, it employs over 100,000 people and operates in over 120 countries. In the early 1990s, it gained notoriety for supplying Libya and Iraq with oil drilling equipment that could be used to detonate nuclear weapons. When Dick Cheney became Halliburton's CEO, he spoke out against export bans to rogue states such as Iran and Libya as being motivated by political pressure groups. During the Iraq War, Halliburton was one of the major beneficiaries of the government's awarding of no-bid contracts for services, and it saw its net profit for the second quarter of 2003 reach $26 million as compared to a second-quarter 2002 loss of $498 million.

Efforts to establish the validity of assertions about the influence of the military–industrial complex on U.S. foreign policy have produced mixed results. General agreement exists on the presence of a military–industrial complex, but there is disagreement on how to interpret its influence. One observer suggests that the competing judgments can be reconciled if we make a distinction between major political decisions, which set into motion high rates of defense spending, and legislative and administrative decisions, which translate them into concrete programs. The influence of the military–industrial complex is greatest in the second area and far less in the first, where it faces strong competition from ideological, economic, and other nonmilitary influences.

ETHNIC GROUPS    The most successful ethnic lobbies have relied on three ingredients to give them political clout: the threat of switching allegiances at election time, either from one party to another or from one candidate to another in the same party; a strong and effective lobbying apparatus; and the ability to build case around traditional American symbols and ideals.[38]

Currently, the Jewish American lobby possesses the most formidable combination of these elements. The centerpiece of the Jewish lobbying effort for Israel is the highly organized, efficient, and well-financed American–Israel Public Affairs Committee (AIPAC), which serves as an umbrella organization for pro-Israeli groups. It "promptly and unfailingly provides all members [of Congress] with data and documentation, supplemented, as circumstances dictate, with telephone calls and personal visits on those issues touching upon Israeli national interests."[39]

AIPAC became an active force in American electoral politics in the 1980s. In 1984, Senator Rudy Boschwitz, who chaired the Senate Foreign Relations Subcommittee on the Middle East, received more than one-third of the $4.25 million that pro-Israeli PACs gave to congressional candidates. During the 1986 election campaign, it was estimated that eighty pro-Israeli PACs donated nearly $7 million to candidates. Incumbents have also felt the wrath of AIPAC. Opponents of Representative Paul Finley, Senator Charles Percy, and Senator Jesse Helms all received hearty backing from pro-Israeli forces. (In Finley's case, 90 percent of his opponent's funds came from Jewish sources.) Finley and Percy were defeated, and Helms became a strong supporter of Israel following his hard-fought reelection victory.

Echoing the observation made by Mearsheimer and Walt at the outset of this chapter, observers of American foreign policy argue that one crucial reason for the strong American Gentile support of Israel is the shared vision of having been founded by settlers who were displaced from their homelands and of a common destiny and mission as a chosen people.[40] While this base of support is widespread, its demographics are also changing. Where once its primary supporters were Liberal Democrats, it is now found among Conservative Republicans and especially evangelical Christians. African Americans were once staunch supporters of Israel but now increasingly align with Palestinian causes. This changed support base led in 2008 to the creation of a Jewish Liberal lobbying group known as J Street to counter AIPAC.[41] The task will not be easy. AIPAC has an endowment of over $100 million, while J Street's first-year operating budget will be about $1.5 million.

No Arab American lobbying force equal to AIPAC has yet emerged.[42] In 1972, a central organization, the National Association of Arab Americans (NAAA), was founded, and in the mid-1980s, it had field coordinators in every congressional district and a membership of some 100,000 Arab American families. In 1984, it founded a political action committee and provided $20,000 in campaign funding to twenty-two Democratic and twenty-four Republican candidates. This compares to the $2.8 million in funding provided by some seventy-six pro-Israeli political action committees.

A major obstacle in the way of creating an effective Arab lobbying force is the ethnic diversity of Arab Americans. Until 1948 most Arabs coming to the United States were Christians from Syria and Lebanon. Since 1978 most have been Muslims. The result is that no single political agenda exists for Arab Americans. A consensus exists only on the broad issues of pursuing a comprehensive peace plan in the Middle East and establishing better U.S. relations with the Arab world. Of special concern in this regard are U.S. foreign aid and arms sales policies.

By the mid-1980s, African Americans had made great strides toward meeting two of the three prerequisites we listed. First, as the Reverend Jesse Jackson's 1984 bid for the presidency made clear, blacks make up an important constituency within the Democratic Party. Second, an organizational base, TransAfrica, now exists. Founded in 1977, TransAfrica now has over 10,000 members and an annual budget of over $1.4 million. The major focus of black lobbying in the mid-1980s was reorienting U.S. policy toward South Africa. With this issue behind it, African Americans have had a more difficult time mobilizing on foreign policy issues.[43] On genocide in Rwanda, the African American community evidenced an overall lack of interest. This has been explained by the absence of a clear-cut black–white dimension to the problem. The crisis in Haiti during the Bill Clinton administration more closely resembled this type of situation, and, in fact, one of the reasons Clinton felt forced to act was lobbying by African Americans led by Randall Robinson, who threatened to go on a hunger strike if actions were not taken to return Jean-Bertrand Aristide to power.

Ethnic diversity is a problem for Hispanic American lobbying on foreign policy.[44] Mexican immigration has been motivated largely by economic considerations, is concentrated in the Southwest, and is largely Democratic. In 1980, Jimmy Carter got 72 percent of this vote. Cuban immigration is concentrated on the East Coast, has been motivated largely by political concerns, and is politically conservative and Republican. Ronald Reagan got 59 percent of Florida's Hispanic vote. To this, one must also add Puerto Ricans, who are concentrated largely in the Midwest and Northeast and who generally vote Democratic.

Two additional fissures within the Hispanic community also make the establishment of an effective lobbying force difficult. One pits American-born Hispanics against immigrants.[45] The only real area of overlapping concerns is immigration policy. When questioned as to their policy priorities, American-born Hispanics give greatest weight to domestic issues such as education, crime, economic growth, and the environment. Only American-born Cuban Americans consistently site foreign policy problems as being important. Immigrants, on the other hand, are home oriented. This is particularly notable in two respects. First, they send considerable amounts of money back to their country of origin each year. In 1999, more than $5.6 billion was sent back to Mexico, $1.4 billion to El Salvador, and $1.5 billion to the Dominican Republic. Second, candidates from Latin America now routinely come to the United States in search of votes and campaign funding from immigrant communities. The second fissure is generational. This came through clearly in the differing reactions to George W. Bush's June 2004 imposition of tight restrictions on travel to Cuba and on the practice of sending money to relatives still there. The ban was supported by the 250,000 remaining "historic exiles" who fled Cuba right after Castro seized power but was opposed by those who fled more recently.

The most successful Hispanic lobby is the Cuban-American National Foundation.[46] It vehemently opposes any change in American policy toward Cuba and has been charged with intimidating and harassing those members of the Cuban American community in Florida who wish to open a dialogue with Castro. Its Free Cuba political action committee (PAC) made $114,000 in campaign contributions in the 1989–1990 elections. In mid-1992, it had contributed to twenty-six congressional candidates and "maxed out" on its contribution to Representative Robert Torricelli, who represented a large Cuban American community in New Jersey and who authored the 1992 Cuban Democracy Act. Passed by Congress in an election year and endorsed by both Bush and Clinton in an effort to gain the support of the Cuban American community, this piece of legislation has been derided by its critics as an "economic declaration of war" against Castro and a violation of international free trade agreements. The act prohibits foreign affiliates of U.S. firms from doing business in Cuba.

The end of the Cold War ushered in a new era of ethnic interest group lobbying. The 1996 senatorial race in South Dakota saw a battle in which the Democratic candidate raised over $150,000 from Pakistani American groups, while the Republican candidate (who authored legislation cutting U.S. foreign aid to Pakistan) raised approximately the same amount from Indian American sources. The influence of these groups is now also found in the halls of Congress. Founded in 1993, the Congressional India Caucus now has some 115 members. Twice in 1999, India's supporters blocked legislation that would have cut off aid to India. Also emerging are signs of joint ethnic group lobbying efforts. In 2003, India and Israel jointly lobbied Congress on the terms of a $3 billion foreign-aid package for Pakistan. They successfully got language inserted that pressured Pakistan to stop Islamic militants from crossing into India. Indian American lobbying was also evident in full force in 2006 when strong effort was directed at Congress to pass the U.S.–India nuclear agreement at a time when its passage was in doubt.[47]

FOREIGN LOBBYISTS. Foreign lobbying has become big business in Washington. In 1988 alone, 152 Japanese firms and government agencies contracted with 113 Washington lobbying firms. And they were not alone. Canada had sixty-one organizations working on its behalf; Great Britain had forty-four. All told, there are now some 8,000 foreign agents registered with the Justice Department.[48] A virtual Who's Who of Washington "in-and-outers" and ex-legislators can be found in the employment of foreign concerns. For example, Bob Livingstone, former chair of the House Appropriations Committee, built the tenth-largest lobbying firm in Washington in 4 years. In 2003, he beat back an effort by Republicans to strip Turkey of $1 billion worth of foreign aid. The Republicans were angered by Turkey's failure to participate more fully in the Iraq War. Livingstone provided Turkey with advice on how to approach members of Congress, personally contacted his former colleagues, and arranged for embassy officials to stand just off the House floor as the vote was being taken.

The strength of Turkish lobbying efforts was sorely tested in late 2007 when, over the objections of the White House, the House passed a resolution labeling as genocide the deaths of Armenians at the hands of Turks during and immediately after World War I. Turkey had spent more than $300,000 per month to stop this resolution. Working in support of the resolution was the Armenian Assembly of America, which in 2006 had a budget of $3.6 million.[49]

Both foreign governments and foreign firms engage in lobbying. The most common concerns of foreign governments are foreign-aid legislation and arms sales. The typical plan of attack involves two steps. First, one must secure the support of the executive branch. The second step is to lobby Congress. The goal here is to prevent resolutions of disapproval or amendments that would block the transfer of aid or weapons. The effort involved is often considerable. Charles Goodell, a former Republican senator and representative from New York, reported having a total of 253 meetings, lunches, and phone calls in his successful lobbying effort to get approval for a Moroccan arms sales package. A favorite tactic is to arrange for "information" trips for members of Congress and their staffs. From 2001 to 2005, the Korea–U.S. Exchange Council and the U.S.–Malaysia Exchange Association sponsored twelve congresspeople and thirty-one staffers and their relatives to nearly $500,000 in trips.

The primary concern of foreign firms is their ability to conduct business in the United States. Accordingly, their lobbying activities are directed at all levels of the American political system. Of particular concern at state and local levels are taxation, zoning, and labor laws. Sony threatened not to go ahead with plans to build new plants in California and Florida unless those states repealed that portion of their state tax codes that would have taxed Sony's earnings based on worldwide sales rather than just on what was produced within the state. Both states succumbed to the foreign lobbying campaign.

A recent addition to the list of foreign lobbyists are the Kurds. They employ former Mossad (Israel's spy agency) officials, Republican Party and White House officials, and an evangelical Christian minister. The services of a Washington lobbying firm cost the Kurds $29,000 per month. One of their first targets was to obtain $4 billion worth of money held in trust by the United States stemming from the UN oil-for-food program. The Kurds succeeded in getting $1.4 billion. Next they sought to obtain $18.4 billion in U.S. construction funds dedicated for Iraq. The State Department opposed their efforts. Kurdish lobbying then switched its target to the Commerce Department in an effort to enlist its help to advertise Kurdistan as an investment area for U.S. businesses. They succeeded here when the undersecretary of commerce paid a visit to Kurdistan and called it the "gateway" for U.S. firms going to Iraq.

IDEOLOGICAL PUBLIC-INTEREST GROUPS    A wide variety of groups fall into this category. At one extreme are highly institutionalized and well-funded organizations that one does not normally think of as interest groups. These are "think tanks" that have as part of their mission the propagation and advancement of ideas on how to address public policy problems. The Brookings Institution was long the most prominent foreign policy think tank advancing a liberal-democratic foreign policy agenda. Over the years it has become more moderate and centrist in its orientation. Two of the most visible think tanks now occupy positions at the conservative end of the political spectrum: the Heritage Foundation and the Cato Institute. The former sees its mission as advancing policies based on free enterprise, limited government, and traditional American ideals and calls for a foreign policy based on a strong military defense, limited involvement in humanitarian undertakings, and advancing free market principles in international trade. The latter is a libertarian organization that has advanced an isolationist foreign policy agenda for the United States.

Think tanks make their mark in Washington in many ways. Their members serve as a source of expertise for administrations and congressional committees to draw on either as outside experts or employees. Less visibly but perhaps most significantly, they serve as a focal point for bringing like-minded individuals together to address common concerns. For example, think tanks were prominent members of the "blue team," a loose alliance of members of Congress, staffers, conservative journalists, and lobbyists for Taiwan who have worked to present China as a threat to the United States. They succeeded in restricting the scope of U.S.–Chinese military contacts, getting the State Department to address human rights concerns, and forcing the Pentagon to do a study of the China–Taiwan military balance.

Also included in this category are more traditional interest groups, the most prominent of which today may be the "religious right."[50] Identifying primarily with the Republican Party, members of the religious right were staunch supporters of Ronald Reagan and found foreign policy a powerful venue onto which to project their values. Pat Robertson's Christian Broadcasting Network gave $3–$7 billion to U.S.-backed anticommunist forces in Central America. In 2003, Robertson defended about-to-be-deposed Liberian leader Charles Taylor against charges that he was a war criminal and urged the Bush administration to stop "undermining a Christian, Baptist president to bring in Muslim rebels to take over the country." More recently, Robertson called for the assassination of Venezuelan President Hugo Chavez. Jerry Falwell emerged as a strong defender of apartheid in South Africa. Overall, the religious right has supported Israel to the point of creating visions of a new crusade in Palestinian minds. The UN and the International Monetary Fund have also become lobbying targets because of their funding of family planning and population-control programs.

Evangelical groups become especially active in shaping U.S. foreign policy to Africa in a number of ways during the George W. Bush administration.[51] The U.S. policy on AIDS was heavily influenced by its beliefs and lobbying by the Focus on Family group. Bush also created a new Center for Faith-Based and Community Initiatives within the U.S. Agency for International Development (USAID). Sudan emerged as a high-priority country in evangelical African lobbying efforts due to limitations it placed on religious freedom and the continued presence of slavery. Christian Solidarity International has been particularly active on questions of slavery.

The religious right does not hold a monopoly on interest group activity by religious organizations. The prelude to the Iraq War found groups active on both sides. Whereas fundamentalist groups tended to support the war, the Catholic Church, the Religious Society of Friends (Quakers), the United Church of Christ, the World Council of Churches, the Muslim Peace Fellowship, and the Shalom Center all spoke out against it.

The wide range of views held by religious groups on foreign policy comes through quite clearly in a poll conducted in 2004.[52] Samplings of its findings are presented in Table 5.3. Eighty-four percent of those identifying themselves as Latter-day Saints (Mormons) agreed with the view that the United States has a special role in the world. This was by far the highest percentage of any religious group. It compares to 41 percent of black Protestants and 62 percent of modernist evangelicals. Identifying the nature of this special role produced quite varied responses. Whereas only 40 percent of Latter-day Saints said that fighting AIDS was a high-priority goal, 72 percent of modernist evangelicals and Hispanic Catholics believed it was. Fighting religious persecution also produced a wide split among religious groups. Only 19 percent of Latter-day Saints rated it as a high priority, compared to 53 percent of Hispanic Protestants. Foreign policy also produced splits within religious groups. Forty percent of traditional (white) Catholics rated fighting religious persecution as a high priority, compared to 18 percent of centrist Catholics and 10 percent of modernist Catholics.

## Impact

Establishing the influence of an interest group on a specific policy is difficult. More is required than revealing the presence of group activity. A concrete link must be established between the group's actions and the actions taken by those who were influenced. Moreover, success is not an all-or-nothing condition. Consider the Jewish lobby and its efforts on behalf of the 1974 Jackson–Vanik Amendment. At the time, passage of this amendment was viewed as a major success and a show of strength. It is now seen by many as a hollow victory

## TABLE 5.3

RELIGIOUS ATTITUDES ON SELECTED U.S. FOREIGN POLICY ISSUES, 2004

| | U.S. Has Special Role in World | Iraq War Justified | Favor Israel in Middle East | Human Rights Is the Most Important U.S. Priority in International Affairs | Economic Growth Is the Most Important U.S. Priority in Internatio- nal Affairs |
|---|---|---|---|---|---|
| All voters | 62% | 58% | 41% | 44% | 27% |
| Latter-day Saints | 84 | 89 | 54 | 31 | 28 |
| Evangelicals | | | | | |
| Traditionalists | 74 | 87 | 68 | 41 | 22 |
| Centrists | 69 | 66 | 44 | 36 | 24 |
| Modernists | 62 | 52 | 50 | 53 | 27 |
| Mainline | | | | | |
| Traditionalists | 66 | 73 | 49 | 50 | 21 |
| Centrists | 59 | 64 | 34 | 42 | 24 |
| Modernists | 51 | 36 | 23 | 46 | 39 |
| Hispanic Protestant | 67 | 72 | 55 | 46 | 20 |
| Catholics (white) | | | | | |
| Traditionalists | 65 | 84 | 49 | 48 | 23 |
| Centrist | 59 | 64 | 38 | 41 | 28 |
| Modernists | 63 | 39 | 35 | 52 | 28 |
| Jewish | 64 | 37 | 76 | 42 | 33 |
| Hispanic Catholics | 64 | 40 | 27 | 42 | 34 |
| Black Protestants | 41 | 34 | 19 | 40 | 33 |

*Source*: Adapted from James Guth, John Green, Lyman Kellsedt and Corwin Smidt, "Faith and Foreign Policy: A View from the Pews," *The Review of Faith and International Affairs*, 3 (2005), 5 and 7, Tables 1 and 2.

that brought with it ruinous costs. The Jackson–Vanik Amendment made freedom to emigrate from the Soviet Union a prerequisite for the granting of most favored nation (MFN) status to Soviet goods. It did not have its intended effect. The amendment strained détente and embroiled the emigration issue in the larger context of rising U.S.–Soviet competition. Human rights remained largely an illusion within the Soviet Union, and emigration quickly became more difficult. From its high of 35,000 in 1973, emigration fell to a low of 13,000 in 1975.

It should also be noted that not all issues lend themselves equally to interest group lobbying. Some issues threaten the unity of an interest group and therefore may need to be avoided all together or at least approached with great caution. Immigration is just such an issue. Evangelical Christian groups can be found in support of legislation that would allow illegal immigrants to become citizens and in support of legislation that focuses on greater border security patrols and deportation. The same is true for business groups. Many businesses support tighter immigration controls, but the National Restaurant Association and the Associated General Contractors of America strongly oppose such legislation, placing the U.S. Chamber of Commerce in a delicate position.

## POLITICAL PROTEST

The public voice on foreign policy matters is expressed not only through offi-cially sanctioned avenues. It can also be seen and heard in a variety of forms that challenge policy makers to take notice of positions that are often at variance with official policies. Such protests range in form from the acts of single individuals, such as Cindy Sheehan challenging President George W. Bush's position on the Iraq War by camping out outside his ranch in Crawford, Texas, to large antiwar marches through Washington, DC, and other cities. Modern technology has added a new dimension to protest movements, the "virtual protest march." In October 2003, when tens of thousands of protesters marched in Washington calling for an end to the occupation of Iraq, other protesters flooded congres-sional offices with e-mails stating their opposition to the war. A similar tactic was used in July 2003 to pressure Congress into investigating the prewar intelligence claims made by the George W. Bush administration, when more than 400,000 people from every state contacted members of Congress.

Although foreign policy protest movements tend to be associated with opposition to war, this does not have to be the case. Protesters clashed with police in Seattle in December 1999 at a meeting of the World Trade Organi-zation and in Quebec in 2001 at a meeting to establish a free trade zone for the Americas. The year 2006 saw rallies and marches across the United States by groups protesting the wave of anti-immigration legislation that was being considered by Congress. That same year also saw five members of Congress arrested outside the Sudanese Embassy for protesting that government's policies in Darfur. Two days later, thousands marched in Washington, DC, calling for the Bush administration to halt genocide in Darfur.

Political protests are valued for their ability to alter the political landscape by bypassing existing power centers and introducing new or marginalized voices into the political debate. In the case of the antiglobalization protests, it ensured that environmental, labor, and democracy issues could not be totally ignored. In the case of pro-immigration forces, it brought many Hispanics into the political process for the first time. Protestors on Darfur hoped to bring greater attention to this issue among an American public that is largely unfamiliar with Africa.

The ability for political protests to have this impact may be especially important today in large part because an "apathetic internationalism" is reshaping American politics, encouraging policy makers to ignore foreign policy problems and empowering "squeaky wheels," those who make the loudest noise about foreign policy problems. More often than not, this condition favors those organized interests who can mobilize their supporters most effectively to pressure policy makers. But when thousands of protesters repeatedly take to the streets, a new element is added to the equation.[53]

There is nothing automatic about the success of protest movements. In fact, for several reasons they face great obstacles. First, policies are not easily reversed. Anti-Vietnam protests did not bring about a sudden end to the American involvement in that war. Second, it is often difficult to sustain the momentum needed to change policies. Cindy Sheehan's first camp-out in Texas became a huge media event. The second camp-out drew far less media attention or support from prominent individuals opposed to the war. Pro-immigration leaders were disappointed by the small turnout at protests organized in fall 2006 compared to the size of those in the spring of that year. Finally, protest movements often give birth to counterprotests that can be cited by policy makers as justifying their policies. Such was the case in September 2005, when pro–Iraq War individuals marched in Washington, DC.

## THE MEDIA AND AMERICAN FOREIGN POLICY

To this point we have looked at how the public conveys its views to policy makers. We have not yet examined how they obtain their information about the world. In looking at this issue we will first examine the sources of information that the public relies upon and then how those sources can shape their thinking.

### Newspapers and Television

The role of newspapers as force influencing American public opinion on foreign policy has long been recognized. At the turn of the twentieth century, the Hearst and Pulitzer newspaper chains engaged in sensationalistic "yellow journalism" to increase circulation. Their accounts of the sinking of the USS *Maine* are seen by many as contributing greatly to the onset of the Spanish–American War in 1898. Newspaper reporting of foreign policy was by its nature slow in its ability to convey information, and it relied heavily on overseas bureaus. Today, newspapers face stiff competition from other news sources and rising costs that threaten their very survival. More and more, they have cut foreign bureaus. A typical bureau costs at least $425,000 per year to operate, with an office in a hot spot such as Baghdad costing four times that amount. Between 2002 and 2006 the number of foreign-based correspondents fell from 188 to 141. Only the *Wall Street Journal*, the *New York Times*, the *Washington Post*, and the *Los Angeles Times* continue to have a sizable overseas presence. As a result, the percentage of front-page foreign news stories in 2007 was at 14 percent, down from 21 percent in 2003 and 27 percent in 1987 and 1977.[54]

In time, television came to replace newspapers as the primary source of foreign policy news for the American public. In 1962, only 29 percent of Americans considered television news to be the most credible source of information, and the network evening news broadcasts on the major networks were only fifteen minutes long and relied heavily on sixteen-millimeter black-and-white footage of international events that were at least a day old because of the need to develop, edit, and transport the film to the United States. By 1980, 51 percent of Americans found television news to be their most credible news source, and that same year CNN came on the air with its twenty-four-hour news format.

The impact was significant. Consider how differently the October 1962 Cuban missile crisis might have been played out had it occurred in the 1990s.[55] Robert McNamara, President Kennedy's secretary of defense, observed, "I don't think that I turned on a television set during the whole two weeks of that crisis." During the 1990 Persian Gulf War, CNN was monitored regularly by government officials. George H. W. Bush's secretary of defense, Dick Cheney, followed CNN in the period leading up to the air war for the first sign of leaks. CIA Director William Webster told National Security Adviser Brent Scowcroft to turn on CNN to find out where Iraqi missiles were landing. A similarly stark contrast exists among the viewing habits of the American people. During the Cuban missile crisis the Kennedy administration knew about the missiles in Cuba for six days before the information was broadcast to the American people. By contrast, President George H. W. Bush was expected to respond almost instantly to Iraq's invasion of Kuwait and to pictures of starving people in Somalia. Using military force was the first option embraced by the Kennedy administration, but it was abandoned as the week progressed in favor of a blockade. McNamara, for one, is uncertain that the same decisions would have been reached in an altered decision-making environment.

Responding to this increased ability to put administration foreign policy decisions under a telescope, it became necessary for presidents to develop a television policy to accompany their foreign policy. The George H. W. Bush administration succeeded in doing so during the Gulf War but failed with its Haitian, Bosnian, and Somalian policies, failures shared by the Bill Clinton administration. In the Persian Gulf War, the administration was able to frame the policy issue on its own terms and to control the media's coverage of it.[56] A key to its success was the Hometown News Project that flew more than 900 members of the press to Saudi Arabia to write stories about local soldiers stationed in the Gulf. Not surprisingly, these human interest stories tended to be positive and served administration interests well.

Uncertain about how to proceed in Haiti, Bosnia, and Somalia, the Bush and Clinton administrations found the media far more troublesome.[57] The inability of U.S. administrations to respond to these images led to a chorus of congressional demands to "do something" and reinforced the view that American foreign policy had lost its sense of vision and competence. A similar failure to frame the issue on its own terms was evident on Haiti, where the media gave extensive coverage to a hunger strike by Randall Robinson, executive director of TransAfrica, who was protesting Clinton administration policy.

Many in the traditional news media responding to administration complaints that they are not fairly portraying American foreign policy or that they are hampering its conduct make two points. First, very often administrations have developed television policies but not foreign policies. They show the American public only what is happening. If that does not correspond to declaratory statements of American foreign policy, it is not the media's fault. Second, the clearest way to limit the influence of the media is to enunciate a clear policy. The media's foreign policy influence is tied directly to the absence of a clear policy and the absence of contextual information with which the watchers evaluate what they are seeing or reading about.

Drawing on his experience as a historian and CNN commentator, Michael Beschloss offers a set of lessons to presidents as they make foreign policy in the television age. A sampling is found in Table 5.4. Following these guidelines is not easy. Consider President George W. Bush's attempt to frame the Iraq War. His administration successfully couched it as the central front in

---

**TABLE 5.4**

MEDIA LESSONS FOR MODERN-DAY PRESIDENTS

1. Television offers presidents a superior weapon for framing issues and selling policy in crisis.
2. Television also amplifies public opposition.
3. Television can encourage presidents to favor crisis management over long-term planning.
4. Television can drastically reduce the time, secrecy, and calm available to a president for deliberating with advisers on an urgent foreign policy problem.
5. Presidents cannot presume that they can maintain a monopoly on information for long.
6. Television allows presidents to communicate with adversary leaders and populations.
7. Television can seriously affect relations with allies.
8. Unexpected events shown on television can have inordinate influence on the public's perception of a foreign crisis.
9. When appearing on television during a crisis, a president and his high officials must be absolutely honest with the public.
10. Censorship can risk a damaging backlash.
11. Television can help create an unexpected agenda, especially during the run-up or endgame of a war.
12. Presidents who fail to craft an implicit or explicit television strategy while dealing with a foreign crisis do so at their own peril.

*Source: Hearings, Committee on Foreign Affairs, House of Representatives, 103rd Congress, April 26, 1994. (Washington, DC: U.S. Government Printing Office, 1994), pp. 52–53.*

the war against terrorism early in that conflict, but then fell victim to its "stay the course" rhetoric as American casualties mounted and calls for changes in Bush's Iraq policy arose.

## The New Media and American Foreign Policy

The nature of media coverage and its impact on foreign policy continues to evolve. The next generation of media coverage of foreign policy is already in place and centers on the ability to send words and pictures over the Internet. Consider the following. A cell phone camera videotaped the execution of Saddam Hussein in January 2007. A Sony PlayStation portable memory drive contained recorded graphic images (so graphic that they were not made public) of twenty-four civilian deaths in Haditha, Iraq, in 2005 for which U.S. Marines were investigated, and evidence of the inhumane treatment of prisoners at Abu Ghraib prison was found on laptop computers.

By 2003, 77 percent of Americans who used the Internet used it to get or share information on the Iraq War, and one in five Internet users stated that it helped shape their thinking about the war.[58] In terms of specific uses of the Internet, 55 percent use e-mail in connection with the Iraq War, and 44 percent use it to look for news. To these numbers we could now add the legion of Internet users who read and write blogs. In explaining why the Internet was used to obtain news about the war, over 60 percent cited the desire to get up-to-the-minute information and to get news from a variety of sources. A majority also cited an interest in getting news from nontraditional and nongovernmental sources. The Internet is not monopolized by either pro– or anti–Iraq War individuals, but they do use it differently. Table 5.5 presents an overview of their Internet activities and compares them to each other.

## Shaping the Public's View

While it has become commonplace to speak of the media as driving foreign policy decisions, that is, "the CNN effect," a more complex relationship exists between the media and policy makers that drives their coverage of foreign events. Evidence suggests that the media does not so much discover foreign policy problems as it cues about what to report from the political debate in Washington. This is referred to as indexing. If there is no debate in Washington, then there is no debate in the media, and coverage of a topic may all but disappear. In the case of the Iraq War, the drop in coverage, from an average of 15 percent of the news content in July 2006 to 3 percent in February 2007 coincided with a drop-off from 35 percent to 23 percent of the number of Americans who could correctly estimate the number of U.S. fatalities in the war.

Additionally, in reporting on foreign policy problems journalists look first to the White House for cues on how to define a problem. This is important because first impressions are often difficult to challenge. With this frame of reference in hand, journalists then go to other, lesser news sources such as members of Congress, ex-government officials, and outside experts for commentary and input. This is referred to as the opinion cascade

**TABLE 5.5**

DIFFERENCES IN INTERNET USE BETWEEN IRAQ WAR SUPPORTERS
AND WAR OPPONENTS

| Topic | War Supporters (Percentage) | War Opponents (Percentage) |
|---|---|---|
| Look at Web sites of American newspapers | 27 | 39 |
| Use e-mail to discuss war with friends | 17 | 22 |
| Look at Web sites known as alternative media sources | 6 | 15 |
| Sign online petitions for/against the war | 4 | 14 |
| Get information online about the country/people of Iraq | 13 | 23 |
| Receive/send patriotic material by e-mail | 30 | 19 |
| Receive/send e-mail prayer request | 27 | 20 |
| Look online for news about the war | 45 | 46 |
| Look at U.S. government Web sites | 15 | 16 |
| Use instant messaging to discuss war | 11 | 13 |
| Get information about preparing for a terrorist attack online | 9 | 10 |

*Source*: Lee Rainie, Susannah Fox, and Deborah Fallows, "The Internet and the Iraq War" (Washington, DC: Pew Internet & American Life Project, 2004), p. 8. Available online at www.pewinternet.org/pdfs/PIP_Iraq_War_Report.pdf.

and according to some, including White House Press Secretary Scott McClellan, identifies the media as a "complicit enabler" of the Bush administration's case for going to war with Iraq.

One recent example of how presidents are able to use the media to influence public opinion is found in the lead up to the Iraq War when the Bush administration used secret intelligence in a public fashion in order to build up support for the Iraq War.[59] Virtually all of the intelligence made public during this campaign was either challenged in secret by elements of the intelligence community at the time, taken out of context so that its importance was overstated, or later proven to be inaccurate.

The Bush administration's campaign began in August 2002. Responding to a question at the Commonwealth Club in San Francisco, Vice President

Dick Cheney said, "It is the judgment of many of us that in the not too-distant future he [Saddam Hussein] will acquire nuclear weapons." In a speech to the National Convention of the Veterans of Foreign Wars on August 26, he referenced intelligence in highlighting the threat posed by Saddam Hussein. Cheney stated, "There is no doubt that Saddam Hussein has weapons of mass destruction." He continued, "We now know that Saddam has resumed his efforts to acquire nuclear weapons. Among other sources we've gotten this from firsthand testimony from defectors, including Saddam's own son-in-law, who was subsequently murdered at Saddam's direction."

President Bush also invoked intelligence reports in seeking to build public support for the war. In an October 7 speech, he stated, "evidence indicates Iraq is reconstituting its nuclear weapons program" and that "satellite photographs reveal that Iraq is rebuilding facilities at sites that have been part of its nuclear program in the past." He also stated, "we have discovered through intelligence that Iraq has a growing fleet" of unmanned aircraft and worried they might be targeted on the United States. His administration also released a white paper based on the classified National Intelligence Estimate it had just produced, entitled, "Iraq's Weapons of Mass Destruction Program." Its lead "key judgment" was that "if left unchecked it [Iraq] probably will have a nuclear weapon during this decade."

Public intelligence was at the heart of Secretary of State Powell's February 5, 2003, address to the UN Security Council. In making his case, he affirmed that "Every statement I make today is backed up by sources, solid sources. . . . These are not assertions. What we are giving you are facts and conclusions based on solid intelligence." At one point he affirmed that "we have firsthand descriptions of biological weapons factories on wheels and rails."

Two very different consequences follow from the manner in which the media frames its foreign policy stories. The first is the **rally-around-the-flag affect** in which the public moves to support the president in times of conflict and crisis. Examples of each can be found in the Persian Gulf War. Initially, the American public was sharply divided on using military force against Iraq in 1991. Support for war hovered around the 50 percent mark until President George H. W. Bush's January 16, 1991, speech announcing the beginning of the bombing campaign. Support then shot up to 72 percent. Support surged again in February, this time to a high of 80 percent, when President Bush announced the beginning of the ground war, and it remained high for the remainder of the conflict. One explanation for this pattern is the "rally-around-the-flag" argument, which pictures the public as being very responsive to cues from policy makers and predisposed to support the president in times of international crisis.

The second consequence is a "**spiral of silence.**" Here, when individuals hold opinions that they do not hear voiced by others they exercise self-censorship as a way of protecting themselves from criticism. The opposite reaction takes place among those who receive positive reinforcement for their views. They become even more vocal and confident in their beliefs, leading the dissenters to exercise even more self-censorship. In the case of the Gulf War, the networks all but ignored antiwar stories. Of 2,855 minutes of network news coverage of the war between August 8 and January 3, only 29 minutes showed popular opposition to the American military buildup. Once military activities designed to liberate Kuwait began, network stories on opinion in the United States were framed in terms of patriotism, militarism, and nationalism. Film clips of war protesters were paired with scenes of Americans praying in churches. The views of members of Congress who opposed the war were defined as "atypical," and the media declared that "of course, the political leaders are falling in behind the president."

Finally, media coverage of the Iraq War also raised issues about its independence and objectivity. Controversy centered on two practices. The first was the dependence of the media on military sources for information about the war. *New York Times* reporter Judith Miller regularly filed reports based on information given her by the military that supported the administration's claim that Saddam Hussein's government possessed WMD. In return, Miller received special treatment by the military. She was the only reporter embedded with the task force looking for WMD.

The second point of controversy was over the Pentagon's public relations program that was designed to produce positive coverage of the war. A key piece of this plan was through the extensive use by the networks of retired military officers who had been specially briefed by the Pentagon as analysts. As many as seventy-five retired military officers were briefed by the Pentagon. Their business links were seldom disclosed to the viewers or even the networks they worked for.

## POLICY-MAKER RESPONSE

The prevailing view among policy makers holds that foreign policy is too important to be left to the uninformed and unstable flow of public perceptions of world affairs. Public attitudes are something to be formed and shaped by the policy makers rather than followed by them. As secretary of defense during the Persian Gulf War, Dick Cheney, when asked about the media and its influence on foreign policy, said, "I do not look upon the press as an asset. Frankly, I look on it as a problem to be managed."[60]

The tendency of policy makers to discount the positive contribution of the public voice to foreign policy making also shows up when they look to uncover the public voice. Our discussion has stressed public opinion polls, election results, and interest group activity. State Department officials emphasize public attitudes as interpreted by personal contacts, other institutions, and the working press. Especially important for the State Department is the view that Congress has of public opinion. As one State Department official observed, "If a given viewpoint different from our own does not have congressional expression, forget it."[61] The inevitable result of this perspective is to narrow greatly the range of public attitudes that are taken into account in making policy.

An even deeper problem may exist. Quite simply, policy makers seek out little information about how the public views foreign policy.[62] A congressional staffer could not remember the last time he was asked to do a foreign policy poll. A member of the executive branch said that most information on this score was anecdotal.

## OVER THE HORIZON

Debate such as that over the degree of influence that the Israeli Lobby may have over American foreign policy is not likely to end soon. The avenues through which the public voice may be heard—if policy makers are listening— are too many and varied to permit an easy answer. It also needs to be kept in mind that impact of public attitudes can be expected to vary from issue to issue. The public's influence is greatest on issues where economic and security concerns are present and when the decision time is long. As these conditions are removed, the public's influence progressively lessens.[63]

Looking over the horizon, commentators see two important developments taking shape. One is the steadily increasing importance of new or nontraditional means of communicating on foreign policy issues. Three examples illustrate this point. First, despite the Army's best efforts to contain their use by mid-2007 more than 7,000 video clips of combat footage from Iraq were available on Youtube. Second, blogging on foreign policy issues is now a prominent Internet activity, and it is not policy neutral.[64] The blogosphere is primarily liberal and Democratic. It is capable of generating huge sums of money for candidates and spreading myths. For some analysts, the blogosphere represents the latest in a long American tradition of populists reaching out to remove foreign policy from the control of elites. Third, the White House arranged for President Obama's June 2009 speech in Cairo to be sent out in text message format in four languages, translated into thirteen languages, and broadcast on Facebook.

A second impending development over the horizon is the loss of the bipartisan liberal internationalist political center on which most U.S. foreign policy initiatives have been built.[65] In the view of some, this has already happened and the challenge now is to rebuild the center. The fundamental unanswered question is how. Can the divergent strands in the public voice come together on their own to create the basis for a new foreign policy consensus, or will this consensus be thrust upon it by either foreign policy successes or tragedies?

## CRITICAL THINKING QUESTIONS

1. Which of the means of exercising the public voice discussed in this chapter (public opinion, elections, lobbying, and political protest) is most effective?
2. Is the media best seen as a threat to the president's ability to conduct foreign policy or an important tool he can use?
3. Should policy makers listen to the public or use their professional judgment in making foreign policy decisions?

## KEY TERMS

CNN effect   134
military–industrial
   complex   122
positional
   issues   118

rally-around-the-flag
   effect   136
spiral of silence   136
think tanks   127
tipping point   116

valence issues   118
Vietnam syndrome   112
yellow journalism   131

## FURTHER READING

Robert Entman, *Projections of Power: Framing News, Public Opinion and U.S. Foreign Policy* (Chicago: University of Chicago Press, 2004).

Steven Kull and I. M. Destler, *Misreading the Public: The Myth of the New Isolationism* (Washington, DC: Brookings, 1999).

Richard Sobel, *The Impact of Public Opinion on U.S. Foreign Policy Since Vietnam* (New York: Oxford University Press, 2001).

Peter Trubowitz, *Defining the National Interest: Conflict and Change in American Foreign Policy* (Chicago: University of Chicago Press, 1998).

Eugene Wittkopf and James McCormick (eds) *The Domestic Sources of American Foreign Policy*, 5th ed, (Lanham, MD: Rowman & Littlefield, 2008).

## NOTES

1. For a condensed version see John Mearsheimer and Stephen Walt, "The Israel Lobby," *London Review of Books*, March 23, 2006. available at www.lrb.co.uk/v28/n06/mear01_.html

2. James Billington, "Realism and Vision in Foreign Policy," *Foreign Affairs*, 65 (1987), 630.

3. Walter Lippmann, quoted in Amos Jordan and William J. Taylor, Jr., *American National Security Policy and Process* (Baltimore, MD: Johns Hopkins University Press, 1981), p. 43.

4. Barry Hughes, *The Domestic Context of American Foreign Policy* (San Francisco: Freeman, 1978), pp. 23–24.

5. Matthew Baum, "Circling the Wagons: Soft News and Isolationism in American Public Opinion," *International Studies Quarterly*, 48 (2004), 313–38.

6. Kathryn Tempas, "Words vs. Deeds," *The Brookings Review* (Summer 2003), 33–35.

7. Robert Erickson, Norman Luttbeg and Kent Tedin, *American Public Opinion (New York: Wiley, 1980)*, p. 44.

8. Hughes, *The Domestic Context of American Foreign Policy*, p. 31.

9. Ole R. Holsti and James N. Rosenau, *American Leadership in World Affairs, Vietnam and the Breakdown of Consensus* (Winchester, MA: Allen & Unwin, 1984), pp. 218–20.

10. Lloyd Free and William Watts, "Internationalism Comes of Age . . . Again," *Public Opinion*, 3 (1980), 46–50.

11. John Rielly, "Americans and the World: A Survey at Century's End," *Foreign Policy*, 114 (1999), 97–113.

12. World Public Opinion.Org, "Americans Assess International Strategy," December 7, 2006, www.worldpublicopinion.org/pipa/pdf/dec06/USIntlStrategy_Dec06_rpt.pdf.

13. Ole R. Holsti, "Public Opinion and Foreign Policy: Attitude Structures of Opinion Leaders After the Cold War," in Eugene R. Wittkopf (ed.), *Domestic Sources of American Foreign Policy: Insights and Evidence,* 2nd ed. (New York: St. Martin's, 1994), 36–56.

14. Shoon Kathleen Murray and Christopher Spinosa, "The Post 9/11 Shift in Public Opinion," in Eugene Wittkopf and James McCormick (eds.), *The Domestic Sources of American Foreign Policy,* 4th ed. (Lanham, MD: Rowman & Littlefield, 2004), 97–116.

15. Miroslav Nincic, "Domestic Costs, the U.S. Public, and the Isolationist Calculus," *International Studies Quarterly,* 41 (1997), 593–610; and Robert Hormats, *The Price of Liberty: Paying for America's Wars* (New York: Times Books, 2007).

16. Bruce W. Jentleson, "The Pretty Prudent Public: Post-Vietnam American Opinion on the Use of Military Force," *International Studies Quarterly,* 36 (1990), 49–74.

17. John Rielly, "The Public Mood at Mid-Decade," *Foreign Policy,* 98 (1995), 76–95.

18. Richard Eichenberg, "Gender Differences in Public Attitudes Toward the Use of Force by the United States, 1990–2003," *International Security,* 28 (2003), 110–41.

19. Leslie Gelb and Richard K. Betts, *The Irony of Vietnam: The System Worked* (Washington, DC: Brookings, 1979).

20. Richard Sobel, *The Impact of Public Opinion on U.S. Foreign Policy Since Vietnam* (New York: Oxford University Press, 2001).

21. Richard J. Barnett, *The Roots of War* (New York: Penguin, 1977), p. 243.

22. Quoted in William Schneider, "Conservatism, Not Interventionism: Trends in Foreign Policy Opinion, 1974–1982," in Kenneth A. Oye, Robert J. Lieber, and Donald Rothchild (eds.), *Eagle Defiant: United States Foreign Policy in the 1980s* (Boston: Little, Brown, 1983), p. 138.

23. Douglas Foyle, *Counting the Public In* (New York: Columbia University Press, 1999), p. 267.

24. Daniel Yankelovich, "The Tipping Points," *Foreign Affairs,* 85 (2006), 115–25; and "Poll Positions," *Foreign Affairs,* 84 (2005), 2–16.

25. Gerald M. Pomper, *Elections in America: Control and Influence in Democratic Politics* (New York: Dodd, Mead, 1968), p. 251.

26. The figures for 1983 are reported in *The New York Times,* July 1, 1983, p. 1. The remaining figures through 1987 are discussed in ibid., p. 19; and Hughes, *Domestic Context of American Foreign Policy,* p. 91. The 1987 figure is from William Galston and Christopher Makins, "Campaign '88 and Foreign Policy," *Foreign Policy,* 71 (1988), 9. The 1993 data are from *Time* (October 4, 1993). The 2003 data are from Kull et al., "Misperception, the Media, and the Iraq War." The 2008 data is from "Awareness of Iraq War Fatalities Plummets," Pew Research Center, March 12, 2008.

27. Erickson et al., *American Public Opinion,* p. 216.

28. Michael Abramowitz, "Terrorism Fades as Issue in 2008 Campaign," *Washington Post,* September 11, 2008, p. A6.

29. Charles Whalen, *The House and Foreign Policy* (Chapel Hill, NC: University of North Carolina Press, 1982).

30. Schneider, *Eagle Defiant*

31. Laurence Radway, "The Curse of Free Elections," *Foreign Policy,* 40 (1980), 61–73.

32. William B. Quandt, "The Electoral Cycle and the Conduct of American Foreign Policy," *Political Science Quarterly,* 101 (1986), 825–37.

33. Bob Woodward, *The War Within* (New York: Simon & Schuster, 2008), pp. 320–21.

34. Kerry Dumbright, "Interest Groups," in Ramon Hawley Myers, Michel Oksenberg, and David L. Shambaugh (eds.), *Making China Policy* (Lanham, MD: Rowman & Littlefield, 2001), pp. 149–72.

35. David Hilzenrath, "From Public Life to Private Business," *The Washington Post*, May 28, 2006, p. A1.
36. C. W. Mills, *The Power Elite* (New York: Oxford University Press, 1956).
37. See Steven Rosen (ed.), *Testing the Theory of the Military Industrial Complex* (Lexington, KY: Heath, 1973).
38. Martin Weil, "Can the Blacks Do for Africa What the Jews Did for Israel?" *Foreign Policy*, 15 (1974), 109–29.
39. Charles McMathias, Jr., "Ethnic Groups and Foreign Affairs," *Foreign Affairs*, 59 (1981), 975–99.
40. Walter Russell Mead, "The New Israel and the Old: Why Gentile Americans back the Jewish State," *Foreign Affairs*, 87 (2008), 28–46.
41. Michael Abramowitz, "Jewish Liberals to Launch a Counterpoint to AIPAC," *Washington Post*, April 15, 2008, p. A13.
42. David J. Sadd and G. Neal Lendenmann, "Arab American Grievances," *Foreign Policy*, 60 (1985), 17–29.
43. Fran Scott and Abdulah Osman, "Identity, African-Americans and U.S. Foreign Policy," in Thomas Ambrosio (ed.), *Ethnic Identity Groups and U.S. Foreign Policy* (Westport, CT: Praeger, 2002), 71–92.
44. Bill Richardson, "Hispanic American Concerns," *Foreign Policy*, 60 (1985), 30–39.
45. Michael Jones-Correa, "Latinos and Latin America," in Thomas Ambrosio (ed.), *Ethnic Identity Groups and U.S. Foreign Policy (Westport, CT: Praeger, 2002)*, pp. 115–30.
46. See Shawn Miller, "Trade Winds Stir Miami Storm," *Insight*, June 7, 1993; and Carla Anne Robins, "Dateline Washington: Cuban-American Clout," *Foreign Policy*, 88 (1992), 165–82.
47. James Kirk, "Indian-Americans and the U.S.-India Nuclear Agreement: Consolidation of an Ethnic Lobby," *Foreign Policy Analysis*, 4 (2008), 275–300.
48. Congressional Quarterly, *The Washington Lobby*, 4th ed. (Washington, DC: Congressional Quarterly, 1982), pp. 155–62.
49. Glenn Kessler, "Leaders at Odds on Armenia Resolution," *The Washington Post*, October 10, 2007, p. A1.
50. William Martin, "The Christian Right and American Foreign Policy," *Foreign Policy*, 114 (1999), 66–80.
51. Asteris Huliaras, "The Evangelical Roots of US Africa Policy," *Survival*, 50 (2008–2009), 161–82.
52. James Guth, John Green, Lyman Kellstedt, and Corwin Smidt, "Faith and Foreign Policy: A View from the Pews," *The Review of Faith & International Affairs*, 3 (2005), 3–10.
53. James Lindsay, "The Apathy: How an Uninterested Public Is Reshaping Foreign Policy," *Foreign Affairs*, 79 (2000), 2–8.
54. Fred Hiatt, "The Vanishing J Foreign Correspondent," *The Washington Post*, January 29, 2007, p. A15; Pamela Constable, "Demise of the Foreign Correspondent," *The Washington Post*, February 18, 2007, p. B1; Jill Carroll, *Foreign News Coverage*, Working Paper, Joan Shorenstein Center on the Press, Politics and Public Policy, Harvard University, Fall 2006. The number of newspaper foreign correspondents does not include the *Wall Street Journal* because it has European and Asian editions.
55. See prepared statement by Michael R. Beschloss, "Impact of Television on U.S. Foreign Policy," Hearing before the Committee on Foreign Affairs, House of Representatives, 103rd Congress, 2nd Session, April 26, 1994.
56. Trevor Thrall, "The Gulf in Reporting the Gulf War," *Breakthroughs*, 2 (1992), 9–13.

57. Jacqueline Sharkey, "When Pictures Drive Foreign Policy," *American Journalism Review,* 15 (December 1993), 14–19.
58. Lee Raine, Susannah Fox, and Deborah Fallows, *The Internet and the Iraq War, The Internet and American Life Project* (Washington, DC: The Pew Foundation, 2004).
59. This case study is drawn from Glenn Hastedt, "Public Intelligence: Leaks as Policy Instruments—The Case of the Iraq War," *Intelligence and National Security,* 20 (2005), 419–39.
60. Quoted in Herbert Abrams, "Weapons of Miller's Descriptions," The Bulletin of the Atomic Scientists 60 (July/August 2004), p. 63.
61. Ibid., p. 117.
62. Steven Kull and I. M. Destler, *Misreading the Public: The Myth of the New Isolationism* (Washington, DC: Brookings, 1999).
63. On the matter of issue areas see Hughes, *The Domestic Context of American Foreign Policy,* chap. 7.
64. David Frum, "Foggy Bloggom," *The National Interest* 93 (2008), 46–52.
65. Charles Kupchan and Peter Trubowitz, "Dead Center: The Demise of Liberal Internationalism in the United States," *International Security,* 32 (2007), 7–44.

# Congress

In February 2009, Senate Judiciary Committee Chairman Patrick Leahy called for creating a "truth" commission to investigate possible Bush administration abuses of power in the war against terrorism. By then, House Judiciary Committee Chairman John Conyers, Jr., had already introduced legislation calling for the establishment of an advisory National Commission on Presidential Powers and Civil Liberties to "investigate relevant facts, circumstances and law" pertaining to Bush administration policies, including the use of domestic warrantless wiretaps and enhanced interrogation techniques. These were not the only congressionally sponsored efforts underway to pass judgment on Bush administration policies. The Senate Intelligence Committee indicated that it too would undertake a review of the Central Intelligence Agency's handling of captured terrorist suspects. Included in its six-month study would be uncovering the extent to which waterboarding and similar interrogation methods produced significant information as the Bush administration claimed. The committee's investigation is not intended to produce calls for legal action against specific individuals.

President Barack Obama's administration responded cautiously to calls for a truth commission, declaring that neither CIA officials who engaged in these interrogations nor the Justice Department officials who authorized them should be prosecuted. CIA Director Leon Panetta indicated that he could cooperate with the Senate investigation because it was a legitimate exercise of Congress' oversight authority and it was important to learn from the past, but he would not support an investigation or prosecution of those individuals involved in the interrogation program. Senator John McCain argued against prosecuting Bush administration officials because of the "deeply chilling effect" it would have on future administrations. In fall 2009, Attorney General Eric Holder appointed a prosecutor to investigate alleged CIA terrorism abuses. His decision went beyond what many in the Obama administration preferred, but was too far for many CIA's supporters

As this debate illustrates, to a president Congress often appears to be an obstacle course through which the administration's foreign policy proposals must first pass. It is an obstacle course made up of two parts: the constitutional distribution of powers between the Congress and the president and Congress's internal structure and operating procedures. This second set of obstacles is every bit as formidable as those obstacles rooted in the constitutional separation of powers.

Before proceeding to examine the nature of this obstacle course in more detail two dissenting views need to be presented. The first is that Congress is in reality not much of an obstacle course for presidents to run. Two scholars who study Congress assert that over the past six years congressional oversight of presidential war power has virtually collapsed.[1] A second dissent argues that even if it is a hard obstacle course congressional participation in foreign policy making is not an evil to be avoided because it raises the public's awareness about issues, provides additional information to policy makers, and, in the long run, may improve the quality of U.S. foreign policy.[2]

# CONSTITUTIONAL POWERS

Congress has four important powers rooted in the Constitution to influence foreign policy: (1) the power of advice and consent in making treaties, (2) the power to confirm presidential appointments, (3) a set of war powers, (4) and the power to regulate commerce. In this section, we look at each of these as well as the way in which the House has become involved in foreign policy making.

## Treaty-Making Power

The Constitution states that the president, by and with the advice and consent of the Senate, has the power to make treaties. The president's role in the treaty-making process has not been a source of serious controversy. The president nominates the negotiators, issues instructions to them, submits the treaty to the Senate for its advice and consent, and if consent is given, the president decides whether to **ratify** the treaty and make it law. Far more controversial have been the nature of senatorial advice and consent, the topics to be covered by treaties, and the role of the House of Representatives in the treaty-making process.

SENATORIAL ADVICE AND CONSENT  Over 1,500 treaties have been ratified by the Senate and only 21 rejected. Fifteen of those occurred from 1789 to 1920.[3] A list of rejected treaties is presented in Table 6.1. These figures do not tell the full story. Omitted in this counting are treaties negotiated by presidents but never voted on by the Senate or those the Senate consented to only after prolonged delays. President Jimmy Carter's withdrawal of the SALT II treaty is only one example of major Senate "nonrejections." Harry Truman negotiated a treaty establishing an International Trade Organization that was to be part of the Bretton Woods system along with the World Bank and the International Monetary Fund. Because of certain Senate opposition, President Truman never submitted the treaty for advice and consent, and the interim General Agreement on Tariffs and Trade (GATT) became the formal international vehicle for lowering tariffs. In 1988 the Senate gave its consent, by a vote of 83–11, to a Convention on the Prevention and Punishment of Genocide that was signed by the United States in 1948 and first submitted to the Senate by Truman in 1949.

An overall tally such as the one in Table 6.1 also makes no mention of senatorial attempts to change the treaties. Between 1947 and 2000, the Senate attached reservations to 162 of the 796 treaties that came before it.[4] In the heated debate over the Panama Canal Treaties, 145 amendments, 76 reservations, 18 understandings, and 3 declarations were proposed.

Studies suggest that the Senate's attachment of amendments and reservations to treaties is far from random.[5] Several factors increase the odds that the Senate will not simply give a straight thumbs-up or thumbs-down vote on a treaty that comes before it. First, the subject matter of the treaty matters. "High politics" treaties—those dealing with national security issues and questions of U.S. sovereignty—are far more likely to be saddled with reservations. Economic treaties are also likely to attract reservations. Second, beginning

## TABLE 6.1

Rejected Treaties

| Bilateral | Multilateral |
| --- | --- |
| Suspension of Slave Trade/ Columbia, 1825 | Treaty of Versailles, 1920 |
| Property Rights/Switzerland, 1836 | World Court, 1935 |
| Annexation/Texas, 1844 | Law of Sea Convention, 1960 |
| Commercial Reciprocity/ Germany, 1844 | Montreal Aviation Protocol, 1983 |
| Transit and Commercial Rights/Mexico, 1860 | Comprehensive Test Ban, 1999 |
| Cuban Claims Commission/ Spain, 1860 | — |
| Arbitration of Claims/United Kingdom, 1869 | — |
| Commercial Reciprocity/ Hawaii, 1870 | — |
| Annexation/Dominican Republic, 1870 | — |
| Interoceanic Canal/Nicaragua, 1885 | — |
| Fishing Rights/United Kingdom, 1888 | — |
| Extradition/United Kingdom, 1889 | — |
| Arbitration/United Kingdom, 1897 | — |
| Commercial Rights/Turkey, 1927 | — |
| St. Lawrence Seaway/Canada, 1934 | — |

Source: David M. O'Brien, "Presidential and Congressional Relations in Foreign Affairs," in Colton Campbell et al. (eds.), *Congress and the Politics of Foreign Policy* (Upper Saddle River, NJ: Prentice Hall, 2003), p. 74.

with the Vietnam War, ideology has been an important factor shaping Senate treaty votes. Today, conservative senators tend to vote for arms control agreements only when the president is a member of their party. Liberal Senators, in contrast, tend to support arms control agreements regardless of what party occupies the White House.

Not all Senatorial changes to treaties are alike.[6] Some senatorial changes are designed to improve a treaty; others are meant to kill it by introducing unacceptable provisions such as occurred during the SALT II treaty debate. Even when the intent is not to kill a treaty, senatorial changes can cause problems for a president. Senatorial changes in a Treaty of Friendship and Cooperation with Spain led to charges of interference in Spanish domestic affairs and almost resulted in Spain's refusal to ratify the treaty. The root motivations behind such changes are many. They include the desire to protect domestic economic interests, reassert senatorial powers by insisting on increased reporting and certification provisions as a condition for giving its advice and consent to a treaty, or make a policy statement—such as the 1997 Chemical Warfare Convention that directed the secretary of defense to increase U.S. military ability to operate in areas contaminated by chemical and biological weapons.[7]

Finally, we should note that the president and Senate may continue to clash over the provisions of a treaty long after senatorial advice and consent has been given. At issue here is who has the power to interpret treaty language and, in the course of doing so, potentially change the meaning of the treaty itself. A significant presidential–congressional clash over the language of a treaty occurred over the Antiballistic Missile (ABM) Treaty. The centerpiece of the dispute was whether a president could reinterpret the language of a treaty without congressional approval. President Reagan did so, and on the basis of this new interpretation his administration asserted that it could legally test elements of his Strategic Defense Initiative (SDI) shield. The controversy continued when the Clinton administration approached Russia about modifying the language of the treaty to permit the deployment of mobile defensive systems against intermediate missiles. The administration said its proposal was intended only to clear up ambiguities in the treaty. Senate leaders responded that the administration should not try to put any change into effect without Senate approval. The Clinton administration ultimately conceded this point in 1997 and recognized the Senate's right to review the revised treaty language. President George W. Bush formally withdrew the United States from the ABM Treaty in June 2002. Thirty-one members of Congress unsuccessfully brought legal action against the administration, asserting that the president lacked the constitutional power to do so.

**THE ROLE OF THE HOUSE**   The constitution gives the House no formal role in the treaty-making process, and traditionally it played the part of a spectator. This is changing as the House has seized upon its budgetary powers as the vehicle for making its will known to both the Senate and the president. Treaties are not always self-executing. They typically require enabling legislation and the expenditure of funds before their provisions take effect. The constitution gives the House control over the budget and in the process the ability to undo what the Senate and the president have agreed on.

A case in point is the Panama Canal Treaties. According to one observer, the House came quite close to destroying these treaties by inserting into the implementing legislation language that disagreed with and contradicted parts of the treaty just approved by the Senate.[8] On September 16, 1977, President Carter submitted one document containing two treaties defining the future status of the Panama Canal to the Senate for its consideration.[9] The Panama Canal Treaty abolished the Panama Canal Zone by terminating the 1903 treaty that had established it. The United States would retain the right to manage and operate the canal until December 31, 1999, through a newly created Panama Canal Commission. A Neutrality Treaty established the permanent neutrality of the canal and guaranteed that it would always remain open. Both treaties were approved by the Senate in 1978 by identical 68–32 votes.

The Carter administration's implementing legislation was assigned to four House committees. Primary jurisdiction was held by the Merchant Marine and Fisheries Committee, whose chair, Representative John Murphy, opposed the treaty. He proposed his own version of the implementing legislation that gave Congress a continuing say in supervising the Panama Canal for many years to come. For example, instead of creating a government corporation to run the canal, which would pay its expenses out of tolls as the Carter administration proposed, Murphy's bill would create a government agency whose budget would be voted on annually by Congress.

Eventually, the Carter administration found it necessary to abandon its own bill in favor of the Murphy bill. In doing so, it angered Panamanian Aristides Royo who cited almost 30 articles of the House bill that violated provisions of the treaty as it had been negotiated. In the end, final congressional approval was given to the implementing legislation only four days before the treaty was scheduled to take effect.

## Appointment Powers

As originally envisioned, the power to approve or reject presidential appointments was closely related to the power to give advice and consent to treaties. By exercising a voice in who negotiated the treaty, the Senate would be able to influence its content. In practice, this linkage was never fully put into place, and it has long since unraveled. The Senate has failed to actively or systematically exercise its confirmation powers. Frequently, it has not hesitated to approve ambassadors appointed solely for political purposes and without any other apparent qualifications for the post. In 1956, a contribution of $22,000 to the presidential campaign of Dwight Eisenhower "bought" the ambassadorship to Sri Lanka. During the Nixon administration, the ambassadors to Switzerland, Austria, and France all made contributions in excess of $100,000 to the Republican Party. At the end of President George H. W. Bush's term in office, 20 percent of the ambassador corps was made up of political or noncareer appointments. About 30 percent of Bill Clinton's ambassadorial appointments could be classified as political in nature. The pattern of using ambassadorships as rewards for political support continues. Under George W. Bush many ambassadorships went to "Pioneers," individuals who had raised a minimum of $100,000 for his presidential race. Included among them were positions in Belgium and the Netherlands.

Typically, when the Senate has raised its voice in opposition to an appointment, the concern has been directed more toward making a policy statement than questioning the qualifications of the nominee. In 2007, George W. Bush withdrew the nomination of Sam Fox as ambassador to Belgium. Fox, a businessman, made a $50,000 contribution to the Swift Boat Veterans for Truth organization, which opposed Democratic presidential candidate Senator John Kerry in 2004. Robert Pastor was nominated by President Bill Clinton to be ambassador to Mexico. Pastor's nomination was withdrawn after it had been approved by the Senate Foreign Relations Committee. This approval came before the 1994 election but was vigorously opposed by Senator Jesse Helms, who became chairperson of the Foreign Relations Committee after the Republicans won control of the Senate in that election. Helms blamed Pastor, a Latin American expert who had served on Jimmy Carter's National Security Council, for the Panama Canal Treaties. A similarly politically inspired challenge occurred in President Obama's first months in office when, after a coup in Honduras, Republican senators sympathetic to the new military government blocked two of Obama's appointments to the region in protest of the lack of U.S. support for the new government.

## War Powers

The war powers of the Constitution are split into three basic parts. Congress is given the power to declare war and the power to raise and maintain an army and a navy, while the president is designated as commander in chief of the armed forces. In the abstract these powers fit together very nicely, but in practice a far different picture prevails. A problem immediately arises over defining when a state of war exists. Is it any instance where U.S. troops are placed into combat, or must a war be declared into existence? In its Prize Cases decision of 1862, the Supreme Court ruled that the existence of a war was found in the prevailing conditions and not in a formal congressional declaration. U.S. practice has borne this out. Congress has declared only 5 of the over 125 "wars" that the United States has fought: the War of 1812, the Spanish–American War, the Mexican War, World War I, and World War II.

In addition, no state today can wait until a war has broken out or has been declared to begin mobilizing its armed forces. Successful military action requires forces in being. The dilemma facing Congress is that once it has created a standing military establishment capable of going into combat without further mobilization, it has lost control over the president. The Cuban missile crisis and the Bay of Pigs invasion were played out without a declaration of war. Jimmy Carter presented Congress with a *fait accompli* with the Iranian hostage rescue effort; Ronald Reagan acted unilaterally in invading Grenada and bombing Libya; and George H. W. Bush did the same in invading Panama and sending troops to Somalia.

President Bill Clinton did not seek congressional authorization for his use of troops to return President Jean-Bertrand Aristide to power in Haiti. In fact, the Clinton administration asserted that the War Powers Resolution should be interpreted as recognizing and presupposing "the existence of a unilateral Presidential authority to deploy armed force." Neither the Clinton administration nor anyone in Congress mentioned the War Powers Resolution in February 1998, when Clinton was contemplating air strikes against Iraq for its refusal to permit UN inspectors to search for weapons sites. President George W. Bush began the war against terrorism in Afghanistan without a declaration of war or any reference to the War Powers Resolution. The single major congressional action was the September 12, 2001, Senate Joint Resolution #22, which "supports the determination of the President, in close consultation with Congress, to bring justice and punish the perpetrators of these attacks as well as their sponsors."

Presidents have defended such uses of force, citing their powers as commander in chief. The exact meaning of these powers is unclear, however. Alexander Hamilton saw them as a symbolic grant of power, with the actual power to decide military strategy and tactics being held by professional soldiers. Yet many presidents have taken this grant of power quite literally. Franklin Roosevelt participated actively in formulating military strategy and tactics during World War II, and Lyndon Johnson participated actively in selecting bombing targets during Vietnam.

The most visible means available to Congress in trying to limit the president's use of force is the 1973 **War Powers Resolution**, which was passed over President Nixon's veto.[10] It requires the president to do the following:

1. "In every possible instance," consult with Congress before committing U.S. troops in "hostilities or into situations where imminent involvement in hostilities" is likely.
2. Inform Congress within 48 hours after the introduction of troops if there has been no declaration of war.
3. Remove U.S. troops within 60 days (or 90 days in special circumstances) if Congress does not either declare war or adopt a concurrent resolution approving the action.

Congress also can terminate the U.S. military involvement before the 60-day limit by passing a concurrent resolution. Such a resolution does not require the president's signature and therefore cannot be vetoed. From the outset, the War Powers Resolution has been controversial. Senator Jacob Javits saw in it the basis for a new foreign policy compact between the president and Congress. Senator Thomas Eagleton, originally a supporter of the legislation with Javits, voted against it because he claimed that it gave the president powers he never had: the power to commit U.S. troops abroad without prior congressional approval.

Presidents have argued that the War Powers Resolution is unconstitutional. The particular object of presidential hostility is the provision granting Congress the right to terminate hostilities through the use of a **legislative veto**. The legislative veto is a device that Congress has relied on to reinsert its voice into foreign affairs decision making. It allows Congress to approve or disapprove executive branch actions after the fact, in a form short of legislation. In addition to the War Powers Resolution, Congress has inserted legislative vetoes into a wide range of foreign policy legislation, including arms sales, the export of nuclear fuel and facilities, presidential decisions not to grant relief to industries injured by imports, the continuation of most favored nation (MFN) status for communist states, the stationing of U.S. personnel in the Sinai, presidential declarations of emergency, and national defense contracts in excess of $25 million.[11]

Presidents have maintained that only congressional action that has been approved by the president or is passed by Congress over a presidential veto is legally binding. On January 23, 1983, in a landmark case, the Supreme Court agreed with the presidential interpretation in making its ruling in *U.S. v. Chadha*. The case centered on the exercise of a legislative veto by the House of Representatives of the attorney general's decision to allow Chadha, an East Indian student holding a British passport, to stay in the United States. The Supreme Court reaffirmed this position 13 days later in a second case and explicitly linked its ruling to the legislative veto provisions of the War Powers Resolution.

It should be noted that a foreign affairs legislative veto has never been exercised. The closest it came to being used was with the transfer of nuclear material to India in 1980 and the sale of an AWACS (Airborne Warning and Control Systems aircraft) and F-15 enhancement package to Saudi Arabia in 1981.

Another sore point with presidents is the 60-day time limit imposed by the War Powers Resolution. From the very outset, presidents have challenged the time limit on constitutional and practical grounds, while at the same time they have acted in accordance with its reporting provisions. Of interest is the language used by presidents in making their reports.[12] In some cases (the transportation of refugees from Da Nang in April 1975, the evacuation of U.S. nationals from Cambodia and Vietnam in April 1975, and the evacuation of U.S. nationals from Lebanon in1976), the president reported his action in a perfunctory manner. In reporting the Mayaguez rescue operation in 1975, President Gerald Ford stated that he was "taking note" of the War Powers Resolution but asserted that he acted on the basis of his commander-in-chief powers. In this case, it is also unclear whether the advance consulting provisions were met. Senator Hugh Scott (R, Penn.), deputy minority leader and a member of the Senate Foreign Relations Committee, stated: "We were informed. We were alerted. We were advised. We were notified. . . . I don't know whether that's consultation or not."

In preparing for the Iraq War, the George W. Bush administration put forward two arguments for why the War Powers Resolution did not apply.[13] First, the administration argued that the 1991 resolution passed before the Persian Gulf War provided continuing military authority to the president. Second, they maintained that the use of force was authorized by the 1998 Iraq Liberation Act, which called on the president to provide for the overthrow of Saddam Hussein. In fact, the act specifically stated that none of its provisions "shall be construed to authorize or otherwise speak to the use of United States Armed Forces . . . in carrying out this Act."

In place of a War Powers Resolution vote, the George W. Bush administration obtained a congressional endorsement for the Iraq War in the form of a resolution authorizing the administration to enforce the UN resolution on Iraq's weapons of mass destruction and to protect the United States from Saddam Hussein. This authorization became the subject of great controversy as the Iraq War dragged on and public opinion turned against it. In summer 2007, Republican Senators John Warner (Va.) and Richard Lugar (Ind.) argued that a new nonbinding resolution was now necessary, because the mission of U.S. forces in Iraq had changed dramatically from that approved in the October 2002 resolution. Democratic Senators Robert Byrd (W.Va.) and Hillary Clinton (N.Y.) called for its repeal and for Congress to vote for a new Iraqi troop authorization. In the end, congressional efforts to force President Bush to begin withdrawing troops or develop an alternative strategy in 2007 failed for a lack of votes.

## Commerce Powers

Two trade issues have dominated congressional–presidential relations in the last several decades. The first has been largely put to rest. It involved extending **"permanent normal trade relations,"** long referred to as MFN status, to communist states. The early focus was on the Soviet Union. Increased trade with the United States was to be one of the main carrots held out by the Nixon administration to the Soviet Union as part of its détente policy. It was to be an inducement for signing arms control agreements and refraining from opportunistic behavior in the Third World. Quickly, however, Congress inserted language into trade legislation through the Jackson–Vanik Amendment, which linked improved trade terms with changes in Soviet domestic human rights behavior, most notably its treatment of Soviet Jews. This angered Soviet leaders who saw it as an unacceptable intrusion into their internal affairs and limited Nixon's ability to use trade as a foreign policy tool.

The focus then shifted to China. For 20 years, Congress held yearly votes on the terms by which Chinese goods would enter and compete in the U.S. market. In September 2000, the Clinton administration scored a major victory when, by a vote of 83–15, the Senate voted to permanently award China normal trade relations, opening the way for China to join the World Trade Organization (WTO). Supporters cited the economic benefits of increased trade with China, while opponents cited its poor human rights record, unfair trading practices, and involvement in provocative arms sales.

The second point of conflict is very much alive. It involves granting the president fast-track authority to negotiate international trade agreements. As we will note later, fast-track authority severely limits the ability of Congress to modify trade agreements when they are presented for its approval. President Bill Clinton was forced to allow this authority to lapse as part of the political price for getting the Senate to ratify the GATT treaty establishing the WTO. In December 2001, the House of Representatives passed a bill restoring fast-track authority (now renamed **"trade promotional" authority**) to President George W. Bush by a vote of 215–214. The Senate, which historically has been solidly pro–free trade, supported the measure with little opposition. In the House vote, only 21 Democrats supported the measure. Many of those opposed represented "high-tech" communities whose firms depend on selling to export markets and who are traditional free traders. Opponents were concerned that trade-offs of environmental protection, intellectual property rights, and labor standards would be made at the Doha Round of WTO talks in the name of furthering free trade. This dispute remains ongoing as on July 1, 2007, Bush's fast-track authority expired.

The president and Congress have clashed over these and other trade matters because the Constitution gives Congress the power to regulate commerce with foreign nations. In theory, this power belongs exclusively to Congress. No parallel statement exists laying out presidential powers. In practice, power sharing between the two branches has been necessary. Congress may have the power to regulate foreign commerce, but only the president has the power to negotiate treaties, and it is the president whom the Supreme Court has designated as the "sole organ of the government in the field of foreign affairs." Interestingly, power sharing in international economics has not produced the same level of conflict between the two branches as it has in other areas. Instead, it has produced a series of innovations that have brought a high degree of continuity and consistency to U.S. policy.

The first innovative power-sharing arrangement is found in the 1934 Trade Agreements Act, by which Congress delegated to the president the authority to "implement into domestic law the results of trade agreements as they relate to tariffs." This authority greatly enhanced the president's power position in multilateral trade negotiations by removing the threat of congressional obstructionism in the formal approval and implementation of the negotiated agreement. Congress periodically renewed this grant of authority for a succession of presidents, changing only the time frame involved and the value of the reduction permitted and inserting legislative veto provisions.

This procedure worked well until the Kennedy Round negotiations (1964–1967), when for the first time nontariff barriers to trade became the major points of contention. The Trade Reform Act of 1974 introduced the second major innovative power-sharing arrangement. It created a "fast-track" reporting procedure we discussed above. Under it Congress was required to vote yes or no within 90 days on trade legislation that came before it and was prohibited from adding any amendments.

The fast-track process and other legislative innovations have allowed Congress to insulate itself from domestic pressures for protectionist trade legislation. The result is that congressional representatives have been able to "advocate, even threaten, trade restrictions, while nicely relieving them of the need to deliver on their threats." The end of fast-track authority removes these barriers and raises the possibility of a lessened presidential ability to enter into trade agreements. Signs that this is taking place surfaced in 2009, when a House economic stimulus bill contained a "Buy American" provision that limited the use of these funds to projects using only American-made equipment and goods. U.S. companies such as General Electric opposed this move, noting that their operations were now global in scope and that such legislation could be interpreted as violating U.S. trade agreements.

# CONGRESSIONAL STRUCTURE AND FOREIGN POLICY

While Congress' constitutional powers provide it with an entry into foreign policy making, its ability to speak with a coherent voice and in a timely fashion are often heavily compromised by its internal structure and standard operating procedures that emphasizes operating through committees and subcommittees as well as respecting seniority. In this section, we highlight four important consequences of congressional structure for U.S. foreign policy: the existence of blunt foreign policy tools, the absence of a single voice who can speak for Congress; the presence of policy entrepreneurs, and the significant power possessed by staff aides.

## HISTORICAL LESSON

### The Nye Committee

Between 1934 and 1936, the seven members of the Senate Special Committee on Investigation of the Munitions Industry held 93 meetings and questioned more than 200 witnesses under the chairmanship of Senator Gerald Nye. Commonly known as the Nye Committee, it was created to investigate the extent to which banking interests and weapons manufactures had been responsible for the United States' involvement in World War I. That this might have been the case, that the U.S. involvement in World War I was not necessary, or that it was not fought for noble purposes had become a frequent theme in books and articles in the 1920s and early 1930s.

Nye was a progressive Republican from North Dakota. He would serve 20 years in the Senate, from 1925 to 1945. A supporter of President Franklin Roosevelt on domestic matters, he had already made a reputation for himself as an opponent of big business by helping to uncover the "Teapot Dome" scandal, in which President Warren Harding's secretary of the interior had given Mammoth Oil Company a no-bid lease on government oil fields in return for contributions to the Republican National Committee.

The Nye Committee issued its report in February 1936. It identified South America and China as the major markets for American weapons. Secondary markets included Poland, Turkey, Siam (Thailand), Italy, and Japan. Among its findings was that between 1915 and April 1917 the United States loaned Germany $27 million compared to $2.3 billion to Great Britain and its allies. It also stated that Electric Boat Co. patents had been sold to German firms and were used in submarines that destroyed American ships and killed Americans. In the final analysis, the Nye Committee concluded that there was no evidence that wars had started just because of the actions of munitions makers, but it did create the impression that they had been a strong force pushing the United States into the war.

The Nye Committee report observed that almost without exception American munitions companies had engaged in bribery in order to secure business and that in doing so they had "sown the seeds of disturbance to the peace and stability of those nations," corrupted officials, and weakened the remaining democracies in the world. The committee's report continued that they could find no evidence of arms manufacturers aiding any proposal for limiting the spread of weapons. Instead they found them to be actively involved in opposing almost all of them. An important part of their strategy for doing so was to obtain the active support of the War, Navy, Commerce, and even the State Department to sell their products abroad. The Nye Committee also concluded that American munitions companies on occasion intensified people's fears about their neighbors in order to make a larger profit. It noted in this regard that at a time when a $617 million naval bill was before Congress, the president of Bath Iron Works approached the publisher of several newspapers to reprint a Japanese war-scare story, even though it had been determined to be false.

The impact of the Nye Committee investigations was felt immediately in the Neutrality Acts that were passed in the 1930s. The first Neutrality Act was passed in 1935 and imposed an arms embargo on all countries involved in war regardless of whether they were the stronger party or weaker one and regardless of whether they were the aggressor or the victim of aggression. The 1936 Neutrality Act continued this prohibition and added to it a ban on loans or credits. It also created a loophole by permitting the sale of material to those involved in a civil war. General Motors, Texaco, Standard Oil, Ford, and others quickly took advantage of it, selling supplies to General Francisco Franco, who was leading right-wing forces in the Spanish civil war. The Neutrality Act of 1937 closed this loophole but did permit President Roosevelt to sell material to those fighting a war on a "cash-and-carry" basis. This provision allowed Roosevelt to send supplies to Great Britain while denying them to Germany. The Neutrality Acts came to an end in 1941 with the passage of the Lend-Lease Act.

**Applying the Lesson**

1. What are the dangers of investigations to assign blame for past foreign policy decisions; what are the possible benefits?
2. Is Congress the proper forum for conducting these types of investigations, or should independent commissions be set up to do this?
3. Many today see the Neutrality Acts as having been a major mistake. What types of mistakes might follow from a truth commission investigation into Bush's policies during the war on terrorism? What benefits might come by it? ■

## Blunt Foreign Policy Tools

Foremost among the tools on which Congress relies to influence policy are its general legislative, budgetary, and oversight powers. While they are formidable powers, Congress often finds itself frustrated in its efforts to fine-tune U.S. foreign policy or give it a new sense of direction, because of their bluntness and essentially negative character.

GENERAL LEGISLATIVE POWERS    Four basic forms of congressional action exist. Included are the *simple resolution,* which is a statement made by one House; the *concurrent resolution,* a statement passed by both Houses; and the *joint resolution,* a statement made by both Houses that is signed by the president. None of these carries the force of law; they are simply statements of opinion by Congress. Last, there is the legislative bill, which is passed by both Houses and is signed by the president (or passed over the president's veto) and becomes law.

An early post–World War II study of Congress found that while presidential policy proposals were primarily presented as bills, congressionally initiated actions tended to be expressed as simple resolutions.[14] The situation today is much the same, with one major exception. Congress still relies heavily on resolutions to express its will, as evidenced by its attempts to influence U.S. policy toward Iraq. It first did so in October 2002, when it passed a resolution authorizing President George W. Bush to use force against Iraq. The original 2002 resolution is presented in Box 6.1. Four years later the Senate passed a resolution calling 2006 a period of significant transition to full Iraqi sovereignty . . . thereby creating the conditions for a phased redeployment of United States forces from Iraq." This Republican-sponsored resolution was voted on and passed after a Democratic-sponsored resolution calling for the administration to outline a drawdown of U.S. forces was rejected.

---

### Box 6.1 EXCERPT: HOUSE RESOLUTION AUTHORIZING THE USE OF FORCE AGAINST IRAQ, OCTOBER 2, 2002

**Section 1:**

This joint resolution may be cited as the "Authorization for the Use of Military Force Against Iraq."

**Section 2: Support for United States Diplomatic Efforts.**

The Congress of the United States supports the efforts by the president to:

a. strictly enforce through the United Nations Security Council all relevant Security Council resolutions applicable to Iraq and encourages him in those efforts; and

b. obtain prompt and decisive action by the Security Council to ensure that Iraq abandons its strategy of delay, evasion and noncompliance and promptly and strictly complies with all relevant Security Council resolutions.

**Section 3: Authorization for Use of United States Armed Forces.**

a. *Authorization.* The president is authorized to use the Armed Forces of the United States as he determines to be necessary and appropriate in order to

1. defend the national security of the United States against the continuing threat posed by Iraq; and

2. enforce all relevant United Nations Security Council Resolutions regarding Iraq.

b. *Presidential determination.* In connection with the exercise of the authority granted in subsection (a) to use force the president shall, prior to such exercise or as soon thereafter as may be feasible, but no later than 48 hours after exercising such authority, make available to the Speaker of the House of Representatives and the president pro tempore of the Senate his determination that

1. reliance by the United States on further diplomatic or other peaceful means alone either (A) will not adequately protect the national security of the United States against the continuing threat posed by Iraq or (B) is not likely to lead to enforcement of all relevant United Nations Security Council resolutions regarding Iraq, and

2. acting pursuant to this resolution is consistent with the United States and other countries continuing to take the necessary actions against international terrorists and terrorist organizations, including those nations, organizations or persons who planned, authorized, committed or aided the terrorists attacks that occurred on Sept. 11, 2001.

c. WAR powers resolution requirements.
  1. Specific statutory authorization. Consistent with section 8(a)(1) of the War Powers Resolution, the Congress declares that this section is intended to constitute specific statutory authorization within the meaning of section 5 (b) of the War Powers Resolution.
  2. Applicability of other requirements. Nothing in this resolution supersedes any requirement of the War Powers Resolution.

**Section 4: Reports to Congress.**

a. The president shall, at least once every 60 days, submit to the Congress a report on matters relevant to this joint resolution, including actions taken pursuant to the exercise of authority granted in section 2 and the status of planning for efforts that are expected to be required after such actions are completed, including those actions described in section 7 of Public Law 105338 (the Iraq Liberation Act of 1998).
b. To the extent that the submission of any report described in subsection (a) coincides with the submission of any other report on matters relevant to this joint resolution otherwise required to be submitted to Congress pursuant to the reporting requirements of Public Law 93-148 (the War Powers Resolution), all such reports may be submitted as a single consolidated report to the Congress.
c. To the extent that the information required by section 3 of Public Law 102-1 is included in the report required by this section, such report shall be considered as meeting the requirements of section 3 of Public Law 102-1. ■

---

The very consideration of a resolution can complicate relations with other states. In 2000, a scheduled House vote on a nonbinding resolution labeling Turkey's treatment of Armenians from 1915 to 1923 as genocide became the focal point of intense politicking between the White House and Congress. It was proposed by Representative James Rogan, who was locked in a tight reelection race and whose district has the largest concentration of Armenian Americans in the United States. Turkey protested the action to the Clinton administration and threatened to deny the United States use of its air bases for staging flights over northern Iraq. To press their case, Turkey made full use of its lobbyists. Under pressure from the White House, House Speaker J. Dennis Hastert cancelled the vote, thereby avoiding the diplomatic confrontation between the United States and Turkey.

The White House was not as successful in blocking such a vote in 2007, when both the Senate and House passed nonbonding resolutions labeling Turkish actions against Armenians during and after World War I as genocide. Congress voted to do so over the objections of President George W. Bush and all eight living former secretaries of state. One-third of the members of the Senate cosponsored the resolution there, and in the House, Speaker Nancy Pelosi (D, Calif.), whose district includes larger numbers of Armenians, was a strong supporter of the resolution.

In 2002, the George W. Bush administration was unable to prevent the House (352 to 21) and Senate (92 to 2) from voting favorably on slightly differing resolutions that endorsed Israel's military campaign to dismantle the "terrorist infrastructure" in its occupied territories. Both resolutions characterized Israel's actions as self-defense and part of the global war on terrorism. The Bush administration argued that these resolutions complicated its efforts at mediating a Middle East peace agreement.

One trend that has become more pronounced over time and stands out as an exception to the early post–World War II years is the amount of legislation that bears on U.S. foreign policy and Congress's use of its legislative powers to limit or amend presidentially initiated foreign policy legislation. The sheer volume of foreign policy legislation has become staggering. The 1960 edition of *Legislation on Foreign Relations* only ran 519 pages; by 1985, it was divided into two volumes with a total of 2,698 pages.

**Barnacles** is the term often used to describe the amendments that Congress attaches to foreign policy legislation sought by the president.[15] One type of barnacle is to earmark or designate funds contained within a piece of legislation for a specific country. In passing the fiscal year (FY) 1990 foreign aid bill, Congress earmarked $4 billion in aid for traditional U.S. ally Israel. Most of these barnacles contain escape clauses that allow the president to get around them. Some of the most prominent barnacles lie in the areas of human rights and drug trafficking. A 1986 law requires that the State Department annually certify that recipients of U.S. foreign aid are "fully cooperating" in eradication efforts and the worldwide fight against drugs. Congress then votes to support or reject the State Department's judgment. If a country fails to win certification, it loses American military and economic aid and trade preferences. In 1988, "national interests" were cited in the certification of Panama and Mexico. Five states, Afghanistan, Laos, Paraguay, Syria, and Iran, were decertified. The Senate voted 63–27 to decertify Mexico, but the House refused to do so, and Mexico was able to continue receiving U.S. aid. An escape hatch also exists in the Burmese Freedom and Peace Act of 2003. It called for the ban of all imports from Burma for one year, but it allowed the president to lift the ban at any time if he concluded that Burma was making "substantial and measurable progress" in ending human rights violations and creating a democratic government or that it was in the U.S. national interest to do so.

**BUDGETARY POWERS** Congress's budget powers are equally blunt and difficult to use. In part this is because using them involves three different sets of decisions. Congress must decide on an overall authorization level for the budget under consideration, authorize the expenditure of funds for the programs contained in the budget, and then allocate funds for those programs. These decisions are made in different settings, at different times, and by individuals and committees that are responding to different sets of outside pressures. The decision on the overall budget ceiling is made by Congress as a whole and takes the form of a budget resolution. Authorization decisions are made separately by the committees with legislative jurisdiction over the policy area. Appropriations decisions are made by the House and Senate Appropriations Committee and their subcommittees.

An additional problem with using the budget as an instrument to shape the direction of U.S. foreign policy is that programs cost money but "policies" may not. What policies are able to do is raise expectations, place U.S. prestige on the line, or commit the United States to a course of action in the eyes of other states. Congress faced this reality in 2007, when it considered reducing funding for a missile defense system the Bush administration wanted to build in Eastern Europe and that Russia strenuously opposed. When this type of situation occurs, Congress tends to find that it has little choice but to support—fund—the policy initiative, at least on a cosmetic basis. Senator John Kerry (D, Mass.) spoke to this point in expressing his opposition to the congressional resolution supporting the Persian Gulf War. He noted:

> I hear it from one person after another—"I do not want the President to look bad. . . . The President got us in this position. I am uncomfortable— but I cannot go against him. . . . Are we supposed to go to war because one man—the President—makes a series of unilateral decisions that put us in a box. . . . Are we supposed to go to war because once the President has announced publicly, to reverse or question him is somehow detrimental to the Nation."[16]

War funding presents particular problems for Congress. A Democratic Congress tried and failed to pass a legislation in spring 2007 that linked funds for the Iraq War to a set withdrawal date. Passed by the House by a vote of 218–208 and the Senate by a 51–46 margin, the legislation was vetoed by President Bush, who asserted that a pullout deadline was the equivalent of setting a date for failure. A subsequent compromise bill funding the Iraq War was passed that set up 18 political and legislative benchmarks for judging the success of the war effort along with requiring periodic reports from the president on the political and military situation in Iraq. Not unexpectedly, the first benchmark assessment report submitted by the administration in September 2007 did not end the controversy over the Iraq War, as the administration's many claims of success were challenged by Congress.

Several factors combine to create problems for Congress in trying to use its budgetary powers to control a president during a war. First, there is the inherent uncertainty over projecting the costs of the war. In the case of the Iraq War, political considerations compounded the matter. During the lead-up to the war, the White House economic advisor suggested the cost of the war would be $100–$200 billion. He was quickly replaced, and the estimated cost was lowered to $50–$60 billion. Second, once a war begins, the actual cost of the war becomes heavily dependent on military decisions made by both the United States and its enemy, none of which can always be fully anticipated.

Finally, there is a problem with presidential implementation of congressional budgetary decisions. In 1971, Congress appropriated $700 million for a new manned bomber. The funds went unspent by the Nixon administration because it opposed the project. The reconstruction of Iraq provides another example of the limited ability of Congress' budgetary powers to influence the implementation of American foreign policy. In 2003, the Bush administration called for a quick infusion of money into Iraq to speed its recovery and transformation in the aftermath of the war. Yet, much to the dismay of many in Congress, in June 2004, just days before power was transferred to a new Iraqi government, only 2 percent of that money had been spent. None of the $500 million for health care, $400 million for roads and bridges, or the $4.2 billion for water and sanitation improvements had been spent. The largest area of expenditure was for security and law enforcement, where $194 million of the appropriated $3.2 billion had been dispersed.

An ironic twist of the budgetary process is that Congress often makes foreign policy bureaucracies spend money in ways that they feel are wasteful. In 2009, the Navy decided to end production of a destroyer after 15 classified studies found it vulnerable to long-range missiles. Seven Democratic Senators and Four Republicans demanded that the decision be reversed or they would cut funding for all surface combat ships. One month later, the Pentagon restored these funds. A similar situation existed with the F-22, a plane that has not been used in Iraq or Afghanistan. Secretary of Defense Robert Gates called for its cancellation, but legislators from both parties united to pass legislation appropriating $523 million as a down payment on parts to build 20 more in 2010. With the threat of a veto by President Obama hanging over its head, the Senate finally voted to end production of the F-22 by a vote of 58–40. Still, the House Appropriations Committee unanimously added $2.75 billion in extra funds to the 2010 defense bill for unwanted weapons systems. About one-half were for projects requested by private firms who gave funds to the political action committees of committee members.

OVERSIGHT   Oversight refers to the actions of Congress regarding the bureaucratic implementation of policies such as those we have discussed. In July 2009, controversy erupted when it was revealed that during the George W. Bush administration the CIA was instructed not to inform Congress about an intelligence program that had been run since 2001 after the 9/11 attacks. Obama's CIA Director Leon Panetta ordered the program ended when he was informed about its existence and subsequently informed the House and Senate intelligence committees. Subsequently it was revealed that the core of the program involved hiring a private firm, Blackwater USA, to assassinate top al Qaeda leaders.

Because of earlier controversies over the quality of information being provided to it by the White House, the House Permanent Select Committee on Intelligence had already passed out of committee proposed legislation requiring the president to give each intelligence committee "general information" about intelligence operations where lives may be lost, sources and methods compromised, or significant funds spent. The committee also sought to make the position of Director of the National Security Agency (NSA) subject to Senate confirmation. This move was in response to the NSA's involvement in a warrantless electronic eavesdropping program directed at Americans suspected of being linked to terrorism. Obama threatened to veto any bill containing these requirements.

As this case illustrates, **oversight** is no easy matter. Congress relies on a number of tools to accomplish it. One of the most frequently employed tools is the use of reporting requirements. As we noted earlier, after failing to cut off funds for the Iraq War, Congress switched tactics and set monthly reporting requirements on the administration as well as periodic benchmark assessments on the progress of the war effort. Few policy areas have escaped the reach of congressional reporting requirements initiatives. Congress has required the executive branch to certify such practices as the human rights records of states, their stance on the nonproliferation of nuclear weapons, their efforts to combat drug trafficking, their efforts to stop human trafficking, and their willingness to comply with trade agreements.

Three major types of **reporting requirements** are used by Congress.[17] Periodic reports are produced in a policy area on a regular basis. For example, each year the State Department is required to submit a country report on human rights practices. A second type is the notification that a particular type of foreign policy action has been taken or will be taken. From Congress's point of view, the absence of presidential notifications of covert action was a major issue in the Iran–Contra affair. Most of these reports, however, are far less politically charged and involve changes in the distribution of foreign aid funds, arms sales, and arms control initiatives. In the mid-1980s, an average of over 700 notifications were sent to Congress. The third type of reporting requirement is a one-time report, when Congress is seeking a particular piece of information from the executive branch. In the 1986 Anti-Apartheid Act, Congress identified 10 issues on which it wanted the president to furnish it with information.

In August 2009, Senator Patrick Leahy used the reporting requirement to successfully block a State Department report affirming that Mexico was respecting human rights in its war against drug trafficking. This statement was necessary for Mexico to continue receiving more than $10 million in antinarcotics assistance. Leahy argued the State Department's judgment was premature, and State agreed to rewrite the report before submitting to Congress.

An important variation on the idea of reporting requirements is found in congressional oversight of intelligence. Initially there was little if any meaningful congressional control over the CIA. When asked if the committee he chaired had approved funding a 36,000-man "secret" army in Laos, Senator Allen Ellender, chairperson of the Senate Appropriations CIA subcommittee, replied, "I did not know anything about it. . . . I never asked. . . . It never dawned on me to ask about it. I did see it published in the newspaper some time ago."[18]

Beginning in 1974, Congress's attitude toward the intelligence community began to change. One factor prompting the new outlook was a series of revelations about CIA wrongdoing and excess. The two most publicized ones implicated the CIA in a destabilization campaign directed at bringing down the socialist government of Salvador Allende in Chile and allegations that the CIA had violated its charter by undertaking surveillance of U.S. citizens inside the United States. In their aftermath Congress passed the Hughes–Ryan Amendment to the 1974 Foreign Assistance Act. It required that, except under exceptional circumstances, the CIA inform members of six congressional committees "in a timely fashion of the nature and scope of any CIA operation conducted for purposes other than obtaining information." According to the terms of the Hughes–Ryan Amendment, the president was also required to make a "finding" that each covert operation is important to national security. **Presidential findings** have included such information as the time and duration of the activity, the risks involved, funding restrictions, the relationship to prior NSC decisions, policy considerations, and the origin of the proposal.[19] This has not always meant that Congress has been well informed by the presidential finding. The presidential finding for the Iran arms transfers carried out by the NSC was signed after the operation began, and DCI Casey was instructed not to inform Congress. It is presented in Box 6.2. The 1975 presidential finding supporting U.S. activities in Angola was so vague that only Africa was identified as the location of the

## Box 6.2 PRESIDENTIAL FINDING ON CIA INVOLVEMENT IN ARMS SHIPMENTS TO IRAN

I hereby find that the following operation in a foreign country (including all support necessary to such operation) is important to the national security of the United States, and due to its extreme sensitivity and security risks, I determine it is essential to limit prior notice, and direct the Director of Central Intelligence to refrain from reporting this Finding to the Congress as provided in Section 501 of the National Security Act of 1947, as amended, until I otherwise direct.

Scope

Iran

Description

[Assist selected friendly foreign liaison services, third countries, which have established relationships with Iranian elements, groups, and individuals] sympathetic to U.S. Government interests and which do not conduct or support terrorist actions directed against U.S. persons, property, or interests for the purpose of: (1) establishing a more moderate government in Iran, and (2) obtaining from them significant intelligence not otherwise obtainable, to determine the current Iranian Government's intentions with respect to its neighbors and with respect to terrorist acts, [and (3) furthering the release of the American hostages held in Beirut and preventing additional terrorist acts by these groups.][a] Provide funds, intelligence, counterintelligence, training, guidance and communications, and other necessary assistance to these elements, groups, individuals, liaison services and third countries in support of these activities. The USG will act to facilitate efforts by third parties and third countries to establish contact with moderate elements within and outside the Government of Iran by providing these elements with arms, equipment, and related material in order to enhance the credibility of these elements in their effort to achieve a more pro-U.S. government in Iran by demonstrating their ability to obtain requisite resources to defend their country against Iraq and intervention by the Soviet Union. This support will be discontinued if the U.S. Government learns that these elements have abandoned their goals of moderating their government and appropriated the material for purposes other than that [sic] provided by this Finding.

[a]Point (3) did not appear in the first draft.

*Source:* President's Special Review Board, *The Tower Commission Report* (New York: Bantam, 1987), pp. 217–18. ■

operation. The stated purpose was to provide "material, support, and advice to moderate nationalist movements for their use in creating a stable climate in order to allow genuine self-determination."[20]

There is nothing automatic, however, about information being furnished to Congress. On November 16, 2006, the Senate gave its consent to a plan to create an India-specific exemption to existing laws that outlaw the transfer of nuclear technology to countries that have not signed the Non-Proliferation Treaty. This was done in spite of the fact that the secret intelligence estimate of India's nuclear capabilities and India's ties with Iran, which had been requested by congressional leaders in January, had not yet been given to Congress. The House approved a similar piece of legislation in July, only to be informed after the vote that the Bush administration had decided to impose sanctions on two Indian firms for selling missile parts to Iran. The Iran–Syria Non-Proliferation Act requires the president to report to Congress on the state of the nuclear arsenals of these two countries. A report was due on July 1, 2006, but had not been issued. In September 2009, the House Armed Services Committee unsuccessfully sought to get General Stanley McChrystal to testify about U.S. policy in Afghanistan despite support from members of both parties on the committee. The Obama administration refused, arguing that it had not yet finished its own policy review.

Confronted with an administration unwilling to provide it with information Congress will often turn threaten a congressional hearing or investigation. A case in point is oversight of the Bush administration's controversial domestic intelligence–gathering program and the interrogation methods.

At the heart of the first dispute was the Bush administration's assertion that the president had the legal authority as commander in chief to engage in secret wiretapping of Americans without a warrant, a position many on the Senate Judiciary Committee rejected. In 2002, Bush had signed a secret order authorizing the NSA to undertake a variety of surveillance activities within the United States, including "data mining" of surveillance targets and monitoring telephone calls and e-mails between the United States and abroad if one of the participants was believed to be linked to a terrorist group. The Bush administration also argued that Congress had given its consent by participating in informal briefing to the "Gang of Eight," the leadership of the House and Senate and the intelligence committees, on its domestic spying program. Under the terms by which this process operates staff members are not present and those briefed are prohibited from discussing the information they receive with other members of Congress, including those who serve on the intelligence committees. After the domestic spying program became public, Senator John Rockefeller IV, the ranking Democrat on the Senate Select Intelligence Committee, revealed that he sent a letter in 2003 to Vice President Dick Cheney complaining that the briefings were unsatisfactory. It stated, "Given the security restrictions associated with this information, and the inability to consult staff or counsel on my own, I feel unable to fully evaluate, much less endorse, these activities."[21]

The second point of contention centered on the legal status of prisoners held at Guantanamo Bay and the interrogation methods used. From the outset the George W. Bush administration claimed that the detainees did not have access to U.S. courts and could be held as long as the president felt appropriate because they were unlawful enemy combatants captured on the battlefield and because Guantanamo Bay was not part of the United States. The administration defended its interrogation tactics as necessary to obtain crucial information about potential terrorist acts and denied that waterboarding and other methods employed constituted torture.

Both these claims were rejected by members of Congress. In 2007, Senate Democrats introduced legislation restoring *habeas corpus* rights to detainees. The legislation would place strict limits on a president's power to determine who is an enemy combatant and when human rights violations have occurred. The year before Congress responded to growing concern about the morality and legality of the administration's interrogation methods by passing the McCain Detainee Amendment to the 2006 Defense Department Appropriations Act. The amendment established uniform standards for detainee treatment and interrogation, based on the Army Field Manual on Intelligence Interrogation, and put forward broad prohibitions on the cruel, inhuman, and degrading treatment of prisoners. While lauding its intent, critics noted that the McCain Detainee Amendment did not cover the CIA or persons not in the custody or physical control of the United States and did not prohibit making changes to the Army Field Manual.

## The Absence of a Single Voice

Traditionally, the work of Congress was done in committees. It was here that the political deals were made and the technical details of legislation were worked out. Congress as a whole was expected to quietly and expeditiously give its consent to committee decisions, and more often than not, it did. Beginning in the early 1970s, the focus of decision making shifted from the full committee to the subcommittee. The result has been an even greater decentralization of Congress, which is visible in a number of ways.

First, there is the increased attention that the executive branch must give to the foreign policy views of all members of Congress. As one State Department official put it, "It used to be that all one had to do was contact the chairman and a few ranking members of a committee, now all 435 members plus 100 senators have to be contacted."[22] The Defense Department has experienced a similar change in its dealings with Congress. In 1964, Defense Department representatives spent 1,575 witness-hours before Congress. In 1976, that number increased to 7,746.[23] As a result, we have to look in many places to find foreign policy legislation, and these pieces are not easily assembled into a coherent whole. In 2000, legislation allowing the sale of food to Cuba was part of an agricultural spending bill. In 1998, Congress sought to limit President Clinton's ability to move forward on the Kyoto Protocol by attaching an amendment to the appropriations bill for the Environmental Protection Agency that prohibited it from spending money on planning efforts related to the treaty.

Second, there is the growing tendency for prospective pieces of legislation to be referred to more than one committee. Multiple referrals are necessary because of the lack of fit between the jurisdictions of congressional committees and policy areas. One study found a dozen Senate committees involved in foreign economic policy and nearly 50 subcommittees involved in foreign policy toward the Third World.[24] Another study found that the House Armed Services Committee had jurisdiction over 13 agencies and departments and 12 legislative areas, while its Senate counterpart had jurisdiction over 10 agencies and 11 legislative areas. Former Representative Lee Hamilton asserts that the greatest concentration of foreign policy power is now in the appropriations committees, where domestic concerns hold greater weight than foreign policy ones.[25]

## Policy Entrepreneurship

A change in attitude has accompanied the trend toward increasing decentralization. Policy individualism has replaced party loyalty as the motivation behind much congressional action. As a result, the long-standing congressional norms of deference and apprenticeship have been replaced by expectations of power sharing and policy input. "Entrepreneurship" is the label frequently attached to this new outlook. A **policy entrepreneur** is someone who is looking for opportunities to make political capital out of policy gaps.[26] The entrepreneur is different from the traditional foreign policy **"gadfly,"** who raises issues in order to influence the terms of the policy debate and is concerned with long-term policy gains.[27]

Policy entrepreneurship surfaced early in the Obama administration. Senate Republicans led by Jim DeMint, who never visited Latin America, began attacking the administration for its failure to support the leaders of the Honduran coup that ousted President Manuel Zelaya in June 2009. The new Honduran leaders quickly spent almost one-half million dollars on lobbying for U.S. recognition, which the Obama administration and other countries have refused to grant. For its part Democrats sought unsuccessfully to block Republican fact-finding trips to Honduras.

Gadflies are found across the political spectrum. Prominent conservatives have included Jesse Helms, while George McGovern was a noteworthy liberal. Among the most outspoken gadflies today are John McCain, Chuck Hegal, and Jack Murtha. The policy entrepreneur is motivated largely by short-term considerations. The primary one is reelection and the belief that the likelihood of being reelected is enhanced if one can claim credit for authoring or amending important bills or publicly exposing a major problem or scandal. As one observer notes, the problem with credit taking, position taking, and self-advertising is that all three are concerned with the public's image of a piece of legislation and not with how it actually turns out.[28]

Foreign policy has always been a major area of entrepreneurial activity. The Senate Foreign Relations Committee has long been a focal point of media attention and a breeding ground for presidential candidates, who used its visibility to their political advantage. "Japan bashing," in the form of harshly worded congressional resolutions, has become a common staple of U.S. international economic policy. In 1995, many in Congress moved aggressively to promote retaliatory trade legislation against those who trade with Cuba and

Iran. Senator Jesse Helms and Representative Dan Burton sought to bar sugar imports to the United States from anyone purchasing or renting property in Cuba that was confiscated after Castro seized power in 1959. Canada saw itself as the target of this legislation and sent a sharply worded protest to the United States stating that Helms–Burton violated North American Free Trade Agreement (NAFTA) and WTO obligations entered into by the United States. At the same time that this legislation was being debated, the Clinton administration and Congress were engaged in a race to see who could propose the toughest actions against Iran. The administration barred Texas-based Conoco Oil Company from developing oil and gas fields with Iran, but Republicans in Congress wanted to go even further. Senator Alfonse D'Amato and Representative Peter King introduced a bill that, according to D'Amato, would force a foreign corporation or individual to "choose between trade with the United States or trade with Iran."

Individual activity, whether as a policy entrepreneur or as a gadfly, has left a distinct mark on the conduct of American foreign policy by forcing foreign dignitaries to expand their negotiating agendas. Seeking to gain congressional support for the Clinton administration's plan to pay off a portion of its UN debt, Secretary General Kofi Annan met with Senate Foreign Relations Committee chairperson Jesse Helms. Annan agreed to the meeting only after President Clinton told him it was essential to gain Helms's support if he hoped to see the United States pay its back dues.

## Staff Aides

Information has always been a problem for Congress when it comes to making foreign policy. Few members can hope to acquire the background and expertise to understand and stay on top of such a wide range of issues as Defense Department appropriations, export controls, world hunger, and recognizing the Transkei territory in South Africa. The emergence of a large and well-informed number of staff aides has given the problem a new focus.[29] The problem is no longer one of acquiring needed information from the executive branch or party leaders. It is now also one of using information in a controlled and coherent fashion. Concerns have been expressed about whether (1) the staffers are serving Congress or just leading willing members from issue to issue as they build their own reputations, and (2) an activist staff might not be overloading Congress with new issues, thereby robbing it of the time needed for debate and deliberation.

The tremendous increase in staff size is visible throughout Congress. In 1947, there were roughly 500 committee and 2,000 personal staffers. In 1979, these numbers had jumped to 3,000 committee staff aides and over 10,000 personal staff aides. Congress as a whole has also increased its information-gathering and -processing capabilities by establishing or increasing the size of the Congressional Research Service (established in 1914), the Congressional Accounting Office (1921), the Office of Technology Assessment (1972), and the Congressional Budget Office (1974). In 1976, the Office of Technology Assessment supervised a study for the Senate Foreign Relations

Committee that estimated the number of American casualties in a nuclear war. Its findings challenged Defense Department assumptions and methodology. It has also studied questions relating to nuclear terrorism and energy policy.

In addition to being able to draw on vast amounts of information from their staffs and congressional research services, representatives and senators can also draw on the products of private nonprofit research institutes and think tanks such as the Brookings Institute, the Cato Institute, and the Heritage Foundation.[30] Until the 1970s, think tanks were relatively few in number. Today, they are prominent fixtures on the Washington, DC political landscape.

## THE INFLUENCE OF PARTY AND REGION

From what we have seen so far, it is clear that Congress has great difficulty speaking with one voice on foreign policy matters. We can bring this difficulty into even greater focus by examining the influence of party and region on foreign policy decisions. The overwhelming majority of votes occur along party lines, and this tendency has become more pronounced since the 1980s. Strong as it may be, party affiliation cannot withstand all of the competing pressures that representatives and senators face when they vote. This is true even when their party controls the White House. Republicans deserted President George W. Bush on two major issues in 2007. The first was immigration reform, where a coalition of Republicans and Democrats united to allow a filibuster to continue and block consideration of reform legislation supported by the president. The second issue was the Iraq War, where during the summer, in advance of the administration's September benchmark assessment report, a series of Republican senators led by Richard Lugar (Ind.) and Pete Domeneci (N.M.) called for a policy change. Electoral considerations are not necessarily a driving force in decisions to abandon one's party leadership. Of the first 13 Republicans to support an antiadministration resolution on Iraq after the 2006 midterm elections, only 3 got less than 55 percent of the vote in those elections.

These splits within the Republican Party are not new. They began to surface in the late 1990s as senior Republican leaders embraced an internationalist outlook rooted in Cold War foreign policy triumphs, while those elected for the first time in the 1990s and later have a different world view.[31] Junior Republicans have opposed supporting loan guarantees to Mexico, favor privatization of foreign aid, oppose expensive new weapons systems, and show little interest in bipartisan resolutions supporting the president in Bosnia or elsewhere. The Democratic Party is also beset with its own internal struggles. The crafting of anti–Iraq War resolutions in 2007 was marked by significant internal party bargaining in an effort to write a document that all Democrats could support.

One area where partisanship appears to trump all other factors in influencing congressional involvement in foreign policy involves controlling presidential war powers.[32] The single best predictor of whether or not Congress will remain quiet or vocally oppose presidential calls for war is its partisan composition. When the opposition party controls, Congress raises its voice. Congressional opposition inspired by party politics may not prevent a president from acting, but it is capable of raising the political costs of military action and lead presidents to alter their plans or abandon them entirely.

Regional interests are also significant factors in influencing congressional votes. Today, as in the 1890s and the 1930s, the changing nature of the global economy and the uneven impact it has on different areas of the United States has produced regional conflict over how to define the American national interest.[33] From this vantage point U.S. foreign policy can be seen as driven by a coalition of the South and the West, regions that benefit from a foreign policy designed to promote free trade and assure international stability. Opposed to it is the Northeast, which, though it once benefited from such policies, now sees itself as economically disadvantaged by them and favors protectionism and cuts in defense spending. This regional alignment of forces, rather than a Republican–Democratic divide, is what steered the Reagan military buildup through Congress.

Geography also influences foreign policy votes in one other important way. The drive for reelection makes members of Congress extremely protective of how any piece of legislation affects their state or district. Long-time senator Henry "Scoop" Jackson, a conservative Democrat from Washington and long-time fixture on the Armed Services Committee, was known as the "Senator from Boeing" for his ability to steer contracts to Boeing aircraft, which was headquartered in Washington. In 1995, the Republican-controlled Senate Armed Services Committee added $5 billion in funds for weapons spending onto Clinton's request. Eighty-one percent of these funds were to go to states represented by committee members. This concern for "pork" extends beyond the committee system. At one time the contract for the B-1 bomber had 400 subcontracts in over 400 of the 435 districts of the House. In 2008 congressional leaders threatened to withhold funding for a $40 billion aircraft construction program because the Pentagon rejected Boeing's bid in favor of one by Northrup and European Aeronautic and Space. In leading the opposition, Rep. Jack Murtha stated, "there is the industrial base you have to consider. The political implications are important."

## OUTSOURCING FOREIGN POLICY

Senator Trent Lott addressed the Senate on September 23, 2002, on the subject of special commissions, specifically the creation of the 9/11 Commission. He observed that, in his opinion, congressional commissions were "an abdication of responsibility." Why, he wondered "do we have an Armed Services Committee, an Intelligence Committee, a Government Affairs Committee, or a Foreign Affairs Committee?"[34] His comments had little impact. Special commissions have become a prominent feature of the Washington political landscape. In recent memory we have had the National Commission on Terrorist Attacks on the United States (the 9/11 Commission), the Commission on the Intelligence Capabilities of the United States Regarding Weapons of Mass Destruction, the United States Trade Deficit Review Commission, the U.S.–China Security Review Commission, and the Defense Base Closure and Realignment Commission.

Congress (and the president) has turned to commissions for a number of reasons. First, the appointment of a commission represents a symbolic response to a perceived foreign policy problem. Second, it reflects the cumulative impact of rising partisanship with the Congress and between the Congress and the president that has frustrated efforts to deal with foreign policy problems in a nonaccusatory manner. Commissions take political pressure off policy makers in both branches by providing them with a political cover for making difficult decisions. Third, commissions provide an opportunity for educating the public and for information gathering that extends beyond the closed network of congressional staffers, committee and subcommittee chairs, and executive branch officials. Their recommendations are not, however, always welcome. Senator John Warner, objecting to the Defense Base Closure Commissions recommendation to shut down major facilities in Virginia, referred to its decision-making process as "rigged."

Establishing a commission is no guarantee that the problem will be solved, or even that its recommendations will be listened to. Many of the recommendations of the 9/11 Commission were ignored. A December 2005 "report card" issued by members of the 9/11 Commission gave the administration 5 Fs and 12 Ds for its follow-through in implementing its recommendations. It received only one A, and that was for its antiterrorism finance efforts.[35] President Bush responded to the Iraq Study Group's recommendations for a phased drawdown of U.S. forces in Iraq by asking for recommendations and studies from within the executive branch and went forward with a surge that increased U.S. forces in Iraq.

## CONGRESS AND THE PRESIDENT: THE CHANGING RELATIONSHIP

The relationship between Congress and the president is not static. Viewed over time, congressional–presidential relations have shown a great deal of variation. One way to capture the changing relationship is by looking at the degree to which Congress has been assertive and active in its dealings with the president on foreign policy matters.[36] Combining these two dimensions produces four patterns. A *competitive* Congress is both active and assertive in foreign policy and thus quite willing to challenge a president's lead. A *disengaged* Congress is neither active nor assertive and tends to readily follow a president's foreign policy preferences. A *supportive* Congress is one that is active but not aggressive. It cooperates with the president on a broad range of foreign policy initiatives without challenging him. Finally, a *strategic* Congress is not particularly active but is willing and capable of challenging a president on specific issues that conflict with its foreign policy agenda.

From the end of World War II until about 1958, a *supportive Congress* existed. Relations between the two branches were largely harmonious. Bipartisanship was the order of the day. The president was the acknowledged architect of American foreign policy, and Congress's role was to reaffirm his policy initiatives and provide him with the means to act. Often its participation took on a plebiscitary character, with the passage of area resolutions such as those on the Middle East, Taiwan, and Latin America. Periods of dissent did occur, such as after the "loss of China" and during the McCarthy hearings, but overall, the Cold War consensus held.

The next decade, 1958–1968, saw the emergence of a *strategic Congress*. The Cold War principles around which the earlier bipartisan consensus was built had by now begun to fray. Congress was not in open revolt against the president; however, proclamations of support were still present, most notably the Gulf of Tonkin Resolution, and failures such as the Bay of Pigs did not evoke partisan attacks. But pockets of resistance had now formed, and Congress did move to challenge the president selectively. Two key points of confrontation were the Vietnam War and the existence of a missile gap.

From 1968 into the mid-1980s, Congress was both active and assertive. This *competitive Congress* not only sought to limit the president's ability to conduct foreign policy by passing such measures as the War Powers Resolution and the Case–Zablocki Act, it resisted many of the president's most important foreign policy initiatives. The Jackson–Vanik Amendment undermined Nixon's détente policy, Carter was challenged on the Panama Canal Treaties, and Ford was rebuffed on an arms sales agreement to Turkey.

The period from the mid-1980s until September 11, 2001, marked a return to a *strategic Congress*. Once again, Congress selectively engaged the president on foreign policy issues. In some cases, such as the annual vote on MFN status for China, the interactions became almost ritualistic. On other occasions, such as the Comprehensive Test Ban Treaty, ratifying NAFTA, and granting fast-track trade authority, the conflicts were highly partisan and spirited.

The terrorist attacks of 9/11 led to the emergence of a *disengaged Congress,* one that was willing to cede the authority to make crucial foreign policy decisions to the president. Nowhere is this more evident than in George W. Bush's ability to obtain a use-of-force resolution from Congress against Iraq by votes of 77–23 in the Senate and 296–133 in the House. Congress was not totally compliant, but it did not directly challenge the president. Objections to the Bush administration's proposed language that authorizing the president "to use all means that he determined to be appropriate" was addressed in behind-the-scenes meetings. In its place was language acceptable to the administration that authorized Bush to "defend the security of the United States against the continuing threat posed by Iraq and to enforce all relevant UN resolutions." Also inserted was reporting language consistent with that used in the War Powers Resolution, language that the administration accepted without at the same time accepting the constitutionality of the War Powers Resolution. Senator Robert Byrd, who opposed the resolution, said, "How have we gotten to this low point in the history of Congress? Are we too feeble to  resist the demand of a president who is determined to bend the collective will of Congress to his will?"[37]

This disengaged Congress did not last long. It soon showed signs of moving back toward a strategic Congress, and by 2005, it was firmly in place. George W. Bush and Congress regularly sparred over the conduct of the Iraq War toward the end of his presidency. Bush did achieve a significant victory in 2008 when Congress approved his controversial nuclear trade deal with India, which gave that country access to use nuclear technology for the first time since it conducted a nuclear test in 1974. Advocates saw it as a means for bringing India's nuclear program more closely under international inspection. Critics argued it undermined efforts to reduce the size of nuclear weapons inventories.

President Barack Obama and Congress tangled early in his administration over his handling of Guantanamo Bay detainees. Obama announced his intention in January 2009 to close the Guantanamo Bay facility and allow prisoners cleared for release to resettle in the United States. Bipartisan opposition caused him to abandon this plan in June. He also encountered opposition to his plan to continue Bush's practice of prolonged detention without trial for those detainees judged to be too much of a risk to release. Some senators led by Russ Feingold argued that doing so would set the stage for future Guantanamo Bays and injure both U.S. national security and its legal system.

## OVER THE HORIZON

The fundamental problem facing Congress in exercising its foreign policy voice in the future is just that which Congress faces in trying to determine how and if it should undertake an investigation in President Bush's counterterrorist policies. At the core of this problem is the challenge of managing the contradictory pressures for efficiency and participation.

In looking over the horizon, one area where we can expect to find a great deal of activity involves the congressional exercise of its war powers. In 2008, a bipartisan National War Powers Commission called upon Congress to pass the War Powers Consultation Act.[38] At its core was the requirement that the president consult with Congress before undertaking any military combat operations expected to last more than one week. A loophole does exist for extreme circumstances. Congress for its part must declare war or otherwise authorize that conflict in 30 days. If it does not, then further steps are called for.

A second area in which we can expect to see increased congressional involvement in foreign policy involves trade legislation. As we noted, Congress' ability to protect itself from voices calling for protectionism has lessened considerably with the failure to renew presidential fast-track authority. The focal point of attention may be the NAFTA. Calls for its renegotiation are already being heard, as segments of the American economy argue it is giving Mexican and Canadian firms an unfair advantage, while others complain about the lax enforcement of labor rights and environmental standards.

## CRITICAL THINKING QUESTIONS

1. Is there a need for a new War Powers Act?
2. Which is a more important influence on how members of Congress with foreign policy issues, party or geography?
3. What changes would you make to Congress's internal structure and operating procedures to make its voice more effective in foreign policy?

## KEY TERMS

barnacles 158
gadfly 165
legislative veto 150
oversight 160
permanent normal trade
  relations 152

policy entrepreneur 165
presidential finding 161
ratify 145
reporting
  requirement 161

trade promotional
  authority 152
War Powers
  Resolution 150

## FURTHER READING

Colton Campbell, Campbell, et al. (eds.), *Congress and the Politics of Foreign Policy* (Upper Saddle River, NJ: Prentice Hall, 2003).

Louis Henkin, *Foreign Affairs and the Constitution* (Mineola, NY: Foundation Press, 1972).

William Howell and Jon Pevehouse, *While Dangers Gather: Congressional Checks on Presidential War Powers* (Princeton: Princeton University Press, 2007).

*National War Powers Commission Report* (Charlottesville, VA: The Miller Center of Public Affairs, University of Virginia, 2008).

Norman Ornstein and Thomas Mann, "When Congress Checks Out," *Foreign Affairs,* 85 (2006), 67–82.

## NOTES

1. Norman Ornstein and Thomas Mann, "When Congress Checks Out," *Foreign Affairs,* 85 (2006), 67–82.
2. Douglas Bennett, Jr., "Congress in Foreign Policy: Who Needs It?" *Foreign Affairs,* 57 (1978), 40–50.
3. David M. O'Brien, "Presidential and Congressional Relations in Foreign Affairs," in Colton Campbell et al. (eds.), *Congress and the Politics of Foreign Policy* (Upper Saddle River, NJ: Prentice Hall, 2003), p. 73.
4. David Auerswald and Forrest Maltzman, "Policymaking Through Advice and Consent: Treaty Consideration by the United States Senate," *Journal of Politics,* 65 (2003), 1102.
5. Auerswald and Maltzman, "Policymaking Through Advice and Consent," 1097–1110; C. James DeLaet and James M. Scott, "Treaty-Making and Partisan Politics: Arms Control and the U.S. Senate, 1960–2001," *Foreign Policy Analysis,* 2 (2006), 177–200.
6. See David Auerswald, "Senate Reservations to Security Treaties," *Foreign Policy Analysis,* 2 (2006), 83–100.
7. Theodor Meron, "The Treaty Power: The International Legal Effect of Changes in Obligations Initiated by the Congress," in Thomas M. Franck (ed.), *The Tethered Presidency* (New York: New York University Press, 1981), pp. 103–40.
8. William L. Furlong, "Negotiations and Ratification of the Panama Canal Treaty," in John Spanier and Joseph Nogee (eds.), *Congress, the Presidency, and American Foreign Policy* (Elmsford, NY: Pergamon, 1981), pp. 77–107.
9. The material in this section is drawn from the accounts by Furlong; and Cecil Crabb, Jr., and Pat M. Holt, *Invitation to Struggle: Congress, the President, and Foreign Policy,* 2nd ed. (Washington, DC: Congressional Quarterly, 1984).
10. Robert F. Turner, *The War Powers Resolution: Its Implementation in Theory and Practice* (Philadelphia: Foreign Policy Research Institute, 1983), presents a thorough

and critical review of the cases to which the War Powers Resolution has been and could have been applied.

11. Congressional Research Service, *Foreign Policy Effects of the Supreme Court's Legislative Veto Decision* (Washington, DC: Congressional Research Service, February 23, 1984).

12. House Committee on Foreign Affairs, *The War Powers Resolution: Relevant Documents, Correspondence, and Reports* (Washington, DC: U.S. Government Printing Office, 1983); Reagan's actions are examined in Charles Madden, "Foreign Policy Report," *National Journal 16* (May 19, 1984), 989–93.

13. On the Iraq War see Louis Fisher, "Deciding on War Against Iraq," *Political Science Quarterly*, 118 (2003), 389–410; and Fisher, "Presidential Wars," in Eugene Wittkopf and James McCormick (eds.), *The Domestic Sources of American Foreign Policy*, 4th ed. (Lanham, MD: Rowman & Littlefield, 2004), pp. 155–70.

14. James A. Robinson, *Congress and Foreign Policy Making: A Study in Legislative Influence and Initiative* (Homewood, IL: Dorsey, 1962), p. 110.

15. I. M. Destler, "Dateline Washington: Congress as Boss," *Foreign Policy*, 42 (1981), 161–80.

16. *The Congressional Record*, January 11, 1991, pp. S250–51.

17. Ruth Collier, "Foreign Policy by Reporting Requirement," *Washington Quarterly*, 11 (1988), 74–84.

18. Quoted in Victor Marchetti and John Marks, *The CIA and the Cult of Intelligence* (New York: Dell, 19080), p. 324.

19. William Corson, *Armies of Ignorance: The Rise of the American Intelligence Empire* (New York: Dial, 1977), p. 472.

20. John Stockwell, *In Search of Enemies* (New York: Norton, 1978), p. 47.

21. Charles Babington and Dafna Linzer, "Senator Sounded Alarm," *The Washington Post* December 20, 2005, p. A10.

22. Roger H. Davidson, "Subcommittee Government: New Channels for Policy Making," in Thomas E. Mann and Norman J. Ornstein (eds.), *The New Congress* (Washington, DC: American Enterprise Institute, 1981), p. 130.

23. Amos A. Jordon and William J. Taylor, Jr., *American National Security: Policy and Process* (Baltimore, MD: Johns Hopkins University Press, 1981), p. 121.

24. Thomas L. Brewer, *American Foreign Policy: A Contemporary Introduction,* 2nd ed. (Englewood Cliffs, NJ: Prentice Hall, 1986), p. 119.

25. Lee Hamilton, *A Creative Tension* (Washington, DC: Woodrow Wilson Center Press, 2002).

26. David Price, *Who Makes the Laws?* (Cambridge, MA: Schenkman, 1972), p. 330.

27. Joshua Muravchik, *The Senate and National Security: A New Mood*, Washington Paper #80 (Beverly Hills, CA: Sage, 1980), pp. 57–60.

28. I. M. Destler, "Executive–Congressional Conflict in Foreign Policy: Explaining It: Coping with It," in Lawrence Dodd and Bruce Oppenheimer (eds.), *Congress Reconsidered* (Washington, D.C.: CQ Press, 2001), p. 301.

29. For a discussion of congressional staffs, see Michael J. Malbin, "Delegation, Deliberation, and the New Role of Congressional Staff," in Thomas Mann and John Ornstein (eds.), *The New Congress* (Washington, D.C.: American Enterprise Institute, 1981), pp. 134–77; and Muravchik, *The Senate and National Security.*

30. James A. Smith, *The Idea Brokers: Think Tanks and the Rise of the New Policy Elite* (New York: The Free Press, 1991), and David Newsom, *The Public and Foreign Policy* (Bloomington: Indiana University Press, 1996).

31. James Kitfield, "The Folk Who Live on the Hill," *The National Interest, 58* (1999/2000), 48–55.

32. William Howell and Jon Pevehouse, "When Congress Stops Wars," *Foreign Affairs,* 96 (2007), 95–107.

33. Peter Trubowitz, *Defining the National Interest* (Chicago: University of Chicago Press, 1998).

34. Trent Lott, "Special Commissions," *Congressional Record,* September 23, 2002, pp. S9050–53.

35. Dan Eggen, "U.S. Is Given Failing Grades by 9/11 Panel," *The Washington Post,* December 6, 2006, p. A1.

36. James Scott and Ralph Carter, "Acting on the Hill," *Congress & the Presidency,* 29 (2002), 151–69.

37. James Lindsay, "Deference and Defiance," *Presidential Studies Quarterly,* 33 (2003), 543.

38. *National War Powers Commission Report,* The Miller Center of Public Affairs, University of Virginia, 2008.

# Presidency

For the Clinton administration, "Black October" began in Somalia on October 3, 1993, with the Battle of Mogadishu between U.S. military forces and guerrilla forces led by the most powerful Somali warlord, General Mohammed Farah Aidid. Two Black Hawk helicopters were shot down by rocket-propelled grenades. While some of the soldiers on the downed helicopters managed to reach safety, some did not. A rescue assault followed. The final tally showed 18 American soldiers dead, 73 wounded, and 1 taken hostage. Scenes of bodies of some soldiers being dragged through the streets of Mogadishu were captured on film and broadcast worldwide. Only days later, on October 12, the USS *Harlan County* attempted to enter Port-au-Prince harbor in Haiti. Its visit was part of a United Nations plan to restore Jean-Bertrand Aristide to power. Elected in December 1990, he was overthrown in a September 1991 coup. Instead of being welcomed with open arms, the *Harlan County* was met by an angry crowd shouting "Somalia, Somalia." After a few days it turned away without docking and departed.

President Bill Clinton struggled to gain control of the decision making in both cases. Virtually, without recognizing what was happening, the Somali mission had gone from one of providing emergency food supplies to capturing Aidid and removing him from power. Clinton's top advisors in Washington were not experts on Somalia, a country that had mattered little to the United States for most of the Cold War, but what they knew made them skeptical, if not opposed, to the U.S military presence there. On the other hand, his key appointee in Somalia pressed for military action against the leading. In Haiti, no one in the administration expected trouble. A July agreement brokered by the United States and the United Nations had put into place an agreement for a peaceful transfer of power and the ending of economic sanctions. The *Harlan County* was bringing in an advance unit of UN police and military forces to train the Haitian police and army and rebuild the country's infrastructure.

## WEAK PRESIDENT OR STRONG PRESIDENT

In the eyes of the public, it is the president who makes American foreign policy. True or not, Somalia and Haiti were seen as Clinton's fault. What has been unclear to the public and debated by scholars is whether we have a weak president or a strong president. The traditional image of the president is that of a weak leader who is often little more than a clerk because he lacks the power to command others to act and must instead rely on the ability to persuade.[1] Far from running the government the president struggles simply to comprehend what is going on.[2] In 2003, President George W. Bush had a conversation with Secretary of Defense Donald Rumsfeld and Jerry Brenner, who headed the Coalition Provisional Authority in Iraq. Bush asked who was in charge of finding weapons of mass destruction in Iraq. Rumsfeld said Brenner was; Brenner said Rumsfeld was.[3] Information does not come to the presidents automatically (Assistant National Security Advisor Stephen Hadley first found out about the orders for de-Baathification and disbanding of the Iraqi military when Brenner publicly announced them), nor can they count on speed and secrecy in making and carrying out decisions.

This view is challenged by those who see the president as at least potentially a strong powerful leader, one capable of unilateral action.[4] Unilateral presidential action is not a matter of presidents usurping congressional powers as much as it is being able to take advantage of ambiguities in the constitutional distribution of powers, the existence of vaguely worded and ambiguous legislative language and the inherent difficulties that Congress, the courts, and other political competitors face in acting in a unified fashion. By acting first and alone, the president places political competitors in the position of having to undo what he has just done. The **unilateral president** has many tools at his disposal ranging from issuing executive orders and national security directives to setting up new organizations and redefining their responsibilities.

During World War II, Franklin Roosevelt issued an executive order relocating and interning over 110,000 Japanese in the United States. In 1948, Harry Truman desegregated the military through an executive order. John Kennedy unilaterally created the Peace Corps after Congress was unable to pass the necessary enabling legislation. Numbered among the national security agencies created by presidential action or the actions of one of his appointees are the National Security Agency and the Defense Intelligence Agency. In March 2008, President Bush took away much of the power of the Intelligence Oversight Board.[5] The board was created by President Gerald Ford after the Watergate investigations as a means for protecting citizen's rights. Under the rules established by Ford, when the board uncovered intelligence actions that were "unlawful or contrary to executive order," it had to report that finding to both the president and the attorney general. Under Bush's executive order, its authority to inform the attorney general was deleted and the president was to be informed only if other officials were not "adequately" addressing the matter.

The debate over whether the president is weak or is capable of exercising unilateral power is ongoing. As noted above, George W. Bush can be used to illustrate both positions. In the remainder of the chapter, we examine three potential sources of weakness and strength: (1) the ability of the president to make foreign policy within the constitutional distribution of powers we introduced in the last chapter, (2) the president's personal traits, and (3) the organizational structure of the presidency.

## THE PRESIDENT AND THE FOREIGN AFFAIRS CONSTITUTION

The president and Congress are both bound by the constitution, yet over time the president has developed a number of strategies for circumventing the power of Congress on those occasions where it is exercised. In this section, we examine four of the most important strategies that are at the president's disposal: using executive agreements, issuing signing statements, using unofficial ambassadors, and engaging in undeclared wars.

## Executive Agreements

The U.S. Constitution specifies that the Senate shall give its advice and consent to treaties, but it does not define what a treaty is or what international agreements are to be made in this form. From the outset, presidents have claimed the constitutional authority to engage in international agreements by means other than treaties. This alternative is known as an **executive agreement,** and over time it became the favored presidential method for entering into understandings with other states.

Unlike a treaty, an executive agreement does not require the consent of the Senate before coming into force. The U.S. Supreme Court has ruled that it carries the same legal force as a treaty. The principal limit on its use is political, not legal. This came through quite clearly in the dispute between President George H. W. Bush and Congress over how best to protect Chinese students in the United States following the Tiananmen Square massacre of 1989. Bush promised to issue an executive order while Congress considered legislation. Each viewed the other's action as misguided. Congress felt the president's action did not make enough of a symbolic statement, and Bush argued that the congressional action was unnecessary and complicated his foreign policy dealings with China. Bush successfully vetoed the legislation.

The number of executive agreements compared to treaties has increased steadily over time. Between 1789 and 1839, the United States entered into 60 treaties and 27 executive agreements. A century later, between 1889 and 1939, those numbers had grown to 524 treaties and 917 executive agreements. Since the administration of Richard Nixon, presidents have favored executive agreements over treaties by ratios ranging from 25.6:1 under Gerald Ford to 9.9:1 under Bill Clinton. In his first two years in office, George W. Bush's administration entered into 21 treaties and 262 executive agreements, a ratio of 12.5:1.[6]

Additional insight can be gained by looking at how heavily the president has relied on executive agreements in various policy areas. One study showed that from 1946 to 1972, 371 diplomatic agreements were entered into by the United States. Only 26.7 percent were executive agreements. However, throughout this period, every president relied more heavily on executive agreements than on treaties for making major military commitments. Numbered among the 99 agreements were establishing military bases in the Philippines (1947); a military security agreement with South Korea (1949); a U.S. military mission in El Salvador (1957); security pledges to Turkey, Iran, and Pakistan (1959); and the military use of Bahrain (1971).

Documents uncovered in the National Archives after the Persian Gulf War revealed a lengthy history of secret presidential agreements with Saudi Arabia.[7] In 1947, President Harry Truman entered into an agreement with King Ibn Saud that stated that "one of the basic policies of [the] United States in [the] Near East is unqualifiedly to support [the] territorial integrity and political independence of Saudi Arabia." The document continued, "If Saudi Arabia should therefore be attacked by another power or be under threat of attack, the United States through the medium of [the] United Nations would take energetic measures to ward off such aggression." In 1963, President John

Kennedy also entered into a secret agreement with Saudi Arabia. On the heels of an Egyptian-inspired coup and the assassination of a member of the Saudi royal family, Kennedy sent a U.S. fighter squadron to train in Saudi Arabia as a public show of support for that government. What was not made public was that Kennedy had authorized these units to use force against Egypt if they were provoked.

On a number of occasions, the Senate has attempted to curb the president's use of executive agreements. Two efforts have been particularly noteworthy. The first was the **Bricker Amendment**. It would have required that executive agreements receive the same two-thirds vote of approval from the Senate that treaties must get. In 1954, the Bricker Amendment failed by one vote to get the two-thirds majority needed in the Senate to set into motion the amendment ratification process at the state level.

The second was the 1972 Case–Zablocki Act, which required that Congress be informed of all executive agreements. The goal was to give Congress the opportunity to take action to block these agreements if it saw fit. According to Senator Clifford Case, this act was needed because there were at least 4,000 executive agreements in effect in the early 1970s that Congress knew nothing about.[8] The Case–Zablocki Act did not end the practice of secret executive agreements. In part, the problem is definitional. In 1975, Representative Les Aspin estimated that 400–600 agreements had not yet been reported to Congress because the White House claimed that they were understandings, oral promises, or statements of political intent but not executive agreements.[9] Included among these were a 1973 secret message that President Nixon had sent to North Vietnam promising reconstruction aid in return for a peace agreement, Henry Kissinger's 1975 understanding with Israel and Egypt that U.S. personnel would be stationed in the Sinai as part of the disengagement process, and the 1975 Helsinki Accords.

## Signing Statements

Passing legislation is not the equivalent of changing the direction of U.S. foreign policy. Presidents still have the ability to resist the will of Congress. Presidents may also act unilaterally to thwart Congress by issuing **signing statements**. Some signing statements amount to little more than claiming credit for a piece of legislation or thanking key supporters. Other times they are statements of constitutional rights and prerogatives. Such was the case in 2005 upon the passage of the antitorture legislation, which contained provisions championed by Senator John McCain and opposed by President George W. Bush. Two weeks after its public signing, Bush quietly attached a statement dealing with the rights of detainees. It read:

> The executive branch shall construe Title X in Division A of the Act, relating to detainees, in a manner consistent with the constitutional authority of the President to supervise the unitary executive branch and as Commander in Chief and consistent with the constitutional limitations on judicial power, which will assist in achieving the shared objective of

the Congress and the President, evidenced in Title X of protecting the American people from further terrorist attacks.[10]

The effect of this statement was to claim presidential authority to ignore the McCain amendment and conduct the war on terror as the executive saw fit.

This was not Bush's only constitutional signing statement. Of 40 foreign policy bills he signed, Bush issued 14 constitutional signing statements, and he also issued 17 such statements in signing 35 pieces of national security legislation.[11] Another prominent example is his signing of the Defense Authorization Act for 2008 on January 25, 2008. Bush objected to a statute that prevented funds from being spent on "establishing any military installation or base for the purpose of providing for the permanent stationing of Armed Forces in Iraq." Such an agreement was under negotiation, and the administration had already indicated that it would not define any agreement as a treaty, thereby getting around Senate approval.

In spite of his criiticisn of Bush's use of signing statements, Obama has not abandoned the practice. In June 2009, Obama signed a spending bill that placed conditions on money given to the World Bank and International Monetary Fund. In his attached signing statement Obama stated he would not allow this legislation to intefere with his authority as president to conduct foreign policy and negotiate with other countries.

## Informal Ambassadors

The Constitution gives the Senate the power to approve or reject presidential appointments. By having a voice in who was appointed to negotiate treaties and run departments it was thought that the Senate would be able to influence policy. In practice, this linkage between people and policy has never fully materialized. Appointees see themselves as agents of the president. It is his agenda they seek to advance and not that favored by members of Congress.

Presidents have also turned the confirmation powers into something less than what was originally intended by using personal representatives as negotiators. President Franklin Roosevelt relied heavily on Harry Hopkins in making international agreements, leaving Secretary of State Cordell Hull to administer over "diplomatic trivia." President Jimmy Carter had Hamilton Jordan conduct secret negotiations during the Iranian hostage crisis, and in the Reagan administration, National Security Council (NSC) staffers and private citizens were relied on to carry out the Iran–Contra initiative. A similar problem confronts the Senate if it wishes to influence the type of advice the president gets. Presidents are free to listen to whom they please. Under Woodrow Wilson, Colonel House, a friend and confidant, was more influential than Secretaries of State William Jennings Bryan and William Lansing. Today it is widely recognized that the national security adviser often has more influence on presidential thinking than does the secretary of state. Yet the former's appointment is not subject to Senate approval. Obama has turned to informal ambassadors by designating special "czars" for foreign policy problems such as those in the Middle East, border security with Mexico, and Afghanistan.

## Undeclared Wars

By one count the United States has used force over 300 times.[12] Only five times has it declared war. The passage of the 1973 War Powers Resolution did little to redress this imbalance. Rather than willingly abide by it, they have submitted reports to Congress declaring that they were doing so voluntarily and characterized their decision to use force as lying beyond the jurisdiction of the War Powers Resolution. Carter did not engage in advance consultations with Congress in carrying out the hostage rescue effort. He claimed that it was a humanitarian action. Reagan used the same logic in bypassing Congress on

### HISTORICAL LESSON

#### Presidents and Haiti and the Dominican Republic

Haiti and the Dominican Republic share the island of Hispaniola in the Caribbean Sea. They have long been the objects of U.S. foreign policy attention. In late 1853, President Franklin Pierce sent an envoy to the Dominican Republic in hopes of arranging for a lease on a naval base. An agreement was reached in 1854, but at the urging of the French and British, who opposed an American naval presence in the Caribbean Sea, the Dominican government added a clause to the agreement requiring that Dominicans "of all complexions" be treated "on the same footing" as U.S. citizens. This clause effectively killed the agreement. American interest in the Dominican Republic did not return until after the civil war. Secretary of State William Seward traveled there in 1866. It was the first trip ever made by a secretary of state outside of the United States. Not only did he agree to recognize Dominican independence but he also authorized negotiations that would lead to its absorption by the United States. These negotiations produced an annexation agreement in 1869. To the surprise of President Ulysses Grant, his cabinet objected to the agreement.

The Dominican Republic next played a major role in American foreign policy in the administration of Teddy Roosevelt when he issued the Roosevelt Corollary to the Monroe Doctrine, blocking a threatened French takeover of the Dominican Republic for its failure to pay foreign debts. He followed this up in 1906 by having the United States take over the job of customs collection in the Dominican Republic. When an insurrection in the Dominican Republic led to the closure of several customs houses in 1912, President William Howard Taft sent in 750 marines to restore order. Domestic unrest continued, however, and in 1916 President Woodrow Wilson dispatched army and naval forces to the Dominican Republic and formally established military rule over the country. It would be 1920 before the United States announced plans to withdraw its occupying army.

In 1930, Rafael Trujillo captured the presidency. He was assassinated in 1961. A period of domestic instability followed, and in 1965 President Lyndon Johnson sent some 22,000 U.S. troops to the Dominican Republic to prevent what his administration described as the further spread of communism in the Western Hemisphere.

*(continued)*

*(continued)*

A slave revolt in 1804 officially established Haiti as an independent state. Haitian independence was not officially recognized by the United States until 1862 when President Abraham Lincoln recognized the free black states of Liberia and Haiti. Racism, both overt and subtle, played into the long delay in recognizing Haitian independence. An 1826 congressional debate over recognition had raised the issue of whether the recognition of Haiti would "introduce a moral contagion." Between 1853 and 1915, Haiti experienced 22 changes in government. This continuing domestic instability, persistent poverty, plus fears of European intervention brought Haiti to the attention of the Taft and Wilson administrations. Taft pressured Haiti into accepting a major loan, but this did not correct the situation. Wilson first tried to obtain a naval base there, and when that failed, he sent in troops in July 1915. The American occupation was marked by continued domestic violence and unrest, but it provoked little public comment in the United States. U.S. forces did not leave until 1933, when Franklin Roosevelt signed an executive order directing them to do so.

During the Cold War, Haiti continued to occupy an uneasy place in U.S. foreign policy thinking. Concerns about widespread domestic violence led John Kennedy to exclude Haiti from the Alliance for Progress. On the other hand, continued concerns over the expansion of communism in the Western Hemisphere led Johnson and Ronald Reagan to give Haiti military aid. One consequence of the political and economic conditions existing in Haiti was a steady stream of refugees to the United States. The first to leave were members of the upper class. They were followed by members of the urban middle class and semiskilled workers. In the early 1970s, many poor and uneducated Haitians began to flee by sea. Known as "boat people," they arrived in southern Florida in large numbers. After Jean-Bertrand Aristide was overthrown, thousands of Haitians took to the sea. Some 40,000 were intercepted and sent back to Haiti. During his presidential campaign Bill Clinton promised to change this policy, but after his inauguration he reversed course and made it known he would continue the policy.

### Applying the Lesson

1. Should the Clinton administration have been surprised by the reception it got in Haiti?
2. What is more important for understanding the reception the USS *Harlan County* received, the failure in Somalia or past U.S. foreign policy toward Haiti?
3. What is the most important piece of information a president needs to have before sending troops into a country? ∎

the invasion of Grenada. He would later argue that because the marines were invited in by the Lebanese government, they were not being sent into a combat situation, and the War Powers Resolution did not apply. About to use military force against Haiti without congressional authorization, Bill Clinton proclaimed that he was prepared to "carry out the will of the United

Nations." George H. W. Bush followed Carter and Reagan's logic, arguing that because Somalia was a humanitarian operation, no congressional approval was needed. He went to Congress for approval of military action against Iraq in the Persian Gulf War with great reluctance, with Secretary of Defense Dick Cheney asserting that no additional authorization from Congress was necessary because the United Nations had sanctioned the use of "all necessary means" to force Iraq to withdraw from Kuwait. Even after Congress passed supporting resolutions in January 1991, George H. W. Bush continued to stress that "I don't think I need it. . . . I feel that I have the authority to fully implement the United Nations resolution."

In a reverse twist, President Grover Cleveland went so far as to tell Congress that even if it declared war against Spain over Cuba he would not honor that vote and begin a war.

## WHEN DOES THE PRESIDENT MATTER?

In a study of twentieth-century U.S. foreign policy, John Stoessinger was struck by how few individuals made crucial decisions shaping its direction.[13] He found that "movers" (exceptional individuals who, for better or worse, not only find turning points in history but help create them) have been far outnumbered by "players" (individuals caught up in the flow of events, who respond in a standard and predictable fashion). One explanation for this imbalance is that there may exist relatively few situations in which the personal characteristics of the president or other policy makers are important for explaining policy.

A useful distinction can be made between action indispensability and actor indispensability.[14] **Action indispensability** refers to situations in which a specific action is critical to the success or failure of a policy. The identity of the actor is not necessarily a critical factor in explaining the action. It is possible that any individual (player) in that situation would have acted in the same manner. **Actor indispensability** refers to those situations in which the personal characteristics of the involved are critical to explaining the action taken. In Stoessinger's terms, the individual involved is a mover. This is someone who increases the odds of success or failure by bringing his or her unique qualities to bear on a problem.

A crucial element of action indispensability is the degree to which the situation permits restructuring. Some situations are so intractable or unstable that it is unreasonable to expect the actions of an individual policy maker to have much of an impact. The most favorable condition for individual actions to have an impact is when a "precarious equilibrium" exists and events are primed to move in any number of directions. This is seldom the case. Many of the foreign policy problems that a president confronts are either highly intractable situations or very unstable ones. Presidents do not ignore these policy problems. Peace initiatives in the Middle East have become a common feature of U.S. foreign policy. Economic summit conferences that bring together the leaders of the advanced industrial states now occur at regular intervals. It is just that either the instability of the situation overtakes policy initiatives, or its persistent features dilute the policy initiative, perpetuating the status quo.

In concrete terms, we can suggest that the identity of the president will have the greatest impact on policy under certain conditions. The first is when the issue is new on the agenda. Jimmy Carter's involvement in human rights policy and Ronald Reagan's championing of the Strategic Defense Initiative are cases in point. The second is when the issue is addressed early in the administration. Carter's decision not to simply wrap up the SALT II package left him by Gerald Ford but to negotiate his own treaty illustrates this point. Bill Clinton's handling of Somalia is another example. Third are those ongoing issues in which the president is deeply involved. Vietnam was such an issue for Lyndon Johnson and Richard Nixon. Release of the American hostages in Lebanon was such an issue for Reagan. Finally, we can expect presidential personality to matter when the issue is in a state of precarious equilibrium. Recent issues that could be classified this way include arms control, the Middle East peace process, Bosnia, and the democratization movement in Russia. All four of these conditions are met by the events of 9/11. The issue was new on the agenda. Although the administration of Bill Clinton had given terrorism more attention than did the incoming George W. Bush administration, no firm plan of action was in place. The attack occurred early in the Bush administration. And certainly from the point of view of key individuals in the administration, the terrorist attacks presented the United States with a unique opportunity to remake the political map of the Persian Gulf.

Students of the presidency have focused most heavily on two aspects of the president as individual in attempting to understand U.S. foreign policy. The first is presidential personality. The second is the president's managerial or leadership style. We will look at each in turn.

## PRESIDENTIAL PERSONALITY

Textbooks and newspaper accounts of U.S. foreign policy are dominated by references to policies that bear a president's name such as the Monroe Doctrine, the Truman Doctrine, or the Bush Doctrine. Personalizing the presidency this way suggests that the identity of the president matters greatly and that if a different person had been president, U.S. foreign policy would be different. Certainly this is the case in terms of how presidents approach certain aspects of their job. Consider the differences between the trips to Africa made by Bill Clinton in 1998 and by George W. Bush in 2003. Clinton spent 11 days in Africa and visited six countries. Bush saw five countries in five days. Clinton spent two days on safari. Bush spent one hour on safari. Clinton traveled with an entourage of 40. Bush brought few guests. Whereas Clinton routinely commented that it was wrong for the United States to have taken slaves from Africa, Bush spoke out aggressively against the failure of African leaders to do enough about AIDS. Clinton toured Nelson Mandela's prison and visited Soweto; Bush went to Pretoria, where the white-only government had ruled.

Yet does any of this matter? Africa was largely neglected by both administrations and continues to exist at the periphery of world politics. Presidents seem to be attracted to it for reasons that have little to do with Africa per se. Clinton's trip occurred against the backdrop of the Monica Lewinsky scandal and was a means of getting out of Washington. Bush was drawn to Africa because of the link between failed states and terrorism, and because his administration was about to reluctantly commit U.S. troops to Liberia. Stated more generally, a persuasive case can be made that situational factors, role variables, and the common socioeconomic backgrounds of policy makers place severe constraints on the impact of personality on policy. In this section, we look first at a leading effort to capture presidential personality and then examine under what conditions we should expect presidential personality to make a difference.

The most famous effort to classify presidential personality and explore its implications for policy is that of James David Barber, who defines personality in terms of three elements.[15] The first element is *worldview,* which Barber defines as an individual's politically relevant beliefs. The second element is *style,* which refers to an individual's habitual ways of responding to political opportunities and challenges through "rhetoric, personal relations, and homework." Both are heavily influenced by the third and most important component of personality: *character,* which develops in childhood. Character is the way individuals orient themselves toward life and involves two dimensions. The first is the amount of energy they put into the presidency. Presidents are classified as either passive or active. The second dimension is whether the president derives personal satisfaction from the job. A president who does is classified as positive, and one who gets no personal satisfaction from being president is classified as negative. Together these two dimensions produce four presidential personalities. Each type of **presidential personality** has different implications for U.S. foreign policy.

*Active–positive* presidents, such as Truman, Kennedy, Carter, Bill Clinton, and George H. W. Bush, put a great deal of energy into being president and derive great satisfaction from doing so. They are achievement oriented, value productivity, and enjoy meeting new challenges. *Active–negative* presidents, such as Lyndon Johnson and Nixon, are compulsive individuals who are driven to acquire power as a means of compensating for low self-esteem. Active–negatives adopt a domineering posture toward those around them and have difficulty managing their aggressive feelings. *Passive–positives* are directed individuals who seek affection as a reward for being agreeable. Passive–positive presidents such as Reagan do not make full use of the powers of the presidency but feel satisfied with the job as they define it. *Passive–negatives* such as Dwight Eisenhower get little satisfaction from the job and use few of the powers available to them. They are in politics only because others have encouraged them to be, and they feel a responsibility to meet these expectations. Their actions are plagued by low self-esteem and feelings of uselessness. They do not enjoy the game of politics. Rather than bargain and compromise, they seek to avoid confrontation by emphasizing vague principles and procedural arrangements.

Carter's handling of the Panama Canal Treaties illustrates the ability of active–positives to engage productively in coalition-building efforts and to accept the compromises necessary to get a policy measure passed. Carter's presidency also illustrates the problem with active–positive presidents: They may overreach themselves by pursuing too many goals at once, and they may be insensitive to the fact that the irrationalities of politics can frustrate even the best-laid plans. Carter was roundly criticized for being too flexible in the search for results and for trying to do too many things at the outset of his administration: negotiate a SALT II Treaty, negotiate a Panama Canal Treaty, and reorder U.S. foreign policy priorities by emphasizing human rights and economic problems over the Soviet threat. Bill Clinton is a second example. Clinton is a perfect fit for classification as an active–positive president. He is a supremely political animal who enjoys the game of politics; when he is defeated, he bounces back; and he displays a fundamental pragmatism in approaching policy problems.[16] The great danger of active–negatives is that they will adhere rigidly to a disastrous foreign policy. Woodrow Wilson did so during the League of Nations controversy; John Adams, with the Alien and Sedition Acts; Lyndon Johnson, with Vietnam; and Richard Nixon, with his actions in the Watergate scandal and the impeachment proceedings.

Passive presidents are especially prone to two problems. The first is policy drift. Problems may go unaddressed and opportunities for action missed. This situation results both from a general disinterest in using the powers of the presidency and a reluctance to engage in the nitty-gritty political work necessary to forge a consensus and move ahead. The second potential danger is the absence of accountability. Without the energetic involvement of the president in making policy, the inevitable question arises of "Who is in charge?"

Placing a president in one of Barber's categories involves a great deal of subjective judgment. Consider the case of Eisenhower, who was defined as a passive–negative president by Barber. Recent evidence suggests that this may not be the case.[17] Eisenhower may have deliberately cultivated the image of not being involved in policy making in order to deflect political pressures away from him. His "hidden-hand leadership" employed a behind-the-scenes activism combined with a low profile in public.

An even more significant complicating factor is that Barber's personality traits may not be as permanent or enduring as the term implies. Change may occur over time because multiple traits are present. George W. Bush is a case in point.[18] Looking first at the active–passive dimension Bush can be seen as passive in his delegation of authority to others, his preference for focusing on a few select themes, and his engaging in binary black–white thinking that allows him to make decisions without getting into the deeper questions involved in an issue. Bush once volunteered to an interviewer that he did not watch TV news or read newspapers other than scanning the front page because "I like to have a clear outlook . . . it can be a frustrating experience to pay attention to somebody's false opinion or somebody's characterization, which simply isn't true."[19]

At the same time, we can see a very active side to Bush. Bob Woodward, who chronicled the Bush administration's decisions to go to war in Afghanistan and Iraq, said that Bush's decision-making style "bordered on the hurried. He wanted actions, solutions. Once on course, he directed his energy at forging on, rarely looking back, scoffing at—even ridiculing—doubt and anything less than 100 percent commitment."[20] Richard Clarke, who worked for both George W. Bush and Bill Clinton on terrorism matters, says of Bush that he "asked us soon after September 11 for cards or charts of senior al-Qaeda managers as though dealing with them would be like a Harvard Business School exercise in a hostile takeover. He announced his intention to measure progress in the war on terrorism by crossing through the pictures of those caught or killed."[21]

Competing positive and negative traits are also present. Bush's positive outlook on politics is evident in his competitive nature, his strong belief that he is right and has the ability to make strategic adjustments in dealing with political opponents. With the Republicans firmly in control of Congress, Bush showed little inclination to work with the Democrats. After the 2006 midterm election, however, Bush displayed a recognition that this strategic posture would no longer work. Yet as one commentator noted in reviewing his 2007 State of the Union speech, "if he was humbler in tone and rhetorically generous to his Democratic opponents in calling for cooperation he was anything but defensive."[22] Days later, Bush reminded Congress that "I'm the decision-maker." Even in summer 2007, with his personal approval rating at historic lows, Republicans in Congress deserting him, and evaluations of his presidency almost certain to focus on failures in Iraq, Bush was described as "exhibiting an inexorable upbeat energy that defies the political storms" and being tranquil and serene.[23]

Early speculation based on his presidential campaign and early life experiences leads to the expectation that Barack Obama will fit comfortably into the active–positive category.[24] Politically Obama has described himself as progressive and pragmatic. He is portrayed as a listener, someone who conveys a sense that he is open to the views of others. At the same time he is seen as being ambitious and fully capable of defending his own interests. More generally, Obama is pictured as one who is highly organized in how he approaches problems and has the ability to recognize and seize opportunities when they present themselves. With this skill comes an ability to avoid being locked into large numbers of losing positions or those where victory comes with a high political price tag.

A potential danger facing Obama is the possibility that pragmatism and compromise will be seen as "flip-flopping" and that it will alienate him from his core political base without broadening his governing coalition through the addition of Republicans. Signs of this scenario potentially playing itself out came early in his administration in announced decisions to break with the Bush administration and close Guantanamo Bay but to follow its policies by blocking the release of secret memos on the details of the CIA's interrogation program and its invoking the "state's secret" argument to block civil liberties groups from gaining access to key information about its program of warrantless wiretaps of Americans.

## PRESIDENTIAL MANAGERIAL STYLE

Presidents do not lead by personality alone. Just as important to the outcome of their presidency is the managerial style they embrace to get others to follow. And, where we might expect presidential personality to have its greatest influence under a limited set of conditions, a president's managerial and leadership style could be expected to have a more uniform effect on U.S. foreign policy. Getting others to follow is not easy. In accepting the resignation of Alexander

Haig as secretary of state, Ronald Reagan wrote in his diary that "actually the only [foreign policy] disagreement was over whether I made policy or the Sec. of State did."[25]

Presidential managerial styles can be described in any number of ways. Zbigniew Brzezinski gave the following thumbnail sketches of how the first three post–Cold War presidents managed foreign policy.[26] George H. W. Bush had a "top-down" managerial style that placed him firmly in command of decisions. This did not mean that he or his national security advisor, Brent Scowcroft, were happy with the way the system worked. Commenting on discussions about dealing with Soviet pressure on Lithuania, Bush later said, "I was dissatisfied with this discussion since it did not point to action and I wanted to take action." Scowcroft said of a meeting before the beginning of the Persian Gulf War, "I was not happy with the briefing. It sounded unenthusiastic, delivered by people [military officers] who didn't want to do their job. The options they presented us . . . seemed to be so counterintuitive that I could not stay silent."[27] Bill Clinton had a "kaffeklatsch" (informal coffee get-together meeting) approach to decision making. His meetings lacked an agenda, rarely began or ended on schedule, frequently were marked by the spontaneous participation of individuals who had little reason to be there, and often ended without any clear sense that a decision had been reached. Clinton's managerial style is also characterized as politically opportunistic and not conducive to strategic clarity. George W. Bush is described as having "strong gut instincts" along with a "propensity for catastrophic decisiveness" and a temperament prone to "dogmatic formulations."

Viewed from a more analytical perspective, we find that four basic managerial options have been employed by presidents to bring order and coherence to their foreign policy.[28] None is by definition superior to another. All have contributed to foreign policy successes and failures. The first is a **competitive system,** in which a great deal of emphasis is placed on the free and open expression of ideas. Jurisdictions and grants of authority overlap as individuals and departments compete for the president's attention in putting forward ideas and programs. Franklin Roosevelt is the only president who successfully employed such a model. Lyndon Johnson is seen as having tried and failed to emulate Roosevelt. A second leadership style involves setting up a **formalistic system,** in which the president establishes orderly routines and procedures for organizing the administration's policy deliberations. The system is hierarchically structured, with the president deeply involved as the final arbitrator in defining strategy and policy choices. Truman, Eisenhower, Nixon, Ford, and Reagan set up formalistic systems. The third management style centers on the creation of a **collegial system,** in which the president tries to bring together a group of advisers to operate as a problem-solving team. Kennedy, Carter, George H. W. Bush, and Clinton set up this type of system.

The fourth management style, a **CEO (chief executive officer) system,** was introduced by George W. Bush. In spirit, it harkens back to a Nixon-style attempt to govern by stressing loyalty, tightly controlling the flow of information, and surrounding himself with an "iron triangle" of aides. In his first term, this consisted of National Security Advisor Condoleezza Rice, Chief of Staff

(COS) Andrew Card, Jr., and Vice President Dick Cheney. There are also noticeable differences. Whereas the Nixon NSC system stressed hierarchy and centralized control, Bush emphasized a management strategy in which the president set the overall tone of the administration and policy agenda establishing the general direction of policy. On top of this was placed a flattened power structure so that responsibility for carrying through on policy could be effectively delegated to key individuals.

Early in Barack Obama's administration two elements of his managerial style had emerged. First, as evidenced by his 2009 White House review of the U.S. goals and military presence in Afghanistan, Obama has embraced a collegial approach to decision making, to the point of holding a bipartisan meeting with members of Congress on Afghanistan. Second, he has shown a predilection for trying to control the policy process through the appointment of czars within the White House. In his first months in office, he appointed czars for Afghanistan and Pakistan, intelligence, Middle East peace, and the U.S.–Mexican border.

Categorizing presidents in terms of shared qualities is useful, because it allows us to move beyond making a series of singular observations. We must remember, however, that placing presidents in categories is only the beginning step in an analysis of their presidency and not the end. Attributes alone do not tell us what to expect from a president in terms of either policy or leadership style. Few would have predicted that Ronald Reagan, the arch anticommunist, would end his administration as an advocate of arms control or would bring about a major improvement in U.S.–Soviet relations.[29]

# THE NATIONAL SECURITY COUNCIL

Leadership requires more than getting individuals to work together toward common set of goals. It also has an organizational foundation. Bureaucracies are needed to provide advice, develop policy alternatives, and implement policies. Experience has taught presidents that bureaucracies are easily moved. As a result, presidents have been forced to look elsewhere for organizations that will allow them to lead. The central foreign policy structure that presidents have grown to rely on is the NSC.

The history of the NSC system can be broken down into four phases, each of which introduced distortions into the operation of the system that ultimately hindered the pursuit of foreign policy goals and its ultimate purpose. According to the 1947 National Security Act, its purpose was to advise the president "with respect to the integration of domestic, foreign, and military policies relating to national security."[30] The first phase of the NSC's history ran from 1947 to 1960. During this period the NSC became overly institutionalized. Truman was the first president to have the NSC, and he was cautious in using it. He particularly wanted to avoid setting any precedents that would give it the power to supervise executive branch agencies or establish a norm of group responsibility for foreign policy decisions, as some had hoped when the establishment of the NSC was being debated. For Truman, foreign policy was the responsibility of the president alone. The NSC was to be an advisory body and nothing more. To emphasize this point, Truman did not attend early meetings of the NSC. The outbreak of the Korean War changed Truman's approach to the NSC. He started to use it more systematically and began attending its regularly scheduled meetings. Organizational changes also took place. All national security issues were now to be brought to his attention through the NSC system, the NSC staff was reorganized, and the emphasis on outside consultants was replaced by a senior staff served by staff assistants.

Institutionalization continued under Eisenhower, who transformed the NSC system into a two-part unit that would be actively involved in making policy. A Planning Board was created to develop policy recommendations for the president, and an Operations Coordinating Board was established to oversee the implementation of national security decisions. Eisenhower also established the post of assistant for national security affairs (commonly known as the president's national security adviser) to coordinate the national security decision-making process more forcefully. Conventional accounts conclude that the NSC system never really functioned as envisioned. Instead of producing high-quality policy recommendations, the concern with touching all the bureaucratic bases produced decisions made on the basis of the lowest common denominator. Rather than increasing presidential options, it limited them. Policy implementation continued to be governed by departmental objectives and definitions of the problem rather than by presidential goals and perspectives.[31]

The second phase of the NSC's history, in which it became overly personalized, began with the Kennedy administration and lasted until 1980. Under Kennedy the formal and hierarchically structured system that Eisenhower had created declined in importance. Kennedy adopted an activist approach to national security management that was grounded on informal operating procedures. The emphasis was on multiple lines of communication, direct presidential contacts with second- and third-level officials, and securing outside expert advice. Ad hoc interagency task forces replaced the formal NSC system as the primary decision-making unit for dealing with such international problems as the Cuban missile crisis, Berlin, and Laos. Within the NSC system, emphasis switched from the council itself to the NSC staff. The staff came to be viewed less as a body of professionals who would stay on from administration to administration and more as a group that identified closely with the current administration and was loyal to it. The NSC staff became the vehicle by which Kennedy could essentially serve as his own secretary of state.

In Kennedy's revamped management system, the national security adviser played a key role. This person was responsible for ensuring that the staff operated from a presidential perspective. McGeorge Bundy held this post under Kennedy and in the first part of the Johnson administration. He was replaced by Walt Rostow in 1966. The change in advisers brought with it a change in operating style. Bundy saw his role as a facilitator whose job it was to encourage the airing of ideas and policy alternatives. Rostow was more of an ideologue concerned with policy advocacy over process management.

Like Kennedy, Lyndon Johnson took an activist stance and favored small, informal policy-making settings over the formal NSC system. Major decisions about Vietnam were made at the Tuesday lunch group that brought together Johnson and his key foreign policy advisers. The Tuesday lunch group was a "procedural abomination" lacking a formal agenda and clearly stated conclusions, wearing on participants, and confusing to those at the working levels.[32] The NSC coordinating system was overwhelmed by the pressures of Vietnam and was often bypassed by the tendency of the White House to make key policy decisions.

Nixon began his presidency with a pledge to put the NSC system back at the center of the foreign policy decision-making process.[33] This was achieved by first selecting Henry Kissinger as his national security adviser and William Rogers as his secretary of state. The combination of a strong, opinionated, and activist national security adviser and a secretary of state with little foreign policy experience guaranteed that foreign policy would be made in the White House. Second, Nixon created an elaborate NSC committee and staff system. Separate bodies were created to deal with SALT-related verification issues, Vietnam, intelligence programs, covert action, crisis management, and defense programs. There also existed an under secretaries committee and several interdepartmental groups. Kissinger, positioned at the center of this elaborate system, was able to direct the flow of paper in the direction he wanted, bringing the NSC system into play on certain issues and cutting it out of others. By the end of the Nixon administration, the NSC was largely on the outside looking in. It met only three times in 1973, compared with 37 times in 1969. Such important decisions as the invasion of Cambodia, Kissinger's trip to China, the Paris Peace Negotiations, bombing in Vietnam, and putting U.S. troops on worldwide alert during the Yom Kippur War in the Middle East were made outside the NSC system.

Carter dismantled the elaborate Nixon–Ford–Kissinger committee system in favor of two committees. The Policy Review Committee was charged with handling long-term projects. A Special Coordinating Committee (SCC) was created to deal with short-term problems, crisis situations, and covert action. Originally, these two committees were to be equally important, but over time the SCC dominated. This was especially true with the advent of the Iranian hostage crisis and the Soviet invasion of Afghanistan. Collegiality was evident in the prominent policy-making roles played by the Friday foreign policy breakfasts (attended by Carter and his key foreign policy advisers) and the Thursday lunch meetings (at which these advisers met to prepare for the Friday meeting). Carter's activism often overloaded the foreign policy agenda and created a number of problems for his NSC system, many of them centered on the workings of the Friday foreign policy breakfasts, which became substitutes for full NSC meetings. The problem was that decisions arrived at there were not always fully integrated into the NSC system, nor did they necessarily produce clearly articulated positions.[34]

During the Reagan administration, the NSC entered a third phase. Pledging to depersonalize the system, Reagan pushed too far in the opposite direction, causing it to go into decline. The national security adviser became a "nonperson" with little foreign policy influence or stature. And, as a direct consequence, the NSC staff ceased to function as either a policy-making or policy-coordinating body. With no force able to coordinate foreign policy, an unprecedented degree of bureaucratic infighting and fragmentation came to characterize (and paralyze) Reagan's foreign policy. Only with the arrival of Colin Powell as national security adviser and the passing from the Cabinet of such powerful and highly opinionated figures as Secretary of Defense Caspar Weinberger and Director of Central Intelligence William Casey did a coherent foreign policy agenda appear.[35] While this was happening, the NSC staff moved in two different directions. On the one hand, it became preoccupied with bureaucratic trivia. (There were 25 committees, 55 midlevel committees, and some 100 task forces and working groups.) On the other hand, it became involved in the actual conduct of foreign policy in the Iran–Contra initiative.

In the George H. W. Bush and Bill Clinton administrations, decision making in the NSC became transformed again, becoming more collegial in nature. Both presidents selected low-key national security advisers who were expected to stay out of the public limelight. The move to collegiality was applauded by most as a necessary step to overcome many of the past excesses of the NSC system. In each case, however, the final result was less than had been hoped for. The primary problem encountered in George H. W. Bush's administration was too much homogeneity in outlook. All of the participants, including the president, were confident that they understood the world, and they were slow to adapt to the end of the Cold War. Clinton failed to make his collegial system work because he was unable to provide a constant vision to guide his team or to construct an effective division of labor among its members.

Upon becoming George W. Bush's national security advisor, Condoleezza Rice expressed a desire to follow in the footsteps of Brent Scowcroft and establish a collegial decision-making system with a low-key national security advisor. Structurally, they created a three-tiered NSC system.[36] Those meetings at which Bush was present were officially designated as NSC meetings. Others were Principals or Deputies committee meetings. Sitting atop this system was an informal committee, the "War Cabinet" consisting of some 12 key Bush advisors on the war against terrorism. It was the group that was charged with making major decisions regarding the wars in Afghanistan and Iraq.

The results in practice were quite different. Instead of operating in a collegial fashion, this system became highly competitive and split over how to conduct foreign policy. One commentator described the NSC as having become one of "unrestrained ideological entrepreneurship," in which collegial scrutiny of policy proposals was replaced by pockets of officials with strongly held views competing to sell their policy preferences to the president.[37] A RAND Corporation study on planning for postwar Iraq concluded that the NSC process failed to resolve differences among rival agencies because "tensions between the Defense Department and the State Department were never mediated by the president or his staff."[38]

Both the president and his national security advisors received blame for the collapse of the decision making process they established. Bush was faulted for adopting a "no-doubt" approach to issues that left little for discussion of alternatives or reconsideration of decisions once they were made. Where some saw this as a sign of strength, others saw it as bullying and evidence of insecurity and unwillingness to deal with the complexity of issues.[39]

National security advisors Condoleeza Rice and Stephen Hadley were criticized for their inability or unwillingness to resolve contentious issues. Under Rice, NSC discussions were often highly formalized with no real discussion taking place about the issues or the implementation of policy. Bob Woodward, who chronicled the Iraq War decision making of the Bush administration, painted this picture of one meeting:

> Rumsfeld made his presentation while looking at the president, while Powell looked straight ahead. Then Powell would make his presentation to the president with Rumsfeld looking straight ahead. They didn't even comment on each other's statements or views. So Bush never had the benefit of a serious, substantive discussion between his principal advisors. And . . . the president did not force a discussion.[40]

One reason for the lack of real discussion was that Rumsfeld and Cheney routinely employed back channels to communicate with Bush privately about policy matters. Loyal to the president, Rice did not feel it was appropriate to criticize this practice. The NSC process changed little under Hadley. He acted as an advocate for the president, not an advisor. His job was determining what Bush wanted and then bringing the NSC into line behind it. Studies of what to do in Iraq, for example, were structured in such a way that the surge was always an option.

President Obama used his first presidential directive to set up his national security system. He added the attorney general, the secretaries of energy and homeland, and the U.S. ambassador to the United Nations to the NSC. Other advisors and officials will attend on a case-by-case basis. It was also determined that many of the functions carried out by the Homeland Security Council, established by George W. Bush, will now be carried out by the NSC. National security advisor James Jones was put in charge of setting its agenda and communicating its decisions to the president and other administration officials. Below the NSC Obama established a complex series of interagency committees to coordinate analysis and review issues for consideration by more senior committees. He also divided presidential national security orders into two groups: One deals with policy directives and the other study directives.

In commenting on Obama's NSC system observers made two points. First, the NSC system was "top heavy" with such powerful figures as Hillary Clinton and Robert Gates holding key secretarial positions at State and Defense, respectively. Second, as we have noted, few presidents have managed to operate for long with the national security advisory system they established upon taking office.

## OTHER WHITE HOUSE VOICES

The NSC system is not the only advisory body close to the president that exercises influence over the making of U.S. foreign policy. Three other voices that have grown in prominence are that of the vice president, the president's COS, and the first lady.

## The Vice President

Political folklore assigns the vice president little more than a ceremonial position in the policy-making process, barring the death of the president. There is often great truth in these images. Harry Truman spoke with Franklin Roosevelt only eight times and knew nothing of the development of the atomic bomb or discussions that Roosevelt had with Winston Churchill and Joseph Stalin on the shape of the post–World War II international system. Of late, however, much as changed. More and more vice presidents are playing important foreign policy roles.[41] Dan Quayle, George H. W. Bush's vice president, became the administration's most active voice on Latin American affairs, and his decidedly pro-Israel position was important in maintaining the Persian Gulf War alliance against Iraq. Quayle also stressed to the president the importance of obtaining congressional support for the Persian Gulf War. Al Gore, Bill Clinton's vice president, established himself as a key administration expert on Russia and some of the important newly emerging states such as Kazakhstan and Ukraine.

The foreign policy roles played by Quayle and Gore, however, pale in comparison to that of Dick Cheney, George W. Bush's vice president. Cheney laid a solid structural foundation from which to exert his influence on foreign policy matters. His national security staff (35) was the largest of any vice president and was larger than that of President Kennedy (15).[42] Cheney also brought a clear-cut perspective on foreign policy matters and considerable foreign policy experience to the vice presidency. He had served as secretary of defense under George H. W. Bush and had established himself as the most aggressive member of that administration's inner circle in dealing with the collapse of communism and the end of the Cold War, arguing that "we ought to lead and shape events."[43]

Before the 9/11 terrorist attacks, Cheney was charged with leading the administration's planning for homeland security, and after those attacks he became a powerful voice for taking the war to Iraq, often engaging in spirited exchanges with Secretary of State Colin Powell, who opposed such a move. This position was advanced in NSC meetings and in private meetings with the president. Both before and after the invasion of Iraq, Cheney vehemently asserted in public that Iraq possessed weapons of mass destruction and that a link existed between Iraq and al Qaeda. His behind-the-scenes efforts to root out intelligence supporting this position and his preoccupation with discrediting opponents of the war are among the most controversial aspects of the Bush administration's handling of prewar intelligence. Defenders assert that it was necessary to overcome the lethargy of the CIA in pursuing intelligence on Iraq, while critics charge that Cheney's actions politicized intelligence.

Joe Biden has continued in the role of an activist vice president as part of the Obama administration, although more in the mode of Al Gore than Dick Cheney. By the end of 2009, he made over a dozen trips abroad, including ones to Iraq, Poland, and the Czech Republic. Biden has also been involved in discussions on Afghanistan, voicing the concerns of skeptics about how to proceed there.

## The Special Trade Representative

Up until the early 1960s, the State Department had primary responsibility for conducting international economic negotiations. That changed with the passage of the 1962 Trade Expansion Act, which created the Office of the Special Trade Representative to head an interagency trade organization located in the White House. The move, which was led by Congress, was seen as necessary because the State Department was not viewed as a strong enough advocate of American economic interests.

The special trade representative is charged with responsibility for overseeing U.S. activity in multilateral trade negotiations, negotiating trade issues with other states, and negotiating trade issues within the UN system of organizations. Thus it was Robert Zoellick, rather than Colin Powell, who accompanied George W Bush to Quebec to meet with Latin American leaders in hopes of laying the foundation for Free Trade of the Americas. It was Zoellick who announced that the United States and the European Union had reached an agreement resolving a long-standing dispute over trade in bananas. It was Zoellick who accompanied Bush to the G-8 Economic Summit in Genoa, and it was Zoellick who supervised U.S. negotiations at the Doha Round of World Trade Organization talks. When President Obama went to Italy in July 2009 to attend the meeting of the G-8 nations, it was U.S. Trade Representative Ron Kirk who accompanied him.

## The White House Chief of Staff

By convention, a division of labor has evolved in White House decision-making circles between the COS and the national security advisor. Each acts as a principal source of advice for the president—the COS for domestic policy and the national security advisor for foreign policy. In addition, the COS acts as a gatekeeper, regulating those who have access to the president. This latter power is seen as making the COS more of a political (and powerful) figure than the national security advisor.[44] Without much fanfare, however, this division of labor is disappearing, and more and more the COS has come to have an important voice in foreign policy matters. This trend began with Alexander Haig, who was COS under Nixon, and Hamilton Jordan, who held the post under Carter. Their efforts have not always been judged a success. For example, whereas Howard Baker, Jr., who was COS under Reagan, is credited with persuading the president to hold frequent summits with Soviet leaders, Thomas McLarty's actions as Clinton's first COS are seen as having threatened congressional approval of NAFTA.

President George W. Bush chose Andrew Card to be his COS. Card defined his role as COS in terms of being a facilitator rather than a micromanager, as John Sununu had been during George H. W. Bush's presidency, or as a prime minister who would act as the president's agent in negotiating with Congress and the media.[45] Card's portfolio extended into foreign policy almost immediately. He was widely associated with an early Bush immigration initiative that was seen as designed to garner Hispanic votes for the Republican Party. After

9/11, he was one of those placed in charge of the Homeland Security Council. As the Bush administration moved toward war with Iraq, Card established the White House Iraq Group to make sure that the various parts of the White House were working in harmony on Iraq. Card was replaced by Josh Bolton in spring 2006 and soon began to exercise influence in foreign policy. He is credited with arranging for meetings between Bush and critics of the Iraq War as part of a strategy of puncturing the protective information bubble that had come to engulf the president.

The influence of domestic considerations as filtered through the COS's office reaches not only to what decisions are made but also to how foreign policy decisions are communicated. Brent Scowcroft, George H. W. Bush's national security advisor, noted that he had expected the NSC to write the first draft of the president's national security speeches because the language was so very important, but that this was not the case. Instead, the White House speech writers, under the direction of John Sununu, took the lead, with the result that foreign policy speeches often sounded like campaign speeches laced with dramatic rhetoric.[46]

Several reasons stand out for why the COS is now a potentially important foreign policy voice. Foremost among them is the blurring of the boundary between foreign and domestic policy. Today many traditional foreign policy problems have characteristics of both and can be characterized as "intermestic" issues. One consequence of this is to make the COS's domestic political expertise relevant for how many foreign policy issues are decided. As Hamilton Jordan recalls, he sought to play the role of an "early warning system" to alert officials to potential domestic political problems embedded in foreign policy decisions. In speaking of the timing of the Iraq War, Andrew Card observed that, from a marketing perspective, it was not wise to introduce a new product in August. A second consequence of the intermestic nature of foreign policy problems is that presidents have increasingly turned to advisory groups to help manage and coordinate policy decisions in these areas. The COS's role as power broker and gatekeeper has become crucial for ensuring that the president stays on top of the policy process. Leon Panetta, Clinton's second COS, insisted that all decision papers, including those from the NSC, went to the president only after his review. If he felt that not enough options were being given to Clinton, the paper was returned.

## The First Lady

In the George W. Bush administration Laura Bush filled the traditional and largely ceremonial foreign policy role bestowed upon First Ladies. She was seen much more than heard but did have a focal point for her foreign policy activities, in this case freedom in Burma. It is important to recognize that this role, while the most common, is not the only role that first ladies have played in U.S. foreign policy making.

First ladies have long been involved informally in making U.S. foreign policy. Abigail Adams lobbied President John Adams on a treaty with the Netherlands in 1799. Edith Wilson served as Woodrow Wilson's communication link with both foreign governments and others in the U.S. government while he was incapacitated by a stroke. While generally neutral on policy matters, she tried but failed to get Wilson to accept Sen. Henry Cabot Lodge's reservations on the League of Nations. Eleanor Roosevelt engaged in a wide series of debates with President Franklin Roosevelt during his presidency.

Two recent first ladies who adopted a much more visible and active role in foreign policy were Rosalyn Carter and Hillary Clinton. The signature foreign policy undertaking of Rosalyn Carter's stay in the White House was a June 1977 trip to Latin America. With Jimmy Carter heavily involved in completing the Panama Canal Treaties, the Middle East peace process, and arms control talks with the Soviet Union, the decision was made to send her to Latin America as a sign of the U.S. interest in the region and its commitment to human rights. In preparation for the trip, Rosalyn Carter met with scholars and representatives from the State Department, Treasury Department, National Security Department, and Organization of American States.

Hillary Clinton's signature foreign policy initiative involved advocacy for women's right and her attendance at the Fourth United Nations Conference on Women held in Beijing in September 1995. In addressing that body she strongly criticized China's treatment of women. Hillary Clinton's preparation for this trip included discussions with representatives from the State Department, the NSC, the office of the U.S. Ambassador to the UN, and nongovernmental organizations.

## OVER THE HORIZON

Pressure continued to build on President Clinton to take steps to return Aristide to power in 1993 and 1994. Randall Robinson, president of TransAfrica went on a hunger strike to demonstrate the importance of action. Yet, opposition also built. Robert Dole, who would be the Republican presidential nominee in 1996, spoke out against using military power. Clinton ultimately accepted the necessity of an invasion and set September 15, 1994, as its date. Earlier that summer the United Nations Security passed authorizing states to use force to restore Haiti's constitutional government. With invasion troops in the air, a last-minute delegation led by former President Jimmy Carter convinced General Raoul Cedras to resign. On September 19, an international force landed in Haiti. Aristide returned on October 15. In March 1995, the international force became a peacekeeping force, and its numbers dropped from 21,000 to 6,000 troops. This number steadily declined, and by January 2000, with Clinton's presidency entering its final year, all U.S. forces departed from Haiti.

In looking over the horizon two trends are worth watching. The first is the further development of what some refer to as the **partisan presidency**.[47] Rather than exist above party politics and serve as a unifying force in American politics, partisan presidents seek to use political party loyalty, patronage, and ideology as the principal tools of governing. This trend to a partisan presidency began in the 1980s and reversed the existing pattern of relations between presidents and their parties that existed from the 1950s through the 1970s. Increasingly political consultants from ideological think tanks rather than nonpartisan experts are relied upon for policy advice. Instead of broadcasting to the public at large presidents use the media to reach out and mobilize their base. Presidents reject bipartisanship in favor of working closely with their own party and select members of the opposition.

A second area of possible change lies in how the president conducts national security policy. The bipartisan Project on National Security Reform released its report in November 2008.[48] Among its key recommendations were replacing the NSC and the Homeland Security Council with a new President's Security Council that would also have jurisdiction over international economic and energy policy. It was also recommended that a director for national security be created within the executive office of the president. The president was also urged to selectively shift management issues away from the President's Security Council staff to interagency committees and create a National Security Professional Corps of specialists who were specifically trained for interagency assignments.

## CRITICAL THINKING QUESTIONS

1. Where does presidential responsibility begin and end in foreign policy making?
2. Is there a "best" type of presidential personality for foreign affairs?
3. What is more important in determining presidential success in foreign policy, the way the NSC is organized or presidential management style?

## KEY TERMS

action
 indispensability 183
actor
 indispensability 183
Bricker
 Amendment 179

CEO system 188
collegial system 188
competitive system 188
executive
 agreement 178
formalistic system 188

partisan president 197
presidential
 personality 185
signing statement 179
unilateral
 presidency 177

## FURTHER READING

Ivo Daalder, and I. M. Destler, *In the Shadow of the Oval Office: Portraits of National Security Advisors and the Presidents they Served—From JFK to George W. Bush* (New York: Simon & Schuster, 2009).

Glenn Hastedt and Anthony Eksterowicz (eds.), *The President and Foreign Policy: Chief Architect or General Contractor?* (New York: NOVA Science, 2005).

William Howell, *Power Without Persuasion: The Politics of Direct Presidential Action* (Princeton: Princeton University Press, 2003).

Richard Neustadt, *Presidential Power* (New York: Free Press, 1960).

Bob Woodward, *The War Within* (New York: Simon & Schuster, 2008).

## NOTES

1. Richard Neustadt, *Presidential Power* (New York: Free Press, 1960).
2. Hugh Heclo, "Introduction: The Presidential Illusion," in Hugh Heclo and Lester M. Salamon (eds.), *The Illusion of Presidential Government* (Boulder, CO: Westview, 1981), p. 1.

3. Bob Woodward, *State of Denial* (New York: Simon & Schuster, 2006), p. 212.

4. Terry Moe and William G. Howell, "Unilateral Action and Presidential Power: A Theory," *Presidential Studies Quarterly* 29 (1999), 850–872.

5. Charlie Savage, "President Weakens Espionage Oversight Board Ford Created," *The Boston Globe*, March 14, 2008, A1.

6. James Pfiffner, *The Modern Presidency* (Boston: Bedford/St. Martins, 2004), p. 187.

7. Walter Pincus, "Secret Presidential Pledges Over Years Erected U.S. Shield for Saudis," *The Washington Post*, February 9, 1992, p. A20.

8. James A. Nathan and Richard K. Oliver, *Foreign Policy Making and the American Political System* (Boston: Little, Brown, 1983), p. 115.

9. Charles W. Kegley, Jr., and Eugene R. Wittkopf, *American Foreign Policy: Pattern and Process*, 2nd ed. (New York: St. Martin's, 1982), p. 418.

10. George W. Bus, "Statement on Signing the Department of Defense, Energy Supplemental Appropriations to Address Hurricanes in the Gulf of Mexico and Pandemic Influenza Act, 2006," *Weekly Compilation of Presidential Documents* (December 30, 2005), 1918–1919.

11. Christopher Kelley and Bryan Marshall, "The Bush Presidencies and the Unitary Executive Theory: The Implications of Presidential Signing Statements," *White House Studies,* 7 (2007), 144–62.

12. Ryan Hendrickson, *The Clinton Wars: The Constitution, Congress, and War Powers* (Nashville: Vanderbilt University Press, 2002), p. 1.

13. John Stoessinger, *Crusaders and Pragmatists: Movers of Modern American Foreign Policy* (New York: W. W. Norton, 1979).

14. Fred I. Greenstein, *Personality and Politics* (Chicago: Markham, 1969).

15. James David Barber, *The Presidential Character: Predicting Performance in the White House*, 3rd ed. (Englewood Cliffs, NJ: Prentice-Hall, 1985). Also see Alexander George, "Assessing Presidential Character," *World Politics,* 26 (1974), 234–82. For other formulations of presidential personality, see Lloyd S. Etheridge, "Personality Effects on American Foreign Policy, 1898–1968: A Test of Interpersonal Generalization Theory," *American Political Science Review,* 72 (1978), 434–51; and Stoessinger, *Crusaders and Pragmatists.*

16. Fred I. Greenstein, "The Presidential Leadership Style of Bill Clinton: An Early Appraisal," *Political Science Quarterly,* 108 (1993/94), 589–601.

17. Fred I. Greenstein, *The Hidden Hand Presidency: Eisenhower as Leader* (New York: Basic Books, 1982).

18. See Ilan Peleg, *The Legacy of George Bush's Foreign Policy* (Boulder: Westview Press, 2009), pp. 75–98. Peleg classifies Bush as an active-negative.

19. Peter Beinart, "When the War Won't Stay at Bay," *The Washington Post*, August 18, 2005, A21.

20. Bob Woodward, *Bush at War* (New York: Simon & Schuster, 2002), p. 256.

21. Richard Clarke, *Against All Enemies* (New York: The Free Press, 2004), p. 287.

22. Dan Balz, "The State of the President: Beleaguered," *The Washington Post*, January 24, 2007, p. A1.

23. Peter Baker, "President Besieged and Isolated, Yet at Ease," *The Washington Post,* July 2, 2007, p. A1.

24. See, for example, Stanley Renshon, "Psychological Reflections on Barack Obama and John McCain: Assessing the Contours of a New Presidential Administration," *Political Science Quarterly,* 123 (2008), 391–433.

25. Ronald Reagan (ed. Douglas Brinkley), *The Reagan Diaries* (New York: Haper-Collins, 2007); also Howard Katz, "Ronald Reagan, in His Own Words," *The Washington Post*, May 2, 2007, p. A1.

26. Zbigniew Brzezinski, *Second Chance: Three Presidents and the Crisis of American Superpower* (New York: Basic Books, 2007), pp. 11, 86–87, 137.

27. George Bush and Brent Scowcroft, *A World Transformed* (New York: Vintage, 1998), 225, 381.

28. Donald M. Snow and Eugene Brown, *Puzzle Palaces and Foggy Bottom: U.S. Foreign and Defense Policy-Making in the 1990s* (New York: St. Martin's, 1994), pp. 44–70.

29. John Lewis Gaddis, "The Unexpected Ronald Reagan," in John Lewis Gaddis (ed.), *The United States and the End of the Cold War: Implications, Reconsiderations, Provocations* (New York: Oxford University Press, 1992), pp. 119–32.

30. Zbigniew Brzezinski, "The NSC's Midlife Crisis," *Foreign Policy,* 69 (1987/88), 80–99.

31. For a reinterpretation of the Eisenhower NSC experience, see Fred Greenstein and Richard Immerman, "Effective National Security Advising: Recovering the Eisenhower Legacy," *Political Science Quarterly,* 115 (2000), 335–45.

32. William P. Bundy, "The National Security Process: Plus Change . . . ," *International Security,* 7 (1982/83), pp. 94–109.

33. On the Nixon NSC system see John P. Leacacos, "Kissinger's Apparat," *Foreign Policy,* 5 (1971), 2–27.

34. Robert E. Hunter, *Presidential Control of Foreign Policy: Management or Mishap,* Washington Paper #91 (New York: Praeger, 1982), pp. 35–36.

35. Terry Diehl, "Reagan's Mixed Legacy," *Foreign Policy,* 75 (1989), 34–55.

36. John Prados, "The Pros from Dover," *Bulletin of the Atomic Scientists,* 60 (2004), 44–51.

37. Colin Campbell, "Unrestrained Ideological Entrepreneurship in the Bush II Advisory System," in Colin Campbell and Bert Rockman (eds.), *The George W. Bush Presidency* (Washington, DC: Congressional Quarterly Press, 2004), pp. 73–104.

38. Michael Gordon, "Army Buried Study Faulting Iraq Planning," *New York Times,* February 11, 2008, P. 1

39. Bob Woodward, *The War Within* (New York: Simon & Schuster, 2008), pp. 407–8.

40. Woodward, *State of Denial,* p. 241.

41. Paul Kengor, "Cheney and Vice Presidential Power," in Gary Gregg II and mark Rozell (eds.), *Considering the Bush Presidency* (New York: Oxford University Press, 2004), pp. 160–176; "The Vice President, Secretary of State, and Foreign Policy," *Political Science Quarterly,* 115 (2000), 175–99.

42. David Rothkopf, "Inside the Committee That Runs the World," *Foreign Policy,* 147 (March–April 2005), 30–40; and the series in the *Washington Post,* "Angler: The Cheney Vice Presidency," June 24–27, 2007.

43. James Oliver, "Pragmatic Fathers and Ideological Suns: Foreign Policy in the Administrations of George H W Bush and George W Bush," *White House Studies,* 7 (2007), 203.

44. David Cohen, Chris Dolan, and Jerel Rosati, "A Place at the Table," *Congress and the Presidency,* 29 (2002), 119–49.

45. Woodward, *State of Denial,* p. 355.

46. Bush and Scowcroft, *A World Transformed,* p. 49.

47. Richard Skinner, "George W. Bush and the Partisan Presidency," *Political Science Quarterly,* 123 (2008–2009), 605–622.

48. *Forging a New Shield,* Project on National Security Reform, November 2008.

# CHAPTER

## 8

# Bureaucracy

In late June 2009, the Pentagon formally moved ahead with plans to create a new unified cyber command to protect the military's computer networks from attacks. As a presidential candidate, Barack Obama had promised to move in this direction because the existing bureaucratic system of the government was not structured to deal with cyber warfare. Dubbed by some to be fought with eWMDs (electronic weapons of mass destruction), cyber warfare is already with us. In the month following this announcement, it was revealed that a coordinated cyber attack had taken place against Web sites operated by the White House, Defense Department, Department of Homeland Security, the Federal Aviation Administration, and others. Damage was minimal, and it was believed the attacks were carried out from North Korea. In spring 2007, Estonia was the target of a monthlong cyber attack that effectively shut down its banking system. In 2008, prior to Russia's invasion of Georgia, Georgia government's Web sites were knocked offline. In both cases the attacks were determined to have originated in Russia and were carried out by nationalistic hacker gangs. The extent to which the Russian government was involved in the planning of these attacks is unclear. Evidence also indicates that hackers have entered the computers used for developing the Pentagon's biggest weapons program and stolen data.

Unclear is the extent to which the cyber command will focus on intelligence gathering, defensive measures, and the development of an offensive capability. The establishment of a cyber command also raises a number of pressing bureaucratic questions that have yet to be answered. One question is, Who will run this program? Will it be the military, the National Security Agency (NSA), or some other member of the intelligence community? A second question involves the fate of the Department of Homeland Security. It is excluded from the program, yet is responsible for the security of the government's nonmilitary computer system. Finally, there is the question, What to do about the private sector? It is the focus of a separate Obama initiative, yet the interface between government and private computer systems is such that some are calling for national standards for computer security.

Our concern in this chapter is with the foreign affairs bureaucracy. And as our cyber command example illustrates, the challenge is not only to  understand the foreign affairs bureaucracy as it exists today and tomorrow but to think creatively and about creating the **military after next**.[1] We begin by examining the three organizations that dominate the foreign affairs bureaucracy: the State Department, the Defense Department, and the Central Intelligence Agency (CIA). We then take a brief look at bureaucracies that have traditionally been classified as domestic but that now also have a foreign policy role: the Treasury, Commerce, and Agriculture Departments as well as the Department of Homeland Security, the newest bureaucratic unit with a role in foreign policy. Finally, we examine how policy makers respond to the challenges of dealing with the foreign affairs bureaucracy.

# THE STATE DEPARTMENT

Three aspects of the State Department are of concern to us: its structure and growth, its internal value system, and its impact on U.S. foreign policy.

## Structure and Growth

According to historical tradition and government documents, the president looks first to the State Department in making foreign policy. The State Department must serve as a transmission belt for information between the United States and foreign governments and as a resource for senior policy makers to

---

**HISTORICAL LESSON**

### Creating the OSS

The United States entered World War II with the bombing of Pearl Harbor. It soon became apparent to many that the U.S. military and foreign policy establishment was ill-suited to the task in front of it, and a number of steps were taken to bring greater coherence and resources to the war effort. One was to create the Joint Chiefs of Staff (JCS). A second was to create the Office of Strategic Services (OSS). President Franklin Roosevelt established it through a military order issued in June 1942. The OSS was assigned two main tasks in support of the work of the JCS. It was to collect and analyze strategic information and to conduct special operations that were not the responsibility of other agencies. For all practical purposes, this made the OSS the forerunner of the CIA.

Prior to the creation of the OSS, the United States barely had an intelligence service. No separate intelligence agency existed within the State Department. In 1922, it had only five employees classified as having intelligence responsibilities. In 1943, there were still only 18 Foreign Service Officers (FSOs) who were its main source of intelligence. The Army and Navy were only marginally better. In the 1930s, naval intelligence employed only 20 permanent civilian employees. The Army was limited by a congressional mandate to having no more than 32 military attachés abroad. The focus of intelligence work was on preventing subversive acts rather than on anticipating enemy actions. The U.S. code-breaking operation known as the Black Chamber had been shut down in 1929 by Secretary of State Henry Stimson, who once famously said, "gentlemen don't read each other's mail." The only active nonmilitary force in U.S. intelligence in the interwar years was the Federal Bureau of Investigation (FBI) under J. Edgar Hoover.

The driving force behind the OSS was William J. "Wild Bill" Donovan, a close personal advisor of Roosevelt. Donovan's thinking about the intelligence and security needs of the United States during wartime was heavily shaped by the British. Great Britain had become frustrated in dealing with the American national security bureaucracies because of the lack of a central point of contact that would permit coordinated planning. Initially the FBI was seen as the most

*(continued)*

*(continued)*

logical partner, but Hoover's personal ambitions and penchant for publicity led the British to explore an alternative channel. Donovan was that channel. He toured Europe in 1940 at the invitation of Prime Minister Winston Churchill as Roosevelt's personal representative and was coached on intelligence matters by William Stephenson, who was a key British intelligence officer operating out of New York City. Donovan came to embrace the British notion of a centralized intelligence service responsible for espionage, intelligence analysis, and subversive operations.

Hoover opposed the creation of such an agency out of fear that it would lead to a diminished role for the FBI in intelligence matters. Hitler's invasion of Russia put an end to this bureaucratic turf struggle. President Roosevelt endorsed Donovan's vision of a centralized intelligence agency and by executive order established the Office of Coordinator of Information, with Donovan as coordinator. A year later this office became OSS.

The OSS was divided into several different functional branches. The Research and Analysis branch carried out economic, political, and social analyses. A Secret Intelligence branch carried out clandestine collection activities. A Special Operations branch carried out sabotage and worked with resistance forces. A Counterespionage branch was charged with protecting American intelligence operations from enemy penetrations. A Morale Operations branch engaged in propaganda activities. The Operational Group conducted guerrilla warfare and covert action operations in enemy territory, and a Maritime Unit conducted maritime sabotage operations. The OSS encountered fierce bureaucratic opposition. The FBI was able to largely keep the OSS out of Latin America, and General Douglas MacArthur excluded the OSS from China. The military did not cooperate fully in sharing intelligence sources and material for analytic purposes.

At the end of World War II, Donovan proposed to President Harry Truman that the OSS be maintained as a peacetime intelligence organization. Truman disagreed. In 1945, he disbanded the OSS. Its various functions were distributed among existing intelligence organizations. The Research and Analysis branch went to the State Department and the Secret Intelligence branch and Counterespionage branch were transferred to the War Department. A centralized intelligence service would be reborn in 1947 with the passage of the National Security Act that created the CIA.

### Applying the Lesson

1. What does the history of the OSS foreshadow for the problems a new cyber command will face?
2. How similar are the bureaucratic problems confronting the CIA today to those that the OSS faced?
3. Was Truman right in his decision to shut down the OSS? ■

draw on as needed. Both of these tasks have become increasingly difficult to accomplish within the ever-expanding agenda of American foreign policy. Annually, the State Department represents the United States in over 50 major international organizations and at over 800 international conferences. The volume of information that it must process has grown at a staggering rate. In the late 1960s and early 1970s, an average of over 4,000 messages was processed each day. Over one-half were classified. By the mid-1980s, approximately 10,000 messages, reports, and instructions were sent and received by the State Department each day. Dean Rusk, secretary of state under presidents John Kennedy and Lyndon Johnson, estimated that he saw only 6 of every 1,000 cables sent to the State Department each day, and that the president saw only one or two. Rusk also estimated that he read only 20 to 30 of the 1,300 cables sent out each day.[2] By the end of the twentieth century, the State Department was electronically processing over 14,000 official records and 90,000 data messages each day along with over 20 million e-mail messages per year.

Management challenges also lie in the number of non–State Department personnel who can be found in American embassies. In 1994, only 38 percent of U.S. government personnel in embassies worked for the State Department; 36 percent worked for the Defense Department, 5 percent for the Justice Department, 3 percent for the Transportation Department, and 18 percent for the Treasury, Commerce, and Agriculture Departments.[3] The concept of a country team has been developed to bring coherence to the welter of agencies and programs that are now represented at an embassy.

As chief of mission, the ambassador heads the **country team**. In practice, ambassadors have found it quite difficult to exercise enough authority to transform a set of independent and often competing policies into a coordinated and coherent program. They have been frustrated by the scope and complexity of the programs being carried out, the access of non–State Department personnel to independent reporting channels, and the needs of these individuals to meet the performance and promotion standards set by their own bureaucracies. A recent example of this phenomenon is a 2005 Pentagon request to be allowed to put special operations forces into a country without the explicit approval of the ambassador. Also complicating the problem is the background of the ambassador. Frequently, the ambassador is not a career diplomat. Under Carter, 75 percent of all ambassadors were career diplomats. This was up from 40 percent in 1955 and 68 percent in 1962, but under Reagan it fell back to 60 percent.[4] Approximately 30 percent of President Clinton's appointments were noncareer diplomats.

The State Department's basic structure remained largely unchanged for the duration of the Cold War. Beneath the secretary of state were a small number of deputy secretaries of state with responsibility for political, economic, international security, and management affairs. The remainder of the State Department was organized around geographical areas and functional tasks. While the number and identity of the regional areas remained steady, the functional bureaus showed considerable change over time, as certain units such as the education and culture bureau disappeared and others such as the refugee bureau and a bureau responsible for human rights and humanitarian affairs were created. Bureaus were also transformed as the international agenda changed. For example, the International Scientific and Technical Bureau to the Oceans became the International Environment and Science Bureau.

In part, this organizational stability was realized by setting up semiautonomous organizations to deal with three of the more pressing problem areas of Cold War diplomacy: foreign aid, arms control, and dispersal of information. Their emergence reflects a trend begun in World War II when, rather than incorporate new foreign policy tasks into the State Department system, separate organizations operating under White House control were established. The United States Agency for International Development (USAID) was established in 1961 and was responsible for administering the U.S. foreign economic aid program. The Arms Control and Disarmament Agency (ACDA) was also established in 1961 and is responsible for conducting studies on arms control and disarmament policies, managing U.S. arms control and disarmament negotiations, overseeing U.S. participation in arms control agreements, and advising the president, the National Security Council (NSC), and the secretary of state on arms control and disarmament matters. The United States Information Agency (USIA) was established in 1953 and is charged with promoting a better understanding of the United States in other countries. The *Voice of America* is one of its best-known undertakings.

Today, the State Department is undergoing two profound changes. One change involves the State Department's "shrinking presence" overseas. Between 1993 and 1996, the State Department cut more than 2,000 employees and closed 5 embassies, 23 USAID missions, and 26 consulates, consulate generals, and State Department branch offices. This reduction is a by-product of a reduction in the international affairs budget from $37.5 billion in 1984 to $18.6 billion in 1996.

The second change is organizational. Already we have seen the formal integration of the USIA and ACDA into the State Department and an end to their status as semiautonomous agencies. The USAID retains its independent status, but its director reports to the secretary of state rather than to the president. More recently, Secretary of State Condoleezza Rice has set in motion a new set of changes. The arms proliferation and arms control bureaus have been combined into a Bureau of International Security and Nonproliferation, and a director of foreign assistance has been placed over all foreign aid programs, whether they are administered by the State Department or by the USAID.

## The State Department's Value System

In order to understand the State Department's value system, we need to look at both how secretaries of state and FSOs have defined their jobs.

THE SECRETARY OF STATE  Capturing the essence of the State Department's value system is best done by looking at how secretaries of state have defined their role and how the FSO corps approaches its job. The job of secretary of state is not an easy one. Cecil Crabb suggests that "almost without exception, every postwar Secretary of State has left under a cloud of criticism." Among the charges that have been leveled are lack of leadership (Dean Rusk), aloofness and arrogance (Dean Acheson), and overly zealous attempts to dominate foreign policy making (Henry Kissinger).

Secretaries of state have also found themselves excluded from key decisions. Cyrus Vance resigned from the Carter administration partly in protest over his exclusion from decision making on the Iranian hostage rescue effort. George Shultz claimed that he was only marginally informed of the NSC plan to sell U.S. weapons to Iran and secure the release of U.S. hostages in Lebanon during the Reagan administration.

In order to participate effectively in foreign policy making, secretaries of state, like their counterparts at Defense and the CIA do, need a power base from which to work. In practice, this has required that they must either become advocates of the State Department perspective or serve as the loyal ally of the president.[6] Each power base has its dangers and limitations. Adopting the first perspective makes one suspect in the White House, while the second makes one suspect within the State Department and runs the risk of letting it drift for lack of effective oversight. The greatest danger comes with the failure to establish any power base, a situation said to have been experienced by Madeline Albright, who served as secretary of state in the Clinton administration.

President George W. Bush's secretaries of state adopted both of these two role orientations. Colin Powell's primary role orientation was as a spokesperson for the State Department perspective. And, while he was credited with "historic" accomplishments in getting resources for the State Department and changing its culture,[5] his was not a dominant voice in foreign policy making. Powell's position repeatedly lost out to more hawkish ones advanced by Secretary of Defense Donald Rumsfeld and Vice President Dick Cheney. So often did this happen that, both before and after 9/11, Powell was on occasion described in the press as "missing in action."

Condoleezza Rice, who followed Colin Powell, built her power base around the close personal ties she had developed with the president during the campaign and as national security advisor in his first administration. Not all went smoothly for Rice. Many at the State Department found her lacking in this regard. Eighty-eight percent of those polled by the American Foreign Service Association did not consider Rice to be their advocate. They saw her as aloof and isolated, in contrast to Powell, who was seen as deeply involved and in touch with subordinates. The most pointed criticism of Rice's managerial abilities involved her advocacy of "transformational diplomacy." Rice did not define the term nor make resources available to implement it. A similar fate befell the Office of the Coordinator for Reconstruction and Stabilization, which was announced in 2004 with great fanfare to be the State Department's lead agency in managing postconflict situations. In 2008, it had fewer than 10 employees.[6]

Secretary of State Hillary Clinton marks a potentially interesting departure from the pattern of seeking a power base within the State Department or in the White House. As a strong political figure in her own right, the possibility exists that she could seek to establish an independent power base from which to operate as secretary of state. Clinton's first months as secretary of state did much to dispel fears that she would not be a team player but also revealed a penchant for speaking out on issues more bluntly than others in the Obama administration or State Department officials would prefer. Notable examples included a blunt call for stopping the construction of Israeli settlements in disputed territory, accusing Pakistan of abdicating to the Taliban in the border region, and comparing North Korea to an unruly child.

FOREIGN SERVICE OFFICERS    In October 2009, an FSO resigned in protest over U.S. foreign policy toward Afghanistan. While the first to do so because of this conflict, he was not the first to take such a drastic step. Three FSOs resigned in protest over the George W. Bush administration's policies leading up to the Iraq war.

At the heart of the State Department system is its FSO corps. The Foreign Service was created in 1924 by the Rogers Act. **Foreign Service Officers** were intended to be generalists, "trained to perform almost any task at any post in the world."[7] The principal organizational device for producing such individuals is to rotate them frequently among functional tasks and geographic areas. The civil service, which existed apart from the FSO corps, was relied on to perform the State Department's "lesser" technical and administrative tasks. In 1954, a reorganization proposal developed by Harry Wriston led to the merger of these two personnel systems. Provisions were also made for widespread lateral entry into the restructured FSO system. "Wristonization" was not a complete success. Integrating the two career tracks did not bridge the differences in outlook that had arisen between them. Some had hoped that lateral entry would "Americanize" the Foreign Service by bringing into the FSO individuals with pasts different from the eastern, Ivy League, and upper-class backgrounds associated with it. Wristonization also created new problems. It created resentment in the ranks of the FSOs, who felt that the corps was being diluted by the addition of outsiders.

Additionally these reforms created overcrowding at the top of the FSO career pyramid, because while the number of FSOs had increased, there was no increase in the number of highly desirable positions. Further reform of the FSO system took place in 1980 with the passage of the Foreign Service Officer Act. It too trimmed the number of positions available for senior FSOs. From 1986 to 1990, between 350 and 450 upper-grade FSOs were forced to retire. The American Foreign Service Association contends that the negative impact of the 1980 reforms goes deeper than number cuts and extends to the quality of U.S. foreign policy:

> No one wants to serve as the political or economic counselor at overseas embassies because these are not management jobs. No one is going to be willing to spend two or three years learning Chinese or Japanese, because it's likely to be regarded as dead time when you come before a promotion board. The word in the corridors now is get a job managing something and forget everything else, or you're dead.[8]

FSO misgivings about their place in the making of American foreign policy have grown over time. Under Reagan and George H. W. Bush the concern was **political creep** By this, FSOs meant the tendency for political appointees to be placed at the assistant secretary and deputy secretary positions. In the 1950s, few political appointees could be found at these levels. In 1973, only 11 of 63 deputy assistant secretaries of state were political appointees. In 1984, almost one-half (59 of 136) were political appointees. Beyond the loss of job opportunities, FSOs complained that the presence of this "new blood" made it difficult to have frank discussions of thorny issues.[9] Under President Clinton, the problem was the potential outright elimination of these positions as part of the effort to hold down costs. The administration's initial reorganization plan called for cutting as many as 40 deputy assistant secretary positions. Under George W. Bush the concern was with the administration's emphasis on military solutions to problems and the dominant voice that gave the Pentagon in foreign policy decision making.

The representativeness of the FSO corps continues to be a major problem. Minorities and women are particularly underrepresented. In late 1993, 56 percent of the FSO corps was white male, 24 percent white female, 7 percent minority male, and 4 percent minority female. The distribution is even more skewed if attention is paid only to the senior ranks of the FSO Corps, from which ambassadors and policy makers are selected. At this same time, 84 percent were white male, 9 percent white female, 5 percent minority male, and 1 percent minority female.[10] Over one 11-year period, 586 appointments were made to the post of deputy chief of mission. Women received only nine of them. At the same time, women were appointed to consular positions (which deal largely with passport and visa matters) as opposed to political posts (where one is likely to be involved in policy making) so much more frequently than men that the odds of being appointed to political posts were one in one million. These revelations came about as part of a lawsuit filed against the State Department in 1976. In 1989, the State Department finally admitted that discrimination did exist and began taking steps to address the problem. In March 2000, the State Department settled the largest employment discrimination case ever, by agreeing to pay $508 million to approximately 1,100 women who were denied employment or promotion by the USIA and the Voice of America between 1974 and 1984.

The State Department is not alone in facing charges of discrimination. In 1993, "Jane Doe Thompson," a CIA professional with over 20 years' experience in the clandestine service and who had once served as station chief, sued the CIA charging sex discrimination. In a separate legal action, over 100 female officers in the clandestine division, almost one-third of all female case officers, joined in a class action lawsuit alleging discrimination. The CIA settled both matters out of court. In the class action suit, it agreed to pay $990,000 in back salaries and to make 25 retroactive promotions.

For its part, the military continues to struggle with questions about the place of gays in the military and the treatment of women. A "don't ask, don't tell" policy was put in place in 1994 that allowed gays to serve in the military. This has not stopped gays from being discharged, however. This number reached an estimated 10,000 in 2005, including 300 language specialists, over 50 of whom were fluent in Arabic. Harassment of women continues to be a major issue for the military. A 2008 government survey of 14 military installations found that one-half of the cases of sexual assault go unreported, with about 34 percent of the women in the military stating that they have been sexually harassed.

The heart of the FSO corps is its value system. The subject of repeated studies, the FSO value system consists of a clearly identifiable world outlook and set of guidelines for survival within the State Department bureaucracy.[11] Agreement also exists in the belief that these qualities are not conducive to the formulation and administration of U.S. foreign policy and that they are one reason for the State Department's declining influence on foreign affairs. Central to the belief system of the FSO is the dual conviction that the only career experience relevant to the work of the State Department is that gained in the foreign service, and that the core of this work lies in the areas of political reporting, negotiating, and representing U.S. interests abroad. The FSO is empirical, intuitive, and cautious.[12] Risk taking in the preparation of analysis or processing of information is avoided. As many as 27 signatures have been required before instructions were sent regarding the Food for Peace program. As one observer put it, the "desk officer 'inherits' a policy toward country X, he regards it as his function to keep that policy intact."[13]

Changes are coming to the FSO system. Under the heading of "transformational diplomacy," Rice had indicated that she was altering the way in which diplomats are posted. No longer will European embassies house as many diplomats. Instead, the focus will shift to the Middle East and Asia. Under Rice's plan, FSOs will no longer be promoted to senior ranks unless they accept assignment to dangerous places, gain expertise in two regions, and become fluent in two languages, with Chinese, Urdu, and Arabic being cited as preferred examples. This policy could affect as many as one-third of the 6,400 FSO positions. Additionally, in mid-2007 Rice announced that all U.S. diplomatic positions in Iraq had to be filled before any other State Department openings in Washington, DC, or elsewhere were filled. Approximately 20 percent of U.S. FSOs had already served in Iraq at the time of her announcement. Rice's announcement of forced postings to Iraq met strong opposition from FSOs. In the end, no one was required to accept an assignment to Iraq under the threat of dismissal, because enough volunteers stepped forward.

Of even greater potential long-term significance is a change in how FSOs are selected. Instead of competing in a national exam covering a dozen subject areas and then passing an interview test, applicants for the Foreign Service will now take a shortened test and be judged on their team-building skills and résumés. This move is necessary, its proponents argue, to attract large numbers of quality applicants to a career that is increasingly taking back seat to private-sector opportunities.

## Impact on Foreign Policy

The State Department, once the centerpiece of the foreign affairs bureaucracy, has seen its power and influence steadily erode. It has gone from being the leading force behind such policies as the Marshall Plan, NATO, and containment to largely playing the role of the critic who finds fault with the proposals of others. It has become defensive and protective in interdepartmental dealings, unable to centralize and coordinate the activities of the foreign affairs bureaucracy. Two complaints frequently are voiced about the State Department's performance. First, its recommendations are too predictable. Regardless of the problem, the State Department can be counted on to advocate minimizing risks, avoiding quick action, and adopting a long-term perspective on the problem. Second, its recommendations are insensitive to the presidential perspective on foreign policy matters. It fails to frame proposals in ways that will produce political support or at least minimize the political costs to the president. The combined result is that State Department recommendations are easily dismissed. In the eyes of many, it has become more of a spokesperson for foreign viewpoints within the U.S. government than an advocate of U.S. national interests. This situation is not condemned by all. To some it is the role the State Department should play (and a role it plays well), and they believe it should stop trying to perform functions for which it is no longer suited.[14]

The State Department's inability to exercise leadership in foreign policy has repeatedly produced calls for reform. Former secretary of state Lawrence Eagleburger asserts that the proliferation of assistant secretaries has "balkanized" the administrative apparatus, making it difficult for the State Department to speak in one voice.[15] Calling the department a "crippled institution," long-time critic and former Speaker of the House of Representatives Newt Gingrich has called for a "top-to-bottom" transformation of the State Department that will place it more effectively under the control of the president and bring it more in line with American values.[16] This is not the first time the State Department has come under fire. In the 1950s, it was a prime target of the McCarthy investigations into un-American activities. In 1953 alone, some 70–80 percent of the highest-ranking FSOs were dismissed, resigned, or were reassigned to politically safe positions.[17]

# THE DEFENSE DEPARTMENT

Just as in our discussion of the State Department, we are interested in looking at the structure and growth of the Defense Department, its internal value system, and its impact on foreign policy.

## Structure and Growth

For most of its history, the military security of the United States was provided by forces under the command of the War Department and the Department of the Navy. No political or military authority other than the president existed above these two departments to coordinate and direct their affairs. During World War II the ineffectiveness of this system became apparent and led U.S. policy makers to take a series of ad hoc steps to bring greater coherence to the U.S. war effort. In 1947 the National Security Act formalized many of these arrangements by establishing a Department of the Air Force and giving legal standing to the JCS. It also created a National Military Establishment and the position of Secretary of Defense. Further changes were made in 1949, when the National Military Establishment was redesignated as the Defense Department.

The dominant reform issue of the early 1980s within the defense establishment was improving the operational efficiency of the armed forces. The failed 1979 hostage rescue effort, the 1983 terrorist attack on the marines in Beirut, and problems encountered in the 1983 invasion of Grenada were cited by many military reformers as proof that reforms were needed, beginning at the very top.[18] Congress shared the concerns of defense reformers. Over the objections of the executive branch and many in the military, in 1986 it passed two pieces of legislation designed to remedy perceived shortcomings in the performance of the U.S. military. The Goldwater–Nichols Act strengthened the position of the JCS relative to that of the individual services. It also gave added weight to those parts of the Pentagon that had an interservice perspective. The second piece of legislation, the Cohen–Nunn Act, established a unified command for special operations and created an Assistant Secretary of Defense for special operations and low-intensity conflict.

Today, two fundamental and underlying issues dominate the military reform agenda. The first is the need to find a response to the personnel crunch facing the military. The Army has experienced this problem most acutely. In 1990, at the end of the Cold War, the Army had 732,403 active-duty soldiers. In 2002, this number was down to 486,542.

The military has sought to soften the blow of these decreased numbers on its operational preparedness through three actions. One was to **outsource** many tasks to private contractors. These ranged from the mundane (feeding personnel and cutting lawns) to the complex (maintaining tactical systems and drone aircraft), to the highly sensitive (interrogating prisoners). During the Persian Gulf War, some military units operated at one contractor for every 25–50 military personnel. In the Balkans, the ratio was 1 contractor per 10 combatants, and this carried over to the start of the Iraq War.[19] The second compensatory action was to rely more heavily on National Guard and reserve forces. By 2005, almost 400,000 of the nearly 870,000 members of the reserves have been activated since 9/11. This represents the greatest proportional use of the National Guard and reserves since World War II.

Third, it has stepped up its recruitment efforts, but this in turn has brought with it new problems.[20] More and more the military has come to rely on young men and women from economically depressed rural areas. More than 44 percent of U.S. recruits in 2004 came from rural areas, compared to 14 percent from major cities. The education level has dropped to a new low. In 2005, 83.5 percent of new recruits were high school graduates. In 2007, it was 71 percent. There has also been a decline in the number of African American recruits. Whereas in 2001 there were almost 51,500 new black recruits, in 2006 that number fell by 38 percent, to less than 32,000. Over roughly this same time period, the percentage of Hispanic recruits increased from 10 percent to 13 percent. A significant factor in the drop in African American recruits appears to be the unpopularity of the Iraq War.

Finally the armed services are increasingly giving "conduct waivers" to enlist individuals with criminal records including felony convictions.

Transforming the mission of the Defense Department is the second major reform issue. In 2001, the Bush administration's **Quadrennial Defense Review** (QDR) moved away from a two-war concept, in which the United States would have to possess the capability to fight and win two major wars at the same time, to one that emphasized the need to defeat two aggressors at the same time but removed the requirement of being able to occupy both countries. Secretary of Defense Gates hopes to use the 2010 QDR to redirect U.S. defense efforts from long-range hypothetical threats such as a rising China to immediate ones like Pakistan and Afghanistan. Among the scenarios under discussion for inclusion in it are the possibilities of militants in Pakistan getting control over its nuclear weapons and a conflict between China and Taiwan.

## The Defense Department's Value System

Understanding the Defense Department's internal value system requires that we look at how secretaries of defense have defined their job as well as how the professional military approach its job.

SECRETARY OF DEFENSE    Secretaries of defense generally have adopted one of two roles.[21] The first is that of the generalist. According to James Roherty, the generalist recognizes and defers to military expertise. He is concerned with coordinating and integrating the judgments he receives from the military professionals. He sees himself as being the Defense Department's representative in the policy process. In contrast, the functionalist is concerned with consolidating management and policy control in the office of the secretary of defense. The functionalist rejects the notion that there exists a unique area of military expertise, and he sees himself as first among equals in defense policy decision making. Above all else, the functionalist seeks to manage the system efficiently in accordance with presidential policy objectives.

James Forrestal, the first secretary of defense, adopted the generalist perspective. As secretary of the Navy he had opposed creating a unified military establishment, and his tenure as secretary of defense was marked by repeated efforts by the services to protect their standing as independent organizations. Robert McNamara, who served as secretary of defense during the Vietnam War, was a functionalist who sought to move decision-making power out of the hands of the military services and into the civilians in the Office of the Secretary of Defense. To do so he brought Planning, Programming, and Budgetary Systems (PPBS) analysis to the Defense Department. As was commonplace in other government bureaucracies, the Defense Department's budget was organized by department (Army, Navy, Air Force) and broken down into such traditional categories as personnel, maintenance, and construction. Under PPBS, "all military forces and systems were grouped into output-oriented programs according to their principal missions [conventional defense of Europe, nuclear deterrence], even though missions cut across traditional service boundaries categories."[22]

Donald Rumsfeld, George W. Bush's first secretary of defense, established himself from the very outset of the administration as a functionalist who intended to alter the fundamental direction of American military policy and organization. Military professionals saw his presence as a "hostile takeover."[23] One of his favored managerial techniques was to send "snowflakes" (short notes written on white paper) demanding prompt answers to questions or complaints about matters both large and small. After snowflakes came follow-on snowflakes. Before the terrorist attacks of 9/11, his outspoken criticism of the military, intrusive management style, and abrasiveness alienated so many that he was widely rumored to be in danger of being forced from office. Victory against the Taliban in Afghanistan and the success of his military strategy of a rapid military advance with minimum forces against Baghdad appeared to vindicate his arguments and greatly elevated his standing in the White House and in Congress. Subsequent problems with the occupation and reconstruction of Iraq led to open questioning of his ideas and management style. This was particularly true with regard to questions about accountability and the chain of command in the interrogation abuses at the Abu Ghraib prison and the inadequate number and overall lack of preparation of U.S. occupation forces.

Immediately after the 2006 midterm elections, George W. Bush replaced Rumsfeld with Robert Gates, who had served as head of the CIA under George H. W. Bush. Gates continued on as secretary of defense under Obama. After he took over, talk of transformation quickly subsided. Gates moved to repair the working relationship between the civilians and the professional military officers in the Pentagon and to restore accountability by removing individuals responsible for the situation at the Walter Reed Medical Center. This did not mean, however, that Gates was a generalist. He quickly established himself as a functionalist, moving aggressively to restructure defense-spending priorities away from advanced technology, high-cost, long lead-time weapons systems as well as such traditional military priorities as aircraft carriers and the U.S. missile defense system to simpler systems that could be put into combat quickly.

**PROFESSIONAL MILITARY**    To understand the system of values inside the Defense Department, we need to examine the outlook of the professional military toward policy making at two different levels. Two different general sets of perspectives exist on the nature of **civil–military relations**.[24] The traditional view of civil–military relations sees the professional soldier as being above partisan politics. A clear line separates military and political affairs, and professional soldiers are expected to restrict themselves to speaking out only on those subjects that fall within their sphere of expertise. In the fusionist perspective, the professional soldier must acquire and use political skills if he or she is to exercise an effective voice on military matters. Moreover, the line separating military decisions from political ones is blurred. No pure area of military expertise exists wherein the professional soldier can expect to find his or her opinion accepted without challenge by civilian policy makers. To the fusionist, military involvement in traditional nonmilitary areas is all but guaranteed by the increasing use of the military as an instrument of foreign policy and by problems of resource scarcity. The challenges to a president created by the fusionist perspective were fully evident in the dilemma facing the Obama administration on how to proceed in Afghanistan. General Stanley McChrystal's public evaluation of the situation there as dire and his call for a significant increase in the U.S. presence put him at odds with many civilians in the administration and helped create a politically charged domestic political climate within which Obama had to make a decision.

If we look down one level further, we see differences in outlook among the military services. They each have different "personalities."[25] The Navy, it is said, worships at the altar of tradition, the Air Force at the altar of technology, and the Army at that of country and duty. They also have different views of their own identities. The Navy sees itself above all as an institution whose stature and independence must be protected. The Air Force sees itself as the embodiment of the idea that air power is the key guarantor of national security in the modern age. The Army views itself as artisans of warfare, whose members are divided into mutually supportive guilds—infantry, artillery, and armor (cavalry). These different traits, combined with other differences, give each service a distinct outlook on questions of war and on peace and on the use of force as an instrument of U.S. foreign policy.

One of the challenges facing the U.S. Army today is to change its thinking about the conduct of war away from a focus on coventional wars to counterinsurgency warfare. One of the strategies being used by General David Petreaus is to promote to brigadier general those colonels who have established themseves as "unconventional thinkers" regarding combat in Iraq. He is supported in this culture-changing mission by Secretary of Defense Gates, who has argued that there needs to be an end to the fascination with pursuing new generations of military technology and a focus on sovling today's problems. The belief that a new generation of military technology particulary in the areas of satellites, weapons-guiding systems, and communications could provide a significant battlefield advantage to U.S. forces had been one of the central tenets of the **Revolution in Military Affairs** (RMA) concept that came to dominate U.S. defense thinking after the Persian Gulf War in 1991 and was seen by many as contributing to the smaller-than-needed contingent of U.S. forces sent out into Iraq after the defeat of Saddam Hussein.

## Impact on Foreign Policy

The professional military's impact on foreign policy is a subject that is often discussed with great emotion. While some believe that military professionals are more aggressive than their civilian counterparts, evidence suggest otherwise.[26] Where the military professional and the civilian policy maker part company is over how and when to use force, not over whether to use it. The military prefers to use force quickly, massively, and decisively, and it is skeptical of making bluffs that involve the threatened use of force. Diplomats, on the other hand, prefer to avoid using force as long as possible, because they see its use as an indication of a failure in policy, but they are positively predisposed to making military threats.

The military's real policy influence comes not through its direct participation in the policy process but through its indirect influence: its ability to get the context of a decision through the presentation of information, capabilities, and tactics. Bob Woodward, author of *The Commanders,* similarly reflects on how variable the influence of the military is on decisions regarding the use of force.[27] The Pentagon, he notes, "is not always the center of military decision making." It was so in the months before the George H. W. Bush administration's invasion of Panama, when the attention of the White House was on other matters. In the case of the Persian Gulf War, the White House paid attention to little else. "When the President and his advisors are engaged, they run the show." The same can be said for the Iraq War. Planning was not taken out of the hands of the military, but their input into the construction of a war plan was highly structured by Rumsfeld. Similarly in 2006–2007 the George W. Bush administration pushed ahead with plans for a surge in U.S. force levels in Iraq in spite of sentiments voiced by many in the military that such a move (which they had once advocated) was no longer desirable or practical.

# CIA AND THE INTELLIGENCE COMMUNITY

Unlike our discussion of the State Department and Defense Department, we are not concerned here with just one bureaucracy, the CIA, but a set of bureaucracies that together make up the intelligence community.

## Structure and Growth

Two points need to be stressed before outlining the makeup of the intelligence community. First, the concept of a community implies similarity and likeness, and it suggests the existence of a group of actors who share common goals and possess a common outlook on events. In these terms the U.S. intelligence community is a community only in the loosest sense. More accurately, it is a federation of units existing with varying degrees of institutional autonomy in their contribution to the intelligence function. Second, the intelligence community is not a static entity. Its composition, as well as the relative importance of its members, has changed over time as new technologies have been developed, the international setting has changed, and bureaucratic wars have been won and lost.

The status of charter member is best conferred on the CIA; the State Department's intelligence unit, the Bureau of Intelligence and Research (INR); and the intelligence units of the armed forces. All of these were given institutional representation on the NSC at the time of its creation. Three institutions that have a long-standing but lesser presence in the intelligence community are the FBI, the Treasury Department, and the Atomic Energy Commission (AEC), which is now found in the Energy Department. The newest addition to the intelligence community is the Department of Homeland Security. It does not possess an independent intelligence-gathering ability. Its primary intelligence missions are to monitor, assess, and coordinate indications and warnings related to terrorist threats against the United States and to gather and integrate terrorist-related information from its component agencies.

Historically, the most significant additions to the intelligence community have been military-related intelligence agencies. The first addition came in 1952, when Truman issued a presidential directive transforming the recently created Armed Forces Security Agency into the NSA.[28] This operates as a semiautonomous agency of the Defense Department and is charged with (1) maintaining the security of U.S. message traffic and (2) interpreting traffic, analyzing, and cryptanalyzing the messages of all other states. In 1961, the Defense Intelligence Agency (DIA) joined the intelligence community as its newest major member. The DIA emerged as part of the centralization process then occurring within the Defense Department. The major objectives behind its creation were to unify the overall intelligence efforts of the Defense Department and to collect, produce, and disseminate military intelligence more effectively. Over the years, DIA emerged as the principal challenger to the CIA in the preparation of intelligence estimates. Under George W. Bush, the challenge to the CIA came from a newly created Office of Special Plans (OSP). Its mission was to provide an independent review of raw intelligence and dispute the mainstream interpretations given to it by the intelligence community. Both the CIA's and OSP's intelligence analyses before the Iraq War came in for criticism, but for different reasons. The CIA was criticized for missing warnings of the 9/11 attack and for its failure to express its doubts over the quality of intelligence behind the decision to go to war. The OSP was criticized for "cherry-picking" intelligence that suited the prowar case being advanced by Rumsfeld and Cheney and "stovepiping" it forward out of normal channels into the intelligence estimating process.

From the time of its creation in 1947 until the establishment of the Office of the Director of National Intelligence (DNI) in 2004, the Director of the CIA also served as the head of the intelligence community, giving the CIA the status of first among equals. Organizationally, there are four major operational components to the CIA. Each is headed by a deputy director who reports to the Director of Central Intelligence (DCI).[29] The Directorate of Support is responsible for recruitment, training, support activities, communications, and the physical security of CIA buildings. The Directorate of Science and Technology (DS&T) is the newest major directorate. It was established in the early 1960s out of the conviction that technology had begun to change the nature of the intelligence function and that the CIA had to stay on top of this trend. The results of these efforts have been considerable. The U-2 and SR-71 spy planes and satellite reconnaissance systems all owe much to the efforts of this directorate.

The third operating unit of the CIA is the Directorate of Intelligence (DI). The DI is the primary producer of government intelligence documents, which range in frequency from daily briefs (at varying levels of secrecy) to weekly, quarterly, and yearly summaries, to occasional special reports. The best known of these reports are the National Intelligence Estimates (NIEs). The most notable NIE was that on the state of Iraq's weapons of mass destruction, which the Bush administration used to support its invasion of Iraq. That NIE was alternately seen as a sign of the politicalization of intelligence or the incompetence of the intelligence community.

The fourth directorate is the National Clandestine Service. It has been the most controversial component of the CIA. The National Clandestine Service has three basic missions: the clandestine collection of information, counterintelligence, and covert action. Within it there exists a staff for each mission. The Foreign Intelligence Service monitors, assesses, and directs the clandestine collection of information; the counterintelligence staff is concerned with protecting the CIA from foreign penetrations; and the covert-action staff plans and carries out covert actions. Its actual operations are grouped on regional lines and subdivided into stations. Each station is headed by a station chief and is generally housed in the U.S. embassy. Their size varies from only a few individuals to several hundred.

Periodically throughout its history, the CIA has found itself an institution under siege. This has usually been because of failings in the area of covert action. Since the 1990s, however, it is the CIA's intelligence failures that have led to demands for reform, restructuring, and transferring its duties to other agencies. Well before 9/11, calls for action came from all quarters. In the Senate, Daniel Patrick Moynihan was so outraged over the CIA's failure to anticipate the fall of communism in the Soviet Union that he called for its abolition. Post–Cold War Directors of Central Intelligence commented publicly on the need for the CIA to undertake institutional changes and reexamine its intelligence priorities.[30] In November 1991, President George H. W. Bush issued National Security Directive 29, calling for a "top-to-bottom examination of the mission, role, and priorities of the intelligence community."

Demands for reform were a common theme in the investigations conducted by the House and Senate intelligence committees, and the special commission set up to investigate 9/11. Included in the commission's recommendations were the creation of a new national terrorism center and the establishment of a cabinet-level post of DNI to oversee the CIA, FBI, and other intelligence agencies. Support was strong in Congress for such reforms, but they were opposed within the executive branch. The CIA called them unnecessary, and the Defense Department feared the budgetary and control implications of a new national director of intelligence. An estimated 80–90 percent of the intelligence budget is allocated to Pentagon intelligence units. Under pressure to act and in the middle of a close election campaign, a reluctant President George W. Bush endorsed the concept of a White House–based national intelligence director in August 2004. The position was officially created in December, with the signing into law of the Intelligence Reform and Terrorism Prevention Act.

## The Intelligence Community's Value System

Criticism of the CIA has not been directed only at its structure. Also coming in for censure has been the manner in which both its top leadership and professionals approached their job. The Senate Intelligence Committee's report placed a major portion of the blame for the intelligence failures on Iraq and before 9/11 on "a broken corporate culture and poor management." It is to this side of the CIA that we now turn.

DIRECTOR OF CENTRAL INTELLIGENCE   The DCI was simultaneously head of the intelligence community and the CIA. Because of this dual position, DCIs had many role orientations available to choose from. Few had sought, and none had achieved, real managerial control over the intelligence community. The most recent to try was Stansfield Turner, President Carter's DCI, who ran into stiff and successful resistance from Secretary of Defense Brown. The DCIs did not give priority to their role as head of the intelligence community because significant weaknesses lie beneath their formal position. Of all the members of the intelligence community, only the CIA exists as a separate organizational entity; all the others are parts of larger departments, most often the Defense Department. Consequently, the other members of the intelligence community look with only one eye to what the DCI demands while keeping the other eye firmly fixed on departmental positions and priorities. As a result, the DCI's budgetary authority over the other members of the intelligence community remained largely unrealized, and his ability to direct their collection efforts was imperfect.

When defining their role as head of the CIA, three outlooks have been dominant: managerial, covert action, and estimating. Only John McCone (1961–1965) gave primacy to the intelligence-estimating role, and he was largely an outsider to the intelligence process before his appointment. Allen Dulles (1953–1965) and Richard Helms (1966–1973) both stressed the covert-action side of the agency's mission. Since the replacement of Helms by James Schlesinger, DCIs have tended to adopt a managerial orientation. Although their particular operating styles have varied, a common theme to these managerial efforts was to increase White House control over the CIA.

Controversy has surrounded the managerial orientations of recent DCIs. One frequently leveled complaint is that the heads of the CIA have politicized the intelligence process. By this it is meant that they have used their managerial control over intelligence products to ensure that its findings are consistent with the policy preferences of the administration and do not reflect the judgment of intelligence professionals. **Politicizing intelligence** was a charge directed at George Tenet. Described as the "ultimate staff guy," his appointment was seen as proof of "the rewards of being a loyal and obedient servant of one's boss."[31] Tenet became DCI under Clinton and retained that position under George W. Bush, quickly becoming regarded as a team player. Tenet resigned in June 2004, after having become a central figure in the debate over whether the CIA as an organization or he personally had overstated the case for war with Iraq.

Leon Panetta, who was named DCI by Obama, fits very much into this mold of director whose primary mission is to control the CIA. Lacking in any background in intelligence, Panetta is a trusted Democratic Party figure who served as Chief of Staff in Clinton's administration. Reasserting control became a paramount concern for the new administration in the aftermath of the political dispute over interrogation methods used against prisoners at Guantanamo Bay and Bush's policy of authorizing warrantless wiretaps against American citizens as part of the war on terror.

DIRECTOR OF NATIONAL INTELLIGENCE   The DNI is torn by the same types of role conflicts that have afflicted DCIs: the need to establish a power base and the need to define an orientation to intelligence. On one level, the DNI has established his position as the spokesperson for the intelligence community. Upon assuming office, John Negroponte, the first DNI, began to give the daily briefing to the president instead of the head of the CIA. Negroponte also dominated the annual threat assessment given by the intelligence community to the Senate Select Committee on Intelligence. Prior to 2006 no single individual from the intelligence community had delivered the global threat briefing. Instead, the heads of the FBI, CIA, INR, and DIA each presented individual statements.

On another level, serious problems remain. Not long after the 9/11 Commission's report was released, Secretary of Defense Rumsfeld announced that he would create an undersecretary of defense for intelligence who would have authority over all of the Defense Department's intelligence units and control their budgets, and the FBI moved 96 percent of its intelligence budget into units that were not under the jurisdiction of the DNI. Second, some observers have expressed concern that although the DNI was expected to be a lean management organization sitting atop the intelligence community, it had already grown to have a staff of 1,539 people. Obama's DNI Dennis Blair quickly clashed with DCI Panetta on control over covert action, with Blain sending out a statement saying his office would now determine who the covert action station chief would be and Panetta countering it with a communication of his own indicating that it would remain a CIA decision. The Senate Intelligence Committee injected itself into the dispute siding with Blair. The final White House decision largely supported the CIA'S position.

INTELLIGENCE PROFESSIONALS   In order to understand how the intelligence professional thinks about intelligence, we first need to note how the consumers of intelligence think about it, because it is their demands and inquiries to which the intelligence professional responds.[32] First is the conviction that analysts should furnish information and nothing more. Analysts are not expected to explore alternatives or come to conclusions—this is the responsibility of the consumer. The underlying assumption is that the facts contain self-evident implications and that if all the facts are known, then any question can be answered. Second is the assumption that experience rather than the application of analytical techniques to a problem provides the most insight into the meaning of raw data. Third is an emphasis on current events. The perceived need is for up-to-the-minute information to solve an ongoing problem. Long-range planning is too academic an exercise and too far removed from the policy maker's most immediate concerns to be highly valued. A final shared attitude toward intelligence is the tendency to treat it as a free good. Intelligence is seen as something "on tap" and always on call.

The views on intelligence within the intelligence community are far from uniform. Differences exist both between and within organizations.[33] With this qualification in mind, it is possible to identify four tendencies in the approach to intelligence adopted by members of the intelligence community.[34] One tendency is to be current events oriented and to be a "butcher," cutting up the latest information and presenting the choicest pieces to the consumer. This perspective appears to be adopted only grudgingly by analysts, out of a desire to participate in the policy process. Analysts see their most important role as that of giving warning, but to stick to this role orientation in the face of policy-maker disinterest condemns them to working on the fringe of the policy process. A second tendency is for analysts to adopt a "jigsaw theory" of intelligence. The analyst here acts like a "baker"; everything and anything is sought after, classified, and stored, on the assumption that at some point in time it may be the missing ingredient to solving a riddle. Like the butcher, the baker's role orientation is consistent with the policy maker's notion of intelligence as a free good and the assumption that the ambiguity of data can be overcome by collecting more data.

A third tendency is for the production of "intelligence to please" or "backstopping." Often, when consumers of intelligence stress current data, they combine it with known policy preferences. The analyst is then placed in a very difficult position. Efforts at providing anything but supportive evidence will be ignored. Decisions on troop strength in Vietnam and target selection for bombing and rescue raids reveal the extent to which pressures to produce "intelligence to please" can be felt and the detrimental effect this can have on the intelligence function. The final role orientation is that of the "intelligence maker," who acts as an organizational broker, forging a consensus on the issue at hand. Because a consensus is needed for action, this role orientation is valuable, but a danger exists in that the consensus does not have to be based on an accurate reading of events. Facts bargained into existence provide an equally suitable basis for a consensus.

Mike McConnell, who became DNI in 2007, identified changing the organizational culture of intelligence professionals as one of the primary means of improving the performance of the intelligence community.[35] He asserted that the mindset of "need to know," which stresses secrecy in collection and analysis, must be replaced by one of "responsibility to provide," and that instead of thinking in terms of vertical lines of accountability and reporting, a horizontal perspective that cuts across organizational lines must be created. An important component of this culture shift, in his view, is new hiring practices to bring a new generation of professionals into the intelligence community.

## Impact on Foreign Policy

The purpose of intelligence is to provide policy makers with enough warning to allow them to act in the face of a challenge to national security. This is not easily done. Surprise is a fundamental reality of international politics, and no foreign policy or defense establishment can expect to escape completely from its negative consequences. Yet intelligence is not easily integrated into the policy process.[36] The conventional wisdom holds that policy and analysis must be kept separate, or policy will corrupt analysis. The alternative view holds that analysis cannot be kept value free or separate from policy making. This position holds that analysts must articulate and evaluate policy options as well as force policy makers to confront alternatives.

The relationship between the CIA and the president is the key determinant of its impact on the policy process. This relationship is marked by a series of tensions that often serve to make the impact of intelligence on policy less than what it could be under optimum circumstances. The first tension is between the logic of intelligence and the logic of policy making.[37] The logic of intelligence is to reduce policy options by clarifying issues, assumptions, and consequences. The logic of policy making is to keep options open for as long as possible. One way to do this is to keep secrets from intelligence agencies. The second tension is between the type of information the president wants to receive and the type of information that the intelligence community is predisposed to collect and disseminate. Commenting on his experience at the INR, Thomas Hughes states that policy makers were most eager to get information that would help them convince Congress or the public about the merits of a policy. They were most frustrated with information that was politically impossible to use and generally skeptical about the incremental value of added information for policy-making purposes.[38] Third, intelligence produced by the intelligence community is not the only source of information available to policy makers. Interest groups, lobbyists, the media, and personal acquaintances all compete with it, and presidents are free to choose which intelligence they wish to listen to. No one can make a policy maker accept or act on a piece of intelligence.

# THE DOMESTIC BUREAUCRACIES

The most recent additions to the foreign affairs bureaucracy are organizations that have been classified traditionally as domestic in their concerns and areas of operation. Their foreign policy involvement parallels a process that happened with the Defense Department. After World War II, the Defense Department rather than the State Department was instrumental in shaping global arms development programs and international security arrangements.[39]

Integrating these newcomers into the foreign affairs bureaucracy has not been an easy task. At the core of the problem is finding an agreed-on balance between foreign policy and domestic concerns. In the early post–World War II period, the foreign policy goal of containing communism dominated over private economic goals, but, more recently, domestic goals have become dominant and are often pursued at the cost of broad foreign policy objectives.

## Treasury, Commerce, and Agriculture

Foremost among the domestic bureaucracies are the Treasury, Commerce, and Agriculture Departments. By the mid-1970s the State Department had become more of a participant than a leader in the field of international economic policy. Its chief bureaucratic challenger is the Treasury Department, and the two approach international economic policy from quite different perspectives. Like the other domestic bureaucracies, the Treasury Department takes an **"America first" perspective** and places the needs of its clients at the center of its concerns. One author describes it as having an "undifferentiating adversary attitude" toward world affairs.[40] This is in contrast to the State Department's tendency to adopt a long-range perspective on international economic problems and one sensitive to the position of other states. A type of standoff currently exists between the State Department and Treasury Department for influence in the policy process. Each exercises a virtual veto over intragovernmental agreements on international economic policy. When disagreements arise, the issue gets kicked up the bureaucratic ladder for a decision by higher authorities. However, it now takes a strong secretary of state to neutralize the influence of the Treasury Department and its domestic allies.[41]

The Commerce Department has also emerged as a major foreign affairs bureaucracy, but its influence is not on the level of the Treasury Department's. It still functions as somewhat of a junior partner and is more involved in operating issues than in policy ones. Until 1969 the Commerce Department's primary foreign policy involvement stemmed from its responsibility for overseeing U.S. export control policy. These controls were aimed largely at restricting the direct or indirect sale of strategic goods to communist states. In 1969, its mandate was expanded to include encouraging "peaceful trade with the East" while at the same time "vigilantly protecting" U.S. national security interests. Since 1980 the Commerce Department has become the primary implementer of nonagricultural trade policy and the chief administrator of U.S. export and import programs. As part of this task, it supervises the enforcement of antidumping regulations and the distribution of assistance to industries injured because of lower-priced imports. Through its Foreign Commercial Service, the Commerce Department has representatives stationed in 66 countries and has become active in export-promotion activities. The Commerce Department is not without its own challengers for influence on trade policy. The Office of the U.S. Trade Representative has also benefited at the expense of the State Department, and it enjoys a great deal of congressional support for its activities.

The Agriculture Department also remains a junior partner in the foreign affairs bureaucracy. It is active in administering U.S. food export programs throughout the world and has representatives in approximately 40 embassies. Its best-known foreign policy role is as the administrator of P.L. 480, the Food for Peace program, which provides for the free export of government-owned agricultural commodities for humanitarian and developmental purposes. In 2003, the Agriculture Department became embroiled in controversy for providing export help to American tobacco companies. The Foreign Agriculture Service provided market information to firms about where the demand for American cigarettes was high and where control laws were weak.

These are not the only domestic bureaucracies that now find themselves involved in foreign affairs. In 2008, the Food and Drug Administration announced that it was halting the import into the United States of 28 drugs made in India because of manufacturing deficiencies. It also opened its first overseas office in China to work with importers and Chinese regulators to ensure the safety of a wide range of products imported to the United States.

## Homeland Security

The Department of Homeland Security is an uneasy fit in the foreign affairs bureaucracy. It has elements of both a foreign policy organization and a domestic one, given the wide range of activities that fall under its jurisdiction. The Department of Homeland Security was established on November 25, 2002, as a response to the terrorist attacks of 9/11. Its creation combined 22 different agencies from eight different departments with a projected budget of $37.45 million and 170,000 employees into one. It absorbed all of the Federal Emergency Management Agency, the Coast Guard, the Secret Service, the Immigration and Naturalization Service, and the Customs Service, along with the new Transportation Security Administration. The FBI and CIA were not directly affected by the creation of the Department of Homeland Security, but the new department was given an "intelligence and threat analysis" unit that would serve as a customer of FBI and CIA intelligence for purposes of assessing threats, taking preventive action, and issuing public warnings.

Conceptually, the Department of Homeland Security is built on four pillars: border and transportation security; emergency preparedness and response; chemical, biological, radiological, and nuclear counterterrorism measures; and information analysis and infrastructure protection. Where the Defense Department has been described as a bureaucratic battleship that can only change directions very slowly, Homeland Security has been likened to a speedboat that keeps turning and shifting gears but going nowhere. In virtually all aspects of its work Homeland Security has encountered problems, beginning with its ineffective color-coded terrorist warning system that was put into place after 9/11.

The explosion of drug-related violence along the U.S.–Mexican border led to demands for action on the part of Homeland Security and caused Secretary of Homeland Security Janet Napolitano to define drug cartels as the country's No.1 crime risk. A central element in the department's proposed response was to send additional soldiers to the border. This brought protests from the Defense Department, which argued that if troops were going to be used, they should be controlled by the Defense Department and not Homeland Security. Other critics of the plan argued that it might be illegal under the Posse Comitatus Act of 1878, which prohibits the use of the military for law enforcement functions.

The Bush administration's inability to coordinate a response to Hurricane Katrina, which hit New Orleans in August 2005, also brought forward concerns about Homeland Security's ability to act effectively. Here the issue was its information-sharing capabilities. Thomas Kean, who cochaired the 9/11 Commission, noted that "on September 11, people died because police officers couldn't talk to firemen, and Katrina was a reenactment of the same problem."[42]

Homeland Security also came under criticism for tracking the activities of peaceful war protestors and passing this information on the Maryland State Police that had identified them as terrorists. Included among those groups placed under surveillance in 2005 and 2006 were Amnesty International, CASA, and People for the Ethical Treatment of Animals.

## POLICY MAKERS' RESPONSE

According to Henry Kissinger, "The purpose of bureaucracy is to devise a standard operating procedure that can cope effectively with most problems."[43] Doing so frees high-level policy makers to concentrate on the unexpected and exceptional and to pursue policy innovations. While true in theory this view is misplaced for several reasons. First, policy makers expect a great deal from bureaucracy—probably too much. Consider President Gerald Ford's statement about the U.S. involvement in Vietnam, which was published after his death: "We could have avoided the whole darn Vietnam War if somebody in the Department of Defense or State had said, 'Look here. Do we want to inherit the French mess?'"[44] The reality of the U.S. involvement in Vietnam is far more complex.

Second, the relationship between policy makers is filled with tension for several reasons. Perhaps most fundamentally, different time horizons govern the thinking of policy makers and expert bureaucrats. Unlike career bureaucrats and military professionals, policy makers cannot help thinking about the next election. The dangers posed 10 years in the future by a problem are discounted heavily compared to those that are visible on the horizon. Similarly, solutions that will take 10 years to work are worth far less than those that offer immediate rewards. Bureaucratic rivalries and concerns for survival also create problems for policy makers. Early in the discussions about the reconstruction of Iraq, Jay Garner, the first head of the Coalition Provisional Authority, and Undersecretary of State Richard Armitage had the following exchange:

> Hey, Jay. Let me tell you one thing. You've got a bunch of goddamn spies on that team of yours. They're talking about you. They are reporting on you, so you better watch your back. Well yes Sir. Garner replied, I'll do that. But you've got some spies over here too. "We know who they are," Armitage said.[45]

Policy makers have adopted three different strategies for dealing with bureaucracies that are perceived to be failing them.[46] The first is to fire senior careerists. The second is to reorganize bureaucracies. Rare is the bureaucracy that is simply eliminated. Instead, the solution is to combine the offender with another or rearrange its internal structure. In the extreme, this solution takes the form of creating a new bureaucracy to address an ongoing problem. Finally, policy makers may simply choose to ignore the bureaucracy, either by becoming their own experts or by establishing an informal in-house body of experts to produce policy guidance.

It also needs to be noted that bureaucrats have their own view of the problem. When asked by President Kennedy what was wrong with the State

Department, career diplomat Charles Bohlen replied, "You are."[47] George Ball, also a career diplomat, seconds this observation by suggesting that the State Department is being used by presidents as a scapegoat for foreign policy failures. Presidents claim all of the successes but none of the failures.[48] Diplomats are not alone in this view that much of what is wrong with the foreign affairs bureaucracy is the doing of elected officials. The professional military view was that escalation in Vietnam would fail. They also believed that when the war ended and the civilians who championed escalation were no longer in office, the professional military would be left to shoulder the blame for what went wrong.[49] Intelligence professionals see their organizations as now bearing the brunt of the blame for the use of interrogation techniques advocated by policy makers.

## OVER THE HORIZON

Viewed solely in terms of lines on an organizational chart, the foreign affairs bureaucracy offers presidents a powerful set of organizations to use in pursuit of their foreign policy agendas. Looked at from the perspective of values and roles, a more challenging picture emerges. The bureaucracy cannot be used as freely as would be liked. Not only must coordination be achieved between and within organizations, the way in which bureaucrats approach their jobs must also be addressed. The problem of forging a consensus is a real and enduring one, and one that the cyber command is likely to face.

In looking over the horizon we can expect continued pressures for change in the foreign affairs bureaucracy to come from two directions. The first is the need for greater policy coherence. Creation of the cyber command reflects this pressure as do emerging calls for reforming the organizational structure of foreign aid and continuing calls for fixing the intelligence community. A major issue here is the size of the DNI's office. Projected to be a small organization it has already grown so large that many consider it to be part of the intelligence coordination problem rather than the solution.

A second issue is cost both in absolute and relative terms. In terms of absolute costs, one observer has noted that "a dangerous game is being played in Washington."[50] It is the notion that a successful foreign policy can be constructed on the basis of about 1 percent of the federal budget. One consequence of rising costs has been the outsourcing of foreign affairs tasks. In mid-2007, the number of U.S.-paid private contractors in Iraq exceeded the number of U.S. military forces stationed there, 180,000 to 160,000. Outsourcing has also become an issue for the intelligence community. The CIA has outsourced intelligence gathering, warning, and briefing tasks as well as covert-action assignments. One published estimate placed covert-action outsourcing contracts at more than $42 billion per year.[51] In terms of relative costs it has led to calls by Secretary of Defense Gates and others to "demilitarize" U.S. foreign policy by reestablishing the State Department as the lead organization in the foreign affairs bureaucracy. This cannot be done without a large infusion of money and people.

## CRITICAL THINKING QUESTIONS

1. What is more important to the quality of bureaucratic performance, its formal structure or the value system of its members?
2. Is there a place for the domestic bureaucracies we identified in making American foreign policy or should their tasks be taken over by more traditional foreign policy agencies?
3. Can the State Department lead in the making of U.S. foreign policy? Should it lead? If not, who should lead?

## KEY TERMS

"America first"
   perspective   222
civil–military
   relations   214
country team   205
Foreign Service
   Officer   208

military after next   202
outsource   212
political creep   209
politicizing
   intelligence   219

Quadrennial Defense
   Review   213
Revolution in Military
   Affairs   215

## FURTHER READING

Morton Abramowitz and Leslie Gelb, "In Defense of Striped Pants." *The National Interest*, 79 (2005), 73–77.
Peter Feaver, *Armed Servants: Agency, Oversight and Civil-Military Relations* (Cambridge: Harvard University Press, 2003).
Paul Pillar, "Intelligence, Policy and War in Iraq," *Foreign Affairs*, 84 (2006), 15–27.
Bruce Stokes and Pat Choate, *Trade Policy: The Changing Context* (New York: Council on Foreign Relations Press, 2001).
Amy Zegart, *Flawed by Design* (Stanford: Stanford University Press, 1999).

## NOTES

1. Paul Bracken, "The Military After Next," *Washington Quarterly*, 16 (1993), 157–74.
2. On the volume of State Department message traffic, see Werner Feld, *American Foreign Policy: Aspirations and Reality* (New York: John Wiley, 1984), p. 61; and Gene Rainey, *Patterns of American Foreign Policy* (Boston: Allyn & Bacon, 1975), p. 175.
3. Henry T. Nash, *American Foreign Policy: A Search for Security*, 3rd ed. (Homewood, IL: Dorsey, 1985), pp. 134–35.
4. Leslie H. Gelb, "Why Not the State Department," in Charles W. Kegley, Jr., and Eugene R. Wittkopf (eds.), *Perspectives on American Foreign Policy: Selected Readings* (New York: St. Martin's, 1983), p. 286.
5. Glenn Kessler, "State-Defense Policy Rivalry Intensifying," *The Washington Post*, April 22, 2002, p. A1.
6. J. Anthony Holmes, "Where are the Civilians: How to Rebuild the U.S. Foreign Service," *Foreign Affairs*, 88 (2009), 148–60.
7. Donald P. Warwick, *A Theory of Public Bureaucracy: Politics, Personality and Organization in the State Department* (Cambridge, MA: Harvard University Press, 1975), pp. 29–30.

8. John Goshko, ""Up or Out in the Foreign Service," *The Washington Post*, March 28, 1986, p. 13.

9. David Corn, "At the Foggy Bottom of the Barrel, Political Hacks," *The Washington Post*, January 10, 1993, p. C3.

10. John M. Goshko, "Foreign Service's Painful Passage to Looking More Like America," *The Washington Post*, April 21, 1994, p. 29.

11. In addition to other studies cited in this chapter, see Andrew Scott, "The Department of State: Formal Organization and Informal Culture," *International Studies Quarterly*, 13 (1969), 1–18; and his "Environmental Change and Organizational Adaptation: The Problem of the State Department," *International Studies Quarterly*, 14 (1970), 85–94.

12. John Harr, *The Professional Diplomat* (Princeton, NJ: Princeton University Press, 1969), pp. 197–98.

13. I. M. Destler, *Presidents, Bureaucrats, and Foreign Policy: The Politics of Organizational Reform* (Princeton, NJ: Princeton University Press, 1972), p. 158.

14. Robert Pringle, "Creeping Irrelevance at Foggy Bottom," *Foreign Policy*, 29 (1977/1978), 128–39; and Warwick, *A Theory of Public Bureaucracy*, p. 72.

15. Lawrence Eagleburger and Robert L. Barry, "Dollars and Sense Diplomacy," *Foreign Affairs*, 75 (1996), 2–8.

16. Newt Gingrich, "Rogue State Department," *Foreign Policy*, 137 (2003), 42–48.

17. Nash, *American Foreign Policy*, p. 141.

18. For a discussion on the pros and cons of reorganizing the JCS system, see William J. Lynn and Barry R. Posen, "The Case for JCS Reform," *International Security*, 10 (1985/1986), 69–97; MacKubin Thomas Owen, "The Hollow Promise of JCS Reform," *International Security*, 10 (1985/1986), 98–111; and Edward Luttwak, *The Pentagon and the Art of War* (New York: Touchstone, 1985).

19. Renae Merle, "More Civilians Accompanying U.S. Military," *The Washington Post*, January 22, 2003, p. A10.

20. Ann Scott Tyson, "Youths in Rural U.S. Are Drawn to Military," *The Washington Post*, November 4, 2005, p. A1; Josh White, "Steady Drop in Black Army Recruits," *The Washington Post*, March 9, 2005, p. A1.

21. James Roherty, "The Office of the Secretary of Defense," in John E. Endicott and Roy W. Stafford (eds.), *American Defense Policy*, 4th ed. (Baltimore, MD: Johns Hopkins University Press, 1977), pp. 286–96.

22. Amos A. Jordon and William J. Taylor, Jr., *American National Security: Policy and Process* (Baltimore, MD: Johns Hopkins University Press, 1981), p. 185.

23. Bob Woodward, *State of Denial: Bush at War, Part III* (New York: Simon & Schuster, 2006), p. 39.

24. John H. Garrison, "The Political Dimension of Military Professionalism," in John Endicott and Roy Stafford (eds.), *American Defense Policy* pp. 578–87.

25. Carl Builder, *The Masks of War* (Baltimore, MD: Johns Hopkins University Press, 1989).

26. Richard K. Betts, *Soldiers, Statesmen, and Cold War Crises* (Cambridge, MA: Harvard University Press, 1977), pp. 4–5.

27. Bob Woodward, *The Commanders* (New York: Simon & Schuster, 1991), p. 33.

28. James Bamford, *The Puzzle Palace: Inside the National Security Agency* (Baltimore, MD: Penguin, 1982).

29. Mark Lowenthal, *U.S. Intelligence*, Washington Paper #105 (New York: Praeger, 1984), pp. 89–92; and Stafford Thomas, *The U.S. Intelligence Community* (Latham, MD: University of America Press, 1983), pp. 45–63.

30. See, for example, Herbert Meyer, "Reinventing the CIA," *Global Affairs*, 7 (1992), 1–13; and Marvin Ott, "Shaking up the CIA," *Foreign Policy*, 93 (1993), 132–51.

31. Tim Weiner, "For the 'Ultimate Staff Guy,' a Time to Reap the Rewards of Being Loyal," *The New York Times*, national edition, March 26, 1997, p. A14.

32. Roger Hilsman, *Strategic Intelligence and National Defense* (Glencoe, IL: The Free Press, 1956), pp. 37–56.

33. For a discussion of these points, see Patrick J. McGarvey, *The CIA: The Myth and the Madness* (Baltimore, MD: Penguin, 1973), pp. 148–59; and Victor Marchetti and John D. Marks, *The CIA and the Cult of Intelligence* (New York: Dell, 1974), pp. 235–77.

34. Hilsman, *Strategic Intelligence and National Defense,* pp. 199–222; and Thomas L. Hughes, *The Fate of Facts in a World of Men,* Headline Series #233 (New York: Foreign Policy Association, 1976), pp. 36–60.

35. Mike McConnell, "Overhauling Intelligence," *Foreign Affairs,* 86 (2007), 49–58.

36. Sherman Kent, *Strategic Intelligence for American World Policy* (Princeton, NJ: Princeton University Press, 1966); and Willmoore Kendall, "The Functions of Intelligence," *World Politics,* 2 (1949), 542–52.

37. Hughes, *Fate of Facts in a World of Men,* p. 47.

38. Thomas Hughes, "The Power to Speak and the Power to Listen: Reflections on Bureaucratic Politics and a Recommendation on Information Flows," in Thomas M. Franck and Edward Weisband (eds.), *Secrecy and Foreign Policy* (New York: Oxford University Press, 1974), p. 18.

39. Raymond Hopkins, "The International Role of 'Domestic Bureaucracies,'" *International Organization,* 30 (1976), p. 411.

40. Stephen D. Cohen, *The Making of United States International Economic Policy: Principles, Problems, and Proposals for Reform,* 2nd ed. (New York: Praeger, 1981), p. 40.

41. Ibid., p. 41.

42. Joby Warrick, "Crisis Communications Remain Flawed," *The Washington Post,* December 10, 2005, p. A6.

43. Henry Kissinger, "Conditions of World Order," *Daedalus,* 95 (1966), 503–29.

44. "No Point in Being Bitter," *The Washington Post,* December 31, 2006, p. B1.

45. Woodward, *Bush at War,* p. 144.

46. Morton Abramowitz and Leslie Gelb, "In Defense of Striped Pants," *National Interest,* 79 (2005), 73–77.

47. Quoted in Destler, *Presidents, Bureaucrats, and Foreign Policy,* p. 155.

48. Quoted in Cecil Crabb, Jr., *American Foreign Policy in the Nuclear Age,* 4th ed. (New York: Harper & Row, 1983), p. 102.

49. Betts, *Soldiers, Statesmen, and Cold War Crises,* p. 11.

50. Richard Gardner, "The One Percent Solution," *Foreign Affairs,* 79 (2000), 2–11.

51. R. J. Hillhouse, "Who Runs the CIA? Outsiders for Hire," *The Washington Post,* July 8, 2007, p. B5.

# Policymaking Models

In anticipation of the July 4, 2009, test firing of an intermediate-range ballistic missile (IRBM) by North Korea, the Obama administration announced that it was beefing up its antimissile defense capabilities in Hawaii. Already under construction was a Terminal High Altitude Area Defense system consisting of four batteries, each with 3 launchers and 24 missiles that have a range of 200 km. The price tag for each battery is $310 million. The U.S. Army hopes to buy at least 18 launchers, 1,400 missiles, and 18 radars. The U.S. Navy is also interested in acquiring an antiaircraft missile capability against a North Korean IRBM. The weapons it proposes cost over $3 million each. The object of concern is the Taepodong-2 missile. North Korea has had it in development for over a decade. A 1998 test flight went 1,500 km. A 2006 test flight barely made it off the ground. A 2008 test flight went 3,000 km. Hawaii is some 7,300 kilometers from North Korea.

Images of Pearl Harbor and the World Trade Center are testimony to the importance of defending the United States from attack. Yet, how do policy makers decide what threats to protect against and how much to pay for added increments of defense? In this chapter, we survey five of the most frequently used models of U.S. foreign policy making.[1] We also illustrate how these models can be used to understand U.S. foreign policy making by looking at the Cuban missile crisis from three different vantage points.

## FOREIGN POLICY DECISIONS AND MODELS

One former foreign policy maker has observed that "the business of Washington is making decisions."[2] But what is a foreign policy decision? What is it we are trying to understand? Answering these questions is complicated by a number of factors. First, the notion of a decision is itself somewhat misleading. It suggests the existence of a specific point in time at which a conscious judgment is made on what to do about a problem. Reality is often far less organized. Decisions are seldom final or decisive; they tend to lack concrete beginning and end points; and they often amount to only temporary breathing spells or truces before the issue is raised again. Decisions are also often made with far less attention to their full meaning and consequences than is commonly recognized. "A government does not decide to inaugurate the nuclear age, but only to try and build the bomb before its enemy does."[3]

A second factor complicating efforts to understand how policy is made is the relationship of the policy process to policy outcomes. Our intuitive sense is that if the policy process can be made to work properly, then the policy outcome should also work. Accordingly, bad policy can be attributed, at least in part, to bad decision making. Unfortunately, the link between the two is imperfect. Good decision making does not ensure good policy. A provocative account of the U.S. experience in Vietnam argued that the fundamental irony of Vietnam is that while U.S. policy has been roundly criticized, the policy-making system worked.[4] It achieved its basic purpose of preventing a communist victory until domestic political opinion coalesced around a strategy of either victory or withdrawal. The political system produced policies that were responsive to the wishes of the majority and near the political center while at the same time allowing virtually all views to be aired. The bureaucracy selected and implemented measures designed to accomplish these ends, and these policies were undertaken without illusions about their ultimate chances of success.

In an effort to make sense out of the complicated business of making decisions, models have been developed to help explain, describe, predict, and evaluate how U.S. foreign policy is made. Models are analytical tools that are designed to serve as simplified representations of reality. As simplifications, they leave out much of the detail and texture of what goes on in the policy-making process, in an effort to isolate and highlight what are felt to be the most salient features. Models can be distinguished from one another in terms of how they seek to capture and depict reality. The critical task for the foreign policy analyst is deciding how to select from the range of models available and combine them in an insightful fashion.

Before turning our attention to the models, two final caveats need to be raised. First, we are not arguing that policy makers consciously choose one of these models and act accordingly. We are arguing only that these models can help us understand what is happening during the policy-making process. Policy makers are not ignorant of the existence of these models, but their actions are far more likely to be governed by the complexities, uncertainties, and time constraints inherent in the policy-making process. Second, these models should not be judged in terms of being right or wrong. A more useful standard is how helpful the model is for explaining, describing, or evaluating the workings of the foreign policy process for the policy you are studying.

## THE RATIONAL ACTOR MODEL

The most frequently employed policy-making model is the **rational actor** model. At its core is an action–reaction process. Foreign policy is viewed as a calculated response to the actions of another actor. This action then produces a calculated response that in turn causes the state to reevaluate and readjust its own foreign policy. In carrying out these calculations, the state is seen as being unitary and rational. By *unitary,* it is meant that the state can be viewed as calculating and responding to external events as if it were a single entity. There is no need for the analyst to delve into the intricacies of governmental organization, domestic politics, or personalities in trying to understand why a policy was selected. The state can be treated as a **black box,** responding with one voice to the challenges and opportunities confronting it. We implicitly employ this model when we speak of Israeli goals, Argentine national interests, or Soviet adventurism. The calculations by which a foreign policy is selected are assumed to be rational. The basic elements of a rational decision process are that (1) goals are clearly stated and ranked in order of preference, (2) all options are considered, (3) the consequences of each option are assessed, and (4) a value-maximizing choice is made. Broadly speaking, there are two ways of carrying out a rational actor analysis of policy making. The first is inductive. It is frequently employed in diplomatic histories. The analyst tries to understand the foreign policy decision by placing himself or herself in the position of the government taking the action. The objective is to appreciate the situation as the government sees it and to understand the logic of the situation. The second approach is deductive. It is best exemplified by game theory and is frequently employed by military strategists and deterrence theorists. Here it is assumed that "a certain kind of conduct is inherent in a particular situation or relationship."[5] Rather than relying on actual events to support its analysis, the deductive approach relies on logical and mathematical formulations of how states should (rationally) behave under given conditions.

The rational actor model is attractive because it places relatively few informational demands the observer. It is also frequently criticized for essentially the same reason: It understates the complexity of foreign affairs and the reality of the policy process. Foreign policy is not just made in response to external events; it is heavily influenced by domestic political calculations, personalities, and organizational factors. In addition, the rational actor model assumes that "important events have important causes." By doing so, it downgrades the importance of chance, accidents, and coincidence in foreign affairs. Critics also contend that the model's information-processing demands exceed human capabilities. Goals are seldom stated clearly or rank ordered. The full range of policy options and their consequences are rarely evaluated. And in making decisions, the need for value trade-offs is denied more than it is faced. In place of the assumption of rationality, many critics advance a model based on an incremental decision-making process in which goals are only loosely stated, a limited range of options is examined, and the policy selected is one that "satisfies" (from satisfactory and sufficient) rather than optimizes.[6]

A final challenge to the rational actor model centers on its methodology. Carried out either inductively or deductively, the rational actor model relies heavily on intuition and personal judgment in interpreting actions or placing weights on policy payoffs. Graham Allison has captured this criticism in his *rationality theorem*.[7] He states that there is no pattern of activity for which an imaginative analyst cannot find objectives that are maximized by a given course of action.

## THE BUREAUCRATIC POLITICS MODEL

Bureaucratic politics is the "process by which people inside government bargain with one another on complex public policy questions."[8] As this definition suggests, the **bureaucratic politics** model approaches policy making in a completely different way from the rational actor model. Policy making is seen as a political process dominated by conflict resolution and not problem solving. Politics dominates the decision-making process because no individual is in a position to decide matters alone. Power is shared, and the individuals who share power disagree on what should be done because they are located at different places within the government and see different faces of the problem.

Using military force to punish terrorists looks different to a secretary of state, who must balance the diplomatic pluses and minuses of such a move, than it does to the military chiefs of staff, whose forces would be used, or to a presidential aide, who is perhaps most sensitive to the domestic implications of the success or failure of such a mission. A concrete example comes from the Middle East, where the future of Iraq will depend heavily on Turkish–Kurdish relations. Inside the Pentagon, Turkey belongs to the European Command, while Iraq belongs to the Central Command. Inside the State Department, Turkey is part of the Bureau of European and Eurasian Affairs, while Iraq is part of the Bureau of Near Eastern Affairs. Thus any discussion of what to do about rising tensions between Turkey and Iraq's Kurds finds military and diplomatic experts starting from very different assumptions about who is to blame or how to solve the problem, depending on whether they are responsible primarily for European or Middle Eastern affairs.

Not everyone in the government is a participant in a particular policy-making "game." The political bargaining process is constrained by the organizational context within which policy makers operate. Fixed organizational routines define the issue, produce the information on which policy decisions are made, link institutions and individuals together, and place limits on the types of policy options that can be implemented. Furthermore, the players in the game are not equal in their ability to influence the outcome of the bargaining process. Deadlines, the rules of the game, and **action channels** confer power to some and deny it to others. Rules determine what kind of behavior is permitted and by whom. Can unilateral statements be made, or must the decision be cleared by a committee? Can information be leaked? Action channels link policy makers together and determine who is in the best position to leak information, make a unilateral statement, or be included in a committee that approves action. Deadlines force issues by accelerating the tempo of the decision making process and creating pressure for an agreement. Deadlines come in many forms: a meeting with a foreign head of state, a presidential press conference or speech, the adjournment of Congress, or the beginning of a fiscal year. Congress may also establish deadlines. It established a recurring deadline in 1977, when it required that the secretary of state report annually to Congress on human rights conditions in every state that receives U.S. development assistance.

Rarely do policy problems enter or leave the policy process in a clearly definable manner. More frequently, they flow through it in a fragmented state and become entangled in other ongoing policy issues. The result is that policy is not formulated with respect to any underlying conception of the U.S. national interest. Instead, its content is heavily influenced by the way in which the problem first surfaces and how it interacts with the other issues on the policy agenda. A recent example is the George W. Bush administration's misstep in handling its decision to withdraw from the Kyoto Protocol. Environmental Protection Agency head Christine Whitman sought to take the lead in this policy area and assured European leaders that the administration would act to control carbon dioxide emissions. Secretary of State Colin Powell also endorsed this position. Yet Bush chose to reject their advice, responding to pressure from congressional Republicans and lobbyists from the coal and steel industries.

Bush's decision placed the United States on the defensive in its meetings over the next several months with European and Japanese leaders, who saw it as another troubling example of the Bush administration's penchant for unilateralism, along with the decision to go forward on a national ballistic defense system and to go slow on talks with North Korea.

In putting all of the foregoing together, advocates of the bureaucratic politics model argue that policy is not, and cannot be, a product of deliberate choice. Instead, policy is either a result of a political bargaining process or the product of organizational **standard operating procedures.**[9] In either case, the new policy arrived at is not likely to differ greatly from the existing policy. This is because bargaining is a time-consuming and expensive process. Not only do policy makers disagree, they are often quite deeply committed to their positions. The need for agreement pushes policy makers toward accepting a minimal decision, one that is not radically different from the existing compromise and one that will allow all sides to claim a partial victory. The inflexible and blunt nature of organizational routines and procedures reinforces the tendency for policy to change only at the margins. Administrative feasibility is a constant check on the ability of policy makers to tailor policy options to meet specific problems. In sum, from the bureaucratic politics perspective, the best predictor of future policy is not the policy that maximizes U.S. national interests but that which is only incrementally different from current policy.

The bureaucratic politics model makes important contributions to understanding U.S. foreign policy by highlighting the political and organizational nature of policy making. However, it has also been the subject of extensive criticisms. First, by emphasizing compromise, bargaining, and standard operating procedures, the bureaucratic model makes it very difficult to assign responsibility for the decisions being made.[10] Second, it misrepresents the workings of the bargaining process by overstating the extent to which policy simply emerges from the policy process.[11] Third, the bureaucratic politics model is chastised for artificially separating the executive branch bargaining process from the broader social and political context. In this view, Congress and domestic political forces cannot be treated as outside interlopers in the policy process. Attention must also be given to the values of policy makers and not just the policy-making games they play. Finally, the model is criticized for being too complex, a virtual "analytic kitchen sink" into which almost anything can be thrown that might be related to how an issue is resolved.[12] The result is a story that may make for interesting reading but that violates one of the most fundamental rules of explanation: All things being equal, simple explanations are better than complex ones.

# THE SMALL-GROUP DECISION-MAKING MODEL

A third policy-making model focuses on the dynamics of small-group decision making. Advocates of this perspective hold that many critical foreign policy decisions are made neither by an individual policy maker nor by large bureaucratic forces. From a policy maker's perspective, small-group decision making offers a number of advantages over its bureaucratic counterpart. Among its perceived advantages are the following:

- The absence of significant conflict, because there will be few viewpoints to reconcile
- A free and open interchange of opinion among members, because there will be no organizational interests to protect
- Swift and decisive action
- Possible innovation and experimentation
- The possibility of maintaining secrecy[13]

Three different types of small groups can be identified.[14] First is the informal small group that meets regularly but lacks a formal institutional base. The Tuesday lunch group in the administration of Lyndon Johnson and the Friday breakfast and Thursday lunch groups of the administration of Jimmy Carter are prominent recent examples. Second is the ad hoc group that is created to deal with a specific problem and then ceases to function once its task is completed. In the first week of the 1950 Korean crisis, six small-group meetings were held. During the Cuban missile crisis, the key decisions were made by ExCom, an ad hoc group of about 15 individuals brought together by President John Kennedy specifically to deal with this problem. The third type of small group is permanent in nature, possesses an institutional base, and is created to perform a series of specified functions. The subcommittees of the National Security Council (NSC) fall into this category. During the Carter administration, two subcommittees were established. One, the Special Coordinating Committee (SCC), was set up to deal with crisis situations when they arose. During the Iranian hostage crisis, Robert Hunter, an NSC official in the Carter administration, reported:

> Throughout the hostage crisis, the SCC met at 9:00 A.M.—at first daily and later less frequently—with an agenda coordinated with the government by the NSC staff in the early hours of the morning. Discussion was brisk, options were presented crisply, and recommendations were rapidly and concisely formulated for presidential decision. . . . The crisis team, with nearly three years' experience of working together, did its job efficiently and with dispatch. . . . Subcommittees of the SCC worked on specialized parts of the problem. The State Department Iranian Working Group worked around the clock all 444 days and fed information back and forth. . . . The results of the days' labors were reported back; new wrinkles in the crisis were assessed; and the SCC was ready to act again the next morning.[15]

Following the terrorist attacks of September 11, 2001, the George W. Bush administration established a "war cabinet" consisting of some dozen people. Almost half had played key roles in Gulf War decisions: Vice President Dick Cheney had been secretary of defense, Secretary of State Colin Powell had been chairman of the Joint Chiefs of Staff, Deputy Secretary of Defense Paul Wolfowitz had been undersecretary of defense, Deputy Secretary of State Richard Armitage had been a special envoy, and National Security Adviser Condoleezza Rice had been a senior official at the NSC. Missing from this war cabinet was any long-time confidant of the president comparable to Secretary of State James Baker III in President George Bush's Persian Gulf War cabinet.

In spite of its advantages, small-group decision making often results in policy decisions that are anything but rational or effective. Pearl Harbor, the Bay of Pigs invasion, and key decisions in Korea and Vietnam have all been analyzed from a small-group decision-making perspective.[16] The Iranian hostage rescue mission and the Iran–Contra initiative can easily be added to this list.

These policy failures are held to result from the presence of strong in-group pressures on members to concur in the group's decision. This pressure produces a "deterioration of mental efficiency, reality testing, and moral judgment" that increases the likelihood of the group's making a potentially defective decision.[17] Irving Janis coined the term **groupthink** to capture this phenomenon. He also identified eight symptoms that indicate its presence. He divides them into three categories: overestimation of the group's power and morality, closed mindedness, and pressures toward conformity. Janis argues that the more symptoms are present, the more likely it is that concurrence-seeking behavior will result and that defective decisions will be made. Table 9.1 presents a series of observations

## TABLE 9.1

GROUPTHINK AND THE IRAN–CONTRA AFFAIR

| Element of Groupthink | Findings of the Tower Commission Report |
|---|---|
| Illusion of invulnerability | The president "was all for letting the Israelis do anything they wanted at the very first briefing." (McFarlane, p. 131) |
| Unquestioned belief in group's morality | The president distinguished between selling someone believed able to exert influence with respect to the hostages and dealing directly with the kidnappers. (p. 39) |
| | The administration continued to pressure U.S. allies not to sell arms to Iran and not to make concessions to terrorists. (p. 65) |
| Collective efforts to discount warnings | "There is a high degree of risk in pursuing the course we have started, we are now so far down the road that stopping . . . could have even more serious repercussions. We all view the next step as confidence building." (North, p. 167) |
| Stereotyping the enemy | Release of the hostages would require influence with the Hezballah, which could involve the most radical elements of the Iranian regime. The kind of strategy sought by the United States, however, involved what were regarded as more moderate elements. (p. 64) |

(continued)

| | |
|---|---|
| **TABLE 9.1** *(continued)* | |

| Element of Groupthink | Findings of the Tower Commission Report |
|---|---|
| Self-censorship | Evidence suggests that he [Casey] received information about the possible divergence of funds to the Contras almost a month before the story broke. He, too, did not move promptly to raise the matter with the president. (p. 81) |
| | Secretary Shultz and Secretary Weinberger, in particular, distanced themselves from the march of events. (p. 82) |
| Illusion of unanimity | "I felt in the meeting that there were views opposed, some (presidential support) in favor, and the President didn't really take a position, but he seemed to, he was in favor of this project somehow or other." (Shultz, p. 183) |
| | "As the meeting broke up, I had the idea the President had not entirely given up on encouraging the Israelis." (Casey, p. 198) |
| Direct pressure against dissenters | "Casey's view is that Cap [Weinberger] will continue to create roadblocks until he is told by you that the President wants this move NOW." (North to Poindexter, p. 232) |
| Emergence of mindguards | "I don't want a meeting with RR, Shultz, and Weinberger." (Poindexter, p. 45) |
| | North directed that dissemination be limited to Secretary Weinberger, DCI Casey, McFarlane, and himself. North said McFarlane had directed that no copy be sent to the secretary of state and that he, McFarlane, would keep Secretary Shultz advised orally on the NSC project. (p. 149) |

Citations from: Robert McFarlane, national security advisor, 1983–1985; Col. Oliver North, national security council staffer; George Shultz, secretary of state; William Casey, director of central intelligence; Adm. John Poindexter, national security advisor 1985–1986; Caspar Weinberger, secretary of defense.

*Source:* President's Special Review Panel, *The Tower Commission Report* (New York: Bantam, 1987).

in the Tower Commission report about the decision making on the Iran–Contra affair against the symptoms mentioned by Janis. Although the match is not perfect (e.g., illusion of unanimity is better seen as an illusion of presidential support), the parallels are striking.

Groupthink is a phenomenon that occurs regardless of the personality traits of group members. It is not an inevitable product of a tight-knit decision group, nor is it necessarily the cause of a policy fiasco. Poor implementation, changed circumstances, or accidental factors also produce policy failures. Groupthink exists as a tendency that is made more or less likely by three sets of antecedent conditions: the coherence of the decision making group, structural faults of the organization, and the nature of the decision context. At its core is the assumption that concurrence-seeking behavior is an attempt on the part of group members to cope with stress by developing a mutual support base. The source of the stress may be internal or external to the group. External stress is conducive to groupthink when it stems from a threat for which there appears to be little hope of finding a better solution than the one put forward by the leader. Internal stress tends to come from feelings of low self-esteem such that "participating in a unanimous consensus along with respected fellow members of a congenial group will bolster the decision maker's self-esteem."[18]

Because groupthink is a tendency and not a condition, it can be avoided. Recognizing that each proposed solution has its own drawbacks, Janis puts forward several measures that he feels would improve the quality of small-group decision making.[19] They include modifying leadership strategies so that impartial and wide-ranging discussions of alternatives will take place, establishing multiple groups for the same task (multiple advocacy), establishing a devil's advocate, and having a "second chance" meeting at which decisions can be reconsidered one final time.

Three general lines of criticism have been directed at the groupthink approach to small-group decision making. First, the proposed solutions probably will not work. Consider the idea of multiple advocacy, which attempts to ensure that all views, "however unpopular," will receive serious attention.[20] Two dangers exist here. In each case, they are brought on by overloading the intellectual capabilities of policy makers and by highlighting the ambiguity of the evidence before them. One outcome is that policy makers will simply choose whatever policy option is in accord with their preexisting biases. If a wide range of options are all made to appear respectable and doubts exist about the effectiveness of each, why not "let Reagan be Reagan" or "Bush be Bush" and select the one that best fits his image of the world. The other, equally undesirable, outcome is paralysis. Confronted with too many policy options, all of which appear to have problems, policy makers may end up doing nothing.

Second, criticism is directed at the criteria used to establish a good decision.[21] The standard used (vigilant appraisal) virtually duplicates the functional steps involved in making a rational decision that we presented in our discussion of the rational actor model. The point remains: If the rational actor model is an unrealistic benchmark against which to judge decision making, isn't the same true for groupthink? A final point is more theoretical in nature. The groupthink approach is grounded in a conflict model of individual decision making. According to this model, individuals often confront decision-making situations in which they feel "simultaneous opposing tendencies to accept and reject a given course of action."[22] Vigilant appraisal is realized when individuals address this stress successfully, and groupthink occurs when they do not. The "cybernetic" approach to policy making suggests an alternative starting point to understanding individual decision making. According to this perspective, individuals do not even attempt to resolve the value conflict and tensions involved in making such a decision. Instead, "the decision process is organized around the problem of controlling inherent uncertainty by means of highly focused attention and highly programmed responses."[23]

Based on this line of argument, John Steinbruner suggests that, in place of the calculating policy maker, we focus our attention on three types of thinkers, each of whom avoids the need for making value trade-offs.[24] Any individual may exhibit these patterns of thinking or switch among them as time constraints and issues change. The uncommitted thinker has difficulty making up his or her mind on an issue and is very susceptible to the arguments and positions of others; the theoretical thinker approaches an issue from an ideological perspective; and the grooved thinker deals with a problem by placing it into a limited number of preexisting categories.

Even with these problems, recent decision-making studies continue to point to the importance of groupthink. One study focused on the relative importance of situational factors such as high stress and time constraints versus variation in how groups are structured and information processed.[25] Its findings suggest that situational factors have little effect on the quality of the decision compared to the other two. Another study reviewed evidence regarding the effectiveness of various ways of combating groupthink's negative tendencies.[26] It found that multiple advocacy did improve the quality of the presidential policy-making process but that its implementation was uneven, making a full evaluation difficult.

## ELITE THEORY AND PLURALISM

We have already encountered the final two perspectives on policy making that we will examine, elite theory and pluralism, though without naming them as such. During the 1960s and early 1970s, these two models served as the focal point for an intense debate that raged among political scientists over how best to understand the process by which public policy is made. Although they are no longer the center of attention, elite theory and pluralism remain important approaches for understanding how U.S. foreign policy is made, and we briefly summarize the arguments that they make.

**Elite theory** represents a quite different perspective on foreign policy making than do the three approaches that we have examined so far. It is not concerned with the details of the action taking place inside the policy process, but it also does not ignore what goes on inside the state. Elite theory is vitally concerned with the identities of those individuals who make foreign policy and the underlying dynamics of national power, social myth, and class interests. From this perspective, foreign policy is formulated as a response to demands generated by the economic and political system. Not all demands receive equal attention, and those that receive the most attention serve the interests of only a small sector of society. These special interests are transformed into national interests through the pattern of office holding and the structure of influence that exists within the United States. Those who hold office are seen as being a stable and relatively cohesive group who share common goals, interests, and values.

Disagreements exist only at the margins and surface most frequently as disputes over how to implement policy and not over the ends of that policy. Those outside the elite group are held to be relatively powerless, reacting to the policy initiatives of the elite rather than prompting them. Furthermore, public reactions are often "orchestrated" by the elite rather than being expressions of independent thinking on policy matters. This explains why certain policy proposals routinely fail to attract serious attention: Ideas that do not build on the relatively narrow range of value assumptions shared by the elite and rooted in the underlying dynamics of the socioeconomic structure are rejected as unworkable, fundamentally flawed, or fatally naive. Elite theory also suggests that the basic directions of U.S. foreign policy will change slowly, if at all.

Within this broad consensus, elite theorists disagree on a number of points. First, disagreement exists over the constraints on elite behavior. Some see few, if any, constraints on the type of policies that elites can pursue. Others see a more open policy process that is subject to periodic "short-circuiting" by the public, as perhaps was the case with the nuclear freeze movement. Disagreement also exists over how conspiratorial the elite is. Some elite theorists pay great attention to the social backgrounds and linkages among members of the elite class, whereas others deemphasize these features in favor of an attention to the broader and more enduring forces of a capitalistic economic system that drives U.S. foreign policy to be expansionist, aggressive, and exploitive.[27]

Several recent administrations, including that of George W. Bush, have been the subject of conspiratorial-style elite analysis. In the case of the Carter administration, the object of attention was on the presence of large numbers of members of the Trilateral Commission in policy-making positions. The Trilateral Commission was formed in 1973 to foster cooperation among the United States, Western Europe, and Japan. In the Reagan administration it was on links between his appointees and the Committee on the Present Danger, a group established in the 1970s to warn against the continuing threat posed by the Soviet Union. In the George W. Bush administration, the focus was the influence neoconservatives had on foreign policy decisions, especially in the Middle East. Unlike the other two groups, the neoconservatives do not have an institutional embodiment.

Rather, neoconservativism refers to a broad philosophical outlook on America's role in world politics. Conservatives are generally skeptical about the ability of American military and economic power to transform the world, whereas neoconservatives are optimistic about its ability to do so and see the United States as having a responsibility to exercise that power even if other states object. With this more comprehensive sense of purpose, neoconservatives have also adopted a more all-encompassing sense of threat to the United States. The enemy is not just al Qaeda but Hamas, Hezbollah, and other terrorist groups as well, along with states such as North Korea, Iraq, Iran, and Syria. The emphasis on threats emanating from the Middle East is also consistent with the neoconservative view that Israel is among America's most valuable allies and must be protected. Key neoconservatives in the Bush administration included Deputy Secretary of Defense Paul Wolfowitz; Undersecretary of Defense for Policy Douglas Feith; Richard Pearle, who headed the Pentagon's Intelligence

Advisory Board; and Lewis "Scooter" Libby, who was Vice President Dick Cheney's chief of staff.

In sum, elite theory is a valuable source of insight into U.S. foreign policy making because it stresses the ties that bind policy makers together rather than the issues that separate them. In contrast to elite theory, pluralism is regarded as the orthodox interpretation of how the U.S. policy-making system works. Just as with elite theory, no single comprehensive statement of the argument exists. Still, six common themes can be identified:

1. Power in society is fragmented and diffused.
2. Many groups in society have power to participate in policy making.
3. No one group is powerful enough to dictate policy.
4. An equilibrium among groups is the natural state of affairs.
5. Policy is the product of bargaining between groups and reflects the interests of the dominant group(s).
6. The government acts as an umpire, supervising the competition and sometimes compelling a settlement.

Pluralists acknowledge that power resources are not evenly distributed throughout society. However, they hold that merely possessing the attributes of power (wealth, status, etc.) is not equal to actually possessing power itself.[28] This is because the economic and political sectors of society are held to be separate. In addition, power resources may be substituted for one another. Large numbers may offset wealth; leadership may offset large numbers; and commitment may overcome poor leadership. **Pluralism** would point to the grassroots movement in the United States to force South Africa to end apartheid as evidence of the validity of their case. What began as a movement on college campuses to force companies to disinvest from South Africa and later took the form of daily, peaceful demonstrations at the South African embassy gradually succeeded in sensitizing policy makers and the American public to the problem, with the result that in 1985 U.S. policy toward South Africa began to show signs of change. More recently, the change in U.S. policy on Cambodia, in which support for the rebel forces (including the Khmer Rouge) was dropped in favor of talks with Vietnam, can also be linked to shifting political power of domestic political forces on this issue.

A number of flaws have been suggested in the pluralists' argument.[29] Pluralists assume that competition between groups produces policy makers who compete over the content of policy. What happens when policy makers do not compete over policy but instead are so fragmented that they rule over separate and self-contained policy areas? Lowi suggests that these conditions better describe the operation of the U.S. government than does the pluralist model, and that when this happens, the government is not an umpire but a holding company. Pluralism then exists without competition as interest groups capture different pieces of the government and shape its policies to suit their needs. New groups or the poorly organized are effectively shut out of the decision making process. Just as important, interest-group liberalism reduces the capacity of the government to plan, because it is unable to speak with one voice or examine problems from a national perspective.

## HISTORICAL LESSON

### The MX Missile

The MX missile, for Missile eXperimental, was a defensive antiballistic missile (ABM) system that was first deployed in 1986. Each MX missile had the capabiity of launching 10 separately targeted nuclear warheads over 8,000 miles and delivering them within 200 feet of their target. Each warhead was about 20 times as powerful as the bomb dropped on Hiroshima. Originally, 200 were to be deployed, but in the end only 50 became operational. The last MX, by then known as the Peacekeeper, was removed from the U.S. nuclear inventory in 2005. By 1998 the MX project had cost $20 billion.

In the early 1970s, the increasing size of the Soviet nuclear arsenal raised concerns about the survivability of the Minuteman missile system that was desinged to protect the United States from a Soviet nuclear attack. The MX was to be the answer to this problem. It was to have a hard target kill capability so that it could destroy Soviet missile sites, and it was to be mobile so that it could avoid being destroyed by Soviet missiles. Survivability had long been a concern of U.S. military planners. The idea of a mobile intercontinental ballistic missile (ICBM) like the MX had been under consideration since the 1960s; other options being investigated included the hardening of missile sites, concealment, deception, and an air defense system. This last possibility was no longer viable because of the Strategic Arms Limitation Treaty (SALT I) that banned ABM defense systems.

In the rush to develop the MX, the Air Force decided to simply place the MX in existing Minuteman III silos, the very silos that were judged to be vulnerable to Soviet attack. Of overriding concern to them was the fear that if they did not act quickly, submarines would become the primary means of defending the United States. The Carter administration did not object to this plan, since studies by his administration were doubtful about the ability of the MX to achieve its stated mission. Carter came to see the MX primarily as a bargaining chip to use in the SALT II arms control talks with the Soviet Union. The problem for Carter was that a bargaining chip such as the MX becomes more valuable the closer it comes to being operational, so further steps to deployment were necessary. Accordingly, in June 1979, Carter approved full deployment of the MX in hardened silos to be built in the West that would be linked by an underground rail system that would move the MX from launch site to launch site, thus greatly complicating any attempt to destroy the system.

This decision set off a new wave of political problems, as opposition arose in those areas set to house the MX. In his presidential campaign, Ronald Reagan criticized the slow pace of MX deployment. Upon becoming president, Reagan announced he was abandoning Carter's plan and would put the MX in Minuteman silos. This plan met with disapproval from those in Congress and the military that valued MX mobility as the key to its survival. The Reagan administration then explored the possibility of an

*(continued)*

*(continued)*

airborne MX system, placing the MX inside large trucks that would travel on the U.S. interstate system, and a "densepack" deployment plan that was a more condensed version of Carter's scheme. It settled on the densepack plan only to have Congress once again raise objections.

In desperation, the Reagan administration created the Scowcroft Commission to break the deadlock over the MX. The commission tended to see the MX as a bargaining chip and called for the immediate deployment of 100 MX missiles in existing Minuteman silos as a sign of "national will." The first MX was deployed in retrofitted Minuteman silos at Warren Air force Base in Wyoming in December 1986, but by then the future of the entire MX project was in great doubt. In 1985, Congress had voted against deploying all 100 MX missiles as the Scowcroft Commission had called for. Yet again the survivability problems of using fixed silos undercut the argument for their deployment. Three former chairmen of the Joint Chiefs of Staff stated it was not necessary. This time the solution was found in the construction of specially designed railroad launch cars that would travel the national railroad system as the means for avoiding detection by Soviet missiles. This system was scheduled to become operational in 1992 but was cancelled before then with the ending of the Cold War and the break up of the Soviet Union.

### Applying the Lesson

1. Do you think the future of the Hawaii anti-North Korea system will come to resemble the history of the MX?
2. Are presidents or the military more responsible for inability to fix or cancel the MX in a timely fashion?
3. Which of the models we present in this chapter are useful for understanding the MX decisions? ■

## INTEGRATING MODELS

It stands to reason that given the complexity of the situations faced and the variety of factors that might go into selecting a course of action, no single foreign policy model standing alone will be able to help us fully understand a foreign policy decision or outcome. This will often require integrating several different models together. Typically, there are four ways in which this integration can be attempted. The first is to shift from model to model as the focus of the analysis changes. For example, from the rational actor perspective, the decision to send U.S. troops to Korea in 1950 is a single decision. From the bureaucratic or small-group perspective, a number of separate decisions can be identified.[30] A distinction can also be made between the sociopolitical aspects of policy making and the intellectual task of choosing a response.[31] The pluralist and bureaucratic politics models help us understand why policy makers act as they do once they are "in place," but they tell us little about how they got there or the values they bring to bear in addressing a problem. To answer these questions, we might want to turn to insights from elite theory or the rational actor model.

A second way to integrate policy-making models is to recognize that some models are more appropriate for analyzing some problems, or issue areas, than they are for others. The general argument is that the more open the policy process and the longer the issue is on the policy agenda (such as is typically the case for structural and strategic issues), the more useful will be the bureaucratic and pluralist models. The more closed the process and the quicker the response, the more useful will be the rational actor, elite theory, or small-group model.

A third way to integrate these models is to shift from one to another, as the policy problem develops over time. Thus, the elite or rational actor model might be especially helpful for understanding how the United States got involved in Vietnam; the small-group or bureaucratic politics model might be most helpful for understanding key decisions during the course of the war; and the pluralist or bureaucratic politics model might be most helpful for understanding the actual process by which the United States withdrew from Vietnam.

A final way of integrating these models is based on the values that guide one's analysis. We have already suggested that although the rational actor model may be deficient as a description of the policy-making process, it is still valuable if the purpose is to evaluate the policy process. One must be careful in using models in this way, for embedded in each are assumptions about how policy should be made that are not always readily apparent. For example, implicit in the rational actor model is a belief in the desirability of a strong president and the ability to act quickly. The model does not place great value on widespread participation in decision making or on a system of checks and balances.

# THE CUBAN MISSILE CRISIS

In this section we examine one of the most important events in U.S. foreign policy, the Cuban missile crisis. For many it was the defining foreign policy crisis of the Cold War. We first present an overview of how the crisis unfolded and then employ three models—rational actor, bureaucratic politics, and groupthink—to show how models can help us understand foreign policy.

## The Crisis: An Overview

The Cuban missile crisis, which took place over 13 days (October 16–28, 1962), is widely regarded as a major turning point in the Cold War.[32] Never before and never after did the United States and the Soviet Union appear to be on the brink of nuclear war. At the time of the crisis, President John Kennedy estimated that the odds of averting such an outcome were between one in three and even.[33]

Soviet weapons shipments to Cuba had been taking place since the summer of 1960. A slowdown in these shipments occurred in early 1962, but the pace quickened again in late July. By September 1, the inventory of Soviet equipment in Cuba included surface-to-air missiles (SAMs), cruise missiles, patrol boats, and large quantities of transportation, electrical, and construction equipment, as well as over 5,000 technicians and other military personnel.[34] The first strategic missiles arrived secretly in Cuba on September 8. They were medium-range ballistic missiles (MRBMs) with a range of 1,100 nautical miles. Forty-two of these missiles reached Cuba before the crisis was resolved. Equipment also began arriving for the construction of IRBMs and IRBM sites, although no IRBMs actually reached Cuba. Finally, Soviet shipments in September included IL-28 jet bombers, MIG-21 jet fighters, plus additional SAMs, cruise missiles, and patrol boats.

Intelligence on the exact dimensions of the Soviet buildup in Cuba came from a number of different sources: refugee reports, Central Intelligence Agency (CIA) agents operating in Cuba, analyses of Soviet shipping patterns, and U-2 spy plane overflights. Not all of the information from these sources was equally reliable, nor did it all come together at the same time and place for analysis. For example, refugees were reporting the presence of Soviet missiles in Cuba before Cuba began receiving weapons of any kind from the Soviet Union, and great care had to be taken in processing reports from agents operating inside Cuba. The United States Intelligence Board met on September 19 and approved an intelligence estimate that indicated the Soviet Union would not introduce offensive missiles into Cuba.

This conclusion was not uniformly shared in the administration. In late August, Director of Central Intelligence John McCone told President Kennedy, Secretary of Defense Robert McNamara, and Secretary of State Dean Rusk that he believed the Soviet Union was preparing to place offensive missiles in Cuba. In late September, others began to agree with McCone, and, on October 4 the Committee on Overhead Reconnaissance (COMOR) approved a U-2 overflight over western Cuba. No U-2 overflights had been authorized over this area since September 5 because of recent mishaps with U-2 overflights in Asia. Fearful that all U-2 flights might be canceled if another incident were to occur, COMOR had decided not to send any U-2s over western Cuba, where SAM sites were known to be under construction. A jurisdictional dispute between the Defense Department and the CIA over who would fly such a mission led to an unsuccessful flight on October 9, and it was not until October 14 that a successful U-2 flight took place. Its photographs firmly established the presence of Soviet offensive missiles in Cuba. On October 22, President Kennedy went on national television to announce their discovery.

Kennedy called together a special ad hoc advisory group known as the Executive Committee of the NSC (ExCom) to deal with the crisis. ExCom's first meeting took place on October 16, and it began to identify the options open to the United States. Six major options surfaced: (1) no action, (2) diplomatic pressures either at the United Nations or at the Soviet Union, (3) a secret approach to Castro with the option of "split or fall," (4) invasion, (5) a surgical air strike, and (6) a naval blockade.[35] The first option seized on was the surgical air strike.[36] The blockade was not lobbied for strongly until the end of the day, and Kennedy's initial response to this option was one of skepticism, because he was not sure how a blockade would get Soviet missiles out of Cuba.

By the end of the first day, Kennedy identified three options. Participant accounts suggest that attention focused primarily on two of these, the surgical air strike and the blockade. (The third option appears to have been invasion.) In his October 22 statement, Kennedy also announced that on October 24 a naval quarantine would be imposed on Cuba, and he threatened future action if the missiles were not removed. The blockade was chosen both for what it did and for what it did not do. It was a visible, forceful, military response, but it did not put the Soviet Union into a position where it had no choice but to fight. In fact, it placed responsibility for the next move back on Soviet Chairman Nikita Khrushchev. A number of additional measures were taken publicly to impress on the Soviets the depth of U.S. resolve and to make credible Kennedy's threat of additional action: Squadrons of U.S. tactical fighters were moved to points from which they could attack Cuba; an invasion force of 200,000 troops was readied in Florida; some 14,000 Air Force reserves were called up; and U.S. forces around the world were put on alert.[37]

The air strike remained a live option. An air strike had tentatively been scheduled for October 20 but was postponed in favor of the blockade. On October 27, one day before Krushchev offered to remove the missiles, Kennedy approved plans for an October 29 air strike on Soviet missile silos, air bases, and Cuban and Soviet antiaircraft installations. At that same meeting, ExCom also concluded that an invasion would follow. McNamara held that an "invasion had become almost inevitable," and he felt that at least one missile would be successfully launched at the United States.[38]

The blockade did bring an end to Soviet military shipments to Cuba, but it did not bring a stop to the construction of Soviet missiles and missile sites in Cuba. SAM missiles became operational during the crisis and shot down a U-2 on October 23. President Kennedy's original orders were that if this happened, the United States would destroy the site that had launched the missile. However, when the incident occurred, Kennedy delayed retaliating in an effort to allow quiet diplomacy some additional time to bring about the withdrawal of the Soviet missiles.

Recent accounts of the Cuban missile crisis suggest that Kennedy would not have ordered an air strike had Khrushchev not responded favorably to U.S. demands, and that the president was prepared to pursue additional negotiations—perhaps through the United Nations—to resolve the crisis.[39] These accounts also argue that U.S. policy makers felt a sense of urgency in their deliberations, not out of a fear that Soviet missiles might soon become operational, but because the longer the missiles remained in Cuba, the more legitimate they would come to be seen by the other states.

On October 28, Khrushchev agreed publicly to remove Soviet missiles in Cuba in return for a U.S. pledge of nonintervention into Cuba. This allowed both sides to achieve their publicly stated goals. The United States got the missiles out of Cuba, and the Soviet Union could claim that it had succeeded in protecting Cuba from U.S. aggression (the justification it gave for having placed the missiles in Cuba when confronted by Kennedy). Recently released documents reveal the existence of a secret agreement between Kennedy and Khrushchev with terms different from those that officially ended the crisis. In order to entice

Khrushchev into removing the missiles from Cuba, Kennedy promised to remove U.S. missiles from Turkey. The secret offer was made by Robert Kennedy to Soviet Ambassador Anatoly Dobrynin on October 27. Dobrynin was also told that a commitment was needed from the Soviets the next day if the crisis was to be ended on these terms. For reasons of domestic politics and international prestige, Kennedy had refused to publicly accept this trade-off, which had been repeatedly called for by the Soviets and suggested to him by some members of ExCom. Implementation of the U.S. part of the agreement was made conditional on the Soviets' keeping the agreement secret.

October 28 marks the conventional ending point for the Cuban missile crisis, but it in fact continued for several more weeks as both sides struggled with the question of how to implement the agreement. Particularly troublesome issues involved defining what was meant by "offensive" weapons—the United States insisted that the IL-28s must be removed—and establishing a date for ending the blockade—the Soviets wanted the blockade ended and a no-invasion pledge issued before they took out the bombers. Within the U.S. government there occurred a repeat of the earlier debate on how to proceed: Take unilateral military action to resolve the issue, tighten the blockade, or concede the point and go on to other matters. Diplomacy again came to the rescue when, on November 20, Kennedy announced that the Soviet Union had agreed to remove the IL-28s and that the blockade was being ended.

## Three Views of the Cuban Missile Crisis

The account of the Cuban missile crisis we have presented is largely consistent with a rational actor interpretation of U.S. foreign policy making. It emphasizes the thorough canvassing of alternatives once a problem has been identified and the selection of a value-maximizing choice. For U.S. policy makers, the goal directing the search for policy options was clear: Get the Soviet missiles out of Cuba without the appearance of having appeased the Soviets and without starting a war. A hard-line stance was in part dictated by domestic political considerations. Cuba had become an important and reoccurring emotional issue in American electoral politics since Fidel Castro had come to power there in 1959, and Kennedy was vulnerable on Cuba. The Bay of Pigs fiasco had made Cuba Kennedy's political Achilles' heel, raising questions about his judgment and leadership. The Republican Senate and congressional campaign committees had already identified Cuba as the major issue in the upcoming 1962 election. Inaction (a possibility suggested at one point by McNamara) and quiet diplomacy, therefore, were not policy options capable of achieving both the removal of the missiles and a demonstration of political resolve. The air strike was rejected because the Air Force could not give Kennedy a 100 percent guarantee that the missiles would be knocked out. Similar problems confronted the choice of an invasion. Coupled with highly visible signals of further military action, the blockade was selected as the option that offered the greatest likelihood of getting the missiles out and demonstrating U.S. resolve without running a high risk of setting off a war between the United States and Soviet Union.

As the rational actor model suggests, the blockade itself was structured to fit the needs of U.S. policy makers. It was not implemented until U.S. officials were sure that Soviet leaders had been able to communicate with Soviet ship captains, and the blockade was placed closer to Cuba than was militarily prudent in order to give the Soviet leadership the maximum amount of time to formulate a peaceful response. The first ship stopped was also carefully selected to minimize the possibility of a hostile Soviet response. Two ships that clearly did not carry missiles were allowed to pass through the blockade. The first ship that was stopped also did not carry missiles. It was a U.S.-built World War II Liberty ship, registered in Lebanon, owned by a Panamanian firm, and under lease to the Soviet Union.

A similar analysis of policy options and consequences late in the crisis would identify Kennedy's secret offer to remove U.S. missiles from Turkey as the logical follow-up move. The blockade did buy time and show U.S. resolve, but, in and of itself, it could not remove the missiles. Domestic political considerations again limited Kennedy's options, as did the continued inability of the military to guarantee that an air strike or invasion would not result in one or more Soviet missiles reaching the United States. Kennedy's publicly announced deadline ensured that the military option, with all of its drawbacks, would be used unless Khrushchev could be convinced to take the missiles out of Cuba. The key was to find a face-saving way out for the Soviets that was also true to Kennedy's stated objectives. The combined secret agreement and public pledge of Soviet missiles being removed from Cuba in return for a nonintervention pledge by the United States accomplished this.

The bureaucratic perspective on decision making during the Cuban missile crisis points to quite a different picture of what transpired. Rather than emphasizing the logic of policy making, it stresses the politics and organizational context of policy making. Politics is evident first in the discovery of missiles in Cuba. Consider the following: As early as August, Director of Central Intelligence (DCI) McCone voiced concern about Soviet offensive missiles being placed in Cuba, but he was overruled by McNamara and Rusk; no U-2 flights were directed over the area most likely to have Soviet missiles from September 5 until October 14; the October 14 flight had been authorized on October 4, but a jurisdictional dispute between the Defense Department and the CIA over who would fly the aircraft and which aircraft would be used delayed it. (The solution agreed to was that an Air Force officer in uniform would fly a CIA plane.) Moreover, evidence now points to the fact that the United States underestimated by one-half the number of troops (42,000) the Soviet Union had sent to Cuba. Had this figure been known or had the United States discovered the missiles earlier, the nature of policy options considered, the reading of Soviet goals, and U.S. objectives might have been quite different.

The "logic" of the blockade also suffers when the air strike option is examined in closer detail. First, the Air Force did not specifically design an option to meet ExCom's goal of removing the Soviet missiles. Instead, it merely dusted off an existing contingency plan that also called for air strikes against arms depots, airports, and artillery batteries opposite the U.S. naval base at Guantánamo Bay. Second, Air Force calculations on its ability to destroy the

Soviet missiles were based on an incorrect labeling of the missiles as mobile field-type missiles, although they were actually movable missiles that required six days to be switched from one location to another. Because the Air Force believed that the Soviet missiles might be moved between the time the last reconnaissance mission was flown and the time of the air strike, it was only able to offer Kennedy a 90 percent guarantee that it could knock out all of the missiles. The limits of rational choice are also revealed in the implementation of the blockade. The Navy, like the Air Force, did not tailor its plans to meet ExCom's needs. After-the-fact reconstructions of the timing of ship stoppings show that, contrary to Kennedy's orders, the Navy did not move the blockade closer to Cuba but placed it where they had originally proposed.

The bureaucratic politics model also raises a number of troubling questions about the logic of the agreement that ended the crisis. One point centers on the nature of Soviet goals. No one in ExCom gave serious consideration to the possibility that the Soviet Union was genuinely concerned with deterring a U.S. invasion of Cuba. Evidence now suggests that, along with balance-of-power considerations, this was one of Khrushchev's goals. Moreover, it appears that it was not the threat of nuclear retaliation but the possibility that the United States might use the crisis as a pretext for invading Cuba that led to the decision to remove the missiles. The formal ending of the crisis on the Soviet side also raises troubling questions. Early accounts suggested that Khrushchev was not in full control of the Politburo, and for this reason contradictory messages were being received in Washington concerning the terms for ending the crisis. Evidence now suggests that this may not have been the case; rather, faulty intelligence may have been responsible. The first and more conciliatory note was sent when Soviet intelligence was indicating an imminent U.S. attack on Cuba. The second and more stringent communiqué was sent once it became clear that there would not be an invasion.

Early accounts of Cuban missile crisis decision making from the small-group perspective praised ExCom for not falling victim to groupthink. Janis credits ExCom with not stereotyping the Soviets but actively trying to understand what led them to try to place missiles in Cuba secretly.[40] Janis cites Robert Kennedy's concern about a Pearl Harbor in reverse as evidence of a sensitivity to the moral dilemmas involved in the air strike option. Janis also notes that members of ExCom frequently changed their minds and eventually came to the conclusion that there were no good policy options at their disposal. President Kennedy is credited with having learned from the Bay of Pigs and practicing a leadership style that maximized the possibility that ExCom would produce quality decisions. To encourage free debate, he did not attend all of its meetings, and he split ExCom into smaller groups to debate the issues and reexamine the conclusions reached by other participants.

More recent accounts of ExCom's deliberations suggest that its escape from groupthink was far less complete than was originally believed.[41] At least three decision-making defects surfaced that are fully consistent with the groupthink syndrome. First, ExCom operated with a very narrow mandate: It was to consider the pros and cons of a variety of coercive measures. Kennedy had declared off limits any consideration of either acquiescence to the Soviet move or diplomacy. ExCom was true to that mandate; 90 percent of its time was spent studying alternative uses of troops, bombers, and warships. Thus, ExCom did not engage in a full search for policy options or operate as an open decision-making forum.

Second, those who sought to expand the list of options under consideration and break out of the group consensus were ostracized. U.S. Ambassador to the United Nations Adlai Stevenson initially opposed the use of force and wrote Kennedy a note cautioning him on the dangers of this option. Kennedy was annoyed by the note and blocked efforts by McNamara and Stevenson to include diplomacy on the options list. Stevenson also suggested a trade of Soviet missiles for U.S. missiles in Turkey or for the Guantánamo Bay Naval Base. For these suggestions he came under sharp personal attack by Kennedy and was frozen out of the core decision-making group.

Third, Theodore Sorensen, special counsel and advisor to President Kennedy, and Attorney General Robert Kennedy acted as surrogate leaders for Kennedy, reporting back to the president on the discussion and pushing group members to reach a consensus. Here, too, the impact was to limit the choice of policy alternatives and to stifle discussion. Stevenson observed that "we knew little brother [Robert Kennedy] was watching and keeping a little list where everyone stood." On Friday night, October 25, President Kennedy informed ExCom that he had chosen the blockade. The very next day, the consensus within ExCom for the blockade began to unravel. At that point Kennedy told his brother to "pull the group together quickly." Sorensen would tell the group that they were "not serving the president well," and Robert Kennedy would tell them that the president could not possibly order an air strike.

## MODELS: A CRITIQUE

As we have seen, decision-making models involve taking apart and dissecting a complex set of political activities. Inevitably, the result is that certain features of the decision-making process receive greater attention and are accorded greater importance than are others. For these reasons, policy makers often are uncomfortable with decision-making models. The models are seen as oversimplifying policy decisions by putting forward a mechanistic and highly segmented interpretation of a process that is better seen as a seamless web of activity involving efforts at consensus building, problem definition, and problem solving. Generalizations about decision making are dangerous, they contend, because of the uniqueness of each situation, in terms of both the problem at hand and the domestic political context in which decisions are made.

For these reasons, many of these policy makers believe that the preferred vehicles for conveying the intricacies of decision making are memoirs or historical narratives of the kind written by David Halberstam on Vietnam and Bosnia and by Bob Woodward on Iraq.[42] Constructed as stories, memoirs, and historical narratives place individuals at the center of the decision-making process, rather than abstract concepts and forces such as value-maximizing choices, bureaucratic routines, mindguards, and elites. Placing individuals at the center of the decision-making process is necessary, because in their view it is personal experience, professional skill, and hard work that allow them to succeed.

Proponents of models acknowledge that the potential for distortion is present when models are used, but that memoir-type accounts also may distort our understanding of events by overemphasizing the role of individuals or their freedom to act. They suggest that the task facing students of foreign policy making is to blend these models together to produce a picture containing the maximum amount of insight and a minimal amount of distortion on the nature of the policy-making process, without overwhelming them with data demands.[43]

## OVER THE HORIZON

As this chapter suggests, there are many different ways to understand why the United States announced its intention of beefing up its air defense system in Hawaii against North Korean missiles. The bureaucratic politics model offers an especially attractive first option since it is frequently used in studies of U.S. defense and weapons procurement policy. The decision-making models we have examined in this chapter are not the only ones that are used. New ones are always being put forward in an attempt to gain a better understanding of how foreign policy decisions are made.

As such, in looking over the horizon we can expect new decision making models to appear. One model already enjoying some support is today is **prospect theory**.[44] It takes exception to the assumptions of the rational actor model, asserting that individuals do not weigh all outcomes and select the strategy that will offer the highest expected utility. Instead, individuals tend to value what they have more than what they do not have; they prefer the status quo more often than one would predict; and they tend to be risk averse with respect to gains and risk accepting when it comes to losses. This implies that leaders will take more risks to defend their state's international position than to enhance it, and that, after a loss, leaders will have a tendency to take excessive risks to recover their positions.

## CRITICAL THINKING QUESTIONS

1. What are the strengths and limitations of using models to understand U.S. foreign policy making?
2. How might the pluralist and elitist models explain the Cuban missile crisis?
3. Which model might be most helpful in trying to understand the foreign policy of China, Iran, or Russia?

## KEY TERMS

action channels   234
black box   232
bureaucratic
   politics   233

elite theory   240
groupthink   237
pluralism   242
prospect theory   252

rational actor   232
standard operating
   procedures   235

## FURTHER READING

Graham T. Allison, *Essence of Decision: Explaining the Cuban Missile Crisis* (Boston: Little, Brown, 1971).

"Policy and Poliheuristic Theory of Foreign Policy Decision Making; A Symposium," *International Studies Perspectives*, 6 (2005), 94–150.

Irving L. Janis, *Groupthink: Psychological Studies of Policy Decisions and Fiascos*, 2nd ed. (Boston: Houghton Mifflin, 1982).

Christopher Hill, *The Changing Politics of Foreign Policy* (New York: Palgrave, 2003).

David Mitchell, *Making Foreign Policy: Presidential Management and the Decision Making Process* (Aldeshot, U.K.: Ashgate Publishing, 2005).

## NOTES

1. A short summary of additional models can be found in Thomas L. Brewer, *American Foreign Policy: A Contemporary Introduction*, 2nd ed. (Englewood Cliffs, NJ: Prentice-Hall, 1986), pp. 26–54.
2. Roger Hilsman, "Policy Making Is Politics," in Charles W. Kegley, Jr., and Eugene R. Wittkopf (eds.), *Perspectives on American Foreign Policy: Selected Readings* (New York: St. Martin's, 1983), p. 250.
3. Ibid., p. 251.
4. Leslie H. Gelb with Richard K. Betts, *The Irony of Vietnam: The System Worked* (Washington, DC: Brookings, 1979).
5. Patrick Morgan, *Theories and Approaches to International Politics: What Are We to Think*, 3rd ed. (New Brunswick, NJ: Transaction, 1981), p. 110.
6. Herbert A. Simon, *Administrative Behavior: A Study of Decision Making Processes in Administrative Organization*, 3rd ed. (New York: The Free Press, 1976).
7. Graham T. Allison, *Essence of Decision: Explaining the Cuban Missile Crisis* (Boston: Little, Brown, 1971), p. 35.
8. I. M. Destler, *Presidents, Bureaucrats, and Foreign Policy: The Politics of Organizational Reform* (Princeton, NJ: Princeton University Press, 1974), p. 52.
9. As originally presented by Allison in his Essence of Decision, two separate models were used to explain foreign policy making through organizational routines and governmental politics. Subsequently, Allison combined them into one model, as is done here. See Graham T. Allison and Morton H. Halperin, "Bureaucratic Politics: A Paradigm and Some Policy Implications," *World Politics*, 24 (1982), 40–79.
10. Robert L. Gallucci, *Neither Peace nor Honor: The Politics of American Military Policy in Vietnam* (Baltimore, MD: Johns Hopkins University Press, 1975), p. 153.
11. Robert J. Art, "Bureaucratic Politics and American Foreign Policy: A Critique," in Robert J. Art and Robert Jervis (eds.), *International Politics: Anarchy, Force, Political Economy, and Deci* Col. Oliver North,, 2nd ed. (Boston: Little, Brown, 1985), p. 471; Stephen D. Krasner, "Are Bureaucrats Important? (Or Allison Wonderland)," *Foreign Policy*, 7 (1972), 159–79; and Jerel Rosati, "Developing a Systematic Decision Making Framework: Bureaucratic Politics in Perspective," *World Politics*, 33 (1981), 234–51.
12. Jonathan Bendor and Thomas H. Hammand, "Rethinking Allison's Models," *American Political Science Review*, 86 (1992), 301–22.
13. Robert L. Wendzel, *International Politics: Policymakers & Policymaking* (New York: John Wiley 1981), p. 439.
14. Ibid., p. 438.

15. Robert E. Hunter, *Presidential Control of Foreign Policy: Management or Mishap?* Washington Paper #191 (New York: Praeger, 1982), pp. 35–46.
16. Irving L. Janis, *Groupthink: Psychological Studies of Policy Decisions and Fiascos*, 2nd ed. (Boston: Houghton Mifflin, 1982).
17. Ibid., p. 9.
18. Ibid., p. 256.
19. Ibid., pp. 172, 262–71.
20. Richard K. Betts, "Analysis, War, and Decision: Why Intelligence Failures Are Inevitable," *World Politics,* 31 (1978), 61–89.
21. Carol Barner-Barry and Robert Rosenwein, *Psychological Perspectives on Politics* (Englewood Cliffs, NJ: Prentice-Hall, 1985), p. 247.
22. Irving L. Janis and Leon Mann, *Decision Making: A Psychological Analysis of Conflict, Choice, and Commitment* (New York: The Free Press, 1977).
23. John D. Steinbruner, *The Cybernetic Theory of Decision: New Dimensions of Political Analysis* (Princeton, NJ: Princeton University Press, 1974), pp. 66–67.
24. Ibid., pp. 125–36.
25. Mark Schafer and Scott Crichlow, "The Process-Outcome Connection in Foreign Policy Decision Making," *International Studies Quarterly,* 46 (2002), 45–68.
26. Alexander George and Erick Stern, "Harnessing Conflicts in Foreign Policy Making," *Presidential Studies Quarterly,* 32 (2002), 484–508.
27. Compare Gabriel Kolko, *The Roots of American Foreign Policy* (Boston: Beacon, 1969), with C. Wright Mills, *The Power Elite* (New York: Oxford University Press, 1956).
28. Robert A. Dahl, "A Critique of the Ruling Elite Model," in G. William Domhoff and Hoyt B. Ballard (eds.), *C. Wright Mills and the Power Elite* (Boston: Beacon, 1968), p. 31.
29. Theodore J. Lowi, *The End of Liberalism: Ideology, Policy, and the Crisis of Public Authority* (New York: N.W. Norton, 1969).
30. See, for example, Glenn D. Paige, *The Korean Decision, June 24–30, 1950* (New York: The Free Press, 1968).
31. Glenn H. Snyder and Paul Diesing, *Conflict Among Nations: Bargaining, Decision-Making, and System Structure in International Crises* (Princeton, NJ: Princeton University Press, 1977), p. 355.
32. For discussion of Cuban missile crisis decision making, see Graham T. Allison, *The Essence of Decision: Explaining the Cuban Missile Crisis* (Boston: Little, Brown, 1971); Theodore Sorensen, *Kennedy* (New York: Harper & Row, 1965); and Richard Ned Lebow, *Between Peace and War: The Nature of International Crisis* (Baltimore, MD: Johns Hopkins University Press, 1981).
33. James A. Nathan and James K. Oliver, *United States Foreign Policy and World Order*, 3rd ed. (Boston: Little, Brown, 1985), p. 275.
34. Allison, *The Essence of Decision*, p. 103.
35. Ibid., pp. 58–61.
36. Walter Pincus, "Standing at the Brink of Nuclear War," *The Washington Post,* July 25, 1985, p. A10.
37. Allison, *The Essence of Decision*, p. 64.
38. "The Decision Would Take Out Only the Known Missiles," *The Washington Post*, July 25, 1985, p. A1.
39. The most important of these is Raymond Garthoff, *Reflections on the Cuban Missile Crisis,* rev. ed. (Washington, DC: Brookings, 1989). The revised edition contains insights into the crisis that came out of a joint U.S.–Soviet conference on the Cuban missile crisis held in 1987.

40. Irving Janis, *Groupthink*, 2nd ed. (Boston: Houghton Mifflin, 1982), pp. 132–58.

41. Lebow, *Between Peace and War*, especially chapter 8.

42. See David Halberstam, *The Best and the Brightest* (Greenwich, CT: Fawcett, 1969), and *War in a Time of Peace* (New York: Touchstone, 2001); and Bob Woodward, *The Commanders* (New York: Touchstone, 1991), *Bush at War* ((New York: Simon & Schuster, 2002), *Plan of Attack* (New York: Simon & Schuster, 2004), and *State of Denial* (New York: Simon & Schuster, 2006).

43. One model that does try is the decision-making model presented by Richard Snyder, H. W. Bruck, and Burton Sapin in "Decision Making as an Approach to the Study of International Politics," in Richard Snyder, H. W. Bruck, and Burton Sapin (eds.), *Foreign Policy Decision Making* (New York: The Free Press, 1963).

44. Jack Levy, "Prospect Theory, Rational Choice and International Relations," *International Studies Quarterly*, 41 (1997), 87–112.

# Diplomacy

A l-Hurra, "The Free One," is the Arabic-language television network created in April 2003 and financed by the U.S. government to help spread democracy in the Middle East.[1] Headquartered in suburban Washington, DC, it broadcasts commercial-free programs 24 hours a day, with content consisting of a combination of news broadcasts; original programming such as the talk show *Town Hall* and *Equality*," a show that stresses women's issues; and Arabic-subtitled standard American TV shows.

To date al-Hurra has struggled in its mission of providing a more positive image of the United States in the Middle East, something advocates of soft power argue is essential if the United States is to achieve its goal of transforming the region. Early executives did not speak Arabic. Many came from the entertainment field with backgrounds in producing *American Top 40 with Casey Kasem* and *The History of Rock and Roll*. On-air broadcasters lacked experience; they came overwhelmingly from Lebanon, with most of their stories being about that country. Reporting errors of omission and commission were common. When an Israeli air strike killed a major Hamas leader, almost all other Arabic news programs interrupted their programming to cover the story, whereas al-Hurra continued with a cooking show. One Easter morning, al-Hurra's news anchor told its Muslim audience that "Jesus is risen today." It also unknowingly broadcast a lengthy anti-Israeli speech by a Hezbollah leader and gave sympathetic coverage to Iranian President Mahmoud Ahmadinejad's Holocaust denial conference.

Content problems have led to viewer problems. Independent viewer surveys find that where 54 percent of those surveyed said they watch al-Jazeera for international news, only 2 percent said they watched al-Hurra. An important exception is Iraq, where it has some nine million weekly viewers.

## PROCESS VERSUS PRODUCT

Our focus in this chapter is on diplomacy. As an instrument of foreign policy, diplomacy is closely identified with **bargaining** and **negotiation.** It is also identified with government-to-government relations. As our story of al-Hurra's struggles indicates, this is no longer the case. Public diplomacy reaches out to the people of a state, speaking to them directly in hopes of laying a foundation that is favorable to U.S. foreign policy initiatives.

Still, for many diplomacy remains the classic policy instrument and the one best suited to producing lasting and workable solutions to foreign policy problems. Others point out that the use of diplomacy is not without its dangers. Negotiations also hold the potential for exacerbating hostilities, strengthening an aggressor, preparing the way for an attack, and eroding the moral and legal foundations of peace.[2] They do so because, in addition to solving problems, negotiations can also be used to stall for time, obtain information, and make propaganda plays.

The tension described here points to the difference between viewing diplomacy as a process and diplomacy as a product or outcome. According to some observers this tension, which has always existed, is growing greater because while interest in diplomacy as talking is on the rise the preconditions needed for diplomacy as product are on the decline.[3] Three of the most important factors standing in the way of the success of diplomatic efforts today are (1) the absence of shared principles on which to base international agreements, (2) the increased presence of nonnegotiable goals, and (3) the growing role of public opinion in foreign policy making. The first two make compromise difficult and greatly reduce the amount of common ground on which solutions can be built. The third complicates the ability of governments to implement agreements.

## BILATERAL DIPLOMACY

The most common form of diplomacy is bilateral diplomacy, in which two states interact directly with one another. These relations occur at varying levels, from heads of government and ambassadors down to junior Foreign Service Officers. They also can cover a wide array of subjects, ranging from sensitive security and economic issues to the routine issuing of visas. Bilateral relations are assuming a new prominence today. In part, this is attributed to the end of the Cold War and the disappearance of the Cold War alliance systems. Without the Cold War to frame its negotiations, diplomacy has become heavily influenced by country-specific considerations.

Historically one of the most sensitive topics in bilateral relations has been the willingness of countries to allow the United States to station its troops on their territory.[4] This remains the case today. In 2008, Ecuador closed a U.S. air base that played a key role in the international war on drugs largely due to rising anti-American sentiment and concerns for sovereignty. That same year Kyrgyzstan threatened to close a key U.S. air base that provided access to Afghanistan. Growing anti-U.S. sentiment was a major contributing factor here, as well as an offer of $2 billion in loans from Russia if the base were to be closed. In June 2009, Kyrgyzstan reversed course and extended the U.S. base contract when the U.S. agreed to pay an additional $180 million for the Manas air base. These bilateral dealings are not new. Between 1947 and 1990, the United States was asked to leave many countries. Among them were France, Yugoslavia, Iran, Libya, Saudi Arabia, Indonesia, Peru, Mexico, and Venezuela. Anti-American protests during this same period allowed Spain, Greece, the Philippines, and Turkey to obtain large concessions from the United States in order to keep its bases. The potential scope of the problem is immense. Where in 1938 the United States had 14 military bases outside of its continental borders, in 2003 it owned or rented 702 overseas bases in some 130 countries.

Basing rights became a controversial issue early in Obama's presidency. The United States and Japan had agreed upon a plan for reorganizing the U.S. military presence there and shifting some marines to Guam. This plan did not receive widespread popular support in Japan and was never acted upon. A new Japanese government announced in late 2009 that it was not going to rush into a decision. The United States sees implementing the agreement as an important sign of Japan's ability and willingness to serve as a major U.S. ally in the region.

A second conflict centered on the establishment of a U.S. base in Colombia. The Obama administration downplayed the move saying it was little more than a formalization of policies in place with Colombia since the early 1950s and will help in the war on drug trafficking. Venezuela, Brazil, and other states in the region questioned the need for a new U.S. military base and threatened to purchase arms from Russia and other states in retaliation.

We can gain a sense of the potential scope of bilateral diplomatic initiatives under way at any one time by looking back to February and March 2007. In March, President George W. Bush made a six-day, five-country trip to Latin America, visiting Guatemala, Mexico, Brazil, Uruguay, and Colombia. Absent on this trip was a visit to Cuba. The United States had closed its embassy in Havana on January 3, 1961, and had withdrawn its recognition from Fidel Castro's government. March also saw Secretary of State Condoleezza Rice make her fourth trip to the Middle East in four months. Finally, a representative from the U.S. Treasury Department traveled to Asia to meet with Chinese officials in hopes of resolving a dispute over the status of North Korean funds held in a Chinese bank, which was creating a roadblock to efforts to deal with North Korea's nuclear program.

As this overview suggests, countries enter into three different types of bilateral relationships, each of which has its own unique set of characteristics: allies, friends, and adversaries. Dealings with allies are marked by high levels of commitment to the negotiation process, a recognition that a wide area of common interests exists, and a willingness to address the specific issues involved in a dispute. Relations with adversaries also are marked by a high degree of commitment and attention but lack any sense of shared interests. Instead, there is an underlying sense of conflict and distrust. As a result, much of the bilateral dialogue centers on finding formula-based solutions for problems. Finally, there are bilateral relations among friends. These are relations between states that are on good terms but lack extensive dealings with one another. As a result, it is often difficult to strike a deal, as each side advances its own particular interest in the absence of widely perceived common interests.

As the Cuba case shows, a fourth category of (non)relations also exists. During the George W. Bush administration, the most prominent countries with which the United States lacked formal diplomatic relations were the three members of the Axis of Evil, Iran, North Korea, and Iraq. Others included Cuba, Syria, and Libya. As the Bush administration ended, steps were taken to reverse this pattern, entering into multilateral talks with North Korea regarding its pursuit of nuclear weapons, announcing that U.S. diplomats would take part in a one-time international negotiating session with Iran, and speaking with Libyan leader Moammar Gaddafi.

The Obama administration followed suit and began to reach out to countries with which the United States did not have formal diplomatic relations. A senior U.S. official met with Burmese leaders in March 2009, and in June it announced that a U.S. ambassador would be sent to Syria, ending a four-year absence, and that talks were under way with Venezuela to restore their ambassadors after a nine-month break in diplomatic relations.

Venezuela broke diplomatic relations as a sign of solidarity with Bolivia after that country's government accused the United States of interfering in its domestic affairs and helping the opposition incite domestic violence and expelled the U.S. ambassador. In September, the administration held six days of meetings with Cuban government officials as well as opposition leaders. This move followed Obama's earlier decision to lift restrictions on family visits and remittances as well as permit investments in Cuba by U.S. telecommunication firms. The following month it indicated a willingness to open a diplomatic dialogue with North Korea if that would pave the way for international disarmament talks.

## Incentives Versus Sanctions

One of the most difficult decisions that must be made in bilateral relations involves the choice between employing sanctions and offering incentives. Sanctions are penalties and thus are generally directed at adversaries. The most frequently employed sanctions are economic in nature, and we will look at them more closely in the next chapter. At this point it is enough to note that often the threat of a sanction may be enough to induce another state to adopt a more cooperative attitude. There are limits to the ability of sanctions to change behavior. When relations are minimal or sanctions are already in place, there may be little additional damage that sanctions can do so there is little reason for states to comply.

The historical record shows that sanctions have also been used against allies and friends. Chile was warned by Secretary of State Colin Powell that a proposed meeting of UN Security Council members opposed to the Iraq War would be seen as an "unfriendly act" and would jeopardize prospects for signing a U.S.–Chile free trade agreement. These threats were soon dropped when Chile's help was needed to support U.S. postinvasion reconstruction efforts in Iraq.

Engagement is relatively understudied compared to sanctions.[5] Incentives can include the removal of sanctions or the offering of additional trade and foreign aid. Diplomatic recognition, joint military training exercises, and building people-to-people contacts are also examples of incentives that can be offered. If engagement is chosen, the key decision that policy makers must make is whether the strategy is conditional on the other state undertaking specific actions or whether it is unconditional.

Offering incentives to a friend or ally is easy. Such a policy is much more controversial when the target state is a foe. Yet it is precisely with these states that the strategy of engagement may offer its greatest benefits, because it provides an avenue for dialogue that did not previously exist. The Clinton administration's policies toward North Korea and Vietnam, for example, were based on engagement rather than sanctions. U.S. policy toward China, with its emphasis on expanding trade opportunities, similarly has a strong engagement element.

The greatest challenge faced by architects of engagement strategies is to avoid the charge that they are appeasing dangerous states rather than providing for U.S. security. The George W. Bush administration faced these very charges from Republicans as it switched strategies in dealing with North Korea, moving from one of confrontation to one that offered incentives or rewards to close down its nuclear facility. Among the rewards offered were movement toward full diplomatic relations, partial payment by the United States for the costs of shutting down its nuclear facilities, and allowing heavy fuel oil to be shipped to North Korea.

This problem arises because approached as a domestic politics problem it is far easier to demonize the other state than to engage in negotiations with it. It helps focus public attention on specific aspects of the problem, moral clarity is retained, and attention is deflected from the inconsistencies and indecisions of policies and placed instead on the actions of the other.[6] The downside to a strategy that relies on sanctions and demonizing an opponent is that it limits options for both the current administration and its successors. No case better illustrates this point than Fidel Castro and American foreign policy with respect to Cuba, toward which a policy of nonrecognition and nonnegotiation has been a constant for over 50 years.

## Bilateralism Versus Multilateralism

In addition to engaging in bilateral diplomacy, or instead of doing so, countries may also engage in multilateral negotiations in which typically many countries participate. A high profile example came in fall 2009, when the Obama administration turned to multilateralism in its efforts to curb Iran's pursuit of nuclear weapons. Faced with threats of economic sanctions and coming under increasing pressure to change its policies, it was announced in October 2009 that Iran would meet with representatives from the U.S., Germany, France, Great Britain, Russia, and China. This was the first meeting between these states in over a year.

Multilateralism is not without its own problems as a diplomatic problem solving strategy.[7] One set is domestic. Public opinion tends to support acting through the United Nations and other multilateral bodies, but only up to a point, because unilateralism runs deep in the American national style. A second set of obstacles is international. With whom does one partner? The choice at its most fundamental level is between **alliance** members such as those in the North Atlantic Treaty Organization (NATO) or those in economic organizations such as the World Trade Organization (WTO) and creating ad hoc **coalitions** of states that share a common interest with regard to specific problems, be it genocide, Iraq, or the environment. Permanent allies and organizations can be slow to respond because of conflicts among members or internal decision-making procedures. There is also the ever-present danger of being rejected on a call for support by allies. Creating ad hoc "coalitions of the willing" gets around these problems, but they provide no firm foundation on which to build long-term solutions. They also require the United States to reinvent the solution each time a new problem arises.

In many respects, the choice between bilateral and multilateral diplomacy is a false one. Bilateral diplomacy can be an important component of any multilateral diplomatic undertaking. Most notably, this was the case in talks designed to denuclearize North Korea. Officially they were conducted under the banner of six-party talks (North Korea, Russia, China, Japan, South Korea, and the United States). Beneath this multilateral façade, a constant stream of bilateral talks took place between the parties, including talks between the United States and North Korea. A second example involves a decision by the Obama administration to begin regular trilateral talks between the United States, Afghanistan, and Pakistan as part of an effort to encourage greater regional antiterrorism cooperation. This decision was followed by U.S. attendance at a UN conference on Afghanistan, on April 20, 2009, in which Iran also participated.

## SUMMIT DIPLOMACY

The most visible of all the forms of diplomacy today is summit diplomacy, in which heads of state meet personally with one another. **Summit conferences** perform a number of valuable services.[8] Foremost among them is establishing a personal relationship between leaders that sensitizes each to the domestic constraints operating in the other's political system. A second valuable service performed by a summit is that it energizes the bureaucracy and sets a deadline for decision making. The benefit here is not so much the summit itself but the preparations for the summit. The SALT I negotiations and the U.S.–Japanese agreement over the status of Okinawa were both carried out under the deadline of an approaching summit conference.

Aligned against these positive virtues of summit diplomacy are a number of potentially negative consequences.[9] First, the personal contacts established through face-to-face negotiations may result in an inaccurate reading of the adversary's character and the constraints unclear which the adversary operates. This appears to have happened at the 1961 Kennedy–Khrushchev summit in Vienna. Khrushchev reportedly came away from it with the impression that Kennedy could be intimidated, and many link the Soviet attempt to place missiles in Cuba to this meeting. Another prime example is Franklin Roosevelt's belief that he could establish a personal working relationship with Josef Stalin as a result of the World War II summit conferences in Tehran and Yalta.

Energizing the bureaucracy does not necessarily guarantee the emergence of a coherent policy. It may only intensify the ongoing bureaucratic struggle so that only a lowest-common-denominator position is taken to the summit. Summit deadlines may also politicize or impede decision making. This point is most forcefully raised with reference to annual economic summitry, but as the many accounts of U.S.–Soviet arms control talks reveal, it is equally applicable to other forms of international diplomacy.[10] Other commentators suggest that periodic meetings are a questionable device for addressing a continuously evolving problem. Agreements reached in April become obsolete in November, but the next summit is still months away. Inaction rather than adaptive problem solving is likely to characterize the bureaucratic process for most of the intervening months. In addition, summit deadlines offer the recalcitrant state a golden opportunity to exploit the other's eagerness for the summit. One observer suggests that this may have happened with the Carter–Brezhnev summit. Carter's desire for a summit is seen as being partly responsible for his supporting a Soviet initiative to reconvene the Geneva talks on the Middle East. The result, had this actually happened, would have been to give the Soviet Union a voice in the Middle East peace process that was denied to it as long as U.S. peace initiatives dominated the agenda.[11]

Summit conferences have also been criticized for unfairly raising public expectations about the potential for a meaningful agreement. Giving attention to a problem is different from discovering a solution. A common criticism of high-level diplomacy is that it is part of a cycle characterized by "a burst of publicity about new initiatives or special envoys, followed by policy drift and an unwillingness to push either side . . . eventually the effort goes dormant, sometimes for months, until yet another approach is crafted."[12] The SALT agreements were negotiated as part of the process of détente, and when détente began to unravel, arms control efforts were one of the main casualties. To deal with many of these shortcomings, President Richard Nixon advocated regular summit conferences as a way of keeping the pressure on the Soviet Union, curbing its behavior, and taking the pressure off getting a major agreement at any one summit.[13]

## East–West Superpower Summits[14]

East–West summit conferences were a frequent, if irregularly spaced, feature of the Cold War. The earlier first summits, from 1955 to 1967, dealt with European security issues. Later they became an important mechanism for institutionalizing détente. All told, they produced more than 24 agreements, including SALT I and SALT II. Reagan and Gorbachev conducted a series of post-détente summit conferences, the most famous of which was the Reykjavik summit in 1986. There, Reagan proposed abolishing all ballistic missiles, and Gorbachev countered with a proposal to eliminate all strategic arms. Nothing came of these initiatives because they would have prohibited Reagan from engaging in Strategic Defensive Initiative (SDI) testing beyond the laboratory, something he refused to do. With the disintegration of the Soviet Union and the end of the Cold War, East–West summits declined in overall strategic importance and increasingly focused on economic assistance rather than arms control. After 9/11, they became a vehicle for George W. Bush to enlist Russian help in the war on terrorism.

## Economic Summits

Beginning in 1975, the heads of state of the seven major Western economies have been meeting at an annual summit conference. Russia joined the summit process in 1998, enlarging the original membership of the Group of Seven, or G-7 (consisting of Canada, France, Italy, West Germany, Japan, Great Britain, and the United States), and making it the Group of Eight (G-8). The President of the European Commission has joined the summit meetings since 1981. At the

Pittsburgh G-8 Summit in September 2009, it was agreed that the G-20 will replace the G-8 as the main forum for international economic discussions. President Obama had pushed for this change, one that brings countries such as Brazil, China, India, and South Africa into the negotiations.

While economic issues dominated the discussions at the first several summits, with the passage of time other issues began to be discussed at them as well.[15] In 1996, at President Bill Clinton's urging, the summit's agenda was broadened to include terrorism and international crime. At the 1998 summit, the heads of state expressed their frustration over India's detonation of a nuclear device, urged the Israelis and Palestinians to resume negotiations, and called for political and economic reform in Indonesia. The willingness to address a broad agenda has not been matched by an ability to reach a consensus on what action to take. In 1996, Clinton was able to get support for a crackdown on terrorism, but in 1998 he failed to get agreement on sanctions against India. Not surprisingly, post-9/11, G-8 summits did not escape the shadows of the Iraq War.

At the 2009 Economic Summit Conference, those in attendance agreed on reducing carbon emissions by 80 percent but failed to establish immediate targets. The G-8 leaders did promise to raise $20 billion in food and agricultural aid over the next three years to help the world's poorest countries deal with the food security crisis brought on by the sudden rise in food prices in 2008. They also agreed to Obama's call for a March 2010 nuclear security summit in Washington, DC, to deal with the problem of nuclear proliferation, which would be attended by some 25 countries. Along with the G-8 Summit, 17 countries (including the G-8) that form the Major Economies Forum on Energy and Climate had a meeting in which they agreed to work to limiting the rise in the earth's average temperature. They were unable to agree on little more than that as rich and poor countries disagree over who should make the largest cuts and who should bear the cost of protecting the global environment.

Another important annual international economic summit conference that the United States participates in is that of the Asian-Pacific Economic Cooperation (APEC) countries. In 2006, major topics of discussion were the need to reenergize the Doha Round of trade talks and North Korea's pursuit of nuclear weapons. The United States and Russia also signed a trade agreement that had eluded them in the 2006 G-8 Summit meeting. The 20th APEC meeting occurred in November 2008 just as the global financial crisis began to make its full effect felt. A major theme that emerged from these talks was to find ways of strengthening the mechanisms of international cooperation.

## CONFERENCE DIPLOMACY

Conference diplomacy starts from the logic that some problems in international politics affect the interests of too many states to be solved unilaterally, bilaterally, or at summit conferences. What is needed is to bring all of the concerned states together. In the examples that follow the issues are global, but they need not be. They may also be regional, as evidenced by efforts to bring peace and stability to the Middle East. In 1991, President George H. W. Bush was the leading force in organizing a conference in Madrid, which he cosponsored with the Soviet Union. Attending were Israel, Syria, Jordan, Lebanon, and the Palestinians. In November 2007, President George W. Bush hosted a Middle East summit conference in Annapolis, Maryland. Representatives from over 50 countries attended, including 12 Arab states. Absent, however, were Iran and representatives from Hezbollah, Hamas, and the Islamic Jihad. The one-day conference resulted in a pledge on the part of the Israelis and Palestinians to begin talking with one another in hopes of settling the issue of Palestinian statehood by December 2008.

## GATT and WTO

The United States has relied heavily on international conferences to accomplish its foreign policy objectives in the area of trade. Historically, the most important of these was the GATT talks. The last GATT conference ran from 1986 to 1994 and was known as the Uruguay Round. It culminated with the signing of an agreement that established the WTO to supervise international trade law and formally bring the GATT process to an end.

From its first meeting in Geneva in 1947, GATT had been seen as a transitional body that would deal with international trade matters only until an International Trade Organization (ITO) was set up. Because of political opposition in the United States to the broad powers that were to be given to the ITO, President Harry Truman never submitted the treaty to Congress for approval. Similar concerns about the loss of U.S. sovereignty were expressed when the WTO was proposed. Only a last-minute compromise reserving the right of the United States to leave the WTO should it consistently rule against the United States cleared the way for the treaty's approval by the Senate.

Two earlier important rounds of GATT trade negotiations were the Kennedy Round (1964–1967) and the Tokyo Round (1973–1977). The Kennedy Round sought to reduce barriers to international free trade and marked the high point of international trade cooperation. By the late 1970s, tariffs averaged less than 10 percent. This compared to 25 percent in 1945 and 60 percent in 1934. The second prolonged negotiating session, the Tokyo Round, was not as successful. The new focus of concern was nontariff barriers (NTBs) to trade. The Tokyo Round made some progress on NTBs. Agreement was reached on such practices as subsidies, dumping, countervailing duties, product standards, and government purchases. The principal failings of the Tokyo Round were that little headway was made on liberalizing agricultural trade, and that questions of trade in services were not addressed.

The Uruguay Round took up these issues. Agriculture pitted the rich countries against the poor and the United States against Western Europe. At the heart of the problem was the need for more markets for agricultural goods, the widespread presence of subsidies and quotas that protected farmers from foreign competition, and the unwillingness of leaders to antagonize the politically powerful agricultural interests in their states. For its part, the

United States was unwilling to stop subsidizing sugar growers and expose them to competition from Third World producers. At the same time, however, it demanded that France stop subsidizing its soybean farmers and open European markets to American soybean producers. A second area of concern to the United States was international protection for intellectual property. American firms charged that Third World states routinely disregarded copyrights and patents in the production of such items as books, compact disks, and computer software. A third area of controversy centered on the demands of the United States and Europe to set international labor standards with regard to child labor, convict labor, minimum wages, and unions. The United States and Europe also pressed, against Third World objections, for the establishment of a body to examine the environmental impact of GATT.

In November 2001, representatives from over 140 states met in Doha, Qatar, and approved the launching of a new three-year round of global trade talks under the auspices of the recently created WTO. Among the topics highlighted for negotiation were agriculture, services, industrial tariffs, investment, and environmentally harmful fishing practices. Representatives met again in Cancun, Mexico, in September 2003 for the purpose of moving these discussions forward. Instead, the talks collapsed, largely over Third World complaints led by China, India, and Brazil, that rich states were subsidizing agriculture at a rate of $300 billion per year, resulting in overproduction that was flooding world markets, artificially lowering the cost of food, and costing farm jobs in their countries. Whereas the Third World press hailed the failure of the WTO Cancun meeting as a "great moral victory for the world's poor," U.S. Trade Representative Robert Zoellick took a different view. He asserted that failure occurred because some countries "used rhetoric as opposed to negotiation." Rich states were pressing poor states to accept new rules on foreign investment and government procure-ment. The Doha talks resumed in 2004, but collapsed again in 2008 over a failure to agree on rules governing agricultural imports. The United States, China, and India continued negotiations on trade on agricultural products after the collapse of the talks, but no progress was made.

## Environmental Conferences

Conference diplomacy also has become a central vehicle for international environmental policy making. However, just as with international economic conference diplomacy, the complexity of these issues, coupled with the imperatives of American domestic politics, has made it difficult for the United States to exert leadership and has often placed it at odds with the rest of the world. This was very much the case during the first Reagan administration, which sought both to weaken domestic environmental standards and to limit U.S. support for international environmental programs. The convergence of many factors brought about a policy shift in Reagan's second term, as the United States assumed a leadership position in international negotiations that led to the signing of the 1987 Montreal Protocol on Substances that Deplete the Ozone Layer. Foremost among these factors were changes in personnel at the Environmental Protection Agency and the State Department, the commitment of leading American firms such as Dupont to support a ban on chlorofluorocarbon (CFC) emissions, growing global concern about the environment spurred by the Chernobyl nuclear reactor accident, and mounting scientific evidence regarding ozone depletion and global warming.[16]

The Montreal Protocol was hailed widely for the real cuts it was able to make in the production and consumption of ozone-depleting materials and for its procedural approach to the problem. Rather than seek a definitive and comprehensive statement about levels of reduction, funding, and the obligations of signatory states, as had commonly been done in the past, negotiators at Montreal established a framework for addressing the problem and committed themselves to periodic review conferences at which target figures and timetables could be adjusted.

The George H. W. Bush administration's principal foray into international environmental conference diplomacy was the UN Conference on Environment and Development. Better known as the "Earth Summit," it took place between June 3 and 14, 1992, in Rio de Janeiro, Brazil. The product of almost two years of advance negotiations and attended by about 35,000 accredited delegates representing over 178 countries, the Earth Summit ended with the signing of seven major pacts and initiatives. It also found the United States on the defensive and the only major state not to sign a biodiversity treaty. The Bush administration objected to the treaty's provisions calling for all states to protect endangered animal and plant species, on the grounds that it did not provide patent protection to U.S. biotechnology firms. The treaty was later signed by the administration of Bill Clinton. The United States was also virtually alone in its objections to a treaty on protection against global warming. It agreed to support it only after references to binding targets, and timetables were dropped in favor of a more general pledge to reduce the emissions of gases that cause global warming.

A major international environmental conference took place in Kyoto, Japan, in 1997. It was agreed there that industrial states would reduce greenhouse emissions of six gases from 1990 levels by more than 5 percent between 2008 and 2012. The Kyoto Protocol was significant because it was the first legally binding environmental agreement, even though no compliance mechanisms were established and Third World states were asked only to set up voluntary targets. The United States signed the agreement, but the Clinton administration indicated that it had reservations and was interested in having parts changed. The George W. Bush administration took a harder stand, terming the treaty "fatally flawed in fundamental ways" and withdrew the United States from it.

In December 2005, representatives from 189 countries and leading nongovernmental organizations such as Friends of the Earth and the Worldwide Fund for Nature met in Montreal at the UN Climate Change Conference. There, countries that had signed the Kyoto Protocol over a decade earlier agreed to begin talks on a new treaty on emissions that would take effect after the Kyoto agreements expired in 2012. The United States refused to sign on to the talks, which would set mandatory limits, and at one point walked out of the conference. The U.S. representative returned after pressure was applied by U.S. allies and 24 senators sent a letter urging him to return. In the end, the United States limited itself to agreeing to enter into a multilateral informal and nonbinding dialogue on what should be done to address the problem of climate change.

Fall and winter 2007 saw the beginning of a new series of environmental summits that were marked by rivalry and animosity. The sequence began in August, when a UN conference on climate change meeting in Vienna ended in a deadlock over how to reduce greenhouse emissions. There followed a September conference in Washington called by the George W. Bush administration. The administration had promised earlier in the year to act on the problem and develop a set of voluntary national "aspirational" goals for reducing greenhouse gases. The sincerity of the Bush administration's efforts was widely questioned and became the focus of concern at a December UN conference in Bali, Indonesia, when the United States refused to accept specific targets on a "road map" to reaching an international climate agreement by 2009. So deep was the conflict that at one point European countries threatened to boycott the next U.S.-sponsored climate meeting.

Global environmental conference diplomacy was reenergized in 2009. Obama and other leaders spoke at a UN "climate summit" held in conjunction with the opening of its fall 2009 session. This was followed by the convening of the Copenhagen Conference in December. In his UN speech, Obama defined global warming an urgent threat and called for a "flexible and pragmatic" response. Two different frameworks for the next round of environmental agreements emerged from the UN meeting. In one, countries would agree to globally negotiated cuts. In the second, countries would make unilateral pledges of cuts setting their own targets.

## Human Rights Conferences

The subject matter of international human rights conferences is quite varied. Topics range from commonly defined rights such as those associated with the 1948 Universal Declaration of Human Rights to concerns of more specific groups of individuals such as women and children or refugees and displaced persons. The United States has been an active participant in these conferences, but at times it has also opted not to participate.

One prominent decision to abstain took place in October 1996 when the United States was absent from the Ottawa Conference on landmines, which resulted in a treaty now signed by over 150 countries. India, China, and Russia have also not signed the treaty banning the production and development of antipersonnel mines. One reason given by the United States for not signing the treaty is the continued need for such mines along the demilitarized zone (DMZ) along the North–South Korea border. An estimated one million mines can be found along the DMZ. It reaffirmed this decision in 2004 by not sending an observer to the first Review Conference, although the George W. Bush administration did promise to remove all persistent landmines from its arsenal.

In April 2009, President Obama announced that while the United States was firmly committed to ending racism and racial discrimination, it was not going to send a delegation to the Durban Review Conference that would meet to evaluate progress toward the goals of eliminating racism, racial discrimination, xenophobia, and related forms of intolerance. The previous conference was held in Durban, South Africa, in 2001. The principal reason given was the conference's equating of racism with Zionism. In making this decision, Obama was following in the footsteps of earlier presidents. George W. Bush administration balked at participating in the 2001 conference because of the language and the inclusion of a proposal calling for reparations for slavery. The United States had refused to participate in earlier international conferences on racism in 1978 and 1983 because of similar concerns over language.

## UN DIPLOMACY

At any one time, U.S. policy toward the UN represents an amalgam of four different roles.[17] First, the United States sees itself as an international reformer. Viewed from this perspective, the UN is an important instrument deserving U.S. support, because it holds the potential to transform world politics. Second, the United States sees itself as a custodian. It sometimes usurps or resists the powers of the UN because its agenda conflicts with the greater purposes identified and defined by the United States. The third role is that of spokesperson for the American public. A problem here is that policy makers do not necessarily have a clear sense of what the public thinks. Finally, the United States finds itself in the same role as other states. It seeks to use the UN system to advance and protect American national interests by such actions as applying international sanctions against Iraq, vetoing resolutions condemning Israel, and opposing an international criminal court. The balance among these four role orientations is not fixed, and changes in U.S. policy toward the UN can be attributed to changes in their intensity and the manner in which they interact.

George W. Bush's UN diplomacy gives evidence of all four orientations. By far the most dominant has been that of international reformer. This outlook allowed the Bush administration to act unilaterally and bypass the UN in going to war against Iraq on the grounds that the UN was not part of the solution but part of the problem to responding to international terrorism. This same outlook allowed it to reverse course and pressure the UN for increased support of humanitarian interventions in Sudan and elsewhere and to lobby for international sanctions against Iran. In 2008, there were nearly 110 peacekeepers in 20 overseas missions. The Bush administration pursued a traditional national interest orientation in returning to the UN after the invasion removed Saddam Hussein from power in order to gain support for its plan to formally end the occupation. That resolution, passed unanimously by the Security Council, approved the transfer of sovereignty to a new Iraqi government, outlined a role for the UN in a posttransition Iraq, and authorized an American-led multinational force. The administration also adopted this role in continuing to demand exemptions for U.S. troops from prosecution by the International Criminal Court and refusing to participate in a UN conference on racism that it considered to be anti-Israeli in spirit.

The United States adopted a custodian role when, in January 2004, it announced that it would demand significant changes in a World Health Organization (WHO) initiative on obesity. The George W. Bush administration stated that the WHO had gone beyond its mandate, and that the United States preferred an approach based on personal responsibility rather than governmental regulation. Moreover, the administration stated that its interpretation of the science in the report differed from that of the WHO. This last critique was not new, as conflicts over the science on which reports are based have been recurring points of controversy in environmental negotiations.

## PUBLIC DIPLOMACY

**Public diplomacy** consists of the statements and actions of leaders that are intended to influence public opinion in other countries. It is alien to classic diplomacy, which emphasizes secrecy and confidential bargaining among government officials and therefore has been largely neglected and often disparaged as propaganda. This fate befell Cold War efforts at public diplomacy, such as the Voice of America or Radio Free Europe, which broadcast into communist-controlled areas. Public diplomacy has received renewed attention largely because of the revolution in communication technologies and the increased roles that public opinion, nonstate actors, and legislatures play in modern diplomacy. Its importance has also grown because of the increased role that ideas are seen as playing in world politics, as evidenced by the debate over the merits of "soft power."

President Bill Clinton is widely recognized as one of the most skilled practitioners of public diplomacy. He brought an American-style political campaign atmosphere to his trips abroad that sought to win foreign publics over to his cause. This stands in sharp contrast to President Reagan's forays into public diplomacy, which tended to have a hit-and-run quality to them. Reagan's references to the Soviet Union as the "evil empire" played well at home but scared the public abroad. A similar problem faced George W. Bush, whose black-and-white image of the world and use of phrases associated with the American frontier has been off-putting to foreign audiences. Obama's mastery of the rhetoric of foreign policy and his ability to locate U.S. foreign policy goals and actions within a supportive international context contributed greatly to his winning the 2009 Nobel Prize for Peace.

Public diplomacy is more than just public statements. At its core is a set of institutions, programs, and practices designed to accomplish four strategic objectives:

1. Inform the world accurately, clearly, and swiftly about U.S. policy.
2. Represent the values and beliefs of the American people.

3. Explain how democracy produces prosperity, stability, and opportunity.
4. Communicate U.S. support for education.[18]

The lead organization in this endeavor is the United States Information Agency (USIA). A mainstay in the conflict with the Soviet Union, its radio broadcasts reached 50 percent of the Soviet population and as much as 80 percent of that of Eastern Europe. Its size declined sharply with the end of the Cold War, from a peak of 12,000 employees in the mid-1960s to 6,715 by the end of the 1990s.[19] The war on terrorism breathed new life into America's public diplomacy. The United States now spends $5–$10 million annually on foreign public opinion polling. It has also developed a number of initiatives targeted at the Middle East. One is a glossy magazine, *Hi*, funded by the State Department and targeted at Arabs ages 15–35. The first issue appeared in July 2003 and was sold on newsstands. Among radio stations in operation are Radio Sawa (broadcasting in Arabic) and Radio Farda (broadcasting in Farsi). Al-Hurra is an Arabic-language TV station that broadcasts to the region.

The newfound emphasis on public diplomacy is not without its critics. One set of complaints deals with the details of its implementation. Sanford Unger, who once served as head of the Voice of America, is critical of the de-emphasis of English in favor of local languages, arguing that there is little evidence that stations such as Radio Sawa and al-Hurra have much of an audience. He is also critical of attempts to use the Voice of America for partisan political purposes, such as presenting President George W. Bush's policies in overly favorable terms or keeping critical stories about the president off the air.[20] A second line of criticism argues that the primary problem faced by public diplomacy is not how it is done but in the fundamental assumption that if the world only heard the American side of the story, they would join us.[21] The problem is that evidence suggests the world does understand and does not like what it sees.[22] Public diplomacy can thus help at the margins but not solve the underlying problem that U.S. foreign policy is not viewed favorably in key parts of the world.

Public opinion polls in late 2007 seemed to bear this out. Despite the efforts of close Bush advisor Karen Hughes, who was Bush's director of communications when he was governor of Texas and then served as undersecretary of state for public diplomacy from 2005 to 2007, 26 countries held less favorable images of the United States in 2007 than they did in 2002. Only in five countries had public opinion of the United States improved.[23]

# THE POLITICAL USE OF FORCE

By its very existence, American military power serves as an instrument of diplomacy. Without ever having to be used or even referred to, it heightens U.S. prestige and gives importance to U.S. proposals and expressions of concern. The knowledge that it exists influences both the manner in which U.S. policy makers approach problems and the positions adopted by other states. In 2008, U.S. helicopters flew into Syrian and Pakistani airspace to launch attacks against terrorists and their supporters. After the Syrian attack, a U.S. official

## HISTORICAL LESSON

### Radio Free Europe, Radio Liberty, and Radio Marti

Radio Free Europe, Radio Liberty, and Radio Marti are three early examples of U.S public diplomacy in action. Today, along with al-Hurra, all three operate under the supervision of the Broadcasting Board of Governors. Radio Free Europe was set up in 1949 by the National Committee for a Free Europe. This group focused its efforts on supporting refugees fleeing communism in Europe, and Radio Free Europe became its flagship operation. Its mission was to broadcast the "truth" into communist-controlled areas in the hopes of producing domestic unrest and creating instability.

Radio Free Europe began broadcasting in 1950 using a U.S. government radio station operating in the American-controlled sector of Berlin as its model. Its broadcasts were often jammed by communist authorities, but nevertheless it achieved a large audience. The CIA secretly provided much of its funding during the Cold War through proprietary or dummy companies, although there is little evidence that the CIA interfered greatly in its programming. The CIA did, however, benefit from the information Radio Free Europe was able to gather from its network of émigrés and defectors as well as its monitoring of East European media outlets.

Among its most notable accomplishments was broadcasting the contents of Soviet leader Nikita Khrushchev's secret speech condemning the excesses of Joseph Stalin after his death. This speech helped set in motion a reform movement in Eastern Europe that would lead to revolts in Poland and Hungary in 1956. The most controversial chapter in its history is linked to these events. During the Hungarian uprising against the Soviet Union, it transmitted back into Hungary, without comment, local broadcasts from Hungary carrying appeals for help from the United States, rumors that such help would be forthcoming, and anti-Soviet stories. Taken altogether, these stories encouraged the Hungarians to continue in their efforts to overthrow communism. When Warsaw Pact troops invaded, however, no U.S. support was forthcoming. In fact, the Eisenhower administration had concluded that it would make no effort to roll back the iron curtain.

Radio Liberty was set up in 1951 by the American Committee for the Freedom of Peoples of the USSR. It began broadcasting into the Soviet Union four days before Stalin's death in 1954. Its broadcasts were jammed until Mikhail Gorbachev ended that practice. As a result, in 1990, Radio Liberty became the most listened to Western radio station in Russia. In 1991, its broadcasts of the attempted coup played a significant role in the ability of Gorbachev and Boris Yeltsin to communicate with the Russian people.

In 1967, Radio Free Europe and Radio Liberty's connections to the CIA were revealed. Congressional hearings followed, and in 1976, they were merged into one organization and openly funded by Congress. For a period of time, government funding decreased. It increased under the Reagan administration but so too did pressures to broadcast stories critical of communism. Today they broadcast to 20 countries in 28 languages. Target audiences include Iran, Afghanistan, Iraq, and Russia.

Radio Marti (and, since 1990, Televsion Marti) broadcasts 24 hours a day into Cuba. Radio Marti was established in 1983 by the Reagan administration and takes its name from the Cuban writer Jose Marti, who led the struggle against Spanish colonial rule and U.S. dominance in Latin America. As with Radio Free Europe, its goal was to provide an alternative source of information to those under communist rule and speed up the fall of communism. The driving force behind its creation was Jorge Mas Canosa, the dominant political force behind the Cuban lobbying group, the Cuban-American National Foundation. Far more so than was the case with Radio Free Europe or Radio Liberty, the content of Radio Marti's broadcasts have come in for scrutiny, and there are complaints about its neutrality and objectivity. A 2009 report by the Government Accountability Office cited the use of incendiary and offensive language and broadcasting of unsubstantiated reports out of Cuba, as if they were factually true. Concerns have also been expressed about its effectiveness. Not unexpectedly, its broadcasts into Cuba are jammed. A 2009 study concluded that its radio and television broadcasts reach less than 1 percent of the Cuban population. An additional problem with Radio Marti is the ban on all public diplomacy stations of broadcasting into the United States. Some of its news broadcasts are carried on U.S. commerical stations, and Cuba's proximity to the United States allows Radio Marti's signal to be picked up in Washington, DC.

### Applying the Lesson
1. How do we measure the effectiveness of public diplomacy radio stations?
2. Radio Free Europe was the model for al-Hurra. Is it a good model?
3. What should be the programming content of public diplomacy stations? ■

stated that their purpose was to send a warning to these governments, "you have to clean up the global threat in your backyard and if you won't do that, we are left with no choice but to take these matters into our hands."[24] The use of force for political purposes by the United States is not new. Researchers have identified 218 incidents between 1946 and 1975 in which the United States did so.[25] To qualify as a political use of force, the military action had to involve a physical change in the disposition of U.S. forces and had to be done consciously to achieve a political objective without going to war or trying to physically impose the U.S. position on the target state.

On average, the political use of force lasted 90 days, with U.S. military forces staying at their maximum force level for 56 days. The actions ranged from a port visit by a single warship to the deployment of major land, sea, and air units in conjunction with a strategic alert and reserve mobilizations. In any one year, as many as 20 incidents and as few as three took place, with the average number of incidents being eight. The greatest number of incidents occurred between 1958 and 1965, when an average of 12 incidents per year took place. In terms of geography, the 218 incidents are spread relatively evenly across the Northern Hemisphere, although the points of emphasis changed over time. Between 1946 and 1948, Western Europe was the primary region in which the United States sought to use military power for political purposes, and Southeast Asia and East Asia were the predominant areas of activity between 1949 and 1955. Between 1966 and 1975, U.S. attempts to use military power for political purposes were divided relatively evenly between Southeast Asia and East Asia, and the Middle East and North Africa. Only South Asia and sub-Saharan Africa have been consistently neglected.

## Post–Cold War Coercive Diplomacy

The end of the Cold War did not end America's interest in using military power for political ends. In fact, a number of factors made the political use of force very attractive. Most prominent among them were the absence of another constraining superpower; the continued presence of serious problems, many of which had deep roots; and an expectation that as the sole remaining superpower, the United States had a responsibility to act to solve world problems. Using a slightly different definition of the political use of force than was used above, a recent study examined instances of **coercive diplomacy** and a series of conflicts with Iraq in the 1990s. These cases, ranging from Haiti to Somalia to the war on terrorism, are important because the causes that gave birth to them are likely to be present for some time to come. The study found that of 16 cases where military power was used to persuade rather than defeat the opponent, success was realized only five times. It clearly failed in eight cases. The limited success rate is not surprising. Studies of a smaller number of attempts at coercive diplomacy during the Cold War documented an even lower success rate.

Three factors seemed to contribute to what success coercive diplomacy enjoyed, although none guarantees success. First, offering positive induce-ments to the other state to adjust its policy was important. Second, the timing of the inducement was important. Inducement was most effective when it was offered after the demonstrative use of force or after threatening of force. Inducements had little positive effect if they were offered in advance of such shows of resolve. Third, it was important to be able to demonstrate clearly to the opponent what would happen to their military forces should war occur, and that their military strategy would fail. Interestingly, the type of demand made by the United States had little relation to success or failure.

## Nuclear Diplomacy

In contemplating using military power for political purposes, American policy makers have not limited themselves to thinking in terms of conven-tional weapons. On at least two occasions, they have threatened to use nuclear weapons in an effort to compel others into action.[26] Evidence suggests that Dwight Eisenhower made a **compellence** threat in 1953 as part of his plan to bring an end to the Korean War. Richard Nixon also made such a threat in 1969 in an attempt to end the Vietnam War. Unlike the Eisenhower case, when the threat of using nuclear weapons was presented as part of a deliberate U.S. strategy, Nixon cast his in quite different terms, telling his chief of staff, H. R. Haldeman:

> I call it the Madman Theory, Bob. I want the North Vietnamese to believe I've reached the point that I might do anything to stop the war. We'll just slip the word to them that "for God's sake, you know Nixon is obsessed about Communism. We can't restrain him when he is angry— and he has his hand on the nuclear button."—Ho Chi Minh himself will be in Paris in two days begging for peace.[27]

On October 10, 1969, U.S. nuclear forces were put on alert "to respond to possible confrontation by the Soviet Union." The actions taken were designed to be picked up by Soviet intelligence but still not be visible to the American press or public. It was Nixon's hope that this would be part of a lead-up to a massive conventional offensive in Vietnam and would stampede the Soviets into working toward a diplomatic solution to the war. In fact, Nixon had already decided against such a military operation because of the domestic opposition it would unleash in the United States and military doubts about its effectiveness. Soviet leaders do not appear to have responded to this political use of nuclear power in any meaningful way. No mention of it was made by Soviet ambassador Anatoly Dobrynin in conversations shortly after it ended. It does appear that Soviet intelligence recognized the change in nuclear readiness.

For those interested in questions of nuclear strategy, two significant points emerge from a detailed look at the history of this episode. First, the military did not automatically and uniformly implement Nixon's alert order. The Strategic Air Command balked, as did Secretary of Defense Melvin Laird, suggesting that Nixon was in far less control of the U.S. nuclear forces than he believed or most commentators thought. National Security Advisor Henry Kissinger proposed this nuclear alert with little regard for other developments in the international system. To the Nixon administration, it was obvious this was nuclear signaling over Vietnam. However, at that very moment the Soviet Union and China were involved in an intense border dispute. Chinese leaders had been evacuated from Beijing, and its nuclear forces were on alert. From both the Chinese and Soviet perspectives, the U.S. nuclear alert could have just as easily been seen in the light of this conflict.

## ARMS TRANSFERS

**Arms transfers** have established themselves as a favorite instrument of policy makers.[28] In 1980, one observer noted that the United States receives annually nearly 10,000 requests from foreign governments for military equipment and services and over 20,000 applications from private firms for export licenses.[29] The Arms Export Control Act of 1976 requires that all arms transfers valued at $25 million or more or those involving the transfer of significant combat equipment be reported to Congress. This same study found that over 100 cases have been reported each year. States sell and buy weapons for a number of different reasons, and the relationship between them has been compared to a reciprocal bargaining process in which each tries to use the other to accomplish goals that are often incompatible.[30] The potential tensions are most clearly evident when each side is driven by strategic imperatives.

For arms sellers, three strategic rationales are most often advanced. First, arms transfers can provide influence and leverage abroad by serving as a symbolic statement of support for a regime and providing access to elites. Second, they can be used to protect specific security interests abroad and further regional stability. Third, they can be used as barter in acquiring access to overseas bases. None of these rationales is without problems. Leverage tends to be a transitory phenomenon in world politics, and an arms transfer relationship can promote friction just as much as it can cement ties. It can also produce a situation of reverse leverage, in which the recipient state, rather than the seller, exercises the most influence. Iran provides a useful example of influence gone awry. The United States sold sophisticated weapons to the Shah of Iran in the hopes that he would use them to contain the spread of communism in the Persian Gulf, while the Shah saw those weapons as a way of realizing his dream of making Iran into a regional superpower. Not only was the Shah quite willing to work with the Soviet Union when it suited his interests, but in the last years of his rule, the large volume of U.S. weapons in Iran created hostility among the people toward the United States.

Efforts designed to improve regional stability can be easily interpreted as an attempt to alter the regional balance of power. The result can be a competitive situation that takes on all of the characteristics of an arms race, such as has become common in the Middle East. Like political leverage, access to bases has proven to be transitory. It can also be an increasingly costly proposition as the host state raises the economic, political, and military favors that must be granted for continued access. In 1985, Turkey publicly stated that the price for renewing U.S. basing rights would be an increase in the value of future Turkish exports to the United States from their 1984 level of $433 million to $3 billion.

There have been five major turning points in the development of U.S. arms transfer policy. The first came in the early 1960s, when the Kennedy administration made a distinction between **arms sales** and arms transferred abroad as foreign aid. Kennedy turned to arms sales in an effort to counter the growing U.S. balance-of-payments problem, which had been brought about in part by the high cost of stationing U.S. troops in Europe. The second turning point came during the Nixon administration. Arms transfers became an important instrument of foreign policy and a cornerstone of the Nixon Doctrine, which stressed the need for Third World allies of the United States to assume the primary responsibility for their own defense. To that end the United States was prepared to channel aid and assistance, but it would not readily intervene into conflict itself. Other changes also took place. Sales replaced aid as the primary vehicle for transferring arms, the Middle East became the primary area of U.S. arms transfers, and the quality of the weapons transferred increased dramatically. No longer were arms transfers dominated by obsolete weapons in the U.S. inventory. Now they regularly involved the most sophisticated weapons the United States possessed. A number of statistics capture these changes vividly. Measured in constant dollars, U.S. arms transfers increased 150 percent between 1968 and 1977.

The third turning point in the evolution of U.S. arms transfer policy came with the Carter administration. It represented a turning point for what the administration sought to do rather than for what it accomplished. Carter sought to replace the Nixon–Ford–Kissinger view of arms transfers as a normal instrument of foreign policy with one that saw them as an "exceptional tool."[31] The Carter policy had an immediate impact. In the first 15 months after it was announced, 614 requests from 92 states for over $1 billion worth of arms were turned down.

Gradually, the Carter administration found it difficult to work within its own guidelines. The first major exception to its own rules was the sale of AWACS (Airborne Warning and Control System) to Iran for $1.8 billion. The Carter administration also agreed to a $1.8 million arms package for South Korea in compensation for the reduction of U.S. ground troops to be stationed there. It soon would completely abandon all signs of restraint by approving weapons sales to Israel and Egypt as part of the Camp David Accords and to Saudi Arabia after the Shah fell and the Soviet Union invaded Afghanistan.

The fourth turning point in U.S. arms transfer policy came with the arrival of the Reagan administration. It moved quickly to use arms transfers as a tool in its global struggle against communism. In its first three months, it offered approximately $15 billion in weapons and other forms of military assistance to other states. The George H. W. Bush administration followed suit. In 1990, it proposed making available $30 billion in arms sales. Key recipients included Egypt, Colombia, Kuwait, Spain, Japan, South Korea, and Norway. In the aftermath of the Persian Gulf War, there was a brief international movement for ending arms shipments to the Middle East. An international registrar of arms was even established to help track arms transfers. However, a reversal of direction quickly ensued, and arms again began to flow into the region. In the Clinton administration, the United States became the world's leading arms supplier, selling over $31 billion worth of weapons to over 140 states.

The current period in arms sales policy began after the 9/11 terrorist attacks. The most notable feature of this period is the embrace of arms transfers to countries that were once on restricted lists. Armenia, Azerbaijan, India, Pakistan, and Yugoslavia, all of which are key allies in the war against terrorism, now receive U.S. arms. In the case of India, 2002 marked the end to an almost 40-year period in which no export licenses were granted. Before 9/11, the last time Pakistan received funds from the United States to acquire American-made weapons, services, or technology was in 1990, when sales totaled $185 million. In 2002, this number had jumped to $690 million. In 2008, a major weapons sale was made to Taiwan, a move generally explained by a desire to improve strained relations between the two. In the works since 2001, the deal had been delayed by political disputes in Taiwan and objections from China, whose help the U.S. needed in dealing with North Korea.

A controversy over arms sales quickly emerged in the Obama presidency. Georgia publicly requested U.S. weapons and warned that not receiving them would invite a Russian invasion. The administration was slow to respond in large part, because, while the United States has been helping to modernize Georgia's army, an international report concluded that Georgia had provoked the 2008 Russian invasion.

Beneath these periodic shifts one can find a great deal of consistency in U.S. arms transfer policy. The United States has retained its position as the world's leading arms merchant. A region-by-region inspection of arms agreements before and after 9/11 shows that in regions farthest removed from the Middle East, little change occurred in who received U.S. weapons. The top five regional recipients are presented in Table 10.1. Consistency is also evident at the global level. Long-standing recipients of U.S. weapons transfers such as Israel, Saudi Arabia, and Egypt continue to hold prominent places. A list of pre- and post-9/11 arms recipients is presented in Table 10.2. Seven countries appear in both lists.

## TABLE 10.1

REGIONAL LEADING PURCHASERS OF U.S. DEFENSE ARTICLES AND SERVICES MEASURED IN TOTAL VALUE OF AGREEMENTS CONCLUDED

| Africa Agreements, 1997–2000 | Africa Agreements 2001–2004 |
|---|---|
| 1. Ethiopia $10 million | 1. Kenya $32 million |
| 2. Ghana $5 million | 2. Nigeria $29 million |
| 3. Kenya $4 million | 3. South Africa $14 million |
| 4. Nigeria $3 million | 4. Djibouti $13 million |
| 5. Senegal $3 million | 5. Uganda $6 million |
| **American Republics 1997–2000** | **American Republics 2001–2004** |
| 1. Canada $280 million | 1. Canada $689 million |
| 2. Colombia $279 million[a] | 2. Chile $552 million |
| 3. Brazil $124 million | 3. Brazil $257 million |
| 4. Venezuela $81 million | 4. Colombia $236 million[a] |
| 5. Argentina $50 million | 5. Venezuela $51 million |
| **Asia Agreements 1997–2000** | **Asia Agreements 2001–2004** |
| 1. South Korea $2.6 billion | 1. South Korea $3 billion |
| 2. Taiwan $1.9 billion | 2. Japan $3 billion |
| 3. Australia $1.3 billion | 3. Australia $1.2 billion |
| 4. Japan $1.3 billion | 4. Taiwan $1.2 billion |
| 5. Singapore $1.1 billion | 5. Singapore $1.1 billion |
| **Near East Agreements 1997–2000** | **Near East Agreements 2001–2004** |
| 1. United Arab Emirates $6.8 billion[b] | 1. Egypt $5.7 billion |
| 2. Egypt $5.5 billion | 2. Israel $4.4 billion |
| 3. Israel $4.9 billion | 3. Saudi Arabia $3.8 billion |
| 4. Saudi Arabia $4.1 billion | 4. Kuwait $1.8 billion |
| 5. Bahrain $640 million | 5. Oman $960 million |

(continued)

**TABLE 10.1** (*continued*)

| Europe Agreements 1997–2000 | Europe Agreements 2001–2004 |
|---|---|
| 1. Greece $3 billion | 1. Poland $3.8 billion |
| 2. Spain $1.3 billion | 2. United Kingdom $2 billion |
| 3. Germany $1.2 billion | 3. Greece $1.4 billion |
| 4. Turkey $1.2 billion | 4. Italy $1.2 billion |
| 5. The Netherlands $930 million | 5. The Netherlands $1 billion |

[a]Includes international narcotics interdiction programs.
[b]Includes $6.4 billion licensed commercial agreement concluded in 2000 for eighty F-16 fighter aircrafts.

*Source:* Robert Grimmett, *U.S. Arms Sales: Agreements with and Deliveries to Major Clients, 1997–2004* (Washington, DC: Congressional Research Service Report for Congress, December 29, 2005), pp. 2–3.

## OVER THE HORIZON

Irrespective of the ability or inability of al-Hurra to duplicate the successes attributed to Radio Free Europe we should expect to see continued emphasis on public diplomacy. The Government Accountability Agency listed improving the U.S. image abroad as goal #5 on the list of urgent problems facing the new

**TABLE 10.2**

WORLDWIDE LEADING PURCHASERS OF U.S. DEFENSE ARTICLES AND SERVICES MEASURED IN TOTAL VALUE OF AGREEMENTS CONCLUDED

| Worldwide Agreements 1997–2000 | Worldwide Agreements 2001–2004 |
|---|---|
| 1. United Arab Emirates $6.8 billion[a] | 1. Egypt $5.7 billion |
| 2. Egypt $5.5 billion | 2. Israel $4.4 billion |
| 3. Israel $4.9 billion | 3. Saudi Arabia $3.8 billion |
| 4. Saudi Arabia $4.1 billion | 4. Poland $3.8 billion |
| 5. Greece $3 billion | 5. South Korea $3 billion |
| 6. South Korea $2.6 billion | 6. Japan $3 billion |
| 7. Taiwan $1.9 billion | 7. United Kingdom $2 billion |
| 8. Spain $1.3 billion | 8. Kuwait $1.8 billion |
| 9. Australia $1.3 billion | 9. Greece $1.4 billion |
| 10. Japan $1.3 billion | 10. Australia $1.2 billion |

[a]Includes $6.4 billion licensed commercial agreement concluded in 2000 for eighty F-16 fighter aircrafts.

*Source:* Robert Grimmett, *U.S. Arms Sales: Agreements with and Deliveries to Major Clients, 1997–2004* (Washington, DC: Congressional Research Service Report for Congress, December 29, 2005), p. 4.

Obama administration. In saying this, it needs to be kept in mind that public diplomacy is more than radio and television. It can be as simple as posters or as technologically sophisticated as internet chat rooms with State Department employees.

In looking over the horizon, we can identify two other developments in the area of diplomacy that hold potential significance for U.S. foreign policy. The first deals with finding new settings for negotiating agreements that do indeed create frameworks for addressing foreign policy problems. In the area of international economic policy, calls have been heard for creating a new Bretton Woods system to replace the existing international finance and trade organizations. Neither the International Monetary Fund nor the WTO with its Doha bargaining rounds are seen as truly capable of providing a context in which the big important economic issues of the day get addressed. In the national security arena, calls are heard for creating a League of Democracies, an international alliance system that would provide security against aggressive dictatorships. Others call for an alliance of English-speaking countries. The basic point shared by virtually all reform proposals is that the United States is seeking to manage the current international system with international institutions built right after World War II and that too much time and effort is going in to fixing them when instead the goal should be to create twenty-first-century international institutions.

Still another development is the possibility of a new arms race in the Persian Gulf, where the Bush administration put together a $20 billion arms package before leaving office. Major purchasers of "smart" bomb weapons technology capable of hitting within four feet of a target when launched from a plane 10 miles away are Saudi Arabia and Israel. The United Arab Republic and Kuwait also hope to buy major U.S. weapons systems.

## CRITICAL THINKING QUESTIONS

1. Are there conditions under which the United States should not enter into diplomatic negotiations with another country or group of countries?
2. Is it wise for the United States to use weapons as an instrument of diplomacy?
3. Confronted with an international crisis, which would you turn to first, bilateral, multilateral, or public diplomacy? Which is most needed to solve the problem in the long run?

## KEY TERMS

alliance   261
arms sale   276
arms transfer   275
bargaining   257
coalitions   261

coercive diplomacy   274
compellence   274
conference
   diplomacy   264

negotiation   257
public diplomacy   270
summit conference   262

## FURTHER READING

Robert Art and Patrick Cronin (eds.), *The United States and Coercive Diplomacy* (Washington, United States Institute of Peace Press, 2003).

Fred Ikle, *How Nations Negotiate* (New York: Harper & Row, 1964).

Charles Kupchan, "Minor Leagues, Major Problems: The Case Against the League of Democracies," *Foreign Affairs,* 87 (2008), 96–109.

Kori Schake, *Managing American Hegemony* (Stanford, Hoover Press, 2008).

Humphrey Taylor, "The Not-So-Black Art of Public Diplomacy," *World Policy Journal* 25 (2008), 51–59.

## NOTES

1. Craig Whitlock, "U.S. Network Falters in Mideast Mission," *Washington Post,* June 23, 2008, A1.
2. Fred Ikle, *How Nations Negotiate* (New York: Harper & Row, 1964), p. ix.
3. Jakub Grygiel, "The Diplomacy Fallacy," *The American Interest,* 3 (2008), 26–35.
4. Catherine Lutz (ed.), *The Bases of Empire* (New York: New York University Press, 2009).
5. Richard N. Haass and Meghan L. O'Sullivan (eds.), *Honey and Vinegar: Incentives, Sanctions, and Foreign Policy* (Washington, DC: Brookings, 2000).
6. Stephen Wayne, "Bad Guys and Bad Judgments," in Stanley Renshon and Debroach Welch Larson (eds.), *Good Judgment in Foreign Policy* (Lanham, MD: Rowman & Littlefield, 2003), pp. 103–26.
7. Jonathan Terperman, "Some Hard Truths About Multilateralism, *World Policy Journal,* 21 (2004), 27–36.
8. For references to the positive contributions of summitry, see Robert Putnam, "Summit Sense," *Foreign Policy,* 55 (1984), 73–91.
9. For a discussion of the negative contributions of summitry, see J. Robert Schaetzel and H. B. Malmgren, "Talking Heads," *Foreign Policy,* 39 (1980), 130–42.
10. Ibid., p. 138, for the case of economic summits; see the discussion in Strobe Talbot, *Deadly Gambits* (New York: Vintage, 1984), for examples from arms control talks.
11. Adam B. Ulam, *Dangerous Relations: The Soviet Union in World Politics, 1970–1982* (New York: Oxford University Press, 1983), p. 186.
12. Quoted in Glenn Kessler, "Road Map Setbacks Highlight U.S. Pattern," *The Washington Post,* October 6, 2003, p. 1.
13. Richard Nixon, "Superpower Summitry," *Foreign Affairs,* 64 (1985), 1–11.
14. For a review of U.S.–Soviet summit conferences, see the various references in James E. Dougherty and Robert L. Pfaltzgraff, *American Foreign Policy from FDR to Reagan* (New York: Harper & Row, 1985).
15. George de Menil, "The Process of Economic Summitry," in George de Menil and Anthony M. Solomon (eds.), *Economic Summitry* (New York: Council on Foreign Relations, 1983), pp. 55–63.
16. Richard Elliot Benedick, *Ozone Diplomacy: New Directions in Safeguarding the Planet* (Cambridge, MA: Harvard University Press, 1991).
17. This discussion is based on W. Michael Reisman, "The United States and International Institutions," *Survival,* 41 (Winter 1999–2000), 62–80, although the definition of roles is slightly different.
18. "Public Diplomacy Campaign to Rebuild U.S.-Muslim Relations," *Frontlines,* January 2003, p. 5.

19. Joseph Nye, Jr., "The Decline of America's Soft Power," *Foreign Affairs,* 83 (2004), 16–20.
20. Sanford Unger, "Pitch Imperfect," *Foreign Affairs,* 84 (2005), 7–13.
21. David Edelstein and Ronald Krebs, "Washington's Troubling Obsession with Public Diplomacy," *Survival,* 47 (2005), 89–104.
22. Humphrey Taylor, "The Not-So-Black Art of Public Diplomacy," *World Policy Journal* 25 (2008), 51–59.
23. Glenn Kessler and Robin Wright, "Hughes to Leave State Dept. After Mixed Results in Outreach Post," *The Washington Post,* November 11, 2007, p. A19.
24. Ann Scott Tyson and Ellen Knickmeyer, "U.S. Calls Raid a Warning to Syria," *Washington Post,* October 28, 2008, A1.
25. Barry M. Blechman and Stephen S. Kaplan, *Force Without War: U.S. Armed Forces as a Political Instrument* (Washington, DC: Brookings, 1978).
26. Scott Sagan and Jeremi Suri, "The Madman Nuclear Alert," *International Security,* 27 (2003), 150–83; and William Burr and Jeffrey Kimball, "Nixon's Nuclear Ploy," *Bulletin of the Atomic Scientists,* 59 (2003), 28–37, 72–73.
27. Sagan and Suri, "The Madman Nuclear Alert," p. 156.
28. For background data on arms transfers, their history, the policies of specific states, and a discussion of their rationale, see Stephanie G. Neuman and Robert E. Harkavy (eds.), *Arms Transfers in the Modern World* (New York: Praeger, 1980); Andrew J. Pierre, *The Global Politics of Arms Sales* (Princeton, NJ: Princeton University Press, 1982); and Michael T. Klare, *American Arms Supermarket* (Austin: University of Texas Press, 1984).
29. Richard H. Wilcox, "Twixt Cup and Lip: Some Problems in Applying Arms Control," in Stephanie Neuman and Robert Harkavy, *Arms Transfers in the Modern World* (New York: Praeger, 1980), p. 32.
30. Edward Kolodiej, "Arms Transfers and International Politics: The Interdependence of Independence," in Stephanie Neuman and Robert Harkavy (eds.), *Arms Transfers in the Modern World* (New York: Praeger, 1980), p. 3.
31. Klare, *American Arms Supermarket,* pp. 43–44.

# Economic Instruments

In early April 2009, Pakistan's ambassador to the United States called for a $30 billion "Marshall Plan" foreign aid package over the next five years to help his country and Afghanistan fight al Qaeda, overcome anti-American attitudes, and stabilize their governments. He argued that the cost will be "negligible" compared to the cost of rescuing failed American banks and corporations.

A little over two months later, in June, the Senate approved a $1.5 billion foreign aid package for Pakistan for each of the next five years. This tripled the amount of foreign aid that the United States was providing to Pakistan. Included in this amount was $400 million in annual military aid plus funds for improving schools, the judicial system, parliament, and law enforcement services. The Senate's bill also established an economic Reconstruction Opportunity Zone along the Pakistani–Afghan border, which will allow duty-free entry of textile products produced in Pakistan and Afghanistan into the United States.

U.S. foreign aid to Pakistan has had a rollercoaster-like history. From 1953 to 1961, Pakistan was seen as a Cold War ally of the United States and received about $2 billion in foreign aid. A dramatic reduction in aid followed due to fighting between India and Pakistan and Pakistani efforts to acquire nuclear weapons. Foreign aid rose and then fell with the Soviet invasion of Afghanistan in 1979. Aid was suspended in 1993 due to its continued pursuit of nuclear weapons. Post 9/11 saw another surge in U.S. foreign aid. The U.S. Agency for International Development (USAID) reopened its Pakistan office in 2002, and between that year and early 2009 an estimated $12.3 billion in aid was given, of which $8.6 billion was military aid. Along with the increase in foreign aid to Pakistan have come concerns over its effectiveness. Corruption is seen as endemic in the tribal areas along the Pakistani–Afghan border, and charges of Pakistan military's misspending of funds have also been widespread.

## ECONOMIC STATECRAFT

Foreign aid such as that given to Pakistan is one of the most commonly employed tools of economic statecraft. Defined as a deliberate manipulation of economic policy to promote the goals of the state, it is an age-old instrument of foreign policy, and one that the United States has used often. Once, the Cold War was the primary reference point for its use. Today, it is the war against terrorism. Once, we spoke of American economic domination (or, according to critics of American foreign policy, **imperialism**). Today, we speak of globalization. No matter the purpose for which it is used or the context in which it is used, American economic power exerts its influence by it ability to attract other countries to the U.S. economic system and then trap them in it. For that reason, many refer to it as America's "sticky power."[1]

If the web that the sticky economic power of the United States weaves entraps other countries in the U.S. system, it also entraps the United States in global-trading relations that span a wide variety of commodities and political relationships. Nowhere is this more evident than in U.S. relations with China, a former enemy and potential military challenger that has jumped to the forefront in recent years as a trading partner and holder of U.S. debt. We begin this chapter by discussing the major strategic perspectives that govern U.S. trade and monetary policy. We then take an in-depth look at two major ways in which economic power is used in foreign policy: economic sanctions and foreign aid.

A major complicating factor in the use of economic statecraft is uncertainty over how to judge its successes and failures. All too frequently its supporters argue economic statecraft is dismissed as ineffective. Advocates of economic statecraft as an instrument of foreign policy make four arguments in its defense.[2] First, day-to-day economic exchanges under the heading of **free trade** are generally defined to be outside the scope of economic power. Second, economic **sanctions** are often said to fail when they do not produce a change in policy in the target state. Underappreciated is the added cost that economic sanctions place on the target state, even if it does not change its policies. Third, economic power has often been judged a failure because it is examined out of context. Policy makers often turn to it when no other instruments are available or to accomplish the almost impossible such as removing Fidel Castro from power or getting the Soviet Union to change its political system. Fourth, economic statecraft suffers because writers on world politics underestimate how important symbolic actions are to policy makers and domestic pressure groups.

# STRATEGIC OUTLOOKS

## Free Trade

Free trade is both an instrument of foreign policy and a strategic orientation to organizing economic power.[3] There is nothing inevitable or natural about free trade. International free trade systems exist because they serve the interests of the dominant power. This was true of Great Britain in the nineteenth century and of the United States in the post–World War II era. From about 1944 to 1962, access to U.S. markets was used as an inducement to get other states to adopt policies favored by the United States. Among those Cold War goals were strengthening military alliances, promoting the economic recovery of Western Europe, ensuring access to strategic raw materials, and stimulating economic growth and political stability in the Third World. American policy makers were also sensitive to the limits of free trade. On a selective basis, they permitted or encouraged discrimination against U.S. goods if it would further these broader U.S. foreign policy goals. At the strategic level, the United States used free trade to create an international system that allowed the U.S. economy to prosper and placed it at the center of international economic trade and monetary transactions.

## Bilateral Free Trade

The most significant use of free trade, of late, at the bilateral level has been establishing normal trade relations with China. In November 1999, after 13 years of on-and-off negotiations, the two countries signed a trade pact whereby China agreed to significantly reduce obstacles to imported goods and foreign investment. The United States agreed to gradually eliminate quotas on Chinese textile imports, although it retained the right to take countermeasures to prevent sudden surges in Chinese imports and to penalize dumping for more than a decade. Most significantly, the United States agreed to support Chinese membership in the World Trade Organization (WTO).

George W. Bush turned to bilateral agreements as a second-best solution to his desire to promote free trade agreements. As we note shortly, Bush had negotiated a series of regional trade agreements, but virtually all of them ran into trouble on several fronts. First, in 2007, Bush lost his **fast-track** presidential authority to sign trade agreements and have Congress take a yes/no vote on the agreement with no amendments. Second, many in Congress expressed concern over the content of the agreements signed, specially those terms dealing with workers' rights, labor standards, and environmental protection. With fast-track authority expired, they were now in a position to demand modification of these agreements.

Key bilateral free trade agreements were approved by Congress with Singapore, Chile, and Australia. Still pending are agreements with South Korea, Colombia, Panama, and Vietnam. During the presidential campaign, President Obama voiced his opposition to the Colombian free trade agreement due to continued antiworker violence. The South Korean agreement, if approved, would be the most commercially significant agreement since the China accord, but has run into problems due to South Korea's ban on beef imported from the United States that has been linked to mad cow disease. The Vietnamese agreement has been held up due to human rights concerns, and the Panamanian agreement was stalled because the president of the National Assembly is charged with killing an American serviceman.

## Regional Trade

The organizing logic of free trade has also been applied at the regional level with the establishment of the North American Free Trade Agreement (NAFTA). The manner by which it came into existence makes clear the extent to which free trade is anyting but natural or automatic. The impetus for NAFTA came from Mexico. In the 1960s, Mexico pegged its development hopes on an import-substitution strategy that would protect domestic industries from foreign competition until they became strong enough to provide Mexicans with jobs. By the 1990s it was clear this strategy had failed. From an economic perspective the most attractive alternative was integration into the U.S. market. Politically, however, this was an unattractive option, given nationalistic sentiments against closer economic ties with the United States and fears that such ties would lead to Mexican dependence on the American economy. As such Mexican President Carlos Salinas de Gortari embraced the idea of a North American free trade zone only after exploring other options. In the United States, the idea of a continental free trade pact had emerged as early as the 1980 presidential campaign, when Ronald Reagan and other candidates endorsed the idea. George H. W. Bush had embraced it in the 1988 campaign.

Salinas now telephoned Bush to determine whether interest still existed, and the answer was positive.

The Bush administration was divided over the wisdom of entering into talks with Mexico. The National Security Council, the Commerce Department, and the State Department supported the idea. The Department of Agriculture and the Office of the U.S. Trade Representative (USTR) were less enthusiastic. Agreement within the administration was reached in fall 1990, and Congress was informed of the administration's intent to join with Mexico and Canada in discussions on a free trade area. This was followed in March 1991 by a formal request for fast-track authority, which was granted in May. In order to secure congressional consent, the Bush administration entered into agreements with Mexican officials dealing with such matters as worker health and safety standards, collective bargaining, and working conditions. Efforts to placate environmental groups included the announcement of an Integrated Environmental Plan for the border.

NAFTA talks began in Toronto on June 12, 1991. On October 7, 1992, the 2,000-page agreement was signed in San Antonio. The Bush administration had wanted to announce that an agreement had been reached before the start of the Republican national convention, but continuing disagreements on its wording prevented this from happening. The administration looked on the NAFTA agreement as a vehicle for generating Republican votes in Texas and California. Together these states led the United States in exports to Mexico, and they possessed 86 of the 270 electoral votes needed to win the presidency. Election results and exit polls showed that the Bush campaign had misread the mood of the American public. By November, only 21 percent of the voters supported NAFTA, and a majority opposed it in Texas and southern California.

NAFTA became a controversial campaign issue. Leading the early charge against it was one-time supporter Ross Perot, who stated NAFTA was the product of a conspiracy among Washington insiders, foreign lobbyists, and huge corporations. Bill Clinton straddled the fence on NAFTA during the primaries and repeated this strategy during the general election. A long-standing advocate of free trade, Clinton softened his endorsement of NAFTA so as not to offend organized labor. When Clinton finally announced his support for NAFTA in October, he conditioned it on the stipulation that the text be improved through the addition of supplemental agreements to cover "serious" omissions. The three side deals required by candidate Bill Clinton involved "surges," or the sudden inflow of large amounts of foreign goods into the U.S. market; the environment; and labor.

Only in late summer of 1993 did the Clinton administration direct its attention to the NAFTA treaty. Three executive agreements were signed dealing with the remaining issues. None of them were formally part of the treaty and were not to be voted on by Congress. Clinton signed them in a highly visible and symbolic ceremony in the presence of former presidents Bush, Carter, and Ford.

The final element of the administration's strategy to win approval for NAFTA involved another round of side deals. Among the bargains struck were the following: Florida legislators were assured that the administration would put in place safeguards for sugar, citrus, tomato, sweet pepper, and asparagus growers; legislators from southern textile-producing states were promised that textile quotas would be phased out over 15 years instead of 10; and a Texas representative received an assurance that a Center for the Study of Trade in the Western Hemisphere would be located in his district. Congress voted on NAFTA on November 17, 1993, with the Senate giving its approval by a vote of 61–38, while the House voted 234–200 in favor of it.

George W. Bush sought to advance regional trade agreements in the Western Hemisphere and Asia. The initial centerpiece of its Western Hemisphere free trade strategy was the creation of a Free Trade Area of the Americas (FTAA). It had first been proposed by Clinton in 1994, but little movement toward making it a reality took place. The Bush administration energized the negotiating process in 2003 but encountered firm opposition to its plans for extending NAFTA to the tip of South America, and the process stalled. Efforts to revive it at the fourth Summit of the Americas meeting in 2005 were unsuccessful. In its place, the administration pursued a more limited regional plan, a Central American Free Trade Agreement (CAFTA) that has since been expanded to include the Dominican Republic and is now referred to as DR-CAFTA. Other members are El Salvador, Guatemala, Honduras, Costa Rica, and Nicaragua. As this initiative faltered, the administration switched to negotiating bilateral agreements.

In Asia, the administration moved in late 2008 to begin negotiations to join the Trans-Pacific Strategic Economic Partnership (TPP) agreement, a free-trade area comprising Singapore, Chile, New Zealand, and Brunei Darussalam. Soon after the Bush administration announced its intention to joint the TPP, Australia, Peru, and Vietnam also indicated interest. The initial start date for negotiations was 2009.

## Global Free Trade

At the global level, free trade provided the strategic foundation for the creation of the WTO. The WTO is a product of the Uruguay Round GATT talks. The first round of WTO talks, launched in Doha, Qatar, in 2001, stalled after a 2003 meeting in Cancun that left rich and poor countries in deep disagreement over free trade in agricultural products. Talks later resumed, but the deadlock continued, and the Doha Round was again suspended in 2008.

One of the most significant structural innovations in the creation of the WTO was its dispute settlement procedures. Under GATT a dispute settlement panel was set up only if requested, and its report was adopted only if there was a consensus in favor of it. Under the WTO a standing dispute settlement panel exists, and its report is adopted unless there is a consensus against it. This change transforms the WTO dispute settlement process into a compulsory and automatic instrument for resolving trade disputes. The operation of the WTO dispute resolution system has become a major irritant to the United States, with fears being expressed about the potential loss of sovereignty and the nondemocratic nature of the decision-making procedures.

In concrete terms, the United States has both won and lost rulings before the WTO. Among the losses is a 2000 ruling against the United States on tax breaks being given to U.S. exporters and for restrictions it placed on lamb being imported from Australia and New Zealand. Another is a 2005 ruling in a case brought by the European Union (EU) and Canada against the United States for tax benefits it gives to exporting companies. The WTO decision allows the EU to impose $28 million in sanctions via retaliatory tariffs on such goods as women's clothing, eyeglasses, and writing pads. Canada was authorized to impose $14 million in sanctions and imposed tariffs on cigarettes, hogs, and fish. A U.S. victory occurred in 2005, when the WTO ruled against a 20 percent tax imposed by Mexico on soft drinks made with imported sweeteners. In late 2008, the Bush administration brought charges against China at the WTO, arguing that Chinese subsidies on a wide range of goods from medicines to appliances and textiles were illegal.

The conflict between China and the United States escalated early in the Obama administration, when in fall 2009 China accused the United States of violating WTO rules by raising tariffs on Chinese tires and the Obama administration asserted that China was illegally subsidizing steel pipe producers. The underlying issues involved were significant as an estimated 5,000 U.S. jobs have been lost as a result of Chinese tire imports, and steel pipe imports rose in value from $632 million in 2006 to $2.6 billion in 2008.

## Strategic Trade

Competing with free trade as the strategic foundation for American international economic policy is strategic trade.[4] Its advocates argue that current U.S. trade policy cannot be sustained politically or economically because the global market is failing U.S. firms. They maintain that the comparative advantages enjoyed by states in international trade is not due to a country's resource base or historical factors, but to imperfections in markets that have been deliberately created by government policy. Only by actively intervening in the international marketplace to create comparative advantages for selected industries can the United States hope to remain a world leader.

Strategic trade policy requires two things of the U.S. government. First, the government must identify high-growth industries whose health is crucial to the overall global competitiveness of the American economy. Most frequently mentioned in this regard are industries such as computers, aerospace, semiconductors, and biotechnology. Second, the government must ensure that these firms are not shut out of foreign markets. Neither task is easy. First, identifying industries for special treatment is a politically charged decision that has huge consequences for states and localities. Just as members of Congress fight to prevent military base closures in their districts, they fight to ensure that their districts will get a fair share of research and development money. A related problem is how to address the problems faced by industries such as steel that are no longer competitive internationally but that retain enormous political clout.

The second problem, ensuring access to foreign markets, is complicated by regional trade agreements that limit access by nonmember firms. An overly aggressive strategic trade policy runs the risk of spawning a trade war in which U.S. goods are singled out for retaliation. In April 2001, a long-running trade war was resolved when the EU agreed to give greater access to the European market to U.S. companies that export bananas. In return, the United States agreed to suspend economic sanctions it had placed on $191 million worth of European products sold in the United States.

The driving force behind strategic trade was the inability of American policy makers (and American industry) to put a dent in the U.S.–Japanese trade imbalance. In 1971, Richard Nixon was moved to act when the imbalance reached $1.3 billion. In 1991, George H.W. Bush was confronted with a $43.4 billion trade imbalance. In 1988, concern with the trade imbalance gave rise to the Omnibus Trade and Competitiveness Act. Section 301, commonly referred to as "Super 301," provides for retaliatory sanctions against states that engage in unfair trading practices against the United States. It requires that presidents identify "priority countries" and set a timetable for resolving the dispute, after which time the sanctions will take effect. In his 2001 report, U.S. Trade Representative Robert Zoellick identified 51 trading partners that, under the terms of Super 301, denied American firms adequate and effective protection of intellectual property rights, or fair access to their markets. His 2003 report singled out, among others, Brazil, Poland, Russia, the EU, Mexico, India, South Korea, and Taiwan for criticism. Ukraine was designated as a "priority foreign country" for its systematic failure to act on U.S. complaints and is subject to $75 million worth of U.S. trade sanctions.

Interest in strategic trade policy increased following the economic crisis of 2008. Elements of it can be found in the stimulus package sponsored by the Obama administration. A prime example is "buy American clauses" such as those requiring using U.S.-made iron and steel in certain infrastructure projects. Additionally, more than 500 U.S. cities and counties have barred foreign firms from bidding on stimulus response-funded projects. The "buy American provisions" have met with a particular sharp and negative reaction in Canada, where even Canadian firms owned by U.S. companies have been targeted.

## Monetary Strategies

The bulk of the discussion in this chapter focuses on trade and aid as the central economic instruments of U.S. foreign policy. It needs to be noted that financial transactions can also be used to further foreign policy goals. For example, the United States moved to freeze the assets of groups suspected of being under the control of, or aligned with, Osama bin Laden, following the September 11, 2001, terrorist attacks. In a similar fashion, it earlier moved quickly to block Saddam Hussein's ability to reach funds in Kuwaiti bank accounts following Iraq's invasion of Kuwait.

The United States played a central role in establishing the **Bretton Woods system,** which provided the framework for international economic transactions from the end of World War II until 1971. The two key financial institutions created under that system were the International Monetary Fund (IMF) and the International Bank for Reconstruction and Development (IBRD or, more commonly, the World Bank). The IMF was to regulate international currencies to ensure that they did not suddenly and violently change value. The World Bank was to provide additional funds that were believed necessary for European economic recovery. Virtually from the outset, the Bretton Woods system did not function as anticipated. American dollars became the international currency of choice, and American foreign economic and military aid provided the necessary funds for economic recovery.

By 1960 the situation began to change, and the outflow of dollars reached the point at which U.S. officials began to worry about the trade deficit. The Bretton Woods system ended in 1971, when President Nixon announced that the U.S. dollar would no longer be convertible to gold. Since then, international monetary management has taken the form of periodic exercises in crisis management rather than systemic reform. The most recent exercise of crisis management came in 2008 with the largest financial and economic crash in over 75 years. Under the prodding of France and Great Britain the G-20 met in a special session in Washington in November 2008 to discuss steps that might be taken to deal with the current crisis and avoid similar crises in the future. The meeting ended with agreement on a broad statement of principles known as the Washington Declaration, covering the causes of the crisis and an action plan. Disagreement, however, continued, as in February 2009 at a meeting of the G-7 in London, the United States found itself in disagreement with key European allies over the extent of a global stimulus package and the need for greater government intervention into financial markets.

Beyond questions of how to respond to the immediate problems created by the financial crisis of 2008, a more fundamental issue also surfaced. In one corner are those who call for a fundamental reform of the way in which international financial and trade relations are managed. Advocates of this perspective call for a new "Bretton Woods." Aligned against it are those who argue that any reform of this magnitude is unworkable in today's globalized international economy. The pace and density of global financial transactions has simply outpaced the ability of national governments and international organizations to regulate them like they did in the immediate post–World War II period.[5] Rather than using a hatchet, they call for using a scalpel to make minor adjustments to the IMF and WTO systems that are tailored to deal with specific problems as they arise.[6] A compromise of sorts between these two reform strategies was agreed to in 2009, when the G-20 replaced the G-8 as the primary international setting for making global economic policy.

## ECONOMIC SANCTIONS

Economic sanctions have become a popular way of exercising American economic power. By one recent count, the United States put into place 33 new unilateral sanctions between 1997 and 2001. According to a United Nations (UN) study, 75 countries were subject to U.S. economic sanctions in 1998.[7] What constitutes an economic sanction, however, is highly contested. We adopt a middle-of-the road definition. Economic sanctions are "the deliberate withdrawal of normal trade or financial relations for foreign policy purposes."[8] It is important to recognize that sanctions are "not forever." They are intended to bring about change in targeted countries, and when that is accomplished, they are to be removed. Determining when that is the case is no easy matter and not without controversy, any more than is the decision to implement sanctions.

In 2004, George W. Bush imposed broad sanctions against Syria for its support of terrorism. Among other measures, the Syrian Accountability Act bars U.S. exports to Syria except for food and medicine. In spite of his administration's hostility toward Syria, Bush delayed implementing the measure and immediately indicated that he would continue to permit the sale of telecommunication equipment and aircraft spare parts. The telecommunication exemption was justified on the grounds of the need to "promote the free flow of information." Critics argued that Bush did this in order to protect the economic interests of the telecommunication industry. In 2007, Bush lifted sanctions against the West Bank Palestinian government of Mamoud Abbas, shortly after the more militant and anti-Israel group Hamas seized power in the Gaza Strip. Supporters and critics of the move saw it as an attempt by the United States to divide moderate and radical Arabs and to build support for an accommodation with Israel in the region. Where they differed was over the wisdom of the decision and its prospects for success.

In the period after 9/11, the George W. Bush administration argued frequently for sanctions even though, even when they were implemented, in most cases the effect was largely symbolic—and deliberately so. One of these, the Iran–Libya Sanctions Extension Act of 2001, kept in effect sanctions approved by Congress in 1996 that were about to expire. The act required that the president impose at least two of six possible penalties to any firm that invested over specific amounts in any one year in the energy sector of these states, unless he finds it in the national interest to waive this provision. No firms have been sanctioned under its terms, largely because of the strong opposition of the EU, which threatened to take the issue to the WTO. Iran is one of the most frequently discussed targets of U.S. sanctions, for its pursuit of nuclear weapons and general opposition to the United States in the Iraq War. The United States has sought to impose both unilateral and multilateral sanctions against Iran. Efforts to work through the UN system were often frustrated by the opposition of Russia and China. As a result, by late 2007 the United States and its European allies began to talk of imposing sanctions against Iran by a "sanctions of the willing" coalition of countries, bypassing the UN. The Obama administration has continued the Bush strategy both in terms of the features of Iran's economy, wherein it is willing to continue to target Iran with sanctions, and its reluctance to anger Russia or China. An overview of the history of U.S. economic sanctions against Iraq is provided in Box 11.1.

## Box 11.1 OVERVIEW OF U.S. ECONOMIC SANCTIONS AGAINST IRAN

**Carter Administration.** Economic sanctions were placed on Iran 10 days after the November 1979 takeover of the U.S embassy in Tehran, when 66 American diplomats and others were taken hostage. They would be held in captivity for 444 days. Sanctions included preventing Iranian access to all properties in the United States owned by the Iranian Central Bank or the Iranian government; an embargo on all imports from Iran; an embargo on U.S. exports to Iran, including financial transfers; and prohibitions on travel to Iran. After the hostages were released, all of the sanctions except for the blocked access to properties in the United States were lifted. The value of these assets was placed at about $12 billion.

**Reagan Administration.** Economic sanctions were placed on Iran after the bombing of the marine barracks in Lebanon in 1983, when the administration declared Iran to be a sponsor of international terrorism. This designation prevented Iran from receiving U.S. foreign and military aid either directly or through international organizations. Iran's continued support of terrorism led the Reagan administration to ban U.S. imports of Iranian crude oil and other products in 1987.

**George H. W. Bush Administration.** Under terms of the 1992 Iran–Iraq Arms Non-Proliferation Act, the administration blocked the sale of dual-use technologies to Iran.

**Clinton Administration.** Bill Clinton's principal foreign policy initiative in the Middle East was *dual containment*, an effort to constrain and isolate both Iran and Iraq. As part of this strategy, in 1995, the administration first prohibited U.S. companies and investors from contributing funds for developing oil resources in Iran and then extended the embargo to include a total trade and investment ban. The following year the Iran–Libya Sanctions Act was passed. It required the president to impose sanctions against foreign firms that invest over $20 million in any one year in Iran's energy industry or over $40 million in any one year in Libya's energy industry. The act gave presidents the ability to waive sanctions if it was believed to be in the U.S. national interest to do so, or if the country agreed to take strong steps to inhibit its pursuit of weapons of mass destruction and support of terrorism. No firms have been sanctioned under this act.

**George W. Bush Administration.** Bush signed an extension of the Iran–Libya Sanctions Act in August 2001, as it was about to expire. After the election of the Ahmadinejad government in 2005, the Bush administration prevented Iran from any dealings, direct or indirect, with U.S. financial institutions. The United States continues to prevent dual-use technologies from being exported to Iran, including aircraft and spare parts for aircraft. In 2007, the administration imposed sanctions on three Iranian banks for their involvement in Iran's nuclear program and labeled the Revolutionary Guard as a proliferator of weapons of mass destruction. In January 2008, the administration imposed sanctions on Brigadier General Ahmed Foruzandeh for fomenting violence in Iraq. ■

## Inventory of Options

Should American policy makers decide to employ U.S. economic power against another state, they have several options at their disposal.

A **tariff** is a tax on foreign-made goods entering one's country. Typically, tariffs are applied to protect domestic industry against foreign competition or to raise revenue, but they can also be manipulated to serve foreign policy goals. Twice in the post–World War II era, the United States made notable efforts to manipulate its tariff structure to accomplish foreign policy goals. First, the United States used its tariff system as a lever in dealing with communist states. The United States excluded communist states from equal access to the U.S. market. During détente the United States sought to use access to the U.S. market and most favored nation (MFN) status as an inducement to the Soviets to cooperate in noneconomic areas such as the SALT negotiations. The second attempt to use tariffs as an instrument of foreign policy occurred in 1971, when President Nixon placed a 10 percent "surcharge" on all imports not already under a quota. The primary objective behind this move was to force major changes in the trading practices of other states. It failed to do so, and created foreign hostility toward the United States.

The primary danger inherent in the excessive use of tariffs is retaliation. The most serious instance of retaliation took place in the early 1930s, after the United States passed the Smoot–Hawley Tariff. The highest tariff in U.S. history, the Smoot–Hawley Tariff taxed imports at an average rate of 41.5 percent of their value. Retaliation by foreign governments led to a sudden and dramatic drop in U.S. exports, which only worsened the ongoing depression, something the Smoot–Hawley Tariff had been intended to help solve. In the first half of 1929, U.S. exports exceeded $2.5 billion; by the first half of 1932, they were valued at less than $1 billion. The Trade Agreements Act of 1934 broke the spiral of raising tariffs that had begun in 1879 and set off a new downward spiral. It authorized the president to lower existing tariffs by as much as 50 percent to those states that made reciprocal concessions.

Manipulating **nontariff barriers** (NTBs) to trade is a modern variation on this theme. Bringing forms ranging from labeling requirements, health and safety standards, and license controls to taxation policy, they have become powerful tools in the hands of policy makers who want to protect local firms from foreign competition or remedy a balance-of-payments problem. U.S. use of NTBs dates at least from the 1930s, when the Buy America Act required the government to purchase goods and services from U.S. suppliers if their prices were not unreasonably higher than those of foreign competitors. Another piece of legislation in the 1930s gave preferential treatment to U.S. shipping interests. It required that goods purchased overseas with U.S. loans or guaranteed funds had to be transported whenever possible in U.S. vessels.

An **embargo** is a refusal to sell a commodity to another state, and it is the third economic instrument of foreign policy. Embargoes (and the more subtle concept of export controls) have long played an important role in U.S. Cold War foreign policy. Building on the Trading with the Enemy Act of 1917, the United States embargoed financial and commercial transactions with North

Korea (1950), the People's Republic of China (1950), Cuba (1962), and North Vietnam (1964). Trade with communist states was also controlled by the Export Control Act of 1949 and the Battle Act of 1950. The Export Control Act denied export licenses for strategic goods intended for communist bloc states. At the outset, practically every commodity that might be considered to have some military or strategic value was placed on the Department of Commerce's Commodity Control List. During the Korean War the list of restricted items reached 1,000 in number.

In the post–Cold War international system, embargoes have become a prominent instrument of American foreign policy. In 1994, the administration of Bill Clinton lifted the U.S. embargo on Vietnam. That embargo was first imposed in May 1964 in response to North Vietnamese attacks on the south. Progress toward lifting the embargo was slow because of questions regarding Vietnam's cooperation in helping locate American prisoners of war. An embargo also played a central role in American efforts to bring down the Haitian military junta and return deposed president Jean-Bertrand Aristide to power. In June 1993, the UN voted to impose an oil and arms embargo on Haiti. The ease with which oil and other goods reached the junta through the Dominican Republic blunted its effectiveness, and in 1993, Clinton got the UN to impose a near-total embargo on Haiti. Only food and humanitarian supplies were exempt.

Perhaps most controversial have been two post–Cold War embargoes in different parts of the world that have been linked politically to Washington. They are the arms embargo against the Bosnian Muslims and the near-total embargo against Iraq. Both were instituted on a multilateral basis, and pressure repeatedly surfaced that they be lifted. An embargo on trade with Iraq was put into place by the UN in April 1991. It was to be lifted only when Iraq met the UN's terms for dealing with its nuclear program. By 1994, France and Russia were arguing that these terms had been met, because Iraq was beginning to cooperate with UN monitors. The United States considered Iraq's action insufficient and continued to view Saddam Hussein as a regional threat to be contained. The United States argued that Iraq still had not met all of the conditions of UN Resolution 687 regarding its invasion of Kuwait, and that until it did, the embargo should remain in place. About the same time as the Iraqi embargo went into effect, the UN also put into place an arms embargo on Yugoslavia. Although the embargo was neutral in its language, it had a far more serious effect on the military capabilities of the Bosnian Muslims than it did on the Bosnian Serbs. The Serbs were able to draw on the military resources of the old Yugoslav army, which was now under the control of the neighboring Serbian government.

A **boycott** is a refusal to buy a product(s) from another state, and it represents the fourth economic instrument available to policy makers. One case involved U.S. participation in UN-sponsored sanctions against Rhodesia (Zimbabwe).[9] Off and on, these sanctions lasted for over a decade. They were first imposed by President Lyndon Johnson in a 1968 executive order, and were finally lifted in 1979. The purpose of the sanctions was to force the Rhodesian government into accepting the principle of majority rule. The U.S. commitment to the boycott was never firm. Congress amended the boycott in 1971 to allow the export of raw chromium and other critical materials to Rhodesia. It closed this loophole in 1977, when the same groups that had lobbied for the exemption objected to the flood of low-priced Rhodesian-processed chromium into the U.S. market. Throughout 1979 the Carter administration fought a holding action against moves by the Senate to lift the boycott until such time as the British were able to mediate the changeover to majority rule.

In 1995, the administration of Bill Clinton instituted a boycott against Iran in response to evidence that it was seeking to acquire nuclear technology and expertise from Russia. Clinton publicly labeled Iran a threat to peace in the Middle East and a sponsor of terrorism. The move came on the heels of an administration ban on trade between Iran and U.S. oil companies and their subsidiaries. Political pressures played a major role in these decisions, as Congress had been pressing the administration for even tougher action against Iran.

The fifth policy tool we examine in our survey is the **quota,** which is a quantitative restriction on goods coming from another state. Because of GATT, quotas have not played a large role in foreign economic policy making for most of the post–World War II era. This began to change as the U.S. balance-of-payments situation continued to deteriorate and as concerns grew over the international competitiveness of U.S.-made products. One notable use of quotas came in 1994, when the administration of Bill Clinton threatened to limit the amount of Canadian grain entering the United States. In 2004, quotas were used in a failed attempt to ease a trade dispute with Canada. In 2002, the United States imposed tariffs on Canadian lumber entering the United States. Now it offered tariff-free access to the U.S. market for Canadian lumber under a quota system.

## Sanctions in Action

REMOVING CASTRO FROM POWER.  Fidel Castro's Cuba was a major irritant to U.S. policy makers in the 1960s, and economic pressure was only one of several policy instruments brought into play. In 1959, the year Castro came to power, Cuba was heavily dependent on the United States: 67 percent of its exports went to the United States; 70 percent of its imports came from the United States; and under the terms of legislation passed in 1934, the United States purchased the bulk of Cuban sugar at prices substantially above world market rates. Relations between the United States and Castro were tense from the very beginning. In February 1960, Castro concluded a barter deal with the Soviet Union that involved an exchange of Cuban sugar for Soviet crude oil. After U.S.-owned oil refineries refused to process the Soviet oil, Castro took them over. The U.S. response was to terminate all remaining foreign aid programs and to cancel all purchases of Cuban sugar for the remainder of the year. Castro retaliated with additional nationalizations of U.S. property. Next, the United States imposed an embargo on all exports to Castro except for food and medicine. Cuba then entered into more economic agreements with the Soviet Union, and, in turn, the United States broke diplomatic relations. Even after the Cuban missile crisis and the Bay of Pigs invasion, the United States continued to apply economic sanctions. The Foreign Aid Act of 1963 required the president to stop U.S. aid to states that refused to restrict their trade with Cuba unless he felt that it was in the U.S. national interest not to do so. The United States also succeeded in getting the Organization of American States first to expel Cuba and then to sever commercial relations with it.

Economic sanctions have remained in place ever since. Periodically, they have been tightened, often as a result of electoral considerations. In 1992, Congress tightened the existing embargo by passing the Cuban Democracy Act. It placed heavy penalties on U.S. firms that engaged in trade with Cuba through foreign subsidiaries. In 1996, the Helms–Burton Act threatened sanctions against countries that provided Cuba with foreign aid and allowed U.S. nationals to sue foreign firms that that now controlled properties seized during the Cuban revolution. Opposition from American allies to this last provision has been intense, and both Bill Clinton and George W. Bush waived it annually. In 2002, George W. Bush announced that Cuban Americans would only be able to visit home once every three years, for no more than two weeks at a time, and they could take with them only a limited amount of luggage and money.

In April 2009, the Obama administration announced a reversal of U.S. policy toward Cuba. It was lifting travel and spending restrictions on trips to Cuba as well as lifting the ban on U.S. telecommunications doing business in Cuba. The administration left in place a series of other trade measures imposed by previous administrations.

**PUNISHING SUPPORT FOR TERRORISM**  Moammar Gaddafi came to power in Libya through a coup in 1969. His nationalization of oil fields produced only a moderate response from the United States in 1973, but relations became increasingly tense as his regime became identified with terrorist attacks and hostility toward Israel. One result was that in 1978 the United States banned the sale of military equipment to Libya. The Reagan administration entered office determined to use its Libyan policy as a means of making a statement about America's renewed willingness to flex its power. In 1981, Reagan placed an embargo on crude oil imports from Libya and restricted the export of sophisticated gas and oil equipment to the North African state. In 1985 the importation of refined Libyan oil products was barred. The following year, after a new wave of terrorist violence, Reagan imposed a comprehensive trade embargo that banned all imports and exports. Libyan financial assets in American banks were also frozen. Later in 1986, U.S. oil companies were forced to leave Libya, but were allowed to sign "standstill" agreements permitting the Libyan National Oil Company to run their affiliates until they returned. In 1993, after Libya was implicated in the explosion of Pan Am flight 103 over Lockerbie, Scotland, and French UTA flight 772 over Niger, the UN Security Council passed Resolution 883, which imposed a global embargo on Libyan oil and gas products and froze Libyan funds abroad. In 1996, the United States enacted the Iran–Libya Sanctions Act, which put stiff penalties on companies that invested more than $40 million in Libya's oil industry. In 1999, after Libya turned over two suspects in the Lockerbie bombing to the World Court, the UN suspended its sanctions. They were lifted entirely in 2003, after

Qaddafi renounced his support for terrorism. The United States and France abstained from this vote; for political reasons, neither country could vote in favor of lifting the sanctions, but their abstentions allowed the vote to pass. In December 2003, Qaddafi unexpectedly announced that Libya had attempted to develop chemical, biological, and nuclear weapons but renounced further attempts to do so. He also welcomed international inspections.

### Smart Sanctions

Dissatisfaction with the success rate of economic sanctions, and growing questions about the ethical justification for inflicting hardship and suffering on innocent people because of what their government has done, has led many to advocate abandoning conventional economic sanctions for "smart sanctions."[10] **Smart sanctions** differ from conventional sanctions in two respects. First, they target decision makers and political elites, not populations. Second, they protect vulnerable social groups. The first aim is achieved by focusing on arms embargoes, travel restrictions, and targeted financial sanctions.

The Bush administration has aggressively employed smart sanctions. In 2003, it froze the assets of Zimbabwe's President Robert Mugabe and other key government officials for undermining democracy and contributing to a "deliberate breakdown in the rule of law." In 2007, it imposed sanctions on Sudan for its failure to put an end to the Darfur crisis. Sanctions were directed against Sudanese oil companies and key individuals whose U.S. bank accounts were frozen. Also in 2007, Bush put in place additional sanctions against Myanmar (Burma) in response to that country's crackdown on pro-democracy supporters. Restrictions were placed on the export of high-performance computers to Burma, and the U.S. bank accounts and assets of 11 senior Burmese officials were frozen. The UN sanctions against Iran passed in 2008 also contained a smart sanctions section. It ordered countries to freeze the assets of 12 companies and 13 individuals linked to Iran's nuclear weapons and ballistic missile programs.

Initial evaluations of smart sanctions are not encouraging.[11] They do not appear to be significantly more successful than conventional ones. The fundamental problem is the same, a lack of political will to enforce them, and no amount of technical refinement can compensate for this shortcoming. Smart sanctions may also cause unanticipated problems. For example, the humanitarian objectives of the "oil for food" program in Iraq were never fully realized because corruption and mismanagement in the UN system allowed Saddam Hussein to siphon off funds for his own purposes and actually strengthened his grip on power.

## FOREIGN AID

A perennial debate exists over the purpose of U.S. foreign aid. Is it a "soft" policy whose primary goals lie in the areas of humanitarian assistance, development, and democratization, or is the purpose of foreign aid to advance core American national security interests? No easy answer exists. Colin Powell, for example, argued that it is the latter, but also went on to note that the United States will not punish people in need because of the actions of bad governments that operate beyond their control.[12] The existence of multiple goals means that foreign aid policy often runs the risk of working at cross-purposes, as in cases where foreign aid given to support governments fighting terrorism may negate efforts to promote democracy.

Several underlying conditions need to be kept in mind in thinking about foreign aid as an instrument of foreign policy. If we look at it from a policy perspective, we find first that the size of the U.S. foreign aid program has varied greatly, from a peak of $35 billion in 1985 to a low of $15.3 billion in 1997 (as measured in constant 2007 dollars). Compared to other areas of government spending, the foreign aid budget is small. Second, we also find that U.S. foreign aid is not distributed evenly around the world but is concentrated on a few states. Egypt ($2.58 billion in 2005) and Israel ($1.84 billion) traditionally have been at the top of the list. Rounding out the top five recipients of U.S. aid in 2005 were Afghanistan ($980 million), Pakistan ($700 million), and Colombia ($570 million). Along with Pakistan after 9/11, India, the Philippines, and Indonesia also experienced significant growth in the amount of foreign aid funds they received. Pakistan's funding in 2000–2001 was $3.4 million, whereas from 2002 to 2006 it averaged $678 million. India's U.S. foreign aid doubled from pre-9/11 levels, whereas that of the Philippines tripled. Tables 11.1 and 11.2, respectively, present an overview of how U.S. foreign aid was distributed around the world by country and purpose in 2007.

Third, U.S. foreign aid is often given with restrictions, although these restrictions may be overridden by national security concerns. President George W. Bush announced in his 2005 State of the Union address that he would seek

### TABLE 11.1

TOP TEN RECIPIENTS OF FOREIGN AID FROM THE U.S. AGENCY FOR INTERNATIONAL DEVELOPMENT (USAID), 2007

| Country | Amount Obligated |
| --- | --- |
| Afghanistan | $1.446 billion |
| Iraq | $1.243 billion |
| Egypt | $606 million |
| Pakistan | $458 million |
| Sudan | $382 million |
| Kenya | $289 million |
| Jordan | $280 million |
| South Africa | $250 million |
| Ethiopia | $214 million |
| Uganda | $204 million |

Source: Frontlines, USAID, March 2008, p. 2

## TABLE 11.2

TOP TEN PURPOSES OF FOREIGN AID FROM THE U.S. AGENCY FOR INTERNATIONAL DEVELOPMENT (USAID), 2007

| Purpose | Amount Obligated |
|---|---|
| Health | $4.328 billion |
| Emergency response | $1.638 billion |
| Good governance | $1.102 billion |
| Infrastructure | $705 million |
| Education | $627 million |
| Financial sector capacity | $497 million |
| Agriculture | $435 million |
| Stabilization operations and security sector reform | $397 million |
| Civil society | $365 million |
| Counter narcotics | $358 million |

Source: Frontlines, USAID, March 2008, p. 2

$200 million to support Palestinian political, economic, and security reforms. Yet when Congress passed the bill, $50 million was given to Israel to help build checkpoints, and other restrictions made it difficult for any money to go directly to the Palestinian Authority. From 1993 to 2005, Indonesia faced congressionally imposed foreign aid restrictions resulting largely from human rights violations by its military. In 2005, Secretary of State Condoleezza Rice certified that Indonesia had met congressional concerns and should now receive access to military aid funds. Fourth, a very high percentage of U.S. foreign aid funds are spent on U.S. products. The Congressional Research Service estimates that 90 percent of food aid is spent on U.S. goods and services. In 2004, U.S. and British firms had obtained 85 percent of the monies in Iraqi reconstruction contracts, compared to 2 percent for Iraqi firms.

It is worth noting that the restrictions attached to U.S. foreign aid may also set of a backlash in the country receiving it. For example, in 2009, Obama approved a $7.5 billion, five-year aid program to Pakistan. Pakistani officials and that country's media quickly characterized the terms as "insulting and unacceptable." Among the conditions attached by the United States were the establishment of monitoring mechanisms to see how the money was spent and establishing procedures for promoting military officers. This conflict erupted just as Pakistan was about to undertake a long postponed major military offensive against the Taliban in the Pakistan–Afghanistan border region.

Two structural factors also bear mentioning in looking at U.S. foreign aid policy. First, the amount of money we are talking about is small from a budgetary perspective. It is less than 1 percent of the overall U.S. budget; national defense spending accounts for 19.7 percent. Second, as small as it is, this money is not distributed by any one bureaucratic unit. At least eight different organizations are responsible for dispensing U.S. foreign aid. Figure 14.1 presents a breakdown of who distributed U.S. foreign aid in 2005 and how much they controlled. The four leading dispensers of foreign aid in 2006 were defense (31%), state (24%), Agriculture (24%), and Health and Human Services (6%)

## Types of Foreign Aid

There is no standard method for categorizing the different types of U.S. foreign aid programs. One approach used by the researchers of the Congressional Research Service identifies six basic categories, and we will follow that scheme here. Before examining the breakdown of official U.S. foreign aid, however, it is important to note that private foreign aid, not from organizations but individuals, is now among the most important sources of funds for Third World states. Known as remittances, in 2006 it was estimated that immigrants sent $45 billion home to family members. This compares with about $2 billion in 1980. Mexico received some $24 billion from immigrants living in the United States, while El Salvador received $3 billion, which equals about 15 percent of its gross domestic product. The downturn of the U.S. economy had a staggering impact on remittances. In 2009, this fell to $25 billion, the first drop since records began being kept in the late 1990s. The consequences for Mexico are significant since, after oil, remittances are the second largest source of hard currency, more even than tourist spending.

The first category of official U.S. foreign aid is *economic aid* given for the purpose of advancing U.S. political and security objectives. This is the biggest category of foreign aid. Monies given in this category have supported such diverse programs as the Camp David Accords negotiated by Carter, the building of democracy in the Russia and Eastern Europe, antinarcotics efforts, antiterrorism plans, and countering weapons proliferation. George W. Bush's 2002 plan to create a U.S.–Mexico Partnership for Progress, which was intended to direct $30 billion to Mexico to create jobs there and discourage immigration here, falls into this category of foreign aid.

The second largest category of foreign aid is *military assistance*. These monies go to help allies maintain and train their armed forces, as well as to buy U.S. military equipment. Included here are Economic Support Funds. These are loans to countries that are not eligible for development assistance, but are considered to be strategically important. Finally, the military assistance grant program provides funds to purchase U.S. military equipment and support military training funds.

Assessing the success of economic or military aid in achieving foreign policy goals is not easy. Often, the providing aid is a necessary part of an explicit or implicit deal. In 2005, for instance, Polish leaders made little secret of the fact that they expected an additional $600 million in military aid, increased trade, and other benefits in return for the presence of Polish troops in Iraq in 2006. Using pro-U.S. votes at the UN as a measure of effectiveness, two researchers found that the more dependent a nondemocracy is on the United States for military or economic aid, the more likely it is to vote with the United States. These researchers suggest that cooperation with other democracies is best achieved by having complementary policy goals.[13]

The third category is bilateral *development assistance*. These aid programs are generally administered by the U.S. Agency for International Development (USAID) and have a long-term development focus on strengthening the economy, environment, health care delivery systems, and political institutions of recipient states. Funding for the Peace Corps and debt relief falls into this category. Economic development aid has become the "ideology" by which most people think foreign aid must be justified. In 1989, Alan Woods, the head of USAID, asserted that U.S. development foreign aid had lost sight of its original rationale: providing transitional help to Third World states to meet their own development needs.[14] Not only had this aid become permanent, it had created a dependency on it that was actually stifling development. In the early 1990s, a new consensus on how development aid should work formed. This "Washington Consensus" shifted attention away from subsidizing projects to establishing free markets.[15] By the end of the 1990s, however, it had also come under attack, for failing to take into account the negative social impacts of free markets in terms of income equality, abuses of labor rights, and large-scale environmental destruction.

A particularly troublesome aspect of economic aid in the 1980s and 1990s was debt relief. The sums were staggering. In 1988, Brazil's outstanding debt was $120.1 billion, Mexico's debt stood at $107.4 billion, and Argentina owed $59.6 billion. At first, the Reagan administration approached the problem as one that was solvable through a combination of austerity measures on the part of countries and the adoption of more prudent lending policies by banks and international organizations. This response proved inadequate, and the Reagan administration sought to increase the level of funding available through the Baker Plan. With the problem continuing, George H. W. Bush devised the Brady Plan, which combined a program of limited and voluntary debt forgiveness with international guarantees of the remaining loan amounts. The Brady Plan also did not solve the debt problem (in 1995, Bill Clinton found it necessary to provide Mexico with $12 billion in loans to stabilize the peso), but it did seem to make it manageable compared to new debt problems that were emerging in Asia as a result of rapidly declining currency values, which reverberated through global stock markets.

The fourth category of foreign aid is *humanitarian economic assistance*. This aid tends to be short term and emergency focused. Refugee assistance, emergency food aid, and disaster relief account for the bulk of this spending. Bipartisan congressional support for this type of aid has generally been high, although the amount of money involved has fluctuated greatly from year to year, largely because of the unpredictability of the natural disasters that set such aid in motion. In general, humanitarian aid has increased by almost 30 percent since 1978. Of late, however, this rate of growth has slowed, such that the FY 2006 humanitarian aid appropriate was below the levels of FY 1999 (Kosovo relief and Hurricane Mitch), 2003 (Africa food relief and Iraq war relief), and 2005 (tsunami relief and Darfur relief).

The fifth category is *multilateral development assistance*. It accounts for less than one-tenth of the foreign aid budget and consists of funds contributed to such international development organizations as UNICEF, the United Nations

Development Plan, the World Bank, and the African Development Bank. U.S. aid to multilateral organizations is affected by a number of concerns, such as the international planning policies of organizations, the implementation of the Iraq Oil for Food program, and the pace and nature of reform efforts at the United Nations.

The final category of foreign aid is *nonemergency food aid*. The Food for Peace program, also known as PL 480, is the primary instrument for distributing this aid. It makes surplus U.S. agricultural goods available to Third World states in local currency and at concessionary prices. Critics of the Food for Peace program have noted that tension has always existed between the humanitarian and political purposes of this aid and that the political purposes tend to triumph. In 1973, only two of the top 20 recipients of PL 480 funds were among the world's 40 poorest states. Under Ronald Reagan, Egypt received the most PL 480 funds ($221 million). India was a distant second ($93.5), followed by El Salvador ($50.8) and the Sudan ($50.7).

## Cold War Foreign Aid

The relative importance of military and economic aid varied considerably during the Cold War. The Truman administration's foreign aid program was dominated by economic development initiatives such as the Marshall Plan, which made $17 billion available in loans and grants for European economic recovery, and the Point Four Program, whose goal was to bring economic development and modernization to the Third World through the transfer of U.S. technical assistance. In Truman's foreign aid budgets, 96 percent consisted of development funds. With the outbreak of the Korean War, a change occurred. Increasingly, policy makers viewed foreign aid as an instrument for furthering American national security. More than 60 percent of foreign aid now was given for military purposes. In the process, the focus of American foreign aid changed as well. Between 1949 and 1952, Europe received 86 percent of U.S. foreign aid. That fell to 25 percent between 1953 and 1957 and then 6 percent between 1958 and 1961. Correspondingly, the share of American aid to the Third World increased during this period to 68 percent.

During the presidency of John Kennedy the proportion of economic aid to military aid changed again, so that by the mid-1970s economic aid accounted for 75 percent of all U.S. foreign aid. Within the economic aid category, however, greater emphasis was given to loans (which had to be repaid) than to grants (which did not). With the deepening American involvement in Vietnam, the balance swung back in favor of military aid. By the mid-1970s it constituted 70 percent of U.S. foreign aid. After the American withdrawal from Vietnam, economic aid reasserted itself, growing to 80 percent of the total. It again faded under the Reagan administration. From 1980 to 1985, economic aid rose from about $7.5 billion to almost $10 billion, while military aid virtually tripled from $2 billion to almost $6 billion.

## HISTORICAL LESSON

### The Marshall Plan

The Marshall Plan, or the European Recovery Program as it was more formally known, was a blueprint for European economic recovery presented by Secretary of State George Marshall at a Harvard University commencement address in June 1947. Marshall asserted, "it is logical that the United States should do whatever it is able to do to assist in the return of normal economic health in the world, without which there can be no political stability and no assured peace."

By 1947 the United States had already provided Europe with approximately $9 billion in loans and grants, but European post–World War II economic recovery was proceeding slowly. German production had fallen to 29 percent of its 1936 level, and the British had just managed to reach their prewar level of production. Concerns in the United States about the political stability of Europe mounted. It was feared that communists might come to power in France and Italy because one-fourth of the French electorate has voting communist and might freely elect a communist government. Concerns were also expressed about the danger posed to the health of the U.S. economy by the large European deficit.

A precondition for the aid package Marshall proposed was European agreement on a plan of action. Europe was to take the initiative identifying common needs and a common recovery plan. In mid-June, the British and French foreign ministers met in Paris to begin formulating a European proposal. The Soviet Union was invited to join them. Evidence suggests that the United States did not want Soviet participation in the Marshall Plan, but for political reasons felt obliged to extend the offer to all European states. A precondition for Soviet participation was that it should agree to abide by the decisions of the planning group and that the Soviet Union contribute raw materials to the recovery effort.

Coming only months after the proclamation of the Truman Doctrine, Soviet leaders were suspicious of Western motives and labeled it "a plan for interference in the domestic affairs of other countries." The Paris Conference reached a deadlock, and the Soviet Union pulled out of further negotiations. It also pressured Czechoslovakia to do the same. As a countermove, it put forward its own Molotov Plan to rebuild the economies of the now communist states of East Europe. It also resurrected the international organization of communist parties. Before World War II, it had been known as the COMINTERN. It now became the COMINFORM.

Discussions continued throughout 1947. The Truman administration submitted a $17 billion aid package to Congress, and in March 1948, Congress approved $4 billion in aid for the first year. The vote occurred against a backdrop of a recent communist coup in Czechoslovakia, pending elections in Italy, and a growing crisis in Germany. Marshall Plan funds were allocated more or less on a per capita basis, with the larger states receiving more money than did smaller ones. Officially, the United States was to be paid back for the money provided through the Marshall Plan, but recipients knew that this would not be the case.

The Marshall Plan ended in 1952, having directed over $13 billion toward European economic recovery. In 1951, the Economic Cooperation Administration that oversaw this effort was absorbed by the Mutual Security Administration, and military aid began to replace economic aid as the centerpiece of U.S. aid to Europe. By 1952, 80 percent of American aid to Europe was military.

The Marshall Plan was an economic success. By 1950, European production exceeded prewar levels by 25 percent. The Marshall Plan also had larger political consequences. It represented a small but important step forward in European economic cooperation and integration that would culminate decades later in the creation of the EU. Politically as well as economically, the Marshall Plan was an important contributor to the dividing of Germany and all of Europe into "East" and "West." This division would take on a military dimension in 1949 with the establishment of the North Atlantic Treaty Organization (NATO).

The success of the Marshall Plan led the Truman administration to try and apply a similar logic to U.S. foreign aid through the 1949 Point Four Program that called for worldwide technical assistance to Third World states for the purpose of promoting economic development and dampening the appeal of communism. While it had its successes, the Point Four Program never approached the level of acceptance in the United States or abroad enjoyed by the Marshall Plan. At home many in Congress saw it as wasteful, and abroad it was overshadowed by U.S. military aid and covert operations.

**Applying the Lesson**

1. Is the Marshall Plan a good model for aid to Pakistan and Afghanistan?
2. What are the requirements for a successful foreign aid program?
3. Would there be any negative consequences of a Marshall Plan for Pakistan and Afghanistan? ■

## Post–Cold War Foreign Aid

During the first decade of the post–Cold War era, three controversies dominated the foreign aid agenda. All of these programs continue to be controversial, but to some extent they have been overtaken by new foreign aid concerns. The first centered on foreign aid to Russia. The United States targeted two areas for assistance. One was funding to help Russia denuclearize, by providing it with funds to destroy chemical and nuclear weapons, establish safeguards against proliferation, and assess the environmental damage done by nuclear waste. Funds were provided for this purpose by the 1991 Nunn–Lugar Threat Reduction Program. The second area of funding was economic development. No one denied the need for Russia's economy to grow, but many argued that widespread corruption and government inefficiency made growth impossible. The George W. Bush administration was not interested in continuing the Nunn–Lugar Program until after the 9/11 terrorist attacks. It had ordered a review of the program upon taking office, but after 9/11, in 2002, it advocated an additional $750 million for 30 different programs.

A second area of controversy surrounded funding for combating HIV/AIDS. Donor states provided about $350 million to fight AIDS in 1999, with about half that amount coming from the United States. The American response to the AIDS crisis has been caught in a political crossfire of congressional opposition to foreign aid in general and opposition to any form of aid for family planning programs. Since the Reagan presidency, U.S. foreign aid legislation has prohibited funding groups that support or promote abortion. In 2007, Democrats in Congress challenged this ban by passing an amendment to a foreign aid spending bill that rescinded this prohibition. President Bush promised to veto any bill that altered the "Mexico City" policy. It is known as such because it was in Mexico City in 1984 that the UN held a population and development conference supporting abortion rights.

Complicating matters further was lobbying by Third World states to be allowed to produce generic versions of the leading AIDS drugs. In trade negotiations, the United States pressed for these states to pay full licensing fees. When South Africa passed a law permitting the government to produce drugs it considered too expensive on the world market, the United States threatened economic sanctions and placed it on a Super 301 watchlist. The George W. Bush administration made fighting AIDS a high priority, but problems such as limited congressional funding and disputes between the administration and nongovernmental organizations over how and to whom such funds should be delivered continued to plague the program.

The third area of controversy involved efforts to stop international drug trafficking. The most ambitious undertaking was Plan Colombia. This is a $7.5 billion aid package, and was intended to advance the peace process in Colombia, strengthen its national economy, stop the production of drugs, promote justice and human rights, and foster democracy and social development. Plan Colombia met with a mixed reception. Seventy-five percent of its initial $1.5 billion in aid was military in nature, and critics asserted that the plan was reminiscent of the 1980–1981 period, when the United States became embroiled in El Salvador's civil war by its overly close identification with the military. It has also been argued that Plan Colombia was not sufficiently sensitive to the complex interactions between the drug war and the guerrilla war, whose roots date back to the 1960s. In January 2004, Secretary of State Colin Powell certified to Congress that the Colombian government and armed forces were complying with human rights standards. This finding was necessary to allow the last 12.5 percent of the Plan Colombia funds to be obligated. Human rights watch groups challenged this assessment of the situation, with some asserting that the human rights situation in Colombia had worsened in parts of Colombia since Plan Colombia began.

In 2007, the George W. Bush administration sought to expand anti–drug trafficking efforts to include Mexico, when it proposed to Congress a $1 billion, two-year foreign aid package. Officially known as the Merida Initiative, it was nicknamed "Plan Mexico." A central part of the initiative, which is 10 times larger than any previous U.S. antidrug policy directed at Mexico, was to provide aerial surveillance aircraft and rapid-deployment troops along with training for court officers and prison managers. Virtually nothing came of this initiative.

In 2009, it was acknowledged that delivery of the aircraft could be as much as two years away. Stung by the rapid increase in drug-related violence along the U.S.–Mexican border, the Bush administration moved an emergency funding bill through Congress in June 2008 that appropriated $400 million of the promised money. Still, by the end of the year, less than half of those funds had been released for spending, and only $7 million had been spent. President Obama sought to demonstrate additional U.S. resolve by issuing an Executive Order placing the three major Mexican drug cartels on a list which prevents U.S. companies from doing business with them and allows the United States to seize their assets.

## Post-9/11 Foreign Aid

Since 9/11, foreign aid has come to be viewed in a more positive light, under the assumption that it can make a major contribution to the war against terrorism. Many, however, are doubtful that its effect will be significant in direct and measurable ways. Interestingly, the interest in foreign aid as a tool against terrorism comes from both national security and economic development perspectives. One consequence of this renewed interest in foreign aid is the heightened involvement of the Pentagon in foreign aid programs. Whereas in 2002 only 10 percent of U.S. foreign aid went through the Pentagon, in 2006 almost 25 percent was funneled through it.

Almost immediately after 9/11, the George W. Bush administration sought authority from Congress to waive all existing restrictions on U.S. military assistance and weapons exports for five years to any country he determined was helping in the war on terrorism. A similar pattern existed in the area of trade. In 2002, for example, the administration proposed dropping trade restrictions on eight Central Asian countries that emerged out of the Soviet Union after its fall. All had questionable records in the areas of human rights and democratization. Only Belarus, which did not offer antiterrorism assistance, was not in line to have trade restrictions dropped. In addition to being used as a carrot, trade restrictions were also used as a stick. In 2003, the administration announced that it would only allow companies from countries that supported the war against Iraq to bid on prime reconstruction contracts. Undersecretary of Defense Paul Wolfowitz justified the decision to limit competition as necessary "for the protection of the essential security of the United States." Also that year, the Bush administration announced that it was suspending military aid to some 35 countries because they failed to meet a congressionally imposed deadline exempting Americans from prosecution in the new UN International Criminal Court. Congress exempted 27 states, including NATO members, Israel, and Egypt, from the loss of aid. Most recently, in 2007, the United States rushed $40 million in military assistance to Lebanon, as its army was engaged in fighting with al Qaida–inspired militants inside Palestinian refugee camps.

The signature development assistance program of the George W. Bush administration was the Millennium Challenge Account (MCA).[16] Targeted toward low-income countries, it was announced in 2002 and began operation in FY 2004 under the jurisdiction of a new independent agency, the Millennium

Challenge Corporation (MCC). One of the defining features of the MCA was to be its narrow focus. Money would be given only to countries that met a demanding set of criteria, and its only purpose would be to support economic growth and reduce poverty. The 16 different indicators used to judge a country's eligibility in 2007 are presented in Table 11.3. They fall into three categories: (1) good government, (2) economic freedom, and (3) investing in people. In its first year of operation, 63 countries were found to meet the eligibility criteria, and 16 were then identified as being eligible to submit applications to the MCC. By the end of 2006, a total of nine compacts were in place. Concerns were raised about two aspects of these compacts. First, they all tended to emphasize agricultural and transportation infrastructure projects. More variety had been expected. Second, the funding levels were not has high

---

### TABLE 11.3

**MILLENIUM CHALLENGE ACCOUNT FUND CRITERIA, 2007**

| Indicator | As measured by . . . |
|---|---|
| **Ruling Justly** | |
| Civil liberties | Freedom House |
| Political rights | Freedom House |
| Voice and accountability | World Bank Institute |
| Government effectiveness | World Bank Institute |
| Rule of law | World Bank Institute |
| Control of corruption | World Bank Institute |
| **Encouraging Economic Freedoms** | |
| Cost of starting a business | World Bank Group |
| Inflation | IMF, World Economic Outlook |
| Fiscal policy | IMF, World Economic Outlook, and national governments |
| Days to start a business | World Bank Group |
| Trade policy | Heritage Foundation, Index of Economic Freedom |
| Regulatory quality | World Bank Institute |
| **Investing in People** | |
| Public expenditures on health | World Health Organization |
| Immunization | World Health Organization |
| Total public expenditures on primary | UNESCO and national governments education |
| Girls' primary completion rate | World Bank and UNESCO |

Source: Millennium Challenge Corporation, *Report on the Criteria and Methodology for Determining the Eligibility of Candidate Countries for Millennium Challenge Account Assistance in Fiscal Year 2007* (Washington, DC: U.S. Government Printing Office, September 8, 2006).

as had been anticipated. Often the new MCA money did not differ significantly from the existing level of U.S. foreign aid being received.

Of particular concern to many was the impact of the MCA foreign aid program on the coherence of U.S. foreign aid initiatives. MCA money was not intended to replace U.S. funding for multilateral foreign aid initiatives or the core development activities of USAID. It is the relationship between USAID and MCA that has received most attention. The two are mandated by Congress to cooperate, and a rough division of labor finds USAID responsible for countries not yet eligible for MCA money as well as those participating in a Threshold Program designed to make them eligible. Consistent with this assignment of responsibilities, Colin Powell described the relationship as one of the MCA "pulling" countries forward and USAID "pushing" them in that direction.[17] Yet this may be easier said than done. Early accounts from Madagascar point to bureaucratic conflict between the two in the field, and MCC executives indicating that countries should not received technical or financial support from USAID in preparing their compact proposals.

The MCC has distributed more than $5.5 billion to 16 developing states. The largest program worth almost $700 million operates in Tanzania. As has been the case with virtually all foreign aid programs, the MCC has not proven to be capable of withstanding political pressures emanating from Congress. In 2008, conservative dislike for foreign aid and Democratic complaints about the program's lack of success caused Congress to cut its funding in half.

## OVER THE HORIZON

As our survey has revealed, U.S. policy makers have used a great variety of economic instruments in order to further U.S. foreign policy goals. It is less clear that any agreement exists on what mixture of economic tools or what amount of aid would be most desirable in seeking to bring stability to Pakistan and Afghanistan, or if it can even be done.

Looking over the horizon, three developments involving economics as an instrument of foreign policy can be anticipated. The first is a reexamination of NAFTA. Calls for doing so were raised by both Hillary Clinton and Barack Obama during their battle for the Democratic nomination. As president, Obama indicated that the time was not right for such a move, and it would have to wait.

The second and third developments involve U.S. foreign aid. Both entail using foreign aid for humanitarian purposes. In 2008, the United States was criticized by a nonprofit group for being among the world's worst countries in delivering foreign aid in an impartial and neutral fashion, and the group placed the United States as 22nd out of 23 countries. We can expect to see an intensified debate over the purposes of aid as the global economy tightens and U.S. military involvements abroad continue. A second area of activity relating to the humanitarian use of foreign aid has been raised by U.S. officials: If a country blocks the delivery of humanitarian aid, can the world intervene? The impetus for this debate was Burma's refusal to allow U.S. aid (along with that from other states) to enter after Cyclone Nargis.

## CRITICAL THINKING QUESTIONS

1. Which type of free trade agreement, bilateral, regional, or global, is of most value to the United States today?
2. Should economic sanctions be used against friends or just foes?
3. What should be the primary objective of U.S. foreign aid, to help the United States or to help the recipient?

## KEY TERMS

boycott 295
Bretton Woods
   system 290
embargo 294
fast track 286

free trade 285
imperialism 284
nontariff barrier 294
quota 296

sanctions 285
smart sanctions 298
tariff 294

## FURTHER READING

Brian Atwood, M. Peter McPherson, and Andrew Natsios, "Arrested Development," *Foreign Affairs*, 87 (2008), 123–32.

David Baldwin, *Economic Statecraft* (Princeton, NJ: Princeton University Press, 1985).

Aaditya Mattoo and Arvind Subramanian, "From Doha to the Next Bretton Woods: A New Multilateral Trade Agenda," *Foreign Affairs*, 88 (2009), 15–26.

Walter Russell Mead, "America's Sticky Power," *Foreign Policy*, 141 (2004), 46–53.

Meghan O'Sullivan, *Shrewd Sanctions* (Washington, DC: Brookings Institution Press, 2003).

## NOTES

1. Walter Russell Mead, "America's Sticky Power," *Foreign Policy*, 141 (2004), 46–53.
2. David Baldwin, *Economic Statecraft* (Princeton, NJ: Princeton University Press, 1985), makes this point throughout this work. The statement is found on p. 115.
3. Ibid., pp. 44–47, 207–09.
4. Theodore Moran, "Empirical Studies of Strategic Trade Policy," *International Organization,* 50 (1996), 175–205.
5. Susan Strange, *Casino Capitalism* (New York: Oxford University Press, 1986).
6. Roger Altman, "The Great Crash, 2008: A Geopolitical Setback for the West," *Foreign Affairs,* 88 (2009), 2–14.
7. Mark Strauss, "Sanctions Soup," *The Chronicle of Higher Education,* 49 (June 13, 2003), B11–12.
8. Meghan O'Sullivan, *Shrewd Sanctions* (Washington, DC: Brookings Institution Press, 2003), p. 12.
9. Stephen R. Weissman and Johnnie Carson, "Economic Sanctions Against Rhodesia," in John Spanier and Joseph Nogee (eds.), *Congress, the Presidency, and American Foreign Policy* (New York: Pergamon, 1981), pp. 132–60.
10. David Cortright and George Lopez (eds.), *Smart Sanctions* (Lanham, MD: Rowman & Littlefield, 2002).
11. Arne Tostensen and Beate Bull, "Are Smart Sanctions Feasible?" *World Politics,* 54 (2002), 373–403.
12. Colin Powell, "No Country Left Behind," *Foreign Policy,* 146 (January/February 2005), 30–35.

13. Brian Lai and Daniel Morey, "Impact of Regime Type of the Influence of U.S. Foreign Aid, *Foreign Policy Analysis,* 2 (2006), 385–404.
14. *Development and the National Interest* (Washington, DC: Agency for International Development, 1988).
15. Robin Broad and John Cavanagh, "Beyond the Myths of Rio," *World Policy Journal,* 10 (1993), 65–72.
16. Gene Sperling and Tom Hart, "A Better Way to Fight Global Poverty," *Foreign Affairs,* 82 (2003), 9–14; and Lael Brainard, "Compassionate Conservatism Confronts Global Poverty," *The Washington Quarterly,* 26 (2003), 149–69.
17. Powell, "No Country Left Behind."

# CHAPTER

## 12

# Military Instruments:
# Big Wars

In January 2004, Pakistani nuclear scientist Dr. A. Q. Khan admitted to having been a central figure in a secret international conspiracy to sell nuclear weapons technology to rogue states, including Iran, Libya, and North Korea. He has also been linked to Pakistani scientists who were arrested in late 2001 for their ties with the Taliban. The Central Intelligence Agency (CIA) became aware of his activities in the late 1990s. In putting together his secret operation, Khan made use of contacts from around the world, working with Germans, Israelis, and South Africans. Production facilities were located in Malaysia. Shipments to Libya were sent through Europe and Dubai. Khan traveled to Egypt and Saudi Arabia, potential purchasers of his services, and the uranium-rich African states of the Sudan Ivory Coast and Niger. His motivations are not entirely clear but appear to be a mixture of a desire to support for Muslim nations, anti-Western sentiment, and personal greed.

Khan is widely known as the father of Pakistan's nuclear program and is widely admired and respected in Pakistan. After his confession, he was pardoned by Pakistani President Pervez Musharraf. Anxious to keep Pakistan as an ally against al Qaeda, the Bush administration announced that it would not impose sanctions on Pakistan. In 2008, Khan recanted his confession, saying that he was being made a scapegoat for actions of the Pakistani government.

The *Bulletin of the Atomic Scientists* displays a "doomsday clock" depicting the time to nuclear midnight prominently on its cover. In 1953, as the U.S.–Soviet nuclear arms race began, it stood at 11:58 P.M. In 1991, with the signing of the Strategic Arms Limitation Agreement (SALT), it moved back to 11:43 P.M. After North Korea's nuclear blast test in 2006, it was moved back to 11:58 P.M. As Khan's efforts and the *Bulletin of the Atomic Scientists'* response to North Korea's nuclear test blast suggest, the specter of nuclear war continues to be a major concern for policy makers. In this chapter, we examine the role that nuclear weapons have played in U.S. foreign policy thinking (both as an instrument of war and a weapon to be controlled) along with the large-scale use of conventional military power. In the next chapter, we continue to look at the military instrument but shift our focus to small-scale wars.

## COLD WAR NUCLEAR THINKING

U.S. nuclear strategy during the Cold War was not static, changing several times. It was also not always internally consistent. There often could be found a distinction between what policy makers said their strategy was and what it actually called for. The former is known as declaratory policy, and the latter as action policy. To fully appreciate this difference, we begin by looking at the development of U.S. and Soviet nuclear arsenals and then examine the strategies built upon them.

## The U.S. Strategic Arsenal

At 5:30 A.M., on July 16, 1945, in the New Mexican desert, the first atomic bomb was detonated. On August 6, Hiroshima was destroyed by an atomic bomb. On August 9, Nagasaki was similarly destroyed by a plutonium bomb. These two attacks effectively depleted the U.S. (and therefore the global) inventory of atomic weapons. The U.S. nuclear arsenal grew slowly. Only 2 weapons were stockpiled at the end of 1945, 9 in July 1946, 13 in July 1947, and 50 in July 1948.[1] None of these weapons was preassembled; it took 39 people over two days to put them together. The year 1949 marked the end of the U.S. nuclear monopoly, as the Soviet Union detonated its first atomic bomb. Estimates suggest that by 1949 the U.S. arsenal had only 100–200 weapons. Part of the U.S. response to the Soviet Union's acquisition of the nuclear bomb was to develop a more powerful weapon, the hydrogen bomb. The United States successfully tested an H-bomb in November 1952, and the Soviet Union duplicated the feat in August 1953.[2] It is estimated that by 1957 the United States probably had 3,000 nuclear bombs, and the Soviet Union had a few hundred.[3]

Reinforcing this U.S. numerical advantage in bombs was a marked superiority in delivery systems. The Soviet bomber fleet was small and could reach the United States only on a one-way mission. The United States did not face a similar handicap, because it could use bases in Western Europe to deliver an attack on the Soviet Union. This advantage disappeared in 1957 when the Soviet Union successfully tested an intercontinental ballistic missile (ICBM) and launched *Sputnik* into orbit. With these two actions the Soviet Union demonstrated the theoretical capability to deliver a nuclear attack on U.S. cities and its overseas military bases.

Fearing the development of a "missile gap" in which the Soviet Union would have a significant advantage over it in nuclear weapons, the United States stepped up production of its own ballistic missile force, constructed new early-warning radar systems, and placed the Strategic Air Command (SAC) on a heightened alert status so that almost half of its planes could take off on 15 minutes' notice. As it turned out, no missile gap developed because the Soviet Union did not engage in a crash buildup of its nuclear forces. The result was an overwhelming U.S. nuclear superiority. At the time of the Cuban missile crisis in October 1962, the United States had an ICBM advantage of 226–75, and it had 144 Polaris missiles to 0 submarine-launched ballistic missiles (SLBMs) for the Soviet Union. It also had a lead of 1,350 to 190 in long-range bombers.

The U.S. buildup continued through the mid-1960s before leveling off in 1967. By the mid-1960s the long-predicted Soviet buildup got under way, and for several years the pace of this buildup exceeded the worst-case scenarios of the U.S. intelligence community. Between 1966 and 1970, the Soviet Union increased the number of its ICBMs from 292 to 1,300. The term *parity* was now used to characterize the U.S.–Soviet nuclear relationship, because while the two nuclear inventories did not match each other weapon system for weapon system, they each had compensatory advantages. Table 12.1 presents an overview of the U.S. nuclear arsenal as the Cold War ended.

**TABLE 12.1**

U.S. Strategic Forces as the Cold War Ended

| | Deployed Under START I | | Planned Under START II | |
|---|---|---|---|---|
| Weapon System | Launchers | Accountable Warheads | Launchers | Accountable Warheads |
| Minuteman III ICBMs | 500 | 1,200 | 500 | 500 |
| Peacekeeper ICBMs | 50 | 500 | 0 | 0 |
| Trident I Missiles | 168 | 1,008 | 0 | 0 |
| Trident II Missiles | 264 | 2,112 | 336 | 1,680 |
| B-52 bombers (air-launched cruise missiles, ALCMs) | 97 | 970 | 76 | 940 |
| B-52 bombers (non-ALCMs) | 47 | 47 | 0 | 0 |
| B-1 bombers | 90 | 90 | 0 | 0 |
| B-2 bombers | 20 | 20 | 21 | 336 |
| Total | 1,236 | 5,947 | 933 | 3,456 |

Source: Amy Woolf, "U.S. Nuclear Weapons: Changes in Policy and Force Structure," *Congressional Research Service Report for Congress*, August 10, 2006, p. 23

# U.S. Cold War Nuclear Strategy

For the first eight years of the nuclear age, virtually no such thing as nuclear strategy per se existed at either the declaratory or action level. The uniqueness of nuclear weapons was not yet appreciated. They were simply treated as the largest explosive devices yet created, and it was expected that the next war would be fought along the lines of World War II. Long-range bombers would deliver these weapons against Soviet cities, industries, and military support facilities. When the small stockpile of atomic bombs was exhausted, plans called for using conventional bombs and a general mobilization of U.S. forces.[4] During the period from 1945 to 1953, a number of specific war plans were drawn up. The first war plan to identify atomic bomb target lists was Broiler in the fall of 1947. It called for 34 bombs to be dropped on 24 cities. Trojan, approved in December 1948, anticipated using 133 atomic bombs on 70 Soviet cities over a 30-day period.

There was a certain degree of unreality to these war plans. Most fundamentally, Bernard Brodie questioned whether nuclear weapons could be used in the same way as other weapons, or if **deterrence** rather than war fighting was their sole credible use.[5] Moreover, if deterrence was to be the principal purpose to which nuclear weapons were put, then some thought was necessary about how to accomplish this purpose. Deterrence could not simply be assumed to exist.

The first formal statement of nuclear strategy was put forward by the Eisenhower administration as part of its new-look defense posture. The nuclear component of this strategy was **massive retaliation**. Massive retaliation was intended to deter a wide spectrum of Soviet attacks, guaranteeing not only the security of the United States but also that of its European and Third World allies. It would accomplish this by threatening the Soviet Union with massive destruction in retaliation for aggressive behavior. No details were given as to what type of Soviet aggression would bring about massive retaliation or what would be attacked; all that was promised was "retaliation instantly, by means and places of our own choosing." The lack of specificity was intentional. The Eisenhower administration felt that the Truman administration's pledge of help for any country threatened by communism had given the initiative to the Soviet Union. Massive retaliation was designed to give it back to the United States.

Two recurrent lines of criticism were leveled against massive retaliation. The first concerned its credibility. Critics asserted that deterrence required more than just the capability to inflict damage. The threat also had to be credible. To threaten the Soviet Union with massive destruction for an attack on the United States was one thing; to make the same threat for attacks on Third World states was quite another. Soviet leaders would find the former credible, but not the latter, and therefore, they would not be deterred. The United States would then be left with the distasteful choice of having to implement its threat or do nothing. To prevent being placed in this position, critics argued that the United States must abandon massive retaliation for a policy with more strategic options. The second line of criticism was that massive retaliation was ill-suited to the changing nuclear relationship between the United States and the Soviet Union. Massive retaliation assumed the existence of an invulnerable retaliatory force, and this was no longer the case because of the growth in the Soviet nuclear arsenal and its development of ICBM technology. The growing vulnerability of nuclear forces to attack transformed deterrence from a certainty into one based on a "delicate balance of terror."[6]

Massive retaliation was U.S. declaratory policy. Action policy was reflected in U.S. war plans. Evidence suggests that U.S. war plans were not being tailored to meet the two primary contingencies spoken of by policy makers: retaliation and preemption (striking first in self-defense). Instead, U.S. war plans had become capability plans. They were constructed in such a way as to employ all of the nuclear weapons in the U.S. inventory and provide a rationale for acquiring additional weapons.[7] The gap between what the war plans would produce and what policy makers wanted was often quite glaring. For example, in 1955, a SAC officer stated that its plan would leave the Soviet Union "a smoking, radiating, ruin at the end of two hours."[8]

The first coordinated effort to establish a nuclear action policy came in 1960 when President Dwight Eisenhower approved the establishment of a National Strategy Target List (NSTL) and a Single Integrated Operational Plan (SIOP) for using nuclear weapons. Planners selected 2,600 separate installations for attack out of an overall list of 4,100 targets.[9] This translated into approximately 1,050 designated ground zeros (DGZs), 151 of which were urban-industrial targets. Plans called for launching all 3,500 nuclear warheads if sufficient warning time existed. If not, an alert force of 800 bombers and missiles would attack approximately 650 DGZs with over 1,400 weapons and a total of 2,100 megatons. According to one calculation, the SIOP assigned 300–500 kilotons of weapons to accomplish the level of destruction caused by a single bomb on Hiroshima. Officially known as SIOP-62, this was the war plan inherited by the Kennedy administration.

The Kennedy administration shared its predecessors' conviction that deterrence was the proper role for nuclear weapons. It differed in how to structure deterrence, and it gave attention to a problem that had never been fully addressed in the 1950s: how to fight a nuclear war. Kennedy replaced massive retaliation with the concept of flexible response under which the United States would have a range of options to choose from in deterring and responding to Soviet aggression, running the gamut from unconventional forces (Green Berets) to conventional forces to nuclear weapons. It emphasized the measured and restrained use of nuclear weapons to accomplish political objectives. To that end the Kennedy administration officially incorporated three new features into U.S. nuclear thinking.

First, prominence was given to the use of tactical nuclear weapons in the hope that, because of their less destructive nature, they might be more manageable. Second, a new targeting policy was adopted that emphasized attacks on military forces and avoidance of population centers. In Defense Secretary Robert McNamara's own words, the counterforce strategy sought to use nuclear weapons "in much the same way that more conventional military operations have been regarded in the past." Third, the Kennedy administration looked into two measures that might limit the damage done to the United States in case of a nuclear war: civil defense and damage limitation.[10] Political and technical problems plagued both of these initiatives, and they were abandoned.

The value of these changes in nuclear strategy was called into question by the Cuban missile crisis in 1962. The way in which the crisis was played out suggested that "deterrence, in practice was less graduated and more absolute than had been imagined."[11] Attention now shifted back to formulating a nuclear posture built less on war fighting and more on the ability to inflict widespread devastation on the enemy. To be credible, McNamara estimated that U.S. forces must have the assured capability to destroy 25–30 percent of the Soviet population and 66 percent of its industrial capacity. Later he lowered these levels to 20–25 percent of the Soviet population and 50 percent of its industry. Assured destruction as this policy came to be known, was not a return to massive retaliation. Massive retaliation rested on U.S. nuclear supremacy and was ambiguous as to where and when the United States would strike. Assured destruction recognized the difficulty—if not impossibility—of defending the United States against Soviet missiles and guaranteed retaliation for a Soviet attack on the United States.

Movement from massive retaliation to controlled response and then to assured destruction implied a parallel set of changes in U.S. targeting policy. Changes in the SIOP did occur, but not necessarily on the scale implied by the change in declaratory policy.[12] One observer noted that "the basic patterns of nuclear strategy it [the SIOP] embodied proved resistant to change." The SIOP remained a capabilities plan rather than an objectives plan. In spite of the change in declaratory policy, attacks on Soviet population centers remained a target of last resort.[13]

Major changes in U.S. strategic thought began to occur during the Nixon administration. And although the names given to the ideas developed here at that time changed and the concepts were refined, they continued to guide U.S. thinking through the 1980s. The first change came in U.S. declaratory policy. In 1970, the Nixon administration introduced the principle of **sufficiency**. It required strategic equality between the United States and the Soviet Union rather than simply the possession of a minimum level of retaliatory threat.[14] This was seen as providing crisis stability, so that neither side had an incentive to go first with its nuclear weapons in a crisis.

The Nixon administration also undertook a review of U.S. action policy. The impetus for change was strategic parity. The existence of a large Soviet nuclear force made it unwise to carry out a retaliatory attack on Soviet population centers because of the Soviet ability to retaliate against U.S. cities. Work on changing the SIOP began in 1974. The new Nuclear Weapons Employment Policy (NUWEP) emphasized the destruction of Soviet economic recovery assets as the primary objective of U.S. nuclear forces. It stipulated that under all circumstances the United States must be able to destroy 70 percent of the Soviet industrial capacity needed for postwar economic recovery.

Neither Carter and Reagan nor George H. W. Bush formally broke away from the concepts laid out in the Nixon years. At most, there were refinements in thinking, changes in priorities, and alterations in rhetoric. Carter's countervailing strategy called for possessing "strategic options such that at a variety of levels of exchange, aggression would either be defeated or would result in unacceptable costs that exceed gains." The major notable and controversial addition by the Reagan administration was the requirement that the United States be able to "prevail" and "force the Soviet Union to seek the earliest termination of hostilities on terms favorable to the U.S."

# POST–COLD WAR NUCLEAR THINKING

The end of the Cold War did not bring with it an end to nuclear weapons, and one of the major criticisms of current U.S. nuclear strategy is that it has failed to address the implications of U.S. nuclear primacy.[15] In particular there is concern that whereas during the Cold War nuclear weapons were seen as a stabilizing force, they may now be the source of instability.

## The U.S. Strategic Nuclear Arsenal

In 1998, the United States had more than 2,300 warheads on alert at any given time. Together, they could deliver the equivalent of 44,000 Hiroshimas or about 550 megatons of TNT. They were aimed at some 3,000 targets,

## HISTORICAL LESSON

### The Baruch Plan

As World War II came to a close, a divided Truman administration looked out to the post–World War II era. Many decisions would have to be made, not the least of which was determining what to do with the nuclear bomb. On one side of the debate was Secretary of War Henry Stimson, who argued that the United States could not for long keep a nuclear monopoly. It would only be a matter of time before the Soviet Union and other countries acquired the scientific knowledge and technological capacity to build nuclear weapons. The answer he favored was placing nuclear power under international control. Aligned against Stimson was a group led by Secretary of State James Byrnes. Distrustful of Soviet motives and fearful of its power, Byrnes argued against any sharing of nuclear secrets. From this perspective, a monopoly over nuclear weapons would be crucial to maintaining the postwar balance of power. Truman was divided on the matter, but ultimately supported Stimson's perspective.

The first international discussions about the future of nuclear power took place in Washington in September 1945 between representatives from the United States, Great Britain, and Canada, all of which had worked on various aspects of the Manhattan Project that developed the bomb. This was followed by a Foreign Ministers meeting in Moscow in December, where the United States, Great Britain, and Soviet Union agreed in principle to the create a United Nations (UN) commission to work for the peaceful use of nuclear power and advise on the destruction of existing nuclear weapons (which only the United States possessed). To help formulate a U.S. position, Stimson appointed Undersecretary of State Dean Acheson to chair a committee in January 1946 that would draft a U.S. nuclear energy policy. Acheson formed a technical advisory group to support his committee's deliberations. It was chaired by David Lilienthal, who also chaired the Tennessee Valley Authority.

The Acheson–Lilienthal Committee issued its report in March 1946. Its fundamental conclusion supported Stimson's position. International inspections of atomic energy facilities were unlikely to stop their spread and the diversion of atomic energy for military purposes. Accordingly, the best solution was to place atomic energy under the control of a new international agency, the Atomic Development Authority, and make it available in small quantities to all countries for peaceful use. In return for the United States taking this step, all other countries would agree not to develop nuclear weapons. The committee's approach was consistent with the prevailing view of the early post–World War II era that the primary obstacles to developing a bomb were not to be found in technological and scientific problems but in the access to the raw materials needed to build the bomb.

After receiving the report, Truman arranged for it to be given to Bernard Baruch, whom he had appointed to be the U.S. representative to the UN Atomic Energy Commission. Baruch proceeded to make important changes in

*(continued)*

*(continued)*

the Acheson–Lilienthal Plan, the most significant of which dealt with changing the enforcement procedures that could be wielded by the new Atomic Development Authority. Baruch eliminated the possibility that decisions by Atomic Development Authority might be vetoed by participating countries. Only then did Baruch believe that the phrase "immediate and direct enforcement" would carry any weight. Additionally, Baruch inserted language that Truman accepted. Baruch's change in wording and the Baruch Plan was presented to the UN Atomic Energy Commission on June 14, 1946. Truman's about-face appears to be tied to steadily deteriorating relations with the Soviet Union that made conflict appear far more likely than cooperation.

Baruch opened his presentation by telling the assembled delegates they faced a choice between the "quick and the dead." His plan called for giving the Atomic Energy Authority the power to inspect nuclear facilities, made it illegal to possess an atomic bomb, and allowed for the seizure of facilities. The United States would end its nuclear monopoly in stages and destroy its nuclear weapons only when the Baruch Plan was fully implemented. The Soviet Union quickly rejected the Baruch Plan, objecting to its loss of a veto and calling for the United States to end its nuclear monopoly as a precondition for participating in the plan. In December, the Baruch Plan was approved by 10–0 vote, with the Soviet Union and Poland abstaining. Since a unanimous vote of all 12 members of the UN Atomic Energy Commission was needed, the plan was defeated. The Soviet Union detonated its first nuclear device on September 23, 1949.

**Applying the Lesson**

1. Could the Baruch Plan have slowed down or stopped nuclear proliferation?
2. Some argue that Truman knew the plan would be rejected and was not serious. What do you think?
3. What would a new Baruch Plan have to look like to stop A.Q. Khan? ■

down from the 12,500 targets of the Cold War SIOPs. Since then, the size of the nuclear arsenal has continued to drop.

In January 2009, the U.S. nuclear inventory contained approximately 5,200 nuclear warheads. Over half, some 2,700, were operational warheads, while the remainder, about 2,500, were defined as reserves. In addition to these 5,200 nuclear warheads, the United States had some 4,200 nuclear warheads waiting to be dismantled. 550 of the deployed warheads are on ICBMs, 1,152 are on submarines and 500 are on bombers.

The reduced size of the U.S. nuclear arsenal has not ended debate over its proper size or makeup. Former Deputy Secretary of Defense and Director of the CIA John Deutch has called for deploying less than 1,000 warheads.[16] Two others with extensive government service call for a nuclear arsenal of 500 operationally deployed warheads plus 500 more in reserve.[17] Both of these figures are far below the limit of 1,700–2,200 warheads that the

United States and Russia have pledged to reach by 2012 under the terms of the Strategic Offensive Reductions Treaty (also known as the Moscow Treaty), which was agreed to in 2002.

Two aspects of how this force is configured have drawn special attention; both relate to nuclear warheads. The first centers on the condition of the warheads. It was first raised by scientists in the late 1970s. At issue is the readiness and reliability of U.S. nuclear warheads, each of which contains thousands of parts. Of particular concern are warheads designed in the 1950s and early 1960s. The deterioration of warheads was not an issue during the Cold War because the United States was regularly modernizing its nuclear arsenal and introducing new generations of warheads. In 2005, Congress began funding the Reliable Replacement Warhead program.

Supporters of the program cite safety problems of having old warheads in storage and the potential for reducing the size of the U.S. nuclear arsenal by replacing existing warheads with smaller numbers of more reliable ones. Critics question whether the program isn't much more than "make work," that the problem is overstated, and whether the risks of accidents in conducting the program are worth the cause. Of particular concern is the question of whether the new warheads need to be tested. The United States imposed a moratorium on nuclear testing in 1992. Congress effectively halted work on this program in 2008, but studies continue, and Secretary of Defense Robert Gates supports it.

The second issue centers on the size and purpose of the warheads. At issue here is the concept of "bunker busters," officially known as Robust Nuclear Earth Penetrators. If they are developed, they would be the first new nuclear weapons designed to implement the George W. Bush administration's new nuclear policy, which stresses preemption rather than deterrence. Bunker buster warheads are small in size, under five kilotons. The need for such weapons is seen as a result of the emergence of rogue states that cannot be deterred and the estimated presence of over 10,000 hard and deeply buried targets worldwide. Questions surround virtually all aspects of the proposed program, including its cost, the need for such a weapon because conventional capabilities already exist for this purpose, the ability to limit fallout and destruction from its use, the procedure for obtaining presidential authority to actually use such a weapon in combat, and the danger of eliminating the long-standing psychological firewall that has existed between nuclear and nonnuclear weapons. At present, work on bunker busters remains in the study stage. At the Bush administration's request, Congress dropped a ban on testing sub–five-kiloton warheads in the fiscal year (FY) 2004 budget to facilitate such preliminary research.

## U.S. Nuclear Strategy

U.S. nuclear thinking continues to bear the imprint of Cold War thinking, with strategic revisions largely being made at the margins. The first presidential statement of U.S. post–Cold War policy came with Bill Clinton's 1997 Presidential Decision Directive 60. According to PDD-60, the U.S. military should no longer prepare to win a protracted nuclear war, as was required by

PDD-13. The military aim of the nuclear arsenal was defined as one of deterring the use of nuclear weapons against the United States and its allies. PDD-60 continued to call for the existence of a wide range of nuclear strike options against Russian nuclear forces and against its civilian and military leadership. It also contained a requirement to plan for nuclear strikes against states that have "prospective access" to nuclear weapons or that may become hostile to the United States.

The George W. Bush administration's Nuclear Posture Review (NPR) of 2002 reaffirmed that nuclear weapons play a fundamental role in U.S. force projection capabilities. His major changes were to operate on the basis of capabilities-based targeting instead of threat-based targeting, as was practiced during the Cold War, and to replace the SIOP with two new war plan documents, OPLAN (Operations Plan) and CONPLAN (Contingency Plan). The goal was to add flexibility to U.S. nuclear strategy by constructing a wider range of scenarios in which nuclear weapons might be employed. In February 2008, it was revealed that OPLAN 8010 contained nuclear strike options against combat forces and options to use support equipment against six potential enemies. They were identified as Russia, China, North Korea, Iran, Iraq, and Syria.

# BRIDGING THE NUCLEAR–CONVENTIONAL DIVIDE

Careful thinking about nuclear weapons is especially important in two of the most controversial areas of contemporary U.S. military strategy: the rejection of deterrence and the embrace of preemption. Neither deterrence nor preemption is exclusively a nuclear or conventional military option. They serve as an uneasy bridge between the two.

## Deterrence

A deterrence policy seeks to prevent something unwanted from happening. At its most basic level, the United States is concerned with deterring attacks both on its own homeland and on its allies. The former is known as *direct deterrence* and the latter as *extended deterrence*. Up until the terrorist attacks of 9/11, it was taken for granted that direct deterrence was more easily achieved than was extended deterrence. Now both are suspect. Deterrence succeeds by threatening a would-be aggressor with an unacceptable level of damage should it engage in the unwanted behavior. It requires possessing a sufficient military power to inflict such damage, the resolve to act in the threatened manner, and the ability to communicate this policy to the enemy.

Two different strategies have been used in the past to try and prevent a deterrence failure. The first is to set up "trip wires." These were, figuratively speaking, lines in the sand that, if crossed, would provoke an immediate American military response. In concrete terms, the trip wires took the form of American troops stationed in Germany and South Korea, who would be in the way of any enemy attack. During the Cold War, the presence of American troops abroad was seen as a sign of strength and resolve. Today, the situation is different. Along with the large number of civilian contractors who now serve with them, they have become targets of opportunity for terrorists and insurgents.

A second strategy was to leave the door open to a nuclear response should deterrence fail. By threatening to take a crisis to the brink of nuclear war, it was assumed that the enemy would abandon its unwanted line of action. Reportedly President Eisenhower threatened the nuclear weapons against China if it did not help bring about an end to the Korean War. Raising the stakes this way may succeed because in the view of some deterrence works like an auction.[18] How much the winning bidder ultimately has to pay is determined by how high the second-highest bidder is willing to go. The more resolute the second-highest bidder, the more dangerous the crisis becomes and the more expensive deterrence (and deterrence failure) becomes.

We can begin to understand the problems faced in constructing a successful deterrence strategy even better if we look at how deterrence has failed in the past.[19] Two primary failure patterns exist. In one, deterrence fails through a *fait accompli*. Hostile policy makers detect no U.S. commitment and feel that they can control their risks in challenging the United States. The 1950 North Korean attack on South Korea is an example of this type of deterrence failure. The attack was not irrational because no clear U.S. commitment existed and the risks appeared to be controllable. Public statements by leading U.S. diplomats (Secretary of State Dean Acheson) and military figures (the Joint Chiefs of Staff) had placed South Korea outside of the U.S. "defense perimeter" and referred to it as a "liability" in the event of war in the Far East. Reinserting U.S. forces into Korea was not expected to be an easy task, so the most likely response to an attack would be diplomatic protest or a minimal military action.

Deterrence can also fail as a result of a limited probe, where the challenging action is easily reversed or expanded depending on the nature of the U.S. response. In these cases the U.S. commitment is unclear, and the risks still seem to be controllable. The Berlin Wall crisis of 1961 illustrates how deterrence can fail through a limited probe. A succession of Berlin crises in 1948, 1958, and earlier in 1961 had demonstrated the existence of a U.S. commitment to Berlin. Yet they had also demonstrated a U.S. desire to avoid a direct military confrontation and had brought home the military reality that East Berlin was over 100 miles into communist territory, making Western military operations difficult but not impossible. From the perspective of the East German leadership, the situation in Berlin had become intolerable. Averages of over 1,000 people were fleeing to West Berlin each day. Included among them were many professionals, whose skills would be needed to build up the East German economy. The Soviet Union and East Germany moved at midnight on May 12 to close the border by constructing a barbed-wire wall on East Berlin territory. Only when the minimal nature of the U.S. response was clear (the Western powers did not make a protest for four days) did they move to construct a more substantial and permanent wall with only a few well-guarded openings.

Problems such as these led the George W. Bush administration to move away from deterrence to **preemption.** Deterrence is not without its defenders. As one observer put it, if deterrence worked against Joseph Stalin, who we knew was determined to get nuclear weapons, why did we think it could not work against Saddam Hussein?[20] Others suggest that the problem is not with deterrence per se but with how the Bush administration is implementing it. Deterrence, these analysts argue, has two dimensions. It contains both a threat, "Cross this line and we will attack," and a promise, "If you do not cross this line, we will not harm you." The Bush administration, with its stress on regime change as a means of dealing with hostile states, has pursued only the first part of the deterrence equation.

## Preemption

Preemption is striking first in self-defense when the threat is imminent. When the threat is not imminent but still held to be real, striking first in self-defense is referred to as a *preventive strike.* Technically speaking, the George W. Bush administration had ignored this long-standing distinction in putting forward its policy of preemption and combining both scenarios under one heading. Bush introduced preemption as a replacement for deterrence in a speech at West Point in June 2002, and it has become the core concept of what is popularly known as the Bush Doctrine. Preemption is not a new strategy by any means. Historical examples go back at least to the Punic War, which was fought in 264–147 B.C. It is also a strategy that the United States has employed in the past. Most recently, Ronald Reagan justified the invasion of Grenada in 1983 as a preemptive move. Lyndon Johnson acted in a similar manner, sending troops to the Dominican Republic in 1965. In the more distant past, one could classify Woodrow Wilson's decision to send troops to Mexico in 1914 as consistent with the logic of preemption.

The Iraq War represents the first attempt by the Bush administration to implement a policy of preemption. Particular attention has been directed at the "shock and awe" strategy used in its opening stage and more generally at the ability of the military to carry it out, given the difficulties encountered in the occupation. During the Cold War, the end-strength number of U.S. active-duty military personnel never fell below 2.0 million. It reached its high point of some 3.5 million during Korea and Vietnam. It has now dropped to 1.4 million. According to its originators, "shock and awe" is designed to achieve rapid dominance of the battlefield and avoid the attrition type of military campaigns that occurred in the past. The expectation was that by rapidly overcoming the enemy's ability and will to fight, the enemy would become immobilized and reconstruction would be less expensive. They maintain that Operation Iraqi Freedom was not a test case for "shock and awe." Because of an inability to control the environment in Iraq and less-than-perfect knowledge of the enemy, it was reduced to a slogan. They cite a conflict with China as a potential case in which it might be better applied.[21]

If the logic of striking first in self-defense is accepted, a series of questions remain to be addressed.[22] First, should nuclear weapons be used? Dating back to the Carter administration, it has been U.S. policy not to be the first state to use nuclear weapons in a conflict. George H. W. Bush went so far as to refer to them as weapons of last resort. Some assert that today only the specter of a nuclear attack on the homelands of America's enemies can deter them from pursuing aggressive foreign policies. Second, should the United States act unilaterally in making the determination that a preemptive strike is necessary? Military effectiveness points to unilateral action, while political legitimacy suggests a multilateral and collaborative decision-making process. Third, is preemption feasible? It demands high-quality and timely intelligence, as well as precise weapons. Finally, can the United States embrace a policy of unilateral preemption but deny it to others?

## USING CONVENTIONAL MILITARY FORCE

Conventional military power can be used for many purposes. In this section we examine the large-scale use of conventional military power for fighting wars. In the next chapter we return to its use in the context of peacekeeping operations and as a stability force.

War fighting has always been the ultimate measure of a state's military power. For much of the post–World War II period American military policy was cast in terms of a two-war capability, meaning that the United States needed the ability to fight two wars at the same time. This has not always been the case. Under Nixon the standard was 1.5 wars. Under Reagan it was 3.5 wars. With the Cold War over in 1996, Congress passed legislation requiring that the Defense Department conduct a thorough review of defense needs every four years. The first Quadrennial Defense Review (QDR) was issued in 1997. The 2006 review put forward a 1-4-2-1 war-fighting requirement. U.S. forces need to be able to simultaneously defend the U.S. homeland, deter aggression in four key areas, stop aggression in two overlapping areas of major conflict, and have the reserve capability to achieve a decisive victory in one of them.

Anticipating where U.S. forces might engage in traditional war-fighting missions has proven to be a challenge for U.S. planners. The 1994–1995 Defense Planning Guidance Document identified seven potential situations where the United States might need to use its conventional military capability. Not surprisingly, all of them placed the United States in a reactive mode, responding to the aggression of others (Russia, Iraq, and North Korea), a domestic coup (Panama, Philippines), or the emergence of an unnamed potentially threatening superpower. None had the United States acting in a preemptory fashion as was the case with the Iraq War. Table 12.2 lists the paths to war identified in the Pentagon's 1994–1999 Defense Guidance Document

Regardless of the military context, two fundamental political conditions frame the large-scale use of conventional forces. The first of these is the domestic political conditions under which conventional military power should be used. This debate has largely been over two different perspectives. During much of the Reagan administration, advocates of both perspectives

## TABLE 12.2

POTENTIAL PATHS TO WAR

| Path to War | Comment |
| --- | --- |
| Russia invades Lithuania | An expansionist and authoritarian government assumes power in Russia. Parts of Poland are also seized. NATO forces win in 89 days of combat. |
| Iraq invades Kuwait | UN sanctions have slackened. Oil revenues are up, and Russia has provided aircraft. U.S.-led coalition wins in 54 days of combat. |
| North Korea attacks South Korea | North Korea launches surprise attack during peace initiative. It possesses nuclear weapons. United States and South Korea win after 91 days of combat. |
| Iraq and North Korea invade at the same time | While the United States is engaged with Iraq, North Korea attacks South Korea. The United States tries to fight one war at a time. The U.S.-led coalition defeats Iraq in seventy days of combat. Another 157 days are required to defeat North Korea. |
| Coup in Panama | Right-wing police alliance with Panama's military and narcoterrorists from Colombia stage a coup. United States wins in eight days. |
| Coup in Philippines | Opposing sides include the police and military against the New People's Army. United States wins in seven days. |
| Reemergence of a hostile superpower | "A Resurgent/Emergent Global Threat" arises that is authoritarian and strongly antidemocratic and is capable of threatening U.S. interests worldwide. No outcome is presented for a global war. |

*Source:* Data from *The Washington Post*, February 20, 1992, p. A1.

were represented in the Cabinet. Secretary of Defense Caspar Weinberger argued that U.S. forces should only be engaged under strictly defined circumstances that included the presence of clearly defined goals, widespread public support, and the clear intention of winning. Secretary of State George Shultz argued for a more permissive set of operating conditions. He stated that the United States must be prepared to act "even without the assurance of victory or total public support."

The second framing political consideration is the extent to which the United States can or should act alone. As we noted in our discussion of the American national style, a preference for unilateralism runs deep in American political and strategic thought. Yet this is not always possible. When the United States chooses not to act alone, it carries out military operations as part of an alliance or coalition. The difference is that coalitions are informal agreements for immediate common action, whereas alliances are more formal agreements and have a longer sense of common purpose. Controversy surrounds both of these options for multilateral action because of the conflicting imperatives of unity of command, speed, and efficiency in military operations, and the often time-consuming need for consensus-driven political consultation.

The most notable American alliance is the North Atlantic Treaty Organization (NATO). It was long a bulwark against communist expansion into Western Europe; with the end of the Cold War, it expanded to take in many of the states of Eastern Europe. In the process, NATO has become an alliance in search of a mission. Its political and military performance in the Balkans crisis left many wondering if it could adapt to a peacekeeping role. NATO was further marginalized in the Iraq War, when France and Germany took the lead in opposing the U.S. calls for action at the UN. The United States turned back to NATO in 2003 when it took over command of the International Security Assistance Force in Afghanistan. This marked the first time that NATO's mission was outside the Euro-Atlantic area.

Prior to Afghanistan we have already seen two major uses of conventional military power in the Middle East. The first came with the 1990 Persian Gulf War when the United States led a UN-sanctioned war against Iraq. Its August 1990 invasion of Kuwait led to the insertion of U.S. ground forces into Saudi Arabia in order to protect its oil fields as part of Operation Desert Shield. It was followed on January 17, 1991, with a massive air campaign that in turn led to offensive military actions under the heading of Operation Desert Storm. Iraqi resistance was ineffective and after 100 hours of the ground campaign, President George H.W. Bush declared a cease-fire. On April 6, 1991, he announced that Kuwait had been liberated.

The second major use of conventional force came in 2003 when the United States put together another coalition, the Coalition of the Willing, to defeat Saddam Hussein. Comprised almost exclusively of U.S. and British combat forces, this coalition army initially engaged in warfare for 21 days. After that it found itself engaged in a protracted unconventional fight against insurgent forces. The invasion began on March 20, 2003, following a short intense period of bombing designed to "shock and awe" the Iraqi military and civilian leadership into surrender. Operation Iraqi Liberation (later known as Operation Iraqi Freedom) encountered little sustained resistance, and Baghdad fell on April 9. Standard accounts terminate the conventional stage of the Iraq War on or about April 30. An estimated 7,300 Iraqi combatants and civilians were killed during this phase, as were about 179 U.S. and British military personnel.

# REDUCING THE DANGER OF WAR: ARMS CONTROL AND DISARMAMENT

In the earliest years of the Cold War, two general strategies, **arms control** and **disarmament,** were pursued to lessen the likelihood of nuclear war. More recently, a third strategy, defense, has also been pursued. We examine each of these now as ways of controlling or preventing big wars.

## The Cold War Record

Arms control seeks to place restraints on the use of weapons, whereas disarmament has as its ultimate goal the systematic elimination of weapons. For the most part, disarmament tended to be pursued at the level of declaratory policy. Arms control efforts were pursued both bilaterally between the United States and Soviet Union and through global agreements. They were also carried out through a variety of means. Arms control did not always take the form of formal agreements or treaties. More flexible and informal "traffic rules" agreements such as an agreement to give advance notification of a test or military exercise to reduce the possibility that these actions might be incorrectly interpreted and spiral into a military conflict. The rationale for pursuing such traffic rule agreements was that a treaty in and of itself did not produce arms control. Arms control was a product of mutual restraint that could be arrived at without explicit negotiations or formal treaties. These multiple paths to arms control continue today, as does the tendency for disarmament to remain at the declaratory level.

From 1946 to 1957, disarmament proposals dominated the international negotiating agenda. Little of significance was achieved, and nuclear diplomacy was not a high-priority item. Primary attention was given to the production of nuclear weapons and the formation of nuclear strategy. As a consequence, proposals were put forward more with an eye to their propaganda and image-creating potential than to their substantive merits. The first nuclear disarmament proposal to command global attention was the Baruch Plan. Presented by the United States at the UN in 1946, it sought to place all aspects of nuclear energy production and use under international control. The Soviet Union rejected it.

Proposals for lessening the danger of nuclear war were not forthcoming again until the Eisenhower administration. Its first proposal was the 1953 Atoms for Peace Plan. This was followed in 1957 by the Open Skies Proposal. The Atoms for Peace Plan was a disarmament plan only in an indirect sense. It sought to get states to cooperate on the peaceful development and use of atomic power. Eisenhower's proposal led to the creation of the International Atomic Energy Agency, but it did not produce movement in the direction of disarmament. The proposed Open Skies Treaty focused on reducing the fear of surprise attack by exchanging blueprints of military installations and allowing each side to carry out aerial surveillance of each other's territory. It too failed to serve as a first step toward disarmament. Rather than accepting the plan as a way of sidestepping the question of on-site inspection, the Soviet Union interpreted it as a device for legitimizing U.S. spying.

The Cuban missile crisis added an element of urgency and importance to arms control negotiations that until then had been lacking. The first major breakthrough came in 1963 with the signing of the Limited Test Ban Treaty, which outlawed nuclear explosions (testing) in the atmosphere, under water, and in outer space. A second milestone was reached in 1968 with the signing of the Nonproliferation Treaty (NPT). Up until then the primary **proliferation** concern shared by the United States and the Soviet Union was in stopping the spread of nuclear weapons in Europe, especially to West Germany. With the NPT, attention shifted to the Third World. The NPT represented an agreement between nuclear and nonnuclear states. Those states that had nuclear weapons promised not to provide them to nonnuclear states and to negotiate in good faith among themselves to reduce their nuclear stockpiles. They also pledged to help nonnuclear states develop nuclear energy for peaceful purposes. In return, the nonnuclear states agreed not to try to obtain nuclear weapons.

In addition to spurring interest in multilateral arms control treaties, the Cuban missile crisis also nudged the United States and Soviet Union toward bilateral arms control efforts. The first major product was the hotline, which linked the White House and the Kremlin. During the crisis it had taken almost 12 hours for a key communication from Soviet leader Nikita Khrushchev to reach President John Kennedy and be decoded. Often described as being a telephone, the hotline was actually a telegraph link. This was deliberate and intended to prevent policy makers from trying to read each other's intentions by evaluating their emotions and voice patterns during a phone call. The hotline was first used in 1967 during the Arab–Israeli war when the Americans and Soviets each informed the other of the movement of their navies.

The negotiation of a formal arms control treaty between the United States and Soviet Union had to wait until their nuclear inventories had grown to the point where each side felt comfortable with the balance of power that existed between them. The breakthrough agreements came with 1972 Antiballistic Missile (ABM) Treaty and the SALT I agreement. The ABM Treaty, which was of unlimited duration and was modified by a 1975 agreement, limited each side to one ABM deployment area, either around its national capital or an ICBM field. It also prohibited the development, testing, or deployment of ABM components, or the development of ABM components on exotic physical principles that would be capable of substituting for ABM launchers. The SALT I agreement on offensive forces expired in 1977. Among its key provisions were limits on the number of fixed launchers for ICBMs (1,054 for the United States and 1,608 for the Soviet Union) and numerical limits for SLBMs (656 for the United States and 740 for the Soviet Union).

The shared expectation was that SALT I would lead to SALT II. A first step toward the SALT II agreement was reached in November 1974 with the signing of the Vladivostok Accords, which set ceilings on the total numbers of strategic launchers that each side could possess (2,400) and the number of vehicles that could carry multiple independently targeted warheads (1,320). Building on the Vladivostok Accords, the SALT II agreement was to have been completed in the summer of 1973. This deadline was not met due to the arrival in Washington of a new administration led by Jimmy Carter and the emergence of two contentious issues: the U.S. cruise missile and the Soviet Union's Backfire bomber. As it finally emerged, SALT II was a complicated, multilayered document to which the U.S. Senate has never given its consent and that has now technically expired.

In his campaign for the presidency, Ronald Reagan attacked the SALT II Treaty as being fatally flawed, because it placed the Soviet Union in a position of military advantage. Accordingly, the first priority of his administration was not arms control but arms modernization and expansion. Only after restoring the nuclear balance and showing evidence of a willingness to match Soviet military advances could a meaningful arms control agreement be reached.

Reagan's first concrete arms control proposal was directed at the problem of intermediate-range nuclear weapons in Europe. These weapons had become NATO's main defense against the conventional military advantage held by Warsaw Pact troops. By the late 1970s their military value was seriously challenged by the Soviet Union's introduction of the mobile SS-20 missiles. After much debate, NATO agreed on a two-track response. It would modernize and expand its missiles while at the same calling for talks to limit the number of nuclear weapons in Europe. In November 1981, Reagan presented his solution to this problem. His "zero option" called on the Soviet Union to eliminate its existing intermediate-range ballistic missiles targeted at Europe in return for a U.S. pledge not to deploy a new generation of missiles there. The idea of a zero option was quickly rejected by the Soviet Union. The resulting deadlock was broken in dramatic fashion when, in September 1987, the United States and the Soviet Union agreed in principle to an agreement covering intermediate-range nuclear forces (INF). These are weapons with a range between 300 miles and 3,400 miles. Under terms of the proposed agreement, the United States and Soviet Union would dismantle more than 1,000 weapons.

In the same speech in which he unveiled his zero option, Reagan indicated that his administration was preparing proposals for a new round of strategic arms talks to be known as Strategic Arms Reduction Talks (START). Little visible movement was forthcoming, and public concern began to mount over the administration's commitment to arms control and its loose language about nuclear war. The nuclear freeze movement became a focal point for efforts to push the administration back to the arms control negotiating table.[23]

To blunt this criticism and regain the political initiative on arms control, the Reagan administration presented a two-step START proposal in May 1982. The Soviet Union found the START proposal unacceptable, but it did not reject it out of hand. In 1983, Reagan put forward a new approach that the Soviet Union also rejected, characterizing it as "old poison in new bottles." Still, negotiations continued, and a basic START framework was agreed upon by the time Reagan left office. The agreement was signed by President George H.W. Bush and Mikhail Gorbachev in July 1991.

## The Post–Cold War Record

The ascension into power of Mikhail Gorbachev, the subsequent collapse of communism, and the end of the Cold War changed the dynamics of U.S.–Soviet arms control. Rather than engaging in a new round of protracted negotiations to further reduce the size of their nuclear arsenals as had been the norm during the Cold War, the United States and the Soviet Union entered into a series of unilateral cuts. For example, in September 1991, Bush ordered that (1) all tactical nuclear weapons, except those dropped from planes, be removed from the U.S. arsenal; (2) all nuclear cruise missiles and bombs be taken off naval ships, attack submarines, and land-based naval aircrafts; (3) all strategic bombers be taken off high-alert status; and (4) development and deployment of mobile ICBMs be halted. Gorbachev responded by calling for the elimination of all land-based tactical nuclear weapons and the removal of all nuclear arms from ships, submarines, and land-based naval aircrafts.

The failed August 1991 coup against Gorbachev also raised concerns in the United States that should the Soviet Union disintegrate, the government and military's ability to exert command and control over the immense Soviet nuclear arsenal would also disappear with potentially catastrophic proliferation consequences. To try and minimize the dangers inherent in thousands of "loose nukes," in November of that year Congress passed the Cooperative Threat Reduction Program, better known as the Nunn–Lugar Program, to help the Soviet leadership secure and dismantle its nuclear stockpile. With the passage of time, the focus has extended to all weapons of mass destruction and the United States now works with Ukraine, Georgia, Kazakhstan, and other countries that were once members of the Soviet Union. As of mid-2009, the Nunn–Lugar Program had deactivated and destroyed over 6,300 nuclear warheads and 530 ICBMs, 35 percent of Russian chemical weapons and four biological weapons sites were placed under heightened security controls.

The United States and Russia returned to formal arms control agreements in January 1993 with the signing of START II. Before Bill Clinton's administration could move to bring the START II treaty to the Senate for its approval, it first had to deal with problems surrounding the ratification of START I. The problem was the breakup of the Soviet Union. Its dissolution had left four nuclear states in its wake: Russia, Ukraine, Belarus, and Kazakhstan. These states expressed misgivings about giving up their nuclear weapons and sought compensation from the West in terms of security guarantees and foreign aid as a precondition for doing so. The last holdout was Ukraine, which did not formally give its approval to the START I treaty and the NPT until November 1994. In December 2001, the United States and Russia announced that the reduction targets set by START I had been met.

START II never came into force, although it was ratified in 1996. Domestic and foreign policy issues in both countries led to the treaty languishing in limbo. Russia delayed final approval as a sign of its disapproval of U.S. military action in the Balkans. In the United States, attention shifted to the politically charged question of whether it should withdraw from the ABM Treaty so that a national missile defense system could be created. Defenders of the ABM treaty saw it as one of the cornerstones of the Cold War arms control regime and of great symbolic value as a statement of U.S. foreign policy goals and priorities. President George W. Bush moved decisively on this latter question in December 2001 when he gave the required six-month notice that the United States was withdrawing from the ABM Treaty.

Russian President Vladimir Putin called the decision to withdraw from the ABM agreement a "mistake," but it did not stop him from signing a new arms control agreement with the United States in May 2002. The Strategic Offensive Reductions Treaty (SORT), also known as the Treaty of Moscow, overtakes the never-negotiated START III treaty. SORT breaks new ground in treaty language. It starts from the premise that Russia is a friend of the United States and not an enemy. The body contains only 10 sentences. It lacks the appendices, caveats, statements of understanding, and covenants found in earlier arms control agreements. In essence, the treaty permits each side to do as it pleases so long as its nuclear arsenal is reduced to 2,200 deployed warheads by December 31, 2012. As one U.S. senator observed, "there are no mileposts for performance. There is nothing really to verify except good faith."

The agreement was negotiated in six months, but it was not without controversy. Putin wanted a treaty that would reduce the number of missiles, long-range bombers, and submarines, because Russia could not afford to maintain its nuclear arsenal at its current size. Putin also sought to insert language that promised an American missile defense system would not be directed at Russia. The Bush administration wanted to restrict deployed warheads. The president had promised to cut the size of the U.S. nuclear weapons arsenal in his presidential campaign and sought the agreement as a means of fulfilling this promise. One particularly troubling issue involved how much notice would have to be given if one side wanted to withdraw from the treaty. The United States wanted only 45 days if the 2,200-warhead limit was going to be exceeded. Russia felt this was too little warning. In the end, a three-month warning period for withdrawal from the treaty was set. SORT is set to expire on December 21, 2012.

START I expired in December 2009. President Obama and Russian President Dmitry Medvedev announced at a July 2009 summit meeting that they had agreed upon the outlines of a new agreement that would continue the verification arrangements of START I as well as reduce the number of deployed nuclear warheads down from the permitted ceiling of 2,200 to 1,500–1,675. Agreement was not reached on reducing the number of delivery vehicles each side could maintain. Russia called for far deeper cuts than were politically acceptable to the United States. The Russians sought deep cuts fearing that the United States could quickly rebuild the U.S. arsenal or be outfitted with large precision conventional weapons and threaten it. The two sides also agreed to explore options for cooperating on missile defense, something Russia had originally refused to consider so long as plans for an anti-Iran system based in Poland and the Czech Republic went ahead as scheduled.

## DEFENSE

According to one observer, "The great missing innovation in the nuclear age is the development of means to defend against nuclear attack."[24] If this capacity is lacking, it is impossible to protect one's population and territory without the cooperation of the enemy. Both parties must agree not to attack population centers. Strategists have established that such tacit cooperation between enemies is possible and often takes place during war.[25] Still, many are troubled that the defense of the United States in the nuclear age is possible only with the cooperation of an adversary. Reagan gave voice to these concerns in a March 1983 speech, when he called on the scientific community to find a way for the United States to escape from this situation.

> What if free people could live secure in the knowledge that their security did not rest upon the threat of instant U.S. retaliation to deter a Soviet attack; that we could intercept and destroy their strategic missiles before they reached our soil or that of our allies? . . . Is it not worth every investment necessary to free the world from the threat of nuclear war?[26]

## THE STRATEGIC DEFENSE INITIATIVE

Reagan' solution to this dilemma was the Strategic Defense Initiative (SDI). He defined it as a long-term research and development program designed to identify viable policy options for creating a nuclear defense system. The decisions as to which system, if any, to pursue were scheduled to be made in the 1990s. However, in early 1987, the Reagan administration began examining the possibility of an early deployment of SDI. As envisioned by most observers, Reagan's SDI system involved a series of defensive systems layered together in such a way as to create a protective shield. Each layer in this system was to perform the same tasks: It would search out and detect targets, track them, discriminate between real targets and dummy targets, and intercept and destroy the real targets. The layers in the SDI system would correspond roughly to the four major phases in the trajectory of an ICBM.[27]

During the Reagan administration, the scope and funding of a "Star Wars" system was progressively cut back, although the goal was never formally abandoned. In 1989, Secretary of Defense Dick Cheney declared that SDI had been "oversold" as a leakproof umbrella (a possibility he described as "extremely remote"). Still, the George H. W. Bush administration continued to seek funding for it under the guise of "brilliant pebbles." Under it, missiles sent into space would be sent into layered orbits and would possess the ability to detect the launch of enemy missiles at a distance of several thousand miles. Upon receiving orders to attack, the missiles would speed toward the enemy missiles and ram them at high speed, thereby destroying them.

SDI's short-lived existence formally came to an end during the administration of Bill Clinton. In May 1993, Secretary of Defense Les Aspin announced that the SDI Office was being closed. It would be replaced by a Ballistic Missile Defense Office, whose mission would be to develop follow-on missiles to the Patriot system used against SCUD missiles in the Persian Gulf War. Instead of constructing a nuclear shield over the United States, the new goal would be to prevent attacks by short-range ground-launched missiles.

## NATIONAL MISSILE DEFENSE SYSTEMS

The death of SDI in the Clinton administration did not mark the end of efforts to establish a national ballistic missile defense system.[28] In one of its few foreign policy statements, the Republican Party's "Contract with America" called for building a national missile defense system by 2003. Clinton not only vetoed the legislation passed in 1995 that would have set this in motion but also proposed an alternative. The "3 + 3" program called for three years of research and development followed by a decision in 2000 on whether or not to go ahead with implementation in 2003. Surprise missile tests by Iran and North Korea in 1998 provided additional political backing for creating such a system, and in 1999, large majorities in both houses passed a bill asserting that the United States should deploy a national missile defense system as soon as it was "technologically feasible." The new target date became 2005.

Clinton's plan relied heavily on ground-based interceptors that would be supported by a network of ground-based radars and space-based infrared sensors. Planning suggested that the first deployment of this system would be in Alaska, where 20 high-speed interceptors capable of shooting down a limited number of incoming warheads would be deployed. This number was expected to expand to as many as 100 interceptors in the first phase and 250 in the second. High-resolution radar installations would be placed in the Aleutian Islands. Support would also come from upgraded early-warning radar stations in Greenland, Great Britain, and the United States.

Clinton's plan for a national missile defense system was thus a significant departure from SDI, which had relied much more heavily on satellite-based weapons systems. The change in technological focus did not lessen the challenges involved in creating an integrated command and control system that would culminate in a missile hitting a missile. The Pentagon scheduled 19 tests to determine the technical feasibility of the proposed system. By contrast, 165 fight tests were conducted of the Safeguard missile system, 125 tests of the Polaris submarine, and 101 tests of the Minuteman missile. The first test of the system in October 1999 was successful despite the failure of the tracking system, but the second test in January 2000 and a third in July 2000 failed. Clinton then announced that he would leave the decision of whether to build a national missile defense system to his successor.

As we noted above, President George W. Bush removed the major diplomatic and legal roadblock to the development of such a system by announcing in December 2001 that the United States was withdrawing from the 1972 ABM Treaty. In December of the following year he signed National Security Presidential Directive (NSPD) 23, which ordered the initial deployment of a set of long-range missile interceptors in Alaska and California by September 2004. The move was billed as part of an evolutionary approach to the development of a missile defense system that would never produce a final fixed system.

The Bush system encountered the same types of technological problems that hindered the development of earlier missile defense systems. A General Accounting Office study released in 2004 concluded that many aspects of the system had yet to be tested. Specific problems identified included the ability to discriminate between decoys and real warheads, the ability to launch multiple interceptors, and the system's ability to perform at night and under adverse weather conditions. Unsuccessful tests were carried out in 2004 and 2005 before a success was realized in September 2006, but even this test did not erase all doubts. The missile interceptor did not have to distinguish between similar-looking decoys or deal with countermeasures. One of the biggest concerns was the repeated failure of the booster to launch the interceptor missile. Problems with the booster had led to a two-year gap in testing and the failure to have an operational missile defense system in place in 2004.

The benefits of a national ballistic missile system continue to be debated.[29] Two issues dominate the discussion. The first is the wisdom of constructing a sufficiently robust system that could potentially negate a Russian or Chinese nuclear capability. Many fear that, should this be the case, it would force these two states to undertake large-scale expansion of their nuclear programs in order to deter the United States from acting unilaterally against them. One study using documents recently declassified reveals that this is how the United States responded in 1968 to the development of a Soviet ABM system. All components of the Soviet system became high-priority nuclear targets, and the goal was to overwhelm it. The second debate is about the value of a more limited system that would be directed at protecting the United States from rogue states with smaller nuclear arsenals. Whereas some see it as a prudent investment in an age of terrorism, others prefer to rely on diplomacy and conventional forces to protect the United States, especially given the types of technological issues that have arisen.

## European Defense Shield

Another dimension to the conflict over the value of a missile defensive system surfaced in 2007, after the Bush administration began talks with Poland and the Czech Republic about allowing the construction of antimissile facilities in those countries to protect Europe from Iranian missiles. Russia responded angrily, claiming that such a move threatened its security, and followed up with three countermoves. First, it announced that it was suspending its obligations under the Conventional Forces in Europe Treaty. Second, Russia tested a new intercontinental missile. It then surprised the Bush administration with an offer to jointly build an ABM system in Azerbaijan, where Russia leases a radar station. Such a project would require an unprecedented level of cooperation between the United States and Russia, making the realization of this undertaking highly unlikely.

In 2008 Bush signed agreements with Poland and the Czech Republic to build this limited missile defense system. Russia responded with threatening words directed at Poland. One of Obama's first foreign policy initiatives was to terminate this project replacing it with one that focuses on Iran's shorter range missiles and begins by using interceptor based on ships.

## OVER THE HORIZON

The activities of Dr. A. Q. Khan plus the pursuit of nuclear weapons by North Korea and Iran raise a concern that nucler proliferation may be entering a new era. Many fear that with it will come the disappearance of the long-standing dividing line between nuclear and large-scale conventional weapons, a dividing line already has become cloudy with deterrence and preemptive strategies. Without a clearly defined **"fire wall"** separating them, the danger exists that we may see a conventional war escalate into a nuclear one.

A second issue we can expect U.S. military strategists to face in the near future is the need once again to adjust U.S. nuclear thinking. In the eyes of many analysts, no matter what is said, the debate over nuclear deterrence has become "lazy,"[30] with U.S. thinking still directed at Russia and with an eye toward realizing a first-strike capability.[31] The central strategic problem is the failure to recognize that with the emergence of Asia as the new center of military power, a "second nuclear age" that requires a fundamental adjustment of Western strategic assumptions has arrived.[32]

Similar conceptual challenges lie over the horizon in thinking about how to protect ourselves from nuclear weapons. Two very different mindsets cloud policy-maker thinking about how to prevent states from acquiring a nuclear capability.[33] Both are rooted in a form of historical amnesia. The first is excessive optimism. We have forgotten just how hard it was to keep peace in the Cold War, and for the United States and the Soviet Union to overcome their differences and negotiate meaningful arms control agreements. The second is excessive pessimism. The history of the nuclear era shows that just because a country could go nuclear, it does not mean that it will, and also that countries that did go nuclear later changed their course and dismantled their programs. A likely battleground between optimism and pessimism is the fate of the Comprehensive Test Ban Treaty that was signed in 1996, which forbids all nuclear testing regardless of its purpose. Rejected by the Senate in 1999 by a vote of 51–48, many now call for its reconsideration. The United States is one of nine states that participated in the negotiations, possesses nuclear reactors, but has not ratified the agreement. The others are China, Egypt, India, Indonesia, Iran, Israel, North Korea, and Pakistan.

## CRITICAL THINKING QUESTIONS

1. Are nuclear weapons a usable military tool? Under what conditions should their use be considered in place of conventional weapons?
2. Should we be optimistic or pessimistic over the future of arms control efforts?
3. Can arms control efforts become counterproductive?

## KEY TERMS

| | | |
|---|---|---|
| arms control   328 | fire wall   336 | preemption   324 |
| assured destruction   317 | flexible response   317 | proliferation   329 |
| deterrence   315 | massive retaliation   316 | sufficiency   318 |
| disarmament   328 | | |

# FURTHER READING

Richard Betts, (eds.), *Conflict after the Cold War*, 2nd ed. (New York: Pearson, 2005).
Sidney Drell and James Goodby, *"What Are Nuclear Weapons for?* (Washington, DC: Arms Control Association, April 2005).
Michael Krepon, "Ban the Bomb. Really." *The American Interest 3* (2008), 88–93.
Janne Nolan, Bernard Finel, and Bryan Finlay (eds.), *Ultimate Security* (New York: The Century Foundation Press, 2003).
Thomas Ricks, *Fiasco: The American Military Adventure in Iraq* (New York: Penguin, 2006).

# NOTES

1. David Alan Rosenberg, "The Origins of Overkill: Nuclear Weapons and American Strategy, 1945–1960," *International Security,* 7 (1983), 124.
2. There is an inherent upper limit to how much power can be generated by fission, but there is no upper limit for fusion.
3. The Harvard Study Group, *Living with Nuclear Weapons* (New York: Bantam, 1983), p. 79.
4. There are a number of excellent volumes dealing with the development of U.S. nuclear strategy. The major ones relied on in constructing this history are David Rosenberg, "The Origins of Overkill," International Security 7 (1983), 3–71; Jerome H. Kahan, *Security in the Nuclear Age: Developing U.S. Arms Policy* (Washington, DC: Brookings, 1975); Michael Mandelbaum, *The Nuclear Question: The United States and Nuclear Weapons, 1946–1976* (Cambridge, MA: Cambridge University Press, 1979); and Richard Smoke, *National Security and the Nuclear Dilemma: An Introduction to the American Experience* (Reading, MA: Addison-Wesley, 1984).
5. Bernard Brodie and others, *The Ultimate Weapon* (New York: Harcourt Brace, 1946).
6. Albert Wohlstetter, "The Delicate Balance of Terror," *Foreign Affairs,* 37 (1959), 211–56.
7. See Rosenberg, "The Origins of Overkill"; and Peter Pringle and William Arkin, *S.I.O.P.: The Secret U.S. Plan for Nuclear War* (New York: W. W. Norton, 1983).
8. See David Rosenberg, "A Smoking Radiating Ruin at the End of Two Hours: Documents of American Plans for Nuclear War with the Soviet Union, 1954–1955," *International Security,* 6 (1982/83), 3–38.
9. Rosenberg, "The Origins of Overkill," pp. 116–17.
10. On the ABM decisions, see Morton Halperin, *Bureaucratic Politics and Foreign Policy* (Washington, DC: Brookings, 1974).
11. Mandelbaum, *The Nuclear Question,* p. 134.
12. Rosenberg, "The Origins of Overkill," p. 178.
13. Desmond Ball, "U.S. Strategic Forces," International Security 7 (1982/1983), p. 34.
14. Warner R. Schilling, "U.S. Strategic Nuclear Concepts in the 1970s: The Search for Sufficiently Equivalent Countervailing Parity," *International Security,* 6 (1981), 59.
15. Kier A. Lieber and Daryl G. Press, "The End of MAD," *International Security,* 30 (2006), 7–44.
16. John Deutch, "A Nuclear Posture for Today," *Foreign Affairs,* 84 (2005), 49–60.
17. Sidney Drell and James Goodby, *"What Are Nuclear Weapons for?* (Washington, DC: Arms Control Association, April 2005).
18. Robert Powell, "Nuclear Deterrence Theory:" Nuclear Proliferation, and National Missile Defense," *International Security,* 27 (2003), 86–118.

19. Alexander George and Richard Smoke, *Deterrence in American Foreign Policy: Theory and Practice* (New York: Columbia University Press, 1974).
20. Morton Halperin, "Deter and Contain," *The American Prospect*, 13 (November 4, 2002), 22–25.
21. Harlan Ullman, "Slogan or Strategy," *National Interest*, 84 (2006), 43–49.
22. For a variety of critiques see the various articles in the symposium, "Is Preemption Necessary?" *Washington Quarterly*, 26 (2003), 75–145.
23. For a statement of the nuclear freeze position, see Randall Forsberg, "Call a Halt to the Arms Race—Proposal for a Mutual U.S.–Soviet Nuclear Weapons Freeze," in Burns H. Weston (ed.), *Toward Nuclear Disarmament and Global Security: A Search for Alternatives* (Boulder, CO: Westview, 1984), pp. 384–89.
24. Michael Mandelbaum, *The Nuclear Future* (Ithaca, NY: Cornell University Press, 1983), p. 43.
25. Thomas C. Schelling, *The Strategy of Conflict* (New York: Oxford University Press, 1960).
26. Reagan's speech is reprinted in P. Edward Haley, David M. Kethly, and Jack Merritt (eds.), *Nuclear Strategy, Arms Control, and the Future* (Boulder, CO: Westview, 1985), pp. 311–12.
27. For a discussion of how a BMD system would work, see Stephen Weiner, "Systems and Technology," in Ashton Carter and David N. Schwartz (eds.), *Ballistic Missile Defense* (Washington, DC: Brookings, 1984), pp. 49–89; Sidney Drell, Philip J. Farley, and David Holloway, "Preserving the ABM Treaty: A Critique of the Reagan Strategic Defense Initiative," *International Security*, 9 (1984), 67–79.
28. George Lewis, Lisbeth Gronlund, and David Wright, "National Missile Defense: An Indefensible System," *Foreign Policy*, 117 (1999/2000), 120–37.
29. Stephen Glasser and Steve Fetter, "National Missile Defense and the Future of U.S. Nuclear Weapons Policy," *International Security*, 26 (2001), 40–92; and James Lindsay and Michael O'Hanlon, *Defending America, Revised and Updated Edition* (Washington, DC: Brookings Institution, 2002).
30. Lawrence Freedman, "Does Deterrence Have a Future?" *Arms Control Today*, 30 (October 2000), 3–8.
31. Lieber and Press, "The End of MAD," *International Security*, 30 (2006), 7–44.
32. Paul Bracken. "The Second Nuclear Age," *Foreign Affairs*, 79 (2000), 146–56.
33. Scott Sagan, "How to Keep the Bomb from Iran," *Foreign Affairs*, 85 (2006), 454–59.

# Military Instruments: Small Wars

In April 2008, the chairman of the Joint Chiefs of Staff, Admiral Michael Mullen, stated that the Pentagon was planning for "potential military course of action" against Iran, action he said would be "extremely stressful" but not impossible for U.S. forces. Still, he stated that he had no expectations of conflict with Iran in the immediate future.[1] Earlier in the week, Secretary of Defense Robert Gates stated that war with Iran would be disastrous on a number of levels but that the military option must be kept on the table, given its destabilizing foreign policy and pursuit of nuclear weapons.

Neither Mullen nor Gates specified what form American military action against Iran might take. They left that to the Iranian imagination. While many remember Operation Eagle Claw, through which the Carter administration sought to rescue the 53 Americans taken hostage in Iran in November 1979 following the fall of the Shah, most do not remember that this was neither the first nor the last time that military force had been used by the United States in a "small war" context against Iran, making Mullen's comments particularly open-ended to Iranian leaders familiar with the past. In the previous chapter, we examined the use of the military instrument in big wars. In this chapter, we continue to look at the military instrument but shift our attention to small wars.

## CASUS BELLI

An obvious difference between big and small wars is the level of societal effort and political commitment that lies behind them along with the level of destruction that they entail. An additional reason is found in the language we use to talk about them. Large wars have combatants and are fought according to generally accepted (in the West) rules of law. Small wars have insurgents and often appear to be wars without rules. Just as importantly, we use different language to discuss why big and small wars happen.

In the case of large wars, we speak of **windows of opportunity**, where leaders calculate they can win; **windows of fear**, where leaders do not believe they can win but see the consequences of inaction as so dire that they feel forced to try to go to war; and accidents, where neither side wanted war but find themselves fighting one. This language also underlies our efforts to stop big wars. Deterrence is intended to convince an opponent that no window of opportunity exists. Arms control seeks to close windows of fear and reduce the potential and consequences of accidents. In all cases, it is assumed that a major threat to one's national interest is at work.

The language of small wars is different. Here, we tend to start by talking about the reasons for wars, the **casus belli**. This is not to say that they do not involve the national interest but that this phrase by itself does not convey a sense of why the war began. They often appear to be wars of choice rather than wars of necessity. In talking about small wars we tend to classify them in terms of the concrete issues that gave them life.

One major source of small wars involves access to energy supplies. Access to clean water and food supplies are also seen as potentially significant causes of small wars. Looking beyond natural resources, it is clear that ethnicity is a cause of small wars. In some cases, this takes the form of separatism, where one ethnic group seeks to leave a state and form a new state in order to better protect itself. In other cases, it takes the form of irredentism, where a state reaches out and tries to bring its kin group into the state by expanding its boundaries. In still other cases, it takes the form of genocide, as one group seeks to eliminate another ethnic group from its territory. While the end of the Cold War may have marked the end of ideological competition between the East and West, ideologies, religions, and belief systems in general continue to play important roles in small wars by structuring the way in which we see the world and determining what is acceptable and what is not. This comes through quite clearly in how different parts of the world view American hegemony and the spread of globalization.

# BRIDGING THE CONVENTIONAL–ASYMMETRIC WARFARE DIVIDE

Two forms of military action, often involving the use of large numbers of conventional forces short of engaging in traditional wars, have had a reoccurring presence on the international scene. They are humanitarian/peacekeeping operations and stability forces. They serve as a bridge for our thinking about the use of military power as we move from big wars (discussed in the last chapter) to small wars.

## Humanitarian/Peacekeeping Operations

Operation Restore Hope (Somalia), Operation Provide Comfort (Northern Iraq), Operation Restore Democracy (Haiti), and sending troops to Liberia are prominent examples of post–Cold War U.S. military interventions that at least in part can be classified as humanitarian in nature. A similar operation took place in Afghanistan after the Taliban regime was defeated by U.S. forces in 2002.

Humanitarian military operations grew out of an earlier generation of efforts referred to as **peacekeeping** operations. Carried out by neutral United Nations (UN) forces, their original purpose was to provide a way to stabilize an international or domestic conflict without involving U.S. or Soviet forces or creating a situation where either side had "lost" the conflict. In this sense, they provided a second-best solution for each side. Peacekeeping forces did not arrive until all sides to the conflict were ready to end the fighting. Over time, the scope of these efforts was expanded to include interventions undertaken outside of the UN system and under conditions where fighting continues.

Opposition to humanitarian and peacekeeping undertakings has been expressed from across the political spectrum. In part, objections are directed at the multilateral nature of these operations. Deeper issues, however, have also been raised. Neoisolationist commentators have questioned whether humanitarian interventions are really in the American national interest. Arguing that U.S. security interests were not involved in the Somalian operation, they compare it to bungee jumping: "A risky undertaking for which there is no compelling need."[2]

Advocates of military humanitarian interventions reject the argument that American interests were not at stake in Somalia, Bosnia, or Haiti. They contend that definitions of American national interest that focus only on the physical security of the United States or the health of its economy are anachronistic. Just as important as these traditional foreign policy goals is the creation of an overall international environment that is supportive of American values. Humanitarian interventions are an important aspect of such a strategy. At the same time, it is recognized that military humanitarian operations are complex endeavors that are fraught with danger. If they are to succeed, care must be taken that the mistakes made in Bosnia, Somalia, and Haiti are not repeated.

It is argued that three lessons can be learned from these experiences that will make humanitarian interventions more effective in the future.[3] First, international military interventions should be timely and robust. Second, because of serious shortcomings in the UN secretary general's command and control system, U.S. forces should remain under U.S. or NATO command. And third, regional organizations are not viable alternatives to the UN for carrying out such missions.

## Stability Forces

Peacekeeping and humanitarian interventions focus on developments in a state and generally occur after a crisis has already begun. **Stability operations** in contrast may focus on internal situations, but may also have a broader focus seeking to prevent interstate violence from breaking out or trying to prevent an international conflict from spilling over into neighboring states. One area in which stability operations are seen as growing in importance to U.S. security interests is Africa. This recognition led in 2007 to the creation of the U.S. African Command or AFRICOM. Its purpose is to work with other U.S. agencies and international organizations to strengthen regional stability and security and, if need be, to deter aggression and respond to crises. In the words of one commentator, AFRICOM's mission is conflict prevention not conflict reaction.[4]

Already AFRICOM's goals are proving difficult to implement, as the marriage of political and military objectives has created concern in many quarters. American embassies in Africa are raising questions about who is in charge of U.S. policy. African governments are raising concerns about AFRICOM signaling a new wave of American imperialism on the continent and questioning American designs on its oil and mineral wealth. Complicating matters even more is the fact that many humanitarian and civic groups are reluctant to become identified with AFRICOM for fear of creating distrust among the people they rely upon to achieve their development and humanitarian objectives.

# COUNTERINSURGENCY WARFARE

In the eyes of many strategists, the greatest military challenge facing the United States today stems from a basic asymmetry in military capabilities between the United States and its enemies. Matching the U.S. conventional strength is simply not an option for them. Instead the United States has to be fought by other means. Where the United States relies on precision air strikes guided by the latest technology and "shock and awe" bombing strikes, the enemy counters with suicide bombers, kidnappings and assassination, and hit-and-run attacks. What type of military forces and strategies are best to use in meeting asymmetrical challenges has been a point of major debate within the military and among strategists. For example, traditional Western "just war" principles stress the proportional and discriminating use of military power. It is unclear what this means in situations in which the enemy may be a stateless actor or is employing all of its resources against the United States and not abiding by these same principles.

George W. Bush entered office as a strong supporter of the Revolution in Military Affairs (RMA) concept, in which precision and lethal technology rather than large numbers and brute strength become the core of the military's power projection capabilities. Such a force posture proved highly effective in removing Saddam Hussein from power but not for fighting the war that followed. The Iraq experience provided the impetus for a thoroughgoing review of U.S. military doctrine and a change in emphasis from fighting conventional wars to fighting counterinsurgencies (COINs) as the primary task of the U.S. military.

The 2006 Field Manual (FM3-34) coauthored by General David Petraeus, who oversaw the change in strategy in Iraq following the surge in forces in 2006, defines **counterinsurgency** warfare as a protracted conflict that involves a mix of offensive, defensive, and stability operations. It requires that soldiers be both "nation builders as well as warriors."[5] COIN differs from traditional peacekeeping operations because in peacekeeping operations the primary objective is the absence of violence. In COIN, the absence of violence may actually hide preparations by insurgents for combat.

COIN is defined as struggle for the support of the people. It requires the coordinated use of military, paramilitary, political, economic, psychological, and civic actions. As such, while the military plays an important role in COIN operations, it cannot succeed itself. Using a medical analogy, COIN operations are seen as moving through three stages. Stage I involves stopping the bleeding by providing the patient with emergency first aid. Here, the goal is to protect the population and break the insurgency's momentum. Stage 2 involves inpatient care. The goal is to restore the patient's health and move it on the way to a successful long-term recovery. Stage 3 is outpatient care. Here, the goal is to move the patient to self-sufficiency, with more and more of the governing functions being carried out by the patient. At each stage, attention needs to be given to a wide range of activities, including providing security, providing essential services, promoting good governance, and promoting economic development.

With the U.S. presence in Iraq scheduled to end in 2010, COIN attention has shifted to Afghanistan. In February 2009, General Petraeus observed that the situation in Afghanistan had deteriorated markedly in the last two years and warned of a "downward spiral." The Obama administration plans to send more than 30,000 additional U.S. troops there, bringing the total U.S. and allied deployment to about 66,000. Germany is the single largest NATO contributor with 3,500 troops. U.S. forces are expected to remain in Afghanistan for three to four years, with the majority of them destined for service in Taliban strongholds in the ethnic Pashtun southern region.

Moving COIN's best practices from Iraq to Afghanistan is anything but automatic. The geography, ethnicity, politics, and economics of the two countries all differ to significant degrees. For COIN advocates, these differences point to a central truism: COIN tactics and strategies must be adjusted to the country and region where they are being applied. To others, these differences in context foreshadow failure. Among those pessimists is former secretary of state and national security advisor Henry Kissinger, who calls for rejecting COIN in favor of a more focused military strategy of working with local chiefs to prevent the emergence of a coherent jihadist state within Afghanistan that can destabilize the rest of the country and the region.[6]

A very different critique of U.S. COIN thinking comes from those who question the logic that guides it. A fundamental problem they point out is with the notion of victory. From the U.S. perspective, wars are fought to be won. Yet, for insurgents, this is not necessarily (or ever) the case. Wars are fought because they are a source of profit and influence. When the war ends, that influence is gone and so is the profit that comes from having received American or terrorist aid. The goal then is to keep the conflict going. In fact, these observers argue, most insurgencies degenerate into criminal enterprises and need to be recognized and dealt with as such.[7]

The specter of possible failure raises the question of consequences. Does it matter if the United States walks away from Afghanistan without "winning"? The absence of an exit strategy and fear of the consequences of a premature departure have long haunted military planners and policy makers. One study of U.S. departures from Lebanon, Somalia, Vietnam, and Cambodia suggests the consequences for U.S. security may be minimal. No dominoes fell. No power effectively rushed in to fill the power vacuum, not that they did not try. What did happen was that the civil conflict often got worse.[8]

## COVERT ACTION

**Covert action** seeks results by altering the internal balance of power in a foreign state. No instrument of foreign policy is more controversial or difficult to control. As the Tower Commission that investigated the Iran–Contra affair during the Reagan administration stated in its report, "Covert action places a great strain on the process of decision making in a free society."[9] Writing in a similar vein, two scholars who have studied the Central Intelligence Agency (CIA) extensively assert that there are only two legitimate reasons to carry out covert action: (1) when open knowledge of U.S. responsibility would make the operation infeasible and (2) to avoid retaliation or to control the potential for escalation.[10]

In popular usage, covert action is all but synonymous with the CIA and secret paramilitary undertakings. Neither is true. U.S. covert action predates the CIA. The first forays into covert action were taken during World War II by the Office of Strategic Services (OSS).[11] After a brief interlude in which the OSS was disbanded and in which no central intelligence organization existed, a permanent covert action capability was created in the newly established CIA. A number of different activities fall within its definitional boundaries, ranging from the clandestine support of individuals and organizations to assassination. In many cases, covert operations are becoming increasingly overt.[12] Today the National Endowment for Democracy (NED) supports political groups just as the CIA once did. It has been active in Venezuela, supporting the opponents of President Hugo Chavez. In the realm of paramilitary operations, estimates now place the number of CIA covert operators at 600–700, while the Pentagon has approximately 10,000 special force combatants. Similar trends exist elsewhere.

## Cold War Covert Action

The most common form of covert action is clandestine support for individuals and organizations. This support takes many forms (financial, technical, or training) and can be directed at many targets (politicians, labor leaders, journalists, unions, political parties, church groups, or professional associations). Clandestine support was the major focus of CIA efforts in France, Italy, and West Germany in the immediate post–World War II.[13] Between 1948 and 1968, the CIA spent over $65 million in Italy on these types of programs. A widely publicized case of CIA clandestine support involved efforts to block the election of Salvador Allende in Chile.[14] These efforts succeeded in 1958 and 1964 but failed in 1970. Between 1964 and 1969, the CIA spent almost $2 million on training anticommunist organizers among Chilean peasants and slum dwellers. It spent $3 million on the 1964 election and almost $1 million on the 1970 election.

Another form of clandestine support is the provision of security assistance and intelligence training to foreign governments. Third World leaders are particularly responsive to offers of training and equipment to help them combat potential coups, terrorist attacks, and assassination attempts. A controversial example of such a training program was "Project X." This was a U.S. military training program in Latin America and elsewhere that included instruction on clandestine activity against domestic political adversaries. Documents indicate that the operation was probably shut down in the early 1980s. In 1999, President Bill Clinton expressed regret for U.S. support of the Guatemalan military during that country's 36-year civil war, which dated back to the 1960s. An independent commission had concluded that the U.S.-backed forces were responsible for the vast majority of the human rights abuses that occurred during this war.

A second category of covert action is propaganda. The CIA has used a number of techniques for dispensing its propaganda. One of the most primitive propagandas involved using balloons.[15] In an effort to exploit dissatisfaction and increase internal unrest in China in the early Cold War era, the CIA loaded balloons with an assortment of leaflets, pamphlets, and newspapers. Presidents Reagan and George H. W. Bush both approved clandestine radio propaganda operations against Panamanian leader Manuel Noriega. Neither effort was particularly successful. Press accounts characterized the former effort as "half-hearted" and the latter as "inept."

A third category of covert action involves economic operations. According to one account, comparatively few economic operations have been undertaken by the CIA, and they have not been very successful.[16] As we have already seen, economic operations were an integral part of the CIA's efforts to stop Salvador Allende. The goal was "to make the economy scream." U.S. multinational corporations were approached and asked to cut off credits and the shipment of spare parts to Chile.

Available evidence suggests that the most persistent target of CIA covert economic operations was Fidel Castro's Cuba. One of the most notorious programs is Operation Mongoose.[17] Authorized by President John Kennedy in November 1961, it was designed to "use our available assets . . . to help Cuba overthrow the communist regime." Operation Mongoose succeeded in getting European shippers to turn down Cuban delivery orders and sabotaging British buses destined for Cuba. Operation Mongoose was canceled in January 1963, but covert economic operations against Cuba continued. As late as 1969 and 1970, the CIA directed a program of weather modification against Cuba's sugar crop with the hope of producing rain over nonagricultural areas, leaving the cane fields parched. The CIA has also been charged with infecting Cuban pig herds with an African swine flu virus. The result was a serious shortage of pork, which is a staple in the Cuban diet.

The fourth category of covert action involves **paramilitary** undertakings. A former practitioner defines paramilitary operations as the furnishing of covert military assistance and guidance to unconventional and conventional foreign forces and organizations. He argues that it represents a highly valuable "third option" between sending in the marines and doing nothing.[18]

Initially, paramilitary operations were targeted against the Soviet Union and its Eastern European satellite states.[19] Almost uniformly, they were failures. Numbered among them were efforts to support resistance fighters in Ukraine (the program ended with their defeat by the Soviet army); an effort to establish an underground apparatus for espionage and revolution in Poland (only after several years did it become clear that the Polish secret service had co-opted the network and was using it to acquire gold and capture anticommunist Poles); and an effort to overthrow the Albanian government (virtually every mission failed, and it later became known that the British intelligence officer in charge of the mission was a Soviet agent).

As the 1950s progressed, the more significant CIA paramilitary operations were taking place in the Third World. In 1953, the United States and Great Britain undertook a joint venture, Operation AJAX, to bring down the government of Iranian Prime Minister Mohammed Mossadeq and return the Shah to power.[20] In 1954, the CIA helped bring down the government of Jacobo Arbenz in Guatemala.[21] Arbenz had taken office in 1950 and set out on a path of social reform and modernization. The initial U.S. response centered on using economic sanctions, but in 1953 President Eisenhower approved a covert action plan (PB/SUCCESS). As was the case with Iran, the paramilitary operation itself was relatively small in scale, and it was preceded by a propaganda campaign designed to frighten Arbenz into fleeing the country.

As the 1950s ended, so too did the string of CIA successes. In 1958, it supported an unsuccessful coup against President Sukarno of Indonesia. A still greater embarrassment came in 1961 with the Bay of Pigs invasion of Cuba. Originally conceived during the Eisenhower administration, the plan was approved by Kennedy in April 1961. Later that month a brigade of some 1,400 Cuban exiles was put ashore in Cuba, where it was expected to link up with Cuban opposition forces and topple the Castro regime. Everything went wrong. On the first day of the invasion, two of the four supply and ammunition ships were sunk, and the other two fled. On the second day, the brigade was surrounded by 20,000 well-armed and loyal Cuban soldiers. On the third day, the 1,200 surviving members of the invasion force surrendered. Almost two years later, most were released in exchange for $53 million in food and drugs.

The Bay of Pigs put a temporary dent in Washington's fascination with paramilitary covert action programs, but it did not put an end to them. By the mid-1970s a controversial covert paramilitary operation was under way in Angola.[22] A 1974 coup in Portugal signaled the beginning of the end of Portuguese colonial rule in Africa. In January 1975, agreement among the three rival independence movements in Angola led to the creation of a coalition transitional government that would rule Angola until elections were held in October. Angola's independence was to be officially realized in November. The United States threw its support behind an alliance between the National Front for the Liberation of Angola (FNLA) under the leadership of Holden Roberto and the National Union for the Total Independence of Angola (UNITA) led by Jonas Savimbi.

Covert operations began seven days after the agreement to establish a transitional government was reached, when the CIA was authorized to pay $300,000 to the FNLA. It was encouraged to attack the Soviet-supported Popular Movement for the Liberation of Angola (MPLA), which was receiving military support from Cuban soldiers. The CIA maintained that no U.S. personnel were directly involved in the fighting or directly supplying the FNLA with funds. Evidence soon surfaced that this was not the case. Funds were being sent directly to Angolan forces, and CIA personnel were in Angola to help manage the war. Congress reacted angrily to these disclosures, passing the Tunney Amendment in1975 and the Clark Amendment in 1976 that attempted to cut off all government spending in Angola.

The most controversial of the CIA's paramilitary programs in the 1980s was its Nicaraguan operation. The impetus for CIA involvement in Nicaragua lay with evidence collected in the late 1970s that the Sandinista government there was increasing its shipments of arms to El Salvadoran rebels, intensifying pressure on domestic opposition forces, and becoming the site of a substantial Cuban-backed military buildup. The Carter administration responded to these events with economic sanctions. They were continued by the Reagan administration, but had little impact. In 1981, the Reagan administration authorized a $19.5 million program of covert action to stop the flow of arms to El Salvador. By November 1981 the program's goals had expanded to include creating an anti-Sandinista force (the Contras) that might effectively challenge the "Cuban support structure in Nicaragua."[23]

The CIA's paramilitary program in Nicaragua has had its successes. It is credited with having slowed down the shipment of arms to El Salvador and with hampering Sandinista offenses in 1983 and 1984. It has also been the object of intense criticism. In particular, Congress became concerned with the scope of the CIA's program compared to the program of action that it had earlier agreed to fund. As a result, in 1982, it passed the Boland Amendment, which forbade funding the Contras for the purpose of overthrowing the Nicaraguan government. In 1984, renewed questions were raised over the mining of Nicaraguan harbors and the CIA-sponsored production of a psychological warfare manual that could be interpreted as calling for assassination. This time Congress responded by cutting off all funding for the Contras. These bans became the center of controversy when information surfaced that NSC staffer Lieutenant Colonel Oliver North had been deeply involved in orchestrating Contra operations and in securing foreign and private funds for them.

The largest, and in some eyes the most successful, Third World paramilitary covert operation program run by the CIA was in Afghanistan. In FY 1985, the CIA spent about $250 million, or more than 80 percent of their covert action budgets, helping the Afghan guerrillas evict Soviet forces. In FY 1989, after the Soviet Union had withdrawn, the CIA was still spending $100 million on the Afghan operation. The Afghan paramilitary operation is also significant because, for the first time, the CIA was authorized to send "made in America" weapons to forces it was supporting. Until then, adherence to the doctrine of "plausible denial" had blocked such transfers.

A final form of covert action involves the assassination of foreign leaders. The existence of a unit for the planning of "special operations" can be traced back to the earliest days of the CIA.[24] By all accounts, no actual assassination operations or planning was ever done by it, but suggestions for assassination were put forward. By 1961, another CIA unit had been established for "disabling" foreign leaders, including assassination as a last resort. A former CIA official has stated that between 1959 and 1962 the White House, the NSC, and the CIA all talked seriously of killing foreign leaders.[25] The most thorough investigation into U.S. involvements in assassination plots was carried out by the Church Committee. It investigated five cases of alleged U.S. involvement:

| | |
|---|---|
| Cuba | Fidel Castro |
| Congo (Zaire) | Patrice Lumumba |
| Dominican Republic | Rafael Trujillo |
| Chile | René Schneider |
| South Vietnam | Ngo Dinh Diem |

The committee concluded that only the Castro and Lumumba cases involved plots conceived by the United States to kill foreign leaders. In the case of Trujillo, the United States did not initiate the plot, but it did aid dissidents whose aims were known to include assassinating Trujillo. In the Diem case, some U.S. officials sought his removal from office, but there is no indication that these officials sought his death. Schneider's death is linked to the Nixon administration's efforts to spark an anti-Allende military coup after he was elected president. In the Congo, it appears that events overtook U.S. policy and nullified U.S. plans to assassinate MPLA leader Patrice Lumumba. U.S. authorities had authorized Lumumba's assassination in the fall of 1960, and CIA officers in the Congo urged his "permanent disposal." Toxic substances had been selected as the method for Lumumba's assassination. CIA planning went so far as to send vials of poison to the CIA's Léopoldville station for an assassination attempt. In December, Lumumba was captured by forces aligned with the United States. Several weeks later his death was announced. It appears that the CIA knew the likely consequences of Lumumba's capture but was not involved in the assassination.

The Church Committee found concrete evidence of at least eight CIA plots to assassinate Fidel Castro between 1960 and 1965. One former CIA official characterized these efforts as ranging from "the vague to the weird."[26] Proposed assassination devices included arranging an "accident," poison cigars, poison pills, poison pens, placing deadly bacterial powder in Castro's scuba-diving suit, and rigging a seashell to explode while Castro was scuba diving. Although most of these approaches never went beyond the planning stage, some were attempted. Twice, poison pills were sent to Cuba, and on another occasion, weapons and other assassination devices were provided to a Cuban dissident. Cuban officials state that the closest the CIA came to assassinating Castro was in 1963, when a poison pill that was to be put into a chocolate milkshake by an assassin/waiter was delivered by a Mafia official. The plot failed when the capsule froze and broke open when the waiter went to get it.

In 1972, following the kidnapping and assassination of Chilean General René Schneider, Director of Central Intelligence Richard Helms issued a directive banning assassinations. This ban has since been included in the presidential executive orders. Following the terrorist attacks on the World Trade Center and the Pentagon, President George W. Bush asserted that the ban on assassinations did not prohibit the United States from assassinating terrorists or acting in self-defense.

## Post–Cold War Covert Action

Covert action programs did not disappear with the end of the Cold War any more than did nuclear weapons. The CIA ran a Cold War–style operation against Saddam Hussein between 1992 and 1996. The goal was to remove him from power by encouraging a military coup and reducing his control over Iraq's outlying regions, such as Iraqi Kurdistan. The cost of the program is estimated to have approached $100 million. Included in the funding was support for a clandestine radio station in Jordan, which blanketed Iraq with

## HISTORICAL LESSON

### Project Ajax

Iran has long been a valued and contested country. Commercially significant quantities of oil were discovered in 1908. By then Iran had already been divided into Russian and British spheres of influence. Iran would be occupied by British and Russian forces during World War I and World War II. It was during World War II, on September 16, 1941, that Mohammad Reza Pahlvai became the Shah. His father had come to power as the result of a coup in 1925 and was now forced to abdicate. United States entered the war. American soldiers were sent to Iran to handle supply operations. By 1944, approximately 30,000 U.S. troops were there, and Iran had received $8.5 million in Lend-Lease aid.

Iran's post–World War II independence and territorial integrity were agreed to by the Allies at the Tehran Conference of 1943. This agreement soon unraveled when, unhappy with Iran's refusal to grant it oil concessions, the Soviet Union organized pro-Soviet independence movements within Iranian territory and refused to pull its troops out as agreed upon. With the backing of the British and Americans, Iran took its case to the UN, where an agreement was reached. The Soviet Union received oil concessions, its troops left, and it sent its forces into the breakaway regions and reestablished its control over them. Soon thereafter, the Iranian legislature rejected the agreement, thus denying the Soviet Union access to oil.

As the Cold War intensified, the Shah came to be seen as a key force in containing the Soviet Union. His rule, however, was challenged by Mohammed Mossadeq, who was Prime Minister of Iran from 1951 to 1953. Mossadeq played a leading role in organizing Iran's National Front, whose goals were to establish democracy in Iran by ending foreign influences on its government and nationalizing the British-owned Anglo-Iranian Oil Company, something he accomplished on May 1, 1951.

Mossadeq's action set in motion a spiraling conflict with Great Britain. It responded by establishing a de facto naval blockade around Iran so that it could not sell any of its oil. Mossadeq expelled all British citizens from Iran, and in October 1952, the two countries broke diplomatic relations. Other oil companies immediately began increasing production elsewhere in the Persian Gulf. British actions brought Iranian oil production to a standstill and led to an economic crisis within Iran. A power struggle with the Shah over the extent of his powers and his nationalization policies led Mossadeq to resign in July 1952, only to be reappointed five days later after mass protests and tepid military support for his position; the Shah reappointed him Prime Minster.

As the crisis progressed, Great Britain approached President Harry Truman about removing Mossadeq from power in order to forestall a possible communist takeover, but was turned down. Great Britain renewed its proposal when Dwight Eisenhower became president and now met with a sympathetic response from his administration. U.S. and British officials met in Cyprus in May 1953 to lay out the basic plan. According to the plan, the CIA would persuade Shah, whose powers were by now largely ceremonial, to issue royal decrees dismissing Mossadeq and appointing a replacement. The army would enforce the decrees, and prearranged rioting by forces loyal to the Shah as well as statements by bribed clerics and CIA-controlled media outlets would give the impression of approaching anarchy, which would allow the military to arrest Mossadeq.

The Shah was reluctant to act, but eventually agreed to issue the decrees. The coup began on August 15, 1953, but Mossadeq had been forewarned and escaped arrest. The Shah then fled to Iraq. The CIA continued with its propaganda campaign and eventually succeeded in isolating Mossadeq from the military, allowing the Shah to return on August 22 and restore the monarchy. Upon his return to power, the United States sent some $70 million of emergency aid to Iran. The CIA also continued its operations against the Shah's opposition, including the establishment of SAVAK, the Iranian secret service. Mossadeq served three years in isolated confinement in prison, and lived under house arrest until he died in 1967.

U.S. sponsorship and involvement in the coup remains a sore point in U.S.–Iranian relations. It emerged as a point of emphasis in the anti-U.S. demonstrations against the Shah in 1979 that led to his downfall and the subsequent creation of a theocracy in Iran. Clinton's Secretary of State Madeline Albright expressed regret over the event and stated she understood why Iranians continue to resent the Americans. She explained Eisenhower's decision as being motivated by strategic considerations.

### Applying the Lesson

1. Would covert action be a more effective way of dealing with Iran than direct military action?
2. What is the lesson of Project Ajax for other covert action plans to change governments?
3. Would it have been better to do nothing in Iran in 1953? ■

anti–Saddam Hussein propaganda. Little was achieved. In June 1996, Saddam Hussein arrested and executed more than 100 Iraqi dissidents and military officers associated with the CIA plan. Political infighting among Kurdish leaders further crippled CIA efforts to remove Saddam from power.

The CIA has also played a pivotal role in the overt–covert operation along the Afghani–Pakistan border to target drones on key al Qaeda figures, an operation that officials characterize as "taking the fight to the enemy." On January 1, 2009, a CIA strike killed two al Qaeda leaders said to be responsible for a series of suicide bombings in Pakistan, the 1998 attacks on the U.S. embassies in Kenya and Tanzania, and a failed October 2007 assassination attempt on former Pakistan Prime Minister Benazir Bhutto.

An additional post–Cold War covert action program became public on September 6, 2006, when George W. Bush acknowledged the existence of a program in which suspected terrorists were kidnapped and taken to prisons located outside the United States, where they were subjected to what he referred to as "tough" but "safe and lawful and necessary" interrogation methods carried out by specially trained CIA officers. Nearly 100 detainees were held in these prisons until they were shut down when Bush made his speech. Fourteen "high-value" terrorist suspects were moved to Guantanamo Bay. Whereas Bush characterized the interrogation methods as legitimate, others condemned them as torture. Interrogation techniques included feigned drowning ("waterboarding"), extreme isolation, slapping, sleep deprivation, semi-starvation, and light and sound bombardment.[27]

The "renditions" program, as this policy of forcibly abducting suspected terrorist suspects and transporting them to non–U.S. prisons for interrogation came to be known, was the product of two different post-9/11 concerns.[28] The first problem was what to do with high-ranking al Qaeda leaders. One option was assassination. Another was to capture and then interrogate them. President Bush authorized both courses of action in a Presidential Finding signed six days after 9/11.

The second concern that led to the renditions policy was what to do with terrorist suspects captured in Afghanistan. At first they were sent to prisons in Egypt and Jordan, but soon the number of captured suspects grew too large, and the decision was made to leave most prisoners under the control of the U.S.-backed Northern Alliance. The first agreements on "black site" rendition and interrogation facilities were reached in mid-2002 with Thailand and an Eastern European country. Publicity about the Thai site in June 2003 led to its closing, and agreements were then signed with other countries. Public reports indicated that Egypt, Indonesia, Poland, and Romania were among the countries to which suspects were taken.

In August 2009, Obama announced that his administration would continue the renditions program but more closely monitor the interrogation methods used by assigning oversight responsibiity to the national security council. He also announced that a new interrogation unit, the High-Value Detainee Interrogation Group, was being created within the FBI to question key terrorist suspects. This removed the interrogation process from the jurisdiction of the CIA.

## The Covert War Against Osama Bin Laden

The CIA's pre–9/11 efforts to capture Osama bin Laden took a number of different forms.[29] Perhaps the earliest involved the recruitment of a family-based team of Afghan tribal members. Known by the code name TRODPINT, they were originally formed to capture Mir Aimal Kasi, a Pakistani national who killed two CIA employees at the CIA headquarters in 1993. Kasi was captured in Pakistan, and TRODPINT was then given the task of trying to kidnap bin Laden so that he could be taken out of Afghanistan by U.S. Special Forces. The last effort before 9/11 involved the recruitment of Northern Alliance guerrilla commander Ahmed Shah Massoud in 1999 by a team of CIA operatives known as JAWBREAKER-5. Massoud had a long history of dealings with the CIA, many of which were not positive. At one point he had been given $500,000 to attack Afghan communist forces, but no attack apparently ever occurred.

In between these two operations, the CIA contacted and recruited at least three proxy forces in the region to try and capture or kill bin Laden. One plan involved using a Pakistani commando team that was trained, supported, and equipped by the CIA. The Pakistani government made the offer as a counter to rising pressure from the Clinton administration to cut its support for the Taliban. The unit was ready to act in October, but a coup brought into power a new government that refused to condone the operation. At the same time, U.S. intelligence officials had grown concerned that the operation was compromised as a result of security breaches within the Pakistani intelligence services.

Formal authorization for the CIA to pursue bin Laden had been obtained in 1998, following the bombings of the American embassies in Kenya and Tanzania, when Bill Clinton signed the first of a series of findings consistent with the Hughes–Ryan Amendment. The original finding emphasized the goal of capturing bin Laden but permitted the use of lethal force. The first Memorandum of Notification expanded the covert operation to include using lethal force against bin Laden and his forces even when there was little chance of capturing him. The second expansion permitted the intelligence community to target his top aides. It is believed that fewer than 10 individuals were identified and that they were to be captured or killed. The third expansion permitted the intelligence community to shoot down a private or civilian aircraft if bin Laden was a passenger.[30]

## Counterproliferation

In the last chapter, we examined arms control and defense as ways of addressing threats to the United States. Both are passive and targeted most frequently on major threats. Another strategy, **counterproliferation**, is the use of military force to deter countries from acquiring and using weapons of mass destruction (WMD) against the United States. Its principal targets are smaller states such as Iran and North Korea. Proponents of counterproliferation start from the premise that nonproliferation efforts have failed. They see the United States as operating in a postproliferation international security environment. It is one in which defense lags behind advances in offensive nuclear, chemical, and biological warfare capabilities and in which inspections do not provide an effective long-term solution to U.S. security needs.

Counterproliferation is not a new strategy. In its short history, counterproliferation thinking has already undergone several changes from when it was first proposed.[31] Bureaucratic infighting within the Pentagon over the costs of proliferation and the military's unease over preemptive war and opposition from arms controllers soon transformed it from an offensive policy to a largely defensive and reactive one. This orientation changed again after the terrorist attacks of 9/11. The George W. Bush administration's embrace of a national ballistic missile defense system and its rejection of deterrence in favor of preemption effectively places counterproliferation at the center of its strategy for dealing with WMD.

In 1993, Bill Clinton's secretary of defense Les Aspin unveiled a "counterproliferation initiative." Its details were never spelled out at the time, but most who embraced the idea identified two prominent features. The first was a military capacity to operate against states that possess nuclear weapons and other WMD. The second was the construction of a defense system against ballistic missiles. Significant challenges exist on both fronts. Constructing a military capability to attack states (or terrorist groups) that possess an immature nuclear or WMD capability is quite different from constructing one to counter an adversary with a robust capability. An additional complicating factor is the timing and political context of the planned military action. Is it part of a prolonged crisis, an ongoing war, or a "bolt-from-the-blue" response carried out in a time of international quiet? Only in the last case can surprise be expected. In the others, the target is likely to have advance warning and will be able to prepare for that contingency and develop retaliatory strategies. Decisions must also be made on what targets to attack. Possibilities range from the WMD themselves to infrastructure and support systems, conventional forces, and the political and military leadership of the adversary.

Few historical examples of counterproliferation exist.[32] The most frequently cited are Israel's 1981 raid on Iraq's Osiraq nuclear reactor, the bombing of Iraq's unconventional weapons during the first phase of Operation Desert Storm in 1991, and U.S. cruise missile attacks on the al Shifa pharmaceutical plant in Sudan in 1998. Contingency plans were also developed for using military force against North Korea in 1994 and against China in 1963–1964. In each case, context-specific considerations make it difficult to develop any clear-cut generalizations as to guiding principles for a counterproliferation strategy. Among the factors that have weighed heavily on engaging in counterproliferation military action are the possibility of triggering a full-scale war, uncertain intelligence, and concerns about high levels of collateral damage to people and the environment.

The most talked about potential target for a counterproliferation military strike is Iran. Israel is believed to be a strong advocate of such a military action. In 2005, it destroyed a building in Syria housing a suspected nuclear reactor that was being built with North Korean help. The Bush administration remained largely silent on the military action, although U.S. intelligence reports were said to have indicated that it had only a low level of confidence that the site was at the heart of the Syrian nuclear program.

The value of military strike against Iran's nuclear facilities is widely debated. Supporters point to the success of the 1981 raid on Iraq's Osiraq nuclear facility. Skeptics assert that Iran's nuclear program could not be dealt a similarly crippling blow. Now largely self-sufficient and with nuclear facilities dispersed throughout the country, Iran's nuclear program would recover fairly quickly following a military strike. In 2009 the Obama administration rejected an Israeli request for deep-penetration bombs that could be used to attack underground and fortified nuclear enrichment facilities.

# ARMS CONTROL AND SMALL WARS

Nuclear weapons receive most of the attention when arms control is discussed, but they are not the only proliferation problem facing policy makers today. The proliferation of chemical and biological weapons (along with the missile delivery systems that they use) and conventional weapons has also been the subject of arms control efforts. Collectively we refer to chemical, biological, and nuclear weapons as **weapons of mass destruction.**

## Chemical and Biological Weapons

Chemical and biological weapons may be constructed around a number of different agents. Among the most significant chemical agents are mustard gas, which causes blistering over the entire body, blindness, and death by respiratory failure, and sarin, which interrupts the flow of oxygen to cells. Significant biological agents and toxins include anthrax, which causes pneumonia and organ failure; ricin, which attacks the circulatory system; and smallpox, which in the view of many is the most deadly biological agent. The modern historical record documenting the use of chemical and biological weapons typically begins on April 22, 1915, when Germany used chemical weapons in World War I. Saddam Hussein employed chemical weapons, principally sarin and mustard gas, against Iran in the Iran–Iraq War as early as 1983. He then used poison gas and possibly anthrax against Kurds in northern Iraq to solidify his hold on power following that war. At the turn of the twenty-first century, it was estimated that about a dozen countries had offensive biological weapons programs. Also, in 2000, it was estimated that at least 16 countries had chemical weapons programs. Great fears also exist that terrorist groups might seek to acquire chemical and biological weapons.

Just as problems stand in the way of producing a nuclear weapon, neither biological nor chemical agents are readily produced. For example, microbes used for biological weapons often lose their effectiveness when exposed to sunlight, water, and other natural elements. They are also difficult to use militarily because of the challenges involved in spreading them out over large areas. Chemical agents, on the other hand, have caused widespread death. An accident at a Union Carbide plant in Bhopal, India, in 1984 killed almost 4,000 people and seriously injured another 200,000. The commercial value of chemicals used for weapons creates significant problems for controlling or eliminating their production. An estimated 850,000 facilities in the United States produce, process, consume, or store hazardous chemicals.

Commonly discussed means for the delivery of WMD include dispersal from an aircraft or drone and from artillery shells, rockets, ballistic missiles, and cruise missiles. Of most concern are ballistic and cruise missiles. With few exceptions, countries in possession of, or seeking, such weapons all have ballistic missiles. Another 15 countries have ballistic missiles but are not seeking WMD. The number of countries with cruise missiles is even greater. Some 80 countries have them, and 18 countries make them.

After the collapse of the Soviet Union, widespread concern existed that poorly guarded facilities and unemployed scientists would become the center for a black market in WMD and missile technology. Revelations in 2003 of the existence of a black-market ring led by Pakistani scientist and director of its nuclear program A.Q. Khan made it clear that a far greater proliferation danger existed.

The principal vehicle in place for controlling the proliferation of missiles is the voluntary Missile Technology Control Regime (MTCR). It was formed in 1987 by the United States and other advanced industrial states for the purpose of developing export policies that restrict the global proliferation of key missile technologies. The original focus of control efforts was on nuclear capable delivery systems; an agreement in January 1993 extended the regime to include systems capable of delivering chemical and biological weapons.

## Conventional weapons

Traditionally, efforts to curb conventional weapons proliferation have focused on restricting the sale or transfer of major weapons systems from one state to another. For a brief period of time, it appeared that conventional arms transfers were becoming less pronounced in world politics. Between 1989 and 1991, worldwide sales fell 53 percent and U.S. sales fell almost 34 percent. This downward trend has since been reversed.

Relatively little attention has been paid to the problem of curbing arms transfers. Conventional Arms Transfer Talks were held between 1977 and 1979, but they ended with no agreement being reached.[33] The United States and the Soviet Union entered these talks with conflicting agendas that prevented any agreement from being reached. In the aftermath of the Persian Gulf War, a new conventional arms control initiative has taken place in the form of a UN Arms Transfer Register.[34] The register identifies seven different categories of conventional weapons, and countries are requested to submit to the UN an annual statement of the number of these items it exported or imported during the previous year. The goal is to bring a heightened degree of transparency to the arms transfer process and thereby reduce the military advantages that arms transfers bring to states. The danger, according to one observer, is that because the system is a control mechanism, it may have the unintended effect of legitimizing those arms transfers that are registered.

Not all conventional arms controllers agree with the focus on major weapons systems. The global scale of small arms trade is also imposing.[35] The Arms Control and Disarmament Agency has estimated that some 13 percent of the global trade in conventional arms is made up of small arms and light weapons. In 1996, the State Department and the Commerce Department approved the export of more than $500 million worth of small arms. One author estimates that 10–20 percent of the $62 billion in U.S. military grants between 1955 and 1994 consisted of these weapons. In addition to direct sales and grants, a third source of small arms is surplus sales. One source estimates that between 1990 and 1996 the United States gave away 200,000 machines through the Excess Defense Articles Program. Recipients included Mexico, Taiwan, Latvia, Bosnia, Israel, Thailand, and the Philippines. In 2001, a voluntary international agreement was reached that was designed to stop the international trade in small arms. The United States blocked efforts to include regulations on civilian ownership of military weapons and to restrict small arms trade to rebel movements.

Yet another dimension to the problem of curbing the proliferation of conventional weapons has also emerged. It involves the globalization of the arms production process. Cutbacks in defense spending and shrinking military establishments have led major arms producers to engage in a growing number of joint ventures, strategic alliances, and foreign acquisitions.[36] This is transforming the security environment facing the U.S. military by placing increasingly advanced military equipment in the hands of potential adversaries. It has also led to the development of sophisticated Third World arms industries. Between 1986 and 1993, there were 27 joint ventures, 23 strategic alliances, and 78 mergers or acquisitions among defense firms around the world. Among others, the United States has entered into coproduction agreements on the F-16 fighter with Israel, South Korea, Singapore, Taiwan, Greece, and Indonesia. About 40 Third World states now possess significant defense industries; almost 100 major conventional weapons systems have been licensed for coproduction in the Third World; and seven Third World states have the ability to produce land, sea, and air combat weapons.

## OVER THE HORIZON

In looking over the horizon, the immediate challenge for U.S. foreign policy in the area of small wars is already evident. It is Afghanistan where many already predict a military presence that will be deadly, longer, and more expensive than Iraq. Looking further over the horizon, we can see potential small wars involving the United States in Pakistan and Africa. Regardless of where and when the United States finds intself involved in such conflicts, three questions will demand answers: (1) what are its boundaries, (2) who is the enemy, and (3) how is the military instrument best used.

In thinking about these questions, we find ourselves back at the beginning of *American Foreign Policy: Past, Present, Future,* where we introduced comments by then secretary of state Condoleezza Rice to the 9/11 Commission. Replacing the reference to al Qaeda with one to the Taliban, we get: you don't have an approach against the Taliban until you have an approach against Afghanistan. And you don't have an approach against Afghanistan until you have an approach against Pakistan. And until we could get that right, we don't have a policy.[37]

## CRITICAL THINKING QUESTIONS

1. How can insurgents be best stopped from acquiring weapons?
2. What types of actions are best taken covertly; what actions should never be taken covertly?
3. What is the most likely cause of a U.S. small war in the next 5 years and in the next 10 years?

## KEY TERMS

## FURTHER READING

Thomas Barnet, *The Pentagon's New Map: War and Peace in the Twenty-First Century* (New York: Berkley Books, 2004).
Max Boot, *The Savage Wars of Peace* (New York: Perseus, 2002).
David Halberstam, *War in a Time of Peace* (New York: Touchstone, 2001).
Michael Klare, *Resource Wars* (New York: Owl Books, 2006).
John Nagl, *Learning to Eat Soup with a Knife: Counterinsurgency Lessons from Malaya and Vietnam* (Chicago: Unviersity of Chicago Press, 2005).

## NOTES

1. Ann Scott Tyson, "Joint Chiefs Chairman Says U.S. Preparing Military Options Against Iran," *Washington Post,* April 25, 2008, A1.
2. Ted Galen Carpenter, "Foreign Policy Peril: Somalia Set a Dangerous Precedent," *USA Today,* May 1993, p. 13.
3. Thomas G. Weiss, "Triage: Humanitarian Interventions in a New Era," *World Policy Journal,* 11 (1994), 59–66.
4. Sean McFate, "U.S. Africa Command: A New Strategic Paradigm?" *Military Review* 88 (2008), 10–21.
5. *Counterinsurgency.* Field Manual 3–24, Department of the Army, December 2006.
6. Henry Kissinger, "A Strategy for Afghanistan," *Washington Post*, February 26, 2009, A 19.
7. Steven Metz, "New Challenges and Old Concepts: Understanding 21st Century Insurgency," *Parameters* 37 (2007/08), 20–32.
8. Bennet Ramberg, "The Precedents for Withdrawal: From Vietnam to Iraq," *Foreign Affairs,* 88 (2009), 2–8.
9. The President's Special Review Board, *The Tower Commission Report* (New York: Bantam, 1987), p. 15.
10. Bruce D. Berkowitz and Allan F. Goodman, "The Logic of Covert Action," *The National Interest,* 51 (1998), 38–46.
11. For comments on the OSS and covert action, see Victor Marchetti and John D. Marks, *The CIA and the Cult of Intelligence* (New York: Dell, 1975); and Richard Harris Smith, *OSS: The Secret History of America's First Central Intelligence Agency* (Berkeley: University of California Press, 1972).
12. Jennifer Kibbe, "The Rise of the Shadow Warriors," *Foreign Affairs,* 83 (2004), 102–15; and Frederick Wettering, "(C)overt Action," *International Journal of Intelligence and Counterintelligence,* 16 (2003), 561–72.
13. Ibid., pp. 228–29.
14. Ibid., pp. 15–29.
15. Marchetti and Marks, *The CIA and the Cult of Intelligence,* p. 167.
16. Marchetti and Marks, *The CIA and the Cult of Intelligence,* p. 72; and Jeffrey Richelson, *The U.S. Intelligence Community* (Cambridge, Ballinger, 1985),

pp. 230–31. Steven Metz, "New Challenges and Old Concepts: Understanding 21$^{st}$ Century Insurgency," *Parameters* (Winter 2007/2008), 37 20–32.

17. Warren Hinckle and William Turner, *The Fish Is Red: The Story of the Secret War Against Castro* (New York: Harper & Row, 1982).

18. Theodore G. Shackley, *The Third Option: An American View of Counterinsurgency Operations* (New York: Reader's Digest Press, 1981).

19. Trevor Barnes, "The Secret Cold War: The CIA and American Foreign Policy in Europe: 1946–1956," *Historical Journal*, 24, 25 (1981, 1982), 399–415, 649–70.

20. Ray S. Cline, *Secrets, Spies and Scholars: The Essential CIA* (Washington, DC: Acropolis, 1970), pp. 132–33; and Barry Rubin, *Paved with Good Intentions: The American Experience and Iran* (New York: Penguin, 1981), chapter 3.

21. Richard H. Immerman, *The CIA in Guatemala: The Foreign Policy of Intervention* (Austin: University of Texas Press, 1982).

22. John Stockwell, *In Search of Enemies: A CIA Story* (New York: W. W. Norton, 1978).

23. Christopher Dickey, "Central America: From Quagmire to Cauldron," *Foreign Affairs*, 62 (1984), 669.

24. U.S. Congress, Senate Select Committee to Study Government Operations with Respect to Intelligence Activities, *Alleged Assassination Plots Involving Foreign Leaders* (Washington, DC: U.S. Government Printing Office, 1976).

25. Cline, *Secrets, Spies and Scholars*, p. 187; Harry Rositzke, *The CIA's Secret Operations: Espionage, Counterespionage, and Covert Action* (New York: Reader's Digest Press, 1977), p. 196.

26. Rositzke, *The CIA's Secret Operations* p. 197.

27. Dan Eggen and Dafna Linzer, "Secret World of Detainees Grows More Public," *The Washington Post*, September 7, 2006, p. A18; and Dana Priest, "Officials Relieved Secret Is Shared," *The Washington Post*, September 7, 2006, p. A17.

28. Dana Priest, "CIA Holds Terror Suspects in Secret Prisons," *The Washington Post*, November 2, 2005, p. A1.

29. Information in this section is drawn from various newspaper accounts. See Barton Gellman, "Broad Effort Launched After '98 Attacks," *The Washington Post*, December 19, 2001, p. A1; Gellman, "Struggles Inside the Government Define Campaign," *The Washington Post*, December 20, 2001, p. A1; Bob Woodward and Thomas Ricks, "U.S. Was Foiled Multiple Times in Efforts to Capture bin Laden or Have Him Killed," *The Washington Post*, October 3, 2001, p. A1; Bob Woodward, "CIA Paid Afghans to Track bin Laden," *The Washington Post*, December 23, 2001, p. A1; and Steve Coll, *Ghost Wars* (New York: Penguin, 2004).

30. For critical accounts of the attempt to capture bin Laden, see Richard Clarke, *Against All Enemies* (New York: The Free Press, 2004); and Anonymous, *Imperial Hubris* (Washington, DC: Brassey's) 2004.

31. Henry Sokolski, "Mission Impossible," *Bulletin of the Atomic Scientists* (March/April 2001), 63–68.

32. Robert Luttwak, "Nonproliferation and the Use of Force," in Janne Nolan, Bernard Finel, and Bryan Finlay (eds.), *Ultimate Security* (New York: The Century Foundation Press, 2003), pp. 75–106.

33. Janne Nolan, "U.S.-Soviet Conventional Arms Transfer Negotiations," in Alexander George, Philip Farley, and Alexander Dallin (eds.), *U.S.–Soviet Security Cooperation* (New York: Oxford University Press, 1988), 27–36.

34. Edward J. Laurance, "Conventional Arms: Rationales and Prospects for Compliance and Effectiveness," *Washington Quarterly*, 16 (1993), 163–72.

35. Michael Renner, "Arms Control Orphans," *The Bulletin of the Atomic Scientists,* 55 (January/February 1999), 22–26; and Lora Lumpe, "The Leader of the Pack," *The Bulletin of the Atomic Scientists,* 55 (January/February 1999), 27–33.
36. Richard A. Bitizinger, "The Globalization of the Arms Industry," *International Security,* 19 (1994), 170–98.
37. Steve Strasser ed., *The 9/11 Investigations* (New York: Public Affairs Press, 2004), p. 233.

# Alternative Futures

"Every Golden Age comes to an end." So it was for the Romans and so it was for the British. And so some say it is about to happen to the United States. In this view we are about to enter the "Post-American World" in which we will see "the rise of the rest."[1] This will not be an anti-American world, just one where the United States no longer stands head and shoulders above others. There is certainly much room to debate this assertion. Talk of the decline of the United States as a world power was heard after Vietnam and during the Reagan administration. Unlike the declinist speculation of the past, the reasons for the possible passing of U.S. golden age today lies not in its failures but in its successes, the creation of a prosperous and largely peaceful international system. This said, it is not at all clear who, if anyone, will join or replace the United States as a dominant power. Nor is at all clear how long the transition to a **post-American world** might take. In fact, if this vision of the future should come to pass, it is not at all clear what the world will look like. Some already speculate that the future international system will more closely resemble that of the 1800s than any other period of time.[2] But regardless of whether or not the post-American world is about to begin, one thing is clear: a business-as-usual approach to conducting foreign policy may not serve the U.S. national interest well. Consideration needs to be given to alternative ways of conducting foreign policy. They need not be adopted, but conversation needs to begin. As Zbigniew Brzezinski, President Carter's national security advisor, notes, while for many 9/11 brought home the need for change, there is still lacking a reasoned dialogue of the wisdom of that change.[3]

## FOREIGN POLICY VISIONS

We close our treatment of U.S. foreign policy by introducing six competing visions, six different choices for U.S. foreign policy for the future. The differences among them are many, but there are also points of overlap. We ask three questions of each alternative future: (1) What is the primary threat to U.S. national security? (2) What responsibility does the United States have to other states? and (3) What responsibility does the United States have to the global community? The answers given reflect different views about the degree to which the United States should be involved in world politics, how much power it possesses, and the extent to which we think the future will differ from the past.

### The United States as an Ordinary State

For some, the key to the future is realizing that foreign policy can no longer be conducted on the assumption of American uniqueness or that U.S. actions stand between anarchy and order. The American century is over, and the challenge facing policy makers is no longer that of managing alliances, deterring aggression, or ruling over the international system. It is now one of adjusting to a new role orientation, one in which the United States is an "**ordinary state**."[4] The change in outlook is necessary because international and domestic trends point to the declining utility of a formula-based response to foreign policy problems, be it rooted in ideology, concepts of power politics, or some vision of regional order. Governments ruling over internally divided societies and those ruling over unified populations are finding themselves forced to pursue narrowly defined national interests at the expense of international collaborative and cooperative efforts. In this altered environment, flexibility, autonomy, and impartiality are to be valued over one-sided commitments, name-calling, and efforts at the diplomatic, military, or economic isolation of states.

As an ordinary state, the United States would not define its interests so rigidly that their defense would require unilateral American action. If the use of force is necessary, it should be a truly multilateral effort; and if others are unwilling to act, there is no need for the United States to assume the full burden of the commitment. Stated as a rule: "The United States should not be prepared, on its own, and supported solely by its own means, to perform tasks that most other states would not undertake."[5] Ordinariness does not, however, mean passivity, withdrawal, or a purely defensive approach to foreign policy problems. The quality of U.S. participation in truly multilateral efforts to solve international problems will be vital, because the core ingredients to international influence in the future will be found in the fields in which the United States is a leader: economics, diplomacy, and technology. The goal of these collaborative efforts should be to "create and maintain a world in which adversaries will remain in contact with one another and where compromises are still possible."[6] The three primary areas for such efforts (and thus for U.S. foreign policy) are to bring about a balance between Russia and the West, between the Arab oil producers and the consuming states, and between the rich and the poor states. To summarize, in the Ordinary State perspective:

1. The greatest threat to U.S. national security lies in trying to do too much and in having too expansive a definition of its national interest.
2. The United States' responsibility to other states must be proportionate and reciprocal to that which other states have to the United States.
3. The United States' responsibility to the global community is to be a good global citizen—nothing more and nothing less.

The imagery advanced by the Ordinary State perspective is one that most Americans find troubling. Its denial of American uniqueness, its lack of optimism, its focus on restraints rather than opportunities, and its admonition not to try to do too much all run against the traditional American approach to world politics. For that reason it is a perspective that is unlikely to be endorsed (at least by this name) by politicians. At the same time, it is a perspective on the future that cannot be dismissed. Political leaders must acknowledge it because it taps into a feeling shared by many Americans that although the United States should not retreat into isolationism, it should not be the first to take risks in places such as Bosnia, Somalia, and Haiti.

## Reformed America

According to proponents of the **Reformed America** perspective, U.S. foreign policy has traditionally been torn between pursuing democratic ideals and **empire**.[7] The United States wants peace—but only on its own terms; the United States supports human rights—but only if its definitions are used; the United States wants to promote Third World economic growth—but only if it follows the U.S. model and does not undermine U.S. business interests abroad. Historically, the thrust toward empire (whether it is called *containment, détente,* or *trilateralism*) has won out, and democratic ideals have been sacrificed or given only lip service. Whether it is foreign aid, human rights, environmental protection, or arms control, U.S. policy makers have given highest priority to maintaining the United States' position of dominance in the international system and promoting the economic well-being of U.S. corporations.[8]

The need now exists to reverse this pattern. Democratic ideals must be given primary consideration in the formulation and execution of U.S. foreign policy. Not doing so invites future Vietnams and runs the risk of undermining the very democratic principles for which the United States stands. Foreign policy and domestic policy are not seen as two separate categories. They are held to be inextricably linked together, and actions taken in one sphere have effects on behavior and policies in the other. Bribery of foreign officials leads to bribery of U.S. officials; an unwillingness to challenge human rights violations abroad reinforces the acceptance of discrimination and violations of civil rights at home; and a lack of concern for the growing disparity in economic wealth on a global basis leads to an insensitivity to the problems of poverty in the United States.

The Reformed America perspective demands global activism from the United States. The much-heralded decline in American power is not seen as being so great as to prevent the United States from exercising a predominant global influence. Moreover, the United States is held to have a moral and political responsibility to lead by virtue of its comparative wealth and power. The danger to be avoided is inaction brought on by the fear of failure. The United States cannot be permitted to crawl into a shell of isolationism or to let itself be "Europeanized" into believing that there are limits to its power and accepting the world "as it is." The power needed for success in creating what amounts to a new world order that is faithful to traditional American democratic values is not the ability to dominate others but to renew the American commitment to justice, opportunity, and liberty. In sum, the Reformed America perspective holds that:

1. The primary threat to U.S. national security is a continued fixation on military problems and an attachment to power-politics thinking.
2. The United States' responsibility to other states is great, provided they are truly democratic, and the United States must seek to move those that are not in that direction.
3. The United States' responsibility to the global community is also great and centers on the creation of an international system conducive to the realization of traditional American values.

The values underlying this perspective were widely embraced in the post–Cold War period, as many commentators urged presidents to move more aggressively toward a neo-Wilsonian foreign policy. Both advocates and critics of the Reformed America perspective wrestle with the question of what specific courses of action and instruments of foreign policy further this vision of the future. Military power tends to be rejected, yet many neo-Wilsonians are adamant supporters of humanitarian interventions. Economic sanctions are a preferred option, yet they have been condemned as having "contributed to more deaths that all the weapons of mass destruction throughout history" during the post–Cold War period alone.[9] Even international institutions are sometimes cited as often contributing to international problems rather than being part of the solution.

## Pragmatic America

The **Pragmatic America** perspective holds that the United States can no longer afford foreign policies that are on the extreme ends of the political spectrum. Neither crusades nor isolationism serve America well. In the words of long-time strategist and policy maker James Schlesinger, what is needed in U.S. foreign policy is "selectivity."[10] The United States, he argues, must avoid impulse and image in formulating foreign policy. What is needed is a strong dose of moderation in means and ends. Above all else, the end of the Cold War is seen as vindicating a policy of moderation.[11] As to ends, some world problems require U.S. attention, but not all do. The United States must recognize that the American national interest is not identical to the global interest, and that not all problems lend themselves to permanent resolution. The most pressing issue on the agenda is for the United States to develop a set of criteria for identifying these problems and then act in moderation to protect American interests.

Pragmatic America emphasizes a utilitarian outlook on world politics and recognizes the lessened ability of military force to solve foreign policy problems. It sees military problems as continuing to be the most threatening ones facing the United States. The nature of these problems is not what it used to be, and thus the remedies must also differ. President Bill Clinton's first director of central intelligence, R. James Woolsey, pointed out that while the Cold War dragon represented by the Soviet Union has been slain, the world confronting the United States is now populated by large numbers of poisonous snakes. For many who embrace this view, the most effective means of countering those snakes deemed to be threatening to the United States is through some form of collective action instead of with unilateral or bloc-based moves.

One national security practitioner suggests that the ideal practical method for moving forward is the creation of international posses.[12] Just as in the old American West, when security threats present themselves, the United States (the sheriff) should organize and deputize a posse of like-minded states that will end the threat. It will then disband. This is far less expensive politically and militarily than acting through standing alliances such as NATO or international organizations such as the United Nations. In sum, the Pragmatic America perspective holds that:

1. The primary threats to U.S. national security continue to be military in nature.
2. The United States has a responsibility to other states on a selective basis, and only to the extent that threats to the political order of those states would lessen American security.
3. The United States' responsibility to the global community is limited. More pressing is a sense of responsibility to key partners whose cooperation is necessary to manage a threatening international environment.

President George H. W. Bush, in his farewell foreign policy address, argued for a position that is consistent with this view.[13] Warning against becoming isolationist, Bush asserted that the United States can influence the future, but that "it need not respond to every outrage of violence." It cannot be the police officer of the world, but it must be prepared to act militarily. Bush went on to note that no formula exists that tells with precision when and where to intervene. "Each and every case is unique. To adopt rigid criteria would guarantee mistakes involving American interests and lives. . . . Similarly we cannot always decide in advance which interests will require our using military force." When force is used, Bush urged that the mission be clear and achievable, that a realistic plan exist, and that equally realistic criteria be established for withdrawing U.S. forces.

The Pragmatic America perspective is seen by some as well suited for an international system in a state of flux. Rigidly applied guiding principles such as containing communism or spreading democracy are held to be of little value in a world in which change is the dominant condition. Henry Kissinger, for example, argues that "conviction on what we are trying to achieve must be constant but their application has to be adjusted to specific conditions."[14] At the same time, its measured approach to solving foreign policy problems is also a fundamental weakness in the Pragmatic America perspective. Because pragmatism can be interpreted differently by different people, the policy it produces tends to move forward in a series of disjointed steps. The result is that whereas defenders see it as producing flexibility and adaptability, detractors see in it a foreign policy by lottery, in which the past provides little guidance for friends or enemies as they seek to anticipate America's position.

## American Crusader

At base, the **American Crusader** sees the United States as having won the Cold War and is now intent on enjoying the fruits of its victory as the dominant global power. But victory does not bring complacency. Rather it brings with it an opportunity to act on America's historical sense of mission. It builds on an important strain in the American national style that defines security in absolute terms. The objective is "unconditional surrender." "For more than two centuries the United States has aspired to a condition of perfect safety from foreign threats," both real and imagined.[15] Unlike the Reformed American perspective, the American Crusader perspective identifies military power as the instrument of choice. It is rooted firmly in that part of the American national style that rejects compromise and seeks engineering and permanent solutions to political problems.

Faint echoes of the American Crusader perspective can be found in post–World War II foreign policy. During the Eisenhower administration, some commentators called for rolling back the Iron Curtain, feeling that containment was too passive and accommodating a strategy. During the Persian Gulf War, there was a moment when defeating Saddam Hussein had the characteristics of a crusade, at least at a rhetorical level. The American Crusader perspective burst on the scene with full force following the terrorist attacks on the World Trade Center and the Pentagon.

In sum, the American Crusader perspective holds that:

1. The international system holds real and immediate threats to American national security that must be unconditionally defeated.
2. The United States has a responsibility to help other states that are allies in its cause, because their security increases American security.
3. The United States' responsibility to the international community is great, but how that responsibility is defined is a matter for the United States to determine based on its historical traditions.

There are some who share the American Crusader view that the international system contains immediate and serious threats to American security but question its wisdom. One concern expressed is that it overlooks the fact that superpower status does not convey total power to the United States. The challenge of bringing means and ends into balance is an ongoing one, and "superpower fatigue" becomes a real danger.[16] A second concern is that by acting in this manner the United States may hasten its own decline. Rather than stay on the American "bandwagon" as an ally, second-order states may decide that because they too may become the object of an American crusade, it is necessary to build up their own power and balance that of the United States.

## America the Balancer

Out of a conviction that unipolarity is bound to give way to a multipolar distribution of power in the international system, some commentators argue that the prudent course of action today is to adopt the role of a balancer. The United States needs to stand apart from others, yet be prepared to act in concert with them. It cannot and should not become a rogue superpower, acting on its own impulses and imposing its vision on the world.

The starting point of wisdom from this perspective is that not all problems are threatening to the United States or require its involvement. The United States has a considerable amount of freedom to define its interests. In addition, the United States must recognize that one consequence of having put a global security umbrella in place is that it has discouraged other states and regional organizations from taking responsibility for preserving international stability. This situation must be reversed. Others must be encouraged to act in defense of their own interests. Otherwise the United States runs the risk of becoming entrapped by commitments to unstable regimes.[17] Finally, the United States must learn to live with uncertainty. Absolute security is an unattainable objective and one that only produces imperial overstretch.

In sum, the **America the Balancer** perspective holds the following:

1. The primary national security threats to the United States are self-inflicted. They take the form of a proliferation of security commitments designed to protect America's economic interests.
2. The United States has a limited responsibility to other states, because the burden for protecting a state's national interests falls on that state.
3. The United States' responsibility to the global community is limited. American national interests and the maintenance of global order are not identical.

Many advocates of balancing see a return to multipolarity as all but inevitable and believe that trying to reassert or preserve American preeminence and suppress the emergence of new powers is held to be futile.[18] There is thus little reason for the United States to become deeply involved in the affairs of other states on a routine basis. What is needed is a **hedging strategy,** one that will allow the United States to realize its security goals without provoking others into uniting against it or accelerating their separate pursuits of power. Blessed by its geopolitical location, the answer for some lies in adopting the position of an offshore balancer. The United States is positioned to allow global and regional power balances to ensure its strategic independence. Only when others prove incapable of acting to block the ascent of a challenging hegemony should the United States step in to affect the balance of power. Given its continued power resources, such an intervention is held likely to be decisive.

One issue that needs to be confronted by advocates of the America the Balancer perspective is how to exercise American military power most effectively. Traditionally, war was the mechanism by which a balance-of-power system preserved stability in the international system. Commentators positioned across the political spectrum have raised the question of whether wars can continue to play this role on a large scale. If they cannot, then how is the balancer to enforce its will? One possibility is that rather than using American power to deter or defeat an adversary, America the Balancer will play a central role in compelling adversaries to change their behavior. The distinction is potentially important. One commentator who has looked at compellence suggests that it is more of a police task than deterrence, which is a military task.

## Disengaged America

The final alternative future put forward here calls for the United States to selectively, yet thoroughly, withdraw from the world.[19] The **Disengaged America** perspective sees retrenchment as necessary because the

## HISTORICAL LESSON

### Nixon's Trip to China

On July 15, 1971, President Richard Nixon announced to a stunned world that he had accepted Mao Zedong's invitation to visit the People's Republic of China, referred to in the U.S. media as Communist China. The visit, which occurred in February 1972, ended almost a quarter of a century of isolation, mutual suspicion, and occasional military crises.

Nixon's announcement resulted in strong public reactions for and against the president's planned trip. Reaction was quick and varied. Senator Humbert Humphrey, whom Nixon defeated for the presidency in 1968, stated that if Nixon used the presidency to promote peace and security throughout the world, the price for his reelection would be small. Republican Senator John Tower asserted that Nixon owed the American people an explanation. United Nations Secretary General U Thant said the trip would open a new chapter in international relations. Taiwanese officials asked Nixon to cancel the trip. North Vietnamese officials said the trip was to divert attention from Nixon's crimes. Pope Paul VI said it could change the face of the earth.

Nixon's diplomatic opening took observers by surprise because his entire political career had been based on demonstrating firm anticommunist credentials. He gained national notoriety as a member of the House Un-American activities Committee that investigated allegations that State Department official Alger Hiss was a Soviet spy. Nixon used this visibility as springboard to the Senate in a race in which he characterized his Democratic opponent as a left-wing communist sympathizer. Once in the Senate, he spoke out often against international communism and criticized Truman's handling of the Korean War.

Nonetheless, there were ample signs of Nixon's interest in dramatically changing the landscape of world politics. One year before becoming president, Nixon wrote on China that there was no reason for its people to live in "angry isolation." Early in his presidency, Nixon communicated to the Chinese his interest in ending this long period of isolation through the Romanian government, the U.S. ambassador to Poland, and through Pakistan's president. He also began to refer to Communist China by its official name, the People's Republic of China (PRC). It was only in December 1970 that these initiatives produced a positive response from China. In late April 1971, China signaled its willingness to invite Nixon, and in July, National Security Advisor Henry Kissinger made a secret trip to China to finalize matters.

Nixon visited China from February 21 to February 28, 1972. The trip ended with the United States and China issuing the Shanghai Communiqué. In this document, the two countries agreed to work toward normalizing their relations, a statement that all understood to mean that the United States would drop its recognition of Taiwan as the government of China and recognize the PRC instead in spite of ambiguous language elsewhere in the document. The PRC and the United States also agreed that neither they nor any other power should

(continued)

*(continued)*

seek "hegemony" over the Asia-Pacific region. The unnamed other power was the Soviet Union, and the Shanghai Communiqué thus served as an implicit alliance against Soviet infringement on Chinese territory or regional interests.

Nixon's diplomatic opening to China came against the backdrop of two significant developments for U.S. foreign policy. The first was growing conflict between the PRC and the Soviet Union. The United States had been slow to recognize the growing animosity in Sino–Soviet relations, but it was now clear that the United States was no longer opposed by a unified communist bloc. The second significant trend was the ongoing war in Vietnam. A widespread consensus existed inside and outside of the U.S. government that after Vietnam the United States would have a difficult, if not impossible, time in opposing Soviet aggression. Its military was strained to the breaking point, and the American public would not support "another Vietnam."

The challenge, as Nixon and Kissinger saw it, was to position the United States in such a way that it would remain the dominant power in the international system but at a lesser cost. The answer they arrived at was a strategy designed to reduce Soviet hostility to U.S. leadership by recognizing the Soviet Union as a legitimate power in world politics, while at the same time finding allies to stand with the United States against the Soviet Union, should that be necessary. No country filled that bill better than the PRC. But being able to play the "China card" first required establishing working relations with it.

**Applying the Lesson**

1. What is the equivalent of the "China Card" for U.S. foreign policy in today's international system?
2. Was Nixon's opening to China forward looking or backward looking in what it hoped to accomplish?
3. Is one peaceful foreign policy initiative really capable of changing the direction of world politics? ■

international system is becoming increasingly inhospitable to U.S. values and unresponsive to efforts at management or domination. Increasingly, the choices facing U.S. foreign policy will be ones of choosing what kinds of losses to avoid. Optimal solutions to foreign policy problems will no longer present themselves to policy makers, and if they do, domestic constraints will prevent policy makers from pursuing such a path. In the Disengaged America perspective, foreign policy must become less of a lance—a tool for spreading values—and more of a shield—a minimum set of conditions behind which the United States can protect its values and political processes.[20] In the words of one commentator writing after 9/11, the purpose of American foreign policy should be security first. Promoting democracy is fine so long as it is pursued by peaceful means and is seen as homegrown.[21]

Becoming disengaged means that the United States will have to learn to live in a "second-best world," one that is not totally to its liking but one in which it can get by. Allies will be fewer in number, and those that remain will have to do more to protect their own security and economic well-being. Nonintervention will be the rule for the United States, and self-reliance the watchword for others. The United States must be prepared to "let" some states be dominated and to direct its efforts at placing space between the **falling dominoes** rather than trying to define a line of containment. In the realm of economics, the objective should be to move toward autarchy and self-sufficiency so that other states cannot manipulate or threaten the United States. If the United States cannot dominate the sources of supply, it must be prepared to "substitute, tide over, [and] ride out" efforts at resource manipulation.[22] World order concerns must also take a backseat in U.S. foreign policy. As George Kennan has said about the food–population problem, "We did not create it and it is beyond our power to solve it."[23] Kennan argues that the United States needs to divest itself of its guilt complex and accept the fact that there is really very little that the United States can do for the Third World and very little that the Third World can do for the United States. In sum, the Disengaged America perspective holds the following:

1. The major threat to U.S. national security comes from an overactive foreign policy. Events beyond U.S. borders are not as crucial to U.S security as is commonly perceived, and, moreover, the United States has little power to influence their outcome.
2. The United States' responsibility to other states is minimal. The primary responsibility of the United States is to its own economic and military security.
3. The United States' responsibility to the global community is also minimal. The issues on the global agenda, especially as they relate to the Third World, are not the fault of the United States, and the United States can do little to solve them.

From the Disengaged America perspective, traditional principles of defense planning are largely irrelevant.[24] Military power should no longer be employed to further human rights or economic principles beyond American borders. Rather than pursue military goals, American foreign policy must concentrate on protecting American lives and property, the territorial integrity of the United States, and the autonomy of its political system. Consistent with these priorities, American military power would be used for only three purposes: (1) to defend the approaches to U.S. territory; (2) to serve as second-chance forces to be used if deterrence fails or unexpected threats arise; and (3) to provide finite essential deterrence against attacks on the United States and its forces overseas.

In the words of Pat Buchanan, the purpose of American foreign policy is "America First—and Second, and Third."[25] The Disengaged America perspective has few qualms with the need to defend American interests or take action unilaterally and forcefully in doing so. Preemption as a means for dealing with terrorists is not a repugnant strategy to them. What concerns them is that the war on terrorism has as its objective not simply the defeat of the enemy but their transformation. Nation building has always been seen by supporters of the Disengaged America perspective as a fool's errand, and they look with great trepidation on the prospects of doing so in Afghanistan and Iraq.

## OVER THE HORIZON

Whether it is preparing for the post-American world or simply looking "beyond bin Laden,"[26] a widely perceived need exists to begin a serious discussion about the United States' global role in the post-9/11 world. The visions presented here can be seen as a starting point for that discussion.

If we look over the horizon, we can anticipate two elements of this discussion emerging that build upon our discussion of foreign policy problems in Chapter 1. First, while foreign policy is about choices, it is also about costs and building consensus. It is not simply an intellectual exercise. Changing directions creates winners and losers. We can expect to see spirited political action by groups, government agencies, and individuals whose interests will be harmed by changing the direction of U.S. foreign policy (or by standing pat and not changing direction). Of special interest will be whether a new winning coalition can be put together in the absence of a major unifying foreign policy crisis.

Second, we can expect to see an intense discussion about the power resources and strategies needed to bring into existence a new foreign policy. The challenge of finding and effectively using new power resources will proceed at three different levels. At a material level, it means acquiring the raw power resources necessary to lead. Whether these resources are primarily hard or soft will depend on the vision selected. Power does not automatically translate into influence. For this to happen, others must adjust their policies and follow the United States. Accomplishing this will demand more than just possessing the ability to dominate others; it will also depend on the ability to get others to voluntarily join with the United States in multilateral settings. Leadership at the institutional level will require that the United States develop a capacity for fostering cooperation among states by framing issues so that joint action is possible and providing the resources needed to implement solutions. Finally, there will be the challenge of finding "good people" with insight into human nature and the dynamics of world politics so that opportunities for action are not lost and threats are met effectively.

## CRITICAL THINKING QUESTIONS

1. In selecting a foreign policy for the future which of the three questions we ask is most important?
2. Identify one foreign policy option that is missing and needs to be added to the list. Why is it needed?
3. What power resources are most needed by the U.S. in facing the future?

## KEY TERMS

## FURTHER READING

Zbigniew Brzezinski, "The Dilemma of the Last Sovereign," *The American Interest,* 1 (2005), 37–46.

Robert Kagan, et al. (eds), *To Lead the World: American Strategy After the Bush Doctrine* (New York: Oxford University Press, 2008).

Christopher Layne, *The Peace of Illusions: American Grand Strategy from 1940 to the Present* (Ithaca: Cornell University Press, 2006).

Anatol Lieven and John Hulsman, *Ethical Realism: A Vision for America's Role in the World* (New York: Pantheon, 2006).

Fareed Zakaria, *The Post American World* (New York: Norton, 2009).

## NOTES

1. Fareed Zakaria, *The Post American World* (New York: Norton, 2009).
2. Robert Kagan, "The September 12 Paradigm," *Foreign Affairs,* 87 (2008), 25–39.
3. Zbigniew Brzezinski, "The Dilemma of the Last Sovereign," *The American Interest,* 1 (2005), 37–46.
4. Richard Rosecrance, "New Directions?" in Richard Rosecrance (ed.), *America as an Ordinary Country: U.S. Foreign Policy and the Future* (Ithaca, NY: Cornell University Press, 1976), pp. 245–66; reprinted in Jeffrey Salamon, James P. O'Leary, and Richard Shultz (eds.), *Power, Principles, and Interests* (Lexington, MA: Ginn, 1985), pp. 433–44.
5. Salamon, O'Leary, and Shultz (eds.), *Power, Principles, and Interests,* p. 443.
6. Ibid., p. 442.
7. On this theme, see Robert A. Isaak, *American Democracy and World Power* (New York: St. Martin's, 1977); and Robert C. Johansen, *The National Interest and the Human Interest: An Analysis of U.S. Foreign Policy* (Princeton, NJ: Princeton University Press, 1980).
8. Johansen, *The National Interest and the Human Interest.*
9. John Mueller and Karl Mueller, "Sanctions of Mass Destruction," *Foreign Affairs,* 78 (1999), 43–53.
10. James Schlesinger, "Quest for a Post Cold War Foreign Policy," *Foreign Affairs,* 72 (1992/1993), 17–28.
11. Robert W. Tucker, "1989 and All That," in Nicholas X. Rizopoulos (ed.), *Sea-Changes: American Foreign Policy in a World Transformed* (New York: Council on Foreign Relations Press, 1990), pp. 204–37.
12. Richard Haass, "Military Force: A User's Guide," *Foreign Policy,* 96 (1994), 21–38.
13. George Bush, "Remarks at the United States Military Academy," *Public Papers of the President* (Washington, DC: U.S. Government Printing Office, 1993), 2230–31.
14. Henry Kissinger, "Universal Values, Specific Policies," *National Interest,* 84 (2006), 13.
15. James Chace and Caleb Carr, *America Invulnerable* (New York: Summit, 1988), 318.

16. Graham Fuller, "Strategic Fatigue,' *National Interest,* 84 (2006), 37–42.
17. Hilton Root, "Walking with the Devil," *National Interest,* 88 (2007), 42–45.
18. Christopher Layne, "The Unipolar Illusion: Why Great Powers Will Rise," *International Security,* 17 (1993), 5–51.
19. On this theme, see Earl C. Ravenal, *Never Again: Learning from America's Foreign Policy Failures* (Philadelphia: Temple University Press, 1978).
20. Ibid., p. 15
21. Amitai Etzioni, "Security First," *National Interest,* 88 (2007), 11–15.
22. Ravenal, *Never Again,* p. xv.
23. George Kennan, *Cloud of Danger: Current Realities of American Foreign Policy* (Boston: Little, Brown, 1977), p. 32.
24. Earl Ravenal, "The Case for Adjustment," *Foreign Policy,* 81 (1990/91), 3–19.
25. Patrick Buchanan, "America First–and Second, and Third," *National Interest,* 19 (1990), 77–82.
26. Stephen Walt, "Beyond bin Laden," *International Security,* 26 (2003), 56–78.

# GLOSSARY

**Action channels** Decision-making linkages between organizations and individuals that determines who participates in bureaucratic politics decision-making games. Important because not every one "plays" in these games. Players and their power are determined by where they fit in the action channels.

**Action indispensability** Decision-making situations in which action by policy makers is critical to success or failure. The identity of the actor is not essential because the response was standard and expected.

**Action policy** U.S. foreign policy as it is actually carried out with respect to a problem. Refers to what is done rather than what is said. Often contrasted with declaratory policy. Originally used in context of U.S. nuclear policy.

**Actor indispensability** Decision-making situations in which not only is action by policy makers critical to success or failure but the identity of the actor is seen as being key to the outcome.

**Alliance** A formal agreement among states to provide military assistance to each other. Alliances vary in the types of aid offered and the nature of the commitment.

**America the Balancer** A possible future foreign policy strategic orientation of U.S. foreign policy that is based on a limited and selective involvement in world affairs.

**American Crusader** A possible future foreign policy strategic orientation of U.S. foreign policy that is based on the idea that the U.S. faces real and immediate security threats and has the power and moral responsibility to lead.

**"America first" perspective** A perspective on foreign policy in which priority is given to the interests of American firms and interests over those of other states. Identified with bureaucracies such as the Commerce and Agriculture Departments.

**Analogy** Central to method of reasoning in which comparisons are made between events or objects as the basis for making judgments about similarities and differences. Foreign policy often involves comparison of present with past events.

**Arms control** Policy designed to bring about restraint in the use of weapons. Generally involves reduction in numbers of weapons but does not have to do this. Often contrasted with disarmament.

**Arms sale** Purchase of weapons by one state from another. The distinguishing feature of arms sales is the quality of the weapons obtained. Unlike in the case of arms transfers these weapons tend to be among the most preferred in the seller's inventory.

**Arms transfer** Process of providing weapons to another state for free or at greatly reduced prices. Typically, these weapons are characterized as being excess defense articles or emergency allocations.

**Assured destruction** Nuclear strategy under Johnson predicated on U.S. ability to destroy a significant portion of Soviet population and economic capability in retaliation for a Soviet attack on the United States.

**Bargaining** Process by which two or more states reach agreement on a policy through a process of give and take. It can take place in formal settings or informally. A subtype of negotiations.

**Barnacles** Riders or amendments that are attached to foreign policy legislation. Often needed to secure its passage, they can result in features being added that complicate the conduct of U.S. diplomacy. Reporting requirements are an example.

**Bipartisanship** Situation in domestic politics of American foreign policy, where a policy is supported by both political parties. Seen as a sign of national unity and communicates resolve to opponents. It came into use following World War II when foundations of containment policy were put into place.

**Bipolar** Characterizes an international system that is conflict prone and divided into two competing and mutually exclusive blocs each led by a superpower. Often subdivided into loose and tight variants, depending on the unity of the blocs and the distance separating them. The Cold War was a bipolar system.

**Black box** Part of rational actor decision-making perspective. Assumes that foreign policy is a response to actions and events in the international system. Therefore one does not need to examine domestic politics, and events inside the state can be ignored or black boxed.

**Blowback** The negative consequences that result from foreign policy actions. Originally used with reference to CIA covert actions but now applied more generally to foreign policy initiatives.

**Boycott** A refusal to buy or sell goods from a company or country. Alternatively, a refusal to attend a meeting or negotiations.

**Bretton Woods system** International economic order created after World War II consisting of the International Monetary Fund, the World Bank, and the General Agreement on Trade and Tariffs. Formally ended in 1974 when Nixon took the United States off the gold standard.

**Bricker Amendment** Failed attempt by Congress in the 1950s to limit the president's ability to use executive agreements in place of treaties as instrument of U.S. foreign policy. It would have required Senate advice and consent to executive agreements before they took effect.

**Bureaucratic politics** Decision-making model that emphasizes the influence of bureaucratic factors, most notably,

self-interest. Policy is not decided upon so much as bargained into existence.

**Casus belli** The factors or events used to justify going to war.

**CEO system** Presidential management system introduced by George W. Bush that emphasizes importance of providing overall direction to policy and selecting qualified individuals and then removing oneself from the day-to-day affairs of governing.

**Civil–military relations** The overarching relationship between professional military officers and civilian policy makers. Involves issues such as who has ultimate authority, the values to be pursued, and political neutrality.

**Closed belief system** A belief system is a set of interrelated mental images about some aspect of reality. A closed belief system is one that does not change in spite of contradictory evidence. Contrasts with an open belief system.

**CNN effect** Phrase designed to convey increased importance of the media for determining the foreign policy agenda of the United States by its ability to arouse and shape public opinion, and to force policy makers to respond quickly to unfolding events.

**Coalitions** Informal alignment of states that come together out of self-interest to deal with a specific problem. Common forms include voting blocs at an international organization and combinations of military forces such as those in the Persian Gulf War and the Iraq War.

**Coercive diplomacy** Use or threatened use of force against another state for political purposes. Typically refers to military force but can include economic force. Purposes can include deterrence and compellence.

**Cognitive consistency** The tendency for individuals to seek out information and stimuli that are supportive of one's beliefs and attitudes.

**Collegial system** Presidential management system that emphasizes cooperation, team work, and problem solving as primary values for top presidential aides and department heads.

**Compellence**  Use or threat of using military force to prompt another state to undertake a desired action. Contrasts with deterrence in which force is used or threatened to prevent an action from taking place.

**Competitive system**  Presidential management system that emphasizes playing off aides against one another and assigning same task to multiple units in order to maximize information flow and freedom of maneuver.

**Conference diplomacy**  Category of diplomacy that focuses on large international gatherings that are generally open to all states. Typically they focus on a single problem or issue and attempt to lay down rules for addressing the problem. Differs from summit diplomacy where only a few states attend.

**Constructivism**  A theoretical perspective for studying international relations that emphasizes the subjectivity of actions. Emphasis is placed on understanding how the developments are viewed by the participants by examining ideas, culture, history, and the dynamics of interaction.

**Containment**  U.S. policy toward the Soviet Union for much of the Cold War. Predicated on the assumption that the potential for Soviet aggression was constant but could be checked by applying constant counter pressure to thwart it. Over time this policy was expected to produce a mellowing of Soviet foreign policy.

**Counterinsurgency**  The military strategy for fighting an insurgency, which is defined as an armed rebellion against a recognized government. While a military strategy counterinsurgency also contains political, economic, and psychological dimensions.

**Counterproliferation**  Military strategy designed to prevent spread of weapons. Most frequently talked about in context of weapons of mass destruction, it can be seen as a preemptive use of force.

**Country team**  Comprises the representatives from all U.S. agencies represented in an embassy. Headed by the ambassador. It is meant to signify that a united purpose exists to U.S. foreign policy in the country.

**Covert action**  Activities to influence military, economic, and political conditions abroad, where it is intended that the role of the U.S. government not be apparent.

**Declaratory policy**  Public statements of U.S. foreign policy with regard to a problem. Refers to what is said rather than what is done. Often contrasted with action policy. Originally used in context of U.S. nuclear policy.

**Denuclearization**  Process by which a state has acquired or is pursuing a nuclear weapon reverses course and agrees to forego it.

**Détente**  Foreign policy associated with Nixon. Rather than contain the Soviet Union it sought to establish a working relationship by treating it as a legitimate power and engaging it in a series of mutually beneficial arms control and economic relationships that would reduce its threat to the United States, thus making global conflicts more manageable.

**Deterrence**  The use of power to prevent an unwanted action from taking place. Most frequently, it refers to the use of military power and in the context of the Cold War, the nuclear stand off between the United States and the Soviet Union.

**Disarmament**  Policy designed to reduce the number of weapons in existence. May be applied to specific weapons or inventories in general. Logical end point is zero weapons but does not need to reach this point. Often contrasted with arms control.

**Disengaged America**  A possible future foreign policy strategic orientation of U.S. foreign policy that is based on minimal global engagement and learning to live in a second-best world.

**Elite theory**  Decision-making model that stresses the overwhelming influence of economic class and ideology on policy. Contrasts with pluralism, arguing that there does not exist a system of checks and balances among competing interests.

**Embargo** A prohibition of selling goods or services to another country.

**Empire** A hierarchically structured grouping of states ruled from one power center. It is debated whether or not the U.S. position of dominance in the world qualifies it to be an empire. Similarly, it is debated how long the U.S. empire, if it exists, can survive.

**Executive agreement** Arrangements entered into with other countries by the president that are not subject to a congressional vote. The Supreme Court has ruled executive agreements hold force of law as do treaties.

**Falling dominoes** Term associated with the Cold War, it denotes the possibility that a U.S. foreign policy failure in a given country or military engagement may set off a chain reaction leading to the fall of many states, resulting in a major national security crisis.

**Fast track** Today known as Trade Promotional Authority. Voted on by Congress for set periods of time, it gives the president the authority to enter into international trade negotiations, guarantees a prompt vote by Congress, and limits Congress' ability to modify treaties that come before it.

**Fire wall** A blockage or separation that is intended to stop the spread of a dangerous condition. In warfare it is often used to signify attempts to create a dividing line between conventional and nuclear weapons.

**Flexible response** Nuclear strategy under Kennedy that called for wide range of military responses, including a variety of nuclear options to deal with Soviet challenges.

**Foreign Service Officer** Professional diplomatic corps of the United States. Has been controversial at times for its

values and degree of separation from American society as a whole.

**Formalistic system** Presidential management system that employs strict hierarchical decision-making structure on decision-making process.

**Free trade** International economic policy based on the principle of the open and nondiscriminatory flow of goods across borders. Achieved through the removal of government-imposed barriers to trade.

**Generational events** Those highly visible and psychologically significant events that influence the worldview of a generation of individuals, whether they were experienced directly or not. The Great Depression, Pearl Harbor, and Vietnam are often given as examples.

**Gadfly** A congressional orientation to foreign policy in which an individual raises concerns about the direction of U.S. foreign policy not out of an interest in short-term electoral gains but with an eye toward affecting the long-term direction of policy.

**Guerrilla war** Unconventional war strategy that emphasizes hit-and-run tactics and prolonged warfare rather than direct engagement of enemy forces in decisive battles. Ultimate objective is to get government to overreact and lose support of the people.

**Globalization** Refers to the process of the growing pace and density of economic, political, and cultural interactions in international affairs. Viewed by some in a positive light as a force that unites peoples; others see it as a threatening condition that fosters conflict among people and countries.

**Grand strategy** Overarching conceptual framework for integrating and applying all elements of power. Establishes the general direction, purposes, and logic of U.S. foreign policy. Often associated with presidential doctrines.

**Groupthink** Common consequence of small-group decision-making dynamics.

Concurrence seeking behavior on the part of group members causes them to reach fundamentally flawed decisions.

**Hard power**  The power to coerce. Generally associated with military power. It seeks to impose an outcome on an opponent.

**Hedging strategy**  A foreign policy strategy in which the United States acts cautiously to ensure that the failure of no single initiative can inflict great harm on U.S. national interests. It requires keeping open lines of communication with all states and not locking the United States into an all-or-nothing situation.

**Hegemony**  Domineering and uncontested leadership that is rooted in the political, economic, and military ability to impose one's will on others. Often used to characterize the position of the dominant state in a unipolar system and with the U.S. position in the world after the end of the Cold War.

**Imperialism**  A foreign policy of domination in which one state controls the people, resources and political activity in other states generally by military force. Critics of U.S. foreign policy have often argued that it has been imperialist in dealings with developing countries.

**Intermestic**  foreign policy problems that contain both domestic and foreign policy dimensions thus complicating efforts to solve them and defy the traditional dichotomy of foreign versus domestic policy.

**Internationalism**  An orientation to world affairs that stresses the importance of taking an active role in global decision making in order to protect and promote national security and economic prosperity. Can be undertaken both in the pursuit of liberal or conservative goals.

**Iraq syndrome**  Much speculated on possible negative public reaction to U.S. involvement in Iraq that will prevent policy makers from using force in the future, just as Vietnam Syndrome did in the 1970s.

**Isolationism**  An orientation to world affairs that stresses the dangers of global involvement rather than its benefits. Strong defenses and unilateral action are seen as necessary to protect the national interest. A sharp distinction is drawn between the national interest and the global interest.

**Legalism**  Part of the American national style. The belief that foreign policy problems can be solved through the application of legal formulas and principles.

**Legislative veto**  A situation where Congress repeals presidential action or the decision of a Federal agency by writing legislation so that it can be overridden by majority of one or both Houses. Contained in the War Powers Resolution.

**Lippmann gap**  The difference between a country's power resources and the goals it wishes to achieve. Named after political columnist Walter Lippmann, who argued the larger this gap, the greater the likelihood that U.S. foreign policy would fail.

**Massive retaliation**  Nuclear strategy under Eisenhower that sought to deter the Soviet Union aggression throughout the world by threatening a large-scale retaliatory strike on the Soviet Union.

**Military after next**  Phrase used to describe need to think beyond immediate problems and focus on long-term bureaucratic requirements of U.S. foreign policy. Can also be State Department after next or CIA after next.

**Military–industrial complex**  A phrase used in Eisenhower's farewell presidential address. Most narrowly used, it speaks to the unchecked influence of industry lobbyists and allies in the military to obtain funds for weapons systems and militarize American foreign policy.

**Models**  A simplified depictions of a complex process or structure used to generate insights into their nature. May be mathematical or descriptive.

**Monitoring** Collection of data about state compliance with an agreement or international obligation. May be done via on-the-ground inspections or by technical means such as satellites. Differs from verification, which involves making a judgment about whether a state is in compliance.

**Moral pragmatism** Part of the American national style. Brings together the belief that foreign policy ought to be driven by the pursuit of principles and that they can be solved by applying an engineering problem-solving logic.

**Multipolar** Characterizes an international system in which there are at least five major powers. No permanent dividing line separates them into competing blocs; rather the major states enter into a series of shifting alliances to preserve national interests. Nineteenth-century Europe is seen as a multipolar period.

**National interest** The fundamental goals and objectives of a state's foreign policy. Used as if it were self-explanatory, it is a contested concept that holds great emotional power in political debates.

**National style** Refers to deeply engrained patterns of thought and action on how to approach foreign policy problems and their solutions. More generally, it establishes the basis for how a country looks out at the international system and defines its role in world politics.

**Negotiation** Broadly defined as a dialogue to resolve disputes. This result may be achieved through mediation, fact finding, or bargaining. On occasion, negotiations are entered into by states not to solve problems but to gain an advantage through obtaining information or the publicity it generates.

**Neoconservatism** In foreign policy, refers to an activist and unilateral orientation to involvement in world affairs for the purpose of promoting

democracy and free trade that stresses the use of military power to defeat enemies. Seen by many as the dominant viewpoint of the George W. Bush administration following 9/11.

**Neoliberalism** A theoretical perspective for studying international relations that stresses the ability of states to cooperate, solve problems, and defend their interests peacefully. Emphasis is placed on the importance of mutually beneficial economic interactions, the peaceful effects of democracy, and the importance of international laws and organizations.

**Noise** Background clutter of irrelevant or misleading data that complicates task of policy makers trying to identify important pieces of information or signals that will help them formulate policy.

**Nontariff barrier** A nontax barrier to free trade. Generally takes the form of requirements to ship of national vessels, purchase goods in a specific country of origin, or safe and health or environmental standards imposed on goods and their production.

**Opportunity costs** In conducting foreign policy states are faced with the reality of limited time and limited resources. The pursuit of any objective necessarily comes at the expense of pursuing other goals that now must be neglected.

**Ordinary State** A possible future foreign policy, strategic orientation of U.S. foreign policy that is based on the presumption that the United States has no greater responsibility for maintaining global order than does any other state.

**Outsource** To rely upon on nongovernmental or private sector agencies to carry out assigned tasks. Found throughout foreign policy area. Became controversial with large scale use of private contractors during Iraq War.

**Oversight** Congressional regulatory supervision of the Federal bureaucracy. The stated objective is not day-to-day managerial control but ensuring accountability of decisions made and improving performance.

**Paramilitary** Operations carried out by forces or groups distinct from the professional military for which no broad conventional military capability exists. They are often carried in hostile, politically sensitive, or denied areas.

**Partisan presidency** View of presidency that stresses a president who is in a combative relationship with Congress and relies on his own party and control of the media for political resources to govern. Rather than operate above politics the president is at the center of efforts to gain political advantage.

**Peacekeeping** Operations conducted in postconflict areas to observe the peace process and implement peace agreements. Although not exclusively military in nature, peacekeeping operations generally build upon a significant military presence in the country affected.

**Permanent normal trade relations** Once known as most favored nations status. It denotes the existence of a nondiscriminatory trade relationship with another state. Only a few states do not have it. In the past, granting of this status has often been quite controversial, especially to China and the Soviet Union.

**Pledge System** Form of international cooperation in which countries promise voluntarily to support an agreement. No enforcement mechanism is created.

**Pluralism** Decision-making model that sees policy as the result of competing interest groups. The government is often pictured as a neutral umpire making policy to reflect position of strongest groups.

**Policy entrepreneur** A congressional orientation to foreign policy, whereby the individual takes positions on foreign policy legislation, primarily with an eye toward the electoral advantage it might bestow rather than a long-rang concern for the issue itself.

**Political creep** The tendency for political criteria and considerations to replace professional ones in assignment of personnel to positions within foreign policy bureaucracy. Once identified with appointment of political fundraisers to ambassadorships, now also an issue at lower levels of bureaucracies.

**Politicizing intelligence** Situation where professional expertise and objectivity of intelligence reports is replaced by partisan political considerations. Associated with phrases such as intelligence-to-please and cherry-picking.

**Positional issues** Refers to foreign policy issues in elections that find candidates taking opposite sides. The dominant logic of primary campaigns. A frequent result is to oversimplify issues.

**Post-American world** An international system some say may come into existence in the near future. It is characterized by the rise in the power of competing states to create an international system in which the United States has reduced influence.

**Pragmatic America** A possible future foreign policy strategic orientation of U.S. foreign policy that is based on the view that the rapid changes in world politics make it inadvisable for U.S. foreign policy to be guided by a broad set of principles. Instead, it should focus on the particulars of each situation as they arise.

**Preemption** Striking first in self-defense. In classical usage, a distinction is drawn between preemption, which occurs when the threat is immediate, and prevention, when it is more long term or generic.

**Presidential finding** Mandated by the Hughes–Ryan Amendment, it requires that except under exceptional circumstances, presidents inform key members of Congress in advance of the scope of CIA operations.

**Presidential personality** Refers to those traits of the president that are important for understanding how he defines problems and solutions as well as his outlook on the use of presidential power.

**Proliferation** Spread of weapons. Two different versions exist. Horizontal, in which weapons spread to additional countries, and vertical, in which case the inventories of states already possessing the weapon grow larger.

**Prospect theory** Decision-making model that sees policy makers far more willing to take risks to defend what they have then to pursue new goals and objectives.

**Proxy war** War fought on behalf of another state that does not actively participate in the war itself. Typically associated with a smaller or regional ally fighting on behalf of a major power.

**Public diplomacy** Diplomatic activity that is directed at the public at large in a target state. Contrasts with classical diplomacy, which is conducted in secret and involves government-to-government relations. Based on the belief that the public can influence the foreign policy decisions of adversaries.

**Public goods** Policy benefits that are not the object of competition among state and cannot be possessed by a state or group of states and denied to all others. Often characterized as goals that are in the global interest such as a clean environment, absence of disease, or an international stable economic order.

**Quadrennial Defense Review** Congressionally mandated 4 years of U.S. defense strategy. Used to identify scenarios that might confront the United States and forces that might be needed to meet that threat. In practice, has often been largely a symbolic exercise.

**Quota** Quantitative restriction placed on the amount of goods allowed to enter a country from another country.

**Rally-around-the-flag affect** Tendency for public opinion to coalesce and support the president's foreign policy position in times of crisis. Reflects both the power of the presidency and media to shape public opinion as well as the lack of in-depth knowledge that many Americans have on foreign policy matters.

**Ratify** To give approval. Treaties in the United States are ratified by the president after the Senate has given its advice and consent by a two-thirds majority.

**Rational actor** Decision-making model that stresses foreign policy; it should be viewed as a deliberate and calculated response to external events and actions. Values are identified, options listed, and a choice made that best ensures that the most important values will be realized.

**Realism** A theoretical perspective for studying international relations that emphasizes the struggle for power carried out under conditions of anarchy. Conflict and competition are seen as permanent features of world politics. Security, not peace, is the central objective of foreign policy.

**Reformed America** A possible future foreign policy strategic orientation of U.S. foreign policy that is based on the belief that the time is appropriate to give preference to traditional American values over narrowly defined security interests in dealing with global problems.

**Reporting requirement** A statement added on to legislation, requiring periodic reports by implementing agencies or the president on the status of a situation. They have been used by Congress as a means of keeping pressure on presidents to carry out foreign policy according to its wishes. Generally, escape hatches are included to give presidents freedom to act.

**Revolution in military affairs** Term used to capture the transformational power that modern information and communication technology was expected to have in conduct of military campaigns. Widely used in U.S. defense planning and weapons procurement decisions after Persian Gulf War. Now challenged by new emphasis on counterinsurgency warfare.

**Sanctions** Penalties or other means of enforcement used to create incentives for countries to act in accordance with international policies or foreign policy edicts of the sanctioning state. Typically involves the use of economic instruments of foreign policy.

**Shock and awe** Massive bombing campaign used by United States in opening of Iraq War. Designed as much to psychologically intimidate enemy as to defeat it on the battlefield. Associated with military logic of Revolution in Military Affairs.

**Signing statement** Comments made by the president when signing legislation into law and used to identify which parts of the legislation he objects to and will not enforce. Effectively allows the president to veto certain parts of a bill without having to veto the entire bill.

**Signal** Piece of information that will help policy makers formulate policy. Often difficult to identify because of the presence of noise that masks their presence and significance.

**Smart sanctions** Penalties or other measures that are targeted on specific groups or individuals in a target state. Adopted out of a concern that sanctions, particular economic sanctions, unfairly punish all individuals in a society rather than just those engaging in the disputed behaviors.

**Soft power** The power to influence and persuade. It attracts others to one side rather than forcing them to support your cause as is the case with hard power. Often associated with diplomacy, positive economic incentives, and, more generally, the attraction of American culture, ideas, and values.

**Sovereignty** The principle that no power exists above the state. The state alone decides what goals to pursue and how to pursue them. Its relevance as an absolute standard is questioned by many in today's world of globization, terrorism, and large-scale power inequalities among states.

**Spiral of silence** Tendency for those holding minority views to remain silent when they fail to see the media report

stories that support their position. Results in an exaggerated sense of national unity.

**Stability operations** Military operations undertaken to restore and maintain order and stability in regions or states where a competent civil authority no longer functions.

**Standard operating procedures** Central part of bureaucratic politics model. States that policy is implemented not with an eye to the particulars of a situation or a problem but in a routine and predictable fashion, with the result that policies often fail to achieve their intended purpose.

**Sufficiency** Nuclear strategy under Nixon that emphasized strategic equality with the Soviet Union and the possession of a minimum retaliatory threat.

**Summit conference** Category of diplomacy that involves meetings of the heads of government of a small number of states. Popularized during World War II and the Cold War. They are now less negotiating sessions and more occasions to sign agreements reached in other settings.

**Tariff** Tax on foreign products coming into a country. May be put in place to raise revenue, protect domestic industries from foreign competition, or punish another state.

**Terrorism** Violence employed for purposes of political intimidation. It may be employed in the support of any set of goals and carried out by nonstate actors or state agencies. It may exist as a strategy in its own right or as the first stage in a larger guerrilla war conflict.

**Think tanks** Generic phrase used to describe organizations that engage in policy analysis and advocacy. They may be nonprofits, represent corporate interests, or funded by governments.

**Tipping point** Term used to describe foreign policy issues in which elite and public opinion is sufficiently divided that a shift in public opinion holds the potential for changing the direction of policy.

**Trade promotional authority** Once known as fast-track authority. Voted on by Congress for set periods of time, it gives the president the authority to enter into international trade negotiations, guarantees a prompt vote by Congress, and limits Congress' ability to modify treaties that come before it.

**Unilateral president** View of presidential power that emphasizes strength rather than weakness. By acting unilaterally to make policy statements, create organizations, appoint individuals to key positions, and take action, the president is seen as able to dominate the political agenda and outmaneuver Congress and the Courts, placing them in a reactive position.

**Unilateralism** Part of the American national style. It is an orientation to action that emphasizes the value of going it alone. When cooperation with others is needed, it must be carried out on one's own terms and with a minimal level of commitment to joint action.

**Unipolar** Characterizes an international system in which one power dominates over all others. No balancing or competing bloc exists. Rare at the international level, it has been more common at the region level such as in Latin America and East Europe. Some see the contemporary international system as unipolar.

**Valence issues** Refers to electoral foreign policy issues which find all candidates taking the same side. Common in general elections. For voters the choice becomes not what position to endorse but who they think is best capable of achieving the agreed-upon outcome.

**Vietnam syndrome** Refers to what many interpreted as the primary lesson of Vietnam. The perception that the American public will not again support long-term military engagements that result in the substantial loss of American lives. Consequently, any military action must be quick and decisive.

**War Powers resolution** The major Cold War attempt by Congress to limit a president's ability to use military force without its approval. Its constitutionality has never been tested. No president has officially recognized its binding nature on their decision making power.

**Window of fear** The onset of a set of short-term conditions that lead policy makers rationally to conclude that military action needs to be taken, regardless of how small the prospects of victory are because conditions will only get worse in the future.

**Window of opportunity** The onset of short-term conditions that lead policy makers rationally to conclude that military actions needs to be undertaken because they possess a clear and distinct military advantage over the enemy.

**Wilsonianism** A set of foreign policy ideas associated with Woodrow Wilson. The core essence of these ideas is contested. Generally seen as foundational is the notion that the United States has a moral and national security obligation to spread democracy and create a liberal international order.

**Weapons of mass destruction** Overarching term used to describe nuclear, biological, and chemical weapons. Radiological weapons and delivery systems are also often included in the definition. During the Cold War the term related almost exclusively to nuclear weapons.

**Yellow journalism** Phrase used to characterize media coverage of foreign policy that stresses a provocative, overly dramatic, and sensationalistic treatment of events over measured reporting and a concern for factual accuracy.

# INDEX